To This High Standard

To This High Standard

The Life of Edwin Denby

John Lodwig

Dedication

To Manley R. Irwin, Professor Emeritus, Economics, Whittemore School of Business and Economics, University of New Hampshire Teacher, Mentor, Dear Friend.

Acknowledgements

My adventure began while attending an early Warren Harding Symposium in Marion, Ohio, held annually under the auspices of The Ohio State University at Marion, the Ohio History Connection, and the Harding Presidential Sites. There I met David H. Stratton, Professor Emeritus of History at Washington State University in Pullman, and author of "Tempest Over Teapot Dome". Professor Stratton was one of the featured speakers, and fortunately he mentioned to me another book, "Silent Strategists" by Manley Irwin. All these new areas of information whetted my appetite to further investigate the Harding years on my own. As I began looking for biographies of Harding's cabinet members, it became readily apparent that there was no biography of his illustrious Secretary of the Navy, Edwin Denby. Then I learned that a very great deal of Edwin Denby's papers were housed in two libraries within minutes of my home.

One day I wandered into the Burton Historical Collection of the Detroit Public Library, and I met a wonderful lady, Ms. Joyce Middlebrooks who pointed me on my quest. Her gentle helpfulness went a long way in keeping me going. Also, Mr. Romie Minor was of great assistance in searching out peripheral information on some of Edwin Denby's friends. When I had exhausted the papers at the Burton, I headed for the Bentley Historical Library on the north campus of the University of Michigan in Ann Arbor. There I met Ms. Karen Wight, senior reference assistant, who taught me how to cross reference other collections with the Denby papers. I began seeing a pattern in these indomitable people called librarians, and that one quality which seems to unite them above all others: their desire to help.

I visited Edwin Denby's home town, Evansville, Indiana, and found the people there the same friendly and ingratiating Midwesterners with whom I had grown up. Ms. Stacy Stratman at the Chamber of Commerce helped me find my way around the strange town. At the Evansville Public Library, Mr. Daniel Smith, Local History Librarian, was of great assistance. At the Willard Public Library, Mr. Gregory M. Hager, its director, Mr. Stan Schmidt, library assistant of Special Collections,, and Ms. Patricia Sides, archivist, all were most welcoming and helpful in my quest for information. The Willard is a very special library, and I highly recommend a visit if you are passing nearby.

Late in my research I visited the beautiful tidewater town of Beaufort, South Carolina. Even with modern populations and heavy tourist traffic, it is easy to see what so strongly attracted the Denbys 100 years ago. Special thanks to Ms. Grace Cordial, Senior Librarian of the Beaufort Public Library for pointing me to great sources for the Denbys' time in Beaufort.

Hearty thanks to longtime good friend, Dr. Richard Maxwell, for all his reading and encouraging moral support through the years of writing.

To Manley Irwin, I owe far more than I could ever tell or repay. One of the great scholars that I have known, and a mentor and supporter beyond compare. Manley and I agreed wholeheartedly that Edwin Denby was our "gift that kept on giving", and we shared many a pleasant and lengthy dinner in Denby discussions, and many long telephone talks as well.

Thanks to the Denby grandsons, Ned, French and Dan Wetmore who travelled twice to sit down with me at Detroit for discussions, and were always ready to assist me in any way.

Lastly, and of course, not least, I have to thank Sherry, my long-suffering wife, for "her forbearance in hearing more than she ever wanted to know about the 1920's during breakfast, lunch and dinner." (quoted from Manley's Strategists) Both she and Mrs. Irwin are glad the books are finished!

Table of Contents

"I believe that the greatest thing a person can do is to live as a lady or gentleman, and I mean by that a lady or gentleman in the truest sense — one who will not wrong his neighbor, one who will not take undue advantage, one who will not lie, one who is true to the code of ethics of his country. That is the kind of persons we want to people the earth, and when we have succeeded in doing that and educating our young people so that they all try to live up to this standard, then the rest is easy. And so it is with nations. A nation, in order that it may write its history clear and clean in the world's records must in like manner measure up to this high standard."

Edwin Denby speech to law students in Japan, 1922

Foreword

There was a time in the not-so-distant past when giants walked among us. Heroes and patriots were taught in our public schools to honor God, family and country, in that specific order. Men and women sacrificed "their lives, their fortunes and their sacred honor" for these principles in order to build a world of safety and prosperity, but most of all, of opportunity for their children, and the children of the following generations.

Men such as Davy Crockett, who really DID die at the Alamo, and Daniel Boone who lost a brother and a son during our Revolution, or Simon Kenton or Lewis Cass, who each performed deeds of valor and vision which helped to carve from the virgin frontier a civilization like no other the world has ever seen. These were the people who toiled in the wilderness to put into practice the stirring sentences, and noble ideals of our founding fathers. Despite what political correctness would have you believe, it really was, and remains, a unique experiment in the annals of humankind. There has never been, and there will never be, another like it.

In our world today we often find it necessary to invent such men, because we do not know, and we have never been taught, that Simon Kenton once actually ran nearly half way across the State of Ohio completely naked in order to escape with his life after being surprised by hostile Indians at a hunting camp deep in Shawnee territory. We do not know that Lewis Cass once strode single-handedly into a menacing Indian encampment and ripped down and stomped upon the Union Jack which the Indians had erected to insult him during treaty negotiations. Or that they signed the treaty the next day, still astonished that a lone man would even attempt such an audacious act! But in those days, "in days of yore" as they are called, people didn't have to invent giants — for the giants roamed the wildernesses, founded our cities, established our culture and our folklore and sometimes gently, sometimes violently, passed into history.

One of the reasons we are so easily confounded by the events of today is that so few of us know anything about the events of yesterday. About those who came here before us, those who literally invented America. Since we don't know how America was invented, or by whom, we tend to believe whatever is said about it and about those who came before us. That our country, or our founders weren't anything exceptional, but in fact, something almost accidental, undoubtedly greedy, and most certainly nefarious. But no matter those nay-sayers of today, giants really did walk among us. Once upon a time our nation fairly teemed with them.

And one of those giants was a man named Edwin Denby.
This is his true and untold story.

John Lodwig
Dearborn
2019

"The lives of great men all remind us
We can make our lives sublime
And, departing, leave behind us
Footprints on the sands of time."

Longfellow

Preface

I grew up in Marion, Ohio, just four blocks away from 380 Mt. Vernon Avenue and the spacious, curving 19th Century front porch where Warren Gamaliel Harding campaigned in 1920 for the Presidency of the United States of America. He became our 29th President, overwhelmingly elected, widely beloved, fiscally sensible, and fiercely determined to return the nation to what he famously called "normalcy". He had a giant heart, and one could certainly say, a passionate one. That his heart led him into forbidden areas seems beyond doubt. That it led him to all the places his critics claim it did remains very much in question.

I was told, even before I was old enough to understand the nuances, that Warren Harding had somehow been a very flawed, and yes, a very "bad" man, and nothing like a President should be at all. I was taught to be ashamed of him and all that he stood for, and all that he "did". It was strongly inferred that it was just better to forget about Warren Harding, as though he had never lived there at 380 Mt.Vernon Avenue along my paper route, or worked so diligently to make something of the Marion Star, his beloved newspaper, or to make something of the rehabilitation of America after the devastating effects of World War I, and eight

17

years of the repressive, domineering, divisive, bullying and racist politics of his predecessor.

You see, he died in office — at almost the EXACT time that they were about to blow the lid off his Presidency. The bastard! And unfortunately for him, his wife Florence — equally maligned — died fifteen months later. And they had no children. The only family he left behind were small town Midwestern hicks. Nobodies. There was NO ONE to stand up for Warren Harding after he died, to defend his honor and his memory, —and no one did. The economy he rescued for us roared along for six more glorious years, and then when it all crashed, no one remembered Warren Harding, except when it came time to place him firmly at the bottom of the list of Presidents. Someone wrote a book — today we call it fake news — and five years later, someone else wrote another book quoting from the first book, and ten years later someone else wrote another book, and cited the first and the second piles of errors and falsehoods until we got to that great revelation, "The Shadow of Blooming Grove" (1968), and it turned out that ANYTHING at all could be written about Warren Harding, and it was, and it was printed, and then it became "fact", and then it became "the truth". Steven F. Hayward says "The harsh summary judgment of Harding reflects the massive ideological and historical bias of the mid-twentieth century, when this image of Harding took root as a result of a relentless onslaught of partisan and sensational criticism." (Steven F. Hayward, The Presidents, Part 2: from Wilson to Obama, p.58) If you don't believe that this is how easily it happened, read "The Strange Death of President Harding" by Gaston Means, 1930. And though it is still to this day occasionally cited as fact-based, and often quoted, it is virtually 100% the wild imagination of a life-long prevaricator. It is fake news. And if you still don't believe the bias under which "historians" write about Warren Harding, then try "The Bloviator: Sex, Drugs, Fraud, Suicide, Murder, Scandal, Adultery, Quackery, Corruption, Superstition and President Warren G. Harding" by Jim Yoakam, 2012.

In 1963 Robert K. Murray wrote his book, "The Harding Era: Warren G. Harding and His Administration", possibly the very first book ever written about our 29th President which was objective, and was not written with the intent to slander him. It was actually based on research and facts instead of rumor and malicious supposition. In no way a whitewash of Warren Harding, it was a refreshingly even-handed story of a human being who loved his country and attempted to serve his fellow man. Mr. Murray's book perhaps started a new era in writing the history of Warren Harding, for since, there have come several books about him far more balanced and fact-based than almost anything written about him in the first forty years after his death.

The honest truth about Warren Harding, as he would be the first to acknowledge, is that he was not perfect, and that he made mistakes. He had faults, and he was human. Just, in fact, like you and me. Not a single one of his critics could have withstood the relentless onslaught of slanderous destruction which was rained upon him, his wife, his lineage, his administration, his cabinet, and his dog. Nothing was sacred, and nothing escaped the vicious scythe of scurrilous defamation.

When Warren Harding died so suddenly in only the 29th month of his presidency, he robbed an awful lot of people of an awful lot of headlines. He wasn't there when they got the goods on him, and so they turned their vitriol and their fuming hatred upon those who were still there: his cabinet. The attacks centered primarily around the former Secretary of the Interior, Albert Baker Fall, who had already voluntarily resigned his position in the cabinet several months before to pursue other matters. When the attacks bore fruit, they next shifted toward Edwin Denby, the Secretary of the Navy who had appeared to have at least cooperated, if not colluded, with Fall. Though not a shred of evidence of any wrongdoing was ever presented against Edwin Denby, the attacks continued until he resigned under the threat to his party and his President. The attacks then shifted to Attorney General Harry Daugherty, who again, though he was tried, was never convicted of anything whatsoever. There were those in and around the cabinet who thought that the attacks would never stop, and would eventually engulf them all. However, after Daugherty left the cabinet and Coolidge won a resounding re-election in 1924, at least they seemed contained.

During the remainder of his life Edwin Denby shied away from any attempt to defend himself or his record, firmly, but naively, believing that history would vindicate him. Though under enormous pressure from his myriad friends to jump back into elected politics in any one of several guises, and though he was popular enough in Michigan to have been elected to any office he chose, he does not appear to have given any more than a studied glance at this possibility. He simply seemed to have no more stomach for the way the swamp worked. Almost certainly he expected to have many more years to ruminate on and rectify this and other inequities, but that option was not to be his. Though he served in this nation's armed forces in two different branches of service, the Navy and the Marine Corps, in two different wars, The Spanish American War, and World War I, though he was Secretary of the Navy, and though he gave the Navy a son who sacrificed his life in the World War Two Submarine Service, there has never been a naval ship named the USS Denby. There should be. Even still today, and proudly, there should be. There should be a U. S. Naval ship named after "the Seagoing Secretary" as the men themselves nicknamed him. And named, also, for his son, Edwin, Jr.

That is the primary reason for this book — to set the record, now one hundred years old, straight. An honorable, upright, noble human being such as Edwin Denby deserves no less than the truth.

Here it is.

Chapter One

Let us then be up and doing
With a heart for any fate,
Still achieving, still pursuing;
Learn to labor and to wait...

Longfellow

Giants Among Us

In March of 1812, just prior to the outbreak of the second war with Great Britain, a young entrepreneur named Hugh McGary, Jr. purchased a tract of land on a magnificent, sweeping oxbow of the Ohio River in the Indiana Territory and named it, prosaically, McGary's Landing. Within two years, hoping to attract more settlers to his fledgling community, he re-named it after one of the war's local boys made good: Robert Morgan Evans. Colonel Evans, originally from Virginia, was intelligent, diplomatic, and an all-around pleasing gentleman who had caught the eye of Major General William Henry Harrison and had been a member of the General's command at the two most distinguishing battles of his career: Tippecanoe and the Battle of the Thames. He had come home to get himself elected to the Indiana territorial legislature. He would buy land from McGary, settle for a time in his riverfront community, move away, serve as the Speaker of the Indiana House of Representatives among several other enterprises, and eventually return to the city by then and to this day known as, Evansville, Indiana.

While Evansville was expanding into a thriving metropolis of over 3200 souls, it got some wonderful news from the Indiana

Legislature which announced, in the 1830's, plans to build the longest canal network in the United States at that time, from Toledo, Ohio, all the way to the Ohio River at Evansville. The great Erie Canal had been completed in 1825, connecting New York City via the Hudson River to Albany and thence the 363 miles of the canal itself, all the way to Buffalo on the Great Lakes. It shortened the time of travel from the east coast to Detroit from three months to five and a half days. Indiana wanted in on this immense improvement in travel and boost to trade and settlement. The race to construct the future in the magnificent heartland of America was in full swing.

Because of some poor planning and execution, the proposed Wabash and Erie Canal, which looked so promising for Evansville's future in the 1830's, was not completed to the Crescent City until 1853. It was in that year on September 23 that the passenger packet Pennsylvania became the first boat to traverse the canal all the way from Lake Erie to Evansville. Unfortunately for canals, in that very year the first railroad to reach Evansville, the Evansville and Crawfordsville Railroad, was chartered, placing canals on the precipice of obsolescence. Though of significant importance to the towns through which it passed, achieving the dream of connecting the Great Lakes with the Mississippi River Valley would be left to the Iron Horse.

Another dream of slightly lesser perspective was also coming to fruition in June of 1853 when a young school teacher from Virginia named Charles Harvey Denby arrived in the little village on the oxbow. Born in Botetourt County, Virginia on June 16, 1830, Charles was the second son of Nathanial Denby and Sarah Jane Harvey. His paternal grandfather had emigrated from England, and his maternal grandfather, Matthew Harvey, was a Revolutionary War cavalry private in Captain Michael Rudolph's Company of Light Horse Harry Lee's Legion of Calvary. Eventually, Charles would have four brothers , John, Wythe, Edwin, and a second John born after the first one had died early, and one sister, Laura. He received his early education at the Tom Fox Academy in Hanover County, Virginia. Later he studied at the College Royale in Marseilles, France while accompanying his father, who had been appointed the first ever United States Consul to that city. Charles became fluent in French, and completed his education at Georgetown College in Washington, D. C., and the Virginia Military Institute where he graduated with high honors in 1850. After a short stint of teaching tactics in Selma, Alabama, at the Masonic University, young Denby, as many thousands of other Americans at this time, headed west to seek his fortune in the vastnesses of the great American Continent. He already had relatives in Kentucky, as well as an uncle, Dr. William McDowell, who lived in Evansville.

In the bustling river town on the Ohio twenty-three year old Charles, a strapping fellow over six feet tall, with movie-star good looks, got himself hired by Captain John B. Hall to edit his newly acquired Democrat newspaper, the Evansville Daily Enquirer. Young Charles worked for the paper for two years during the short period in American politics when the Whig Party was disintegrating and the Republican Party not yet formed. Sometimes called the period of "Knownothingism". But Charles, never known for indecisiveness, knew exactly what he wanted, and very soon he began studying law in the offices of Conrad Baker and Thomas Garvin.

Conrad Baker, originally from the not-yet-famous sleepy hamlet of Gettysburg, Pennsylvania, was a Whig who joined the newly formed Republican Party in 1854, and after active participation in the Civil War, became Lt. Governor and later Governor of Indiana. Re- elected in 1868 in the closest governor's race in Indiana history, his most difficult task in his second term was getting the ratification of the post-war amendments to the Constitution which banned slavery and gave the newly freed slaves the vote. The Democrats in the Indiana Legislature resigned en masse to deny a quorum for ratification, but the Republicans passed the amendments anyway. When the democrats retook the legislature in the next election, they voted to revoke the ratification of the two amendments, but the attempt failed, as the amendments had already been added to the Constitution by the

To This High Standard

Federal Government.

Thomas Garvin, Charles' law partner, was a graduate of the University of Michigan Law School, and became Charles Denby's lifelong friend. It would be said in later years that Charles Denby knew every good fishing hole along the "Belle Riviere" for miles in either direction, and that on more afternoons than could be counted, good friends Charles and Thomas could be seen slipping off along the riverbank with rods or shotguns. Young Charles, diligent, affable and quick to learn, was admitted to the bar in 1855. A Democrat, he entered politics in 1856, and served briefly as Surveyor of the Port of Evansville under President James Buchanan. He was elected from his county to the Indiana Legislature in 1857-8. While serving there, he met Martha Fitch who was visiting friends in Indianapolis. She was the eldest daughter of a Logansport, Indiana physician named Graham Newell Fitch who was soon to be elected to the United States Senate. They courted for two years and were wed in September, 1858, in the Trinity Episcopal Church in Logansport.

Although the Denby lineage was gallantly patriotic, that of his new wife would match it, and then some. Both Martha's great-great grandfather, Peletiah Fitch, and her great grandfather, Elisha Fitch, served with distinction in Webster's Regiment, New York Militia during the Revolution. Indeed, Elisha had the misfortune to be among those captured during British General Carleton's raid from Canada, and spent 18 months in a Canadian prison before escaping and making his way home. Martha's paternal grandfather, Frederick Fitch, served in the War of 1812 at age 28, fought at the battle of Queenstown, and lost his leg in the service of his country. Martha's father, Graham Newell Fitch married Harriet Valerie Satterlee in 1832, and began his medical practice in Logansport, Indiana in 1834. In 1836 and 1839 he was a member of the Indiana State House of Representatives. From 1849 to 1853 he was elected to the U. S. House of Representatives as a Democrat, and later he was elected to the U.S. Senate from 1857 to 1861 to fill a vacancy. In addition to his political achievements, Dr. Fitch also served as a professor of anatomy at the Rush Medical College in

24

Chicago, and also at the Indianapolis Medical College.

On Christmas Day, 1859, fifteen months after their marriage, the newlywed Charles Denbys of Evansville were blessed with their first child, a son whom they named after Martha's father, Graham. At the height of the "state's rights" controversy and the coming presidential race of 1860, the Whigs, Democrats, Knownothings, Republicans, Wide Awakes all boisterously campaigned, nominating no less than four candidates, with the result that on November 6, 1860, the rail-splitter from Illinois was thrust into the seat of power with 180 electoral votes out of 303. On March 4, 1861, Abraham Lincoln became our 16th President.

On April 12, 39 days later, Confederate forces fired on Fort Sumter in Charleston harbor, thus opening hostilities in the great conflict between the States. Charles Denby lost no time in raising a company of volunteer soldiers who guarded the powder magazine near Evansville. On September 12, 1861, Denby received his commission as Lieutenant Colonel of the 42nd Indiana Volunteer Infantry Regiment, and was later mustered in at that rank on October 10. Only a month later, on November 14, 1861, the Denbys were blessed with the second addition to their budding family, as Charles, Jr. was welcomed into the fold. Of all the Denby children, Charles Jr. would most closely follow in his father's footsteps.

On October 8, 1862 Union forces under Don Carlos Buell met the invasion forces of Braxton Bragg at a tiny Kentucky hamlet called Perryville. During the battle, Charles Denby was wounded in the lip, was struck by a mini ball which bruised his leg, had his coat ventilated with bullet holes and his horse shot from under him. The Union held the field by the next day, as Bragg faded away into Tennessee, securing the Sate of Kentucky for the North for the duration of the War. The fighting was so serious that the 42nd lost one third of its complement killed and wounded.

On October 21, 1862 Charles was rewarded by Governor Morton with command of the 80th Indiana Volunteer Regiment. While marching his men from Nashville to Murfreesboro, Tennessee, the Regiment passed by a home where several

Confederate women sat on the front porch waving Confederate flags and shouting, "hip hooray for Jeff Davis and the Southern Confederacy!" Commanding his men to halt, he pivoted them so abruptly to face the startled women that his own men thought he was going to order a volley. Instead he loudly called for them to join him in gallantly saluting the women for their bravery. (*"The Man Behind the Cigar", a talk given by Virginia Powell Parkinson at the Reitz Victorian Museum, Evansville, Indiana, November, 2008.)

On January 17, 1863 Charles resigned his commission in the Union Army with a surgeon's certificate of disability. At the same time that Charles Denby was serving his country and his State, his father-in-law, Graham Newell Fitch was also serving in the Union Army. At war's inception Fitch raised the 46th Regiment of Indiana Volunteer Infantry at Logansport for a three year enlistment, and served as its colonel from 1861 to 1862. While leading his men in 1862 he was thrown from his horse sustaining injuries which precluded his continued service. Graham Fitch would return to Logansport and continue his medical practice, living to the ripe old age of 82.

Meanwhile, in Evansville, Charles Harvey was getting back into his law practice and local Democrat politics. He also returned to his family-building duties, as his third child, this time a girl, was born on October 22, 1863. Named for her maternal grandmother, Harriett Ethel would be the first of Charles and Martha's three daughters, but the only one to survive childhood.

The Denbys fourth child, their second daughter named Mary was born in January 1866. Unfortunately, the child lived only a fortnight, succumbing to what was then described as 'congestive fever'. Wythe, named after one of Charles' younger brothers, was born to the Denbys on December 1, 1866.

Affairs of the Clan Denby would settle for a short period, until that fateful day, on February 18, 1870 when the next and most famous of the Denby children was to be born.

Chapter Two

"America! America! God shed His grace on thee!" from
"American the Beautiful"

Katherine Bates, Samuel Ward

The America of 1870

At the dawn of 1870, America was full of bustle and an almost explosive expansion. Still struggling to heal, it was at the same time bursting with hope. Only five short years had elapsed since Appomattox and the end of the great conflagration which had torn the country apart. Only five brief years during which our nation suffered its first Presidential assassination, followed by the torturous years of the overwhelmed Andrew Johnson presidency. Only seven months before, in the past decade, on May 10, 1869, the silver spike was driven into the railroad tie at Promontory, Utah, creating not only the transcontinental railroad, but the geographical completion of the umbilical cord of the American dream. Not only was the United States of America politically unified and whole once again after the war's devastation, but it was also now connected in a way that would help to drive the creation of the greatest economic force in the history of the planet. America had arrived, and by 1870, most of its citizens felt and knew it. A "manifest destiny" was reverberating throughout the land.

The previous year had seen the election of the most popular military hero since Andrew Jackson, the 21st President of the

United States, Ulysses S. Grant. Kansas, West Virginia, and Nevada had joined the Union during the war, Nebraska had been welcomed into the fold in 1867. Tennessee became the first confederate state to rejoin the Union in 1866, followed Louisiana, Arkansas, Alabama, Florida, and the Carolinas in 1868. Virginia, Mississippi and Texas would all be readmitted by March 30, 1870, and Georgia would come back last on July 15. As the Union had been before the conflagration, so it was now again: whole, but by no means complete, nor unified. Not yet.

In January of this great year 1870, in New York City, work was begun on one of the most iconic of all structures in the nation: the Brooklyn Bridge. In the world of that year there were no telephones, no lightbulbs to create artificial light, no phonograph. Women wore bustles which trailed around behind them to keep the hem of their floor-length skirts from dragging on the ground. The "old west" was still in its infancy as a young Constable named Wyatt Earp was married in January and quickly became a widower when his new wife died shortly after of typhoid fever. Henry McCarty, sometimes known as William Bonney, but immortalized for all time as "Billy the Kid" was five years away from his first arrest, and a 33-year-old sheriff named James Butler Hickok overpowered two 7th US Cavalrymen who had jumped him in a saloon, killing one and shooting the other in the knee. He was not re-elected as Sheriff of Hays, Kansas. It was also during this year that Crazy Horse, the Oglala Lakota, ran off with the wife of another brave and was shot in the face for his theft, while Sitting Bull kept himself busy harassing wagon trains and area forts. The Great Sioux Wars and the folly of George Armstrong Custer were still six years in the future.

Railroads were the number one industry of the burgeoning nation, and during the year 1870 a full 54 new ones were to be established. The "block signal system" was just coming into use on the nation's nearly 53,000 miles of track, a way to safely space trains to avoid collisions. The railroad strikes, which would plague the nation on and off for many decades to come, were just beginning. Standard time was not agreed upon by the railroads for several years, so in the world of 1870 wherever you stood was "standard" time. Within twenty years railroad mileage would soar by 2 1/2 times and continue to expand even further for another three decades after that. Cornelius Vanderbilt consolidated two of his railroad lines into the world-famous New York Central and Hudson River Railroad, one of the first conglomerates in United States' history. John Edgar Thomson, who built the legendary Pennsylvania Railroad into the largest business enterprise in the world, was nearing the end of his illustrious twenty-two-year career as its leader. The first railroad car to travel from the Pacific to the Atlantic arrived in New York City on July 24, 1870.

John D. Rockefeller established the Standard Oil Company in Cleveland, Ohio en route to becoming the richest man who ever lived. Thomas Nast drew his first political cartoon depicting the Democrat Party as a donkey ("A Live Jackass Kicking a Dead Lion") which was published in Harper's Weekly Magazine. Around the nation many innovations were beginning to accelerate the pace of change. The U. S. Army established the first weather bureau on February 9, and on November 1st, issued its first forecast. The fireman's pole was invented in Chicago, Illinois only one year before that city would be engulfed in the catastrophic conflagration which nearly consumed it. Postage for a first-class letter was two cents.

The United States Census of 1870 was the ninth census in the nation's history, and the first one to provide detailed information about African Americans. The population was tabulated as 38,555,983 individuals, a 22 percent increase over 1860. New York City was the most populous in the Union with yet less than one million people, while Evansville, Indiana came in at 60th with a population of 21,830, barely edging out Atlanta, Georgia by 41 souls. The Fifteenth Amendment to the United States Constitution prohibiting the denial of the right to vote based on race was ratified on February 3 with the vote of the State of Iowa, and was certified by the Secretary of State, Hamilton Fish on March 30th. The United States Department of Justice was created in June, as was the Office of the Solicitor General. Congress, in the heat of the summer of this illustrious year, on June 28, passed the law which made Christmas a federal holiday. On February 23, Hiram Rhodes Revels, a minister, a politician, a college administrator, and a Republican, was elected to the United States Senate from the State of Mississippi, the first African American to serve in the United States Congress, and thus became one of only two African American men to serve in that body until 1967, and the only African American man to serve from a southern state until Tim Scott of South Carolina in 2011.

Because of the Civil War the national debt was still as high in 1870 as it would be until the great surge caused by World War II, nearly seventy years into the future. Old Faithful was discovered and named in September, and only one year later Congress would create the first national park in the United States, Yellowstone National Park, which is widely believed to be the first national park in the world. One month later, in Lexington, Virginia, the indomitable Robert Edward Lee, General of the Army of the Potomac of the Confederate States of America, died at the age of 63. In one of history's minor ironies, his famous and faithful horse, Traveller, outlived him by several months.

In the wider world of that year infanticide was first banned in India. The circle of the sun, later to become the terror of the pacific, was adopted as the national flag of the merchant ships of Japan. Queen Victoria of Great Britain was in the 33rd year of her reign with a mere 31 years to go. The Franco-Prussian War broke out in July on the continent, lasting ten months, bringing the Third Republic into being in France and costing Napoleon III his crown and his country. On September 20, with the fall of Rome, the unification of the modern state of Italy became complete. The Papal States ceased to exist, thus ending eleven centuries of Papal temporal power. On December 30, the Prime Minister of Spain, Juan Prim, was assassinated, thus introducing a constitutional monarchy to the country of Spain. On June 9, arguably the greatest novelist of all time, Charles Dickens, died at Gad's Hill Place in Kent, and on December 5, perhaps France's greatest raconteur, Alexandre Dumas pere, joined him. John Singer Sergeant, Maxfield

Parrish, John Ruskin, John Atkinson Grimshaw were all active artists. Rimsky-Korsakov, Borodin, Franz Liszt, Tchaikovsky, Brahms and Verdi were all composers. The great Richard Wagner was knee deep in "The Ring of the Nibelung", whose parts were published in 1869, 1870, 1871, and 1876. War and Peace from Tolstoy debuted in 1869, and "The Idiot" that same year from Fyodor Dostoyevsky. In 1870 readers would thrill to the latest offering of Jules Verne (still being re-created in motion pictures to this day), "Twenty Thousand Leagues Under the Sea", while Lewis Carroll gave the world the second installment of Alice's adventures in "Through the Looking Glass."

The Charles Denbys of Evansville, not finished doing their part to bring additional settlers to the Indiana Territory, added their fifth child, the fourth boy, on Friday, February 18 and named him after another one of Charles' brothers, Edwin. In a family of illustrious and cultured, educated and accomplished, patriots and public servants, Edwin would become the best known, and for many reasons. He was also the most loving and giving of the Denby children, and for as long as he lived would not fail to aid his siblings in any way that he could. In a March 11, 1870, letter to distant cousin Captain David E. Moore in Lexington, Virginia, the proud papa wrote two pages of newsy news, mentioning that he had hired a young graduate of Michigan Law School, Daniel B. Kumler, and that his brother Ned was planning an April wedding in Philadelphia, and then casually disclosing on page three: "I had another boy who arrived three weeks ago. That makes four boys for me. I am hesitating about a name. We already have Graham, Charles and Wythe. There are so many Harveys that I am deterred from that and think that I will call him Edwin, and hope that my imagination will never be challenged in this regard again, as I have now a striking resemblance to the old woman who lived in a shoe." (Box #1 ED Jr. Papers, DPL) Such were the mores of the time that he did not feel it necessary to remember that family creation was a joint effort, or that his wife had had decidedly the most strenuous part of the contribution to the affair. Nor did he feel it necessary to mention that he also had had a daughter in his family for seven years. Boys mattered, since men oversaw everything, and all was exceedingly well in Charles Harvey Denby's domestic life.

A third daughter, Jessica, arrived in 1872, and unfortunately, did not survive the year. Then, in 1878, the Denbys would produce the final member of the family, their fifth son. Despite his earlier pronouncement, Charles would be challenged once again to produce a boy's name, and would christen the newborn Thomas Garvin, after his law partner and mentor. The Denbys did not know it in 1878, but Garvin, as he was to be called, would become the typical "baby" of the family, a person who would spend most of his life trying to find his "niche", a task which had come so much easier for his older siblings, and yet would largely elude him. He rejected the law and diplomacy as careers, the first choice of his father and three of his older brothers.

The Denby Family of Evansville was now complete. Charles and Martha had produced a duplicate of the family brought into the world by Charles' parents: five sons and one daughter. By 1878, with the birth of their last child, the Colonel had lived in Evansville for twenty-five years. He was recognized as a pillar of the bar, President of St. Paul's Episcopal Missionary Society, member of the upper echelon of the town's elite. In 1873 Charles was one of a committee of five appointed by the Evansville Bar to petition the County Commissioners of Vanderburgh County to replace the old courthouse with a newer and more modern building. The same committee was then tasked by the Commissioners to locate a site for the new courthouse, which was completed in 1890 and occupied in early 1891. In the late 1870's he was named as a trustee of the newly formed and still operating Willard Library, founded, and funded by Mr. Willard Carpenter, a town benefactor and staunch believer in free libraries. The Willard stands to this day as a testament to the foresightedness of all those who were involved with its inception. On November 10, 1878, the Evansville Daily Journal noted that a good-sized group of prominent men met in the St. George Hotel in Evansville to form a 'dancing club'. Twelve 'receptions' were envisioned to take place at the St. George during the coming year, and Charles Denby was elected as their President. It appears there was nothing he could not accomplish.

Charles' next to youngest son would have noticed all of this, every one of the beloved Colonel's posts, honors, and positions in his profession and in society, and he would one day emulate nearly every step of the Colonel's civic life. The newspapers from those days chronicle several of the Colonel's hunting and shooting trips, sometimes with different members of his family, sometimes with Tom Garvin, his almost constant companion, or others from the legal/ judicial group of the town. Once again, young Ned would take notice, and one day would follow these steps as well, joining more than one prestigious hunting and fishing club, and spending his fair share of time at these same manly sporting pursuits.

It seems that at some point in 1878 Evansville's designation as a "port city" had come under review in Washington, D. C., and appeared in some jeopardy. A two-man committee from Evansville consisting of General James M. Shackelford (the same Union General Shackelford who put an end to Morgan's raid into Ohio at the Battle of Salineville on July 26, 1863) and Colonel Charles Denby were immediately dispatched to the capital to work with Indiana Senators Voorhees and McDonald, as well as the Congressman from their district, Hon. Binoni Fuller. On April 19 the Senate confirmed J. C. Jewell as the Surveyor of the Port, thus assuring Evansville's distinction as a port of entry for the time being. In addition, the Colonel and General Shackelford met with Rutherford B. Hayes' Secretary of War to argue for the distinction of having Evansville made a signal service station. These stations, along the coastlands and on important rivers, were early governmental attempts to create a weather forecasting system, as well as aid stations for those in waterborne distress. By this time there was a teeming traffic of riverboats, both passenger and freight, which plied the giant river highways of the central states and relied upon information from the ports about conditions on their section of the river. The Belle Riviere was a constantly moving and ever-changing highway which had to be always monitored for commercial success and safety. Though the Evansville delegation was unsuccessful at its second objective, it was hopefully reported that only a small increase in the national budget would be needed to affect the goal.

In early May, 1880, several of the town fathers suddenly realized that it was time to begin preparations for what was becoming an ever-larger annual holiday. Decoration Day, as it was being called, had been celebrated in certain southern states for some years, and a few northern states more recently, but two years before, in 1868, General John A. Logan, the Commander-in-Chief of the Grand Army of the Republic had called for a National Decoration Day to be fixed on May 30 each year. Some believed that May 30 had been selected since no other holiday fell near that date. Others decided it would be a good time to decorate soldiers' graves because abundant varieties of flora would be available. At an early organizational meeting in Evansville it was carried that Colonel Charles Denby would be the Grand Marshall for the parade, and would be invited to select as many ex-enlisted men as he felt necessary for his assistant marshals. An unexpected controversy erupted in early meetings over the propriety of celebrating a national holiday on Sunday, and the discussions became so polarized as to jeopardize the solemn ceremonies. The Christian population of Evansville, decidedly the majority, seemed dead set against the Sunday celebration, while the workers and those who sympathized with them, noted that Saturday being a day of work for many of its citizens, would preclude their taking part in the festivities. Finally, in an unusually sudden move toward amity, Sunday was declared acceptable.

A temporary speaker's stand was erected in Oak Hill Cemetery, and Charles published his list of twenty-four young men who would act as assistant marshals, and, the order of the parade. There would be two city bands, Warren's Crescent City Band, and Schreiber's Band, the Evansville Rifles, the local Turnerverein (a German-American gymnastic club), the Hibernian Society, separate contingents of Civil War and Mexican War Vets, the City Police, City Council and other city officials, The Evansville

Light Guard, the Ancient Order of United Workingmen, the International Organization of Odd Fellows, the Crescent City Artillery, and bringing up the rear, the Evansville Fire Department sporting their popular, recognizable bright red shirts. At the cemetery gate, however, the bulk of the firefighters would return to their station houses leaving only a token presence to attend the ceremonies, it being felt that it would never do to have the entire force so out of place in case of an emergency. Two local railroads operated excursion trains on that day to bring people into town from the surrounding villages; riverboats brought in even more from nearby towns along the river. The Evansville and Terre Haute Railroad made five trips with a nine-car train from the E. & T. H. Depot in town to Oak Hill.

At promptly two in the afternoon, a mounted Colonel Charles, with aides, led off the parade and hundreds of citizens followed its progress through town toward the cemetery. The Journal described the scene for posterity: "The sidewalks on both sides of Main Street, from First Street for several squares beyond the E.& T. H. Depot were densely packed with spectators, of both sexes and all ages and classes. They crowded against the houses and along the curbstone, leaving a small pathway for the crowding throng that pressed its way through en route to the cemetery, and the procession thus marched through a living lane of human beings." Along the route, the assistant marshals were posted to maintain a dignified order, and when the throng had gathered at the temporary speaker's platform at the highest point of the cemetery, it was estimated that seven to ten thousand people had gathered to hear the oration of General James Shackelford. "The skies were never brighter, the air balmier, nor the sward and foliage greener. All nature seemed to smile approvingly upon the occasion," said the Journal. In a pleasant twist of fate that could, and probably was, interpreted in different ways, the weather on the previous day had been almost gale-force rains and wind. Ceremonies all over the Midwest which had been stubbornly and piously held on Saturday had been wiped out, postponed, or moved indoors into whatever space at hand might accommodate.

Speaking of the children who would, as the last official act of the day, assist in the spreading of the flowers throughout the hallowed graves, General Shackelford said

"The willing little hands that gather those offerings are taught to emulate the courage and patriotism of the dead. We are giving them a lesson that may someday be useful to their country. We are teaching them what they will teach their children and their children's children, and thus keep the fires of liberty burning down the ages on the vestal altars of young and innocent hearts. It is a sacred task that we perform today, and year after year it will recur till generations yet unborn shall feel its influence and gather from it a purer patriotism and a more earnest devotion to liberty and country." (EDJ 5-31-80) 1880

A young boy among this great throng, tall for his ten years of age, the fifth child of the man on the great horse who had led that solemn procession to the sacred ground of Oak Hill Cemetery, would never forget what he had been taught that very day. That liberty made America great; that it cost a very great price, indeed, to establish, to preserve and protect that liberty; that real, true, proud Americans would always stand ready to pay that ultimate price; and that those left, those spared, those protected, should NEVER forget. WOULD never forget.

It defined him.

1880, when Ned Denby was an inquisitive and growing young fellow, was a Presidential election year. The Charles Denby household of Evansville was a Democrat enclave of the first magnitude, the Democrat party at that time being popularly referred to, mostly by themselves, as "the Democracy." It was a point of pride. However, the fortunes of the democrats on the national stage had been less than stellar, and for quite some time.

There were some sound reasons why.

The entire South was controlled 100% by the "Democracy" before, during the Civil War, and for generations afterward. The simple fact of the matter is that "the Democracy" was not much trusted on the national level for years after the Civil War and did almost nothing to improve that trust. It is so little a theme in the politics of today that almost no American knows that at every turn, every election, every event, and for decades it was "the Democracy" which thwarted and obstructed the progress of liberty, and the principle of equality. During the sixty-two years from the Presidency of the first Republican, Abraham Lincoln, to the greatest Democrat, FDR, "the Democracy" held the White House a mere 3 times: during the separated terms of Grover Cleveland, and during the war-torn eight years of Woodrow Wilson.

In 1876, the first year that Charles participated in a National Convention, "the Democracy" ran Samuel J. Tilden, the Governor of New York against the Ohio Republican Governor, Rutherford B. Hayes. The election was so close that its outcome came down to the last twenty electoral votes which were in dispute from the states of Florida, South Carolina, Louisiana, and one elector from Oregon who had been disqualified. The flak rained down for two whole months until President Grant agreed to submit the question to a bipartisan Electoral Commission which it was agreed would consist of 5 Representatives, 5 Senators, and 5 Supreme Court Justices. This commission was equally balanced with seven Republicans, seven Democrats and one Independent Supreme Court Justice, David Davis, who was widely respected and acceptable to both parties. But once again the applecart got tipped over when the Illinois Democratic Legislature promptly elected Justice Davis as a Senator from Illinois, hoping thus to tip the numerical balance to "the Democracy." Then, to complicate matters further, David Davis refused to sit on the commission, necessitating another selection from the Supreme Court. As all the remaining Justices were Republicans, the most widely believed evenhanded of them, Joseph P. Bradley, was selected. It cannot come as a surprise that all twenty contested electoral votes went to Hayes. But now, with a clear majority, "the Democracy" was still unwilling to accept him as the elected President, and it was not until the "Compromise of 1877" was hammered out behind closed doors that the election finally was concluded. The Compromise called for five conditions to be met, only two of which were: 1) All remaining Federal troops were pulled out of the South which allowed the southern Democrats to once again disenfranchise whom they pleased for the next eighty years, and 2) Hayes appointed a southern Democrat to his cabinet. So, in order to keep the peace, the Democrats insisted upon the Jim Crow South, and the Republicans, hardly any better, took the White House, and acquiesced.

After Hayes' vehemently contested election, it was not surprising that "the Democracy" would spend the next four years claiming his Presidency was stolen, calling him 'Rutherfraud' or 'His Fraudulency'. However, Rutherfraud did them one favor and remained true to his word that he would serve only one term, and therefore threw the race wide open again in 1880 for all comers. It appeared that John Sherman, brother of the famous Civil War General, would get the Republican nomination, but in a year of contentious factions within the Republican party, the dark horse James Garfield was dragged to the fore on the 36th ballot. A Civil War general, he faced another Civil War general, Winfield Scott Hancock, one of the heroes of Gettysburg. We know that James Garfield won by the slimmest of popular vote counts, though by a comfortable margin in the electoral college, and became the 20th President of the United States, and that his Presidency lasted only six months and fifteen days, when he was cut down by the second assassin to overrule the will of the American people. Succeeded by his Vice President, Chester A. Arthur, the nation had four more years of Republican administration.

Once again, however, as Hayes before him, Arthur let it be known that he did not seek his party's nomination for a second term due to his poor health. He would, indeed, die within twenty months of leaving office at the young age of 57. One thing accomplished during his single term of office, however, was the passage of the Chinese Exclusion Act of 1882, a bill he vetoed the first time it passed, and nearly vetoed again when it had been amended. It is still the only immigration ban ever passed by Congress against a single nation. We will look at it again in the following chapter.

In 1884 Charles Denby was once again selected as a delegate from his State to participate in the national Democratic Party's convention in Chicago. The convention, without much ado, selected Grover Cleveland, the popular and successful governor of the State of New York to head its party's ticket in the upcoming election. Thomas A. Hendricks, a long time Indiana Democrat well known to Charles Denby was selected as Cleveland's running mate. They were pitted against a weak Republican ticket consisting of James G. Blaine of Maine and his running mate John A. Logan of Illinois. Blaine was controversial in his own party, and a faction of them split and supported Cleveland. It was the first crack in the Republican Presidential dominance since Abraham Lincoln, and the Democrats were overjoyed at their success. With a Hoosier cheerleader as the Vice President, and most of the rest of the State's Democrats rallying to his cause, it became a foregone conclusion that Charles Denby would be rewarded by the new administration in some significant way.

At noon, on May 29, 1885, the telegram arrived in his Evansville home from the State Department in Washington, D. C. Would Charles be interested in taking a little trip abroad?

Chapter Three

"Experience is a comb which nature gives us when we are bald."

Chinese proverb

Adventures in China

The Qing (pronounced 'ching', meaning 'pure') Dynasty, the last Imperial Dynasty in Chinese history, was established in stages from 1636 to 1683, reached its zenith in the late 18th Century, and was in ever-increasing decay by the time of the Opium Wars in the middle of the 19th. Europe had become eager for Chinese silks and porcelain, but the British were voracious for the number one export of China: tea leaves. At the height of this trade in 1867, the Chinese supplied 90% of the tea consumed by the Western world. (Chang, p. 126) The Chinese, who passed laws to keep the "barbarians" at bay, who allowed only the single trading port of Canton, also insisted that the British pay for Chinese exports in silver, thus quickly putting in jeopardy nearly the entire silver supply of the British Empire. Familiar to current American ears, an alarming trade imbalance quickly imperiled Great Britain, and the British cast about for the swiftest way to reverse it. They fell upon the nefarious plan to sell cheap, but huge, quantities of opium to local middlemen traders, who in turn sold it on the Chinese mainland in exchange for payment in silver. This clever but unscrupulous strategy now reversed the direction of the silver stream and turned a large swath of the Chinese population into

drug addicts. It could not be allowed to go on, and when Chinese
Imperial officials took steps to alter the situation, they suddenly
found themselves peering down the barrel of a British naval
gun. A whole fleet of them, in fact. The Chinese, credited with
inventing gunpowder, were still using it for firecrackers, while
the British had developed it into a far more lethal and persuasive
tool of commerce and conquest.

The result of the First Opium War (1842), China's initial military
clash with the West and a resounding and humiliating defeat,
was the opening of four additional Chinese ports to the hated
barbarian trade, millions of dollars of reparations (in more silver),
and the 99-year lease of what would become the unbelievably
lucrative Island of Hong Kong as a British trading colony. But
the British weren't even half satisfied with this windfall. Having
sanctified the notion of "fair play", they promptly proceeded to
use any and every means but "fair" to further the growth and
security of their own hallowed Empire. They moped along for the
next several years, spoiling for any opportunity to humiliate the
Chinese Dragon with yet another bloody nose. It came in the form
of a minor incident with a British-flagged ship called the Arrow
in 1856. Because of the unfortunate distraction of the catastrophic
Mutiny on the Sub-continent, the British didn't get around to
slapping the Chinese Dragon's snout until 1858. However, when
they did commence hostilities, they had the help of the French,
the Russians and the Stars and Stripes. And, as if the Imperial
Government of the Manchu did not already have enough on its
plate, it was at this time, from 1850 onwards, that they were also
dealing with the Taiping Rebellion, which was every bit as serious
a threat to the ruling Manchu as the barbarian invaders. Owing
to these rebel incursions, by 1854 the Imperial Government was
no longer able to collect maritime duties in the Shanghai area and
was facing the loss of a great deal of income. The solution was to
delegate authority to the French, British and American consuls to
collect the Chinese taxes. While the French and Americans soon
dropped out of this complex and thankless arrangement, the
British forged stolidly ahead.

The Imperial Maritime Customs Service (IMCS), created in 1854, was a function of the Chinese Government headquartered at Peking. However, the Inspector General of the service and nearly all its top functionaries were foreigners. The first Inspector General of the Service, Horatio Nelson Lay, also served on the British delegation to the peace treaty which concluded the Second Opium War and was instrumental in browbeating the Chinese into signing a treaty so humiliating that the Qing negotiator was afterward sentenced to death and was allowed to commit suicide for his efforts.

With the signing of the Convention of Peking in 1860 to end the Second Opium War, the drug trade was made legal, China paid Great Britain and France 8 million taels each in indemnity, British ships were allowed to carry indentured Chinese to the Americas in something euphemistically called "the coolie trade", the Kowloon District was added to the British colony of Hong Kong, Tianjin (Tientsin) became yet another trade port, and in an almost inconceivably hypocritical turn of events, freedom of religion was forced upon the Chinese for the first time. So Christians were granted full civil rights, including the right to own property, and the right to evangelize, while the British were free to enslave such Chinese as they desired by kidnapping or drug addiction. As we shall repeatedly see throughout this book, there is nothing new under the sun, and the politics and the greed of today has not one step on the sins of our great-great grandfathers.

In 1863 the imperious Horatio Lay was fired by the Chinese Government in a dispute over naval vessels which China had attempted to purchase from Great Britain. The Chinese next asked a twenty-eight year old British civil servant then working in Chinese Customs to become the second Inspector General of the IMCS.

Born in February, 1835, in Portadown, Northern Ireland, about 24 miles southwest of Belfast, Robert Hart came into a family of twelve children. After a slow start in school, he became a standout student, so much so that when the British Foreign Office offered a post in the consular service in China to three Irish colleges, after

Hart applied for it, it was granted to him without examination over 36 rival applicants. (Bredon, p.8). Hart arrived in China in 1854, first serving in the legation at Ningpo and being made Acting Consul in 1857 when his boss was suspended because of a dispute with the Portuguese. Hart was still in Ningpo during the massacre in June 1857 when the Portuguese Consulate was sacked. It was to be only the first of many dangerous, often life-threatening episodes in the long career ahead of him in this strange and violent country. Conditions in China were frequently unstable, and when they were not, it seems that one nation or another was trying hard to stir them up.

Hart was next transferred to Canton in 1858 where he worked under Sir Harry Parkes, the man who almost single-handedly started the Second Opium War. He learned a great deal about the consular service and China by traveling about with Parkes for some months. In May of 1859, at the invitation of the Chinese government, Hart resigned his post in the consular service so that, with the permission of the British Government, he could enter the employ of the Imperial Maritime Customs Service. He would be employed by the Chinese Government in this service for the remainder of his life.

Hart was universally recognized by the Chinese and Europeans alike as a man of scrupulous honesty and integrity. He became the most energetic, intelligent, patient and creative mind in the history of the IMCS. "In five years," Jung Chang reports in her "Empress Dowager Cixi", it [the IMCS run by Robert Hart] delivered to Beijing duties of well over 32 million taels. The indemnities to Britain and France [for the Second Opium War] were paid out of the Customs revenue and were completely paid off by mid-1866, with minimal pain to the country at large." (Ibid. p.64) He assisted the Chinese Imperial Government, not only in the collection of customs duties, but with internal taxes, with setting up a postal service, as well as establishing a series of lighthouses along her coast to aid in navigation. He also helped to establish schools to train Chinese diplomats, and encouraged the Chinese to send representation to world trade expositions, even leading the delegation himself upon occasion. When Hart became IG there were only a handful of customs offices in China, and when he retired, there were 38 stations on the mainland, 2 in Taiwan and 3 in Korea, including some internal stations on the Pearl and Yangtze rivers. For forty-five years, Robert Hart became one of the most decorated servants of the British Empire, receiving four hereditary titles, fifteen orders of knighthood, and many other accolades, not only from Great Britain and China, but from Sweden, Austria-Hungary, France, the United States, Netherlands, Prussia, Japan, Portugal, Russia, Norway and the Holy See. He became so powerful within China that when the British Foreign office asked him to become Britain's Minister Plenipotentiary at Peking in 1883, after four months of deliberation he concluded that it would be a step down for him. He managed the careers of thousands of young men who came from literally all over the world to serve in the IMCS. A prolific writer, he "once wrote a famous paper called "Pang Kwan Lun" (What a Bystander Says), full of useful criticism and suggestions on Chinese affairs. Some were followed, others were not, but he had the satisfaction of hearing the Empress Dowager Cixi herself—when she received him in audience in 1902 — say that she regretted more of his advice had not been taken, subsequent events having proved how sound and useful it all was." (ibid.p.43-44) Charles Denby described "the great service which has been at once the most potent civilizing agency in the Empire, and upon more than one occasion the strongest prop of a tottering dynasty." (Denby; China and Her People, p116) In an era that the Chinese still refer to as the "Century of Humiliation", Hart was without question and at all times the loyal friend of the Chinese, while remaining a true son of the British Empire.

No discussion of the China of this era could be complete without an introduction to the last and perhaps the greatest of Chinese rulers who never sat upon the Imperial Throne: the famous Empress Dowager Cixi (also spelled Tzu Hsi, meaning kindly and joyous). (Jung Chang, p 3) Nine months after the birth of Robert Hart in Ireland, Cixi was born in Peking in November, 1835, to a minor government official. At the age of sixteen she was selected from among a group of Imperial concubines to take up residence at the Forbidden City, and on April 27, 1856 gave birth to Zaichun, the Xianfeng Emperor's only surviving son. When Xianfeng passed away in 1861, Cixi became co-regent with the dead Emperor's widow on behalf of the young emperor. But from this time on and until her death in 1908, it was Cixi who ruled China from behind the scenes. Interestingly, in 1861, at almost the same time that Cixi was coming to power, Robert Hart was gaining in stature and making a name for himself. Though she would share power initially with the Xianfeng Emperor's widow, and later with her son, and still later with an adopted son, it was primarily the iron-willed Cixi who ran the country. She acknowledged during her life that she had made many mistakes, but she was just humble enough and certainly intelligent enough to learn greatly from them. While ruling from behind the scenes, literally holding audiences behind screens and curtains through much of her rein, and having to deal almost exclusively with men in a predominantly male environment, she would drag China almost kicking and screaming into the modern world.

"Under her leadership the country began to acquire virtually all the attributes of a modern state: railways, electricity, telegraph, telephone, Western medicine, a modern-style army and navy, and modern ways of conducting foreign trade and diplomacy. The restrictive millennium-old educational system was discarded and replaced by Western-style schools and universities. The press blossomed, enjoying a freedom that was unprecedented and arguably unsurpassed since. She unlocked the door to political participation: for the first time in China's long history, people were to become 'citizens'. It was Cixi who championed women's liberation in a culture that had for centuries imposed foot-binding on its female population - a practice to which she put an end." (Jung Chang, p371)

Because she did not write the history of her reign, others who followed her and some who opposed her, were free to limit the credit she was given, often resorting to disparaging her or discounting her completely. It was in April, 1908 when Sir Robert

Hart, covered in glory and titles, took his leave of China and returned to Ireland. He would formally retire in 1910, and die from a bout with pneumonia at the age of 76, in 1911. The Empress Dowager, knowing that she was in failing health, appears to have poisoned the Guangxi Emperor, her adopted son, some speculate because she knew he was weak-willed and feared that he would wreck her life's work which was to modernize and Westernize her beloved backward empire. She was deathly fearful that he would fall under the influence of the unscrupulous Japanese, who had already humiliated China in 1894, and relentlessly pursued their goal of complete hegemony over the Celestial Empire all the way to their defeat beneath the mushroom clouds of 1945. Cixi died one day after her son, on November 15, 1908, at the age of 72, and less than seven months after Sir Robert Hart had departed China for the last time. Thus two of the giants of the last half of 19th Century China passed from the Chinese Imperial scene.

One further legendary giant from this time and place was Charles George Gordon, best known to the swashbuckling history he helped to create as "Chinese" Gordon. Young Gordon fought in the Crimea at age 22, and when given tamer duties after that war, begged the British War Office to send him anywhere in the world where there was fighting. He arrived in China in 1860, at the ripe old age of twenty-seven, the old man to Hart and Cixi who were each a mere twenty-five. Hart was about to embark upon his life's career, and Cixi was beginning to consolidate her power behind the throne. Gordon was put in charge of a small Chinese army which he led successfully against the Taiping Rebellion, largely unheard of in the West because it took place entirely within the forbidden kingdom, "it turned out to be the bloodiest civil war in human history." (Asher, Khartoum, p. 71). Between 20 and 30 million Chinese lost their lives in this civil war, while Chinese Gordon and his "Ever Victorious Army" slashed their way through 33 straight battles to the successful conclusion of the war and the salvation of the Qing Dynasty itself. The Chinese Government was giddy with gratitude and British society lionized the dashing, quixotic Gordon, while his name became synonymous around the world with dangerous glory. His military prowess and sagacity would add fifty years to the Manchu rule of China. He refused monetary reward from the Qing and also from the merchants of Shanghai, and a journalist of the time reported that he was "a brave man who acted with humanity in an otherwise ghastly conflict, standing out from the other mercenaries, adventurers and cut-throats in wanting almost nothing for himself." His military bravado and overdrawn sense of the heroic, however, would bring him an early grave just days shy of his 53rd birthday in Khartoum, Sudan.

Meanwhile, in the security of peaceful Evansville, Indiana, Charles Denby busied himself with his law firm and working at the State level in Indiana politics for the Democratic Party. His eldest son, Graham, followed him into the legal profession, also becoming a practicing attorney. After a brief and unsuccessful attempt to forge out on his own in Seattle, Washington, he returned to Evansville where he again hung out his shingle. Graham married Olga Caroline Reis, daughter of a wealthy Evansville family, on September 27, 1900, had three daughters and would spend the balance of his entire career in Evansville. Charles Jr. went to Princeton University, matriculating in 1882. In 1883 he became secretary to the Evansville Metropolitan Police Commissioners, and secretary of the police trust fund. At the same time he was studying law in his father's practice. Wythe, Hattie, Edwin and Garvin attended the public schools of Evansville, although Hattie would later be sent to the Helmuth Ladies College in London, Ontario.

Charles Sr. became a delegate to the 1876 Democratic National Convention, and again in 1884 where he did his best to assist in the nomination, and subsequent election of the 22nd President of the United States, Grover Cleveland. At noon, on May 29, 1885, as a reward for his untiring efforts on behalf of the grateful new President, Charles received a telegram from Assistant Secretary of State James D. Porter informing him that he had been appointed Envoy Extraordinary and Minister Plenipotentiary to the court of the Celestial Empire of the Manchu. Just as he had accompanied his own father to a diplomatic assignment overseas to Marseilles, France in an earlier time, so now three of his sons, Charles, Jr., Edwin and Garvin, and his daughter Hattie, would accompany him and Martha to China. Charles would be paid a salary of $12,000 per year, or just over $317,000 in today's currency.

In his book "China and Her People" p.103, Charles Denby claimed that "except the Embassy to England, that of China is and has been, the most important of all our foreign missions." Official representation of the United States to China began in 1843 with the first United States' Commissioner, Caleb Cushing, of whom the Colonel wrote "that America has produced no brighter intellect or accomplished scholar than Caleb Cushing." Eleven commissioners or Ministers would follow, including the notable Ansom Burlingame, appointed by Abraham Lincoln as Minister in 1861, who was the first minister from any western power to insist upon fairer treatment of the Chinese in treaty negotiations. His evenhandedness was so appreciated by the Qing Dynasty that at the close of his service to the U.S. government, the Chinese appointed him as minister plenipotentiary to head a delegation to the western powers on their behalf. The list also included James B. Angell, who took leave from his position as President of the University of Michigan. So Charles Denby would take his place as the thirteenth representative of the United States to the Celestial Empire. Interestingly, he was the second Ambassadorial 'son' of Evansville currently serving in a foreign post. John Watson Foster was Ambassador to Spain, after having already served as Ambassador to Russia and Mexico. He would later become Secretary of State during the last few months of the Presidency of Benjamin Harrison, and still later he would grandfather the future Secretary of State John Foster Dulles, and his brother Allen, the first civilian Director of Central Intelligence. Of further note, on the same day the Evansville Courier reported the appointment of Charles Denby, it ran another story describing the United States Cavalry's pursuit of Geronimo into the mountains near Silver City, New Mexico. The renegade Apache would not officially surrender to the United States Army for another sixteen months.

Two days after Charles received his good news from Washington, a notice appeared in the Evansville Daily Journal to all of the members of the McDonald Club, comprised of dozens of youthful male Evansville Democrats, to meet promptly at "7 1/2 o'clock Monday evening June 1" to participate in a serenade to be given the Honorable Charles Denby at his home on Upper 2nd Street. The Journal later reported that nearly a hundred men arrived that evening to sing his praises, and "the parlors were filled with the finest ladies of our city." Charles thanked them profusely, calling them "the young Democracy of Evansville" and giddily reminded them that for the first time in twenty-four years they had a Democratic President. But he was also careful to thank "my Republican friends and neighbors who received the news of my appointment with so much pride and pleasure." (EDJ 6-2-1885)

Not all was hearts and flowers, however, as the Journal reported on June 7 that a story had surfaced, apparently in certain Washington newspapers more than twenty-two years after the fact, that Charles had resigned his Civil War commission because of his displeasure at the emancipation of the slaves, and went on to explain that "some of the newspapers do not like any of President Cleveland's appointments." It would be the only sour note ever mentioned in connection with Charles Denby's name in a long and illustrious career of service to his country. It was also entirely unsubstantiated.

On the evening of June 11th, the local Farragut chapter of the G.A.R. held a raucous reception in Charles' honor. Eleven of the town's most influential citizens arrived at the Denby home and escorted Charles and Martha through the streets of Evansville to the hall over the First National Bank where speeches were given by both Democrats and Republicans lavishing praise upon the local recipient of Grover Cleveland's favor. The next day Charles was off to Washington, D.C. for final instructions from the State Department, and the President. As the Colonel's train sped eastward through the great republic, the staunchly Republican Journal added its own flourish to the glowing compliments of the previous evening: "The Journal takes great pleasure in saying good words of Colonel Denby and rejoicing in his well-deserved promotion, and while politically opposed to Minister Denby, remembers that he has ever merged the politician in the patriot." (EDJ 6-12-1885) A few days later, when the Colonel was en route home, it further pointed out that alone among the ambassadorial appointments of Grover Cleveland, Charles had according to protocol visited the Chinese Ambassador to the United States. Though newly appointed ambassadors would soon be leaving for the countries of Great Britain, Russia, Spain, Austria and others, it was left to a Hoosier to maintain the diplomatic rectitude of the neophyte Cleveland Administration. In New York on his way back to Evansville, the New York Herald interviewed him about his coming assignment. "I am going to China with the hope that I may be able to return and enlarge the commercial relations between the two countries. We do not want to lay tribute on China or to rob her of any of her territory. We want simply reciprocity in commercial relations." (New York Herald, as reprinted by the EDJ 6-24-1885)

Perhaps it was just as well that Cleveland had selected a man who minded his P's and Q's for the subject of Chinese immigration was at least as explosive then as anything concerning immigration in our day. Dating back to the aftermath of the Opium Wars, the Burlingame Treaty of 1868 was a unilateral attempt by the United States to foster fairer, more humane treaties with the Chinese government. It was brought about by the then ex-Minister to China, Ansom Burlingame's desire to introduce a new era of humanity into the Western Powers dealings with the Chinese. Coming ten years after the Treaty of Tientsin (1858) which was another product of the Western Powers' efforts to defraud and humiliate the Chinese and was the low spot in the degradations heaped upon China by the West, the Burlingame Treaty sought to guarantee the Chinese Government's sovereignty over its own territory, grant religious freedom to both Chinese and Americans of whatever faith, and to grant the Chinese most favored nation status. During the time of the California gold rush from 1848 through 1855, and the subsequent building of the Transcontinental Railroad which culminated with the "Golden Spike" in 1869, California saw an influx of thousands of single Chinese males which flooded the American labor market and alarmed American workers far more than was perhaps necessary. After further provocations seemed only to inflame American workers' prejudice even more, the United States passed the Page Act of 1875 which restricted the immigration of Chinese women. Seven years later, in 1882, under the administration of Chester A. Arthur, the Chinese Exclusion Act banned immigration of all Chinese. Some in Grover Cleveland's new administration wanted a Californian appointed Minister to China, feeling the safest way to police this threat was with someone who lived nearest the problem. It appears that for this exact reason the newly minted President decided to choose an unquestionably honorable man above reproach who haled from a state nowhere near the sensitive area. When a bipartisan group of Indiana legislators and dignitaries began to agitate on behalf of the spotlessly even- handed lawyer from Evansville, he appeared to be the perfect choice.

On July 1, President Cleveland named Charles Jr. 2nd Assistant Secretary of his father's Legation. In addition to his duties at the Legation, Charles Jr. was also dispatched to the Orient by the State Department in order to become fluent in Chinese. Two weeks later the Denbys were feted at a sumptuous banquet at the St. George Hotel in Evansville by over 125 of the most prominent citizens of the town. Two days later, Charles and Martha slipped off to Logansport for a final visit with Martha's father, Doctor Fitch. During this sojourn with Martha's family, Ulysses Grant succumbed to the throat cancer which had conspired to torment him throughout the last months of his heroic and very public life. Returning to Evansville on the 27th, Charles received word that the outgoing Minister, John Russell Young, was ill in San Francisco on his way home from Asia, and that it would be necessary for him to depart immediately for the west coast to meet with him. In a prudent nod to the possible dangers he might face in China, Charles purchased a $5,000 life insurance policy before leaving. (Evansville Daily Journal 8-23-1885) On the evening of the 28th, the family held an informal reception at their home for all in Evansville who wished to bid the Colonel adieu. The next morning he boarded the train for San Francisco.

There had been much speculation in the California press about just what sort of fellow this Charles Denby was, and how he would handle the explosive matter of Chinese immigration. Or, if he would be able or prepared to handle it at all. Understanding more than the Californians gave him credit for, Charles was determined to meet them on their ground and terms, and learn all he could from their perspective. That was why he wanted to arrive in San Francisco well ahead of his family, and with all the time he needed to meet with the local politicians and to educate himself. At the time Charles was headed to China, nearly one third of the entire male work force of California was Chinese. At first the local San Franciscans showed Charles "a number of cigar, boot and shoe, and clothing manufactories" where his only reported comment was surprise at so many men working in such close quarters. But then, gloves off, they escorted him through "A colony of Chinese located two stories underground, where they were sleeping, smoking, choking and gambling; the rooms unventilated, half lighted, and the atmosphere overpoweringly foul and crowded with men," which caused Denby to exclaim, "No description can give any idea of this." It was a threatening enough remark to cause the Indianapolis Times to "take alarm at Colonel Denby's expression of disgust," and to cry foul. "It is to be hoped," they sniffed, " he will remember that he goes to China as the representative of the United States Government and not of the city of San Francisco, or that portion of its population who make it a part of their religion to hate the Chinese." It seems there have always been alarmists and in lockstep with them, overwrought, hand-wringing do- gooders. "It is not hatred of the Chinese," countered the Evansville Courier, in defense of the favorite son, "but love of the Anglo-Saxon race that prompts those who denounce Chinese immigration as one of the gravest of perils." (Evansville Courier, August 11, 1885)

The family, consisting of Martha, Charles Jr., Hattie, Ned and "Master" Garvin, left Evansville on August 5th for the great eastern adventure. Graham would of course remain with his own practice in Evansville, while Wythe, following a summer job at the Rose Polytechnic Institute in Terre Haute, came home for a brief visit before leaving to inaugurate his studies at Cornell.

With the Colonel ensconced in San Francisco feted and fatigued among the foes and friends of the Chinese question, the family was launching out upon the trip of a lifetime. Traveling north from Evansville, and then west through St. Louis and Kansas City, they had been persuaded to take the Denver and Rio Grand Western narrow gauge route through the Rockies for the fame of its vistas. The D&RGW advertised itself as the road which went "through" the Rockies, and its roadbed was fully 2,000 feet higher than any other road traversing the Rockies, boasting the steepest gradients in the world at that time. Unfortunately, their train was delayed for thirteen hours on account of a collision at Canon City, Colorado, a hamlet of only about 1800 souls in 1885, which Martha called "a beautiful and romantic place among the mountains." Eventually, the train headed westward to pass through the nearby famous "Royal Gorge", still a tourist attraction today. At Grand Junction, two hundred and forty miles further west, the party was delayed for another three days because of a washout of track. The D&RGW had been constructed on a limited budget, which was the reason for the narrow gauge and also the use of sand ballast. Although sand ballast was much cheaper to install, it was far more easily destroyed by the sudden squalls which sometimes inundated the area. There was no indication from correspondence how Martha entertained the eight year old Garvin in a western town of less than 2000 which had only been incorporated three years previously. Eventually the Denbys were reunited in San Francisco with the Colonel, and could do some sightseeing there for themselves.

In a letter home to George Hewitt, a Captain of police in Evansville, Charles Jr. reported that their stay in San Francisco was brief but enjoyable. "They consider the Minister to China a much more important personage than the people of the Middle States do. The Chinese question to California is one of life or death," he said. Because of his connection with the Evansville Police Department, he went to the cops in San Francisco and they provided him with two officers for a tour of Chinatown at night. "I cannot tell you all we saw, but can only tell you to believe all you hear bad about the place. Think of 30,000 people living in twelve blocks in the heart of a city as large as San Francisco." After describing the prostitutes and how they live, he said, "It was the worst sight I ever saw and I never want to see it again." He conceded, "It is only right to say, however, that I also saw some Chinese gentlemen, the equal of any in the world. They were dressed in purple and crimson, talked English well, and were as polite and respectable as any white man." (Evansville Courier 10-10-1885) So both of them, the minister and the second secretary of the American Legation in China, were treated (or mistreated) to graphic displays of the darkest side of Chinese life in America. That they both were able to avoid any negative feelings they may have had seems a testament to their Christian upbringing, and their inherently American sense of fairness and inclusiveness.

Embarking from the port of San Francisco on Thursday, August 20, 1885, the Denby family sailed on the mail packet SS City of Rio de Janeiro, an iron-hulled steam- powered passenger ship owned and operated by the Pacific Mail Steamship Company. Pacific Mail was the first steamship company to offer regularly scheduled trans-Pacific steamship service between San Francisco, Hong Kong and Yokohama. The 'City of Rio' was only seven years old at the time the Denbys came aboard. In his book Charles wrote of their harrowing trip across the sometimes treacherous Pacific, during which they spent three days in a typhoon. The winds were so strong at one point that they had to sail in the opposite direction for twelve hours, receding waves left staterooms awash in two feet of water, and smashed several of the lifeboats. On one occasion a wave swept the men out of the smoking lounge onto the open deck.

Charles Jr. wrote the Evansville Courier a letter after reaching

China some weeks later describing their steamer and the passage. He said, "the ship rarely carried more than 12 to 20 cabin passengers, though on their trip the number was 42, representing many nationalities, but he said, only four classes of profession: "missionaries, teachers, merchants and members of the foreign service of various nations." But, he added, "this does not include the Chinese, of whom there were 480 in the steerage."

How one passes the time on a very crowded vessel of this size for the nearly three week journey, Charles is quick to explain:

"In the charming moonlight nights of August, with a soft breeze blowing from the ocean, we gathered in a merry circle on the quarterdeck, sang songs, cracked jokes and told stories with the rocking of the vessel and the splashing of the waves to lend a stimulus to the slowest imagination and a charm to the dullest tale. During the day we read until the common stock of novels was exhausted, and then resorted to the livelier expedients. The ship's deck was laid off in a race course around which twenty-four times made one mile, and America, Germany and England divided the athletic honors of the day. The prizes offered in the various events were liberally devoted by the winners to the purchase of champagne, in which at dinner that evening we drank to the health of countries, rulers, sweethearts and relatives in all corners of the globe. There were musical scores, where each sang a song, and literary entertainments, where each read a piece of his own contribution." (Evansville Courier & Press 1-3-1886)

Under the title "Old Neptune", the Evansville Journal for October 13, 1885 published in full a letter that fifteen-year-old Ned had written home to his Sunday School teacher, Mrs. Tabor. Ned was proud of the fact that almost everyone had gotten seasick soon after leaving the Golden Gate except for himself. "I did not miss a single meal," he brags, "which boast no one else in the family can make." He reported seeing a whale, several porpoises, another day a school of flying fish, "a handsome, three-masted British brig" and an American vessel from Honolulu. "Every night we see any amount of phosphorescent insects, " he says with boyhood wonder, and "Every night we have beautiful sunsets."

He reported the same storm his father mentioned saying that it had begun to blow Friday night and that by Saturday morning,

"I got dressed with great difficulty and went up into the upper cabin. The door was open and some ladies and myself were looking out, when suddenly, without warning, a wave dashed in and drenched us all. Then all the doors and windows were closed over the whole ship. Looking up through the skylight of the cabin, which is the highest part of the vessel, nothing was seen but the green seawater. As the skylight is forty or fifty feet above the sea, you can appreciate the size of the wave. Of course the water poured in through the cracks and crannies and soaked the room. The ladies were below under the lower cabin skylight, and they of course received a wetting. Several times afterwards this performance was repeated. I should have said, instead of storm, typhoon, for that is what it was."

He said that he had thought just a few days previously that what he had seen in the Rockies could never be equalled, but that the typhoon had easily done just that.

"Imagine, if you can, enormous masses of water fifty feet high, capped with snowy foam, rolling and tumbling in grand confusion, keeping time to the roaring of the wind through the rigging; sometimes they would roll over the deck, and again the ship would quiver as one struck her squarely. In the distance we would occasionally see a wave more majestic than its fellows raising its crested head and then falling beneath the pressure of others. You may think me a crank when I say that it reminded me irresistibly of human greatness, as man rises in glorious majesty and stands for a short time towering above his fellow man, and then crowded out he sinks beneath the surface of public thought, and another takes his place."

How prophetic those words would one day become for himself the poetic fifteen-year-old voyager could not know. But he wasn't quite finished, so vividly would he recall this first great adventure of his young life.

"You can conceive the difficulty of doing anything in the storm when I tell you that often the ship would roll so that the edge of the upper deck, which is thirty feet above the sea, would be under; that is, the ship would roll at an angle of more than forty-five degrees. Of course, the ladies cried, but considering what a terrible thing a typhoon is, the ship was lucky to get off with a thousand dollar loss, which is what she sustained. The loss consisted in the destruction of one life-boat, another carried away and minor losses." (EDJ 10-13-1885)

A final note about the Pacific crossing: the SS City of Rio de Janiero continued to ply the oceans for the next sixteen years. During the Spanish American War she was leased by the Federal Government to carry troops to the Philippines. On February 22, 1901approaching San Francisco she struck submerged rocks in heavy fog, which ripped out a large section of her hull allowing her to sink in less than ten minutes. Only eighty-two of the total of two hundred ten people aboard were rescued. Rounsevelle Wildman, the United States Consul General at Hong Kong, along with his wife and two children perished. They had been returning to the United States for a rest and vacation. At the time of the Denbys travel in 1885, the Pacific Mail Steamship Company was one of two operating across the Pacific Ocean linking the United States with China. By the time the Colonel was writing his book in 1904 about his adventures there, he noted that the number of steamship companies had grown to thirteen, a reflection of the burgeoning volume of U.S.-China trade which the Colonel himself had spent fourteen years working diligently to foster.

Arriving in Yokohama, Japan on September 13, the Colonel found his old friend Commodore John Lee Davis waiting aboard his flagship the U. S. Naval screw steamer, USS Trenton, and in overall command of the U.S. Asiatic Squadron. Commodore Davis was one of seven children of the Honorable John Wesley Davis of Indiana, who served four terms in the U.S. House of Representatives, including Speaker of the 29th Congress, and as the United States Commissioner to China from 1848 to 1850 during the Administration of President Zachary Taylor. Commodore Davis was born in Carlilse, Indiana, had served with great distinction during the Civil War, and one month after meeting the

Denbys in Japan would receive his commission as Rear Admiral. According to plan, the Denbys continued on the next leg of their asian trip as guests of the United States Navy.

In a letter to older brother, Graham, Charles Jr. undertook to present his version of the family's journey half way around the world. He somewhat breathlessly began, "The wonder is that we got here at all." They had come 2700 miles by train from Evansville to San Francisco, another 4800 miles by ocean to Yokohama, and are now looking at a further 1800 mile trip in the Trenton "through inland seas, gulfs, straits and bays to Taku Bar, China."

He continued,

"The man-of-war is delightful. The feeling of absolute security from all harm, whether from nature or man; the large and comfortable quarters; the ardent hospitality of admiral, officers and men, and finally the most excellent table, combine to make a war vessel the perfection of locomotive contrivances. We all regretted to leave the 'Trenton'. In fact all of us were on the verge of tears. As we left the guns boomed out the minister's salute of fifteen guns, the band played 'Auld Lang Syne', the officers crowded the quarterdeck, and the men, of their own accord, manning the rigging, gave three cheers which very nearly made babies of us all. You meet an American naval officer in these remote waters and you have a friend whom death cannot win away." (EDJ 11-18-1885)

Charles Jr. was certainly not alone in feeling the great and comforting security of the officers and men of the "man-of-war". Hattie as well found one officer in particular to her liking, the dashing twenty-two year old Ensign, Gilbert Wilkes, a native of Salt Lake, and an 1881 graduate of Annapolis. Grandson of the famous Admiral Charles Wilkes whose Expedition was credited with the discovery of Antartica, and son of an Army Major, young Gilbert fit in very well with the Denby/Fitch lineage of military service and patriotism. The two would correspond, fall in love, and marry four years later in Logansport, Indiana, so that Hattie's aging grandfather could give the bride way — as her father was still the serving United States Minister in China.

While traveling on the Trenton, the two youngest boys, Ned and Garvin, struck up a friendship with a young seaman from the Trenton's crew which had been two years on the Asiatic Station, far from home. Later, seven-year-old Garvin, with the help of his older brother, Ned, sent the sailor the gift of a tobacco box as a token of friendship. The sailor, touched by the thoughtfulness of the gift, wrote the boys a lengthy letter in return, filled with many details about naval life in the late 19th Century. Seaman J. W. Wallace told them first that "all signs of contagion has left our ship and the crew are in the finest health. Unfortunately," he lamented, "we leave the remains of one of our crew out here, who died of the fell disease, and while we thank God that He dealt so leniently with such a large crowd of men who has (sic) to live within the small confines of a ship, yet we cannot but feel a deep sympathy with the parents and relatives of the deceased, as they, like our own, were probably looking forward to the end of 1886 which would bring their wanderer back to them." The Trenton left Yokohama, where it had apparently been quarantined, on May 8, stopping at Nagasaki for mail, and for recently- promoted Rear Admiral John Lee Davis to transfer his flag from Trenton to the USS Omaha. Telling of the disappointment the men felt at learning there was no mail for them on the incoming steamer at Nagasaki, Seaman Wallace then described the chaos which broke out as they spied the signal flags from Omaha with the order to "prepare for sea." It meant they were going home at last!

"Then all became excitement and 'we're going home,' 'we've got our orders,' 'we start tonight!' ' we start tomorrow,' and a hundred other conjectures were passed from one to one in rapid succession, and when you imagine four hundred men, all talking together, each one having his own 'yarn' as to the probable future movements of Trenton, and each man telling it according to his own peculiar style, you can readily perceive what a pandemonium was around decks." Two more hours elapsed as the men prepared the ship, and then "up went the signal from the flagship, 'start fires,' and again, 'departure 4 PM."

After further preparations by the crew he continued, "At 1PM the homeward bound Persuant [a long, thin signal flag] was 'broke' and as the three hundred sixty five feet of bunting floated to the wind and trailed astern of the ship, another yell issued from the crew, given with such a will that many of them aver that they saw the snow crack and slide from the top of Fujiyama, which as you know is from the anchorage sixty miles distant. Of course, I cannot vouch for the truth of the latter assertion but it would not at all be safe to contradict the Blue Jacket who gave it to me and I consequently give it to you."

He next described for the delight of his youthful correspondents that at 330pm, as the signal was given to "Up anchor for the United states", three stuffed dummies were dropped from the masts in celebration: from the fore yardarm a "Chinaman" made of canvas and stuffed with manila shavings, from the main yard a monkey made of the same materials, "while at the miz was sent out a nondescript composed of sailor's pants, Marine's coat, and coal heaver's cap," and all were made to dance jigs to the music of the band, with the maneuvering of attached ropes and rigging." Seaman Wallace, however briefly he touched upon the lives of Ned and Garvin Denby promised to write again at another time, but if he did his further correspondence was not preserved. However, it is safe to say that his amusing 'yarn' of a letter was in all probability never forgotten, certainly not by the young man who was later to sail into battle for his country on a ship very much like the USS Trenton, and later still, to lead the entire naval service so colorfully introduced to him by this friendly and instructive Jack Tar. (Letter from J. W. Wallace, Box #1, Edwin Denby Papers, The Bentley Historical Library, University of Michigan)

A final note about USS Trenton. She was the first US Naval vessel to bear the name, in honor of the city of Trenton, New Jersey. She was "laid down" in 1875, launched in 1876, commissioned in 1877, with our familiar then Captain John Lee Davis as the first to command her. She was the first US naval vessel to use electric lights, which were installed in 1883. After seeing service in many parts of the globe, she returned to the Asiatic Station in 1888 and took up her place with the Pacific Squadron in Samoa on March 10,

1889. She joined in what was then termed as the "Samoan Crisis", a standoff between the German and the United States Navies monitored by the British, which lasted for two years (1887-1889).

And here is where we must insert another story of a very unique Naval Officer, Richard Harrison Jackson, a "passed cadet" from the Naval academy's graduating class of 1887 whose poor grades did not allow him to expect to be commissioned in the regular Navy, but who was sent on his two year qualifying cruise on the high seas anyway. After serving aboard the protected cruiser Boston, he was transferred to the USS Trenton, headed for Samoa.

Though the United States had not yet entered into its "imperialistic" era which was to come in a few short years, she was not ready to cede potentially strategic islands to any nation, particularly in the Pacific. Six days after Trenton took up her station in Samoa, a cyclone stuck the main island of Apia. During the thirty-six hours of the storm, almost all vessels which had been in port were driven onto a reef or into each other and wrecked. At one point Trenton's commander used the highly innovative tactic of ordering his crew to stand on deck and spread their coats to act as a sail, but the courageous Dick Jackson immediately climbed into the rigging, and joined by others at his example, actually formed enough of a windbreak to help "steer" the Trenton. Thus gaining some control, Trenton was able to 'sail' into the USS Vandalia and rescue many of the men from that foundering vessel who would certainly have perished otherwise. Among those rescued from the Vandalia was Naval Cadet John A. LeJeune, future Commandant of the Marine Corps, who left a breathtaking account of the entire affair in his "Reminicscences" (pp 68-80). Of the seven naval vessels from three nation's navies which were in the harbor during the storm, only HMS Calliope survived largely unscathed, two were beached and repaired, and four, including Trenton, were wrecked and later scuttled. Grateful for the heroic action of the "passed cadet", the United States Congress enacted a special bill which granted young Jackson his commission as a Naval Ensign. Ensign Jackson went on to serve the United States Navy for forty-seven years, attaining the rank of Admiral. In retirement, he resided in Hawaii near Pearl Harbor, and witnessed the Japanese attack on December 7, 1941. He lived for many years in retirement, and died in California at the age of 105 in 1971. At the time of his death, he was the oldest military officer in the United States. Giants among us.

From Taku Bar on the coast of China, the family boarded a steam tug which took them sixty miles to Tientsin, and from there by houseboat another one hundred and fifty miles up the Peiho River to Tungcho. There they transferred to ponies and sedan chairs for the thirteen mile journey to Peking. Charles Jr. and Ned were given the ponies and arrived about two hours ahead of the rest of the family who followed in the chairs. They first saw the Chinese capital on the last day of September, forty-one days travel from San Francisco, having managed to traverse, according to Charles Jr.'s calculations, 9523 miles from Evansville. As reported by the traveller, the population of Peking at this time was somewhere between 500,000 and a million souls — with approximately 125 foreigners in their midst at that time. He said, "The city is the dirtiest, shabbiest and stinkingest in the world," and concluded,

"Our legation is on Legation Street (so-called —streets in China and Japan have no names), with all the other legations not far away. It is surrounded with a high wall, four feet thick at least, with an immense archway for an entrance and an iron gate — not iron rails, but solid. This gate has a keeper who oversees all ingoing and outgoing, and without whose knowledge no one can enter. Inside the wall are very pretty but small grounds called the American 'compound'.

There are four houses in the compound — the minister's of ten rooms and kitchen, etc., all on one floor; the secretary's of five or six rooms; the interpreter's of three rooms, and the 'guest' house of three rooms. In the rear of the grounds are stables."

After the physical layout, he explained the servant situation: two cooks, four or five "(no one knows which)" coolies, three house servants, a washerwoman, and a waiting woman, and after they acquire the horses they will need, two hostlers. That is ten servants for a family of five. Charles explained further about the horses and the hostlers, "you must have them because it is impossible to walk in Peking." (EDJ 11-18-1885)

Concerning the sights and sounds of their strange new home, the Colonel would later write,

"One never tires of the strange sites in the streets of Peking: the crowds training birds, each man throwing his bird in the air to have it return to perch on his finger; the kite-fliers rivaling each other in the distances to which they can send their kites; the extempore kitchens covering the sides of the streets; the barbers' boxes which are carried from place to place, and on which the customers sit while their heads are shaved; men playing battledore [a forerunner of badminton] with their feet; archers practicing at shooting at a mark, as graceful as Apollo; great funeral processions bearing chicken cocks, with horses and camels marching along, and numerous retainers of the family of the dead in pompous or uncouth array; wedding processions with gifts of all kinds, such as fruit furniture, great boxes filled with domestic articles, the red sedan of the bride closed and locked, and in front the roasted pork to tempt the evil spirits to feed on it; companies of Manchu soldiers bearing spears and swords; endless lines of carts, some with the wheels placed at an unusual distance behind, a token of princely rank; and sedan chairs borne by two, four or eight men; the imperial chair seen by stealth from a crack in a window, borne by sixteen men instead of the chariot drawn by elephants, which was formerly in use; riders of ambling mules which may have cost 500 taels or more, or Manchu ponies or donkeys; here and there gatherings of attentive listeners to hear the story-tellers recite their wondrous romances; acrobats, or jugglers, performing wonderful feats; fanatics with iron spikes stuck through their cheeks, or seated in a box studded with nails, which pierce them when they move." (China and Her People, p62-3-4.)

And if that wasn't enough for a casual afternoon stroll, he then reminded the reader that China at that time consisted of eighteen provinces, plus the subject nations of "Tibet, Ili, Burma, Manchuria, Mongolia, Korea, Nepal." Ibid., P 64.

Ned's older brother, Charles, Jr., worked as second secretary in the American Legation in Peking, and in 1894, was promoted to first secretary. He would become one of the United States' leading Sinologists of his day, working in China for twenty-four years until 1909. Garvin was only eight years old when he first went to China, and was sent home for a time for educational purposes. Ned was fifteen years old arriving in China, and one can only imagine the awe which life in the Peking of 1885 would have conjured in the adventurous mind of a teen-aged boy. For his first two years in China he would continue his schooling under tutors with the sons of the British Diplomatic Corps. The Qing Dynasty had not as yet entered into the great modernization programs which would characterize the latter years of the Empress Dowager's "reign". The China of 1885 was a helpless backwater, but it was endless, covering five million square miles of territory with over 400 million people. The possibilities, the romance, the mystery, the danger — all were limitless, sudden and deadly. It was going to be a bully time for adventure.

Charles, Sr., though new to the diplomatic game, became a widely respected diplomat who quickly familiarized himself with the territory, particularly becoming well versed with the Christian missionaries which prior to this time had flooded into and throughout China. Widely misunderstood, held in great superstition and even fear by the Chinese populace, and often unfairly criticized, the missionaries found a staunch, supportive friend in Charles Denby. In the Spring of 1886, the Colonel arranged to use the USS Marion, a third-rate US Navy screw steamer on the Asiatic Station, to ferry him to all the treaty ports in China where he set up shop in each consulate and asked the local Americans to call on him. He wanted to know what the missionaries were accomplishing, and he wanted to see it for himself. "What I saw," he would report to the Evansville Courier twelve years later, "astonished me." In addition to the coastal ports, the Colonel also traveled up the Yangtze River to personally inspect those missions as well. He found "hospitals, schools, universities, medical colleges which were sending native Chinese out as doctors among the Chinese people, as well as churches and Sunday schools." (EC 9-26-1898) He was impressed, and forever impatient with "the flippant and ignorant criticisms of missionary work." In fact, when the Denby family arrived in China, missionaries far outnumbered American merchants, as he told the later-to-be-famous Reverend Doctor Frank Gamewell "that at that time there was just one American merchant in the great city of Canton." Dr. Gamewell would later become the hero of the siege of the Legations during the Boxer Rebellion, and was to become widely known and well honored throughout the United States.

Many years later in a letter to then Secretary of State Walter Gresham, Charles stated, "China, before the advent of the foreigner, did not know what surgery was." After the advent of the missionaries, there were over twenty charity hospitals in China. (EC 11-21-1896)

Minister Denby was careful to learn not only about the American missionaries in China, but also to educate himself about the Buddhist religion. "I took some pains," he would write, "to find out in conversation with Chinese, who were not Christian converts, what their religious views were, and I never found one who had any religious belief whatever." (China and Her People, p.67) Keep in mind, this was written after his having spent fourteen years in China!) During the summer heat it was the common practice for the foreign diplomats to spend their time living in Buddhist temples west of Peking. Apparently there was no sacrilege in this, and it seemed to have been perfectly accepted.

"I passed my summers in a Buddhist temple," the Colonel says, "and except a few formal observances, there were no religious exercises of any kind. The system of going to church does not exist except on rare fetes, and these are converted into fairs where peddlers congregate in large numbers. The priests at my temple never fulfilled any religious function, except to beat a block of wood at sunset. They never visited the sick or interested themselves in the affairs of the people, and their lives were simply an unbroken series of eating and sleeping. I had long conversations with them, and strove strenuously to find out what their raison d'être was, and they did not make the least effort to show that they rendered any service whatever to humanity, but they uniformly protested that their work was exactly the same as that of the Christian missionaries — so little did they know about it." (Ibid. p.68.)

When claiming to be just like the Christian missionaries did not seem to convince the Westeerners, there were times when more drastic measures were employed to project the perceived threat of the Christian intruders. Charles describes an incident from 1896 when:

"A scoundrel whom the American missionaries had offended sought revenge by burying the body of a dead child in their compound. He then accused the missionaries of kidnapping and killing the child, and he led a party of men to the place where he had buried the body. Immediately a terrible riot arose, and the missionaries had to flee for their lives, and all their property was destroyed. After things had quieted down, a legal investigation was held, at which it conclusively appeared that the man himself had buried the body in the missionary compound for the purpose of inciting violence against its occupants. The man was condemned to death, and was executed, although the missionaries tried at the last to have the sentence of death commuted." (Ibid. p98-9.)

"There is a better understanding and a kindlier feeling toward missionaries and their work on the part of other foreign residents in China than existed fifteen years ago," stated the eminent Dr. Gamewell in a magazine article some years later, "and Colonel Denby's intelligent, discriminating and loyal friendship, which silenced flippant criticism and unwarranted attack in the social circle — criticism and attack so often based upon ignorance and prejudice — by his fair-minded statement of first-hand facts, has been a very considerable influence in bringing about this better state of affairs. By his writings and addresses he has exerted a large influence in the United States." (Article from "The Christian Advocate" of March 10, 1904, by Frank D. Gamewell, D.D.) Indeed, the elder Denby would travel far and wide giving lectures on China for the benefit of his countrymen to the very day he died in Syracuse, New York, literally hours after addressing an Episcopalian gathering.

Not long after settling into the unfamiliar routine of Occidentals engulfed in a sea of the strange, the brutal and the breathtaking milieu of Chinese life, the Denby's daughter, Harriet Ethel, aged twenty-two, tried her hand at communicating with the folks back home by writing her own descriptive letter to the Evansville Daily Journal, February 10, 1886. She first described the monumental walls which surround the city, giving a feeling of security. "At each of the many gates," she said, "there is an immense watch-tower where, in times of war, soldiers are stationed, and there, in times of peace, thousands of crows make their abode." She said the crows have a strange custom of keeping perfectly silent in their roosts until the gates are swung open for the morning hustle and bustle into and out of the city. The "crows consider themselves at liberty to fly screaming and cawing over the wall on their foraging expeditions. The Chinese," she added, "who call them 'birds of wisdom and love', believe that even the fowls of the air dare not break the laws of the emperor."

Next she described in some detail the customs surrounding the finding of a bride for the fourteen year old Guangxu Emperor, Zaitian (1871-1908), who had now reached the "mature" age of fourteen. Hattie said "it is time for him to choose a wife — or rather about twenty wives." She explained "that all the young girls of suitable rank and age shall be sent up to the palace for approval. Hundreds of little girls clad in exquisitely embroidered, loose-sleeved, satin gowns that hang straight below the knee, with loose trousers of a contrasting shade in pale silk, bound closely around their slender ankles, will be sent in closed chairs with a large escort to the emperor's presence." After suitable inspection "the Empress [Cixi, the current Emperor's aunt, regent and real power behind the throne] herself will solemnly select one for the first or real wife, who may become the mother of a future emperor. Then the emperor is allowed to select the others himself, as they are comparatively of small importance."

After enlightening her readers further with stories about

Chinese ice skating ("While sliding on one foot, the left for instance, they hold the right leg bent at an angle of forty-five degrees in the air in front of them, and vice-versa.), the Chinese New Year (every debt must be paid before the New Year starts, so strictly enforced that the suicide rate of those who cannot pay goes up at this time of year), she concluded

"Our winter has passed delightfully away and we are looking forward to a pleasant summer to be spent in a temple up in the hills, about twelve miles from the city.

This temple life will, according to report, be extremely novel and charming; but I will write home about it after actual experience has shown us what it is like. Harriet Ethel Denby" (EDJ 4-12-1886)

Young Ned was ready by the age of seventeen to begin his career in a diplomacy of his own style for by watching his father at the myriad tasks to which he had aspired throughout Ned's life, and also looking up to his older brother, Charlie, it was obvious that Ned would find some way to make diplomacy a priority in his life. It just wasn't going to be in the exact manner in which his father and brother had chosen, but more of a broader approach to his entire life. Edwin Denby would be the consummate diplomat: joiner, leader, conciliator, lecturer, teacher, toastmaster, mentor, counselor in every facet of his life. If there was an organization doing good or accomplishing the needful, Ned would not simply join it, he would usually lead it. The only organization he did not lead was the first one he joined: the IMCS, for by age 17, he was ready to face the world and make his own way, and with the help of his father and some British diplomats, he secured a position as "Assistant" in Robert Hart's Service. From this time forward and for the rest of his life, Ned would support himself, and never look back.

The IMCS had its pros and cons, just like any large and complex institution. Work went on seven days a week in this Buddhist/Confucian country, but the hours were short and there was a lot of free time. There was also opportunity to travel, posts to fill and many chances for promotion. Since the enclaves where foreigners lived were confined and close-knit, there was of necessity more than ample social life, including dances, teas, plays, sporting events, card playing, shooting, tennis, archery and other celebrations for various occasions. Another pastime of the foreigners was something the British called "stiffening", or the sharing of light lunch and pleasant conversation and gossip. Best of all, after serving for seven years in the Service, one was given the opportunity to return home for up to two years at half pay. After this first hiatus, a leave of two years was granted for every ten years of service. Working for Sir Robert Hart was not overly taxing, but it had requirements. For Robert Hart expected his young men to learn Chinese, and to young Ned Denby, Chinese might just as well have been Greek. It is not certain how well Ned mastered the language as he mentions that he had taken the test several times, but he was able to get through his first seven years and was liked by all who knew him. A colleague's letter from Tientsin dated 31 May 1887 congratulates him on his appointment to the IMCS saying that it must have been because of his "successful labors in Chinese." This was surely an inside joke.

On August 21, 1888, at the age of eighteen, and with a little over a year of work in the foreign service under his belt, he wrote to his older brother Wythe who was studying in his senior year at Cornell. After expressing his hope that Wythe wasn't too disappointed to be in the last year of his college journey, he confidently enunciated his outlook on life: "As for myself, I am firmly convinced that what is to follow in my life, even though my cherished hopes and schemes for success and betterment should fail, will be far happier than what has gone before. That is, it rests with me to make it happy." (Box #1 BHL.) Ned Denby would grow to a physical and a moral stature which few men could hope to attain, but it seems that even at such a callow age he was getting glimpses of his destiny.

He further wrote in this same letter that he was sure that Wythe was "absorbed in the discussion of politics", because he felt "Probably no presidential election ever before so concerned the Denby family as this one does, involving as it does, father's continuance in or exit from office." He said that he read two different stateside papers, but "as both these publications are Democratic and present only one side of the question, it is difficult to really tell how things are going. However, Cleveland's reelection seems to be considered as certain, but it will not be by any overwhelming majority." After categorizing a list of Benjamin Harrison's and Levi P. Morton's faults, he opined that "Cleveland, Thurman and the Platform, clean records, upright men and sound political doctrine, will be victorious." But then he admitted parenthetically, "The above is quite in the style of the inflated editorials which now fill our daily partisan press and give us distorted views on politics." As Ned astutely and correctly judged, the editorials that he had been reading were distorted, and his candidate of choice was defeated and would sit home for four years until winning the presidency once again in 1892. True to Ned's greatest fear, the newly elected Benjamin Harrison decided to replace his father as Minister to China with a Republican Senator, Henry William Blair, from New Hampshire. But since Blair had been a big supporter of the Chinese Exclusion Act of 1882, the Chinese government let it be known that he was persona non grata. In addition, many of the American missionaries whom Charles had graciously and fully supported, now petitioned the new President to retain him. Seeing the obvious favor in which Charles stood with the Chinese, the diplomatic corps and the Americans who were in China, the President followed their advice and accepted Charles' retention. The Denbys' sojourn in China would be safe for another four years. However, that did not stop the almost continuous rumors for the remainder of his tenure in China that he was imminently to be recalled and replaced. Even after Grover Cleveland reclaimed the White House in 1893, speculation continued concerning the replacement of the Colonel for any one of hundreds of political motives. Newspapers must be sold. Some things never change.

Twin among the challenges of life in the diplomatic service in China seems to have been the boredom and the heat. One of the friends Ned had met in China, G. S. Saunderson, wrote him in 1891, "The lack of news is becoming positively painful, something MUST [his emphasis] happen soon to disturb the fearful monotony

of life here now. There is absolutely no [IMCS] service News of any kind. It is becoming fiendishly hot now as I suppose it is in Tientsin. Here! I call that last sentence a jewel, it is what I put in my home letters when there is a lack of interesting news......
Verily the weather is a great boon to letter writers. What I should do without it I tremble to think. I fancy my letters would become beautifully less and very much smaller by degrees until I arrived at that stage where a letter of mine would read thus — 'Dear

— Okay, Yours…..'" Two weeks later Saunderson was back at it with more news, or non- news, this time telling Ned about a doubles tennis match he has played against Ned's older brother, Charlie. "There was a large gallery of ladies who comprised the rank, fashion and beauty of Peking. I wished we had charged for admission." (BHL, Edwin Denby Papers, Box #1)

As an afterthought, he closed each letter, "Your people are very well." We know where "his people" stand in the schemes of young men's dreams, but there is no confusion about what the important subjects were, and certainly near the top of the short list were the women. Throughout his life Ned would never fail to appreciate an attractive, accomplished woman. For two years of his service in the IMCS, he served in Macao, many hundreds of miles to the south of Peking where his mother, father and older brother continued to live, and from numerous letters from several of his peers, co-workers, as well as daughters of diplomats with whom he was acquainted, we can easily get the picture of the young teenager, well-liked by his friends and associates, dutiful to parents, respectful to his elders. From comments made by them in their letters to him it becomes evident that he was a creative writer whose letters were anticipated and enjoyed. In addition to honing his diplomatic side, he was perfecting communications skills which would stand him in good stead for the rest of his life.

In a June, 1888, letter from a friend in Tientsin (Tiangin), he heard about a "Race Ball" which had just taken place and that ….
"it was a night of rare pleasure. The floor, music and supper were all good, the ladies numerous and in high spirits and there was any amount of dancing. It was indeed a time to be remembered."

Aside from the women, most of the talk in letters from his friends concerned who was getting transferred where, and who was newly arriving. There were the usual likes and dislikes shared with his closer friends concerning those unpopular. Curiously, though China would on many occasions turn out to be a very dangerous place, talk of this aspect seems almost to have been taboo, for it is never discussed.

To that point, in early February, 1889, a riot broke out at Ching Kiang over a severe injury inflicted upon a Chinese national by a Sikh policeman in the employ of the British concession. When the British refused to turn the offending officer over to the mob, the riot was on. "The mob then burned and demolished the police station, the British Consulate, several foreign Hongs and several houses of American missionaries. The American Consulate," also, "was burned, but not looted." The British and Americans only escaped by hiding on a "hulk lying in the river, and afterwards passage on a steamboat to Shanghai." Though there were injuries, no lives were lost. "Mr. Denby speaks of this affair as furnishing another lesson of the danger in which foreigners continually live in China. There is no telling the moment when like events may transpire in any part of the empire," Charles remarked. (EC 4-7-1889)

At about this time, Martha, Hattie and Garvin journeyed back to the States for Hattie's marriage to Ensign Gilbert Wilkes from Salt Lake. The wedding took place at 730pm, Thursday, April 25 at Trinity Episcopal Church in Logansport, Indiana in the same church where Hattie's parents had been married thirty-six years before. The wedding party consisted of six bridesmaids and six ushers, including two of Hattie's brothers, two cousins and a sister-in-law. The Reverend Charles Morris of Evansville officiated, assisted by Reverend B. F. Miller. "The bride is a beautiful young lady," the Evansville Courier gushed, "vivacious, well educated and quite a favorite in her circle." (EC 4-26-1889) The couple went to live in Baltimore, Ensign Wilkes' next duty station, and by August, the Courier reported, they had been transferred to Washington, D. C. Martha visited her daughter and son-in-law in Washington at the beginning of 1890, and then spent three months in Logansport with her father. Leaving Logansport in March, she headed for the Celestial Empire via Salt Lake where Wythe was now working in mining. Next, she visited her eldest, Graham, who had moved his law practice to Seattle in 1889. In a letter home in May, 1890, Graham reported he was not having a lot of success in Seattle, and by early the following year he was working for a newspaper.

On March 5, 1891 the entire diplomatic corps in China, including the Colonel, were received in audience by the Guangxu Emperor, nephew of the venerable Cixi, then just nineteen years of age. With extravagant pomp and ceremony, the ministers were escorted by Chinese officials of the court to the "Pavilion of Purple Light", for the first such audience in eighteen years. The correspondent of the Evansville Courier took pains to describe the entire event in minute detail, especially a description of the young Emperor himself: "He looks younger even than he is, not more than sixteen or seventeen. Although his features are essentially Chinese or rather Manchu, they wear a particular air of personal distinction. Rather pale, and dark, with a well- shaped forehead, long, black arched eyebrows, large mournful dark eyes, a sensitive mouth and an unusually long chin, the young emperor, together with an air of great gentleness and intelligence, wore an expression of melancholy, due, naturally enough, to the deprivation of nearly all the pleasures of his age and to the strict life which the hard and complicated duties of his high position force him to lead." EC 4-30-1891

On January 9, 1892, Ned's older brother, Wythe married Miss Lucia Hayes in Milwaukee, Wisconsin. Wythe was then working near Denver, Colorado as a civil engineer. The Courier reported Wythe's bride was "from one of the oldest and wealthiest families of Milwaukee." (1-10-1892). The Journal called her "a handsome young lady and a leader in society.....and is in every way a fit companion of the man she has chosen as her liege lord." Thus, the peculiarly descriptive phrases of the day. On November 8 of that year Grover Cleveland was elected to his second term as President in what was reported as one of the cleanest and quietest races in memory. Because Benjamin Harrison's wife was critically ill with tuberculosis the President declined to campaign, and after her death on October 25, Cleveland suspended campaigning as well. It should have secured Charles Sr.'s place in China for the next four years, but the ever-present hydra of politics kept speculation running rampant that he was to be recalled at any moment. Yet speculation being what it was, it simply filled the newspapers of that day exactly as fake news fills the airwaves in ours.

In later November 1892 Martha again arrived in San Francisco on the RMS Gaelic from Hong Kong. She had been summoned to Logansport, Indiana where the gallant old soldier, doctor and reluctant politician, Graham Newell Fitch, her beloved father, lay dying. Just shy of his eighty-third year, Graham had outlived his son by 21 years and his wife by eleven. Only his daughter Emma, married to a local doctor like himself, was left in Logansport to sustain him. But Martha arrived from half way around the world on November 23, just six days before the elderly Dr. Fitch breathed his last at 630 Tuesday morning, November 29. After some time with her sister in Logansport, Martha traveled to Washington, Chicago, Evansville, back to Logansport, and eventually, to Detroit to spend the summer of 1893 with Hattie and Gilbert.

In a letter to his mother from June of 1892 Ned described a recent evening when he had planned to "dine quietly at home, have an hour or two for study, and go to bed early. I dined at home as proposed, refusing several invitations with commendable stoicism — and then fell victim to the 'Virginians' [Thackeray's novel] over the dinner table and read the book until twelve o'clock, despite the prickliness of an outraged conscience."

In the same letter he mentioned riding horses. "I rode with Dora and her father two days ago and go again today. Dora has been promoted to a big pony, her mother's, and presents a tremendous appearance upon him, with her hair in a knot to keep it free of dust, a style she has just adopted [and a style in accord with the dictates of the time which indicated that Dora was now to be viewed as a woman rather than a schoolgirl], and which I hardly know whether improves her or not (did I say knot? — strike me blind but 'tis a scurvy jest.) She is handsome in whatever attire," he boldly asserted, but quickly amended this comment, noting that he must call "a truce to such praises [because] I am well enough acquainted with the family Denby to know that one more word of rhapsody and they will rise as one man and hoarsely proclaim that the youth of the immortal 18th of February [his birthday] is 'gone again' — an insinuation which the youth must indignantly repel." He explained to mama that it is really Dora's family in which he is interested, saying, "His admiration is for the family, even more slavishly manifested towards her younger sisters than La Perla del Querida herself, and at least as fervid in the case of her parents." Later he waxed poetically, "Too long has this staunch heart withstood the battle and the breeze, the dulcet eye, the piercing voice, to fall victim now at this eleventh hour to anything in petticoats." Perhaps to divert her attention he then launched directly into a fraternal chiding of his younger brother: "But Garvin now — if he hadn't been so quick to fall before the ruthless Wysie's machinations, he might have plucked and worn this glorious May blossom, instead of the demented old turnip he has chosen to surround himself with." On the back of this letter, in Martha's handwriting is the note: "Wysie is a Miss Wyatt as old as I am nearly, whom Garvin hardly knows. But he has to endure a lot of cuffing from Ned about her." (Box 1 Edwin Denby Jr. papers, DPL.) All his life Ned would be known as a man of ready wit, with an enduring love of jest and comedy.

On January 2, 1893, Ned wrote to her in Logansport, Indiana, an extremely poetic description of winter in Peking. On the eve of his 23d birthday, it is easy to see that the young Ned could have ventured into many different career fields had he chosen to do so.

"Christmas and New Year have come and gone, and 1893 has been ushered in with the fitting honors of bright sun, cloudless sky and calm atmosphere — a model Peking winter day the beauty of which you will remember. Queen Nature has shown herself a potent, but a kindly mis- tress. She swirled the dust about our ears in clouds for a day or two before the year's end, then called in her tricksy spirits, proclaimed a truce between the warring winds, and with all the sweetness of her softest mood she smiled upon our dawning year. It ill becomes the mortal worm who profits well when the Queen of Nature arrays herself in all her charms to criticize the lady's motives, but it must be said that this rare maid is, like some other sweet creatures we mortals know, but a petulant flirt at best. With cuffs and buffets, taunts and gibes, she heartlessly dismissed the fond old lover who for twelve months had borne each strange caprice and cranky whim her girlish fancy chose to gratify, and then the maid, with a change of gown, went forth with all the fair seeming of innocence and truth, with smiles and offerings, to greet her new wooer. Why not, with a kindly tension have bade adieu, to the old and with sullenness and anger welcomed the new? Ah, yes! Fair and fickle, fickle and fair, they're all alike. Fairy nymph in woodland dell, dark-tressed mer-maid under the sea, lisping spirit of the air, and the best of all, the mortal maid are all the same, fair and fickle, fickle and fair!" (Ibid)

Once again he lamented that he was completely unable to get himself to make time to study for his Chinese examination, apparently taking, and failing them, every six months. He accused himself of loafing, — "I love to loaf, first of all for loafing's sake, and secondly, because by so doing I avoid Chinese." He told his mama that he had another examination the next day, and said he will not close up this letter until he reported to her. In his post-script he then admitted , "I made, as expected, a feeble showing at the examination." He then launched into a lengthy description filled with great detail of an amateur play, "Cinderella" which he had just seen, and then closed his letter by saying that it is a frivolous one about frivolities, but that there isn't much else going on in China. (Ibid)

Later in the year, in May, 1893, we get a long, newsy and very intimate look into the life of the budding youth, this time in a six page letter to his mother, addressed in care of his brother-in-law, Gilbert Wilkes, in Detroit, Michigan. Ned began this long letter just beneath "Peking" and the date with the plaintive question: "When are you coming back?" Then he launched into the disappointment felt by the Chinese branch of the family when receiving her telegram announcing the fact that a "Mr. Bascomb" had been appointed the new First Secretary of the American Legation in Peking, and not, as had apparently been anticipated, their very own Charles Jr. "The appointment of another man over Charles' head is a blow to his hopes and a disappointment to us all. It was perhaps not to have been expected that they would appoint Charlie First Secretary in the Legation where his father lived as Minister. I suppose," he conceded, albeit reluctantly, "Legations ought not to be made family affairs. But a Consulate or some other reward should have been given Charlie for his very good service. He has done better than Bascomb or any other man is likely to do. He has thoroughly mastered, and now speaks with fluency [which Ned never would], two languages, Chinese and French, and with this equipment and his great natural ability, his social gifts and popularity, and his devotion to and level-headed transactions of business, he would have been picked out among all others as the best available man for First Secretary. He is a specialist, prepared by eight years of training for the very position to which he must now see a man who never saw a Chinese character in all probability, and who equally probably knows no French, and most likely has no qualifications for the office but a local 'pull', appointed over his head." Too bad Charles Jr. had not his younger brother writing his resumes. He reported that Charlie was so incensed at developments that he was thinking of leaving the diplomatic service, and "perhaps he will come into the Customs, but he himself has not the faintest idea of what his course will be. I think Sir Robert [Hart] wants him and would take him at the drop of a hat. Sir Robert has known him eight years and I am sure can have formed none but a high opinion of his abilities and character, besides which he cannot be blind to the special equipment which would make Charlie a valuable man in the service. And Charlie would accept the appointment if offered." he believed. "But like two bashful lovers," he added, "both are shy of making advances."

He continued, in his best philosophic mode, "However, time

and destiny, to them let us leave the future, destiny the architect and time the builder. I wonder what sort of structures they are building for Charlie and me, palaces or hovels? I am inclined to hope for the mean, a strong and goodly home, not gorgeous enough to court the envy of men, not so poor as to claim their pity, but where love, peace and happiness may dwell until the last sands of time slip through the glass." Spoken by the lips of a young man, reverently loved, respectfully reared in just such a home as he so eloquently describes. Ned told his mother that he thought Charlie was, however, a fatalist who believes that he cannot change what is going to be, while he, Ned, is a pragmatist who believes he is in charge of his house, and the dimensions which it will take in his life. But just after having said this, he admitted that he viewed "with far less enthusiasm now than formerly the prospect of cutting adrift from my safe and pleasant moorings in China and embarking upon the troubled sea of life at home. I feel the responsibility of a captain. What if my ship founders in those unknown waters? It will be small satisfaction that I sought for richer cargos and larger markets when my ship is wrecked. Would it not be better to keep to the certain safe anchorage, even at the risk of being gradually smothered in decay? I think my ship is strong enough to prevail against the waves if her captain were not such a lazy fellow. But you know him and must realize how little dependence is to be placed upon him. However, I am fortunate in being able to make an exploratory voyage of two years' duration, beginning 1st June next, and until that voyage is well begun this question of go or stay need not agitate me." Here he refers to the two year leave of absence at half pay after seven years of service, which he will complete in the following year.

So, almost a full year before leaving China for good to return to the United States for a more formal educational experience, young Ned is prudently making his plans, and contemplating his future. "There is one thing I can and do congratulate myself upon," he continued, "which is that I have as yet no fair convoy to go down with me if I sink, and to suffer the pangs of poverty with a failing man. But if I do come back, after my leave, to China,

I hope the passenger list will contain the names 'Mr. and Mrs. Denby', for I am satisfied that I and all the other bachelors in China ought to get married when they can afford it." Graciously, maybe hopefully, he informs her, "You must select the girl, you know, unless I should happen to remain as badly smitten with the girl who visited Sir Robert as I am now. She is a splendid girl and knows all about China, so there would be no danger of disillusionment, which threatens every man who brings a wife from home. I have her London address and am going to visit her on my way home next year. How would 'Laura Denby' sound?" he teases her gently, and then as if to emphasize this teasing, he adds, "As well as, 'Dora Denby' for instance?" One has to wonder a little about Dora Drew, whose family (as he carefully assured his mother) was his REAL interest. We know that Dora had three sisters, Elsa, Lucy and Kay, and a little brother, Lionel, and there are letters from father E. B. Drew, Elsa and Lucy — but none from the handsome and ethereal Dora. Over thirty years later Ned received a letter from Mrs. Anna Drew, informing him of the death of her husband, and bringing him up to date with the lives of her daughters. One is invited to wonder if Ned had fond thoughts of Dora in his later years. Certainly they all shared memories of family get togethers, pleasant gatherings with cherished friends, and oh, those wonderful, leisurely horse rides through the Chinese countryside.

After offering Laura and/or Dora in combination with his last name, however, he reassured his mother, "But you must pay no attention to my present state — it will have passed off probably before you get this letter — and must proceed with the selection." However, after carefully assuring her he is only pipe-dreaming, he next told her, at least half-seriously, "Put the names of the list of attractive girls you meet upon paper with their qualifications and submit the list to me when I come home. Perhaps a few suggestions will assist you in selecting: age between 15 and 23, personal appearance pleasing (details immaterial), must be strong and good tempered, sensible; religion immaterial but must not be bigoted nor want to go to church too often, must neither be an idiot nor a blue-stocking, some accomplishments such as singing, dancing, piano playing preferred but not absolutely necessary, small fortune, say $1000 per annum, desirable but can be dispensed with — large fortune need not deter applicants, it will not necessarily be fatal to their chances — must not chew gum nor tobacco, must treat parents well and show pleasing disposition — with these hints you ought to be able to make a good sized list."

Perhaps tellingly, his next sentence after this outlandish teasing of his mother, begins with, "The Drews...." and said they are comfortably placed in Canton and seem to like it. One can only guess what amusement his mother found here, or how deep the affection ran between these two obviously intimate pen pals.

His next: "No news." speaks again to the boredom which often plagued those in China. And then he signed, "Your son, Edwin Denby" presumably so she wouldn't send his "list" to the wrong son. * Box #1 DPL Edwing Denby Jr. Papers)

During her trip home in 1892-3 Martha not only visited friends and relatives in several locations, she also managed to visit the Chicago World's Columbian Exposition, the largest World's Fair ever held to that date. In August she was in Vancouver and sailed on the Empress of Japan to Shanghai. On October 6, Charles Jr.'s name was submitted to the Senate by the Cleveland Administration for confirmation as First Secretary of Legation.

As 1894 dawned, Graham was back in Evansville again practicing law, and advertising daily in the local newspapers to try to re-establish his clientele. Plans were being made in the Denby household in China for the Colonel, Martha and young Ned, twenty-four in February, to return to the United States in June. Ned had completed his initial term of seven years of service with the IMCS, which allowed him two years' leave on half pay. The next plan for Ned was University of Michigan Law School. Charles Sr. had suffered from bladder stones and had already had one operation in China by a Russian physician without significant success. After sailing to London via Suez, the Denbys journeyed to Paris where Charles Sr. underwent a second operation for his bladder stones. The Denbys then arrived in New York on July

12th, two days after Graham, their eldest son in Evansville, was reported seriously ill with inflammatory rheumatism, and in the hospital in Evansville. The Colonel traveled to Washington D. C. for meetings with the State Department and the Administration, while Ned and his mother went to Detroit to visit Hattie's family. Martha then made a trip to Evansville, staying at the Thomas Garvin home, while Charles Sr. joined Ned and the Wilkes at a summer cottage on the shore of Lake Michigan. The Colonel needed the recuperative rest, and for young Ned, it would be his last respite before two years of law school in nearby Ann Arbor. After assuring herself that Graham was on the mend in Evansville, Martha joined the Denby clan on the Lake Michigan shoreline.

Hardly had the Denbys and the Wilkes had the opportunity to get reacquainted with each other, however, than toward the end of July Charles Sr. was ordered to make himself ready to return to China immediately on account of the heated hostilities which had broken out in east Asia between the Qing Dynasty and the Japanese. Known to history as the First Sino- Japanese War, the shooting lasted from June of 1894 until April of 1895. Both nations had assiduously courted the favor and claimed the tribute of the Korean nation, and when the King of Korea requested Qing troops to quell a local rebellion, the Japanese cried foul and sent their own troops to intervene. In a lopsided series of engagements on land and at sea, won most conclusively by the modernized Japanese military over the antiquated forces of the Chinese, once again the bankruptcy of the Qing government was exposed. Almost a foreshadowing of the Russo-Japanese conflict which would erupt ten years later, the world was given the spectacle of what happens to Empires which do not keep up with the times. Alarmed at the constant threat of appropriation of Chinese territory which was a staple of the relations of almost all nations with the Chinese at this time, Foggy Bottom wanted their man, the Colonel, at the helm in Peking to guard against the depredations of another humiliating defeat of the inscrutable Flowery Kingdom.

Ironically, the August 15 edition of the Evansville Courier contained a glowing article about Charles Jr. and what a stellar job he had been doing handling American interests in China in his father's absence. Furthermore, it mentions that only recently had Charles, Jr. become reacquainted with Martha Orr, a young lady of Evansville society whom he had known for most of his years growing up. It seems that Ms. Orr had been a member of John W. Foster's globe- circumnavigating party, along with her father, sister and others. Apparently it was love, if not at first sight, at first sight as mature adults, for it took the couple no time at all to announce wedding plans for that very autumn. The Courier, as newspapers then so often seemed to do, gushed over Martha, saying she is "beautiful, has travelled a great deal, and is wealthy." What more could you want? Oh, yes, she was Presbyterian, as well, the close cousins of the Episcopalians — a match truly, made in Midwestern heaven.

Though friends had urged the young Ned to remain in China and make his career in the Customs Service with Sir Robert, it was obvious that given his talent and personality he would want a greater challenge. and on a larger stage. Already interested in the field of law (his father, and older brothers had paved this street ahead of him), with his two year leave at half pay now at hand, Ned made himself ready for the next great adventure of his life. Though he would return to China as Secretary of the Navy many years later, and though he would remain a friend of China throughout his life, there is no evidence that he ever questioned his decision to return to America. China was dangerously fascinating, but America was the land of the free and the home of the brave. America was unabashed, unbridled, opportunity. And most of all, America was home.

Chapter Four

"Here's to the college whose colors we wear,
Here's to the hearts that are true!
Here's to the maid of the golden hair,
And eyes that are brimming with blue!
Garlands of bluebells and maize intertwine,
And hearts that are true and voices combine;
Hail! Hail to the college whose colors we wear;
Hurrah for the yellow and blue!"
"The Yellow and Blue"
Michael W. Balfe, Lyrics: Charles M. Gayley, Class of 1878

Michigan Man

When Ned Denby returned to the United States in June of 1894 he had never used a telephone, or ridden in a trolley car. He was twenty-four years and four months old, stood six feet one inch tall, weighed 286 pounds, and his hair had begun to recede dramatically due to a childhood injury to his left forehead. He had already traveled more than most adults in that era would travel in their lifetimes. He had had world-broadening, mind-expanding experiences that made him quite unique for his age. That he was headed to Ann Arbor, Michigan, to the University of Michigan Law School seemed almost preordained. His father's law partner and mentor, Thomas Garvin, had graduated from Michigan Law, and the men were close enough that Charles had named his fifth and youngest son, Thomas Garvin Denby. Some years later, a second law partner and another UofM grad, Daniel B. Kumler, joined the Colonel's law firm, and had died suddenly of inflammatory rheumatism only the year before, tragically at the tender age of forty-seven. Ned's sister, Hattie and her husband had been living in Detroit since 1892, when Gilbert had taken a position as the Chief Engineer of the Detroit Electrical Works. By 1894 Gilbert had set up shop in the McGraw Building in his own business as a consulting electrical engineer. With his sister and her family in Detroit, and his parents still in China, Ned had as much family in Detroit as in Evansville. We know from extant China letters that Ned was interested in law, particularly international law. And we know from a biographical sketch written by his widow after his death that "Ned had always wanted to go to the University of Michigan." (Denby Family Papers, uncatalogued) Ann Arbor, Michigan, then, was his logical destination. That he would reject the temptation to simply come home to the United States to find a wife suitable to take back to a comfortable job in China should not come as any surprise. Ned Denby knew that he wanted more out of life, and it is reasonable to assume, given his success in the Customs Service, and his upbringing by forward-thinking and civic-minded parents, that his aim would go much higher than a clerking job in China.

He had come home via the Suez, Paris, London and New York. By the time he had barely turned twenty four, he had circumnavigated the globe, still a fairly unique achievement for someone of any age in that time. He spent part of the summer of 1894 with his sister Hattie and brother-in-law in Detroit and vacationing on the Michigan lakeshore with his parents. He made a trip to Evansville, visiting family and friends, and undoubtedly dropped by Logansport to see his Grandfather Fitch. But before he achieved the full stature of the man he would become, he would next learn what it meant to be a "Michigan Man".

Not that he had headed to Ann Arbor to play football. He hadn't. He didn't even know what football was. In an article for the October 1921 edition of The Michigan Chimes, many years after his college days, he reminisced ".....one day the football scouts discovered that there was 'beef' in hiding, and spied it out. Alas! It was I. I didn't want to play football, I had never seen a football. They knew all that. They cared nothing for my yearning for knowledge. My career was nothing to them. They cared only for football. They wanted weight in the line. They cared not whether I could really play or not. I need be only my sweet, overburdened self, like poor Meretino's wound, 'neither so deep as a well nor so wide as a church door, but 'twill suffice.' I wailed that I didn't want to play football, or marbles or tiddledywinks. I wanted to loaf and learn.

"I became a football player. I have my picture in togs to prove it. I played football. I became glad of it then and I have been glad ever since. I went forth and grappled with the enemies of my university." (Palladium, Vol. 38, Varsity Football Team) Though he made much of his inexperience and his reluctance, it must've been quite gratifying to find a niche into which he could fit his huge size so promptly and so popularly.

There is a mystique in Ann Arbor about something known as a "Michigan man". He is big, maybe even larger than life. He is valiant — he never quits, never gives up. He may lose, but he will do so in a manner which lets his opponent know he has been in a battle, and he will do so with grace and style. However, he will mostly be a winner. Savvy, sure of himself, well prepared to meet any challenge that life will offer him. Though the University traced its origins from Father Gabriel Richard in Detroit in 1817, it did not actually become an institution of higher learning until the 1840's. It's first class graduated in 1845, its college of law was instituted in 1859. By the time Ned arrived on campus twenty-five years later, it was the largest law school in the country housed in one of the largest universities. It had already graduated the first African-American law student, as well as the first female law student, Sarah Kilgore, who was also the first woman admitted to the bar in the United States.

The University in 1894 was headed by the longest serving President in its history, the venerable James Burrill Angell, who presided, with some leaves of absence, for 38 years, from 1871 to 1909. During President Angell's tenure, the university saw its faculty grow by a factor of ten, and the student body by a factor of five. Coincidentally, James Angell had been dispatched to China in 1880, only five years before the Denbys arrived, nominated by President Rutherford B. Hayes as United States' Minister, and one third of a U. S. Commission to negotiate an update of the Burlingame Treaty of 1868. After Angell's commission had negotiated two treaties with the Chinese, he remained in China as minister for another year before returning to his duties in Ann Arbor. Additionally, President Cleveland later appointed him to serve on two different commissions, the first to negotiate a treaty with the British concerning fishing rights off the coast of Canada, and the second, the Deep Waterways Commission, to create an ocean-going waterway on the Great Lakes, which would not come to fruition until the Saint Lawrence Seaway Project in 1959. In 1897, President McKinley appointed Angell minister to Turkey, his final diplomatic foray, which lasted once again a single year.

It seems almost unthinkable that President Angell and young Ned did not find time to swap China stories, as the number of Americans who had travelled to China by 1894 would have been exceedingly small. Not long after entering the law school, Ned joined the Phi Delta Phi Fraternity, the oldest legal organization in the United States, predating even the American Bar Association. Formed on the campus of the University of Michigan in 1869, it can claim as past members five Presidents of the United States and 14 justices of the Supreme Court.

A fun-loving young man who once loaded a piano onto the back of a truck and drove around the campus serenading young ladies, the youthful Ned had what one of his admirers in later years would describe as an "exceptionally engaging personality." To his great advantage, that winning personality was housed in a very sizable frame, and it did not take certain other young men at Michigan long to tap him for membership in a brotherhood on the gridiron of Regent's Field.

Football had been played in the United States, in several primitive versions, for many years before what is recognized as the "first" American football game took place between Rutgers and Princeton on November 6, 1869. In that game each team fielded 25 players, the ball was round, and could not be picked up or carried. Obviously, American football had many tweaks and improvements to go before reaching the game that would be recognized by American fans of today. In 1880 Walter Camp proposed the reduction of the number of players per team from the then 15 to the current 11, and also introduced the 'snap' of the ball from a line of scrimmage to put more structure into the game. However, in practice these changes allowed teams to hold the ball from their opponent for an entire half thus causing games to conclude in 0-0 ties. In 1882, Camp again provided the innovative solution by inventing the down and distance aspect of the modern game, using five yards as the distance, and thus marking the field for the first time with the lines which formed a 'gridiron' pattern.

By 1894, three men came together at the University of Michigan to begin the creation of the legendary Michigan football teams which were to come. The foundations laid at this time gave Michigan such an unbeatable trajectory that to this day it still is the winningest football program of all time in the United States. First, in 1893, Charles A. Baird, at age 23, became the manager of the team, a position he held until 1895. In 1898 and until 1909 he was Michigan's first Athletic Director, and during this portion of his Michigan career, his teams and programs became so successful that he was accused of "professionalism" by drooling rivals. The second man of this triumvirate was the third coach of the Michigan football team, William L. McCauley, who played tackle for and graduated from Princeton in 1894 before heading to Michigan for medical school. McCauley only coached Michigan for two seasons, 1894-5, the two years Ned Denby joined the team to play the position that was then called 'center rush'. In 1894 McCauley took charge of a team which averaged a mere 170 pounds. During his two years as head coach and with young Denby on the team, Michigan compiled a record of 17-2-1, losing only to Cornell in 1894 and Harvard in 1895. In 1894 Michigan played Cornell twice in the same season. Losing the first contest at Cornell by a score of 0-22, when the teams met again on the Detroit Athletic Club field, the Wolverines triumphed 12-4, the first time a 'western' school had been able to best an invincible team of the 'east'. It was heady; it was history. It made memorable names for many members of the team for the rest of their lives.

The third member of the Michigan football troika of Denby's time, and easily the most accomplished, was Keane 'Fitz'

Fitzpatrick. Born in Massachusetts in 1864, Fitz found early success as a sprinter for a professional New England sports team known as the Natick Hook and Ladder Company. One of several of this organization's members to enter the field of sports training, Fitz would head for Michigan when a friend of his recommended him to the Detroit Athletic Club for an open position as its resident trainer. From there he was hired in the same capacity at the University of Michigan in 1894. During this time (1894-95) he trained the football players to a peak of stamina which allowed them for the first time to compete against the older and more established teams of the east. As already mentioned, in these two years Michigan only lost two games, and during this period outscored their opponents 510-98. Following this first stint at Michigan, Fitz was hired back to Yale for two years. In 1898 when Charles Baird was named Michigan's first Athletic Director, he immediately re-hired Fitzpatrick from Yale, and when, in 1901 he hired Fielding Yost as the football coach, the Michigan football legend would take another leap almost completely off the page. Though it is about another era, it is worth mentioning that the Yost/Fitzpatrick football teams (1901-1905) were quickly dubbed the "Point-a-Minute" teams, and were the envy of every football program in the country. In the nine years the two men worked together at Michigan, the team amassed a record of 75-6-2 (.903), and outscored their opponents 3248-193. And Fitzpatrick was every bit as successful during these same years with Michigan's track team as well as training several Olympians.

So, it was into this atmosphere, in a time when football was growing into a more carefully controlled sort of mayhem, when games were decided by scores of 0-4 (the game Michigan lost to Harvard in 1895), when sometimes teams played each other twice in a single season (as Michigan split decisions with Cornell in 1894), when attendance at games was moving regularly from the hundreds of spectators to the thousands, that young Ned, fresh off his sojourn in southeast Asia, stepped with manly confidence. A self-effacing, but gifted and intelligent young man, Ned joined a team of stalwart, even legendary men, much as he was to do twice more in his life in the years to come. Both times in the future he would join bands of brothers in two different military branches of his nation's armed forces, but until that time, his war- fighting was going to take place on Walter Camp's gridiron on a plot of grass in Ann Arbor, Michigan named Regent's Field.

In the two seasons Ned played football for the Wolverines, a touchdown was worth 4 points, and the kick after the touchdown was worth two. Teams often played home and home games, as they do today, but played them in the same season. Thus, in the 1894 season, Michigan played the Michigan Military Academy [today St. Mary's Preparatory, founded in 1877 in Orchard Lake, Michigan; at the time Ned played against them was home to student Edgar Rice Burroughs, the creator of Tarzan, who graduated there in 1895], as well as Cornell, twice. Michigan Military Academy tied the Wolverines in the first game of the season when it was said that Michigan had only been practicing for four days before the game. When they met the second time, the Wolverines trounced them, 40-6. Attendance at the games ranged from 900 to 6000, and even reached the 10,000 mark when the team played Chicago in 1895. During the 1894 season, the Wolverines traveled all the way to Kansas to play the Jayhawks for the second time. They had won the first contest in 1893 by a score of 22-0, and they prevailed again in 1894, 22-12. They would not play Kansas in football again for 85 years. They played eleven games in 1894 and only nine in 1895. Scheduling was done in a far less structured way as Michigan had yet to join an athletic conference. However, long before Michigan/ Ohio State became "THE GAME" in all of sports, in the 1890's Michigan considered its chief rival the University of Chicago Maroons, which at this time was coached by another legend of the early years: Amos Alonzo Stagg. During Ned's tenure the Wolverines bested their rival in both years.

And all the games were played without helmets; not winged, not plain, not at all.

The Quarterback of the team for both years that Ned played, as well as the 1894 team Captain, was James Baird, brother of Charles Baird, who went on to become an assistant coach at Michigan in

1897 & 8, and later a civil engineer. In 1899 Baird went to work for the George A. Fuller Company, and was directly involved in the construction of the Flatiron Building and the Commodore Hotel (now the Grand Hyatt New York) in Manhattan, the Lincoln Memorial, Arlington Memorial Amphitheater, and the Tomb of the Unknown Soldier. Interestingly, as Secretary of the Navy, Ned would be present at the dedication of the Tomb of the Unknown Soldier. There were several other notable accomplishments among Ned's teammates. Seven of them, including Ned, would go on to careers in law, including John W. Reynolds, Sr. who after his Michigan undergraduate studies, went to the University of Wisconsin Law School, and later became Wisconsin Attorney General from 1927 to 1933. Two future doctors played on these teams, and three individuals who later panned for gold in the Klondike in 1900. The story is told that one of them, Gustave Ferbert, halfback, became fabulously wealthy from his strike, but this story appears to have been a tale too tall for truth. Henry M. Senter, from Houghton, Michigan, one of the more heralded ends in the game of his day, came from a wealthy family and after college went to Columbia, South America where he owned and operated a large coffee plantation for many years. As Michigan teams of today, the majority of players were Michiganders, however, somewhat surprisingly, 13 members of the teams of these two years came from states all over the Union, from Vermont, Idaho, Montana, Wyoming, New Mexico, Alabama, and even Walla Walla, Washington, among others.

Perhaps predictably, four of these young men went on to become football coaches, including Ferbert, who before setting off for the Klondike, was Michigan's coach in 1897-8-9. Harry Haddon, a tackle, coached the Fighting Irish in 1895 before returning to Michigan as an assistant. Bill Morley, the backup quarterback to Baird, would later coach Columbia from 1902 to 1905 before settling on a ranch in New Mexico. Probably the most interesting coaching career was that of John W. Hollister, a halfback, who interrupted his playing at Michigan in 1894 to accept a one-year stint to inaugurate a program for Beloit College, as both athletic director and coach. He returned to Michigan Law School, graduated, and then went on to another one-year stint as head coach at Ole Miss in 1896. He then went back to Beloit as football coach and athletic director from 1898 to 1903, and later coached Morningside College from 1908 to 1910. In later life he worked in publishing and accounting, and seems not to have ever practiced law.

In 1890 funds were allocated to buy land, and later still more funds designated to turn the land into the first official football field used by the Michigan Wolverines. It was called Regents Field, having been purchased by the Board of Regents. The Field opened in 1893 and the first game was played there on October 7. The field was located in the area south of Ferry Field where Schembechler Hall stands today, along south State Street. Originally, the Field had seating for only 400 spectators, but after fire destroyed them, the replacement bleachers were double the capacity. Eventually, with the addition of more and larger bleachers, as well as "sloping platforms" which could seat 8000, the overall capacity reached 15,000 seats. The largest crowd ever to watch the Wolverines play at Regent's Field is reported to have been 17,000 people who saw the home team defeat the Wisconsin Badgers in 1905.

In the 1896 edition of "The Palladium", the annual of the University, Ned wrote the article on behalf of the 1895 football season. The team had played nine games, and as Ned pointed out, their goal line had only been crossed three times, once by Harvard in their only loss, and twice by Purdue in the only win of the season which was not a shut-out for Michigan. Ned began his article by reminiscing about the victory the year before over Cornell, a momentous occasion much worth reliving, and chided Cornell for not finding the "time to arrange the usual series this year." The football players weren't the only ones to rejoice in victory, he said, "there was much enthusiasm and bubblings (sic) of joy heard in Detroit and on the campus." He mused with wistful youth, and — "There were bonfires." (One can almost see Dick Powell and Rudy Valley with megaphones, in turtleneck sweaters.....)

Ned continued, saying he didn't believe the record of the 1895 team would soon be eclipsed, and that "the season of '95 was one great tidal wave of success, and in that year Michigan, as a blushing debutante, made her bow to the country at large and claimed a place as a first-class expert in modern football." There were a lot of sports writers (for that profession would grow as rapidly and as exponentially as the popularity of the game itself) and a ton of fans who agreed with him. He attempted to reconcile the Harvard loss in several ways, but ended by admitting "the fact that we were beaten, and record our intention of turning the tables next year." He mentioned another quirk of 1890's football in writing about the closeness of the hard-fought win over Purdue, stating that "we played under rules different from those we had been using — and changing rules isn't as easy as changing sweaters." He also took a swipe at his own play, for he was backing up the regular center, Bert Carr, who had been injured in the Harvard game, by mentioning that "everyone knows we played a lot of substitutes....." Ned would surprise people all of his life with the frankness of his humility.

He ended his opus by placing credit where he felt it belonged: "If to any one man above another credit is due for this result, McCauley should receive it. Not only his splendid coaching, but his quiet gentlemanly, kindly manner, his forbearance, and his abstention from the use of language too strong for the public prints, all had their good effect upon the team." He said the next season the torches are being passed, for the Captain, "Pa" Henninger, would be replaced by Henry Senter; Buck Richards was taking over the athletic director's job from Charlie Baird, and McCauley was being replaced by a Mr. Ward from Princeton. Only Fitzpatrick, the genius trainer, would remain. Ned didn't feel it important enough to mention that of those passing on to the next chapter of their lives was he himself.

He had come to Michigan, never having set foot in the State before 1894, in search of an official cap to the fabulous education he had received by living and working in China for nine years. He had come to the University of Michigan seeking the imprimatur of an LL.B., for he now desired to follow in his father's and two of his older brothers' footsteps, and practice the law. What he left at the University was a solid foundation for the legend which was to grow for decades to come as one of the early giants who literally wrote the definition of what it meant to be a "Michigan Man".

As 1895 dawned and Ned was finishing up his first year at Michigan, Charles Jr. arrived in New York in early February along with his mother. The First Sino-Japanese War had scotched his and Martha Orr's plans for a wedding the previous fall, and as Charlie talked to reporters about the War, the Orr family was busily making preparations for the March nuptials in Evansville. On February 7, Emma Coleman, Martha Fitch Denby's only remaining sibling, died suddenly in Battle Creek, Michigan while taking a cure. Charles Jr. arrived in Evansville on February 24, the first time he had been home in nearly ten years. Like his father the year before, he remarked how different the city looked with the large number of newly paved streets. On March 3d the entire Denby family rejoiced at the birth of Charles Denby Wilkes in Detroit, the first son of Hattie and Gilbert, and first grandchild of Charles Sr. and Martha. It would be weeks before Grandpa Denby would receive the news in China.

On March 19 the Evansville Courier reported "the most important social event of the present season" took place in Evansville, as Charles Jr. and Martha Dalzell Orr celebrated their marriage at 8 o'clock in the evening at the Walnut Street Presbyterian Church. Graham acted as Charlie's best man, while Garvin was an usher. Ned also attended, as the Courier reported, "from Ann Arbor University." Missing were Charles Sr., tied up with the precarious diplomatic situation in the East, Wythe working out West in mining, and of course, the new parents Hattie and Gilbert tending their newborn in Detroit. (Evansville Courier 3-20-1895) The Journal described the bride as having "a beautiful contralto singing voice," while also playing the violin which she studied while completing her education in Washington, D. C. It was also noted that Martha Orr spoke French and German. The groom, naturally fluent in Chinese [quite unlike his younger brother], "has made several translations of Chinese books into English." After the ceremony, over two hundred guests were feted at a brilliant reception at the Orr mansion on Upper First Street. Early the next morning the happy couple departed on the early train for Detroit to visit the new parents and infant nephew, prior to a quick trip to Washington, D. C. and then a return to the Orient. (EvansvilleDailyJournal 3-20-1895)

Ned and his mother departed Evansville on March 24, also for Detroit; Martha to spend some time with her grandson, while Ned would return to Ann Arbor for the last weeks of his first year of law school. In July the newly married Denbys were accorded the signal honor of an audience with the Emperor and Empress of Japan, en route China, an honor, the awed Courier reported, never before shown the wife of a Secretary of Legation. (EC 7-21-1895) Later, in October of the same year, while Ned was making his reputation on the gridiron, William Curtis, special correspondent of the Chicago Record was quoted in the Evansville Daily Journal as saying that Mrs. Denby Jr. "is quite the belle of the foreign colony, which consists of the diplomatic corps and the customs staff." (EDJ 10-23-1895) He would go on to report that at that time Sir Robert Hart maintained a Customs staff of between three and four thousand men, and the Customs Service for which he was responsible had collected approximately $33 millions in the year 1894 alone.

No one who knew, or studied the life of, Ned Denby would ever make a footnote out of his law degree. Every bit as much as football made him popular, accepted, even lionized, Ned himself would have told you that it was all secondary to the real reason he came to Michigan, and to its flagship university (forgive me Spartans) in the first place. Michigan Law School, as has been noted, was the largest law school in the country by 1894. There were well over 1000 law students in Ned's time, and 318 in his 1895 graduating class, including one woman. Many famous people have attended the hallowed halls of Michigan Law, including Charles Augustus Lindbergh (father of the famous flyer); Larry Elder, radio talk show host; Jimmy Hoffa, famous teamster; Clarence Darrow, of "Monkey Trial" fame; Gerald Ford, the 39th President of the United States; Valerie Jarrett, advisor to President Barack Obama; Harry Daugherty, who would serve with Ned in Washington D. C. as Attorney General in the cabinet of Warren Harding; and Ann Coulter, noted author. Ned was at Michigan to get a great education to top off the "world-class" one he had already received. He made many lifelong friends at Michigan, and for the remainder of his life, would never fail to do anything in his power to aid or assist his alma mater, joining both the University Club of Detroit, and the UofM Alumni Association. In his later years he would not miss any opportunity to return to his beloved school, and even to its gridiron.

Two friends from law school days would be extremely close to Ned in all the years to come. James Orin Murfin was born in Portsmouth, Ohio, but from the time he came north to attend Michigan Law, he was a true Wolverine. After graduation, Murfin came to Detroit, exactly as and when Ned Denby did, and entered law practice in July of 1896. He ran for and was elected to the Michigan State Senate in 1901-2, and practiced law in Detroit from 1896 to 1908, during which time he was one of Henry Ford's attorneys. He became a circuit court judge 1908-1911, and a University of Michigan Regent from 1918 to 1934. Like Ned, he was a member of the Sons of the American Revolution, the Detroit Club and the University Club. In addition, he was president of the Detroit Lawyers Club from 1925 to 1933. He died in 1940 at the age of 65, having spent 45 years of his adult life in Michigan. His body was returned to Portsmouth, Ohio where he was buried.

Henry Laurence Lyster was another Michigan Law friend of Ned's, who was born in Detroit December 22, 1872, and graduated in the same class as Ned. Undoubtedly, Ned spent a great deal of time visiting the Lyster household in Detroit where he took his place among the active and patriotic Lyster family, becoming as Winifred Lyster would later claim, her "fourth son". Dr. Henry Francis LeHunte Lyster came to Detroit after the Civil War, married Winifred Lee Brent in 1867, and would raise his family while practicing medicine in Detroit for many years. The Lysters had three sons and two daughters. Their oldest son, William, became career Army, attaining the rank of Colonel. Their second son was Ned's friend, Henry, who, like Ned, would join the Michigan Naval Brigade and serve in the Navy during the Spanish American War, and later distinguish himself as Adjutant of the First Pursuit Group of the Air Service in World War I, which also included pilots Eddie Rickenbacker and Quentin Roosevelt. Dr. Lyster passed away in Detroit in 1894, the same year Ned came home from China, and Winifred would outlive her husband by thirty-six years. When Winifred was a young girl of twenty she wrote the song, "Michigan, My Michigan", which became popular with Michigan troops during the Civil War. In later life she was greatly revered by Detroit residents. After Ned became Secretary of the Navy, he invited Mrs. Lyster to Washington to be present at a dinner given by the Denbys on behalf of President and Mrs. Harding. "At the dinner she sat next to the President who asked her what had brought her to Washington, to which she replied, 'To see my friend, Edwin Denby, whom I have watched advance from State Legislator to Secretary of the Navy and also to see whether you are as good looking as even your political opponents say you are." Once honored at a civic dinner where she was toasted by General of the Armies John Joseph Pershing, she confessed that she had been puzzled about why she had been invited to the dinner. "I came because I wanted to see General Pershing, and having done so, consider my evening well spent." It was said of her that she was the great-granddaughter, daughter, wife, sister-in-law, mother-in-law, mother, and grandmother of men who served in the Army or Navy, and that America had never fought a war in which she had not had a relative in the ranks. She was said to have kept the following Longfellow quotation, written in her own hand, affixed to the mirror above her dresser:

'Look not mournfully into the Past, It comes not back again.
Wisely improve the Present, It is thine.
Go forth to meet the shadowy Future Without fear, and with a manly heart.'* (Detroit Free Press July 26, 1936)

She wrote Ned letters during his adult life, and outlived him by fourteen months. One additional life-bond between the Lysters and the Denbys would occur on June 8, 1937, some years after both Ned and Winifred were deceased, when William Lyster's only daughter, Elizabeth, married Edwin Denby, Jr. Ned's very good friend, Henry, would never marry, and would live to the ripe old age of 75, passing away in 1948.

At the end of his time at the University of Michigan, Ned had three options for the future: he was still within his two year period of grace and could have returned to his job with the Customs Service in China. He could have returned to his boyhood home in Evansville where his older brother Graham was practicing law and raising his own family. Or, he could head for the bright lights and the great promise of Detroit, already known as "the Paris of the West" for its broad boulevards. By 1896 Detroit's population was well over 200,000 souls, and it was also known as the "Stove Capital of the World." Most of the railroad cars used by American railroads were being built by Detroit industry, and until recently, Detroit had built more shipping than any other 'port' in the country. Tobacco, and pharmaceuticals were growing in importance, and in that fateful year of 1896, when Ned Denby made his choice and moved to Detroit, Charles Brady King drove the first gasoline powered vehicle seen in Detroit down Woodward Avenue, and later that same year, Henry Ford would duplicate the feat. Though the explosive growth of the automobile industry in Detroit was some few more years away, the machine shops and the pool of skilled labor to operate them were already in place, awaiting the next giant leap into the industrial future.

On September 5, 1896, the Denby Clan was blessed once again with an addition to the younger generation, as the Charles Jr. Denbys of Peking welcomed James Orr Denby into the world and the family. Only a few days prior to this happy event, terrible tragedy was narrowly averted as Charles and Martha were on a houseboat being towed up the Peiho river to Peking when the motor launch doing the towing suddenly lurched, capsizing the Denby's craft and dumping them, and all their belongings, into the Peiho River. It was only with great difficulty that Charles, who had been on deck, was able to make it safely ashore, then return to the capsized boat to cut a hole in the bottom and rescue a barely conscious Martha. It is certain that all Denbys breathed a sigh of great relief at the news. (EC 9-12-1896)

Meanwhile, Ned found his way in Detroit, in all probability with the help of some of his University of Michigan friends, to an apartment building at 550 Jefferson Avenue where he joined a group of young professional men of his age called "the Bachelors". Though different members would come and go over the course of time, there were usually ten of them in residence at any one time, with both a cook, and a housekeeper to keep the place going. Because of the address, the men were sometimes referred to as "the 550's". It was during his time here that Ned's friends first began referring to him as "Duke", a nickname which would stay with him in certain circles for the rest of his life. Charles Beecher Warren (4-10-1870 to 2-3-1936), born in Bay City, Michigan, and a graduate of the University of Michigan, became a prominent Detroit attorney. In later life he would be Ambassador to Japan and later Mexico. He was nominated twice by Calvin Coolidge to be his Attorney General, and was twice refused by a stubborn and recalcitrant Senate. Harry Worcester would one day become Vice President of the Big Four railroad. James Orin Murfin, Ned's UofM classmate, we have already seen above. George W. Alexander would become Treasurer of the Grand Trunk Railroad. William E. Strong went on to become an engineer in New York. Andrew H. Green became Vice President of the Solvay Process Company, a chemical company headquartered in New York. B. C. Cobb would become Chairman of Allied Power and Light Company of New York. Walter M. Parker became a Detroit oculist. W. E. S. Strong became a consulting engineer for J. P. Morgan and Company.

Nice neighbors. Bully pals.

Settling in to the rhythm of Detroit, Ned soon passed the bar and joined the law firm of Keena and Lightner. Having been raised in the Episcopalian faith, he joined Christ Church, Detroit, the home church of the Lyster family since the church was founded in the 1840's. Indeed, its very first rector was the Rev. William Lyster, and Winifried Lee Brent Lyster was a member for over seventy years. In 1899 one of the men's clubs at Christ Church was reorganized as 'the Trowbrige Club' with a membership of 78 men. In 1900 Ned was one of the young men who contributed a lecture for this club on the subject, 'Causes and Incidents of the South African War'. Also in 1900 the Men's Parochial Club was formed with Ned as its President. Its stated purpose was 'enhancing the interests and mutual benefit as well as being the means of bringing together the men of the Parish for conferences concerning matters of progress or improvement.' This club heard lectures from various people, but seems to have died out after 1903, a time when Ned was involved with other occupations in Lansing and Washington, D.C. (Christ Church, Detroit, by Rev. Ervin A. Brown, 1995, p 54-55 & p60-61.)

And, best of all, Detroit was home to his own cherished kin, sister Hattie, brother-in-law Gilbert and their young son, named Denby Wilkes. Ned obviously liked and admired his brother-in-law, for in less than a year he would join the Michigan Naval Militia which had only recently been created in Detroit, with brother-in-law Gilbert one of its founding members.

On November 3, 1896, William McKinley was elected the 25th President of the United States. Though it became known within days that the New President would at last replace Charles in China, that would not happen for some months, as the filling of offices more important would take precedence. Further, McKinley's first choice to replace the Colonel was Charles Page Bryan, but Congress objected to Bryan's lack of experience, and William H. Conger was chosen instead. It was not until July of 1898 that Conger would arrive in Peking to relieve the Colonel. At the same time, Charles Jr., perhaps seeing the writing on the diplomatic wall, and almost surely more interested now to secure his own fortune, was busy in the United States building a syndicate of American businessmen for whom he would return to China to represent. In May 1898, Martha left China for the last time, headed stateside. Charles would follow in three months. Though Charles Jr. would remain in China for another eleven years in various posts, both in government and the private sector, the Denbys' family sojourn in the Celestial Empire was at a close.

Ned was busy in his new home in Detroit. Working at his law practice, already an active member of the Episcopal Church, he was also involved in may extracurricular activities. As his life-long friend and some time law partner, Hugh O'Brien would later write about him:

"His fair-skinned face was singularly expressive, yet it never quite lost a certain boyishness that seemed to reflect the spirit of perpetual youth within him. Perhaps his greatest physical charm was an illuminating smile altogether indescribable, alternately kind and mischievous, which instantly dissolved suspicion and won undying allegiance. A delightful storyteller, his companionship was universally sought and treasured for the wealth of lore and brilliant repartee which he prodigally dispensed. He was a man of strong convictions which once formed he esteemed it cowardly not to declare and stand by, if necessary, alone and against the world." (ED Papers, Burton Collection, Box #10)

Ned Denby would one day stand against the world, or so it would seem to him and to his family. But before that time, he would thrill to the blast of the trumpet, the lure of the sea, and the deafening clash of battle.

Chapter Five

Michigan Naval Militia
"Eternal Father, strong to save,
Whose arm hath bound the restless wave,
Who bidd'st the mighty ocean deep
It's own appointed limits keep;
Oh, hear us when we cry to Thee For those in peril on the sea!"
The Navy Hymn, William Whiting, 1860

The Navy

At the foot of Townsend Street in downtown Detroit, hidden behind the abandoned Naval Armory Building, buried under tons of now-dried and forested mud lie the mouldering ruins of a once-beloved naval vessel, the USS Yantic. Originally conceived as a Presidential yacht for Abraham Lincoln, the wooden hulled gunboat, constructed from live African oak, was built at the Philadelphia Navy Yard. Launched on March 19, 1864, and commissioned on August 12, she was named after the Yantic River in Connecticut. One day after commissioning, she raced out of Philadelphia in company with two other U.S. ships in pursuit of the Confederate privateer CSS Tallahassee. After five days at sea, she returned empty-handed. Early in 1865 she participated in two major landing operations to capture Confederate forts, and for the remainder of the War she was on blockade duty.

She had come into the world as a three-masted sailing ship, 186 feet in length with 32 feet of beam. She carried a horizontal steam engine amidships with two tiny boilers that didn't give her much speed, and she only had bunker space for 90 tons of coal. She was built with a four-foot keel running her entire length which gave her the ability to sail as well as a Yankee clipper.

After spending over thirty years on nearly every station the U.S. Navy frequented, including over four years on the Asiatic Station, she sailed in 1884 as part of the American rescue operation which was dispatched to northern waters to search for the missing and overdue Adolphus Greely expedition. Although the six survivors of that expedition were rescued by another ship, Yantic took pride in carrying out every assignment which was given to her.

The United States Navy first proposed the organization of a Naval Reserve Force in the 1880's but Congress voted this early measure down. The idea became popular in several states, however, and the first state naval militia was formed in Massachusetts in 1890. New York State followed suit the next year, and Michigan was soon after, in 1893. Butler Duncan, a graduate of the U.S. Naval Academy and Herbert Satterlee were two of the principal organizers in New York. Butler was a shipmate and friend of a young electrical engineer who had recently moved to Detroit named Gilbert Wilkes. Wilkes, himself an 1881 graduate of Annapolis, had left the Navy to pursue a civilian career, but became interested in this new idea of a reserve naval militia. He was the grandson of Rear Admiral Charles Wilkes who had commanded the United States Exploring Expedition (known as the Ex-Ex) of 1838-1842, which was credited with the discovery of the Continent of Antarctica. (Philbrick, p. 171) His expedition also mapped and charted hundreds of Pacific islands, including the Hawaiian Islands, and mapped and charted much of the coastline of the American Pacific Northwest. Though he was widely heralded for his many contributions to the advancement of several sciences, he was also court-martialed twice during his colorful career, yet would die honored as a Rear Admiral, and be buried in Arlington National Cemetery.

Years later during annual reunions, the list of those who were instrumental in the formation of the Michigan Naval Militia would seem to grow, but it was apparent that one of the moving forces was Truman H. Newberry, later to become Secretary of the Navy under Theodore Roosevelt, and serve in the United States Senate. Another Detroit resident and Annapolis graduate, Charles C. Poe was the militia's first commanding officer, with Gilbert Wilkes second in command. Like Gilbert Wilkes, Lt. Poe was also descended from illustrious military stock, being the son of Civil War officer Brigadier General Orlando M. Poe, who served as Sherman's chief engineer during the March to the Sea, and following his Civil War service was responsible for designing and building many lighthouses in the upper Great Lakes, as well as the Poe Lock at Sault Ste. Marie. This first great lock of the American Soo Locks, completed in 1896, allowed larger vessels to ply the upper Great Lakes, making possible the American steel industry. Like Charles Wilkes, O. M. Poe would be buried in the nation's hallowed ground at Arlington. His son, Charles Poe was further distinguished by being the nephew of Winifried Lyster, whose second son, Henry, Ned's classmate, would join the militia as well.

The early men of the Michigan naval militia would pay their own expenses for the first couple of years as they travelled back and forth to Lansing to lobby the Michigan Legislature for a bill which would legitimize their endeavors and fund them as well. Act 184 of 1893 of the Michigan Legislature officially created the Michigan Naval Militia. They were finally accepted by the state, financed by the legislature and became for many years a pillar of the local military scene.

In 1897 USS Yantic was ordered home from service on the South American Station for the purpose of decommissioning. However, in the summer of that year, as luck would have it, then 39 year old Assistant Secretary of the Navy, Theodore Roosevelt, sailed from Mackinaw to Detroit on the side-wheeler USS Michigan with several members of the Michigan Naval Militia. For some years the USS Michigan had hosted the Michigan Militiamen for their summer cruise which caused uncomfortable overcrowding on the naval vessel. Some of the regular sailors interested Mr. Roosevelt in the idea of providing the militia men with their own vessel. When Teddy returned to Washington he found that a perfect candidate for such service was the USS Yantic, which was at that time at the Boston Navy Yard awaiting orders for her demise. Hence, Roosevelt arranged for her to be loaned to the State of Michigan, and the last chapters of Yantic's career were set in motion.

After an eventful passage from Boston to Detroit, during which she was laid over in dry dock in Montreal to have her four-foot keel removed, and also 15 feet nipped from her stem so she would fit through the existing locks of the St. Lawrence, she arrived too late in the season for her reassembly, which did not take place until the following Spring. When reassembled and refurbished, officially Yantic became the training ship of the Michigan Naval Militia just in time for the outbreak of the Spanish American War.

Young Denby had joined the Michigan Naval Militia soon after graduating from the University of Michigan, and moving to Detroit. His brother-in-law, Gilbert Wilkes, was one of the Militia's prime movers, and given Ned's patriotic background, it was only natural for him to join the young men from the area in what proved to be a heady adventure. The nation had been flexing its nationalistic muscles for several years over the mistreatment of the Cubans by their Spanish masters. Real or imagined, offenses were loudly and tenaciously trumpeted in the many dailies of William Randolph Hearst and Joseph Pulitzer for a long time before that fateful day when the USS Maine exploded in Havana Harbor. But on February 15, 1898, 266 crewmen of the Maine lost their lives in an explosion whose cause to this day has created more controversy and disagreement each time it has been investigated. The certainties are, however, that the Maine DID explode, 266 members of the United States Navy were killed, and both Spain and the United States were now on a collision course for war.

The Spanish American War and the USS Yosemite

On March 30, 1898, the United States requested Spain grant Cuba its independence. One day later the Spanish refused. On April 6 the Pope, and a day after that the ambassadors of England, Germany, France, Italy, Austria and Russia all asked the United

States for peace. However, on April 11, President McKinley requested Congress declare war. But instead of declaring war, on April 19 the U. S. Congress first declared Cuba independent. On April 22 the U. S. Navy began to blockade Cuba and the next day Spain declared war. The United States followed suit on April 25, firing the first shots in Matanzas, Cuba harbor, but backdating the declaration to April 22. Youth all over America were hankering for a fight, as Marine General Smedley Butler would attest many years later, "....we built bonfires and stamped around shouting, 'Remember the Maine — to hell with Spain.'" (Thomas, p. 13). The boys in Detroit were about to go to war, and they hung out anxiously aboard the Yantic awaiting orders to come from the Navy. By April 29, they were in Norfolk being sworn in aboard the USS Franklin for the service of one year. According to his enlistment physical, Edwin Denby stood 6 feet and one eighth inches in height and weighed 286 pounds on the day of his enlistment at the age of 28. His eyes were blue and his hair light brown. He had a distinguishing scar on the left side of his forehead, and his health was reported as good. The Militia was transferred to their permanent ship, the USS Yosemite, on May 7, and Ned Denby was promoted to the rating of Gunner's Mate, 3rd Class on the following day. The Michigan Naval Militia was ready to go to sea in the country's service.

There were 304 men of the crew of the USS Yosemite. Thirty four of them were United States Marines, and the balance US Navy. Only four of the crew were regular Navy. Forty six of the naval militia men were either alumni, students, or, in the case of Mortimer Cooley, faculty, of the University of Michigan. Lt. Chief Engineer Cooley, himself an 1878 graduate of the Naval Academy, would return after the war to his job at the University of Michigan, and would eventually become Dean of the School of Engineering. The bulk of the crew were from the Michigan Naval Militia, and would continue holding reunions in Detroit for many years into the future. Two of the crew, Lt. (jg) Truman Newberry and Gunner's Mate Edwin Denby, would become Secretaries of the Navy. Landsman Albert H. Stanley was a public transportation specialist who worked for the Detroit United Railway. Following the war, he worked for a time in New Jersey transit and then was hired to revitalize the underground in London for which he was knighted by King George V. Chief Coxswain's Mate Henry B. Joy later became one of the principle organizers and president of the Packard Motor Company, while Ordinary Seaman J. Walter Drake would become president of the Hupp Motor Company, and later Assistant Secretary of Commerce under Calvin Coolidge.

USS Yosemite was originally built in 1892 as "El Sud" for the Morgan Line of the Southern Pacific Railroad. The SP had acquired the Morgan Line in 1885, and ran ships from New York to New Orleans, Galveston and Houston. At New Orleans passengers connected to the Sunset Limited (rail passenger train) for the balance of the cross country trip to California. Yosemite was acquired by the U.S. Navy for $575,000 in April 1898 and commissioned as an auxiliary cruiser on April 13, with Commander William H. Emory in command. She was part of the U. S. Navy's build-up before the war in which it bought or leased over 100 additional vessels to beef up the capabilities of the wartime Navy. She was 389 feet long, 48 feet abeam, capable of making 16 knots. She carried ten 5 inch guns, six 6-pounder rapid fire guns and 2 Colt machine guns. After getting fitted for naval service at Philadelphia and Newport News, she headed to Key West, Florida on May 30, was assigned to duty with the Eastern Squadron off Cuba, and departed US waters for the war in the Caribbean on June 7.

She arrived in Havana the same day, then almost immediately was dispatched to Santiago de Cuba where she joined up with USS Panther who carried a landing party of 677 Marines, the 1st Marine Battalion, bound for Guantanamo Bay. Arriving there on the 10th, one of USS Yosemite's landing boats carried the first group of Marines ashore on the Cuban mainland, and reportedly, a Michigan man was first to hoist the US flag over Cuban soil.

In subsequent actions against the Spanish while defending their Guantanamo base, we have the unforgettable picture of Marines, hot, tired and dirty, being surprised by Spanish troops while they skinny dipped in Guantanamo Bay. Many of the Marines, having no other recourse, fled the waters in birthday suits, plucked weapons from wherever they could be found and attacked au natural until the enemy was beaten back and withdrew. Stephen Crane, the famous novelist, and feature writer working for Blackwoods Magazine would leave us his memorable portrait of "Marines Signaling Under Fire at Guantanamo" from this same action.

After Guantanamo Bay, Yosemite made a brief stop at Santiago and then headed for Jamaica for the next few days. In the early morning hours of June 16 occurred a most controversial and curious incident involving Yosemite. She came upon a Spanish troopship, Purissima Concepcion, which was headed for Cuba and reported to be carrying $100,000 in gold for payment to Spanish troops. Observing the enemy combatant the Officer of the watch, Lt. Gilbert Wilkes, notified Commander Emory who was sleeping in his cabin on the deck below the bridge. There being no response from the Captain, Lt. Wilkes called to him again. After getting no answer the second time, he made one more and final attempt to rouse Captain Emory. However, the Purissima Concepcion slipped past Yosemite without drawing a shot.

No mention of this incident appeared in Yosemite's log, yet the story got into the newspapers stateside and there was natural speculation about the possible intoxication or impairment of Captain Emory. The log entry for that morning reported the weather as "clear". Yet in captain Emory's memoir, "The Life of an American Sailor", that same morning was described as "weather so thick as not to be able to distinguish objects." This may not have created the controversy, however, another book by yet another Yosemite crew member, Landsman Joseph Stringer, entitled "The Story of the USS Yosemite" blamed officers of the watch (Lt. Wilkes) for Yosemite's missing the capture of such a lucrative prize. As Wilkes was quite popular with the crew, having come from Detroit like almost all the rest of them, another book would follow giving an alternative view. "The USS Yosemite, Purissima Concepcion Incident, June 16, 1898" written by Chief Boatswain's

Mate Henry B. Joy, claimed that he was part of the deck crew at the time of the incident and that the enemy ship had been clearly visible. Joy also stated that he had personally seen Captain Emory at the porthole of his cabin, but that the Captain had remained in his quarters. He further added that the facts of the incident "reflect no discredit on Lt. Wilkes, the officer on watch." Joy laid the fault of the failure squarely and solely upon Captain Emory. In later years, as an attorney, Ned was involved in taking statements from crew members determined to see justice done and Wilkes' name cleared, but no further action was ever forthcoming.

After returning briefly to Cuba, Yosemite headed for Puerto Rico on June 23. The final chapter of her War cruise was about to take place.

Describing the June 28th action in a letter to his younger brother Garvin in Detroit, Ned told him, "In the gray dawn, misty and rainy, about 5 o'clock, a cloud lifted and showed a large steamer close in shore, and making full speed for San Juan." It was Yosemite's third day of blockade duty outside San Juan harbor, and she had spotted the Spanish troopship, Antonio Lopez. "We turned upon her," Ned continued, "and when about four miles distant we fired a five-inch shell across her bow and a second, to which her only response was a black cloud of smoke from her funnel. She was running for it in full earnest. Then, from Capt. Emory on the bridge came the thrilling order, 'Sink her!'" The Spanish blockade runner, a converted ocean liner carrying half a million rations, guns, projectiles and 50 tons of gunpowder, was attempting to sneak into the harbor unnoticed. Within two miles of her goal, Yosemite opened fire, raking the Lopez with her five inch and six pounder guns. Whether intentionally or not, Antonio Lopez went aground before reaching safety and was virtually destroyed by the guns of Yosemite. Ned's letter continues to describe the action: "In the meantime a great cloud of white smoke had risen from the gaunt fortress, and a distant roar told us that Morro [El Morro, the citadel fortress guarding the entrance to San Juan harbor] had opened on us. We were well within range, and you can imagine how interesting it was waiting for that shot to strike! It did strike in perfect line, but far afield. The next was nearer, and the next, until they were whistling through our rigging. Then the gunboats came out of the harbor, all gallantly arrayed in flags the size of acre fields. They thought probably we would flee like a frightened deer. But Capt. Emory had business where he was and regretted his inability to leave. Instead, we turned upon the gunboats and poured in a terrific fire. The Ship shook from stem to stern. She was at times almost hidden in powder smoke, but we knew that above it all our battle flags were waving. Of course, the gunboats were firing vigorously at us all the time and with great skill. But the Lord God of battle was with us yet and though every man on the spar deck had a sore neck after the action (on the gun deck we could not hear the whistling as plainly and did not have to dodge) not a single shot struck us. One splashed water on the ship I was told, another is said to have passed between one of the small boats and the deck, but none struck.

"The gunboats fared badly, however. They were struck repeatedly, and finally one turned tail and staggered back into the harbor. The lookout reported her as sinking, and at St. Thomas we were told she had gone down. We shall probably never know for certain." With some modest bravado he next related "At eight bells [toward the end of the morning watch] we withdrew some distance , not quite out of range of Morro's vaunted Krupp, and squatting around the deck amid the glistening shells provided for the guns we partook of beans." But the day's action was not quite finished. "Then we returned to the attack. The remaining gunboats had discreetly withdrawn nearer the fort, but they continued to pour in a vigorous fire. We maintained our position, filling the transport with shot, until we judged her to be destroyed and then we withdrew. It was time; Morro's guns were dropping shells with most painful accuracy all around." (EDJ August 14, 1898 Ned Denby to Garvin Denby, letter quoted)

The destruction of Antonio Lopez being nearly completed, Yosemite withdrew beyond the range of enemy guns, and took up her blockade duties once again. She had faced the enemy guns of three combatants and the guns of the castle as well, and had come away unscathed. By July 15 she was relieved of blockade duties by USS New Orleans, and after a three day stopover in Danish St. Thomas (the United States did not purchase the Danish Virgin Islands until 1915), she headed back to Virginia. She arrived at Hampton Roads July 22, and stayed there until August 15. Her crew was discharged from the naval service on August 22, 1898, the war having been brought to a very successful American conclusion several days earlier. Yosemite remained an active naval vessel for the next two years, serving much of her time as a station ship at Guam, another newly acquired American possession from the recent war. On November 13, 1900 a large typhoon struck the island and Yosemite was blasted loose from her moorings, first aground, and then out to sea. Badly damaged in the storm, the Navy decided she was not worth repairing and she was towed out into the Pacific and scuttled.

In 1902 the United States Navy awarded the sailors of Yosemite's crew the Congressional Medal (not to be confused with the Congressional Medal of Honor), and the Admiral Sampson Medal for their part in the action off San Juan. They also received, a bounty of three month's pay for combat against a superior foe, the only such reward of the Spanish American War, and the last time in history that the Navy made such a "prize" award. In a January 23, 1902 article describing the action, a Detroit Free Press writer reported, "The Yosemite was doing duty on blockade for which she was not fitted or intended. Had she been struck by a single projectile she would probably have been destroyed."

The Michigan Naval Militia returned to Detroit and their beloved Yantic. It seems the old girl had a couple more chapters in her story before going the way of all ships. She remained the floating home of the Militia from 1899 to 1907 when a larger vessel was requested from the Navy and subsequently the USS Don Juan de Austria was dispatched to Detroit to take her place. The Yantic was assigned duty in Hancock, MI. until World War I when she became the training vessel at the Great Lakes Naval Training facility. The Don Juan had also been sent into the Atlantic during the Great War, leaving the Michigan Militia without a training ship until 1919. The Navy offered the USS Yantic once again, with the stipulation that the Michigan Militia fetch her from Chicago.

After years at Great Lakes the Yantic was in dire need of major repairs and the story of the trip back to Detroit was filled with harrowing mishaps which easily became many a salty yarn. Including two nearly fatal storms and an embarrassing passage through the St. Clair Flats ship canal which, due to the fact that she was being gingerly towed at a snail's pace, bottled up nearly ten miles of Great Lakes shipping. The Yantic's boiler was repaired and she managed to do some cruising in 1920, and put in a full season in 1921. However, by 1922 she was again replaced by a more modern ship, the USS Dubuque, a gunboat built in 1904 in Morris Heights, New York.

From a newspaper article in 1929,

"She was tied up at the foot of Townsend Avenue adjoining the Naval Reserve Armory and was used as a heating plant for that building and for the Dubuque during winter months, an arrangement that was more economical than using the Dubuque's boilers.

"For more than seven years the old ship dozed at her dock dreaming of the days when all the world knew her. Then on the night of October 22 she gave up the ghost. Three men were sleeping on her the night she died. Chief Machinist's Mate Nelson was one of these. He awoke to find his hand was in cold water and when he got up to see what it was all about he found that the water was knee deep on the berth deck. By the time he had made his way to the companionway it was up to his armpits. He awakened the other men who were sleeping on the gun deck and all of them were able to make their way to the dock before Yantic settled into the mud with a gurgle. The water was up level with the main deck when she finally came to rest." (Detroit Saturday Night, December 21, 1919)

The same article went on to report that no one could have regretted her demise more than Lt. Commander Brodhead who had been an apprentice seaman when Yantic had arrived in Detroit in 1897. It had been Cmdr. Brodhead who had so tenaciously persevered in bringing Yantic back to Detroit in 1919. After Yantic settled into her final grave, the Detroit Naval Armory would be built on the same parcel of land up the bank toward Jefferson Avenue, in the following year of 1930.

Though Ned Denby did not live to see the sparkling and spacious Detroit Naval Armory, he surely must have visited the proud but aging Yantic in her last years, for it is known that he attended many reunions of Yosemite's crew, and that he never failed to remember or to help a shipmate in need. Nor did his shipmates ever forget him. When the new armory was completed in 1930, on the south side of the building facing downriver they would erect a memorial to their friend, who certainly must have contributed his share of the over 250 shells that Yosemite had lobbed into Antonio Lopez. Behind that now-closed naval armory building, the graveyard of the Yantic has become completely overgrown, fenced off and unrecognizable. There are probably few Detroiters who know of the glory that is buried there in the mud — but Ned Denby would not mind. For him it was never about the glory or the recognition. It was all about the nation, and about serving it, and preserving it. And that is exactly what he and his generation did.

In point of fact, it is what Ned Denby gave almost all of his life doing. That was why they loved him so.

THE YOSEMITE

Many a fathom down she lies, With her forefoot buried deep;
And we like to feel it's on even keel That she rests in her last,
long sleep.

O, the fish will swim where our hammocks swung.

And down in the silent sea

The waters blue will swash where you, My shipmate, talked
with me.

And down in the deep where the mermaids keep Their tryst,
its laughter ringing,

Perhaps some ghostly Johnnie Burns Will report: "The devils
are singin'."

Though her decks be wet, her guns are set Just as they always
were;

And at every watch will come the report: "They're ready for
action, Sir,"

She carried her country's flag so fair, And she did her share in
the fight,

And she only bowed her fore-top proud To the storm king's
dreadful might.

When the waters lash and the lightnings flash, There will
sound in brazen tones

The Yosemite's bell as she rings her knell In the locker of Davy
Jones.

by
Samuel S. Harris
Petty Officer 2nd Class Gunner's Mate
USS Yosemite 1898
Michigan Classmate Yosemite Shipmate

Chapter Six

*"I believe that if we should assert today that the sun had shown,
the Democracy would totter to her feet and feverishly proclaim that it
was all a mistake — that the heat and light and comfort that seemed to
come to us from that great luminary was in reality the after-glow from
the prosperity left by the last Democratic administration."*

Edwin Denby, Campaign Speech, November 3, 1904

Congressional Years
Michigan House

During the fateful year while Ned was fighting the nation's sea battles in the sun-swept Caribbean, his parents returned to the United States. Despite Ned's misgivings in 1888 about his father's job security in China, his services were retained by the Republican Administration of Benjamin Harrison, and retained again when Grover Cleveland was re-elected in 1892. It was not until William McKinley was elected in November of 1896 that it became apparent that Charles' sojourn in the Far East was coming to a close. He had been the longest serving United States minister to China in our history, and remains so to this day. In June Charles Jr. was on his way back to China as the representative of an American business syndicate. He and his father nearly passed each other going in opposite directions, as the Colonel was on his way to Washington, D. C. to report to the state Department. Perhaps to show no hard feelings, perhaps because he greatly valued the loyal support of a life-long Democrat, perhaps both, by September of 1898 President McKinley had appointed Charles Sr. to the "Commission Appointed by the President to Investigate the Conduct of the War Department in the War with Spain." As in any endeavor the size of a nation going to war, there had been massive mistakes made, particularly in the area of supply, or the quality thereof, and McKinley and the public wanted answers. And even before finishing this assignment, the President next appointed Charles to the Philippine Commission on January 16, 1899, officially known as the "First Philippine Commission". The Philippine Commission's job was to examine conditions in that country, which had just become a United States' possession at the close of the Spanish American War the previous year, and to make recommendations about the government of the new colony going forward. So close did the appointment to the Philippine Commission follow on the previous investigative work that the Colonel was held over in Washington to complete the first report which was handed to McKinley February 9, 1899. Stopping in Evansville for one day on their trip west, the Denbys were treated to a Midwestern winter's delight of 8 degrees below zero. They sailed from the West Coast on the America Maru on February 22, once again headed to a wildly strange and dangerous far eastern location in the service of the United States. Garvin, now twenty-one, accompanied them as Charles' secretary.

Ned returned from the Navy to a Detroit which was teetering on the edge of explosive growth. Having lived in the Orient, having fought in the Caribbean, having honed his manhood in the exotic east and the cauldron of battle, he was well poised for the next meaningful experiences of his young life. He opened up his own law practice in the Hammond Building, but by 1902 he had formed a law partnership with Samuel L. May, one of his Yosemite shipmates who was at that time Circuit Court Commissioner for Wayne County, and M. Hubert O'Brien, a young Democrat who would remain one of his closest friends for the rest of his life.

By this time his circle of friends and supporters had grown enough that he, following closely in the path of his father before him, decided to test the waters of political office. Unlike his father, however, he would not enter the fray as a Democrat for one apparent, and another very practical reason. His father was beginning to find himself increasingly on the side of the so-called 'expansionists', or those who favored the nascent formula of America claiming or annexing foreign territory, primarily for strategic defense purposes. Charles understood far better than others in his party the value of expansion, not only for national defense, but primarily for protecting international markets and trade routes. He was open to the cautious approach which McKinley advocated on how best for the United States to handle the Philippine question. America had stepped into a very tricky situation in the Philippines, and while honestly attempting to formulate the surest way to lead the Philippine people to a form of democratic self-governance, had become embroiled in local hostilities which were taking a far greater toll in lives and lucre than had ever been foreseen when we started the process. Of course, there were many who wanted the Philippines, and any imagined responsibility of the United States for them, to simply go away. But with the almost complete destruction of the Spanish Navy during the recent war, a power vacuum had been created in the Far East, and McKinley knew that some nation was going to fill it. He was determined, however reluctantly, that that power was NOT going to be any OTHER than the United States of America. Having served for so many years in the east and knowing its problems, challenges, strengths and limitations, the Colonel came down strongly on the side of what had come to be labeled "the Imperialists". It was an entirely new argument for American politicians. America had talked herself (thanks to Pulitzer and Hearst) into "saving" the legitimately mistreated Cuban people, had resoundingly won this "splendid little war", (John Hays in a letter to Theodore Rossevelt) and now had to step up to the plate to face the responsibility of becoming the world power that her military success had obtained. One major responsibility seemed to be the occupation, for however short or long a time, of the Philippine Islands, or some portion of them, if for no other reason than to prepare them to govern themselves, and to keep them from falling into the clutches of a power inimical to American interests.

In addition to siding politically with his father against the Democrats, Ned was also faced with the blunt fact that Michigan was at this time a heavily Republican state. Anyone wishing to enter politics might want to at least consider this very plain political reality: the Governor, the Lt. Governor, the Secretary of State, the Attorney General, the Treasurer, the Auditor General, 31 of 32 State Senators, all 100 state representatives, both U.S. Senators, and 11 out of 12 U.S. Representatives were Republican in 1903. For a successful political life in Michigan, one had far better chances with the elephant than the donkey.

But before his political ambitions advanced to this state, let us look at one or two events which helped Ned Denby arrive at the conclusion of running for political office himself. Eight American Presidents have died while serving in the office of the Presidency. Four from natural causes, and four from the dastardly hands of assassins. Ned was only eleven when James Garfield had been gunned down at the train station in Washington, D. C. But he was a fully mature thirty one years old when the next assassin shot William McKinley at the Temple of Music at the Pan-American Exposition in Buffalo, New York. In October, 1901, Ned received a letter from his friend A. P. Glenour from Glasgow, Scotland. He had met Glenour through mutual Detroit friends, and the two shared an apparently lively correspondence, at least for a time. After commiserating with his friend over their shared loss of a hero, the recently deceased President, Glenour went on to tell Ned that of all the tributes to the late President that he has read, the one Ned penned in his last letter is as "grand and beautiful an appreciation" as anything he had seen. He continued, "You do have a gift for writing (and speaking) splendid English...... Some of these days, if we don't have you in Washington doing your country good service, we must insist that you pass a part of your time in your library following in the footsteps of Rhodes, Fiske, Bancroft, Prescott and the others, for you must employ this talent - and it is indeed an unusual talent - for your countryman's edification and delight!" This is not the first, not the last, and certainly not the only testimonial from those who knew him concerning his talents along these lines. Ned seemed always to have been recognized as a natural orator and a born leader.

In addition, then, to the lead his father's example provided him, and in addition to the promptings of his own heart, Ned had the gentle, and sometimes not so gentle, nudging of many who knew him best, and sensed the path he was to follow. One such friend, or more accurately, family of friends, was the William Pegram Hamilton family. Born in Owensboro, Kentucky in 1864 of Scottish parents, Will Hamilton was educated at the Larchmont Academy and the University of Glasgow. He came to Detroit in 1883, and in time married Mary McClellan Farrand, the daughter of Dr. and Mrs. David Osbourne Farrand of Detroit. The Hamiltons had three children, all creative offspring of their very artistic mother. Two were published authors, two artists and all three wrote poetry. Their father, Will to all his friends, rose to become the President of the Clinton Woolen Manufacturing Company of Clinton, Michigan, and eventually would also hold positions in two of Detroit's prominent banks. He was Vice President of the National Bank of Commerce (on whose Board Ned served), and a Director of the Union Trust. An avid 'clubman' as it was called in his time, he belonged to the Detroit Athletic Club, University Club, Huron Mountain Club, Grosse Point Club and the Grosse Pointe Hunt Club, among others. During World War I he was a Michigan director of the American Red Cross. There were many opportunities for Ned and Will's paths to cross, but it is most likely that they met at the University Club, which was one of the first organizations that Ned joined when he arrived in Detroit. Just as he had so admired the entire Drew clan in China, in the same manner he seemed to have a genuine affection for each member of the Hamilton family, and was welcomed as one of them. It was once again the same familial acceptance and atmosphere that Ned found among the five siblings of the Lyster family — something always called to him from the days of his own five siblings in Evansville. Though he would only bring two children into the world himself, people who were familiar with Ned's immediate family in later years would often remark with envy the closeness of their family unit.

Ned also took his place rapidly in the varied social atmosphere of the bustling metropolis, becoming involved for several years in the Annual Charity Ball to benefit the Women's Hospital and Infants Home, "the Ball of St. Valentine", as well as private parties where his name was included among society elite. By 1900 he was a frequent cast member in plays produced by the Detroit Comedy Club which were held in the Detroit Opera House. He was a member of the cast of "Aunt Jack", described by the Detroit Free Press as "a roaring farce comedy in three acts by the English playwright Arthur Lumley. (DFP 12-12-1900) By 1901 he is listed on the "executive board" of the Club, and he would appear in several theatrical productions over the next few years.

As early as May of 1900 he was selected as a delegate to the State Republican convention, and by November he was beginning to give speeches before various groups, political, commercial, as well as social. In June he was a member of the committee of the University of Michigan Association tasked with the job of collecting money to send Michigan's Track Team to the Paris Exposition Olympic games, and by November of that year he was listed on the board of governor's of the University Club as they were about to move into their new accommodations in Detroit. In June, 1901, he spoke to over 450 guests at the National Association of Manufacturers on the lawn of the Country Club of Grosse Point Farms.

Throughout 1902 as he practiced law to make his living, he remained socially active, and ever more politically active. Not forgetting his military service, on March 25 he became 1st Lieutenant in the founding of the Gilbert Wilkes Command of the Spanish American War veterans. In October he gave a theater party to the Detroit Opera House chaperoned by his friends Will and Mary Hamilton, followed by supper at the Russell House. Attending were a Miss Avery, Miss Longyear, and Miss Tapping, along with his brother, Garvin, and good friend Henry Lyster. It was not the first time his name would appear in society notes along with that of several eligible young women. On the same date as his theater party, the Detroit Free Press in discussing Republican candidates for the upcoming mid-term election, remarked that the candidate "against whom no one is talking is Edwin Denby the well known young lawyer." On October 18 of that year, the Republicans held the first ever direct voting primary for political candidates in the State of Michigan. The Democrats would soon follow. A surprise consequence of the direct ballot of candidates, however, left no African American or Jewish candidates on the ballot; the former process of hand-picking candidates had tried to include them. Unsurprising was the garnering of enough votes for the young Mr. Denby to be placed on the ballot. On November 4, 1902, Ned was elected as a member of the 42nd Michigan House of Representatives, in the first of his five political contests. Later that month, he found himself on a committee of three from the Michigan Alumni Association in a spirited debate with officials from the University of Michigan concerning where the impending championship football game between Michigan and Minnesota would take place. Either on the University's

Regent's Field, which was currently being expanded to meet the growing demands of a burgeoning number of football fans, or on the antiquated Bennet Field in Detroit which had been constructed as a baseball venue, and whose seating capacity appeared to the University men as far too limited. The Detroit contingent wanted the prestige of having the important game played in their city, while the Michigan men fretted that the lack of seating would end up reflecting badly on the University if fans had to be turned away. It certainly was a time when Ned found himself on both sides of a question, and it would not be the last. After a lengthy debate over each field's merits, the university men won out, and the game was played on the campus on the upgraded Regent's Field. Michigan defeated Minnesota by a score of 23-6, winning its second straight Western Conference Title (later known as the

Big Ten), its second National Title, and its twenty-second straight victory. The Fielding Yost years were in full flower.

It was a surprise to no one that Ned Denby had won his seat in the Michigan Legislature. Even his opponents liked him; it was difficult, if not impossible, to find his enemy. While in Lansing, he served on the Judiciary committee, as chairman of the University Committee, and on the Military Affairs committee. He wasted no time in making his name by sponsoring bills almost immediately on such various subjects as water and sewage systems to building a hospital devoted to tuberculosis patients. In February Ned made a sensation in the House when he spoke of his bill to change the tax law in order to stop millions of dollars of property taxes due Detroit from being lost because of estate trustees choosing to live in a suburb where taxes were lower. This was especially astonishing, the Detroit Free Press gushed, coming from Ned Denby who was "figured among Detroit's four hundred." Ned went further: "Nothing tends more toward making socialists and anarchists than the spectacle of the rich and powerful evading their just share of the public burdens." (DFP 2-12-1903) The bill passed the House almost unanimously and went to the Senate where it ran into considerable resistance.

Surprisingly, one of Ned's best friends, James O. Murfin, a UofM Law graduate and "Bachelor" pal, had been hired to lobby against the bill in the Senate, which he did so skillfully that it was defeated in committee and not heard of again. However, as in many cases of this nature Ned did not let political disagreement cost him friendships, and he and James Murfin would remain close to the end of their days.

Most usually remembered today, Ned sponsored and shepherded through the legislature the Denby Act, which raised the capitalization limit of industrial and commercial organizations from $5,000,000 to $25,000,000. Michigan, like many western states, had harbored a suspicion of large corporations, fearing that they would exert undue influence over government affairs. But Ned realized that without this new law, many of the industries

124

coming into being, particularly in this new-fangled automobile business, would simply locate in states which allowed the greater capitalization which such corporations were beginning to need. The bill was modified several times, but finally passed the House on May 6. On May 14 the Free Press noted that "there was an unusual demonstration this afternoon when Speaker Carton called Representative Denby, of Detroit, to the rostrum [to preside over the committee of the whole], showing the great popularity of the capable young man from the metropolis. With the usual pounding with paper weights there were cheers for Denby, and calls for a speech, but Denby modestly assumed the gavel and went on with business." Indeed, within thirteen years, Michigan would be looking to increase even the Denby Act's limitations on capitalization. "When I introduced that bill," Ned told The Detroiter in 1916, "it did not seem possible that we would ever need a larger limit than $25,000,000. The consequences of this act were feared at that time, and two Detroit newspapers cartooned it as an octopus clutching the State of Michigan and leading it on to its prey. Today this limit is entirely inadequate, however. The Ford Motor Co., for instance, has already exceeded it, and other companies such as the Packard, are approaching that limit." The Denby Act of 1903 would help lay the foundation for Michigan's success in becoming the auto capital of the world.

As he would later do in the United States House, he ingratiated himself with the movers and shakers in the Michigan Legislature. Admired for his integrity, hard work, and probably more than any other of his admirable traits, for his loyalty, he became life-long friends with John J. Carton, Speaker of the House, and was told in no uncertain terms, that the Speakership of Michigan's House would be his if he would run for a second term. At the end of the Legislative session in June, the Free Press was profuse in its praise for the novice congressman.

"He has a ready wit and inexhaustible good nature. His views of every public question have proved broad and cosmopolitan. His geniality made him friends with both the farmers and the city members, and it is doubtful whether any other man could have put through the bill liberalizing the Michigan law as to corporations. The farmers are naturally suspicious of anything of this kind, but when the first bill on this subject was found to be defective, it required nothing more than Denby's word that the second bill contained nothing new to give it the unanimous vote of the house, without even a reading of the measure.

Denby's career makes it certain that if he wants another term he can have it, but people in Detroit are talking of running him for congress in the first district, and if he wants to make the run, he will have plenty of backing financially as well as otherwise, from all cases of the Republicans of that district." (DFP 6-7-1903)

At a Municipal League meeting held in November, Charles Hampton, chairman of the Democratic state committee, made a critical and unflattering comment about the Michigan Legislature from the past session which caused an immediate response from Ned.

"I want to enter protest against the slurs thrown at the members of the last Michigan legislature when my friend here called them 'sapient gooseberries'," fired back Representative Denby. "Those men in the legislature were an honest body; while I was there I never saw any evidence of crooked work. There was no wrongdoing as far as the lower house is concerned; I will assure you of that...When men show themselves as contemptible, treat them with contempt. But when men are subject to all those temptations, and pass through them unscarred, they should have more than ordinary credit." Mr. Hampton replied: "....I give Mr. Denby credit for what he did; I will say that had I been in the last legislature, I should have voted upon every question just exactly the way Mr. Denby did. That's a good deal for a Democrat to say of a Republican." (DFP 11-21-1903)

It was that, indeed, and printed in a Democrat newspaper to boot! As early as May of 1903, it was already being talked about publicly, as it was to be printed in the newspapers a little later, that a man of Ned Denby's obvious caliber, though lauded in Lansing, was even more needed in Washington. In December, Ned spoke at a gathering at the Unitarian Church in Detroit on the same dais with W. E. B. Dubois. Organized by the Twentieth Century Club, the gathering was held to publicize, and raise money for, the work being done at Atlanta University, one of the oldest African American centers of learning in the country. On December 5, he presided as Toastmaster over the annual banquet of the Kent Chapter of Phi Delta Phi, his law fraternity from Michigan.

A seminal event which would have great influence on the next several years of his life was the founding of the Detroit Board of Commerce. The great, civic organization was officially founded on June 30, 1903 when a group of 253 Detroit men gathered in the Turkish Room of the Cadillac Hotel and each paid $100 to join. Early in its work the Board was instrumental in bringing the Packard Motor Car Company to Detroit from Warren, Ohio through the auspices of investors Henry Joy and Truman Newberry, two of Ned's Yosemite shipmates and friends. The Board of Commerce "brought into one association the members of three former bodies, making a compact organization with civic as well as commercial aims. The Board ... brought into active co-operation nearly all the leading businessmen of the city and many of the professional men," so noted the 1911 Edition of the Encyclopedia Britannica. The 1900 Census revealed a Detroit population of 285,704, of whom 96,503 were foreign born, many with little or no English skills. By 1907 the Board of Commerce was working directly with officials of Ellis Island to urge incoming skilled immigrants to head for Detroit where workmen were needed on an ever-growing basis. After joining during the first year of its existence, Ned would realize through this body an unending source of friendships and working relationships, and many opportunities to contribute to the advancement and well-being of his fellow man. Indeed, in just a few years, he would rise to lead this several thousand strong business networking behemoth, and it would help point him in directions which would aid in his varied endeavors for years to come. So integral to the rest of his life, it would be The Board which would fete him in the most stupendous homecoming that had ever been mounted for any American to that date in March of 1924, when he returned to Detroit bloodied, but unbowed.

Having served Michigan well, on the football field, in the law classrooms, in the naval militia and at war, in his law practice and his fledgling business interests, as well as in the Lansing legislature, it was now time for Ned to turn his attention toward a higher goal: the U. S. House of Representatives. But before that goal was sought, or reached, a lightning bolt exploded from an unexpected source.

Chapter Seven

Congressional Years
Family Affairs

After Charles Denby had concluded his work on the First Philippine Commission, he returned to the United States in October 1899. Once again Charles was delegated to complete the Commission's Report in Washington, and by February of 1900 was already being mentioned as a member of the Second Commission. This second commission lasted for sixteen years and became the governing body of the Islands. After serving his country continuously abroad for just over fifteen years, Charles, probably with some reluctance, declined work on the second commission. Some rumors had it that he was to be its head. However, that honor went to an upcoming federal judge from Ohio named William Howard Taft. It would serve to launch Mr. Taft's national reputation. In April the Colonel traveled to Evansville where the city fathers threw a splendid banquet at the St. George Hotel in honor of his and John W. Foster's prestigious diplomatic careers. Garvin headed to Detroit at this time to go to work for his brother-in-law, Gilbert Wilkes. By early May, the Commission's report finally completed, the Colonel was back in Evansville, this time seemingly, for good.

However, the peace of the family was once again to be disrupted, as in early June the first rumors of the great upheaval in the Celestial Empire began to reach the family in Evansville. The Boxer rebellion had begun in 1899, and for nearly a year had been building momentum throughout the north of China. Directed against foreigners, and in its early stages, primarily against the Christian missionaries, by the middle of 1900 it had grown to the point of threatening the Legations in Peking, and the consulates in other cities.

The Colonel had just begun writing a series of articles for Evansville Newspapers, and explained his feelings about the origins of the unrest, even while the Denbys anxiously awaited word on the safety of Charles Jr. and his family. The Colonel laid the beginnings of the problem firmly at the doorstep of Japan. "But the Japanese War of 1894 rudely broke into the pleasing contemplation of national progress [under the Dowager Empress Cixi's attempts to modernize the extremely backward empire]. It dissolved all illusions and left the great giant shriveled into a pigmy. Let Japan take to her soul the wretched lesson that for monetary glorification she wounded to death her Eastern sister." Once the Japanese had set the stage for appropriating whole sections of China, by 1897 the Germans were following suit, followed closely by the British, the French and the Italians. The Boxer backlash was the result. By August 15 the Eight Nation Coalition had invaded China and rescued the Legations in Peking and by September the Denbys were finally receiving letters explaining how close run a thing it had been. Charles Jr. and Martha Orr were living in Tientsin, and Charles reported that a Marine had been killed directly at his side. "A vase was broken at my feet by a Mauser bullet, a shell struck a wall five feet above my head. A shrapnel burst in the air above me and fell in a shower all about."

"M ___was splendid," he continued, speaking of his wife, Martha. "She never complained, she never gave up. She was never exacting, she was always cheerful and she was as brave as any hero of the war. They all said at Von Hanneken's where twenty-seven of us were gathered that M___ was the hero of the

party. Mr. Detring told her she deserves the medal for bravery."
(Evansville Courier 9-9-1900)

In August of 1900 the Colonel wrote a letter to a local newspaper calling out the Democratic Presidential candidate William Jennings Bryan for voting for the ratification of the Treaty of Paris of 1898 which ended the Spanish American War, and ceded the Philippine Islands to the United States, and then campaigning against the Republicans using the "anti-Imperialist" theme. To Charles it seemed as though Bryan had voted for the treaty only so he could then during the campaign outspokenly oppose it — while American soldiers were dying in the early stages of the insurrection. The Republican National Committee quickly endorsed Charles' letter, reprinted it, and naturally made the most of it during the campaign. That autumn, Charles allowed no opportunity to escape him to tell anyone who would listen that the United States must hold onto the Philippines, if only from the aspect of its being a gateway to far eastern trade, and protecting America's share in what he correctly saw as the limitless market that Asia, and particularly China, would one day provide. Only the Japanese incursion into China in the 1930's, followed by the World conflict of the 1940's, and the Communist xenophobic bloodletting of the 1950's and 1960's would push back the promise of that market which Charles foresaw in the late 19th Century, nearly a hundred years before its realization. In September Ned's eldest brother, Graham, married his long time sweetheart, Olga Reis, after a courtship lasting a bit over three years. In February, 1901, Charles Jr. and Martha welcomed their second son into the world, Charles Denby III. That joyous news had hardly settled into the family psyche when the terrible tragedy of the sudden death of Gilbert Wilkes, Hattie's husband, descended upon them. He had passed away in Denver, Colorado on March 12, 1901 of hemorrhage of the lungs. Martha rushed to Denver to be with her only daughter in this mournful time. Young Wilkes was only thirty-eight years old, and had left his wife of eleven years with two small boys, Denby and Gilbert. Martha stayed with her daughter and grandsons in Denver until May. By late May

Hattie moved with her boys to Salt Lake City, Utah to live for a short while with Gilbert's parents. The cycle of life and death, birth and passing would continue, however, as August brought Ned's oldest brother, Graham and his wife Olga, the first of three daughters, Caroline Fitch, born August 17.

On September 6, 1901, Leon Czolgosz, an anarchist, shot President William McKinley twice in the abdomen in the Temple of Music at the Pan American Exposition in Buffalo, New York. In agony from his wounds, the President begged those about him to break the news gently to his invalid and beloved wife, and to stop the mob from murdering his assassin. He lingered, for six days, and even appeared to improve, but died on September 14, at 215am. For four years Charles had worked quite hard, and in several capacities, to assist McKinley in his efforts to find America's way in its chosen path of non-colonial imperialism. He had visited McKinley's White House on many occasions, prepared and presented two reports to him, stumped for his positions, written dozens of articles and given as many speeches in support of his plans. When Evansville held its own civic farewell a few days after the President's death, it was Charles Denby whom they appointed as key note speaker. In part, he said, "No man who has ever conducted important affairs of state with the President left his presence without an increased respect for his intellect, his judgment and his honesty of purpose. He was conscientious and clean handed.

"Never was his private character assailed. He will go down to history as one of the greatest men that this country has produced." (Evansville Journal-News, 9-19-1901) William McKinley was not a flamboyant man, nor a man given much to tooting his own horn. To understand how beloved he was by millions of his countrymen helps to bring him back a bit into a focus he has lost in our time. He presided over at least a part, and a very important one, of the expansion of America's role in our world, the ramifications of which are still being revealed and realized to this day. Great mutual respect cemented a relationship between Charles and the President which was, while not intimate, profound and enduring.

In November of 1901 the Denbys entertained a daughter of Sir Robert Hart, who was married to the Honorable William Beauclerc, Ambassador from the Court of St. James to Peru. Mrs. Beauclerc was traveling across the United States en route to join her husband. Surely many of the family had much to discuss and reminiscences to share. By Christmas things had begun to settle somewhat for the family as Garvin and Ned both journeyed from Detroit to Evansville for the holidays.

The Colonel spent the winter lecturing, working on his book, "China and Her People", and writing lengthy and astute articles for both of Evansville's dailies, as well as other papers who sought his opinions. In May, 1902, Martha was again traveling to Denver where she collected Hattie and her boys and took them for a visit to see their two uncles in Detroit. On May 16, Martha learned that she had been elected as Indiana's Vice-Regent for the Mt. Vernon Ladies Association, the non-profit group of women who have owned, operated, restored and preserved the home of George Washington since 1858, and still do to this day. Martha's mother, Harriet Valerie Fitch, had been Indiana's Vice-Regent from 1859 to 1880. Martha journeyed shortly after to Mt. Vernon for the annual meeting. That August, Charles and Martha went north for an extended vacation in Michigan. Martha joined Hattie and her sons at Hattie's summer cottage on Lake St. Clair north of Detroit, while Charles went fishing with Ned at the Huron Mountain Club in northern Michigan. The family remained on its extended northern vacation into October, after which Hattie moved with her two sons back to the family home in Evansville. In late December Wythe and Olga arrived from Alaska for the holidays at home. Wythe was a superintendent of mines in the Juneau area. They were joined by Ned and Garvin from Detroit. Except for Charlie's family, still in Tientsin, the Denbys were once again nearly all together.

In January of 1903 the Detroit Free Press announced the engagement of Miss Ester Jewel Strong of Detroit to Ned's younger brother, Thomas Garvin. In June, Charles and Martha journeyed to Detroit to attend the private ceremony at the bride's home.

Ned acted as Garvin's best man, and the bride was unattended. The following December Ned once again joined his parents and Hattie's and Graham's families in Evansville for the holidays. Garvin and his new wife joined the family for the New Year's celebration. Ned was now the lone sibling unmarried, and would remain so for a few more years. The family did not know it, but 1903 would be the last Christmas that the Colonel would be with them.

A robust and energetic public servant seventy years of age in 1900 when he declined participation in the Second Philippine Commission, Charles realized that the next and final chapter of his life would be the education of his countrymen concerning China, and the Far East. It was the age of Chautauqua, when learned and talented Americans toured the country edifying, enlightening and entertaining fellow citizens on all manner of subjects. Though others had served in China as missionaries, businessmen or government officials, no official minister had ever served as long as the Colonel, and few could command the august respect which attended the last years of his life. After almost two decades of public toil, he was still at times restless about contributing to the common good. He was working on his opus, "China and Her People", which was not to be published until two years after his death, but he was the type of man who needed to be useful. In January of 1904, he had accepted a request to travel to Buffalo, New York for a pair of lectures, and while there, he had unexpectedly run into an old friend in the person of Rev. Otis Smith, formerly the Pastor of the Walnut Street Presbyterian Church in Evansville, who prevailed upon the Colonel to accompany him to Jamestown, New York to deliver another lecture to his current congregation. The Colonel wrote his family that he would return home for a few days' rest right after Jamestown, and before heading westward for a speaking engagement in Kansas City, and then to Detroit for a series of five more appearances. After his lecture in Jamestown, he retired for the night to his room in the Sherman Hotel and about midnight of Wednesday, January 13, he began suffering from acute cardiac failure. He was able to summon help, and a physician arrived and remained with him through the night, but was unable to offer much relief. At 745 in the morning, the Colonel breathed his last. Ironically, before leaving on this last of his many speaking trips, he had confided to his old friend, mentor and law partner, Thomas Garvin, how worried he was about his wife's heart condition, and the unthinkable possibility that she might precede him in death. Almost as ironic was the fact that his personal physician had known for some time that the Colonel was not in the best of health, but this information was kept from him by the doctor and the family so as not to worry him unduly, or mar the remaining months of his life. The simple fact of that time was that medical science had progressed to the point of diagnosing problems which it had little idea of how to effectively treat.

The authorities in Jamestown first telegraphed his life-long friend in Evansville, James L. Orr, at 815am with the news of his passing, who in turn went straight to the offices of Graham Denby, several blocks away. It was Graham who then had the unenviable task of reporting his father's death to his mother. A delegation of civic dignitaries and friends was dispatched to Terre Haute, the nearest major east-west rail junction to meet the body and escort it south to Evansville.

The funeral was held several days later in St. Paul's Episcopal Church, with burial in Oak Hill Cemetery. Neither Charles, Jr., in China, nor Wythe, in Alaska, would be able to attend. However, Graham, Hattie, Ned and Garvin would be there to help their mother through her grief.

Less than a week after the funeral Ned wrote Mary Hamilton in Detroit, describing the shock and the grief with which they were all dealing. "It has been a terribly sad time," he says. "Mother bears her grief with splendid, womanly strength and courage. I am proud of her." He mentioned that they have spent the morning cutting clippings from newspapers, some of which he forwarded, but cautioned her not to believe everything she read, particularly the mention of the hymns his father allegedly selected for his own funeral. "He never made any request of the kind," he scoffed.

Charles left no directions, he claimed, saying his father felt the survivors were in charge and would make the best decisions. "In such matters he was supremely sane and sensible." He said they had been every day to the cemetery except the day he was writing. They are homebound because of heavy rain. "Hattie and Mother and I spend the day together somehow. Mother talks much about Father, but always quietly," he said mournfully, and added, "I have had little time or inclination for grieving. I think of Father as he was, in the prime of his intellect, high in the love and admiration of his fellow citizens, a splendid gentleman who had no old age, but died in the pride and fullness of his strength." He said he knew that both she and her husband, Will, "know it is not easy to lose a father, and it is not easy to write or talk about it for a while." (DPL Edwin Denby Jr. Papers, Box #1)

In 1903 Martha Fitch had written to the Hamiltons, inviting them to stop off at Evansville on their return to Detroit from a vacation in the south. She mentioned how proud they were of Ned's recent political achievement (his election to the Michigan House in 1902), as she cajoled "his dearest friends in the world" to come to stay with them. Perhaps Ned had had time to discuss with his father his ambition to run for the greater prize in Washington in 1904. Given the nearly coast-to-coast newspaper coverage of his prestigious father's demise, it certainly would have been important to Ned then and for all of his life to live up to the Colonel's standards, reputation and achievements. Colonel Charles Harvey Denby had established a reputation both accomplished and unassailable. From his southern heritage and civic-minded, deeply patriotic ancestors he brought his nonpareil sense of public duty, integrity, honor, and service to every endeavor of his life. It was bound to become the benchmark for his most outgoing and ambitious son.

By early March the papers were announcing Ned's firm decision not to return to Lansing, but to make the bid for the Congressional seat from Michigan's 1st district. Surprisingly, his opponent over the tax dodger's bill, his old friend Jimmie

Murfin, was heading up his campaign. Another Yosemite friend, wealthy socialite and businessman, Truman Newberry, decided later in the same month to enter the Republican primary for the same congressional race. Ned surely turned some heads when he categorically announced that he would not be bowing out of the race, despite Newberry's ability to greatly outspend him. The well-connected socialite also had the backing of two of the major Republican caucus organizations. During the election Ned came out strongly in favor of tariff status quo and also in favor of the United States negotiating with Panama over the Canal Treaty, instead of Columbia.

In early July 1904, the Vice Presidential candidate, Charles W. Fairbanks, along with Speaker of the House Uncle Joe Canon and Secretary of State John Hay all arrived in Detroit en route to the 50th Anniversary Celebration in Jackson, Michigan of the founding of the Republican Party. In an oak grove on what was called "Morgan's forty" then on the outskirts of Jackson, a group of like-minded anti-slavery people met to select candidates for state offices. Memorialized as the "Under the Oaks" celebration, the prestigious Republican Washington visitors were on hand to help the Michiganders pat themselves on the back. However, before the festivities in Jackson, the visiting dignitaries were invited to cruise the Detroit River on Truman Newberry's yacht, cleverly named the Truant. In an age which would be called chivalrous compared to those that followed, the gallant Newberry invited not only his Republican competitor, Ned Denby, but their Democrat rival, Alfred Lucking, as well.

Later in the year, Ned spent some time in Evansville during the month of July. While visiting with his family, he took a side trip to see some of his relatives from his father's side of the family who lived in the Lexington, Kentucky area. Undoubtedly, returning the favor of some of the relatives who had attended his father's services. While in Lexington, he wrote one of his lengthy and descriptive letters to his home in Detroit, addressed to Mary Hamilton, but obviously meant for the whole Hamilton family in his open and amusing way. He stayed with a friend of the

Hamiltons, Alan, an attorney and bachelor like himself, who in the custom of the day rented a large, spacious room from an older couple in the town. Ned described the home "on a nice shady street. His own room is finely furnished, high ceiled (sic) and roomy. His bed is one of those enormous mahogany affairs with a canopy and high side boards over which you have to hurdle ungainly to your rest. A delightful bed, so big, that as we reposed upon it, we could only communicate by telephone." He next described how Alan carted him about the town introducing him to several of his friends: "After lunch, the handshaking began. We went from office to office and met lawyers, we chased them into corners on the street, we waylaid them in dark places, and the timid visitor from the North was cast in their teeth at every turn." Later that evening they drove into the countryside to visit with several of Ned's female cousins, the McDowells. "We arrived hot and tired, and I fell into the arms of Cousin May, Cousin Madge, Cousin Nettie, and Cousin Julia, none of whom, except Cousin May (an old lady, my father's first cousin) had I ever seen before. I took to them at once." He went on to tell them about the old Southern manse in which these women lived: "Ashland is a delightful place of which, of course, all Kentucky is proud. [Ashland was the residence of Henry Clay for over forty years until his death in 1852, was briefly owned by Kentucky University, was re-purchased by Henry Clay's granddaughter, Anne Clay McDowell and her husband in 1883, and passed to their daughter Nanette (Cousin Nettie of Ned's letter), who lived there until her death in 1948.] There is nothing especially striking about it, only the charm of glorious lawns and trees and driveways. The house is a brick mansion, vine clad and possessing that something Southern so indefinably charming."

He went on to tell her of the following day's events: "At one o'clock the McDowell carriage came for us....." They dined with all four of the cousins at Ashland and then, "Cousin Madge took Alan and me driving in the afternoon. We went for a very pretty drive among the beautiful bluegrass landscape winding up at the much boasted cemetery where Henry Clay lies in state, while his headless figure in stone surmounts a beautiful, giant monument. His head was knocked off by lightning, and they have never appropriated the money to fix it on again, though the legislature set aside $20,000.00 for a monument to shameless Goebel. This is one of Kentucky's favorite whinings."* *[William Justus Goebel, the 34th Governor of Kentucky, after a checkered political career, to say the least, was assassinated only four days after assuming the State's highest office, in 1900, a mere five years before Ned visited his Kentucky relatives.]

"After the drive," he said, "we shook a few more legal hands, had dinner, and in the evening called upon the famous beauty Pat was reserving for me and with whom I was supposed to fall in love on sight. She is Miss Belle deLong, very pretty and very charming in every way, but I am ashamed to say I did not fall in love with her." It was not the first attempt on the part of friends to make him a match, nor would it be the last. Ned would take all such heavy-handed maneuvers in stride, and in the end, when the time came and the perfect girl arrived, he would know her immediately.

Though he seemed to genuinely enjoy himself on his Kentucky visit, and considered his new friend, Alan, a boon companion, after a few days' visit he confessed "I am a bit out of sympathy with the excessive conceit of Kentuckians. Alan amuses me immensely with his talk. Everything was so fine. An ordinary cornfield was hailed with, 'Ah, look at that, there's one of our rich Kentucky corn fields.' Everything was 'our Kentucky," or 'our blue grass' as if the state had a monopoly not only of the human charms but the beauties of nature as well. I almost rebelled when he remarked the first time we went to Ashland that we might expect an invitation to tea or something, for that was Kentucky style! Considering that the people were my cousins and that aside from that fact, hospitality isn't wholly unknown in Indiana or even as far north as Michigan, I thought 'our Kentucky style' was in danger of becoming mere brag."

Later in the visit he had another opportunity to become smitten with Miss deLong, but apparently it was not to be: "We dined very pleasantly with the deLongs and I still came back whole from the presence of the fair Belle though I must confess she is a most charming young woman." Just not quite charming enough. "I had my dessert," he said with his tongue in his cheek, "out of a Confederate souvenir spoon which I think improved the flavor of the ice." That evening he went alone back to Ashland to have tea with the family. There he met another member of the famous family Breckenridge. "Desha Breckenridge was back from St. Louis and I fell quite in love with him. He seems to me a splendid fellow and the vagaries of his horrible old dad must be a sore trial.

"I met the old man also (W. C. P. Breckenridge), who is most courteous and kindly in his manner and appearance, but a wrinkled, old rascal, as we all know." [William Campbell Preston Breckenridge, at this time nearly sixty-seven years of age, was just four months from his death; a lawyer and Democrat, he broke with much of his family to serve in the Confederate Cavalry, and acted as a bodyguard for Jefferson Davis toward the end of the war. He was married to a granddaughter of Henry Clay who died after barely a year of marriage; his second marriage produced his three children; in 1893 he married for a third time at the age of 56, and was shortly thereafter sued for breach of promise by his mistress, Madeleine Pollard. It is unclear whether Ned's reference to his friend Desha's "horrible old dad" was because he was a Democrat, a Confederate, a philanderer — or all three. In fairness to, and some defense of, this Breckenridge, he completely reversed himself on his feelings for the freed slaves and became a fierce advocate for African American rights in his later years. As well, both his daughter and his daughter-in-law became nationally known suffragettes.] It would seem that Ned's short visit to ante-bellum Kentucky was peopled with the interesting, the irritating and the infamous.

At the end of his stay in Lexington, he and Alan drove to Louisville and boarded the river steamer, Tarascon for the trip downstream to Evansville. He records it as "one of the most pleasing journeys I have ever taken. The weather was cool, cold in the evening, the steamer not crowded, the table good, the staterooms and linen clean and comfortable, and the river scenery simply beautiful." He mused about taking the trip again, it was so enjoyable, and then reports, "At Owensboro [birthplace of Will Hamilton] Alan pointed out to me the place where Will's house ought to show and we saluted the historic spot. He showed me also the island at Owensboro where he and Will potted a flock of quail most shamelessly some centuries ago." He told Mary Hamilton that they had now returned safely to Evansville, and that Wythe was there, probably the earliest he was able to get home from Alaska after their father's passing. He mentioned further that Wythe had just returned from the Post Office and handed him a letter from her husband, Will.

(Box #2, Edwin Denby Jr. Papers, DPL)

Chapter Eight

Congressional Years
First Term

In running for the honor of representing the first Michigan district in the lower house of the most prestigious legislature in the world, Ned Denby had, as the proverbial real estate meme goes, three things going for him: his friends, his friends, and his multitude of loyal friends. According to Pipp's Weekly of May 8, 1920, Ned was "so poor that he had to beg the newspapers for 'free' publicity'". [Davis, Conspicuous Production, p93.] More importantly, what he also did was form the Edwin Denby Club of boosters which eventually throughout his congressional race grew to a membership of over eight thousand, and incredibly lasted even after his demise in 1929, comprising members who had never met or known him. Though he would run against an incumbent, Alfred Lucking, who had served one term in the Fifty Eighth Congress, Ned first had to face the wealthy and much more extensively connected Truman Newberry in the Republican primary. Due to his army of dedicated workers, however, he was able to defeat Newberry by nearly a 1000 votes. According to the Detroit Journal,

"For three days prior to the primaries, and every day this week,

Denby headquarters on the fifth floor of the Hammond building have been crowded day and night by men not usually seen taking an interest in any political campaign.

"They are the young men more often seen assembled in the clubs. They are the young attorneys, young engineers, professional men of all sorts, prominent young businessmen, young men who have won recognition among their fellows by their own efforts. There were broad-shouldered athletes just out of college and older and more dignified alumni. Many were college men, all were staunchest friends of Denby. An old politician looked over the crowd about 2 o'clock in the morning and said, 'If I had a machine like this I could be President of the United States.' They were working for 'the Duke'. That was all. Some of them worked for sixty-six hours at a stretch. Some didn't have their clothes off for three nights...... 'You can't beat a man whose friends sit in a voting booth for forty-eight hours to watch the count—just out of friendship,' said one of Mr. Denby's opponents, who thought he knew politics. 'It is the most remarkable tribute to a man from his friends that I ever saw,' said another politician. 'I wonder if there are any more men who could without a word cause a hundred of the foremost young men of Detroit to neglect their business and go without sleep and rest for three days?' said one of Mr. Newberry's friends.But most everybody was too busy to answer the question." (reprinted from the Detroit Journal in the Evansville Courier 10-26-1904)

Told that he had come up short in the primary count, the unfazed Mr. Newberry remarked, "Then they have nominated a good man." As to whether he would support Ned in the general election, he was quick to reply, "You bet I will."

In the world of 1904, Teddy Roosevelt was nearing completion of William McKinley's second term in office. He had no Vice President. The Chief Justice of the Supreme Court was Melville Fuller, a Democrat from Maine, who had presided over the articulation of the doctrine of 'separate but equal", and had supported the "Jim Crow laws". He would swear in five U.S. Presidents. The Speaker of the House was the venerable, (some would say 'execrable') Uncle Joe Cannon, one of the most powerful Speakers, and one of the longest serving members of the House in its history. Henry Ford, who had incorporated the Ford Motor Company only the year before, his third attempt at corporate endeavor, set a new automobile land speed record in January with a blazing 91.37 mph. On February 7th, the Great Baltimore Fire destroyed over 1500 buildings in that city in about 30 hours. Not quite as devastating as the Great Chicago Fire of 1871, it still roasted its share of marshmallows. On February 23d, after much wriggling and wrangling, the United States finally gained control of the Panama Canal Zone, clearing the way for construction to begin on Teddy Roosevelt's most cherished project across the isthmus of Panama. On April 8, Longacre Square in New York City, was given its more enduring moniker of Times' Square, and on December 31 of that year, the New Year's celebration was first held there. The St. Louis World's Fair, immortalized by Judy Garland forty years later in song and film, officially known as the Louisiana Purchase Exposition, opened on April 30. On May 5, Cy Young pitched a perfect game for the Boston Americans who were playing the Philadelphia Athletics. Curiously, because of the bitter rivalry between the American and the National Leagues, the New York Giant's owner, John T. Brush refused to play the Boston Americans in the 1904 World Series, but the backlash which erupted prompted rules changes which allowed the fledgling Series to resume in 1905. In October the first underground line of the New York city subway system opened for business.

On November 8, Theodore Roosevelt was elected to his only full term as President. In the days long before everything was polled and predicted to death, there seems to have been scant indication of the thundering victory for the Republicans in general, and Roosevelt in particular, in the 1904 elections. He defeated his opponent by over 2,500,000 votes, the electoral count tallying 336 to 140. The Grand Ole Party easily kept its

Senate majority and gained 42 seats in the lower chamber. It was a smashing political performance. Teddy wrote to his son Kermit. "I am stunned....." (Gwin, p91.) Lacking the knowledge of the impending Roosevelt victory, local pundits around Detroit had declared that all indications favored Alfred Lucking to return to Congress for his second term. But when the votes were counted, Ned had beaten his Democrat contender by over 8000 votes. His "victory, however, was largely due to the tremendous efforts of his personal friends. Never before was there such an exhibition of enthusiasm for a single candidate, and there seems to be no limit to the sacrifices that Denby's followers would make in time, energy, or money, and he probably had more workers at the polls than all the other candidates put together." (DFP 11-09-1904) Though the Democrat Free Press had endorsed Ned's opponent, Lucking, primarily because of his experience, as well as his party, after the voters had spoken, it graciously congratulated Ned, saying that "the people yielded to the magnetism of the Denby personality".

In November Ned travelled with his friends Will and Mary Hamilton and Henry Lyster to Evansville to spend a fortnight's vacation over Thanksgiving with his mother. They surely reminisced at the poignancy provided by his triumph coming at a time when his father was no longer there to share in the family joy.

The Fifty Ninth Congress into which Ned was elected on November 8th consisted of members from 45 states, as Arizona, New Mexico, Oklahoma, Hawaii and Alaska were yet territories. Not only was the occupant of the White House a Republican, but Republicans held the majority in the Senate by a margin of 58 to 32, and in the House by 251 to 135. Southern States were still, thirty-nine years after the Civil War, almost exclusively Democrat. Alabama, Arkansas, Florida, Georgia, Kentucky, Mississippi, Texas and South Carolina had no Republicans in the House, and North Carolina had only one. In the Senate, these Republican-less States were joined by Louisiana, North Carolina, Tennessee, and Virginia.

Among the more colorful characters to be found in the House

in which Ned took his place were members such as William Randolph Hearst, probably one of the most notorious persons ever to serve in that body. Born into extreme wealth and privilege, already immensely successful in the newspaper business, by the age of 39 he had convinced himself that the 'common man' needed another elitist, and self-appointed champion. With the support of the Tammany machine of New York, he was elected to the 58th and the 59th Congresses as Representative from New York's 11th District. He would also run for President of the United States in 1904, Mayor of New York City in 1905 and 1909, and Governor of New York in 1906, losing all four contests. During his political years he espoused the principles of the Left wing of the Progressive Movement. "The publisher gave the impression through his newspapers that he was an exceedingly active member of Congress. The reverse was true for he was seldom present." (Gwin, p96.) Growing older, but arguably little wiser, in his later years he found himself sliding hard right in his political views.

John Nance Garner, best known as the 32nd Vice President from 1933 to 1941, had also served in the House from 1903 to 1933, including a stint as Speaker from 1931 to 1933. By 1937 as Vice President he had broken faith with FDR's runaway spending and his attempts to pack the Supreme Court, and was thus dropped from the ticket. By 1939 Garner had decided to run for President himself, presuming that FDR would adhere to the then unwritten rule of serving a maximum of two terms. But at the Democratic convention in 1940, FDR arranged to derail him, and gain the nomination for his third term. He promptly replaced Garner on the ticket with Henry A. Wallace. Garner went on to outlive almost everyone from his world, surviving to his nineties well into the 1960's. Famously, John F. Kennedy phoned him with birthday congratulations on his 95th birthday, and then left his hotel to join his motorcade in Dallas, to be assassinated only a few hours later.

Another colorful character serving with Ned in this Fifty-ninth Congress was Nicholas Longworth III, first elected to the U.S. House from 1903 to 1913, and then again from 1915 to 1931, the last six years of which he served as Speaker. Arriving in Congress

147

as a heart- throbbingly eligible bachelor, he was eventually snagged by Theodore Roosevelt's outspoken and sometimes controversial eldest daughter, Alice, in a White House ceremony in 1906. "Nick" was a conservative Republican who favored a strong tariff and came down on the opposite side of the split of the Republican Party from his father-in-law and his wife. He lost his seat during this controversy in 1913, regaining it in the election of 1915. The Longworth's had one child, a daughter, Paulina, born in 1925 who was widely accepted as being the daughter of William Borah, United States Senator from Idaho from 1907 to 1940. Upon his return to the House, when Nick later became the powerful Speaker, he regained much of the power that had been lost when the House revolted against Uncle Joe Cannon. He also punished the Progressives in his party who had done so much to splinter it. He was known for his cooperation and unfailing gentlemanliness to his political opposites, even forming an informal club with John Nance Garner made up of Republicans and Democrats who became known as the "Bureau of Education" and met regularly to get to know each other and to learn to work together. Debonair, aristocratic, he often wore spats and carried a gold-headed cane. He died suddenly in 1931 at the age of 61.

Andrew John Volstead served in the House from 1903 to 1923 from the 7th District of Minnesota. Volstead sponsored and worked for the passage of the Volstead Act which will forever be remembered in American lore as "Prohibition". After being defeated in 1922 in his bid for his eleventh term in Congress, Volstead stayed on in Washington as an attorney for the National Prohibition Enforcement Bureau, where he remained until the repeal of Prohibition in1933. He then returned to his native Minnesota where he lived until his death in 1947.

John Wingate Weeks graduated from the Naval Academy in 1881 and served two years in the Navy. After becoming wealthy from a successful banking career, he entered Republican politics, first being elected alderman and then Mayor of Newton, Massachusetts. He served in the U. S. House from 1905 to 1913, in the Senate from 1913 to 1919, and then served as Secretary of War under Warren Harding and Calvin Coolidge. While in the House, he most notably sponsored the Weeks Act of 1911 which allowed the federal government to begin the purchase and protection of over 20 million acres of forest in the Eastern United States. After a stroke in 1925, he resigned from Coolidge's cabinet and passed away several months later. Ned Denby formed a close friendship with Weeks which would last for twenty years.

The best known politician of the Fifth-Ninth House of Representatives was its Speaker, the venerable Joseph Gurney Cannon. From Danville, Illinois, his congressional tenure stretched over 46 years from the 1870's to the 1920's. He was Speaker of the House from 1903 to 1911, and many consider him to have been the most powerful Speaker in history. Among the many notable distinctions of his long life is the curious fact that his likeness graced the very first cover of Time Magazine on March 3, 1923. As a young man he became enamored of Abraham Lincoln after hearing the Lincoln-Douglas debates, and he died during the Presidency of Silent Cal Coolidge, fifteen presidents later. A conservative, "standpatter" (a political term given to those who wanted to protect the Constitutional status quo), though he was vilified for his methods, he was universally respected for his integrity, his fierce loyalty to his Party and his unquestioned love for his country.

The biggest issues of the day, as Theodore Roosevelt began his second term as President and Uncle Joe Canon his second term as Speaker [and Ned Denby his first term in the House of Representatives], were the tariff, and conservation. As horrifying as gun control to a Republican of today, or Pro-Life arguments to a Democrat, these two issues made the blood run cold in political discussions of that day. Of course, there were other issues on the table, including railroad regulation, but of the make-or-break issues of the time, most important were how to create and preserve American prosperity (through the lowering and/or raising of tariffs), and how to preserve the vast, almost unheard of, natural resources which Americans were only beginning to realize were a part of their heritage.

The other seismic idea of this era was the Progressive Movement, and specifically, how it impacted and for a time, nearly destroyed, the Republican Party. That it did was mainly due to the fact that Theodore Roosevelt was not only the President, the leader of the Republican Party, and a living, fire-breathing force of nature — he was also a full-blown Progressive in his ideas, his political passions and goals. As with Grover Cleveland, who was sometimes considered more conservative than his party, at times the leaders of the two major parties seemed to reflect more the ideals of the opposing party than their own. TR believed wholeheartedly in a liberal interpretation of the Constitution, was in favor of the income tax, the inheritance tax, in tariff reform, and almost certainly above all else, in his brand of conservation— all more on the liberal side of arguments of that day than on the conservative. In only eight years' time, this deeply patriotic, but altruistic, President would rip his party in two over Progressive issues, and insure the election of only the second Democrat President since the Civil War.

In fact the whole story of the politics of the time, for the most part, may be told through the dichotomy of its two most influential Republicans: Theodore Roosevelt, and Joseph Gurney Canon. Teddy was a Republican by lineage, but "Progressive" by inclination, leaning definitely toward the positions of the Democrats of his day more than the Republicans. There certainly were other influential Republican Progressives, such as Robert LaFollette, but the majority, though slim, of Republicans of this time were of the traditional nature, far more conservative, and were at the time labeled "standpatters". The leader of this group was Joseph Gurney Canon, the ultra-powerful Speaker of the House for the last six years of Teddy's presidency. When Teddy got too far to the left of issues, Uncle Joe simply put the brakes on legislation, and reigned him in. Probably the only politician of his day to whom Teddy deferred, it was Cannon who kept the Republicans honest and truly conservative, despite Teddy's flights of activism. It was only during the last two years of Uncle Joe's tenure as Speaker, 1909-10, when William Howard Taft, Teddy's hand-picked successor, failed to toe the Progressive mark, that the rupture of the Republican party took place. It seemed that no one, not even the almighty Uncle Joe, or the wildly popular Rough Rider himself, could prevent the chaos which engulfed the Grand Ole Party in 1912.

But that was in the future yet, and we are talking about the Congress as it appeared when the thirty-five year old freshman representative from Michigan took his seat in the House. In his own Michigan delegation young Ned joined eleven other Republicans which included three Civil War veterans, and two veterans of the Spanish American War, including himself. There were eight lawyers, including Ned, one who was also a minister, five teachers, three affiliated in various ways with railroading, one grocer, three bankers, and two men from the lumber industry. This totals more than the twelve because several members had more than one profession, including Washington Gardner who practiced law in Grand Rapids, was a minister in the Methodist Episcopal Church, and a professor at Albion College. Among his fellow representatives from Michigan was William Alden Smith who would later become a Senator from Michigan and would distinguish himself by being on the Senate committee which investigated the Titanic disaster. Of the twelve Republican men in the Michigan delegation to the 59th Congress, Ned was the youngest member. Elected in November, 1904, there were no legislative duties to perform for several months. Sessions of Congress in that day were far shorter than today, and except for Presidential election years (of which 1904 was one), or special sessions (which may only be called by the President), legislative duties were not slated to begin until December of the following year. In the Presidential election years, Congress convened for only a few days in March to attend the inauguration of the new President. Then everyone went back home for several months, and re-convened for legislative duties in December of the year after they had been elected.

Ned made the most of his "free" time before being required in Washington, D. C. He spoke at literally scores of banquets of every conceivable size, type and nature. In the days before radio, television and social media, Americans entertained themselves in varieties of ways which are almost completely forgotten today. There were social organizations, spiritual groups, self-betterment opportunities, informational gatherings, professional and political affiliations, memorial meetings — and all of them held banquets, and banquets required speakers, entertainers, enlighteners, informers. In the early part of 1905, Ned spoke on the Hay Doctrine at the Young Men's Club of the Westminster Presbyterian Church, otherwise known as the "Open Door Policy" and calling it, "the surest guarantee of China's future that can be given." He also noted that "Our policy is highly beneficial to us, and almost vital to China." (DFP Jan 9, 1905) He spoke again on China to the Newsboys Association, and again on the Hay Doctrine to the Gridley Republican Club of Ionia, Michigan. He spoke before the Detroit Club, the Bay County McKinley Club, the Railway Mail Association, Detroit Branch, the Grand Rapids Lincoln Club banquet, the Men's Club of the Trumbull Avenue Presbyterian Church and the Postal Clerks Banquet.

He was in Washington in January and on the 20th met with Speaker Canon, letting him know that he preferred to be placed on the foreign affairs committee. Also in January, plans were announced for a Special Train of pullman cars to carry the Governor's party, and the Denby Club members who wished to go to the Inauguration in March. They would travel over the Pere Marquette and the Baltimore and Ohio to Washington with no stops.

As early as February, Senator Russell Alger announced that he would be sponsoring Homer Warren to replace the incumbent Detroit Postmaster whose term was expiring in the following year. This was directly at odds with Ned, whose job it technically was to pick this successor, and who had already advanced the name of his good friend, Will Hamilton, for the political plum. The 'disagreement' over who would pick the new man would bounce around the newspapers for weeks, creating fillers for slow news days. On Thursday, March 2 at 400pm, the Michigan Special departed Detroit, with seven pullman sleepers, a baggage and a diner car, sold out and on a direct route for the capital. Governor Fred Warren with his military escort, and Ned Denby with nearly two hundred Denby Club members, as well as other Republican supporters filled every berth of the special. Though rain had been predicted in Washington, Saturday, March 4 turned out clear and cold with unexpected gusts of wind which de-hatted men and women alike. The immense crowd included spectators clinging to every niche and roof balustrade of the capitol building which today would have given presidential security details heart failure. "Much has been given us," the Rough Rider said that day, "and much will rightfully be expected of us." (Morris, Theodore Rex, p376) No ears in the enormous sea of Americans listening on that day could have been more in agreement than those of the young congressman-elect from Michigan's first district. Later Ned was quoted as telling a story about Uncle Joe Canon. "Ex-Congressman Lucking and I went over to meet our honored friend to make the day complete," Ned explained. "He wore a pleasant smile when he saw us coming. 'Hello, boys,' he called out, kindly, 'Glad to see you. I'm only sorry you both can't represent Detroit.' No wonder the old man retains his grip on the affections of the officials and the public," Ned concluded. (DFP 4-1905)

Back in Detroit, on March 20 he attended a banquet in honor of perennial Democrat presidential candidate, William Jennings Bryan. Held at the Light Guard Armory for over twelve hundred guests, Ned was introduced to the throng by his late opponent, Alfred Lucking. Bryan graciously recalled aloud having known Ned's father in Washington years before. In April Ned journeyed to Evansville to meet with his brother, Charles, newly arrived from China. The Evansville Courier, another Democrat organ, ran an effusive congratulatory editorial about another one of the Colonel's sons who had made good.

"We think Evansville ought to be proud of this big young man. We take pride in asserting our prior claim to Detroit. He is bound to reflect credit on the city of his nativity in the future as he has in the past in his public career. He stands for the things Roosevelt does in public life — honesty and decency. He may not be on our platform on the protective tariff and the holding of the Philippine Islands, but he is in these things, which count for a good deal... As long as he is not a democrat, we are glad to see such a good man on the Republican side." (EC 4-30-1905)

At the end of May, he took part in Detroit's massive Decoration Day celebrations, his memory undoubtedly filled with reminiscence of his father astride his great horse at the head of Evansville's stirring parade. In June he rented a summer cottage on Grosse Isle along with Garvin and his wife. His mother already had a cottage there, and Charles Jr. and family would also rent a cottage and join them. Charles at this time was between jobs, and casting his eye toward Washington and the State Department as possibly his next employment. On the 8th Ned was in Flint, Michigan to celebrate the city's Golden Jubilee, where Vice President Fairbanks dedicated the new federal building. Ned marched in the parade with newly appointed Secretary of the Navy, his old friend, Truman H. Newberry. On the 14th Ned was back in Washington and dropped in at the White House to pay his respects. Two days later he became a charter member of the Michigan American Red Cross, whose national entity had recently been wrested from the inefficient hands of Clara Barton, its founder, by scientific progressives bent on turning it into a far more organized institution.

At the end of June he attended the 2nd anniversary banquet celebrating the founding of the Detroit Board of Commerce, which was held aboard the lake steamer, Pleasure, for a five hour river cruise. Charles Jr. was invited to speak on China; J.L. Hudson, owner of Detroit's largest department store and former President of the Board, as well as Ned, offered remarks. Detroit, perhaps under the auspices of the Board, was beginning to be called the "City of the Straits". In July the venerable Winifred Lyster with Ned's great college friend, her son, Henry, joined the Denbys for two weeks on Grosse Isle. In October Ned joined the speaker's table at the Detroit Club's banquet to wish 'god speed' to Truman Newberry upon his departure for Washington and the job that one day in the future Ned also would hold.

By November 12, Ned was in Evansville for a vacation before finally heading to Washington. He would spend Thanksgiving with his mother. Also, on this day, his older brother, Charles Jr. was finally named chief clerk of the State Department, giving him a sinecure stateside. On November 26 Ned publicly announced that he would now back Charles F. Mellish, a local businessman who had headed up his congressional campaign, to become Detroit's new Postmaster. Will Hamilton had made it known that he would decline the post, but Senator Alger had not yet agreed to defer to Ned's choice. All indications pointed to an untying of this knot by the President.

On December 5, 1905 the 59th Congress met in Washington to hold its first legislative session. On that day Ned was formally appointed as a member of the foreign relations committee, the spot he had wanted all along. Both brothers, Ned and Charles Jr. were in Washington together for the first time, and the newspapers did not miss the opportunity to mark the event. "The two sons [of the Colonel] have made splendid impressions here. They are robust specimens of manhood, as was their father, and they are impressing Washington as men of unusual ability." (Washington Correspondent of the Indianapolis News, as quoted in the Evansville Courier, 12-10-1905) While Garvin and his wife traveled to Evansville to spend Christmas with Martha, Ned was back in Detroit by the 23rd for a holiday rest.

After the holidays, the Congress was quick to get into business. By January 8 of the new year of 1906 Ned was already being recognized by Speaker Cannon by being called to the Speaker's Chair to preside over the committee of the whole. Some political wags got a kick out of claiming that they thought for a moment that old "Czar Reed" of Maine was back to lord over the House. Big and burly, with a superficial but recognizable resemblance to Ned, the former Speaker had been the most powerful leader of the House before the elevation of Uncle Joe, but had not frequented its chambers since 1899, and had passed on in 1902. On January 11, TR put to rest the conjecture about Detroit's next Postmaster by

To This High Standard

siding with Senator Alger and selecting Homer Warren. Always knowing prudently when he was outgunned, Ned was quick and sincere with congratulations to the victor.

On Saturday, February 17, Ned attended what was described at the time as the "wedding of the season", only the fourth time to that date that the daughter of a U.S. President was married in the White House. Just over a thousand invitations had gone out to only the highest of government officials and the closest of friends and family for the wedding of America's Princess, Alice Lee Roosevelt to U.S. Congressman and Cincinnati playboy, Nicholas Longworth. Ned owed his invitation to the most prestigious social event of the year to the fact that he had only the month before joined the Foreign Affairs Committee of the House, whose members also included the dashing groom. How bemused the freshman congressman from Michigan must have been to have found himself automatically on a guest list so coveted by hundreds of disappointed socialites.

On March 19 Ned secured passage of the Consular Bill in the House after a great deal of effort. It provided for a system of inspection of consular services overseas, as well as a much needed increase of pay for Americans in consular service. "I say in regard to our present consular service, it is the best in the world, and I think there are in the service many men looking after the interests of their fellow citizens in the obscurity of foreign ports, who have carried the flag for us under inadequate salaries and under very great discouragement for years." (DFP 3-20-1906) Sounds very near like a man who had spent nine years in China and knew quite well from first hand experience what he was talking about.

Later in March Ned also introduced a bill to create a United States Court for China. At the time court cases in China brought by Chinese against Americans were heard by Consular officials, usually untrained in legal proceedings, and perceived by the Chinese to be highly prejudicial against them. Cases brought by Chinese against Americans in Chinese courts often failed to find justice due to an undue influence by the Americans. Like the consular bill, Ned's Chinese Court was reforming in nature, aimed at correcting longstanding grievances by both parties.

In addition to Nick Longworth, who was for the next several weeks on his extended honeymoon, Ned was joined on the Foreign Affairs Committee by its Chairman, Robert H. Hitt, the Republican representative from the 13th District of Illinois. In 1892, when the Chinese Exclusion Act came up for renewal, Hitt had had reservations about the bill. Hitt was seventy-two years old in 1906, had been Chairman of Foreign Affairs in the 51st Congress (1889-1891), and again from 1895 to his death in September of 1906. In failing health, much of the leadership of the committee fell to Robert Adams, Jr. from the 2nd District of Pennsylvania.

Adams had been in congress since 1893, and had been United States Minister to Brazil for a little over a year before being appointed to Congress to fill a vacancy left by a preceding member's death. In an unusual turn of events, toward the end of the session in June 1906, Adams committed suicide, leaving Ned to tie up the business of the committee before recess. Throughout much of the congressional session, Ned also battled against the Foster Bill, which was aimed at greatly liberalizing the Chinese exclusion laws, offered his own very thoughtful revisions, but as is often the case, nothing came of this legislation in this session. By May he was home for a needed rest, and on the 6th dined with his oldest friends, the Hamiltons. He next travelled to Evansville to visit his mother and to see his older brother Graham, recuperating from a kidney operation in St. Mary's Hospital. On May 25th the Foreign Affairs committee gave a favorable report to his bill to create the United States Court for China. In June he missed the 8th Annual reunion of his Yosemite messmates in Detroit, sending his greetings by wire, as did the Assistant Secretary of the Navy, his pal Truman Newberry. Seventy-seven out of a total ship's complement of 337 attended the affair, giving a hearty "thumbs-down" when their old and unpopular CO, Captain W. H. Emery was toasted.

The first session of this 59th Congress had been extremely productive. Not only had Ned seen the Consular Bill pass, but also his bill for the establishment of the United States' Court for China. Also passed was the Antiquities Act, which gave the President discretion to set aside lands as national monuments, and has been used over a hundred times by all but four U.S. Presidents. Also passed was the Hepburn Act designed to give the Interstate Commerce Commission more authority over U.S. railroads; the Pure Food and Drug Act of 1906, and the Meat Inspection Act. All four of these major pieces of legislation were passed in June. On June 30th, Congress recessed for the summer months, and for all house members to go home and run for re-election.

On July 3, Ned received an important piece of correspondence from then Secretary of State, Elihu Root, a man whom Theodore Roosevelt felt was "the greatest statesman of his time." (Zimmerman, First Great Triumph, p472). Root was about to depart on an extended good will trip through Latin America to reassure American neighbors of United States' good intentions, when he took time out to pen thanks to the freshman congressman from Michigan.

"I do not wish to leave for South America without expressing to you in some degree my very high appreciation of the work that you have done during the last session of Congress," he wrote. "Under the distressing circumstances of Mr. Hitt's illness and Mr. Adams' obscuration of mind and death I do not know what the State Department would have done if you had not been a member of the Foreign Affairs Committee of the House and had not taken such an active and intelligent interest in the important subjects which were before the Committee; or if you had not put your strong personality behind the many things which required to be done to secure effective administration in your foreign affairs. This has been especially noteworthy from the fact that it was your first session as a member of Congress. It may gratify you to know that I have heard comment from many sources upon the evidence you have given of great capacity for usefulness in the House." (BHL, Edwin Denby Papers, Box #1)

Ned was so proud of this endorsement that he quoted it verbatim in his very next letter to the Hamiltons.

On August 16, he filed papers declaring himself for the upcoming congressional contest for the first district, and on August 23, his opponent, Democrat Frederick F. Ingram, did the same. In early October his headquarters was opened, once again in the Hammond Building, with Charles Mellish as chairman of his campaign. In the article about the opening of his campaign headquarters, the Detroit Free Press was lavish in its praise of the novice congressman. "Few first term men in congress succeed in attaining the prominence that came to Mr. Denby, his knowledge of important legislation and the hard work he brought to bear in carrying through, winning him the thanks of the state department."

The great Speaker of the House himself, the venerable Uncle Joe Cannon arrived Detroit on October 22 over 5 hours late from Buffalo to speak on behalf of Ned at a rally at Detroit's packed Light Guard Armory. A freight train wreck on the Wabash had delayed him, but even at the age of 70 hadn't slowed him down, as he insisted on going straight to the armory for the meeting. Becoming an honorary member of the Edwin Denby Club, he spoke for over an hour about the tremendous blessings of prosperity which the country had enjoyed for the past several years. Roundly endorsing the local native son, he also made it clear that Republican policies had been a large factor in that wonderful prosperity. "Our product today is equal to that of Great Britain, Germany and France combined. Let me put it another way. Our product of factory, mine and farm, is equal to one-third of the product of the world," he boasted.

The crowd did its best to stir up the speaker by asking him his opinion of their man Denby. "All wool and a yard wide," Cannon said, "If he does as well in years to come and grows as he has grown during his first session of congress, in the fullness of time he will be buried at public expense." (DFP 10-23-1906) Despite the strenuous schedule and his age, Uncle Joe was at the train station and on his way to Chicago by eleven pm.

Fifteen days later the voters of Michigan's first district cast their ballots to send Ned back for another two years to Congress.

His winning margin was 6766 out of 40,621 votes cast, or 58.25% of the vote, only 0.25% less than his 1904 win. Later in the month he retired to Evansville for a rest with his mother, a short hunting trip, and a visit with Graham. Being interviewed by the Evansville Courier, he stated that he believed the President, despite his pronouncements to the contrary, would be drafted to run for and be elected to another term as Chief Executive, that he expected the upcoming session of congress to be mostly about appropriations. "This is an eight hundred million dollar country now, you know," he stated to obviously astonished readers, "and it will take considerable time to pass all the appropriation measures." He also felt there would be some work on immigration laws, which he felt necessary, but did not believe there would be any revision of the tariffs. (EC 11-22-1906)

Ned was back in Washington in early December for the opening of the second and shorter session of the 59th congress, which was scheduled from December 3 to March 3, and with time off for the Christmas and New Year Holidays. On December 4th the President's annual message to congress was read, and well received by Democrats, including the Detroit Free Press, which crowed: "The President's views on the inheritance and income taxes pleased the Democrats. Representative Champ Clark (D), of Missouri, expressing the sentiment that 'President Roosevelt had stolen, taken away, and converted to his own use another plank of the Democrats.'" For all time it is to be wondered how Theodore Roosevelt remained the most admired man in the country, by people of all creeds and beliefs, when he was so obviously, tirelessly, and unrepentantly, a liberal Democrat.

Though Martha Fitch had been ill while Ned was home over Thanksgiving, it was obviously hoped that she was on the mend when he returned to Washington for the opening of the congressional session. However, by the second week of December, Martha was still ill enough that Hattie left her home in Detroit to rush to her mother's bedside. By December 23, Charles Jr. and Martha Orr, as well as Ned, had all arrived from Washington, while Garvin and Lucy joined the family from Detroit. Only

Wythe, still in Alaska, was not yet present, as Martha's condition became grave. Though she was reported on Christmas Day to be "resting easy", Martha passed away at 7 am on the following morning, Wednesday, December 26. On Friday the last rites were held at St. Paul's Episcopal Church, just three blocks away from the Denby home. Martha was two months shy of her 71st birthday. It would be a sad Christmas the entire family would never forget.

On January 19 of the new year, 1907, Ned's great friend and law partner, M. Hugh O'Brien was named Marshal of the United States Court in Shanghai. O'Brien had graduated Michigan Law two years after Ned, and had also been a member of the Michigan Naval Reserve. By March 4, Ned was appointed by Uncle Joe to the 'joint committee to revise the laws" along with Representatives Moon of Pennsylvania, Parsons of New York, Sherley of Kentucky and Houston of Tennessee. Also, in early March big news in Detroit was the formation of a new bank, one of the early "automobile" banks, to be called the National Bank of Commerce. By May Ned was announced as one of the bank's directors, and a week later his good friend, Will Hamilton, was named the bank's First Vice President. Though the bank did not officially open until early June, by the second day of business, it boasted over $1 million in deposits. In April Ned announced further ambitious plans, this time to publish his own magazine to be called "The Pacific Era." The new magazine was planned to "be at once the historian and the interpreter of the New Far East, of its political, commercial, financial, religious progress and achievements." (EC 9-9-1907) Like the new bank, Ned's magazine had an impressive list of investors including Will Hamilton, James Inglis, Truman Newberry, and his inseparable friend from the House, J. Sloat Fassett of New York.

Wonderful family news came in 1907's Spring when Charlie was notified that he was being tapped for the American Consulate in Shanghai. It represented a substantial increase in salary, and the opportunity for America's "leading sinologist" to return to the land of his expertise. Charles and family left the United States in June, this time heading east to Hamburg, Germany, where his family took up a temporary residence, while Charlie proceeded to Russia, and from St. Petersburg, traveled the trans-Siberian Railway to China.

On September 28, the first issue of "Pacific Era" was published, containing a wide variety of articles by American, Japanese and Chinese authors, including President Roosevelt who contributed a revised, updated speech; an article that had been written some years earlier by Ned's mother, Martha Fitch entitled "Impressions of Old Pekin", and contributions by the magazine's manager, Adachi Kinnosuke.

In October Ned was approached by a committee of striking telegraphers' to use his influence on President Roosevelt to intercede on their behalf. In his usual firmly straightforward way, Ned refused. "I would rather have it out squarely than beat around the bush," he said. "I told the committee that I did not think the President had any right to interfere." The union members protested that business was being hurt, and Ned replied, "I admitted that, and asked them why they had not thought of it before they stuck, and why they had not sought the good offices of the president before an open breach was declared, when he might have been able to do something." It became a clear case of a bitterly divided argument which would rage for another two generations in American politics, and the following day Ned issued a statement of his position:

"My views upon the question of unions are simply expressed — I believe in unions. I believe that if rightly conducted they do a great deal of good but I do not believe in the prevention of men from working for an employer, unless they become members of a union, nor do I believe in any strike based upon the refusal of union men to work with non-union men. To say that I shall not secure employment in the city of Detroit unless I associate myself with a union, is to restrict my liberty and the liberty of my employer. If my work is good, I have a right to employment, if I can get it. If an employer pays good wages and treats his men well, he has a right to employ whom he chooses. Any other course is totally contrary to the genius of our civilization and to the spirit of American liberty. "Unions have come to stay; they are good, but they must base their hopes of success upon something besides forcing men to join their ranks. "That means opposition to the closed shop. I do not deny that or seek to evade it. It is entirely in accordance with my past statements, and known attitude. I could not favor the closed shop without betraying my trust in this great industrial community." (DFP Oct 3, 1907)

There will certainly be people to the end of time who would condemn Edwin Denby for the above remarkably clear and concise words, but no one can say that he was just another politician who wanted nothing more than to evade a straight answer. To the end of his days, Ned would hold his ship on the steady course he felt was true, and even to his detriment, would never alter it. In the very same newspaper, the Free Press offered its own criticism, "Congressman Denby's attitude favoring the open shop, shown in an interview in regard to the telegraphers' strike, does not appear to have made him many friends in local labor circles. Leaders in the federation of labor last night expressed themselves very bitterly against him, and it looks as though the support of organized labor may be taken from the congressman." (DFP 10-3-1907) On the 6th it also published two letters both pro and con from readers. From Oscar Willits of Alpena, Michigan, came a heartfelt, interesting letter of support. Oscar began by saying that he had known Ned's parents in China, that;

"Mrs. Denby was a woman of piety, generously endowed with good sense and practical sympathy with every effort to benefit the less favored races or classes. Mr. Denby was a fine example of an upright judge—frank, outspoken, independent, just. These qualities explain his long continuance in public life. Though he is a Democrat of the old school, President Harrison retained him in his post, and so did President McKinley until advancing years claimed a rest and the fight of retirement.

"It was never my pleasure to meet Mr. Edwin Denby and I have no acquaintance with him whatever. Since his election to congress I have often wondered whether he had the moral stamina of his beautiful mother or the manly outspokenness of his father. But his recent announcement of opposition to the 'closed shop' has answered my query. He is a 'chip off the old block'." (DFP Oct 6, 1907)

In October Ned spoke at the Detroit Tigers' end of season banquet held at the old Cadillac Hotel downtown on the corner of Washington Blvd and Michigan Avenue. The Tigers won the American League pennant, but lost the World Series to the Chicago Cubs, 0-4-1. Over two hundred guests crowded into the Cadillac ballroom for a raucous several hours. The Chicago Cubs would win the World Series once more in 1908, but then not again for another one hundred and eight years. Ned next addressed the state convention of Federated Women's Clubs in Flint, a gathering of nearly four hundred women. He spoke on "Our Relations with the Orient."

The 60th United States Congress opened its first Session on Monday, December 2nd. Ned had moved up two spots on the foreign affairs committee, as Nick Longworth had moved to Ways and Means, and Henry Allen had been defeated. Ned was also appointed to the committee on militias, and revision of laws. It is worth noting that on December 16, Theodore Roosevelt's great gamble with the United States Navy, known as the "Great White Fleet" departed Hampton roads, Virginia on its 43,000 nautical mile journey to circumnavigate the globe with 14,000 sailors manning 16 battleships. A similar voyage by another once-powerful navy had ended in disaster for the Russians in 1905. It would be fourteen months before Americans would learn if the voyage of their navy would be more successful.

On Christmas Day it was announced in the papers that Truman Newberry, then Assistant Secretary of the Navy, was opening his bid to become elected as the delegate-at-large to the next Republican National Convention which would be held the following June in Chicago. He would be supporting William Howard Taft's candidacy. It was further announced, in a show of party loyalty, that Arthur L. Holmes who had assisted in Ned's first election triumph over Newberry in 1904, would be Newberry's chief lieutenant, and that Ned himself would actively assist in the campaign. Asked about their former contest against each other, Newberry remarked, "Denby and myself had a contest which left us better friends than ever, and I see no reason why it should be otherwise." DFP 12-25-1907)

Once again, as several times in the past, Ned was scheduled toward the end of December to address the Detroit newsboys regular gathering. Just before that date it was announced that he was sponsoring seventeen-year-old Humphrey Shaw for a page-ship in the lower House in Washington. Shaw, for ten years a popular, well-known newsboy in Detroit, whose post was on Griswold just down the street from Ned's law office, had not only educated himself while holding his job, but had become so successful selling his papers that he employed assistants who sold papers for him. He was in the early stages of living his American dream, just as was the young congressman so willing to lend him a hand.

Chapter Nine

"I am a Republican because, among other things,
that party has a genius for sanity and a habit for efficiency."

from a letter to Harriet Taylor Upton, 14 January, 1922

Congressional Years (Continued)

In early January 1908, Truman Newberry settled the opposition to his becoming a delegate to the Republican National Convention by withdrawing his name from consideration. Three days later Ned introduced a joint resolution in Congress to secure three obsolete cannon for the planned statue commemorating Major General Alexander Macomb, a native Detroiter, hero of the Battle of Plattsburg in the War of 1812, and later Commanding General of the United States Army for thirteen years. The statue stands there today, just in front of the Westin Book Cadillac Hotel, at the foot of Washington Blvd, facing Michigan Avenue; Ned's three cannon are there as well, guarding the haunting statue which predates Darth Vader by nearly a hundred years. About this time his widowed sister, Hattie, seven years his senior, with her two young sons, moved to Washington D. C. to act as his hostess and social organizer. In a later January letter to his friend Mrs. Hamilton, he mentioned their attendance at a "Musicale" at Theodore Roosevelt's White House, "which we enjoyed very much," he told her, "though I nearly went to sleep during some of the 'musics'. Afterward we had a little talk with the President and saw many people it is always a pleasure to meet.

"We both fell in love with Mrs. Hobson, who is very pretty and attractive. I like Hobson also very much. He is a gentleman and a very nice fellow, and I am sure we shall become good friends."[Richmond P. Hobson was a national hero from the Spanish American War. He survived a suicide mission by sailing an American collier into Santiago harbor in an effort to block the channel, thus trapping the Spanish Fleet. Captured by the Spanish, he became heroically famous in the American press, and toured the country after the war making speeches and kissing multitudes of eagerly scandalized young women all across America. Exceedingly handsome, in fact, he became known as the most kissed man in the country. On one of these tours he stopped and spoke in Evansville, Indiana, and stayed overnight with Ned's parents. He married his wife, Griselda, in 1905 and served in Congress from his home state of Alabama from 1907 to 1915. Notably, he was the only congressman from the deep south to vote in favor of women's suffrage in the 1915 bill which was defeated.] Ned reported to Mrs. Hamilton that since Hattie had come to stay with him, he had learned a lot more about Washington society. "Hattie took me calling to some of the Embassies and Legations which my position on Foreign Affairs makes it incumbent on me to call," he said. " and incidentally, I am by proxy doing my social duty like a little man. Hattie distributes my pasteboards lavishly where they should have gone long ago l appreciate as never before the real value of having a woman in the house." Ned had been in Washington long enough to have begun to move up in social circles, and he next confided, "Tonight I go to a 'small dance' -what do you think of that for a sober and industrious member of congress! It is at the John R. McClean's, who are quite the unofficial beacon lights here, and I was so flattered to be invited without having first called or met them that of course I accepted." [John R. McLean, owner and publisher of the Washington Post and the Cincinnati Inquirer, along with his wife Emily, were the quintessential hosts of the Capital smart set of the day.] He also mentioned how swamped he was in his congressional duties, as the bill codifying the penal code for the China court on which he was working was being debated and he felt it would "hold the floor for some time to come." In addition, he was "Chairman of the subcommittee having in charge the Resolution providing for the release of China from the half of her indemnity." [According to the peace agreement concluding the Boxer Rebellion, China paid the seven nations involved millions of dollars indemnity for losses incurred by them. The U.S., led by Teddy Roosevelt, decided to return a great portion of this money in the form of a scholarship program to educate Chinese youth in the United States. Following the boldness and the obvious merit of this plan, Japan, France and Great Britain all decided upon a similar course of kindness. So much for the 'ugly American'!] (Edwin Denby Papers, DPL, Box #1)

A measure of the good will and honest affection for Michigan's largest and youngest congressman is easy to find in the manner in which he was almost invariably treated in the press. They adored teasing him. Apparently, shortly after arriving back in the capital in early January, the Denby angora cat had somehow gone missing. The police were notified, and the neighborhood diligently searched, but it was not until late February that an Officer Scott brought the wayward feline back to its home-sweet-home. A lot of fun was had with the story of how Officer Scott dutifully turned in to his superior the $1 reward he had received from the parsimonious congressman, and how it had been passed all the way up the line to the "commissioners of the District of Columbia" for a decision about whether or not Officer Scott would be permitted to keep the reward. He was. The following day, at the very bottom of a long list of items of interest throughout the city of Detroit, the Free Press took one more jab: "But the main thing," it assured its subscribers, "is that the Denby cat came back."
(DFP 2-27 & 28-1908)

The first judge for the United States Court for China, Lebbeus R. Wilfley, appointed by Theodore Roosevelt in July of 1906, began almost immediately acquiring enemies for himself in China among certain shady and unscrupulous Americans who were making money in illicit, and sometimes immoral, ways. Judge Wilfley had begun a good, old fashioned 'clean-up' which didn't sit very well with some. He was accused of misconduct in office by a group of American lawyers who resided in China, and by March of 1908 Speaker Cannon appointed a special committee to investigate whether there were grounds for impeachment, selecting George E. Waldo, Representative from New York to act as prosecutor, and Ned to assume the duties of the defense. The judge was charged with "acts of gross favoritism, neglect of duty, prejudice and abuse of power." By March 24, the subcommittee investigating Judge Wilfley hadendered a 'scotch' verdict, the intent of which will be entirely familiar to modern ears: there was not enough evidence (read, "none") to impeach, but just enough to 'roast'. In addition to that equivocal verdict, the report had been leaked to the press, which in that day being a bit more honorable than today, was sitting on it. In fact, someone slipped the judge a copy of the leaked report, and he and Ned went immediately to the committee to inform them that if the report was made public, the judge would demand impeachment to exonerate himself. Ned asserted that the committee had "made up its report solely on the ex parte statements of bitter enemies of Wilfley, without giving him a chance to rebut the testimony." There just does not seem to be anything in political shenanigans of today which is truly rlew. It happened then that the committee "accordingly expunged from its report the objectionable matter and will report adversely on the demand for impeachment." (DFP 3-10-1908) This, after Secretary of State Elihu Root had already held his own investigation of the matter within the State Department and had completely exonerated the judge.

Shortly after, Ned travelled to Boston with a group of congressmen headed by William E. Humphrey of Seattle to appear at the Norfolk Republican club dinner held at the Hotel Brunswick. The others were John Weeks, Ned's friend from Massachusetts, and Jack Beall of Texas. Congressman Humphrey, like Ned, was a staunch supporter of a far tronger United States merchant marine, and his topic was "Our Merchant Marine and the unpreparedness of the United States for war". "If we should have a war on the Pacific Ocean toctlay Russia's fate [Tsushima, 1905] would be ours," Humphrey boldly stated. "I do not believe We are going to have war with Japan, but if war should come, I want my country to be preparbd for it." He further explained that, "Russia and the United States are the only nations of the earth that have committed the colossal folly of spending enormous sums to build up a great navy without at the same time building up a great merchant marine to support and man it."

This idea of a strong merchant marine was quite contentious for one glaring reason: money. According to the Seamen's Act of 1915, strongly supported by labor unions, merchant ships became much more highly regulated, and as always is the case with greater regulation, more expensive to operate. The United States simply did not have and was not prepared to pay for a merchant marine as large as other countries, notably the possible antagonist, Japan. Many politicians and others as well saw the solution to this problem being a goverriment subsidy to encourage the growth of this necessary arm of a nation at war. Congressman Humphrey was correct that not many people felt that the United States was in danger of war with Japan, or anyone else for that matter, and yet many forward-thinking people of the time speculated that if a war were to come, it would most likely be against Japan.

The Japanese had stunned the world in 1905 in their war with Russia, and most experts and the public at large, believed that had Theodore Roosevelt not stepped in to mediate a peace, that instead of humiliating the Russians, Japan would have utterly devastated them. However, few foreigners realized at the time the staggering burden of Japanese debt, and the massive press of taxes upon its own people that had been necessary to finance the war; the Japanese debt had doubled between the years 1905 and 1908. In an article in Collier's Weekly magazine, reprinted in the Evansville Courier, Ned stated that given Japan's massive foreign debt from the Russo-Japanese War, her large, expensive standing army of 300,000 men and her equally expensive first rate navy, and the amount of taxation her government was willing to put upon its population, her choices going forward were three: disarmament, repudiation of her foreign debt, or war. No one believed that the Japanese would disarm; culturally, no one believed the Japanese would incur the humiliation that the repudiation of foreign obligations would entail. That left only the third option, and while Ned scorned the idea of Japan attacking the United States, he was absolutely correct in his assessment that they would gladly, and eagerly, attack the Celestial Empire of China. (EC 5-19-1908)

April saw Ned's bill to provide an additional federal judge for eastern Michigan hopelessly stalled in committee, but in May the Foreign Affairs Committee ordered a favorable report on his code of laws for the recently created Chinese court. May 1st, Ned announced that he would again be a candidate for Michigan's 1st District in Congress. Just shortly before this he had made a flying trip home from Washington on Saturday, April 18 to address a group of Spanish American War veterans at the Light Guard Armory. He left the capital late Saturday evening, arrived in Detroit Sunday afternoon driving straight to the armory for his speech, then directly back to the Michigan Central train station on Michigan Avenue for a 345pm train departure back to Washington. While in Detroit he quashed rumors that he was about to be named to an important foreign post and that ex-mayor, George P. Codd (R) would replace him on the ballot for the 1st District. He also told the press that it seemed unlikely that Michigan would get its additional federal judgeship that year. "I really do not believe that I will succeed at this session," he said of the bill. Once again the press could not resist the golden opportunity to tease the jovial congressman, as it seemed that Ned had been well on his way on his flying trip home to Detroit when he realized, only after the conductor had requested his ticket, that he had inadvertently left it on his dresser in his quarters. After fumbling through his pockets to no avail, "the embarrassed national lawmaker paid his fare rather than be dumped off at the next water tank." How the reporter must have guffawed at constructing that image!

But there was more. It seems that Ned had also forgotten to

pack a fresh collar for his shirt, and upon learning this, decided he would simply purchase one at the nearest store. Arriving in Detroit, however, he found all men's clothing stores closed (Sunday), and had to wear his "soiled collar". Not particularly national news, but too good for the Detroit Free Press to pass up an opportunity to poke some good-natured fun. (DFP 4-20-1908).

The United States had gained control of the Panama Canal Zone via the Hay-Bunau-Varilla Treaty of 1904 with the newly formed and hastily recognized country of Panama, and for the past four years had been making great strides in the construction of the sea link between the oceans. The President himself, considering the Canal was the crowning achievement of his Presidency, visited the Zone in 1906 and as was his habit, manfully crawled all over the muddy ditch posing for photographs in a white suit. On May 19, 1908, Ned was named as one of two United States Representatives on the International Commission for Land Claims in Panama. The other American was Judge E. C. Bumpus from Boston, Massachusetts. A few days later, the two Panamanian members of the commission, Gil Ponce Jaen and Santiago de la Guardia, were also announced. Since the United States was digging a massive trench straight through the Panamanians' back yard, it became necessary to compensate some local citizens for their property. The current session of Congress was scheduled to end on May 30, and after that date Ned would be free to travel south. The selection of Judge Bumpus and Ned for this important work had come from Secretary for War, William Taft in a letter to the Secretary of State, Elihu Root. In his second congressional term, and known as an active participant in legislative matters, with a background in law and foreign affairs, Ned seemed a natural choice.

Before heading south, however, both Ned and Hattie travelled to Philadelphia with the entire Michigan delegation from both houses of Congress, as well as the Secretary of the Interior, James Garfield and his wife, and certain military officers at the invitation of the Acting Secretary of the Navy, Truman Newberry, for the christening of the Navy's newest battleship, the USS Michigan (BB27) at the Camden, New Jersey shipyards. The second of her class of South Carolina battleships, built as the U.S. answer to the British HMS Dreadnought, the Michigan displaced 16,000 tons, was scheduled to carry a complement of 869 officers and men, and cost the American taxpayer a whopping $3,585,000. The entire party travelled to Philadelphia on a chartered railroad car to watch Truman Newberry's daughter, Miss Carol Barnes Newberry smash the bottle on the giant bow.

At the end of May Hattie travelled to New York with Ned to see him off on his Panamanian adventure. Hattie spent a few days in New York, then returned to Washington to close up Ned's house, and then headed for Grosse "ILE" in Michigan, and her summer cottage. The Free Press' special Washington correspondent noted that Hattie had become "one of the most popular of Michigan hostesses and especially as a dinner hostess has she made a success." Also noted was the confusion sometimes about her relationship with her burly bachelor brother, saying that she was "far more often called Mrs. Denby than Mrs. Wilkes."
(DFP 6-13-1908)

About a month into the land claims work in Panama, Ned took time out to write a long, newsy letter to his friends, the Hamiltons. Ned stayed at the Tivoli Hotel, on the Pacific side of the country, where Theodore Roosevelt had stayed in his November, 1906 trip to the canal zone. Though homesick for familiar territory, he was still able to appreciate the beauty of the tropical country.

"This is a strange place," he wrote. "It is only nine degrees from the equator. A straight line across the Pacific following the meridian of Panama would cross the extreme southern end of the Philippine group. About 350 miles due south, less than the length of Michigan, would place the traveller astride the equator. Yet today (July 16) is as cool as a fine summer day up north and so was yesterday and so will tomorrow be. It never gets nearly as hot as it used to be in Macao, and sunstroke, from which unhappy New York suffers so much, is practically unknown. The average temperature is about 80 degrees and seldom does it vary more than a degree or two." Except for a sometimes oppressive humidity, he predicted that the canal zone "is destined to be a winter resort for our people when the work is finished. The little Panama Railroad will be one of the world's scenic routes. Where else will the traveler be able to look from his car window down upon the masts of mighty ocean liners or the decks of battleships deep in the cut below, while all around lies the rich beauty of Isthmian vegetation. It is all wonderful, beautiful and surprising. Nothing was as I expected."

He next discussed the health issues which Americans were sure to have read about. While the French certainly paid a heavy price during their stay in Panama, they built excellent hospitals which the Americans inherited; and the steady advance of medicine rendered conditions far more amenable than when the French were doing the digging. He reported that "yellow fever is unknown. No case has been reported for about two years." Malaria, however, was a different story, and though they had not eradicated it, most cases were of the milder type. Unfortunately, his partner, Judge Bumpus, "is now in hospital convalescing from an attack of malaria." But, "his case was not serious."

He took advantage in his spare time of the opportunity to observe as much of the construction work on the canal as he was able. He spent several days with Colonel George W. Goethals [Chief Engineer of the construction; he brought the canal to completion two years ahead of schedule; was appointed first civil governor of the Canal Zone by Woodrow Wilson] "walking through the Culebra Cut and over the Gatun dam site. These are the new centers of the canal system, the noblest and most difficult works in the entire enterprise."

Of the claims process he reported, "Our work goes on vigorously and is nearing completion. I could not refuse the great compliment tendered to me by the Panamanian government and claimants, when they asked me to act as umpire to settle the old cases on which the last Commission failed to agree. Our government has now cabled its approval and I shall get at these

175

cases soon and dispose of them somehow. I hate the job and am simply sick at the prospect ahead. But it will soon be over and I shall be satisfied if when all is over I can hold the confidence of these people and still retain the good opinion of our government. But the umpire, like the peacemaker, seldom pleases anyone." (DPL Edwin Denby papers, Box #2)

Despite his misgivings, he and Judge Bumpus managed to dispose of their cases in a short time and for a great deal less money than had been anticipated. It had been estimated that it might cost the United States as much as $2 million to settle land claims, and before Ned and the Judge were finished, it appeared that the total would be closer to one-eighth of that sum. As in most cases when a government is about to make a monetary settlement, Ned was credited with spying out some greatly inflated claims.

"One owner claimed his estate contained a coal mine. Mr. Denby and the Panama commissioners went to see this estate and this mine. After walking several miles in the mud through a jungle they reached the man's domain and a river. 'Where is the mine?' asked Mr. Denby. 'Oh, that is across the river,' replied the owner. Mr. Debby said he would cross. Everyone told him the old foot bridge would not hold him. The owner cheerfully said he would have a new one built. Mr. Denby said, 'No.' He started to cross, fell through into water waist deep, regained his feet and waded across. 'Where is the mine?' he again asked. 'Oh, we must be in the wrong place,' said the owner, who was spared the additional humiliation of hearing what was thought of him and his fraudulent claims."

Another Panamanian claimed that a gold mine was located on his property. Further, he claimed that the vein was fifteen feet in diameter! When the commissioners examined the land they found "placer ore in quantities so small that $1 or $2 might possibly be washed by a hard day's work." (EC 8-16-1908)

By August 13, Ned telegraphed that he was already on his way home. Arriving in New York, he went directly to Sagamore Hill on Oyster Bay to report first to President Roosevelt, and then to Washington to stop by the State Department and the

War Department. He arrived in Detroit on August 25, just in time for him to file as a candidate for re-election to Congress. He would be opposed in this election by W. D. Mahon, president of the International Association of Street Railway Employees.

"Campaign Will Be Stiff" warned the Detroit Free Press, glad at last that perhaps a Democrat was found who could stand up to the Republican giant.

"Mahon's entry into the congressional race indicates that there will be a stiff campaign. He has already been endorsed by the Detroit Federation of Labor and the fight is quite likely to be conducted along union lines. By his work in settling street railway disputes, he is widely known throughout the country and he has acquired a reputation for conservatism.

"It is no secret that Congressman Denby has incurred the enmity of union men generally and Mahon's friends are exceedingly hopeful of his chances."(DFP 8-28-1908)

Mahon announced that he had not yet heard from the members of the board of directors of his union, and therefore had not made up his mind to run. It seems that he had been drafted by a petition instigated by one of the Democratic caucuses of Detroit. When pressed, however, he had no trouble taking a swing at his possible opponent. "I don't think that he properly represents the mass of the people of this district, or the rank and file of the people of the country. He represents the rule of wealth that is threatening the republic. When the working people are faced with the proposition that they cannot legally organize and fight for their own rights, then the republic is in danger-if I understand the principles of the republic," declared Mr. Mahon.

Ned was not shy in firing back.

"If the Democrats raise the labor issue in this campaign I shall meet it squarely at every point," said Congressman Denby, "for I am not the enemy of labor that, for campaign purposes, the Democrats would have me appear. On the contrary, I consider myself as true and sincere a friend of labor as ever represented this, or any district in Congress. The only difference between me and any of the working men is one of policy, or the question of what is the best policy from the standpoint of their own interests. I am opposed to the closed shop, the sympathetic strike and the boycott, because I believe they are wrong in principle, and all history teaches us that no cause can triumph in the long run unless it be founded on the right principles. The principle of the privilege of laboring men to organize for mutual protection and advancement is everlastingly right, and on that basis I have always been and am now an ardent friend of labor union organizations. It is only when they adopt policies that I do not believe are right, for the reason that they conflict with the rights of others, that I disagree with them." (DFP 8-30-1908)

The patriotism of the city of Detroit was once again put on great display on Friday, September 11 at four o'clock in the afternoon. Hundreds of troops from local military organizations such as the Loyal Legion, the Grand Army of the Republic, the Light Guard Naval Reserves, and Light Infantry, as well as 300 troops from Fort Wayne and 400 from other parts of the State of Michigan gathered at the junction of Washington Blvd. and Michigan Avenue to help the Daughters of 1812 dedicate the magnificent statue honoring General Alexander Macomb, a hero and a native son. It was still a day when history was not only taught and known, but remembered and revered, on this 94th anniversary of the Battle of Plattsburg in New York, which preserved America's exclusive right to Lake Champlain, and further, equal rights with Great Britain upon all of the Great Lakes. It stifled any chance the British thought they had achieved for territorial gain against the fledgling United Staes. In his remarks during the keynote address, Ned made reference to a famous Revolutionary American: "Somebody once mentioned the war of independence in Franklin's hearing, meaning the war of 1776," he told them. "Franklin said, 'You mean the revolution. The war of independence is yet to come.'" Ned also spoke of the "black humiliation" which was the cowardly surrender of Fort Detroit in August of 1812, early in the War, and "declared that Macomb wiped out the insult on the tablets of history" by his action at Plattsburgh.

October saw Ned's reelection campaign, as well as the

178

campaign of his opponent in full swing. Ned was addressing groups almost nightly, and giving sometimes two speeches an evening. On October 15, the Democrats brought in their 'big gun', president of the American Federation of Labor (AFofL), Samuel Gompers who appeared before a packed house at the Light Guard Armory. Though Ned was hit hard by Gompers and candidate Mahon, as they attempted to paint him as a wealthy "capitalist" against "labor", the Free Press dutifully reported a few days later that "some of the union labor men of the city take the view that a snap judgment was pronounced against Congressman Denby in the effort to line up union labor for the Democratic nominee without any effort to give him a local hearing on his attitude." At one meeting of labor men a resolution was adopted, "Resolved, that having heard the Hon. Edwin Denby we are satisfied that his attitude towards organized labor is perfectly fair and just. We assure him of our hearty support." (DFP 10-17-1908)

The next day Ned again spoke at the end of the season banquet for the Detroit Tigers, who had won the American League pennant; and once again had lost to the Chicago Cubs in the World Series, or, as it was called in that day, the "world's series". For his participation in the series, each Tiger was paid the handsome sum of $870.66. Interestingly, the season did not end with the world's series, for other series were being negotiated to follow it, including a possible one in New York at which the players eagerly hoped to make over $1,000 each.

In late October Ned received the endorsements, by way of letters printed in the Detroit Free Press, of Secretary of State, Elihu Root, Congressman Robert Cousins, chairman of the committee on foreign affairs of the house, and congressman R. 0. Moon, chairman of the committee for the revision of laws of the house. Once again the Edwin Denby Club had reached a membership of over 11,000 and predicted to go well above twelve by election time.

As a measure of the man which Edwin Denby was, and more to the point, what type of politician, the day before 1908's presidential election, the Free Press ran an article which flatly stated, as had Ned himself, his adamant opposition in favor of the open shop, "and particularly declaring against the unionizing of government establishments." You might heatedly disagree with Ned Denby, but you knew precisely where he stood. However, when his opponent was asked, "Do you believe that government establishments should be unionized?" Democratic candidate Mahon exclaimed, "That is not an issue in this campaign."

"Mr. Denby says the matter of an open shop in government offices and shops is an issue of the campaign," suggested the interviewer."

"Mr. Denby lies," blustered candidate Mahon. "I say again, I stand on the Democratic platform. I am running for congress not as a union man but as a Democrat and a free American citizen. I utterly refuse to answer your question or discuss the subject of the open shop."

"As a general proposition do you favor the union shop?" the reporter again asked.

"I have nothing to say on that subject," Mahon declared. Mahon seemed to prefigure some of the political eloquence of our own day and time. (DFP)

Early returns on Wednesday November 4 indicated that Taft would beat Bryan, that Michigan's Republican governor, Fred Warner would squeak through, that the Republican candidate for Detroit's mayoral election, florist Philip Breitmeyer would win, and that the citizens of Michigan's 1st congressional district would once again send Ned Denby back to Washington. Later in the day, Taft's victory became clearer, and though his popular vote was not an avalanche, his electoral college margin, 321 to 162, was more than comfortable.

Ned was summoned to consultations with the State Department in Washington the day after the election. Once again the press did not miss an opportunity to tease him. He remarked while in Washington that he did not know his margin of victory, and someone understood this to mean that he had headed for Washington without knowing if he had won the race. "I guess they were trying to have some fun with me,' the jovial congressman said. "I saw the president while I was down there," he continued. "Naturally, he was very much pleased at the outcome of the election."

Two days later he was off partridge and quail shooting with Will Hamilton, trying to get some much needed rest after his recent campaign and his many trips back and forth to the nation's capital.

Oldsmobile had been the first automobile company to be founded in Michigan at the end of the 19th century. Henry Ford's first attempt at a car company, Henry Ford Company, had folded when Ford left the company in a dispute with his partners, but was then resurrected as the Cadillac Motor Company when the remaining investors hired Henry M. Leland, a genius automotive engineer, to run their concern. By 1908, approximately seventy five automobile companies had been established in Detroit, some of which did not last longer than the year in which they were founded. However, in early November, Bobby Hupp, a thirty-one year old designer who had worked for Olds and Ford, developed his own prototype, an inexpensive two-seat runabout which he called the Hupmobile. Early investors were the Drake brothers, J. Walter and Joseph R., along with John E. Baker and Charles Hastings. Before long, Walter Drake, who became President of the Company, interested his Yosemite shipmate and friend, Ned Denby, to join up with a $7,500 investment, for which he was made treasurer of the company. Introducing their new car at the Detroit Auto Show early in 1909, they "got orders for 500, and collected $25,000 in deposits." (Davis, Conspicuous Production, p.92) So explosive was the growth in this industry that by May 1909 the Hupp Motor Company revealed plans to build a major, modern car-building facility in the city and would turn out 5000 cars in their second year of production.

Over the next 30-plus years the Hupp Motor Car Company would distinguish itself in many ways. From the oft-quoted remark of Henry Ford to a friend that he wished he could build a car as cheap and as good as Bobby Hupp's, to the company's claim that the 1909 model was the Detroit Police Department's first automobile, Hupmobiles made news at every turn. (Ward, Three Men in A Hupp, p21) In 1909 a policeman arrested a Hupmobile driver, claiming that he was doing 60 miles her hour. The directors reportedly said "it was news to them that it could do more" than the 50 miles per hour it was manufactured to achieve. (DFP 4-25-1909)

Carl Wickman of Hibbing, Minnesota, strapped with a seven passenger Hupmobile Touring Car which he could not sell, began ferrying passengers around and began to make so much money with his fledgling bus line that he eventually parlayed it into the Greyhound Corporation. Ralph E. Hay began selling Hupmobiles and Pierce-Arrows in Canton, Ohio, and in 1918 he purchased the Canton Bulldogs, a professional football team, to help promote his car sales. After some years in the football business, Hay became the central figure in the establishment of the National Football League. To honor Hay's role in its creation, in 1961 the NFL decided to build the Professional Football Hall of Fame in Canton, Ohio. So the NFL was created from an idea to advertise Hupmobiles!

In mid November came the startling news from China that both the Guangxu Emperor, and the Dowager Empress Cixi, the most powerful woman who had ever ruled China, were dead. The nephew whom Cixi had put in place after the death of her own son had suddenly died at the age of 37, one day before the Empress herself. Suspicion was rampant, and remains to this day. Interviewed by the local press because of his years of experience in China, Ned said it would be impossible for anyone outside the country to have any idea what was happening. "At any rate," he said, "it is certain we know next to nothing about what is taking place there now," and he added that both imperial person's deaths were "shrouded in mystery." (DFP 11-17-1908)

Later in November Ned addressed a gathering of over 1400 Masons at their annual banquet, again speaking on the progress in

Panama. And toward the end of the month a new real estate firm was launched by several prominent Detroit businessmen, named the State Security and Realty Company with Ned as a director. Late November saw him traveling to Syracuse, New York, to visit his younger brother. Garvin had taken a job in Detroit with the Solvay Process Company of Syracuse, which also had offices in Detroit. One of Ned's Bachelor pals from the 550 Jefferson group, A. J. Green, prominent in the company, had gotten Garvin the job. Ned went to Syracuse for a two day visit, and while there was interviewed by a reporter from the Syracuse Journal. Ned spoke about the tariff, the revision of which had been a major campaign promise of Taft in the recently concluded election, about Uncle Joe Cannon and how he hoped and believed that he would again be elected as Speaker of the House in the congressional session about to start in early December; and then he turned to a subject near and dear to his heart: football. It seems that earlier in the month Syracuse had beaten his old alma mater on the local team's home field, 28 to 4. It may have been thirteen years since the congressman donned the maize and blue, but he didn't miss a game or a score, or the opportunity to let others know there would be a payback in the future. "We hope to reverse the result next year," he said. He next turned to the news from the far east which was the Root Takahira Agreement which had just been signed between the United States and Japan. Basically, this agreement acknowledged on paper the status quo in the eastern Pacific between the growing power of the United States post 1898, and the equally growing power of the Japanese Empire post 1905. "It is too soon to fathom the depths or measure the result of this recent joint note between Japan and the United States regarding our relative purpose in the Orient. But I cordially hope that the Root-Takahira agreement will take its place beside the open door policy of Secretary John Hay as a guiding star to our future course." (Syracuse Journal December 3, 1908) Garvin wrote his brother to tell him how much he and his wife had enjoyed having him. "You seem to have made your usual excellent impression on everybody," he told him. "I hear your praises sung on all sides, and many regrets expressed that you were not here long enough to allow of entertainments for you." He also included greetings for Hattie, who was again in Washington to act as her brother's social secretary, and to look for a house of her own. (DPL, Edwin Denby Jr Papers, Box #2)

From Syracuse, Ned went on to Washington for the opening on December 7th of the shorter and last session of the 60th Congress. There was a lot going on. Though Teddy had less than four months left at the helm, he was not about to relax. In his eighth and final message to congress, delivered on December 8th, he sent the military and the congress into a tailspin over his order that the U.S. Marines be removed from naval vessels, leaving the Corps stranded on land for the first time since its inception at Tun Tavern in 1775. Members of congress, as they often do, nearly fell over each other to voice their opposition to the President's rash and ill considered order.

However, that matter paled in comparison with the real issue which had ignited a firestorm under the entire House. Representative James Perkins of New York offered a resolution that the House appoint a special committee to investigate Roosevelt's comment in his annual speech, "that congressmen who had voted to limit activities of the Secret Service 'did not themselves wish to be investigated.'" (Morris, Theodore Rex, p 542.) Many of the Representatives had interpreted the President's remark as a threat against them, and they were ready to load rifles. When no one dissented, Perkins' resolution passed, and Speaker Cannon appointed a committee of five, including Perkins, Weeks of Massachusetts, Williams of Mississippi, Lloyd of Missouri and Ned to investigate the matter. Thoroughly piqued now, the House further reported that one of its subcommittees was investigating the President's order to have the old Pennsylvania train station torn down during the past summer, as if there had been something sinister in that decision, and even further, they were objecting to a commission appointed by the President on country life having franking privileges, and even questioned this commission's right to exist at all.

On December 15, Ned introduced a bill "prohibiting the

importation, manufacture, sale or gifts of opium, for other than medicinal purposes. Seizure of the drug by the government is provided for." (DFP 12-16-1908) The following day the Free Press ran another article which declared that the Denby bill was "likely to involve the government in the greatest fight it ever has had with the patent medicine manufacturers of the country." Prior to Denby's bill, patent medicine labels had only to state that a drug was present in a medication. "Such an act of congress would be as far-reaching and even more effective than the existing law which compels the proper labeling of proprietary goods and probably would drive a number of patent medicines off from the market or put the manufacturers to their wits' end to secure a substitute." (DFP 12-18-1908)

Cornered a few days later by the Free Press correspondent in Washington, Ned provided insight into his committee's investigation into the President's offensive remarks in his annual message. With a moral rectitude imbibed from the Colonel, Ned unabashedly declared, "The character and views, and past conduct of these representatives have been subjected to careful scrutiny in bitter political contests throughout the country. If the bulk of these men are either fools or rascals it must be assumed that the people know it. And if this be true, there is a least a serious doubt concerning the capability of the American people for self-government." Of course, Ned was speaking directly to the intentions of the founding fathers, and the integrity of the principles which they expounded. He was also engaging in an archaic form of social commerce known as 'the benefit of the doubt." Some in Detroit had speculated that Ned's presence on the sub-committee to investigate the President's remarks would serve to spoil the excellent relationship he had always enjoyed with the President. Ned seemed to address this head-on, "The question at issue is not whether the president has a right to object to an act of congress. The question concerns simply the president's reflections on congress." (DFP 12-22-1908)

Fears that Ned's congressional antipathy would spoil his relationship with the President seemed unfounded just days later as he called at the White House with Dr. and Mrs. E. T. Tappey of Detroit to present them to the President. "The president showed no sign of displeasure over the speech delivered by Mr. Denby in reference to the secret service matter, and the meeting was in every way pleasant." (DFP 1-14-1909)

The social season in full swing, Ned and Hattie held two dinner parties in early January, the first was for two departing United States ministers and six congressmen. At the end of the same week, they again hosted another dinner party for a newly married couple who were friends of Will and Marry Hamilton's oldest daughter. The following week Ned travelled to Augusta, Georgia to lobby President-elect Taft concerning his retention of Truman Newberry as Secretary of the Navy. Though Taft refused to be cornered, Ned made the point that all Michigan was behind him. On January 20th his opium bill was favorably reported out of committee.

February brought a flurry of activity, beginning on Tuesday the 2nd when Ned and Hattie attended a small gathering of Yosemite shipmates at the home of still Secretary of the Navy and friend, Truman Newberry. Present with Detroit guests were the outgoing President and his wife. Several days later Ned, along with a group of Michigan legislators, met with Gifford Pinchot, Chief of the United States Forest Service, to lobby for placement of a government forestry laboratory at the University of Michigan. They were in hot competition with a corresponding group from the University of Wisconsin. In the next year, Ned would have a merry time playing his part in deciding the great controversy between Pinchot and Ballinger. A week later another minor spark erupted when it was learned that Judge Taft [throughout his public career and life, William Howard Taft was called "Judge" Taft almost more frequently than any other title he would wear during his long and illustrious career. That is because of all the hats he wore during his life, that of his judgeships, particularly his last one, meant most to Taft himself.] was leaning toward appointing Philander Knox as his Secretary of State. Knox was a Senator from Pennsylvania whose term did not expire until

1911, and who had recently voted for pay raises for cabinet officers making him ineligible to become one. His buddies in the Senate quickly passed a bill which returned the salary to its previous level in his case only, but several members of the House objected to what they saw as a degrading of the office. Ned was among them, and felt strongly about his position, even though he ended up in the minority on this point. John Sharp Williams, Democrat Representative from Mississippi claimed the bill was "a clear, plain, palpable, obvious and manifest case of a direct and expressed constitutional inhibition." Representative Henry S. Caulfield, Republican from Missouri stated "that it was a case of constitutional jugglery of legislative favoritism." (DFP 2-16-1909) After amending the rules to allow passage of the bill in the House by simple majority, it finally went through 173 to 117. Mr. Knox would head the Department of State.

On a rainy, foggy Monday at Hampton Roads, Virginia, President Roosevelt performed one of the proudest functions of his presidency, welcoming home the Great White Fleet. The fleet had sailed successfully around the world, calling at twenty ports on six continents, all without a major breakdown in the impressive American naval display. Reviewing the breathtaking site of America's naval power steaming by his Presidential Yacht, Mayflower, TR remarked, "I could not ask for a finer concluding scene for my administration." (Morris, Theodore Rex, p549) Ten days later Thursday the 4th of March dawned frigid and blustery, as Mother Nature unleashed a winter tantrum to usher in the reluctant Presidency of William Howard Taft. It was the heaviest snow in the nation's Capital in twenty years. (Rosen, William Howard Taft, p.50.) Describing the scene to Mrs.Hamilton two days later, Ned called it "a bad dream in part and very pleasant in part. The weather was horrible beyond words. Mr. Taft took the oath inside [in the Senate Chamber] while thousands waded in ice water outside. Ugh!" (DPL Edwin Denby Papers, Box #1)

Ned and Hattie had hosted a pleasant dinner the evening before with guests "Mr. and Mrs. O'Laughlin (1st Asst. Secy of State), Mr. and Mrs. Fassett [congressman from New York and Ned's close ally in the House], Mr. and Mrs. Hippisley (under whom I served for two years at Macao, China in my former existence in the Customs), Miss Campau-Thompson and Miss Palms-Campau (about whom the only thing I dislike is their wretched hyphens), my brother Wythe, and Joe Stringham of Detroit." The next day they were to meet at the Capitol and then proceed to a window overlooking the parade route on Pennsylvania Avenue which Ned had rented for their party.

"Then came the blizzard and all plans went wrong. Nobody met anybody and everybody was sore. Hattie, Wythe, the two boys and I managed to get to the window, but I left immediately on a telephone call to try to bring the two ladies from Detroit to our place. I got across the street and got the ladies, but could not get back across Pennsylvania with them. Then I went home in disgust, determined never to be President until the Inauguration date was changed. Pneumonia is the chief beneficiary of the present idiotic system." He next engaged in political comments about the Taft cabinet. "Well, it's over, and Mr. Taft is in, and so is Meyer [George Meyer whom Taft had selected as his Secretary of the Navy], and Newberry is out. I am sorry and so is the service. "I am sure a mistake was made in the case of Knox, but it is done and can't be undone and I have been doing all I could to strengthen the hand of Mr. Knox and give him the staff he needs in the Department. He and I are good friends. He told me the other day that he had that morning told Mr. Roosevelt that he wished my argument against his becoming Secretary of State and my argument in favor of the creation of the office of Under Secretary had both prevailed. [neither did]

He cannot help but continue: "In the meantime, I learn that John C. Spooner, Joseph Choate, Milburn and others whose names are great in the law world, believe Mr. Knox ineligible. Nothing will convince me to the contrary." (Ibid.}

On March 15, 1909 the Congress convened in Special Session called by the new President to fulfill one of his most ardent campaign promises: tariff reform. Arguing tariffs and what they do, what they do not do, who they benefit and who they penalize, is like arguing the chicken and the egg. Semantics do almost anything to any argument, as any half-decent politician knows full well by the time he enters his first race. High tariffs protect domestic production against cheaper foreign goods being dumped into an economy for the purpose of capturing a market. Lower, or no tariffs allow free-market trade, which initially benefits workers with more affordable products to buy, but eventually stifles business in the domestic market, causing companies to fold who cannot compete, and thus increases joblessness. High tariffs do tend to make business owners wealthier, but at the same time, with the protection of domestic production, they protect domestic jobs. Too much tariff: exorbitantly wealthy business owners, high domestic prices making life more difficult on the lower end of the economic spectrum; too little tariff: market flooded with cheaper products from overseas, businesses fold, unemployment rises.

Historically, the United States leapt to the forefront of world production, in part, by utilizing the tariff to protect American industry. By the time of McKinley, Cannon, and Aldrich, opposed by Theodore Roosevelt, Bryan, and Lafollette, over a hundred years later, the tariff question remained one of the major sticking points between the parties. The basic argument all the way into the 21st Century remains the same. For the past two decades we have had low to no barriers to foreign goods, and American industry has been eviscerated, allowing millions of American jobs to evaporate overseas. This process began to be reversed in January 2017, and the economy fairly exploded with a growth unparalleled in our history. In seven and a half years in the Presidency and with astonishing popularity, Theodore Roosevelt never attempted what Judge Taft walked directly into with his insistence upon calling the Congress to meditate upon what he had promised the American voter: tariff reform. But, being a strict constitutionalist, after calling the congress and suggesting what was to be done, the Judge was not about to involve himself in any way with Congress' deliberations. The Judge was a constitutional jurist. TR was a progressive idealist.

The first items to make news were gloves and hosiery. The

ladies of Detroit heard that Congress was looking at raising the tariff on these articles and vehemently protested by writing to Ned. Caught by a newspaperman, Ned diplomatically stated that he did not think he would be able to change anything concerning these items, and the Free Press, a few days later, gleefully responded, quoting the Adrian Times, "Congressman Denby of Detroit dares to talk back to the ladies who sent him a monster protest against the increased duties on gloves and hosiery. Denby is a bachelor." (DFP 4-16-1909)

While the Congress bear-wrestled with tariff reform, another lightning bolt struck the family from far left field. The first inkling of trouble came, as it often does, in the form of rumors and gossip, as the Evansville papers seemed to ferret out information which indicated that Charles Jr. was being accused of improper actions in Shanghai, and was being dismissed from the consular service. This was borne out by a State Department cipher sent to Charles in Shanghai dated April 22 simply stating that "The President directs me to inform you that your resignation is accepted to take effect June first or upon the arrival of your successor if earlier." (BHL Edwin Denby Papers, Box #1) Speculation centered once again around the person of Lebbeus R. Wilfley, the man who had been the first judge of the United States Court for China, whom Ned had defended the preceding year during his impeachment trial before the House. It turns out that Judge Wilfley had gone back to China after his exoneration, that even though a newspaper editor was convicted of criminal libel against him in the British Court and spent two months in jail, the Judge was so unhappy with conditions in China that he resigned his post at the end of 1908 and went home. The details of the charges against Charlie were never made public, but rumors swirled about a real estate deal which the Judge had felt was not in the best interests of the State Department, and Charles was dismissed without investigation or due process.

But then Ned got involved in Washington, and brought the power that he had accumulated in two and a half terms as a very active and popular Representative to bear upon the problem, and the State Department, including his old friend, Philander Knox, decided to investigate after all. It is difficult to understand why men such as William Taft and Philander Knox would have apparently jumped to conclusions about Charlie's behavior, and seemed to act by denying him the benefit of his constitutional rights, but they quickly came to their senses and by May 12, Knox himself sent a cipher to Charles informing him of his immediate appointment as consul general in Vienna. He was told that he might announce this "at once" and "proceed to your post upon the arrival of your successor." Knox was careful to include the following caveat: "The circumstances are understood by your brother here." (Ibid)

Ned also confidentially wired his brother: "Vienna best that can be done. I would advise you to accept. Department of State will send man from here to investigate Wilfley charges. After six months if the President is not satisfied you are expected to resign." So, it wasn't dismissal, but it also wasn't over. Ned added, "Don't talk. Don't worry. I hope for favorable outcome. Ned" (Ibid) Ned's long time friend, Hugh O'Brien, who was still working for the Court in China wrote him on May 11. "Your brother's dismissal has been deeply resented here, and a big send-off is contemplated which will take the form of an international dinner probably larger than anything of it's kind ever held here." In the same letter he told Ned that he was resigning his post effective August 1, and that he enjoyed working with the New Judge who had taken Wilfley's place, Rufus Thayer, but that it was time for him to get back to his practice in Detroit.

Early June saw the U.S. Naval Academy's graduating class of 1881 celebrate their reunion at the Metropolitan Club in Washington, D. C. The event was as well a diplomatic affair given the attendance of retired Japanese Admiral Baron Uryu Sotokichi, a member of the class. Along with many other military and political leaders of the American government who attended to help fete the venerable Japanese Admiral, Ned was included on the guest list, and later as Secretary of the Navy, would one day carry this entire celebration to the shores of Japan. As a measure of how diligently America courted Japanese favor at this time, President Taft broke precedent by attending the dinner party himself and giving remarks in honor of the guest. Taft had visited Japan on several occasions, and certainly considered himself fortunate to be in a position to foster harmonious relations between the two countries. Baron Uryu remained a life long friend of the United States, and unfortunately died in 1937, as another faction of Japanese influence was taking control of the government of the Rising Sun.

When Ned's feet hit the floor on the morning of June 1, 1909, it is virtually certain he had no idea that the coming day would not only significantly alter the remainder of his life, but quite surely in his own opinion, turn out to be the very best day he would ever know. Having saved Charlie's bacon, for now; having helped fete a retired Japanese Admiral; having assisted his congressional colleagues in wrestling with the all-important tariff bill, Ned took time out on this day to stand as best man for one of his good friends, Henry Sanger, the Cashier of the National Bank of Commerce. The wedding took place at St. John's Episcopal Church in Detroit, and the bride, Miss Margaret Snow, was sister to one of Ned's Yosemite shipmates. Much more notable, however, was one of Miss Snow's four attendants, Miss Marion Bartlett Thurber, a fetching and vivacious twenty-four year old Detroit society girl, wearing a "large hat of white Neapolitan straw, trimmed with a bow of white and champagne colored tulle and a large deep pink rose," when first meeting the giant congressman looked up fetchingly at him from beneath the straw and said, "Hello, I'm Marion." To which, the thoroughly captivated and always jovial congressman answered glibly, "Why, I'm marryin', too!" The young lady was at once amused, and it is certain that in their first conversation they found much in common. Years after, Marion loved to tell the story of that fateful meeting, and her grandchildren would always remember it. "I liked that man!" she unabashedly exclaimed to little ones forty years later. (Private conversation with Ned Wetmore, grandson, April 2019)

Born February 22, 1885 in Detroit, she was second in order of birth of five children of Henry Thomas Thurber and Elizabeth (Lizzie) Brady Croul. Lizzie Croul, an heiress in her own right, had descended from one of Detroit's important families. Henry Thurber, a dapper, hard-working fellow from Monroe, Michigan, graduated Michigan Law School and headed for Detroit in 1875 to establish himself. A loyal Democrat in a sea of Michigan Republicans, he joined what would become the prestigious Detroit law firm of Dickinson, Thurber and Stevenson. In 1880 he married Lizzie Croul and in 1883 they welcomed their first child, Donald M. Dickinson Thurber into the world of polite Detroit society.

Henry's law partner and mentor, Donald M. Dickinson, had helped organize the Democrat Party in Michigan in 1872, was a member of the Democratic National Committee from 1880 to 1885, and had been Grover Cleveland's Postmaster General in 1887. It was almost a given, then, that when President Cleveland was looking for a new personal secretary for his second term, Donald Dickinson told the President he had just the man. Marion was eight years old when the family moved to Washington, D. C. The Thurber's rented a home on I Street, three blocks from the White House, in 1893, by then with a total of four children, Henry Thomas born in 1890 and sister Elizabeth born in 1892 having joined the group.. The office of Personal Secretary to the President was in those days nearly a cabinet-level appointment, had its own oath of office, and the men occupying this position were among the most coveted societal guests of their day. The Thurber children attended the White House school, summered in Buzzard's Bay, near Grey Gables, the Cleveland's Summer White House retreat, and welcomed a final addition to the family in 1895 in the form of a third son Cleveland Thurber. After Grover Cleveland's second term expired on March 4, 1897, the family returned to Detroit where father Henry. financially comfortable, interested himself in investments and other business interests. He was a large stockholder in the Ward Lumber Company, and the Detroit, Ypsilanti and Ann Arbor Railway. The idyllic childhood of Marion Thurber came to an abrupt end, however, on May 3, 1898 when her beloved mother was taken suddenly in death at the age of thirty-nine. Marion was thirteen, and became the oldest female member of the family, presiding over younger siblings ages eight, six and three. But tragedy had not yet done with the Thurber family, as scion Henry, widely respected and revered by everyone who knew him, was stricken with an appendectomy in February of 1904, and eighteen days later he succumbed at the age of fifty. In that same year, Marion, now nineteen, graduated from the prestigious Liggett School in Detroit as an orphan.

It may be imagined how difficult it was to have lost both beloved parents by the age of nineteen, but Marion showed her resilience and careful breeding by taking everything as it came, without complaint, with grace and stoic composure. She lived with her Aunt Molly and enjoyed a lively social life with many friends and relatives. Summers were spent at the family's cottage at Point Aux Barques, at the north end of Michigan's thumb on the shore of Lake Huron.

She was twenty four years old when she met the well known congressman, and he thirty nine. Besides political families, a common Detroit heritage with Washington D. C. connections, the two shared a great love of humor, and also theatrics. Marion performed in local plays, and Edwin had once been heavily involved in the Detroit Comedy Club. They were both from families of lawyers and they moved in the upper social strata. They were both Episcopalians. They were both vivacious and engaging people who loved to have a good time. They were both self-sufficient; Ned by choice was proud of the fact that he had gotten his Customs job at the age of seventeen and had never needed further assistance from his father. Marion had certainly had much responsibility in her family with her parents dying at such young ages. They were ideally suited, and they seemed to know it from the start.

"A day later Ned was back in Washington where Garvin and Ester came for a visit with him and Hattie. The four of them took an auto tour through Virginia and the Shenandoah Valley — in 1909 a fairly new form of entertainment — the motor vacation. In the middle of June the Detroit Tigers were in Washington for

a game with the Nationals, The team was visiting the Capitol Building at Ned's invitation and Speaker Cannon met the team and shook every hand. Uncle Joe confessed he didn't know much about baseball, admitting that he had only attended a single game since a boy. He was immediately pressed into joining the team at the ball park that afternoon. On the way, running a little late, the Speaker's car was stopped by the police for speeding, but once it was ascertained who was in the car they were released to make it to the ball park in the nick of time. Later, Ned escorted the team to the White House where they met President Taft. "When Ty Cobb was presented to him, the president grasped the hand of the Georgian warmly and said, 'I believe you and I are fellow citizens of Augusta, Mr. Cobb.' Cobb modestly replied that he was proud to be a citizen of Augusta and a fellow citizen of Mr. Taft. 'The only difference between us,' responded the president, 'is that down there they think you are a bigger man than I am.'"
(DFP 06-15-09)

In July the House of Representatives announced a political baseball game to be held between the Republicans and the Democrats. Apparently Joe Cannon had enjoyed his time with the Tigers. When the game was played, on July 17, the Democrats trounced the Republicans by a whopping score of 26-16. Organized by Representative John Tener of Pennsylvania, this was the maiden outing of what became the annual Congressional Baseball Game which has been played nearly every year since 1909. It was during a practice for this game in June, 2017, that a shooting occurred perpetrated by a crazed gunman wounding four people, including Congressman Steve Scalise, all of whom recoverd from their wounds.

In mid-July Ned wrote his brother Graham in Evansville, bringing him up to date on Charlie's status with the State Department. "The whole matter has been unspeakably disappointing to me, and has certainly prejudiced my heretofore high opinion of president and Secretary of State. I cannot conceive why a man of judicial training could condemn and execute without giving the accused even an opportunity to be heard," he wrote. He next informed his brother that "Hattie is located in a very attractive old farmhouse in Warrenton, Virginia. She is very comfortably located in a beautiful country, and has in prospect apparently a delightful summer. The climate is much cooler than here and there are absolutely no mosquitoes. She has a cow which amply supplies the family with milk, cream and butter, and a vegetable garden yielding all the fresh vegetables they can eat." He also mentioned that he had slipped off to upper Michigan July 1st expecting to get in about ten days of fishing on Lake Superior, but due to the Senate's unexpected passage of the Tariff Bill, he was called urgently back to Washington for the final passage of the bill.

On Thursday, August 5, the Payne-Aldrich Tariff Bill was finally passed, and signed into law by President Taft. Representative Sereno Payne of New York had introduced the bill in the House in early March, and it had passed the House on April 9. However, in the Senate it met a buzzsaw of revisions, led by Senator Nelson Aldrich of Rhode Island, which rendered it all but unrecognizable. After three more months of wrangling, the combined House-Senate bill was finally passed. Surely the President breathed a sigh of relief as "all things considered, the bill represented a downward revision: there were 654 decreases, 220 increases, and 1150 unchanged items, and the average duty on imports was 21.09 percent, whereas under the Dingley law [the bill it replaced] it had been 24.03 percent." (Rosen, William Howard Taft, p63)

Taft may have been relieved to be able to claim he had fulfilled his promise to the American voter, but almost no one in Congress was happy. The divisions created in this debate were to crystallize the factions of political thought in the country for years to come. Some Republicans favored a modest reduction of tariffs, another group known as Insurgents favored even lower tariff rates to "increase competition and lower consumer prices" (Ibid p.60) and an entirely third group of Republicans wanted the status quo, led by Speaker Cannon. This third group became known as the 'standpatters'. Then, in addition, many on the opposite side of the aisle favored no tariffs at all. The Payne-Aldrich Tariff Bill was the first time the Republican Insurgents (Republicans who favored revision of House rules and opposed Speaker Cannon) made their influence count, and Joe Cannon was swift in his retaliation. One day after the bill passed, Uncle Joe released the committee assignments for the next session, penalizing insurgents by dropping Representatives Charles Fowler (NJ), Augustus Gardner (MA) and Henry Cooper (WI) from committee chairmanships. In addition to his past committees, Ned was now placed on the Judiciary Committee.

In September Ned joined Charlie's family vacationing at Roaring Brook, Michigan where they had a cabin for the summer. After the ordeal of his exit from China, Charles was taking the summer off. In November Ned visited his favorite hunting venue, the exclusive Huron Mountain Club on Lake Superior to hunt quail. Toward the end of the month after he had returned to his office in Detroit he received a visit from an extraordinary caller. A landsman, a shipmate from his Yosemite days, George Winter, who had cooked aboard the ship, dropped by "for a friendly chat and his bounty money," reported the Free Press. It had been years since the bounty money had been awarded, but George Winter had been all over the world and had arrived to tell "a tale of adventure beside which Robert Louis Stevenson's pages look insipid." It seemed the sailor had been shanghaied at Seattle and was taken on a full-rigged sailer to Cape Town, South Africa, where he joined the British South African mounted police. "Winter told of his part in the Boer War, a coaling trip to Alexandria, and his unwilling service aboard a vessel carrying the yellow fever flag." He spoke several languages, the Press reported, and it is certain that the small article told only a fraction of the tales that were audibly placed before a rapt Ned Denby. (DFP 10-29-09)

On October 18 the annual Tigers' Banquet was held in the Ponchartrain Hotel, where again hundreds of guests gathered to fete the American League Champions, who went on to lose their third consecutive World Series, this time to the Pittsburgh Pirates. Again Ned was on hand and called upon for remarks. By November 1 Hattie was back at the Connecticut Avenue house she shared with her brother, getting ready for the influx of temporary Washington. By the 18th Ned had joined her, needing to get back before the start of the 2nd Session in order to attend meetings on the joint committee on revision of the laws. At their previous session, Ned told the Press, they had revised the criminal code, and at the coming session they were going to tackle the civil code. "The laws of the United States have not been revised in 30 years and we hope to agree soon upon a plan for a compete revision of the federal statutes," he told the Press. (DFP 11-18,1909)

As the congress gathered up its skirts, preparing for an extremely busy session, the Free Press ran an article describing just how busy it was going to be.

"Despite the fact that President Taft called congress in extra session on March 15 for the purpose of giving consideration to the passage of a tariff bill, and it was the understanding of the leaders at the time that no legislation other than the tariff should be enacted unless it was of the most pressing character, no less than 15,000 bills were introduced by the various mem bers, 3,195 in the senate and 12,384 in the house."(DFP 11-21,1909)

These numbers equate to 35 pieces of legislation per senator, and 32 per representative. The bulk of them, most probably, were pensions requested by members for meritorious constituents, and simple matters of that nature, but the numbers were staggering. Ned alone presented 52 pension bills, a bill to place Capt. William S. Biddle on the retired list of the army; a bill to amend the act prohibiting the issuance of free passes on railroads, and a measure to repay the duties on equipment for vessels. The Free Press continued, "Naturally, the Michigan senators and representatives are not even dreaming that all their measures will be enacted into law. The committees will go over all the bills, pick out the most meritorious ones, make favorable reports on them, and in course of time, if the speaker so wills, they will be passed through the house. Once through that body, they will not have very much trouble in the senate." (Ibid)

Early December found Charles and family visiting Ned and Hattie on Connecticut Avenue, after which they travelled to

New York on Wednesday, December 8 and sailed for Europe the following day. The same evening Ned and Hattie entertained Major Theodore Lyster who was visiting in Washington from his post in Panama. The brother of one of Ned's Yosemite shipmates, and son of Ned's great friend Winifried Lyster, neither the Major nor Ned could imagine that one day the offspring of Denbys and Lysters would join the families in marriage. The Drake brothers also visited Ned and Hattie just before Christmas, after which Ned headed to Detroit for the holidays. Tigers were in Washington for a game with the Nationals. The team visited the Capitol Building at Ned's invitation and Speaker Cannon met the team and shook every hand. Uncle Joe confessed he didn't know much about baseball, admitting that he had only attended a single game since a boy. He was immediately pressed into joining the team at the ball park that afternoon. On the way, running a little late, the Speaker's car was stopped by the police for speeding, but once it was ascertained who was in the car they were released to make it to the ball park in the nick of time. Later, Ned escorted the team to the White House where they met President Taft. "When Ty Cobb was presented to him, the president grasped the hand of the Georgian warmly and said, 'I believe you and I are fellow citizens of Augusta, Mr. Cobb.' Cobb modestly replied that he was proud to be a citizen of Augusta and a fellow citizen of Mr. Taft. 'The only difference between us,' responded the president, 'is that down there they think you are a bigger man than I am.'" (DFP 06-15-09)

Humphrey Shaw, the young newspaper boy whom Ned had gotten appointed to the Paige corps made news on his own when he anchored the last leg of a YMCA marathon team, which won the prize for becoming the first team to finish the twenty mile race. Hattie leased a country home near Warrenton, Virginia for the summer, and by July the House announced a political baseball game to be held between the Republicans and the Democrats. Apparently Joe Cannon had enjoyed his time with the Tigers. When the game was played, on July 17, the Democrats trounced the Republicans by a whopping score of 26-16. Organized by

Representative John Tener of Pennsylvania, this was the maiden outing of what became the annual Congressional Baseball Game which has been played nearly every year since 1909. It was during practice for this game in June, 2017, that a shooting broke out by a crazed gunman wounding four people, including Congressman Steve Scalise, all of whom recovered from their wounds.

In mid-July Ned wrote his brother Graham in Evansville, bringing him up to date on Charlie's status. "The whole matter has been unspeakably disappointing to me, and has certainly prejudiced my heretofore high opinion of the president and Secretary of State. I cannot conceive why a man of judicial training could condemn and execute without giving the accused even an opportunity to be heard." He next informed his brother that "Hattie is located in a very attractive old farm house in Warrenton, Virginia. She is very comfortably located in a beautiful country, and has in prospect apparently a delightful summer. The climate is much cooler than here and there are absolutely no mosquitoes. She has a cow, which amply supplies the family with milk, cream and butter, and a vegetable garden yielding all the fresh vegetables they can eat." He also mentioned that he had slipped off to upper Michigan July 1st expecting to get in about ten days fishing on Lake Superior, but due to the Senate's unexpected passage of the Tariff Bill, he was called urgently back to Washington for the final passage of the bill.

On Thursday, August 5, the Payne-Aldrich Tariff Bill was finally passed, and signed into law by President Taft. Representative Sereno Payne of New York had introduced the bill in the House in early March, and it had passed the House on April 9. However, in the Senate it met a buzzsaw of revisions, led by Senator Nelson Aldrich of Rhode Island, which rendered it all but unrecognizable. After three more months of wrangling, the combined House-Senate bill was finally passed. Surely the President breathed a sigh of relief as "all things considered, the bill represented a downward revision: there were 654 decreases, 220 increases, and 1150 unchanged items, and the average duty on imports was 21.09 percent, whereas under the Dingley law [the bill it replaced] it had been 24.03 percent." (Rosen, William Howard Taft, p63)

Taft may have been relieved to be able to claim he had fulfilled his promise to the American voter, but almost no one in Congress was happy. The divisions created in this debate were to crystallize the factions of political thought in the country for years to come. Some Republicans favored a modest reduction of tariffs, another group known as Insurgents favored even lower tariff rates to "increase competition and lower consumer prices" (Ibid p.60) and an entirely third group of Republicans wanted the status quo, led by Speaker Cannon. This third group became known as the 'standpatters'. Then, in addition, many on the opposite side of the aisle favored no tariffs at all. The Payne-Aldrich Tariff Bill was the first time the Republican Insurgents (Republicans who favored revision of House rules and opposed Speaker Cannon) made their influence count, and Joe Cannon was swift in his retaliation. One day after the bill passed, Uncle Joe released the committee assignments for the next session, penalizing insurgents by dropping Representatives Charles Fowler (NJ), Augustus Gardner (MA) and Henry Cooper (WI) from committee chairmanships. In addition to his past committees, Ned was now placed on the Judiciary Committee.

In September Ned joined Charlie's family vacationing at Roaring Brook, Michigan where they had a cabin for the summer. After the ordeal of his exit from China, Charles was taking the summer off. In November Ned visited his favorite hunting venue, the exclusive Huron Mountain Club on Lake Superior to hunt quail. Toward the end of the month after he had returned to his office in Detroit he received a visit from an extraordinary caller. A landsman, a shipmate from his Yosemite days, George Winter, who had cooked aboard the ship, dropped by "for a friendly chat and his bounty money," reported the Free Press. It had been years since the bounty money had been awarded, but George Winter had been all over the world and had arrived to tell "a tale of adventure beside which Robert Louis Stevenson's pages look insipid." It seemed the sailor had been shanghaied at Seattle and was taken on a full-rigged sailer to Cape Town, South Africa, where he joined the British South African mounted police. "Winter told of his part in the Boer War, a coaling trip to Alexandria, and his unwilling service aboard a vessel carrying the yellow fever flag." He spoke several languages, the Press reported, and it is certain that the small article told only a fraction of the tales that were audibly placed before a rapt Ned Denby. (DFP 10-29-09)

On October 18 the annual Tigers' Banquet was held in the Ponchartrain Hotel, where again hundreds of guests gathered to fete the American League Champions, who went on to lose their third consecutive World Series, this time to the Pittsburgh Pirates. Again Ned was on hand and called upon for remarks. By November 1 Hattie was back at the Connecticut Avenue house she shared with her brother, getting ready for the influx of temporary Washington. By the 18th Ned had joined her, needing to get back before the start of the 2nd Session in order to attend meetings on the joint committee on revision of the laws. At their previous session, Ned told the Press, they had revised the criminal code, and at the coming session they were going to tackle the civil code. "The laws of the United States have not been revised in 30 years and we hope to agree soon upon a plan for a compete revision of the federal statutes," he told the Press. (DFP 11-18,1909)

As the congress gathered up its skirts, preparing for an extremely busy session, the Free Press ran an article describing just how busy it was going to be.

"Despite the fact that President Taft called congress in extra session on March 15 for the purpose of giving consideration to the passage of a tariff bill, and it was the understanding of the leaders at the time that no legislation other than the tariff should be enacted unless it was of the most pressing character, no less than 15,000 bills were introduced by the various mem¬bers, 3,195 in the senate and 12,384 in the house."

(DFP 11-21,1909)

These numbers equate to 35 pieces of legislation per senator, and 32 per representative. The bulk of them, most probably, were pensions requested by members for meritorious constituents, and simple matters of that nature, but the numbers were staggering.

Ned alone presented 52 pension bills, a bill to place Capt. William S. Biddle on the retired list of the army; a bill to amend the act prohibiting the issuance of free passes on railroads, and a measure to repay the duties on equipment for vessels. The Free Press continued, "Naturally, the Michigan senators and representatives are not even dreaming that all their measures will be enacted into law. The committees will go over all the bills, pick out the most meritorious ones, make favorable reports on them, and in course of time, if the speaker so wills, they will be passed through the house. Once through that body, they will not have very much trouble in the senate." (Ibid)

Early December found Charles and family visiting Ned and Hattie on Connecticut Avenue, after which they travelled to New York on Wednesday, December 8 and sailed for Europe the following day. The same evening Ned and Hattie entertained Major Theodore Lyster who was visiting in Washington from his post in Panama. The brother of one of Ned's Yosemite shipmates, and son of Ned's great friend Winifried Lyster, neither the Major nor Ned could imagine that one day the offspring of Denbys and Lysters would join the families in marriage. The Drake brothers also visited Ned and Hattie just before Christmas, after which Ned headed to Detroit for the holidays.

Chapter Ten

"I stand on the record I have made."

Ned Denby to the Detroit Free Press July 7, 1910

New Directions

Those who don't believe that history repeats itself don't know much history. Though William Howard Taft and Theodore Roosevelt were best of friends, though Teddy had selected the "Judge" to follow him into the White House, though the two men shared great areas of common belief, there was one glaring difference between them: Teddy Roosevelt believed that the President could do anything the Constitution did not prohibit, and Judge Taft believed that the President could only do what the Constitution specified. Just before leaving office, therefore, Teddy, not completely trusting his successor's conservation commitment instructed his Secretary of the Interior, James R. Garfield, to remove over a million acres of land from public use. Though Taft had at one time mused that he might keep Teddy's entire cabinet, by the time he was elected Chief Executive, he had come to realize that this would not be possible. Conservationists were dismayed when he appointed Richard A. Ballinger, a former Mayor of Seattle, and also a former judge like himself, to take over the Department of the Interior. Though Ballinger had previously been Commissioner of the General Land Office in the Roosevelt administration, though his objectives were not that different than their own, though Ballinger considered himself a "Roosevelt man", he was disliked from the start because he was someone new. And also because both Taft and Ballinger believed that the late-night withdrawal of millions of acres of land by the Roosevelt Administration had been illegal, and began within weeks restoring them for public use. Those who had distrusted Ballinger now came to despise him.

One man in particular despised Richard Ballinger more than all the others, and this was Gifford Pinchot, the first head of the U. S. Forest Service. Not only appointed by Theodore Roosevelt, he was a close personal friend of the former president, a carefully selected member of Teddy's "tennis cabinet". From a background of wealth and privilege, Pinchot was a dedicated conservationist of the type who brooked no interference or disagreement with his point of view. Ballinger, in his former position in the Land Office had already clashed with Pinchot over methods, and was now put firmly into Pinchot's gunsights as Public Enemy No.1. From the moment that William Howard Taft began to deviate from the previous administration's guidelines, no matter how small the deviation, those left over from the previous administration, led by Pinchot, were out to do whatever was necessary to sabotage his efforts. This included the destruction of his loyal subordinates.

It was really less about policy than power. Almost everyone in both administrations would claim to be conservation-minded, but only the chosen were supposed to hold the positions. What a scalding brew began to boil when the Judge appointed an outsider to Interior would end up making a Czarist Russian police plot look like a child's game. Goaded by Pinchot, an investigator named Louis Glavis, who had previously worked in the Land Office under Ballinger, wrote a 50-page report of charges against his former boss which the two of them managed to get before Taft. After reading the report and consulting with his Attorney General, Taft decided to fire Glavis for insubordination.

"In all, the story which Glavis laid before the president was a fantastic perversion of the record, marked by disingenuous and at times whimsical selection of evidence. Where a fact disputed his case it was suppressed; where it reinforced, it was given extensive prominence. In some (though by no means all) of the allegations against Ballinger, there was an element of questionable judgment. In the distorted image projected by Glavis there was only collusion or condonation of fraud, purblind folly and deliberate deceit." (Penick, Progressive Politics and Conservation. p.114)

From there, matters escalated when the charges against Ballinger were then delivered to Colliers Weekly Magazine. Deep State. Leaked information. False charges. Fake news. Soon major publications across the country were rushing to judgment. Exasperated, Ballinger himself appealed to the President to request a full-blown, bipartisan, joint committee of Congress to investigate everything. Congress thus created the Joint Committee to Investigate the Interior Department and the Forestry Service. Since Pinchot had kept up his non-stop barrage of accusations and denunciations against Ballinger for months, at this juncture, Taft fired him as well. So Pinchot got his wish to attempt the destruction of his enemy via congressional investigation, but he also opened up his own department to the same intense and bitter scrutiny.

Thus by the third week of January, 1910, Congress selected six Senators and six Representatives to sit on this pressure-cooker committee: Republican Senators Root (NY), Nelson (MN), Sutherland (UT), Flint (CA); Democrat Senators Purcell (ND) and Fletcher (FL); Democrat Representatives James (KY) and Graham (IL); Insurgent Representative Madison (WI); and Republican Representatives McCall (MA), Olmstead (PA), and Ned Denby. Seven Republicans, 4 Democrats and 1 Insurgent Republican. Senator Knute Nelson from Alexandria, Minnesota acted as Chairman. The committee sat from January 26 to May 20, meeting in forty-five sessions, and because of partisan politics in the extreme, issued three reports: The Minority Report, the lone Insurgent's Report, and the Majority Report.

As a measure of how incendiary the conservation movement was in those days (think "global warming"), by early February

Ned had received a letter from a woman purporting to be the secretary of the Federation of Women's Clubs of Michigan, threatening dire consequences should he not find it in himself to exonerate Gifford Pinchot. The writer claimed to represent over three thousand women members, all supposedly poised to work against his reelection in the fall if he did not tow the line. Suppressing his immediate impulse to scorch the woman in reply, he merely invited her to submit to the committee any information she might have pertaining to the matter. (DFP 2-4-1910) The following day the Press reported that another prominent women's group not only disavowed this position, but resolved to condemn it, and further stated that the woman suspected of having written the letter was a member of another group altogether, and was "very active in forestry work and who has at heart the exoneration of Gifford Pinchot." (DFP 2-5-1910) On February 8, Ned answered his feminine attacker, in a public letter with words firm, but gentle. "I can only regard the pre-determination of the case by your association or any other body, as unfortunate, and the communication of that decision to me as capable of the most unhappy interpretation." (DFP 2-8-1910) Since the final report (Majority) of the committee was not issued until late in the year, let us leave that for a bit later, and continue with the rest of the events of Ned Denby's journey through this pivotal year of his life.

Early March saw the defeat in the House of the Embassy Bill which would have set aside sizable amounts of money to build embassy, legation and consular buildings overseas. Heavily favored by Ned and his friend, Nicholas Longworth, it was opposed by those in the House dedicated to protecting the budget at every turn. One of the few times Uncle Joe found himself partnered with parsimonious Democrats and against his young protege from Michigan. But the disagreement between Ned and Uncle Joe would remain of the passing nature and affect their long-term friendship not at all. A week later Ned was back in Detroit with Senator Burrows and his friend, Representative Sloat Fassett of New York, to act as Toastmaster at a banquet of the Wayne County Republican Club. Speaking to over 800 of the party faithful, Ned began by announcing his candidacy for reelection in the coming autumn, spoke out strongly for the Payne-Aldrich Tariff Bill and for the Speaker of the House, calling Uncle Joe an "...able, upright, conscientious man." It was his opening shot against the insurgents, the Republican split whose most vociferous plank was their opposition to "Cannonism". To a man of Ned's loyalty, attacking the boss was blasphemy. To the Insurgents it was necessary, and long overdue.

Also in March, James Breck Perkins, Representative from New York, chairman of the House Foreign Affairs Committee died suddenly at the age of 62. There was speculation in the Detroit Press about the possibility of Ned being slotted there, but it did not happen. One reason may have been because there were also rumors afoot that Ned was being groomed by the powers that be to step into the Speaker's Chair whenever Uncle Joe decided to relinquish it. In any case, the Free Press, on March 17, printed an opinion piece highly favorable to the jovial congressman's integrity:

"Some perhaps may not admire 'Cannonism' so called, but they must respect Mr. Denby because unlike some congressmen he is the same at home and in Washington. One always knows where to find Mr. Denby. He stands squarely upon his platform and there is no side-stepping or hedging. This is a refreshing thing about his career. His present outspoken endorsement of the speaker of the house of representatives recalls an episode of his last campaign. He stood for the open shop for government establishments partly because in his opinion the closed shop would constitute class legislation. He never failed to explain where he stood, whether among employers or whether in a 'closed' shop meeting. Everyone knew that he approved of unions, but not of unionized government establishments. This is simply a matter of history that speaks for itself." (DFP 3-17-1910)

In the same month Gifford Pinchot headed for Europe to confer with Theodore Roosevelt who was still hob-nobbing about the Continent visiting sundry potentates, giving speeches, and variously trying to remain as aloof as it was possible for him to be. In the States the newspapers began writing about a "return from Elba", meaning that Judge Taft was going to be spanked when the Big Man found his way to Columbia's shores once more. Or, some hoped he would be. Garfield, the ousted Secretary of the Interior, was in Ohio giving a speech attacking Taft for imagined ills and proclaiming that he could not in good conscience head the Republican movement for his reelection in the State of Ohio. It didn't make sense, it didn't have to. It was pure politics. In addition to resisting the current, elected administration, it was also helping to fuel the Insurgent rebellion. It was beginning to look like the splitting of the Republican Party, and Ned sat on the committee smack in the middle of it all.

Around April 10, the every 75-76 year visitation of Halley's Comet began to become visible with the naked eye from the earth, and several unique things happened in relation to it. Not least of which was that this was the first visitation of the comet to be photographed. It was also, by the author's own declaration, to herald the demise of the world famous Mark Twain, who had been born under the sign of the comet in its last sighting in 1835, and duly died on April 21st. During this unusually close visitation, the earth actually passed through the comet's tail, but as had been predicted by one notable scientist, it failed to eradicate all life on the planet. Whew!

June saw the President tour the Midwest, speaking in Ohio, and Michigan. On June 3 his train arrived at the Michigan Central Station, where he was greeted by over 30,000 Detroiters on his route to the Light Guard Armory. There over 800 members and guests of the Detroit Board of Commerce feted the Chief Executive at a sumptuous banquet. In our day of tele- prompters and speechwriters, it is interesting to note that the Press mentioned the President while sitting at the head table "doing justice to the menu, found time to chat and laugh with his friends, while between times he busied himself with writing notes for the speech which he delivered later." (DFP 6-4-1910) He spoke on, of all things, conservation, and again the Press pointed out what it thought was the most important line in his 43 minute remarks.

"It is of the utmost importance that those executive dispositions and reservations should be affirmed and ratified by act of congress and that the executive should be given express power to make future reservations of the same kind when the occasion arises." (Ibid)

In other words, yes, it's alright to protect millions of acres of land in the name of conservation (the Judge would set aside, legally, far more land in his four years in office than Teddy did in almost eight), but let congress first give me the legal right to do so. They did, and he did.

Later that month, Ned was again put on a special commission, this time to investigate the subject of employers' liability for a growing number of industrial accidents, and what congress should do about it. Fellow members of this committee were Senators Warren and Hughes, and Representative Brantley of Georgia. On June 25, Congress adjourned for the summer. After some traveling, to New York to see Garvin, and to Pennsylvania where he visited his friend Olmstead from the Ballinger-Pinchot Committee, Ned was home in Detroit by July 7. "It was a case of hard work," he told the Free Press. "For the present I do not want to think of politics and as to my own re-election I stand on the record I have made. I voted as my conscience dictated and I would not have been true to myself or my constituents if I had done otherwise." (DFP 7-7-1910)

Political pundits predicted in early August that Ned's opponent in the upcoming election would be the once-defeated Alfred Lucking. Politics were changing at this juncture of the Republic, and no one was better aware of it and Ned Denby. Theodore Roosevelt had returned in June; the conservationists were in full frontal attack, and the anti-Cannon sentiment seemed to be growing in the House of Representatives, as well as in the country, on a daily basis. Insurgents; standpatters; reactionaries; these were the terms defining a game which no longer seemed to find footing in loyalty, honesty or integrity. Before the democratic ticket was solidified, however, before the battle lines were clearly drawn, the Press ran an interesting endorsement of the popular incumbent.

"Congressman Edwin Denby's very frank reply in answer to questions concerning his attitude toward the speakership and the estimation in which he holds the incumbent, is thoroughly characteristic of the man. It is so refreshing in its straight-forwardness, sincerity, and courage, that approval of the sentiments expressed in the statement becomes a matter secondary to admiration of the man who makes it. "One of the fine things about the representative from the first is this, that the public always knows where to locate him. It is certain, too, that Mr. Denby is always to be found occupying a position which he believes to be right, and that he takes this position entirely without reference to whether it happens to be for the time popular or otherwise. Men may differ from Mr. Denby, but no fair, thinking man can doubt him. This calm, unwavering integrity, which never allows him to temporize, combined with good sense has made the congressman, in a comparatively few years, one of the leading figures of the national house of representatives." (DFP 8-19-1910)

In August it was rumored that a Detroit Republican attorney would oppose Ned in the Republican primary, running on an anti-Cannon platform. Though this did not materialize, it was announced in early September that his Democrat opponent would be Frank E. Doremus, a former, and very popular, Detroit comptroller. Recognizing the important issues right from the start, the savvy Doremus shot right out of the gate by offering to define 'insurgency'. Before he could publicly do that, however, the Free Press reported: "If he defines an 'insurgent' as one who is an ally of the Democrats he will get close enough to the fact to meet all ordinary requirements." (DFP 9-3-1910) Only days later, at the conservation congress being held in Minneapolis, Minnesota, the Democrats on the Ballinger-Pinchot committee, allied with the lone 'insurgent', found themselves in a temporary majority of the committee members (most Republicans not having attended, or not having yet arrived at the congress). To the horror of the Committee Chair, Republican Senator Nelson, the minority members voted to accept their own 'final report' on the Ballinger-Pinchot controversy roundly criticizing Ballinger and calling for his dismissal. They did this specifically because it was well known that the Republican majority had no intention of submitting the final report until after the congressional elections. Before the final vote on the minority report could be taken, the Republican members who were present simply walked out to prevent a quorum. "Their proceeding was the most extraordinary, indefensible, unjudicial, that partisan politics could devise," declared Ned. (DFP 9-9-1910) The minority members of the committee knew that Republican Senator Flint of California was traveling abroad and would not be available for a vote, and knew as well that their minority report had no real weight. For this reason, then, and strictly for publicity, they simply released it to the press, before bothering to give it to congress, which body had commissioned it in the first place.

Beyond the controversy at hand, Ned recognized that the GOP was in trouble. "Conditions affecting the republican Party are grave," he said, "for the reason that the party is divided against itself. So far as I understand insurgency it simply means the advocacy of some doctrine which all accept as correct, but which is expressed by insurgents in a form that appeals to the prejudices [read: emotions] of the people. This insurgency is rapidly spreading, and men have been defeated who are of the best blood and brains of the Republican party, for no other reason than that they refuse to discard the name Republican which for 60 years has stood for the best, most progressive and enlightened legislation, and assumed the name insurgent, which has no meaning whatever."

"Is there any question that we all believe in conservation of our natural resources," Ned continued in the same article, "in destroying illegal and dangerous combinations of capital, in an honest tariff as low as is consistent with protection and reasonable profits, and in keeping public life free from capitalistic or other selfish interests? These things which are made to appear as the basic principles of insurgency have been the basic principles of the Republican Party for 50 years. The Insurgents have repudiated

Speaker Cannon, and the regulars refused to admit that after 30 years of service he had suddenly become a monster of iniquity, and they declined to consent to his public humiliation. However it looks as though the question of a Republican candidate for speaker will be of no importance in the sixty-second congress.

For myself, I have done my best fairly to represent this district, and I have done what I thought was right. I have not been a blind or slavish adherent to any man or faction. I have been a Republican congressman for six years. I shall not now masquerade in any false face to secure votes. If I have been a good congressman and an honest man in public office I should be reelected. One thing is sure. If my ship goes down, the flag that I have raised will be the last thing seen above the waters." (DFP 9-16-1910)

Though much has remained exactly the same in the political games that are played and have been for the past millennia, some things have changed, and one of them is the way our fourth estate has covered political events. One day after Ned's above unequivocal remarks, the Detroit Free Press was swift in editorial admiration. As a measure of that golden rule of fair and balanced reporting which once guided newspapermen all across America, and equally as much a measure of the profound integrity of Edwin Denby, the entire editorial is reproduced here:

Courageous Edwin Denby

"A few months ago the country was assured that the Ballinger investigation was to be a 'whitewash'. Very recently, until a bare week ago, the statement was being made freely that the verdict of the Democratic and insurgent members alone would be in accordance with the real opinions of its framers and that the majority would 'play politics' and exonerate the secretary for party purposes.

"It is only necessary to contrast the finding of the four Democrats and the one insurgent on the committee with that of the Michigan member, who as yet is the only majority member to speak, in order to realize how far from the mark these forecasts came. The minority has distinctly 'played politics'. It has given a 'snap verdict' that has been denounced by even Democratic critics

214

for its evident partisan bias and the unnecessarily hasty manner of its publication. Mr. Denby, on the other hand, has spoken out his opinion at a time and in a manner that makes a suggestion of any covert motive on his part; simply absurd. If he had wanted to aid his party he could not have taken a more impossible way than to exonerate Ballinger, for he has flatly defied public opinion and has put his own election in jeopardy by doing so.

"The most earnest opponent of the congressman from the first district must concede to Mr. Denby a courage that arouses admiration, however much he may question the gentleman's judgment in taking the stand he has adopted.

It would have been easy for a trimmer to have evaded this issue, to have concealed his opinion until after the election or even to have given out a misleading utterance for the purpose of catching votes that will be sorely needed in November. But Mr. Denby has not shirked this or any other question. He has sturdily spoken out his true opinions, and has elected to stand or fall by them. It is the course that Detroit has learned to expect of Edwin Denby. It is a course, too, that in most years would bring to his side such strong support that his success would never be in a moment's doubt. What the effect will be this year upon his fortunes must remain for November to disclose. But if there is respect still left for manhood in this congressional district, if the voters here want sober facts and not myths and dreams, the startlingly unusual policy of Mr. Denby ought to prove advantageous to him." (DFP 9-17-1910)

On the same day that the above editorial appeared, Ned's campaign headquarters in the McGraw building opened for business, with Orvice Leonard and C. F. Mellish in charge of the campaign. In response to a claim that his campaign was being funded with a $60,000 contribution from someone who benefitted from the Payne-Aldrich Tariff law, Ned made it clear that his campaign was soliciting no outside funds whatever for the campaign. He said he would accept contributions, but not solicit them. "Neither the national committee nor any interest protected or otherwise has sent me a cent," he declared. (DFP 10-11-1910)

Though Ned had been unopposed in his own primary, on a

national scale, "when the primary contests were over, it was evident that the Insurgents or Progressives had administered a licking to the Old Guard. By the end of September forty-one incumbent GOP Congressmen had been defeated." (Gwen, Uncle Joe Cannon, p 235) The outlook for "regular" Republicans, and especially those such as Ned who remained loyal to Uncle Joe, was becoming more bleak by the day.

Ned did not as of yet believe himself to be among those critically threatened, he wrote a heartfelt letter to his patron on October 4th at his home in Danville, Illinois. Reading the situation correctly, he predicted that even if the GOP retained possession of the House, it would be retention in name only — that insurgent Republicans would be against Cannon, and side with the Democrats. For this reason, he strongly suggested that Joe Cannon declare himself "for whatever reason you choose to give," not a candidate for the Speakership of the next Congress. It was a plea for the Party, for unity, and not the individual. "It is hard for a man pure in heart and conscious of no wrong doing, to yield to the assaults of his enemies. But will there be any gain for you in not so yielding at this time. Will you not by yielding give one more splendid proof of your fidelity to the party and your anxiety to serve it always, even to your own cost." He could not know how deeply these words of his would one day apply to himself. Ned summed up his feelings by concluding, "You have a right to expect candid views from one who has so long enjoyed your friendship." (BHL Edwin Denby Papers, Box #1)

On October 17 he addressed over three hundred at the North End Taft Club stating that "The protective tariff is designed to protect the American workingman especially, and to preserve to him steady employment at good wages and the standards of living that are so necessary to his happiness. We don't want to go back to the conditions that prevailed under the last Democratic measure in 1893, 94, and 95, when however cheap things were, thousands of our fellow citizens in Detroit had not even that little money necessary to buy cheap things." (DFP 10-18-1910) The following week the Republicans held a rally in the Light Guard Armory which was packed with over 2500 screaming faithful. Again, the subject was the tariff, which had been in effect for some months. "In a little over one year it has converted the national deficit of $58,000,000 into a surplus of $20,000,000, under it no mills have closed, no business suffered, no wage scale been cut." Here Ned pointed out the second great value of protective tariffs, and one the United States had used from its very inception: the raising of revenue with which to run the government.

In the meantime, Ned's opponent, Doremus, came out strongly "in favor of untaxed food, reciprocity with Canada, and free raw materials." Even the Free Press was quick to point out that the only tariff restrictions Doremus was willing to lower were on goods which did not pertain to his own district.

A week later, on October 30, Nicholas Longworth, accompanied by his ever-popular wife, Alice Roosevelt Longworth, headlined another huge Republican rally at the Light Guard Armory. Both Ned and Longworth spoke in favor of the tariff, and the bill which the Republicans had passed earlier in the year. Longworth was effusive in his praise for Ned. "There is no man in either branch of congress, be he Democrat or Republican who has attained the respect of his colleagues than Edwin Denby. In some branches of the public service he has a deeper knowledge than any other member of congress. One result of the tariff is our increased trade with the Orient, and no man has a greater and more thorough knowledge of that subject than he. In fact, it got to be that whenever congress struck a knotty problem, we used to say, 'Let Denby do it.'" He wrapped up his speech in saying, "I am proud to call one of my best friends, Edwin Denby." (DFP 10-30-1910)

In November the Free Press published a long letter to the Editor from Judge E. C. Bumpus, the Boston lawyer who had worked with Ned on the Panamanian Commission. The judge first iterated that the commission on which he and Ned had served had been preceded by one which had largely failed to come to agreement and had fostered thereby a great deal of ill feelings on the part of the Panamanians. "For this reason when your member of congress, Mr. Denby, with the writer, was appointed to a successive commission, we found upon arrival at Panama, the Panama authorities in a very doubting mood as to whether any action could be taken to reach satisfactory results, so much so that they hesitated for some time as to whether they would carry out the provisions of the treaty and appoint their commissioners.

"It was at this point that I began to appreciate the character and capacity of Mr. Denby. Instead of doing what many of our officials would have done, holding himself aloof from these people, showing no interest in their welfare and taking a partisan view of the situation, he at once called upon the president, his cabinet, and the other Panamanian officials, and entered into the closest personal and social relations with them. If this had been done merely to get their good will, these sharp-eyed people would soon have found him out. They learned very shortly, however, that here was a fair minded man, one actuated with the capacity and courage to give them their dues, and who would forget, in the service he was called to perform, any prejudice because of his citizenship and look only to right results. Thereupon, two very capable lawyers [Panamanians] were joined with us on the commission. We elected Mr. Denby chairman, and from that time proceeded without dissension to pass upon many perplexing questions until we came to a unanimous conclusion."

The Judge summed up by saying, "I feel somewhat justified in sending this letter from a remark made to me by a Panama official not long since — that the work of the commission has never been known or appreciated in the United States — and so that my friend, Mr. Denby, may get his just due, I have taken the liberty to send this communication to your paper. E. C. Bumpus Boston, October 21, 1910 (DFP 11-03-1910)

In last minute rallies and speeches, Ned hit hard on the tariff arguments, citing numerous facts and figures to prove his point. There had been a great, emotional cry over the tariff on wool, and the argument was made that this caused the price of ladies' hosiery to leap out of the financial reach of the common woman. In fact, the argument was made that the Payne- Aldrich Tariff bill had raised the cost of living. Once again, facts and figures to the

218

contrary, the political attacks were all couched in appropriate language ("protected interests", "privileged interests", "the workingman", etc.). When you don't have the facts and figures, then be sure to pander to the emotions of the masses.

In October Ned and Marion became engaged, and though they originally decided to announce their engagement after the election, it appears that Ned was sensing the election defeat on the horizon, and it became pointless to hold back the joyous news for a time that was likely to be anything but joyous. On Sunday, two days before the election, they released the announcement to the press. In keeping with their usual habit of banter and teasing, the headline of the Press article read "Detroit Congressman to Become Benedict", and reported therein that he had "held his rank as head of Detroit's eligible bachelors even longer than his post in congress, which makes his sudden resolve to become Benedict, a delightful defection." The Press went on to graciously describe Marion as being "regarded as one of Detroit's most attractive and cultivated young girls." (DFP 11-06-1910)

Detroiters went to the polls on Tuesday, November 8, and early on the 9th the word was that the voting had been heavy, and the races close. By late afternoon on the 9th, campaign headquarters in the McGraw Building was deserted, and Ned called his opponent to concede. Magnanimously, Frank Doremus declared, "Mr. Denby is a splendid gentleman and personally I like him very much." He had prevailed over the incumbent by just 2,000 votes out of 32000 cast. Ned had no comment for the press, saying only that the voters had spoken. He thanked his supporters and said that "instead of feeling blue, he preferred to think of the rousing victories that had come his way in the past." (DFP 11-10.1910)

The Grand Rapids Press, another Democrat organ, was quick to note that;

"The only regret that can be felt in his (Doremus') victory is that another man, equally honorable and straightforward, had to suffer defeat. Mr. Denby was a contrast to every other member of the Ballinger investigating committee in that he dared to tell his honest belief before election. His action in thus risking his political fortune is the more commendable in that the shoddy trickery of his colleagues on the committee offers such a marked contrast. It is doubtful if this defeat can permanently eliminate such a high type of man as Edwin Denby." (Reprinted in the DFP 11-12-1910)

Nationwide, the GOP lost 58 seats in the House, including two of the Michigan delegation, and 10 Senatorial seats, The Republicans managed to retain control of the Senate by a 51 to 41 margin, but lost the House 228 to 161. It was the first time the Democrats controlled either house in sixteen years, and their largest majority in the lower chamber since 1890. Turns out those emotional words such as "reactionary", "standpatter", "special interests" all worked well in turning the tide.

Within days his name was found in print speculation that the U. S. Senate would be his next adventure. On the 27th of the month he acted as Toastmaster at the University of Michigan football team's annual banquet in Ann Arbor. Surely he was able for a moment on this night to forget the fickleness of Detroit voters, and to bask in the memories of his gridiron glories. They had called him the most famous bald football player in the country. Now, an ex-congressman, he was in all probability eagerly looking forward to a new chapter in his life. This one was going to be brighter than the last, and more fulfilling than anything to date. This new chapter was going to include his soul-mate.

On December 3 he arrived back in Washington for the final congressional session of which he would be a part, and before the day was over, he was writing to his "Little Pirate". He said that , "All afternoon I spent with the Ballinger-Pinchot Committee, trying to concentrate my mind on a stupid report, but in reality thinking mainly of you. Then after dinner, I lost eight cents to my sister at double dummy bridge — and now again you come demanding my attention." He told her that he wished he had insisted on a Christmas wedding, but that he had wanted to let her take her time, "Please note that I was a fool," he declared, "but I didn't realize how my heart would cry for Marion and my empty arms would long for Marion and my brain would think only of Marion." She would reply, setting a date for the wedding in March, and in his December 9th reply, he concurred. "It's alright about March," he said, "I want you now, but I'm not going to sulk about it. You are the doctor and I can take a licking. Dearest, you are worth waiting for. I may go crazy in the meantime, but that is immaterial." (DPL Edwin Denby Jr. Papers, Box #1)

On December 8, the Majority Report of the Ballinger-Pinchot Committee was submitted to Congress, and released to the public. The Committee reported that "the evidence has wholly failed to make out a case. Neither has any fact proved nor all the facts put together exhibit Mr. Ballinger as being anything but a competent and honorable gentleman, honestly and faithfully performing the duties of his high office with an eye single to the public interest." (NYTimes, Thursday, Dec 8, 1910) The Times went on gleefully to emphasize, however, that the committee disagreed with Ballinger on the side issue of the sale of coal lands in Alaska, preferring, with the President, that the claims upon those lands be adjudicated for lease, rather than for sale. On another side issue concerning the Pinchot policy of logging and lumbering on Indian reservations, 'the committee says the Secretary [Ballinger] found that operations were being carried on by the Bureau of Forestry of a wasteful and extravagant nature, and entailing loss to the Indians." So, although Ballinger was perhaps not supported in the manner he would have liked, neither was Pinchot. The Democrats made it crystal clear, since they had won the House the previous month, that the hounding of Ballinger was not to cease any time soon. By March 6 of the coming year, he had asked the president to be relieved because of health reasons, but not before he had assisted Taft in securing a new law which gave him the power to withdraw nearly twice as many acres of land in one term than Teddy Roosevelt had withdrawn in two. But Mr. Taft, and Mr. Ballinger, did it legally.

On December 8, Ned resigned his position on the commission to investigate liability of employers for workers hurt on the job. A day later newly elected Congressman Doremus filed a campaign expenses statement, revealing that he had spent a whopping $1,357 to defeat Ned the previous month. The records show that the Republican congressional committee spent $1,000 on Ned's loss, though Ned did not declare expenses of his own since the law did not require it of defeated candidates. On December 17, letters went out to all his friends and Denby Club members in thanks and appreciation for their unfailingly loyal support. "I thank you cordially for your support during the congressional campaign. I am deeply grateful to yourself and the members of the Denby club for their attitude toward me during my political career, and while we could not always win, we need not be grieved over defeat.

"I have tried so to live in my public career that the friends who supported me will at least have no cause for shame. There is no humiliation in honorable defeat, and my principle regret is only that my friends have worked for victory in vain."
(DFP 12-17-1910)

By the end of the week he was back in Washington where he spent Christmas with Hattie and his two nephews.

Chapter Eleven

To love all ages yield surrender;
But to the young its raptures bring
A blessing bountiful and tender
As storms refresh the fields of Spring.
Pushkin

Marriage

The social season was in full swing in Washington for the 1910 holidays. Ned was in Detroit spending what time he could with Marion, and formulating plans for what they finally decided would be a Saturday, March 18 wedding during the coming year; a date comfortably beyond the final chapter of his Washington political career. Hattie and her sons entertained Garvin and his wife Ester at the Washington home which she would maintain to the end of Ned's bachelorhood. On Monday, January 2, 1911, the President and Mrs. Taft held a brilliant reception at the White House for official Washington, being greeted first by the new dean of the diplomatic corps, Baron Ladislas Hengelmueller, the ambassador to the United States from the Austro-Hungarian Empire. It was noted by the press that his wife, the Countess Marie, owing to ill health, did not attend. Following this reception, the vice president and all the cabinet members scurried to their homes for their own individual soirees, leaving little time for a breath or a chat or a how-do-you-do. The previous Monday, December 26, President and Mrs. Taft, along with many other Washington dignitaries, had visited Admiral George Dewey, hero of the Battle of Manila Bay during the Spanish-American War, on the occasion of his 73d birthday. All during the week between Christmas and New Years, the young people of Washington had enjoyed dinners, dances and parties each night, culminating in a White House gala held by the President's nineteen year old daughter, Helen. One of Helen's guests that evening was Theodore Roosevelt's youngest daughter, Ethel, also nineteen. In addition to the young people's frivolities, the adults of Washington were engrossed in their own social whirl, and would not note the absence of the jovial Michigan congressman.

Nor did he miss them. His world was changing in rapid and dramatic ways, and though the political loss had initially stung him, it took but seconds to realize that what Marion brought into his life was going to be infinitely more satisfying. And he was going to have time for it! From a dramatic defeat, he would rise phoenix-like into a dawn he had only dreamed about as a younger man. Though he chastised himself before her, calling himself a "discredited politician," when she objected, and she did, he quickly corrected his remark to "misunderstood statesman." (DPL EDJr. Papers, Box #1) He was not much for self pity, and what little he did allow himself, Marion decidedly did not. She would be his staunchest supporter to her last breath.

It seems that others in the capital and in Michigan were having a difficult time wrapping their minds around the idea of a Denby-less Washington D. C. looming only weeks away. One rumor, claiming "the highest authority", reported breathlessly that he would become one of three United States' Commissioners on the International Joint Commission of the Boundary Waters Treaty of 1909 between the United States and the then Dominion of Canada. When that did not materialize quickly enough, another rumor reported that he would become Secretary to the President, replacing Charles D. Norton, who was retiring. (DFP 1-14-1911, & 1-21-1911) In mid-January, the Evansville Courier solemnly declared "Edwin Denby Is To Be Sent To China", and went on to explain that while "the nature of his assignment is not made public by the administration," that Ned would "undertake an important mission to China during the coming summer." On

January 16th, Frank Doremus, the man who had unseated him, was Ned's guest at the Capitol where he introduced his replacement to many prominent members of the house on both sides of the aisle, including the outgoing Speaker, Uncle Joe Cannon. The next day Ned also escorted Doremus to the White House where he introduced him to the President. The two congressmen, despite obvious differences, became cordial friends for many years to come.

Apparently the last measure achieved by the noble congressman was the passage in the House of his bill extending the extradition laws to China on February 8. The small Free Press article mentioning it also reported that it was the first time in several days the congressman had been seen on the floor. (DFP 2-8-1911) In his March 1 letter to Marion he admitted that "these last days drag" and yet he also added his awareness that "the march of time brings us nearer and nearer together." In the same letter he further confessed his deepest feelings to the young woman who had so recently conquered his heart and soul, who was already, and would be for the rest of his life, his closest confidant. "Dearest," he says, "there is a sting in it, this laying down the work, man's work, work worthwhile that I have been doing for six years." He assures her that no matter how much he will miss it that she will make up for all of the loss he felt. "I only wish I could have come to you with banners flying, and WITH my shield, not ON it. [italics his] But believe me, darling girl, I know myself, my temptations in public life and my victories over those temptations, and I tell you that I bring you a better man defeated than I could have brought you victorious by the only methods that would have brought victory last fall." He knew full well that he could have saved his seat had he sacrificed his loyalty, his friendship and his honor, and turned on Uncle Joe Cannon as so many of his colleagues had done. But he had, as he always had and always would, chosen the nobler path, and so now he was ready to "lay away in memory the congressional life, lay it away with a sigh and a smile but without a tear. Tears come with sorrow, shame and remorse," he told her, "and these are strangers to my conscience. I have been through the fires of politics and I have not been harmed. Thank God for both our sakes that as Representative of my people I am clean in heart. I have never betrayed those who trusted me and who looked to me to keep in public life the same faith common among gentlemen in private affairs. So with head ever erect and unashamed, I come to you, and your beloved father, if I have appreciated him aright, would have been better pleased to give you to me as I am than as I would have been, by hateful necessity, if I had won my last fight. "

"Dearest one," he continued, "I have written out my heart to you today because I know you have already read it and you want my confidence. Perhaps I dwell unduly upon and exaggerate the importance of public honor, though I do not think so. Besides I have not much else to glory in, not much else to feed my pride, And always I have made almost a fetish of honesty in the public service, real honesty I mean, honesty of mind and soul. It seems to be an attribute of my people. However bad they have been in other ways, and many of them, myself included, have been bad enough, I have yet to learn of one who betrayed his trust. So you will understand that I must cling fondly to this one little flower that has grown amid the weeds. When I meet my fathers face to face, I want to be able to say 'I have kept the faith. The flower still blooms.'" (Box #1 EDJr. Papers, DPL)

Ned remained in Washington until the bitter end, leaving the capital as a congressman on the noon train on Saturday, March 4, arriving in Detroit as an ordinary citizen at 745 the following Sunday morning. The following Thursday Ned visited the marriage license clerk's office causing quite a stir when his name was mentioned aloud. After everyone in the place surrounded him offering congratulations, he beamed, "Well, boys, I am mighty glad you are pleased, but I want to tell you right now I am pleased most." (DFP 3-10-1911)

The following week a family-only wedding took place at noon on Saturday, March 18 at Marion's home, just a block up Jefferson Avenue from Ned's. It was a Presbyterian service officiated by the Reverend A. H. Barr, rector of the Jefferson Avenue Presbyterian church, the same pastor who had officiated at both Marion's parents' untimely funerals. Marion's younger sister, Elizabeth, was Maid of Honor, and Ned's closest friend, Henry Lyster, served as Best Man. Marion wore a gown of white satin with a long train, the gown trimmed in old point lace which was a family heirloom. Within days the Denbys were on their way to Europe for an extended honeymoon.

On the wedding day, the Denbys shared the limelight in the city of Detroit with perhaps the, most famous democrat of his day, William Jennings Bryan. The three-time standard bearer of the Democrat Party visited Detroit at the behest of friends, rather than at the invitation of the party. He spoke in the evening at the North Woodward Avenue Methodist Church predicting, among other things, that Irish home rule was very close [it did not come for another ten years], that direct election of Senators was a done deal [17th Amendment passed the following year and was ratified by the States in 1913], and answered that he did not know if he would run again for the Presidency [he did not].

Perhaps, in addition to consoling himself over his political loss with the anticipation of his marriage to Marion, Ned might also have realized that he was now free to pursue a whole host of other activities, including ones of far more financial benefit. He had served in Congress at a time that it was not only still possible, but it was expected that a man left Congress no wealthier than he had entered it; in some cases, with even less than he had possessed arriving Washington. He must certainly have been aware that, in an odd turn of events, on the very day he was being defeated at the 1st District polls, three gallant, intrepid adventurers were departing the Motor City in a 1911 Model 20 four-seat Hupmobile to circumnavigate the globe. Planned as a trip to demonstrate the wonderful endurance of their economically-priced car, the approximately 40,000 mile journey was also intended to publicize the company, as well as establish dealerships in even more locations than the company already enjoyed. The three men included Joseph R. Drake, one of the original investors and secretary of the company, Thomas Hanlon, a company mechanic and an expert driver, and Thomas O. Jones, a Detroit Free Press reporter; they were setting out on the trip of a lifetime. Hupmobiles had been entered in previous long distance marathons, already garnering their share of the publicity which surrounded them, but this was to be the supreme contest, not for speed, but for endurance.

Given the significance of this round-the-world endeavor by an automobile company in which he had been heavily invested from the beginning, given the adventurousness of his own character and equally that of his young bride, it should not be surprising that Ned and Marion decided to add some spirit to their European honeymoon by having a Hupmobile shipped to Italy, and then touring parts of the continent on their own motoring adventure. The newlyweds sailed for Naples, Italy in late April with their own Hupmobile Model 20 Runabout which landed with them. Meeting up with the Hupp Sales Agent for Italy, Count Daniele Pecorini, they rested up with sightseeing in Naples for a few days and then departed on Friday, May 5 for Rome. Count Pecorini accompanied them in his own Hupmobile touring car. Just as Jones was included in the round the world trip so that he could keep the newspapers apprised of their progress, so Ned wrote a whole series of letters to the Hupmobile directors of their own progress across Europe, and the performance of the car.

The Denbys took the scenic, coastal route from Naples, traveling at a leisurely pace over yesterday's roads, stopping to spend the first night in the provincial city of Formia where they stayed at an old inn named "The Oak". While there, they also visited the ruins of an ancient villa once belonging to statesman and scholar, Cicero. Starting out the second day, Ned noted that over a large portion of their trip they traversed the Roman Appian Way, "built some three centuries before Christ, and today the finest piece of highway I ever saw. In one stretch it runs straight as a cannon shot for forty miles across the Pontine Marshes between superb rows of beeches, with many colored fields and marshes on either side and in the distance mountains of azure hue. Here," he gushes, "we let them out [the Hupmobiles] and went for long stretches, thirty miles and over per hour." (DPL EDJr. Papers, Box #1) After crossing the marshes, he noted, "we lunched at a primitive little inn in the village of Cisterna." By the time they reached Rome, he informed the directors, he still had two gallons of petrol left in his fuel tank. The Hupmobile was not only rugged, dependable and affordable, but economical to operate as well.

His next letter describing their three day trip from Rome to Florence is filled with descriptions of the beautiful Italian countryside through which they were driving. He reported that the livestock were an almost constant problem since there were very few automobiles in Italy at this time, and little need to be concerned about animals wandering in the road. At one location they inadvertently killed a farmer's goose, and Ned joked the creature had appeared suicidal, but duly reported that they stopped and gave the man more than a fair price for the errant bird, "which he accepted, though he recognized that death was due to the folly or intention of the deceased. We noticed that he kept the remains and we suspected that there was feasting and revelry on the country side that night." The Denbys spent a week in Florence touring the magnificent sites and visiting with his aunt, Mrs. Edwin R. Denby and her daughter, who inhabited a twelfth century palace. From Florence they travelled to Venice, leaving on May 31st and arriving on June 3. After four days in Venice, they left on the last leg of their journey, the three day trip to Vienna. Recapping for the Board of Directors his European itinerary, Ned summed it up thus:

Naples to Rome   150 miles
Rome to Florence   235 miles
Florence to Venice 178 miles
Venice to Vienna   380 miles
TOTAL 943 miles

In Vienna the Denbys stayed with Charlie, who had been posted there since his difficulties with the State Department in 1909. Vienna at that time was a sprawling, ancient city of over two million souls, and much to his chagrin, Ned admitted that he had forgotten Charlie's address. Seeing a shop called the "Columbia Phonograph Agency" and guessing that English might be spoken there, they stopped and sure enough received not only directions but an employee who was lent to them to guide them through the twisting medieval streets. He told his directors that his was the first Hupmobile that had been seen in Vienna, and he wondered why their nearest agency had been established in Budapest, rather than the larger city of Vienna. "I have driven the car around the city a good deal and always it has attracted much attention. We can do business here if we go at it right."

He concluded his tales of the road with a curiously scolding question at the end of his last letter. "What's the matter with you fellows? I haven't heard from any of you. Have you received my letters from Rome, Florence, Venice?" One wonders if the directors were distracted by the news coming from the round-the-world travelers who were in the Far East at this time. Or perhaps Ned simply was writing to mechanical, practical types who didn't share or understand his poet's heart. In any case, they were working diligently to grow their business, and to keep up with the demand which was being generated by exactly such advertising stunts as he and Marion had just completed, and the three men in the Hupp who were currently on their monumental trip around the world. Events would one day show that the company was better at creating interest than producing enough cars to keep up with the orders.

On the steamer crossing back to the United States, the story is handed down through family members that one night the indomitable Marion noticed that the ship's engines had stopped. The following morning she queried the Captain about this. "Why were the engines stopped last night?" she wanted to know. The Captain explained that there had been reports of ice bergs in their path, and he was simply being cautious. In a matter of months, with a different Captain at the helm, the Titanic would not be so fortunate. (Private conversation with the Wetmore Grandsons, September 15, 2022)

In September the Free Press was once again reporting that Ned would be appointed by President Taft as a commissioner on the International Joint Commission on the Boundary Waters on account of the death of one of its members, Senator Thomas H. Carter of Montana. In trying to keep geographic equality on the commission, it was felt that the President would have to go with Ned, as a "western' commissioner. Ned had already emphatically stated in an earlier letter to Marion that the president had not offered him anything because he had not requested anything. Apparently nothing had changed, including the fact that newspapers had to make things up to increase sales. In October, however, Governor Chase Osborn of Michigan did appoint Ned to be a delegate to the meetings of the American Society for the Judicial Settlement of International Disputes being held in Ypsilanti November 7 and 8. He would serve with four other delegates, including the President of his old alma mater, James Angell of Ann Arbor.

October brought news that Ned had purchased a handsome home in Grosse Point, one of Detroit's more exclusive neighborhoods of the day. In the latter part of the year Ned penned a lengthy letter to the Editor of the Detroit Free Press. It is not certain that he ever mailed it, since it does not appear to have been published, and almost certainly would have been had he mailed it. But he saved it, and in it he vented his frustrations with the recalcitrant members of his party who seemed ready to split the ranks over "catch-words and war-cries rather than principles." Still struggling with the loss of his seat, he flatly declared why he believed he lost it, and how this endangered the party he served.

"The great rout of the republican party last fall seems to have been due more to the fact that the members of the so-called regular wing of the party declined to utter certain phrases or to repudiate certain friends than to any other cause. I, for instance, though opposed by a good man, would, I think, undoubtedly have been re-elected, had I but proclaimed myself not a 'republican', but a 'progressive republican', had I denounced a distinguished associate, and had I consented to break an oath, and proclaim guilty of dishonor and official malfeasance a man whom I deemed innocent [Uncle Joe Cannon]. There was no question of principle involved in all of this, there was no question of my integrity, so far as I knew, nor of my fitness for the post; but I would not recant heresies I had never cherished, nor mouth phrases, to me, meaningless - and so I am in the enjoyment of a deeply appreciated private citizenship for the first time in eight years."

His letter further stated that he would not be a candidate for any office in the coming fall of 1911, and he concluded that he passionately believed "that the party must come to judge its servants, not by the phrases they utter, but by the real principles they adhere to and the acts they do." Clearly he did not hold his progressive republican peers in much esteem. Clearly, he was then, had always been, and would always be a man of principle, and a man who would remain loyal to his friends no matter what the cost. And clearly his warnings would fall upon deaf and suicidal ears as the republicans rushed toward the disaster awaiting them in 1912.

On December 15 a meeting of the friends of the conservation of wild animal life was held in the rooms of the Board of Commerce, and Ned was elected as one of the directors of the proposed Detroit Zoological Society. Though this endeavor had been studied and talked about for many years, this was the first really solid beginning of a permanent solution. In time the Detroit Zoo would become one of the premier gardens of its type anywhere in the world, and remains so to this day. Further in the month, just after the Denbys celebrated their first Christmas together, Ned was named one of three delegates from Wayne County to the Republican National Convention for the coming year of 1912.

The year had been dismaying, discouraging, electrifying, disappointing, exhilarating and several other adjectives which Ned would gladly have supplied. Life had set him a new course, one that he was adjusting to, as he always did, with great alacrity. His parents were gone, his siblings greatly scattered, and his Washington mentor a much subdued power in the nation's capital. But Ned had cemented the life-long bond with his soul mate, had readily shifted gears in his professional life and would be in cruise control for the next six years of his adventurous life.

Chapter Twelve

"Where are our men of abilities?
Why do they not come forth to serve their country?"

George Washington

Businessman, Father, Family

Early in January, 1912, Ned let it be known that he would not be a candidate for delegate at large to the Republican National Convention. Lest anyone doubt his loyalty, however, he added a very strong statement of support for the current President, Bill Taft.

"I appreciate the spirit of my many friends,' he said, 'and while I cannot be a candidate for delegate, I shall do all in my power to aid in securing a solid Taft delegation from Michigan. Not only do the people expect his nomination, but President Taft has shown himself to be honest, capable and courageous, and he should be given every assistance in completing the great things in which he is engaged." (DFP 1-6-1912)

In March he was sufficiently pressed that he felt it necessary to publicly and unequivocally announce that he would not be a candidate for Governor of Michigan that year. "Deeply gratified as I am at the expressions of friendship and offers of support that I have received, and personally pleasing as it might be to permit them to continue, it would not be fair to my friends or my enemies, to the public or to other candidates, to do so. Therefore, please

233

state that I shall not, under any circumstances, be a candidate for governor this fall." (Detroit Journal, as reprinted in the EC 3-16-1912) Also in March came the saddening news of the passing of Thomas E. Garvin, long time intimate and law partner of the Colonel, the man whose name was given to the youngest Denby sibling, Thomas Garvin Denby. The venerable Garvin passed away at the age of 85, having lived in Evansville, Indiana for sixty-eight years.

Marion was eight months pregnant when the world began trying to process the horrific news of the Titanic disaster on April 15. The repercussions of that event were still fresh in everyone's mind when on Friday, May 31st, the Denbys welcomed their first child into the family. The arrival of Edwin Denby, Jr. surely fulfilled one of the fondest dreams of his father, and it is certain that the big man's deepest regret was that his parents were not there to see it.

Six weeks later, the Denbys traveled to the far north of Michigan's Upper Peninsula to the exclusive Huron Mountain Club where Ned had members' privileges for several years. Created by a Marquette, Michigan entrepreneur in 1889 as a hunting and fishing club, the ultra private establishment stretches over 24,000 acres containing several lakes and approximately 10,000 acres of 'primeval forest', and is still in existence today. The Denbys would vacation there until September amidst the quiet splendor of the Huron Mountains. They could not know it then, but the infant which had just joined the family in May would honeymoon twenty-five years later in the very cabin where they were vacationing.

Shortly after returning to Detroit, the Denbys learned that younger brother, Garvin, had left his position with the Solvay Process Company of Syracuse, New York and had joined the Federal Motor Truck Company headquartered in Detroit. Garvin became the secretary- treasurer in charge of the sales department. In this endeavor, he joined his older brother who had been invested in the truck company for some years. This also brought the younger Denbys into the same social milieu as Ned and Marion, which put them at times on opposite sides of political questions. Both Garvin and his wife Ester were adamant anti-suffragists.

Early October brought the delegates from the International Congress of Chambers of Commerce to Detroit for two days during their visit to America. Over 400 delegates from 45 countries were met in Buffalo by a committee from the Detroit Board of Commerce who passed out programs for their Detroit visit which were printed in French, the language of the International Congress, and the first language of Detroit. On Thursday, October 3rd, the delegates were given a tour of Detroit automobile factories in over 150 automobiles supplied by Board of Commerce members. That evening they were feted at a dinner at the Hotel Ponchartrain where the speakers included the Mayor, and dignitaries from Brazil, England and China. Ned was also on the dais that evening, and gave a heartfelt speech whose main topic was how commerce fostered civilization. However, he started out in his characteristic way by poking fun at himself. Suggesting an inability to rise to such an august occasion, he opined that the members were probably quoting to themselves Mark Twain's famous line: "He was always the same, always consistent, always an ass." He continued, "And if you are saying that, do me the justice to remember that I at least have sense enough to agree with you. And remember, too, gentlemen of Detroit, that of all the many occasions when I have performed that agreeable feat, I never made an ass of myself in more congenial company."

Several paragraphs later he reached the crux of his message: "If we can bring ourselves to admit, not with our lips alone, but in our hearts, that we are but individual parts in a mighty brotherhood of states, made up of men like ourselves, 'fed with the same food, hurt with the same weapons, subject to the same diseases, healed by the same means, warmed and cooled by the same winter and summer' how wondrously far shall we have gone on the road that we must assume destiny intends us to travel toward peace, justice and brotherhood. And on that road it is your object to help our race to travel. I do not know all the media by which you propose to further the great pur- pose of your organization, the encouragement and simplifi- cation of international commerce, but I do know that, as you increase worldwide commerce, so do you extend civilization, do you carry forward sciences and hygiene to the uttermost parts of the earth." (BHL, Edwin Denby Papers, Box #1)

Early in the new year of 1913, both Ned and Garvin were involved in a two-day meeting of Federal Truck dealers from around the country. In February Ned gave a speech on Abraham Lincoln at the Detroit Post of the G.A.R. He would continue to be one of Detroit's most sought after keynote speakers. In early March Ned attended a regular meeting of the Lawyers Club and heard Dr. William H. Browne, then former medical examiner for Detroit's Juvenile Court, speak on the problems of juvenile delinquency in Detroit. Refuting some rosier statistics from previous speakers, Dr. Browne did not mince words in calling the juvenile detention center a "chamber of horrors", and intimating that Detroit had a serious problem on its hands. The lawyers agreed to form a committee to study the problem and make recommendations for solutions, with Ned being appointed one of the five men chosen to investigate. It would presage important and pioneering work in which he would become involved in post-war years.

In testimony to his wide range of interest and talents, it was announced on February 11 that he had been named as a new member of the Board of Directors of the Michigan State Life Insurance Company which had just been purchased by the Lincoln National Life Insurance Company of Fort Wayne, Indiana. There did not appear to be anything that did not interest him.

In character with his public speaking habits, Ned was kept busy regularly making speeches to church and civic groups concerning the Panama Canal, China, and more recently having been elected President, the Detroit Zoological Society. After a fitful start in 1883, the idea of a zoo for Detroit had foundered for several years until at last in early 1911, several civic-minded Detroiters gathered to form the Society. By this time Ned had been elected its president, with Henry Ford acting as vice president of a fairly large group of determined businessmen who wished to see the dream of a zoological garden materialize for their beloved city. With Ned, as with many interests, the zoo became nearly a crusade. On March 6, he spoke at a University of Michigan Club luncheon, claiming a zoological garden would do wonders to appeal to children, thus helping with the delinquent problem which had recently caught his attention. (DFP 3-6-1913)

On the same day, the the Free Press reported that Ned had garnered sufficient votes to be one of the three highest totals in the running for the Detroit Charter Commission. As in so many other affairs of the city, this had not been something sought by the burly attorney. Detroit had been lumbering along under its original charter which had been presented to it by the state government. Due to a change in state law, it was now eligible to write its own governing document, and who better to join this effort than Edwin Denby? In fact, he would lead it.

In April he composed a lengthy, written response to Mrs. H. G. Sherrard, Vice-Chairman of the Speakers' Committee of the College of Equal Suffrage League, in order to give his opinion on this highly volatile subject of that day. However, before he began his answer, he made mention of how exacerbating he viewed the controversy to be. "I have never observed on any political issue so much ill feeling engendered, so many friendships threatened, and bitter and unkind things said. Slurs and personalities too often take the place of that calm, judicial searching for the truth which should distinguish the discussion of so grave an issue as the doubling of the electorate, the conferring of the right to vote upon half the population." He then mentioned that the New York State Association Opposed to Women Suffrage had issued a pamphlet listing the several top arguments against suffrage, and he went through each one telling why he believed it was incorrect. After which he stated, "If I were a woman I would be for suffrage." However, since he was not a woman, he further stated, "Whether you win at this election or not, I believe the ultimate success of your cause is inevitable. I hope you will win, and that the ballot may become in your hands an instrument of great good to humanity." (BHL Edwin Denby Papers, Box #1)

The suffragists wasted no time in forwarding his letter to the newspapers who thoroughly enjoyed publicizing this pinning of the ex-congressman down. With equal speed, the anti- suffragist forces placed a large ad in the Free Press the very next day. Prominently listed as chairwoman of one of the committees of the Michigan Women's Association Opposed to Women Suffrage was his sister-in-law, Ester Jewel Strong Denby, and below that, in the ad from the Michigan Association of Men Opposed to the Further Extension of Suffrage under the listing as its treasurer, his own brother, Ester's husband, Garvin. It must've made family get- togethers interesting.

Only two days later, after the city elections, it became clear that Ned would garner enough votes to become a commissioner at large on the Detroit Charter Commission. Though at first a colleague seemed to be favored to head the commission, because of a minor conflict of interest, once again Ned Denby was tapped to do the honors. The commission was made up of 14 Republicans, 6 Democrats and 1 Progressive. Given the dominance of Republicans in Michigan state politics of the time, the Democrats were probably glad they had at least six of the commissioners.

The very next day Marion appeared in an original skit during the Detroit Theater Arts club gala, one half of a duo which also included the authoress of the skit, and Marion's childhood friend, Mrs. George Harrison Barbour, Jr. The skit, entitled 'Beatin' the Angels to Heaben', reported the Free Press was 'quite the hit of the evening', and that 'it was at the close of this act that enthusiasm reached its height , and cries of 'author' rang through the hall. Mrs. Denby's acting in the part of Ezekiel Daniel Hosea Johnson, with his aeroplane, would have done credit to an actress of experience." (DFP 4-11-1913)

The Charter Commission began its deliberations April 15,

scheduled to sit for 90 days, meeting each day at 1 o'clock. The commissioners would serve at a salary of $5 a day, and when it was learned that they had been granted expenses of a mere $500, three commissioners, including Ned, offered to donate their salaries. It was also learned that there was nothing in the law which prevented them from exceeding their 90 day mandate. Many issues would divide the commissioners and prolong deliberations. There was the issue of running the city through commissions (its current mode), or through departments controlled by the mayor. The number of council members became an issue. The number of wards was in question, as well as whether council members should be elected from each individual ward (the current mode), or elected at-large. There was the issue of the board of estimates, the current way the Detroit council allocated monies, or its abolition. There was the issue of the recall of politicians, of term of office, and of remuneration for offices. Needless to say, the commission did not meet its 90 day goal, as deliberations slogged through the summer and the autumn before the commission finally announced in October that they had reached agreement on a new City Charter. The vote had been by a bare majority.

Ned spoke to a noon meeting of over 800 members of the Board of Commerce, which had heavily supported his work, on November 5, outlining many of the changes. It was his opening shot in the campaign to "sell" the charter to the public before its upcoming referendum in the new year. The new charter called for many changes, but probably none more unpopular, especially among current aldermen, than the reduction in the size of the Detroit Council. Some politicians were going to lose their jobs. To know anything at all about politics, or politicians, one first must learn that the most sacrosanct tenet on earth to a politician is job security.

In September the Zoological Society announced intentions to purchase 150 acres of prime property north of the city with an option to purchase 115 more adjoining. For the remainder of 1913 Ned and all the other members of the commission who had

239

voted for the new charter spent their nights and days speaking to any and every group of citizens who would listen to them. They spoke to civic groups, to labor organizations, in factories, and in churches.

Special attention was given to wooing the labor vote, which Ned realized had turned against him in his last election. Only one week before the vote Ned spoke at the Board of Commerce once again, this time to over 700 members, extolling the new charter; a straw vote taken showed the businessmen in favor at a rate of 20:1.

As 1913 slipped into 1914, the charter commissioners in favor of the new Charter kept up their relentless campaign for its passage, but as in all matters of public debate were met with opposition and question marks at almost every turn. In the waning days of the debate, Corporation Counsel Richard I. Lawson, in response to requests by opponents of the charter to state his opinion, declared that he felt certain points of the Charter were "of dubious validity." (DFP Feb 7, 1914) When dawn arrived on February 11, the day after the vote, it was abundantly clear that the Charter had met a dismal defeat. The vote was not even close: 15,974 in favor, and 25,207 against. In a light turnout under clear and mild weather, the labor vote which had been so assiduously courted failed to materialize. In fact, it may be said that civic interest in the charter and its importance, failed to materialize as well, It was not only a crushing defeat, it was a thoroughly discouraging one. It represented ten months of work which vanished in a single day of voter apathy.

Early in 1914, in January, an event occurred that would have far-reaching consequences for Detroiters of the future. C. M. Burton, a local businessman and historian as well as a fellow Charter Commissioner with Ned for the past few months, donated his entire collection of memorabilia and rare books, mostly devoted to the subjects of Michigan and Detroit history, to the Detroit Public Library. The gift, representing over 40 years of collecting, included 30,000 bound books, 100,000 pamphlets,

100,000 manuscripts and 27,000 photographs. Further, it also included the deed to Burton's Brainard Street home where much of the collection had been housed in fireproof construction. It would one day fill an entire new wing of the majestic marble main library home on Woodward Avenue, just across the street from the Detroit Institute of Arts. The Burton Collection is today home to perhaps the largest collection of Edwin Denby's papers in the country, donated by Marion in the years after his death.

In mid February the Denbys gave a dinner-dance at the Country Club in honor of their debutante sister, Elizabeth Thurber. The Free Press called it "quite the smartest affair of the debutante set," It went on to explain that "Mrs. Denby, who was a great belle, was known also as possessing a very clever wit. She and Mrs. George H. Barbour, Jr. were inseparable as children and after their debuts were especially popular as dinner guests, as their teamwork in repartee was irresistible and you may be sure that no man ever uttered a groan when he chanced to be a dinner partner of one of them, unless he doubted his ability to maintain his end of the conversation. But what man ever possessed such a thought?" (DFP 22 Feb 1914)

April brought news that Ned had again been tapped to head another civic committee, this time a group of six who would confer with Governor Ferris over what sort of representation Detroit, and therefore, Michigan, should contribute to the upcoming Panama-Pacific International Exposition to be held the following year in San Francisco. It would be this international fair which would leave for the city of San Francisco the incomparable Palace of Fine Arts which still graces a public park in the Marina District.

Also in early April the Free Press reported that Ned had "secured holdings in the Century Electric Car Company," and had been elected Vice President and chairman of the executive committee of the company. Garvin, never far from his brother's footsteps, was named to the board, as well. (DFP 5 April 1914) At the same time that he seems to have been waist deep in civic projects and automotive endeavors, the Press reported that he was toying with the idea of running for Congress once again, to challenge the unfulfilled promises with which Frank Doremus had defeated him in 1910. The man was so ever-present in Detroit doings that this would become almost an annual ritual for the remainder of his life: predicting what office he would run for in what upcoming election. (DFP 3 April 1914())

At the end of May, both Ned and J. Walter Drake sold their shares in the Federal Motor Truck Company to its shareholders. At the same time, Garvin resigned his post as Vice President of the company. On June 10, an interesting article appeared in the Press, reporting that labor organizations which had opposed Ned in 1910 had been impressed at how firmly he had stood in favor of the charter provisions which the unions had sought. In addition, some labor leaders seemed less than enamored of Frank Doremus' habit of seeming to be absent in Washington when labor votes were about to take place. Even though labor had been against Ned in 1910, one current leader remarked that "He was with us in the charter fight, and showed then that, while he is against the closed shop, he is not an enemy of the unions. Also we always knew where he was, because he never sidestepped when we went to him. But Mr. Doremus, who made all sorts of promises before he was elected, has been principally conspicuous by the way he has been absent when labor legislation was up for a vote." (DFP 10 June, 1914)

On the 8th of July it became apparent why Ned and Walter Drake had dumped their shares of Federal Truck, as it was announced that day that the Denby Motor Truck Company was now open for business. The new concern had acquired 20,000 square feet of production space, and had already purchased material for the first 500 trucks to be produced that year, with an estimated 1000 coming in the next. Garvin was named as President, Walter Drake as Vice President, Arthur Webster, a member of Ned's law firm, was secretary, and Ned assumed the duties as treasurer. There had apparently been some difference of opinion, some disagreement with the management at Federal, as several of their other officers and employees would join the new firm. "L. C. Freeman, engineer, was formerly engineer of the Federal Motor Truck Company and connected with the engineering forces of the E. R. Thomas Motor Car Company and the Hudson Motor Car Company. R. P. Spencer, sales manager, was formerly sales manager of the Federal Motor Truck Company, and at one time sale manage of Gauder, Paeschke & Frey, of Milwaukee. R. F. Moore, advertising manager, formerly filled the same position with the Federal Motor Truck Company.

"M. E. McKenney, assistant sales manager, was formerly in a like position at the Federal Motor Truck Company. H. L, Constant, secretary to the president, also was with the Federal Motor Truck Company." (DFP 12 July 1914) One wonders who might have been left at Federal, besides possibly the janitor.

All this and much more would be completely overshadowed in just under three weeks when Gavrilo Princip, a Serbian nationalist, brutally assassinated the Archduke Franz Ferdinand and his wife Sophie, in Sarajevo on Sunday, June 28, ushering in the diplomatic maelstrom which would plunge the entire world into war within the next weeks. Coincidentally, Charlie happened to be in the United States at the time, visiting relatives and friends in Evansville, and also conferring with state department officials in Washington. In an August 7 letter to brother Wythe in Chicago, Ned reported that Charles had just left the day before on the Battleship North Carolina on his return to Europe. He had received word that Martha and the boys were all well. Ned further reported that Garvin had just had an operation, not specifying its nature, but that their youngest brother was doing well. He also mentioned that Hattie and her sons were in Lausanne, Switzerland and not near any of the European danger, and there seemed to be no concern about their safety. Copying a page from the Hupp playbook, two hardy men departed from the Ponchartrain Hotel in downtown Detroit on September 29 for a planned three year, round the world trip to promote the Denby Motor Truck Company, and to establish new dealerships. Two hardy men, C. T. Chenevert, a truck salesman, and his assistant, Beckwith Havens had already honed their skills on a driving trip though Cuba, and were now ready for the great global adventure.

Women challenging the status quo on many fronts were undoubtedly encouraged in November to read that three Detroit women had been granted hunting licenses for the upcoming season. First on the list was Marion Denby who was accompanying her husband on a shooting expedition in the north country. Marion kept good company, as one of the other two women was none other than Mrs. Anna Ricker Vogel, champion woman live bird shot of the world. (DFP 11-13-1914)

In December, Charlie returned home to Detroit, announcing that he would be retiring from the consular service after twenty two years. The Press reported that he was in "negotiations with his brother, former congressman Edwin Denby, and Walter Drake, both of the Hupp Motor Car Company, to take charge of the corporation's export trade." (DFP DEC 15, 1914) The plan was for Charlie to return to Europe after the war.

Chapter Thirteen

"Where the way is hardest, there go thou;
follow your own path and let people talk."

Dante Alighieri

Denby Truck, Hoosiers and Defence

1915 had hardly introduced itself when the Detroit Times reported that former Speaker of the House of Representatives and current Illinois congressman, Joseph Gurney Cannon (Uncle Joe) was coming to town January 7th for a speech before the banquet of the Detroit Real Estate Board. The event, held at the Hotel Ponchartrain was billed as "an informal talk" to be given by the fiery and controversial politician. Though Ned was not a member of the real estate board, he was invited especially because of his close friendship with Uncle Joe, and in order that he might give the introductory remarks. Ned used the occasion, as was his wont, not only to tell a story about his subject, but also to poke fun at himself.

"As though it were yesterday, I feel that I am standing in the doorway of the House of Representatives, a happy, carefree new Congressman, one of 65 who had entered that Congress, doing my duty as I saw it, and remaining as obscure as I could, and that in the Congress of the United States represents some obscurity. Suddenly I heard vaguely out of one ear, from the Speaker's lips the words, 'Mr. Denby of Michigan', and one of the officials at the desk hastened to me and told me I had been called to the chair to preside over the Committee of the whole House. If he had said called to the electric chair, I would have gone more gladly and welcomed him, but to be summoned for the first time in the great House to occupy the chair and preside over Congress utterly without warning, utterly without preparation, was something so horrible that I could not have borne it if I had time to think. I shall not use the language of literature to describe my condition, but simply say that my heart froze in my breast, mechanically my feet carried me to the speaker's platform, in frozen and utter despair I received the gavel and courteous gesture from the speaker, and hopelessly turned to face the Congress of the United States, little knowing how well the ways are greased for the new Congressman. I don't mind telling a secret of Congress here. Before I had time to speak a word, the parliamentarian at the Speaker's desk whispered with moveless lips the correct phrase to use and I used it. Being dead, my voice was without emotion. The wheels began to run. That same sphinx-like face appeared opposite me at every juncture and always told me what to do and what to say. I know I was a hypocrite, and he knew it, but the new members of Congress didn't know it, and I, having the first call to preside, received much enthusiastic congratulation upon the ease and skill with which I had guided the deliberations of the day. Afterwards the Speaker was asked by my sister, who lived with me at the time, why he had not given me the usual warning which it is customary to give, and his reply was significant and characteristic of the man. He said he wanted to see if I had any heart......" (Detroit Times 1-8-1915)

He concluded his remarks of the evening by adding, "He has been accused to be a stand-patter. Probably he is, but remember he who is a stand-patter in regard to certain

policies which he believes in is likely also to be a stand-patter in regard to personal integrity and public righteousness." Uncle Joe kept his remarks for the most part historical and general rather than partisan and political. However, he did take a jab at certain people with whom he heartily disagreed. "When I hear the conservationists talk I'm almost afraid to eat for fear of robbing the earth; of using a scuttle of coal for fear of depleting the mines." Erect, pugnacious, profane, the same Uncle Joe who had spent over 40 years already in Congress, and at the age of seventy-eight, would still be there for another eight years.

In February Ned was in New York on Hupp business. While there he also met with an old "Bachelors" pal Bert Cobb, now head of a large electrical consortium. He wrote home and asked Marion to "write me and tell me how the boy is...", and two days later, on April 23, he told her he had picked up a new toy for the baby from a street merchant, "but don't tell him." Back in Detroit later in the month, he helped preside over the first annual meeting of stockholders of the Denby Motor Truck company. Officers were re-elected, with the addition of a new vice president, Henry Lansdale, an efficiency expert with several years of experience with the National Cash Register Company, Cadillac, and the K.R.I.T. Motor Car Company.

On April 10, the board of Commerce, which had long since become his main nucleus of operations, named among its new officers Ned as chairman of the committees for public affairs, and for national legislation. That same month came the announcement that 30 Denby Trucks had been sold to the Post Office in New York City for parcel post deliveries, marking the first time trucks were to be used by the postal service. In the same month, in a letter to his friend the orthopedic surgeon in Manhattan, Dr. Russell Hibbs, he stated that the Hupp was going great guns, paying dividends, and also that :"The Denby is doing very well indeed. We have a great many orders, including 30 for the parcel post, or mail pick-ups in New York." (BHL Edwin Denby Papers Box #1)

All the civilized world gasped in horror when, on May 7, a German submarine torpedoed the Cunard Liner Lusitania on her 202nd Atlantic crossing, just 11 miles off the coast of Ireland and merely hours before her scheduled docking in Liverpool. 1198 souls were lost, including 128 Americans. To this day the

To This High Standard

British Government is mum about many aspects of the sinking, continuing to fuel theories that she carried contraband munitions, and perhaps, that the British Government allowed her to stray into the path of the submarine which the admiralty may have been able to prevent. Contrary to popular belief, the sinking did not propel the United States into the war as Britain had hoped, and America's entrance into the hostilities would not happen for nearly two more years, and then only after the Germans declared unrestricted submarine warfare against the Americans, and after the diplomatic disaster of the Zimmerman telegram.

At a Detroit City Council meeting in May, Ned watched helplessly, after pleading his cause, as the council voted to refuse acceptance of a 106 acre plot of land a mile west of the city which had been offered free of charge with the single stipulation that the council invest a mere $25,000 in improvements to show good faith. As with politicians sometimes, the council could not see beyond the noses of their faces and felt the money was too much to spend on undeveloped land. That month he and Walter Drake visited a new sports club in the north, called Turtle Lake, which was considerably closer than the Huron Mountain Club. Four days after his arrival he wrote Marion that he had gotten up early before the others in order to write her. Curiously, after two pages of married intimacy, he signed his letter, "Your loving husband, Edwin Denby." Oh, the idiosyncrasies of the age!

World War I had been raging on the continent for nearly a year, and the Wilson administration was not unmindful of the possibility of sabotage in American industry, but since the United States was at peace with the belligerents, the government could do little to defend against it in any overt way. Therefore the administration reached out quietly to Democrats in different states in order to form citizens groups for this endeavor. When men in Detroit were approached, they immediately deferred to certain leading citizens known for their stand on "preparedness". It sounds innocuous today, but in that time the mild word was beginning to become a catchword for defense-minded businessmen/patriots who wished to protect their businesses and their country. In the afternoon edition of the Detroit Times for July 31, 1915, a front page article first reported the formation of a local Branch of the National Security League, which was designed to urge stronger defenses, create a reserve, and educate the public on the country's military needs. Given the gigantic budgets of military spending of today, it is almost impossible to imagine the level of neglect which the armed forces had experienced at this time. Charles Warren, another of Ned's "Bachelors", then President of the Board of Commerce, was appointed temporary president, Ned was named a director of the new organization which had been organized by William B. Brewster, field secretary of the League. After establishing the local Branch, Mr. Brewster quickly left Detroit for Chicago, in his quest to organize many branches in the Mississippi valley and the midwest. Said Mr. Brewster, "I found Detroit ripe for organization. This city, being on the border, is more alive to the country's need of defense than inland cities." The League proposed the following suggestions for its Branches:

1. To adopt a definite military and naval policy.
2. To establish the budget system for appropriations.
3. To increase the regular army by 25,000 (currently at 10,000)
4. To help and strengthen the national guard.
5. To create and maintain an organized reserve.
6. To abolish useless navy yards.
7. To abolish useless and obsolete army posts and concentrate the army in a few posts strategically located. (Detroit Times July 31, 1915)

On August 1, Denby Truck bought 5 1/2 acres of land complete with manufacturing buildings from the defunct Briggs Detroit Motor Company. The increased floor space would allow them to build more trucks and also a wider range of product. Earlier in the year they had already introduced two new lines of trucks.

Two weeks later Ned penned a jubilant letter to his friend, Dr. Hibbs. Marion had given birth that very morning of August 13, to their second child. He told his friend that Marion had had a difficult pregnancy but that "nature was merciful at the end. The Doctor arrived at 320am and told me we would probably be out of the woods about 9. At 505 the baby was born and Marion had a comparatively easy time of it. It was scheduled for July 22."! Only then in his excitement does he think to tell Russell that it is a girl, and they think they will call her Marion. He asked the Doctor to share godfather privileges with his brother Garvin. He also reported that Mrs.Sage, the midwife, had come for this birth, but that since the baby was so late, she had departed only two days before.

He then informed Hibbs that he and Drake had joined the Turtle Lake Club where they had hunted in May, and that what it lacked in comparison with the Huron Mountain Club, it gained in accessibility. Next came a discussion of finances, as Ned was always ready to help friends of his invest in what he saw as great opportunities. "Hupp has had a great boom on the local market lately. I think I can sell your stock for about $55,000. The stock is undoubtedly worth that and more, but would it not be well to sell 1200 shares? If you did so at 25, you would get back your original investment of $30,000 and have still 1000 shares which, in my opinion, will never be worth less than they are today. These shares will yield you at a conservative estimate I think $3,000 to $4,000 per annum." At this time Hupp was about seven years old, so the good doctor had nearly doubled his original investment in that time. The great automobile business was rapidly making Ned Denby more than financially comfortable.

Newspapers in Detroit and Evansville reported in mid August that Charles Jr. had just returned from an extended trip to the orient. He had visited Hawaii, the Philippines, Japan, China and Korea. With his contacts and experience in Vienna as well, it was easy to see what an asset he was to Hupp's overseas enterprise.

In mid September, Ned journeyed to Fort Wayne, Indiana to give an impassioned speech before the annual banquet of the Lincoln National Life Insurance company on the subject of national preparedness. He entitled his address "Insurance for the

Nation" and it was his strongest statement yet on his views of the country's apathy toward the all-important goal of preparedness. He boldly proclaimed that the American people were "drunk with prosperity," foreshadowing not only his, but many American generations of apathy to come. He called Americans "the keepers of the ark of the covenant of liberty," and continued....

"The great experiment of democracy, the ability of the people to rule themselves, is peculiarly our experiment. Yet we garner our wealth, proclaim our greatness, and, drunk with prosperity, we take no reasonable steps to protect our own, to guarantee the success of the great experiment, nor to assure our descendants the blessings we enjoy. Do we not dwell in a fool's paradise?"

What, exactly, was this "fool's paradise" of which he was speaking? The Austrians had diplomatically protested Americans doing munitions business with their enemies in a time of war. Wilson's second Secretary of State, Robert Lansing, publicly answered in a diplomatic note that it had always been the policy of the United States to "remain at peace with all nations and to avoid any appearance of menacing such peace by the threat of its armies and navies." In other words, —no, let's let Lansing's own words explain this statement...."In consequence of this standing policy, the United States would, in the event of attack by a foreign power, be at the outset of the war seriously, if not fatally, embarrassed by the lack of arms and ammunition and of the means to produce them in sufficient quantities to supply the requirements of national defense." In plain English, the United States was totally, possibly FATALLY, defenseless. This was the public, official statement of the Secretary of State. So Ned and his fellow advocates for preparedness were perhaps rightfully aghast at such a naive and dangerous policy publicly stated. He told his audience, "We have not enough soldiers in the country to defend Fort Wayne, let alone New York."

He concluded his remarks with three suggestions:

"First, urge congress to get the best advice from experts on the national defense it can get, and then support congress in taking that advice.

Second, proclaim and insist that for Americans there is no fatherland but the United States.

And last, discourage disparagement of other peoples and undue self aggrandizement. Cultivate less brag and more brotherhood." (DFP Sept 14, 1915)

In October the Denby Motor Truck Company initiated a new sales program which was pure Ned Denby in its emphasis upon educating those involved. The New York Sun on October 15, reported the company's new effort to help small businessmen "to increase the area in which they can sell goods at a profit." Claiming that "A motor truck will accomplish this," but adding that there is more to learn in exactly how to use the vehicle.

"The Denby Business Building and Sales Efficiency Service, just put into operation by the company, is designed to accomplish just this. It is a correspondence course in retail salesmanship, consisting of thirty-six lessons and covering one year. The course has been prepared by the best experts obtainable and takes up in detail every branch of business building.

How to secure new customers; how to increase the size of orders; how to introduce new goods—a hundred different factors of salesmanship are taught. Every truck owner is allowed to nominate one man to take the course free of charge." (New York Sun October 15, 1915

In the 1940 Christmas movie, "Remember the Night", the girl, Barbara Stanwyck, is dancing with the guy, Fred MacMurray, who has just asked the waiter to have the band play "My Indiana Home". When the song starts, she glances up at him and asks, "Why did you have them play this piece?' He tells her because he is going there, Indiana, tomorrow, and she exclaims, "No!?! You're a Hoosier?!?" It may be difficult in the 21st Century to recall the Americana of earlier times. And in the first half of the 20th Century, nothing seemed more American to the country than the Midwest, and nothing about the Midwest was more American than the Hoosier state of Indiana. There were Indiana Societies in both Chicago and New York, and it certainly must have been on one of his travels that this came to the attention of our gigantic Hoosier, Ned Denby. Sometime in 1914, the "great networker" approached other Hoosiers, and shortly a Hoosier Society of Detroit was formed. No fair trying to guess who became its first president. So it should be no surprise that by October of 1915, when the Society was a year old, that Ned would be called upon to address its first anniversary banquet in the Statler Hotel. And it should also be no surprise that the topic of his address was "National Preparedness." In remarks very similar to those he delivered in Fort Wayne, Ned told his audience, "If the United States navy were to participate in a general engagement, all of the ammunition now held in reserve would be exhausted in 30 minutes, and it would be impossible to replenish the supply."

"The indifference and attitude of the American people on a question of such importance as this is simply appalling," Ned blustered.

Additionally, the newspaper article reported that the 'Hoosier Poet", James Whitcomb Riley, had telegrammed his regret at not being able to join them for the occasion, and plans were promptly entertained to hold the "Second Annual" on the anniversary of the poet's birthday, October 7, 1916. (DFP 10-22-1815)

A month later it was announced that "The Monahan Express Company, Eastern distributors of the Denby truck, won the salesman's contest, conducted over a period of seven months by the Denby Motor Truck Company of Detoirt, for the largest number of trucks sold within that period by any of their dealers." The Monahan Company had won out over second place Detroit, and third place, Honolulu. The employees of the Monahan Company were treated to a banquet in New York and the president of the company, Thomas Monahan was presented with a silver cup. The paper further reported that "representatives of the Denby company from all the leading cities in the United States were present, as well as those from Honolulu." (New York Tribune, Nov 21, 1915)

To This High Standard

On December 6, Ned was greeted with cheers as he addressed a packed house of over 1600 enthusiastic attendees at the Broadway-Strand Theater, for the Detroit debut of the documentary, "Battle Cry of Peace." For the first time Ned called for greater attention to the newest of war technologies, the air corps. "Our aviation corps is a negligible quantity. The warring nations of Europe have 20,000 aeroplanes in the field. The aeroplanes are the eyes of the army; if we went to war, we should be sending but a blind army to meet an army," Ned declared. Many of Ned's longtime friends were also behind this effort, including Mr. and Mrs. Henry Joy, Mr. and Mrs. Hugh Chalmers. Judge and Mrs, James Murfin, another of the old Bachelor clique. Governor Ferris, a democrat, sent a note of regret.

The Free Press seemed awed in its description. "The performance began on a signal from buglers in the rear of the theater. An American flag was hoisted from the stage while Captain Stanley Huntley Lewis, of the Arizona Rangers, stood at salute as officer of the day and the strains of "the Star-Spangled Banner" broke from the big orchestra. The audience rose and cheered as the national anthem was played. It is certain that Ned had visions from his youth of Memorial Days in Evansville, watching the great horseman on the white stallion leading the parade. The Press further reported that the line had already formed outside the theater for the first public showing and had grown so large that "Extra police were called out to keep the waiting crowds in line." (DFP 12-6-1915)

To round out the year, on December 19, the Press ran a story about the upcoming plans which the Hoosier Society had been working on for the coming months. Giving a modicum of background on the society, it reported that it had first been organized on October 21, 1914, and had since grown to a membership of 500. Furthermore, "it is expected this will increase as conservative estimates show 4,000 former residents of Indiana now living in Detroit. " Also stated was the fact that at the anniversary banquet in October, the society had elected new officers, including a new president, Charles A. Macauley. Ned had been made "honorary" president. The society had further organized into five committees: membership, entertainment, speakers, boosters, and publicity. Various committees and officers were working on plans for rallies, banquets, smokers and other events "for the sons of Indiana that will rival the gatherings of the New York and Chicago Indiana societies which have already attained national prominence."

In today's world of social media, repeat, "media", it is hard to imagine a time when social media meant meeting in a physical room full of other people. It is even harder to imagine inventing more and more reasons for such gatherings, and continuing to be enthusiastic about them for longer than five minutes. It is hard, in fact, almost a lost art, in fact, to imagine at all.

Chapter Fourteen

"Go forward bravely. Fear nothing.
Trust in God and all will be well."

Jean d'Arc

Board of Commerce, War Plans

Nineteen hundred and sixteen was ushered into Detroit with a mild, misty and then rainy, and extremely foggy, winter day. It reached a high of 39 degrees by eight o'clock in the evening and promised to plunge the following day, with snow on the way. There is a saying in Michigan that if you don't like the weather, wait a minute and it will change. However, later in the month of January, the tiny hamlet of Browning, Montana would experience the largest 24 hour temperature drop ever recorded on the planet from, January 23 at 44 degrees above to January 24 at minus 56. While the cataclysmic struggle raged overseas on the continent, necessitating the cancellation of the 1916 Summer Olympics in Berlin (the Olympics would not return to Germany until Adolf Hitler got burned by Jesse Owens in 1936), the United States, comfortable or uncomfortable in its isolation, went about the business of the mundane, the unusual, and the utterly common. The 40 hour work week would come into being during the year in the western New York factories of Endicott-Johnson, while congress would call into being the National Park Service in August. Georgia Tech's football team would beat Cumberland College in

October in the most lop-sided score ever recored on the gridiron, 220-0. Not all was isolationist smugness in America, as March saw Black Jack Pershing ordered into Mexico to stamp out the bandit, Pancho Villa, while in May, the President ordered the United States Marines to invade the Dominican Republic to restore order after years of assassinations and political turmoil. Including Haiti in 1915, it was the third time in two years that Woodrow Wilson had seen fit to send U. S. troops streaming into a foreign country. In the same year, the United States' congress further tantalized the Philippine people with the Jones Act, another in the interminable steps toward full Philippine independence that would not come to fruition with glacial ineptitude until after World War II. The Battle of Jutland, the largest naval battle of the war, took place in May to a stalemate the British would always claim as victory. In November, the largest ship to be sunk in the entire war, the HMHS Britannic, sister of Titanic, would strike a mine and go to the bottom of the Aegean Sea in fifty-five minutes. And rounding out the year of international mayhem, Grigori Rasputin, one time advisor to Russian royalty was unceremoniously slaughtered in St. Petersburg on the next to last day of December — having been shot, strangled, poisoned and dumped into the Neva where it was later discovered he had died from drowning.

Everyone seemed busy. But no one was busier than Ned Denby. On the second day of the new year the New York Sun ran an article in its automobile section praising what it called the three top men of the Hupp Motor Car Company, J. Walter Drake, President, Joseph R. Drake, Secretary, and Edwin Denby, Treasurer, who had presided from the beginning of the enterprise and were indispensable in its meteoric rise. From a capitalization of $25,000 in 1908, the Hupp now boasted $8,000,000, and from an initial production of 500 vehicles, it was now pumping out 20 to 25 thousand annually from three factories. One in Detroit, one in Windsor, Canada and a parts plant in Jackson, Michigan. January 14 saw Ned addressing the officers and committee heads of the Hoosier Society at a luncheon at the Statler. "'Hoosier' ought to be made so illustrious a term throughout the nation that every time an Indianan rises to speak at a public gathering the band will strike up 'On the Banks of the Wabash'," Ned declared. (DFP1-15-1916)

The old rumors of Ned running for Congress had resurfaced in January, and were being reported both in Detroit and Washington with almost breathless certainty. The only ingredient the rumors lacked was any confirmation from the man himself. In February Ned travelled to Washington to attend the national convention of the Chamber of Commerce U. S., where nearly a thousand representatives from over 700 organizations nationwide gathered. "Men high in the business and political life of the nation, including three cabinet officers, will deliver addresses on legislative and commercial topics now under general discussion," the Detroit Free Press reported. The event was scheduled to conclude with a banquet Thursday evening where Woodrow Wilson gave the address. (DFP 2-7-1916) No sooner back in Detroit than he attended and addressed the 13th annual banquet of the Michigan Manufacturers, again at the Statler. It must have seemed to Ned that he ate more of the Statler's chef's cooking than his own wife's. He spoke very vigorously in favor of a stronger merchant marine, one of his favorite topics through the years. He told the group that in 1810 American ships carried 90% of American commerce on the high seas, and that currently that percentage had dwindled to 9. With much of the world at war, and many believing that it was only a matter of time until America joined them, it was a sobering statistic. Five days later he spoke once again on the subject of preparedness before over 200 members of the Detroit Naval Militia. He was adamant, he was passionate and try as he might, he could not understand his fellow Americans' apathy.

Early March saw Ned once again lending his expertise in raising money for a worthy cause, as he became head of the men's teams of the 250 workers who organized themselves to raise

$300,000 in eight days for a new Y.W.C.A. building. The event was a smashing success, as the committees reported eight days later they had raised well over the mark in their endeavors. At the banquet in the Board of Commerce auditorium amid raucous cheers and hurrahs, it was revealed that they had raised $318,276 in the eight day campaign. (Detroit Times 3-11-1916)

Wednesday March 8 at the noon meeting the Directors of the Board of Commerce elected Ned as the new President of that illustrious body. He took the reins from Charles Warren, the only two-time president in the board's thirteen year history. He would be presiding over an organization of 3800 of Detroit's leading citizens, in what was recognized as one of the most active and innovative organizations of its kind in the country. He had been so involved in Board activities for thirteen years, the wonder was that it took them that long to elect him. Merely three years before the Board had built a new office building which gave them more than enough room for their activities, and even allowed other organizations to use their facilities upon occasion. For Ned, it was a culmination of where the strands of his life had been leading him for quite some time, away from the political, and more toward the civic and altruistic side of his nature.

By March 25, the Free Press was reporting that Ned had finally declared himself in his struggle to decide where he would be able to do the most good. He would not oppose his old political foe, Frank Doremus, for his former seat in Congress. Surprisingly, he admitted that he had accepted the Board of Commerce presidency "with the distinct understanding that his incumbency would not be permitted to interfere with any political plans he might make."

In his remarks, however, he plainly revealed that he understood what a turning point this would be for his life:

"I would like to enter the contest," he explained. "I feel that it is distinctly a day for Republican principles and return to control of the government. Much as I regret it a number of conditions have compelled me to give up the idea of seeking to return to Washington. I feel, too, that as President of the Board of Commerce I shall be able to do as much or more good for Detroit than by going to Washington, provided I were elected." (DFP 3-25-1916)

Once again, his final choice rested upon what was best for Detroit, not what was best for Edwin Denby. It was a trait of long-standing, and would never leave him.

At the same time he was invited to be part of a major effort of America's Jews to raise about $5,000,000 to aid the estimated 7 to 8 million impoverished Jews in war-torn Europe. Detroiters had pledged to raise $100,000 of the money sought. Furthermore, he was also at this time deeply committed to the great partnership which the board of Commerce had undertaken the previous year with the Detroit Board of Education. In 1915 the Board had established an Americanization Bureau to aid foreign workers in becoming more fully acclimatized American citizens. In several Detroit city schools night classes were attended by thousands of these men and women, supported by many of the businessmen who owned the companies where they worked. Recognizing the further need for broader vocational training, as President-elect of the board, Ned lent his great influence to the drive to raise $450,000 for an addition to Cass Technical High School, and also to help raise the salaries of Detroit's high school teachers. The Americanization Bureau was a first in the country, and the night classes model was studied by many of other cities in the United States. Along with Frank Cody, the Detroit City School's forward-thinking assistant superintendent, Ned was determined to find every way to aid Detroit's immigrant population in assimilating into the great American dream. Cody, just as committed to this partnership, joined the Board of Commerce, and went on the annual cruises.

On Tuesday evening, April 4, the reins of the Detroit Board of Commerce were officially passed from Charles Warren to Ned's capable hands. The incoming president made it clear he had no plans to alter the course on which the board was already so ably fixed. Two days later Ned acted as toastmaster at a stag banquet and entertainment of the combined Ohio, Indiana, New York and Kansas Societies held at the Hotel Tuller. Toward the end of April, Denby Motor Truck added a new 2 1/2 ton truck line which the company claimed would allow their dealers to "fill the requirements of practically 75 per cent of the motor truck buyers." (DFP April 23, 1916) A short time later the Press was reporting that Denby trucks were being shipped to virtually all parts of the globe: "including 24 to England, a fleet of 13 to India, four to Rangoon and two to South Africa. Denby trucks were also shipped to Japan, Korea and Fiji Islands." (DFP May 7, 1916)

In May, in response to a letter of invitation from 40 prominent Detroiters, former President Theodore Roosevelt came to Detroit to deliver a speech on preparedness. Ned was a member of the greeting committee at the Michigan Central station, as well as of the greeting committee at the Detroit Athletic Club where Teddy was taken for a lavish breakfast. Crowds estimated at over 50,000 lined streets to get a glimpse of and to welcome the Rough Rider. In the afternoon he was driven to the Detroit Opera House where he spoke to a packed crowd, after thousands more had been turned away. In a quaint description of the day the Detroit Times reported that "motorists created a loud commotion with the warning horns of their cars."

June 9th saw the departure of the Fifteenth Annual Board of Commerce Cruise aboard the lake steamer, City of Detroit III. Nearly 600 members crowded the ship as it headed for Sault Sainte Marie and a grand reception by the Commercial Club. Famed Arctic explorer Admiral Robert Peary joined the cruisers shortly after their arrival at the Soo Locks and was warmly greeted by the Detroiters. In a brief note penned late at night to Marion, Ned told her that though it was raining, the group had been very enthusiastic and he doubted that the inclement weather could dampen their spirits. "Love to Ned, and to 'the little thing'", he referred to ten month old Marion, "and to you, my darling, all the love in my heart." (DPL Edwin Denby Jr. Papers, Box #1) Later in the month of June the family vacationed for a week at Huron Mountain.

On July 4th, Ned spoke at a conclave of well over 20,000 people on Belle Isle where 3000 brand new American citizens took the oath of allegiance. Owing to the overall quiet nature of the day, the Detroit Times remarked, "On the whole it was about the sanest Fourth in the history of the city." (Detroit Times July 5, 1916) Six days later Detroit was favored by a visit from the President of the United States who had come to address the World's Salesmanship

Congress at a noon luncheon at the Detroit Athletic Club.

"The president opened his address with a jocular reference to Edwin Denby, president of the Board of Commerce, who was two seats away from him at the speakers' table.

"I am glad to be in Detroit and among the men who have helped make her the great city that she is,' he said. 'Among other things that have interested me is the shameful admission by Edwin Denby that he is enjoying the company of Democrats." (Detroit Times July 10,1916)

Interviewed by the Free Press in August, Ned had much to say about the success of the Americanization program of the previous year.

"Last year Detroit was the center of interest to all those concerned in the problem of Americanizing the non-English speaking foreigner. This city was the laboratory for a gigantic experiment in citizenship. Detroit was the first city to take a definite step toward uniting the seventy and seven tribes of old Europe that are represented in every large manufacturing city of the north."

So successful had their efforts been in 1915 that "thousands were turned away because of insufficient room"

In the current year "Every agency in the city which comes in touch with the foreigner is preparing to co-operate." Handbills were inserted into library books taken home by foreigners; the foreign press in Detroit was enlisted to help; playground children were given handbills to take home to their parents; posters were hung in employment offices; foreign sections of the city were circularized; employers inserted instruction slips into pay envelopes of foreign workmen. All of this effort was geared to "tell the foreigner of his opportunity not only to learn English and become a citizen, but in addition to acquire a little of the knowledge that perhaps was denied him in his own country." Ned concluded the interview by saying that Detroit was "proud of its preeminence in the motor car industry," and that "it is now endeavoring to show the world that it can make something of far greater importance, which is an American citizen out of the crude material of the immigrant." (DFP August 10, 1916)

On Tuesday, October 3, after driving in to work at his office in the Dime Bank Building, Ned felt compelled to pen a quick note to the beloved of his life. "My Darling," he began, "Driving in this morning I remembered that yesterday was our engagement anniversary." Not only was he far ahead of most married men in recalling the wedding anniversary, he remembered the day they were engaged, albeit, one day after the fact. "Just a word to tell you how dear the remembrance is to me and how much I love my darling wife who has brought me happiness. It has been a happy marriage, dearie, hasn't it? And so will it continue, I devoutly pray and earnestly believe, so long as we shall be together on this earth."

He mentioned the fact that he was writing these sentiments even though he had wanted to phone her, but then remembered that in his day there was no privacy on telephone lines, "so unhappily there are ears on wires. Hence this note." He signed off with "Goodbye dearest sweetheart, now as you were six years ago....." (DPL Edwin Denby Jr. Papers, Box #1)

Later in October Ned delivered brief comments at a civic luncheon held by the women of the Twentieth Century Club. The featured speaker was Mrs. Albion Fellows Bacon, a renowned housing expert who spoke on "Women in Housing Reform". The Board of Commerce was on the threshold of attacking this very problem of Detroit's critical shortage of affordable housing, and it was quite dear to Ned's heart. Interestingly, earlier in the year the Evansville Journal (26Mar1916) had run an article on famous people who had all come, not only from the same town, but from the very same neighborhood and within just a few years of each other. The article, naturally, mentioned Ned's father and his older brother Charlie, each of whom had made international names for themselves in China. It also listed John W. Foster, Secretary of State under Benjamin Harrison, and Minister to Spain, Russia and Mexico; Frank Kramer, world champion cyclist; Henry A. Lozier, a sewing machine and bicycle manufacturer who invented the Lozier automobile, for a time the most expensive automobile produced in the United States; Annie Fellows Johnston, authoress of children's books including "The Little Colonel" series which was the model for the 1935 Shirley Temple movie. Lastly, Annie's sister, Albion Fellows Bacon who became a recognized expert in the field of housing reform, and joined Ned Denby on the speakers' platform at the Twentieth Century Club . Not a bad list for a sleepy Hoosier town on an oxbow of the Belle Riviere in southern Indiana.

On a beautiful, fair autumn day, Tuesday, October 31, Ned addressed a very large gathering of Board of Commerce members in the auditorium of the Board's headquarters on the corner of Lafayette and Washington Boulevards. It was to be a major speech, introducing an important enterprise which would benefit the people of Detroit. Ned began with a broad opening statement about the overall aims of the Board.

"Our attempt is to do the greatest good to the greatest number, and in making American citizens out of foreigners, helping provide school facilities, getting jobs for the needy and feeding the helpless, creating and protecting a trade mark for our commerce at home and abroad, as well as helping solve transportation and other great questions affecting business interests, and in general, giving intelligent aid where public interest is concerned. We feel that we are serving the whole community. There are no special interests in the Board of Commerce." (BHL Edwin Denby Papers, Box #1)

After that introduction, Ned told his listeners that there was a real problem with housing in Detroit, and that certain conditions were "rotten." He then explained that the Board had already conducted its own research, carried out by Secretary of the Board Walter Cole and five members of his staff. "From their investigation Mr. Cole and his aides found that rents had been increased variously from 20 to 50 per cent and in many instances nothing more than a situation enabling landlords to take advantage of a crowded housing condition was the motive." (Detroit Times, Oct 31, 1916) Ned further warned that if this problem were not addressed, and promptly, Detroit stood a very good chance of losing skilled workmen to other cities better equipped to provide decent housing for the men and their families.

However, Ned told the members that he was not there simply to point out the ills without offering some suggestions. The Detroit Board of Commerce had already been in partnership with the Detroit Real Estate Exchange, and the solution offered was to start their own Society of Savings, "that being a form of building and loan association, and that has been done," he told them. Furthermore, the new Society had already taken over the charter of an existing company, elected directors, and was ready to begin operations. For the time being, they would operate out of temporary space in the Board of Commerce Building itself until their permanent quarters were ready in the People's State Bank Building. (Ibid.) Finally, on December 4, the fledgling Society of Savings took up offices in their new location under a deluge of applications from not only people who wanted to take out loans to build their own homes, but also for others who wanted to start up savings accounts where they knew the capital would be put to use for the good of their fellow citizens. This may be where the phrase, "win-win" was first invented, but if it was not, it should have been.

Saturday, December 10, Ned addressed the Schoolmen's Club at a noon luncheon meeting in the grill room of the Board of Commerce Building. His topic was "The Place of the School System in the Community." He was joined by his friend, Frank Cody, who was chairman of the executive committee of the club, as well as assistant superintendent of education, and who outlined for the 287 members "the campaign to obtain an increase in the salaries of Detroit high school teachers." (DFP 12-9-1916) No matter what your need might be, almost anyone in Detroit with an honest cause had a friend in Ned Denby. An ally. A tireless advocate. A loyal supporter. A Good Samaritan. It may be said with complete truth that the needs of others defined him.

Chapter Fifteen

Parris Island
From the halls of Montezuma
To the shores of Tripoli,
We fight our county's battles
On land and on the sea.
First to fight for right and freedom,
And to keep our honor clean,
We are proud to claim the title
Of United States Marine!

War Years, Marine Corps

When war broke out in Europe in August, 1914, Major General George Barnett had been Commandant of the United States Marine Corps for barely six months. He was 55 years old, born in Wisconsin, and graduated from Annapolis in the Class of 1881, the first class which provided officers to the Marine Corps, as well as the Navy. During the Spanish American War in 1898 he served aboard the cruiser USS New Orleans and participated in several bombardments of Spanish forts in Cuba. When Barnett was appointed Major General Commandant on February 25, 1914, the Marine Corps consisted of a fighting force of 343 officers and approximately 10,000 men. This would swell during the war to many times that number, and General Barnett would be lauded for the excellent and highly successful way he molded this great influx of raw civilians into the most elite fighting force on earth. The truth was, he had the help of a few good men.

The war raged on the continent for nearly 33 months while President Woodrow Wilson hand-wrung his way along the slippery path of neutrality. Many Americans would be quick to claim that the sinking of the Lusitania was the straw that broke

Wilson's wrists, but they would be wrong. America managed to remain isolated and uninvolved in war for another 23 months after the great liner went to the bottom. It also remained shockingly unprepared.

However, on February 1, 1917 the Germans reintroduced unrestricted submarine warfare, in direct violation of promises which had calmed American anger after Lusitania. Then later in February the British released a highly sensitive communique which they had intercepted from Germany to the government of Mexico, now famously remembered as the "Zimmerman telegram". The Kaiser's Government was prepared to guarantee large chunks of the American Southwest to Mexico in exchange for Mexican participation against the United States in the war effort. In late February, this telegram was shown to Wilson, who had campaigned for his second term on the slogan, "He kept us out of war….." By March, the Germans themselves were openly admitting the validity of the Zimmermann telegram. Safely sworn in for his second term on March 4, Wilson called for a declaration of war on Monday, April 2, and Congress obliged, on April 6. The World was at war.

Edwin Denby, as was his habit, had not been idle. As President of the Detroit Board of Commerce during 1916-17, because of his great love for his country and at the instigation of the Federal Government which was not yet at war with Germany, he became Chairman of the Defense Council of Michigan, which was an unofficial group of Detroit businessmen who banded together to search out any indications of enemy activity among businesses or manufacturing enterprises; men who helped keep a strong vigil against sabotage in any form. He also maintained contact with others in similar positions in other states, such as the Milwaukee attorney, Wheeler Bloodgood, who was acting in his home town as Chairman of the Wisconsin Defense League. Known for his fierce patriotism, it came as no surprise to anyone who knew Ned to hear, shortly after Wilson's declaration of war, that he was headed back into the Armed Forces of his beloved nation.

Close friend, fellow Michigan Law School graduate and USS Yosemite shipmate, Henry Lyster would also go back to war, as a distinguished pilot in the rapidly forming American Air Service. Others like them would follow.

On Sunday, April 22, 1917, after mulling his options, Edwin Denby drove downtown and headed for the US Navy recruiting office. There is some indication that he had intended to join the Marines all along, but nevertheless, the story of his enlistment would be re-told along more dramatic lines: entering the naval recruiting office on Grand Circus Park, he presented his six foot one inch bulk for enlistment at age 47. He was, at 245 pounds, a bit overweight, a prosperous attorney, and a married man with two children. Purportedly, a doctor had already told him it would be a miracle if he made it through boot camp alive. The recruiter rushed into a back room and called his superiors to report that "Denby is here...", and it appeared they were ready to bestow rank and privilege upon his towering frame. Realizing what was about to happen, the big man marched directly out of the Naval office and straight into the enlistment office of the Marines. The Leathernecks were only too happy to sign him up. The story is told that he passed the physical with flying colors, but whatever was the truth, he passed it. He was told that he would be notified if Washington decided to waive his age restriction. They were currently taking men no older than 40 years of age, and he was seven years past that. On Wednesday, word came down that the Commandant had waived his age restriction, and the following day, on Thursday, April 26, Ned drove downtown to Grand Circus Park where a famous photograph of him was snapped, stepping back and raising his hand, in full enlistment mode. Out of sight, but standing next him were Marion and Ned Jr. The story made headlines around the country. Ex-US Congressman, prominent attorney, wealthy businessman, landowner, ex-Navy Gunners Mate shuns cushy desk job in the rear to join the United States Marine Corps as a private! There would be no bennies handed to Edwin Denby and none were expected. He was out to set an example of patriotism and valor, courage and manliness that would elevate him at least in his own mind very near the pedestal of his father the gallant Colonel Charles. Years later, in 1933 and over four years after his death, Marion would be invited to preside over the unveiling of a granite memorial marker placed in Grand Circus Park at the exact spot where Ned had raised his hand in enlistment. Arranged by the Edwin Denby Club, some of whose members had never met Ned, the slab was removed in subsequent years as modernizations took place, and appears now to have disappeared into the shadows of forgotten history.

He later said that he had enlisted as a private to show the manhood of America both the seriousness of the challenges which he believed the country now faced, and to set an example of patriotism and sacrifice that could be, and certainly would be, emulated by many young men, and admired by many more. "I profoundly feel that the future of the United States is at stake. Victory or destruction are our only alternatives. Therefore, no sacrifice that any man can make, nor any woman, is too great at this time," he would write some months later. (BHL, Edwin Denby Papers, Box #1, undated correspondence) Praise and accolades poured in from all over the country, not only to Edwin himself, but to his wife as well, offering support and any succor that might be needed by his family while he was serving the nation. His resignation from the Board of the Detroit Bank of Commerce was promptly and emphatically rejected in the strongest terms of support and respect. "Probably nothing has made such a profound impression in this community since war was declared as your high sense of duty which led you to march with the humblest of your fellow citizens to the country's defense. Therein lies the spirit of true democracy and your high example will doubtless lead many others into the service of the United States," wrote Richard P. Joy, President of the bank in his letter to Ned in early May. "Four of our directors have enlisted in the service of their country," he went on to say, not mentioning that no other of them were entering the service as Marine privates. In a separate letter to Marion he told her that, "If at any time this bank or the officers thereof can be of service to you, please do not hesitate to command us....." (Ibid)

The Monroe, Michigan Chamber of Commerce was so moved by his act that they sent him a telegram insisting that "you have set the greatest example of patriotism" and praying "the everlasting God that He may protect you and yours and that the name Denby be printed in capital letters in the history of the United States of America." (Ibid)

The Marines were almost giddy at the prospect of securing the enlistment of such a prominent figure. The local recruiters were quick to pen a head's up to their counterparts at the recruit depot at Port Royal. "Mr. Denby is asking for no favors whatever; he did not apply for a commission in the Corps, as many of our applicants are doing, but wants to go the (sic) through the regular course of instruction etc. that every Private must pass through. At the same time, without any solicitation from him, I think he is entitled to special consideration in some respects, in payment for the sacrifice he is making to become a member of the Marine Corps. He is leaving his law practice and his family behind to become a Private in the Corps because he wants action and he feels he can secure it in the Corps more readily than in any other branch of the service." (Ibid.)

In his first letter home to Marion after a long, adventurous train ride south through Cincinnati to Atlanta, he told her he had allowed himself the luxury of a room alone "where I would think of my darling and write to my darling and love my darling without the more or less trying conversation of the boys as a running commentary." He reassured her by mentioning that he had run into some recruiters in Cincinnati who told him that he should be able to withstand the rigors of the physical training at Port Royal, what the Marines were at that time calling the recruiting depot on the eastern coast which would become more famous later under a different name. The recruiters also told him that he wasn't going to need, or be allowed to keep, most of the articles he had taken with him, and so he informed Marion that "I have promptly sent back by Southern Express C.O.D. my suitcase with everything in it except my toilet articles, pills, handkerchiefs, wrist watch and your most cherished gift, the pictures." By the first day he had already met a Texan whom he liked very much, a Potawatomi Indian, a French Canadian and two young men of Polish descent, all headed for service with the Leathernecks. He reported that he found the men from Detroit "simply perfect', but that at Cincinnati seven more recruits joined them "some of whom had been drinking heavily and are armed with quantities of whiskey. We had the car almost entirely to ourselves and the night was one long hell for me."

It seemed "(t)he man in charge took a berth in another car and left his lambs to gambol at will," but apparently Ned stayed with the boys and was able to "turn over to the recruiting office here today seventeen more or less clean and sober 'accepted applicants'." He listened to their stories, so foreign to his own, and seemed to notice almost immediately that the men were eager to confide in him and that he was able to offer them valuable advice from the life-lessons which were second nature to him but still shrouded in mystery to them. "With these men I am a pal whom I know they greatly like, and yet so far they cannot call me anything but Mr. Denby.

"I have been trying to spur him on to ambition and to teach, what I must strive hard to practice, the simple creed of the soldier, to be clean and true, obedient and industrious. I have treated the men well, stood up for them, and they have given me their confidence and their respect. But tomorrow I become simply an aged and obese private soldier, greatly the inferior of these youthful athletes. What then, I wonder?" He was very soon to find out.

A recurring theme of his letters shows up already in this first one, and belies what must have been the source of many conversations between them. "Sometimes my heart sinks like lead when I wonder whether or not I have been justified in hurting you so. But, after a little comes the answer full and clear, and I know that I am serving my country faithfully and effectively in what she does not yet recognize as her hour of need. But Oh! I long to be back with you and our little ones." He finished his first letter, far away from her for many weeks to come, "Goodbye dearest, you must be happy. I shall be wretched if you are not. And besides you must show people that the pride and the glory of doing hard things for the nation's sake does not make one sad, but smiling." (BHL ED Papers, Box #1, April 28, 1917)

He mentioned that they had another hard day of travel, and they did not arrive at their destination until later in the afternoon. At the time that Ned arrived, the only way to the Marine Corps Recruit Depot was by ferry across Archer's Creek from Port Royal Island to the base itself, located on Parris Island. It was first settled by French Huguenots, led by Jean Ribault, in 1562, who built a settlement known as Charlesfort in honor of the French King. Failing to gain proper support from France, the French abandoned the site by 1563, and it was later inhabited by the Spanish from 1566 to 1587. England gained control of the region, and Parris Island was purchased by Alexander Parris, treasurer of the South Carolina colony in 1715. The English divided the island into several plantations growing both indigo and cotton. During the Civil War the island was settled by freed slaves, and Union forces captured Port Royal Sound in 1861. Subsequently, Parris Island became a Naval coaling station, which duty was extended past the duration of the war due to the efforts of a former slave named Robert Smalls.

Smalls was born in Beaufort, SC and after the Civil War became a Republican in the South Carolina Senate, and member of the U.S. House of Representatives; he founded the Republican Party of South Carolina & was the last Republican to be elected from SC's 5th District until 2010.

Smalls lobbied for the creation of a permanent federal installation on the Island, but it was not until 1891 that Marines were assigned duty there as a detachment arrived, consisting of

First Sergeant Richard Donovan, two corporals and ten privates. This unit provided security for the Naval Station at Port Royal. On November 1, 1915, with the foresight and planning of Major General Commandant Barnett, Parris Island was officially designated as the Marine Corps Recruit Depot, and would eventually grow to become an 8,095 acre installation. In early 1917 Barnett also dispatched a board to investigate sites in the Washington, D. C. area, and the sprawling base at Quantico was established. Also under Barnett's purview, Marines began to establish a presence in the San Diego area, and by 1923, MCRD San Diego became the Marine recruit training facility for the western half of the United States.

In his first letter to Marion from Parris Island at the end of April Ned reported that he was doing well and that the "non-comms" (non commissioned officers) were taking care of him. "This is a wonderful place, a man-making place if ever there was one. I may not be able to stand the work that is to come, but I am quite sure that I will not be hurt. All the non-comms will look after me if I do need looking after, which at present I do not anticipate." He continued, "The men all know who I am and whether else my enlistment may have done good, if anywhere, there is no doubt that in this camp it has been of great value. These rookies like it, they seem proud to be here with me. They express it in a variety of kindly and uncouth ways. They have the flame." He's speaking here of the type of patriotism of which he is the standard bearer. "One boy (recruit) is one of eleven brothers, nine were in the British service. Three of them have been killed in France. Two are in the British Navy off our coast. Several others have not been heard from for quite a while. Now, the tenth comes here......"

On May 1 he told her that the base which was initially designed to handle up to 1500 recruits at a time now housed over 3400, and that that number would grow even larger as the war progressed. On May 2 he said that he had received his first letter from her, and said, "When you spoke of your first prayer being answered and of your being given strength, it rejoiced me more than I can say, filled me with a deeper joy than I have known for many days. Not even the solemn satisfaction of doing my duty at whatever cost can begin to equal my pleasure in the assurance from you that you have found strength to endure and smile upon the world to the end, whithersoever that end may be found. It has helped me even more than you can imagine. It gives me strength and courage to face everything. Nothing will be too hard if you approve and hold up my heart with your strength and cheer." Not only do we find a bygone patriotism in the breasts of this passionately married couple, but also an enduring love which seems almost anachronistic by modern standards. They would love each other in exactly this manner until his death.

By May 6, he had been sworn in and had now become a full-fledged Marine. For a man who was absolutely a "joiner" and belonged to dozens of organizations during his lifetime, his association with the Marine Corps was on a par with the life-long friends he met and made on the Yosemite. He would grow to love these young men with whom he trained and served and it would change the course of his life after the war. For the moment he informed his wife, "(y)ou will be interested but not surprised, I am sure, to learn that Uncle Sam had no trousers and no under drawers big enough for me. I have on an old pair left by some other big guy, and specials are being ordered for me. The only things that really fit were shoes and hat, so I am alright below and aloft, but in between I am a sight. In two wars now I have put the government on the blink for clothes. I should think they would begin to learn something by now."

Within the first week of training he talked about his "favorite Captain", a man named Smith. He particularly liked and admired the Captain, one of whose jobs was to introduce the new recruits to the basics of Marine Corps life, and to straighten out enlistment difficulties. The Captain had already approached him about the possibility of his taking over some of these responsibilities and he said, "I must admit that this job is peculiarly adapted to my powers, and there is no one else (besides the Captain) who could do it as well. In fact, I think I can beat him at it." He also told her that he was invited to mess with the non-comms, but declined. "I want no privileges," he told her.

Two days later he reported that he had been inundated with letters from friends and relatives, also including the Detroit News — all requesting a photo of him in uniform. "There is nothing here," he told her, "no photographer, no stores, no town, no nothing. It is a tidal island given up to training Marines. It is overcrowded and rough as can be. When I get my full uniform, I mean a complete set of khakis which is all I will get here, I'll get my picture taken for you and my babies and the families. You can publish it if you want to."

At this time, new recruits arriving at Paris Island were billeted in tents, and then were moved to "maneuvering grounds", and only then moved into spartan barracks, which he described as "comparative comfort." Despite Commandant Barnett's efforts, he told her, "this whole establishment illustrates the country's utter lack of preparedness as well as anything I know. They are short on rifles, uniforms, tents — everything. And men are coming in at the rate of 100 to 200 per day. The first quarantine is a dreadful place now, perfectly sanitary, but a bedlam, a swarm of men running around in the restricted quarter like flies. Some are kept there two or three days after they have taken the oath, because of the lack of uniforms and equipment."

On May 20, he described his first Sunday off, and a church service, organized by the men themselves, and how much he enjoyed it. "At the service," he said, "I could not help thinking of what the scene meant — America training to defend the right and save the world. The boys were coarse, common fellows mainly, from all over the U.S., rough, but of good character according to their lights. In a month or two they will be scattered to the four winds all over the world. Whatever they are like individually, it is well to remember that to them and their like are confided the honor of the flag and the protection of a great nation. And I know what they go through to earn the right to take up the country's

276

burdens. Never can I look upon the uniform again without deep respect. I said once in one of my letters to you that most of these boys 'have not the flame', but on nearer acquaintance I find that in their own primitive way they have the flame. I have come to have a great affection for the Boots, and thank heaven, they like me."

By May 24, he had been made acting corporal with the responsibility of marching his company in drills, to and from the mess hall, on marches and work details. "It relieves me of some of the hard manual labor and puts a little responsibility on me." A few days later he indulged in the age-old practice of making a list of "requests" from a relative in civilian life. Among the razor blades, cigarettes and candy is also included "the volume of Edgar Allen Poe which contains the story of 'The Gold Bug'. I think I told you in an earlier letter how this island with its ocean tides, its marshes, its wild sea shore and its mingled palms suggested to me at once a hiding place for pirate's gold and made me think of Stevenson. Well, it seems," he confided, "it has a traditional legendary fame as a pirate's resort, and is said to be the scene of 'The Gold Bug'. I want to read the story again to see what there is in the statement." He worried why he had not yet heard from his little brother Garvin, and suggested that perhaps Garvin is sore at him for resigning his directorship of Denby Trucks, of which Garvin is president.

By May 28 he said he had gotten lucky, that he had gotten a second shirt from the Quartermaster's Department, which now means, over a month after having arrived on the island, that he will have one clean shirt to wear while he is washing the other one, and won't have to go around in his undershirt while his only shirt is drying. He lamented, "Unpreparedness is certainly criminal! Will our country never wake up and furnish me with pants!?"

On June 2, he wrote that he had heard from Olga, his older brother Graham's wife. "But not a word from Garvin. He probably does not know that I resigned from every directorate on which I served when I enlisted. I do not know which have been accepted.

G. probably thinks I only resigned from the Denby. Talk it over with Charlie and see if G. is sore or what. It is most strange that he has not written me a line."

In the same letter he also said that the Sergeant Major, "the queer old Swede who is ranking non-comm and is said to run the whole show", has also approached him with the information that the Colonel and Major Beadle both want him to consider taking over "the job as recruit instructor relieving Captain Smith." He said it was the same old thing which they keep talking about and never doing anything about it. The Sgt.Major says he supposes that Denby wants to get to France, and on this subject, he is frankly blunt as he tries to reassure Marion. "No," he answers, "I have no right to want to go to France. Wherever ordered I shall of course go, but I shall not ask to be sent." He has, deep at heart, no delusions about actual combat being a younger man's game, or about committing deeds of valor in excess of his physical abilities. "The old Swede was evidently much pleased that I was willing to undertake the recruit job. And today I was told that I was to be examined for Corporal very soon. I guess that settles it, and you may very soon be addressing me as Corporal Denby. I am told I shall have a separate tent, and no assigned duties except the instruction of recruits, and if I want it, some drilling of rookies.

"In this new work (if I get it) I shall be the last man to talk to the citizen and the first to talk to the enlisted man."

On June 6 he reported that the first of his new clothing has actually arrived. "Unfortunately," he says with obvious disappointment, "they fit very badly."

On June 11 he allowed a moment of sarcastic criticism to enter into their dialogue, as he ventures a jab at an old political competitor: "I am glad Truman Newberry has been given a commission in the Navy. All he has to do is keep sober and he will make a good officer. Wonder what his job will be? I was amused by your statement that with $150 given by the Department and what he could put in, he might have 'some uniform'!" He had heard from his old friend, Winifred Lyster, mother of his Law

School and Yosemite pal, Henry Lyster. "It seems Tom (another Lyster brother) goes to France soon. So she will have two sons and one grandson in the service. The Lysters have never been laggard in their country's wars."

After six weeks on the Island he reported that he had been promoted to Corporal, but not gotten his stripes as yet, and had been reassigned to "First Quarantine" for his new duties. He also breathed a sigh of relief that he has finally gotten "one long, long letter from Garvin, setting at rest all my doubts."

On June 21 he recounted that Captain Smith accosted him and told him the Major General Commandant was on base and that he should go back to Quarantine Barracks in case Barnett stopped by there. "So I toddled back," he said, "and all the applicants were gathered together outside the office porch — 440 about in number. Presently the automobile truck drew up. I was on the porch as General Barnett, Colonel Macauley and the staff of the local and visiting officers got out and came on the porch. I saluted, like the rest of the non-comms, in strict military fashion, and I stood at attention. But nothing doing, the General came up to me all smiles and cordially shook hands and said nice things. He said this visit to Quarantine was expressly for the purpose of seeing me and was very complimentary. Col. Macauley was equally cordial. All this in the presence of the applicants and our own men. The General said he was a classmate of Gilbert Wilkes at the Naval Academy and asked after Hattie. He also said he sailed on a warship as a midshipman when Father, then Minister to China, was a passenger. He said he supposed I did not want to go to France. I said, as I have said before, that I am perfectly ready to go where ordered, but had no right to ask to go nor to want to go, that I expected to go without question when the need arose, but was not trying to be sent now. All of which he cordially approved and said with truth that I would be of much more use at home ("Here", I think he said — ouch! That means Parris Island). He also said he saw Charlie in Washington recently.

"The General could not have been more friendly, and seldom is an enlisted man given such honor. You know Barnett is like Joffre or Pershing down here — the head of the Corps and personally very popular. Of course, this great attention to me, so conspicuous, spontaneous and unexpected, made a deep impression on officers and men alike — and I must say gratified me."

In July he traveled to Washington, apparently on an extended weekend pass. He had plans to meet there with his friend from New York, Dr. Russell Hibbs, but when he arrived, Russell was out and so he headed over to Marine Headquarters. Dropping into the Commandant's office without an appointment, he persuaded the Corporal on duty to take his name in anyway, and then seemed amused at the astonished look on the young Corporal's face when he was summoned directly into the inner sanctum. He chatted with Barnett, Macauley, a General Lancheimer and Colonel Porter whom he had known from Detroit, and was presented to all the other officers on hand. Everyone knew the story of the great patriot who was working his way through Parris Island, and all wanted to meet him. "Everything was delightfully informal," he afterward told Marion, "and a good time was had by all — with no tangible results whatever, except that I am still headed for Port Royal with the evident desire on the part of the authorities that I stay there until the Corps is recruited up and the rush is over." He said that there is no word of a commission for him and sounds almost bitter that one has not been offered. He referred to the newly minted young officers as "Babes in diapers", and said that he really didn't want a commission, but that it would be nice if they offered him one. "The net upshot of everything is that they want me at present on Parris Island and then [when the appropriate time comes] I am to ask for what I want. Another thing is they WILL NOT (his emphasis) treat me like the ordinary enlisted man." He insisted that he wanted to earn what he got from the service. His pride coveted the privilege of commission, but his honor insisted on service.

He hooked up with Russell for lunch, and then the two of them headed up to the Capitol Building, his old stomping grounds.

Though the House was not in session, as it was Sunday, they visited "dear old Uncle Joe", Joseph Cannon, his longtime pal. Uncle Joe and retired fellow Republican congressman from New York, John Wilbur Dwight, took the two visitors for an extended automobile ride all over Washington, including stops at the Soldiers' Home and Arlington. "Russell simply fell head over heels in love with my blessed old man, who is the most lovable old gentleman I have ever met."

He mentioned that Hibbs commented upon the queer workings of destiny, adding that "if I had done what he wanted me to do I would now be President of the United States, instead of Corporal of Marines." Apparently this had been a running, chiding disagreement between them, but he added, "He forgives me everything, even for refusing to be President at his desire."

After Russell had returned to his practice in New York, he told her that on Monday, July 25, he had again visited Congress. "On that day I went up to the House and Senate to see old friends in their committee rooms, I saw John Weeks [then Senator from Massachusetts, and later to be Secretary of War in the same cabinet with Ned], Speaker Clark [Champ Clark, speaker of the House from 1911 to 1919] (who was very nice and said he had always had a very warm feeling for me, etc.). Then I saw Uncle Joe and had quite a chat with him. He is still not quite reconciled to my being a private and wants me kept safe — 'for the country' etc. etc. (I'm too sweet, you know.) I told him that seldom in my life had I met a man for whom I felt so great an affection and I wanted him to know it and to remember it always. We parted quite sadly." Joseph Cannon, served for another six years in congress, and at the time of this parting, was 81 years old. He would die in his home in Danville, Illinois in 1926 at the age of 90.

"I went through a back door into the Republican Cloak Room and met a number of old friends then. Longworth [Nicholas Longworth, congressman from Ohio and married to Teddy Roosevelt's daughter, Alice — later to be Speaker of the House], Billy Wilson [William Warfield Wilson, congressman from Illinois and fellow University of Michigan graduate], and others of the younger men threatened to drag me on the floor, but I told them to take a door, [and] remember that I came from a training camp — and come if they dared. They did not come out, and I did not go out on the floor. So I lost another chance to be a hero, but I think they all respected me for it. I simply couldn't put over the spectacular play when the time came." Honor trumped privilege, and humility trumped grandstanding.

Two incidents which he mentioned to her round out this eventful trip to the nation's capital: "At the station in Washington," he said, "I saw a handsome Marine Officer whom I duly saluted and passed by. He came after me and said, 'Are you going to Quantico, Corporal?' I said, 'No, sir, I am going to Port Royal.' He then asked my name which I told him quite truthfully. He laughed and said, 'I knew it! No other corporal in the service would have a porter carrying his suitcase!' It was a fair, and as it happened, correct deduction," he admitted, "but many corporals on furlough would do the same." Hardly.

After boarding his train he said he spent a very pleasant evening "with a First Lieutenant of Artillery, and also Governor Stuart of Virginia, a nice old geezer, nephew of J.E.B. Stuart, the great Confederate Cavalry leader. [Henry Carter Stuart, governor of Virginia from 1914 through 1918.]

Two days later he wrote to her about another relative of a famous person. One of the new applicants that day was "Edgar Allan Poe, Jr., a descendant of the great writer and related to all the football Poes of Princeton. This boy is a junior at Princeton, and seems like a very nice fellow. He is good looking and reminds me of the pictures of the great Edgar." In the same letter he mused, "Honestly, this island wasn't meant for humans to live on. That's why the Marines took it."

The next day, complaining about all the construction and other noises all about him he waxed poetic:

"Carpenters hammer,
Applicants yammer,

And there is no glamour
In the military service
But God reigns
And our country needs us all."

He again mentioned Poe: "I had a long talk with Edgar Allan Poe, Jr. last night. He is a very refined, well educated man — possibly a little bit affected in spots. He says 'clark' for 'clerk', for instance, a la anglais. But seems to have the real stuff in him. He speaks French and German. We talked of everything under the sun, Japan, the war, literature, much about his illustrious namesake and collateral ancestor. The first Edgar was not his lineal ancestor, of course, because he died, like Nathan Hale, childless. Poe is, after all, one of the Reserve Officers." Later in the letter, he added, "I forgot to mention in regard to Poe that his uncle was an officer of U. S. Marines. He went to England during the war, joined the Black Watch and was killed in Europe. Two cousins are also in the Allied Service." For Ned, nothing defined quite like service to country, nor curried respect like military service.

At the end of July he lamented, "The military situation in Europe is, I think, very, very bad, and I should not wonder if our situation at home would become bad before we are many months older. I hate to be pessimistic," he said and then went right into it, "I only pray that we may not be too late, and that 'finis' may not be written after America, before we can recover and protect ourselves." He was further upset that , "At this moment, the greatest newspaper power in the world perhaps, the Hearst combination, is urging peace between the Allies and Germany, and blaming the United States for doing anything to prolong the struggle — on the ground, supported by well written and most plausible arguments, that we are too late to give aid in time and that we cannot beat Germany. So they want the United States to urge peace upon Europe! And make peace itself. Millions of persons will be convinced of their propaganda, and, if they are wrong — which they seem to me to be — the harm done will be incalculable. William R. Hearst is the Kaiser's most efficient servant at this moment!" Some things are simply NEVER new, and history DOES repeat itself.

Almost in vindication of his fears, by August 5th he was talking to her about rumors he had heard of riots that had broken out in some places protesting service in the military. He mentioned Oklahoma, and young men refusing to register for the draft, saying that they would rather die in America than be killed in France. This upset him greatly. "How the cable will sing with this news if the half I have heard is true, and how Berlin will rejoice! 'Americans refuse to fight!'," he speculated, and 'Revolution threatened!!' he imagined the screaming Berlin headlines.

At the same time he settled into his new duties. He developed the lengthy lecture that he gave to all new recruits about what it meant to be a Marine. Part of his duty was also to ferret out those young men who had enlisted fraudulently — being underaged, or enlisting without parental or marital consent. Here he told her that he had just been interrupted by another "yellow spot" (coward) — "….he came into my room. I had my eye on him before, marked for a quitter. He said he came to me because I was bighearted and he wanted to talk to me. And he began his story by saying he was a 'German sympathizer'. He got no farther. I interpreted him to himself. Finally I warned him that if he repeated such a statement to anyone else he would assuredly go to a military prison, but that I wanted to give him the benefit of the doubt, because I knew he was not a German sympathizer, but was merely lying to try to avoid the oath. He will take the oath tomorrow." One of the hundreds of youngsters he was to help in the next few months.

Later in August he heard from his older brother Charlie, who had long been a bit of a misanthrope. After a paragraph of news about his recent vacation at the private Huron Mountain Club in the Upper Peninsula and having visited Marion and the children on the way home through lower Michigan, he says, "business continues fine, shipments and orders are both satisfactory…" But it is not business that has him down, it is life itself. "I am filled with personal uneasiness and vague apprehension, but the causes do not arrive from material nor describable grounds. I am feeling my age, brother Ned! The time for great accomplishments is passing or past — I shall never be great nor rich and many aspirations will die unattained — and the worst of it is that it is of no importance that they should be attained — This war has made everything human of no importance. I believe in fact that I should be more contented if I had accepted that quartermaster appointment. Activity and performance of duty fill many soul gaps. I congratulate you Ned on your choice of a role in life." Charlie had been ground up a bit by the mill and disappointment of life. In time it will come for his brother as well, only a few more years in the future.

In mid August he was notified of his promotion to Sergeant, which had to make him feel better since two of Marion's brothers, in the Army, had already attained that rank. He half jested, "Both he (her brother Cleve) and Tom are away ahead of poor Brother Ned — but they are not regulars and particularly they are not Marines. Some day I'll surprise them by being a Sergeant, too."

On Tuesday, August 21 he was again hit with a wave of loneliness, missing her. "My darling," he started his second letter of the day, "This is just a little extra letter. I just wanted to drop you a line to tell you I love you. Once the idea took root in my mind, I had to do it. I was reading over the drill manual when it came over me that it would be nice to chat a minute with you again. My regular letter was written and mailed this a.m. So this one doesn't count — Only I love you, you see, in the afternoon as well as in the morning......."

The same day a Colonel McLemore arrived on Parris Island inspecting the troops, heard Denby's name mentioned and came over to him to shake his hand. "He knew Charlie," he explained to her, "was shipmates with him and Martha and Mother across the Pacific in 1895 when they were on their way back to Peking after C. & M. were married. Then he noted my corporal's chevrons and said, 'You are a Sergeant now, aren't you?'" Everyone seemed to know Denby's business, and presumably all were in some awe of him. It was no secret that they all wanted to meet him.

The next day he wrote that the Detroit Free Press Sunday paper had come with her last letter and that he had "carefully read all the special articles about the war. Evidently the Allies are winning — to judge from allied newspaper reports. And quite evidently the world will not refuse to think peace at the slightest opportunity. If they ever declare a truce to discuss peace the war will never be resumed. Pray for a truce!" he begged, and yet understood already what a two-edged sword it might turn out to be. "That is," he equivocated, "if the preliminary lessons are satisfactory. I do not want to have to lick Germany a second time, or," much worse, "make Ned [Jr.] do it."

He found several verses of the military song taps from a non-comm's Manual he had been reading. Taps, the official bugle call to signify lights out, found its present form during the days of the Civil War, arranged by Union Army Brigadier General Daniel Butterfield. Within months of its debut, this popular tune was being used by both Union and Confederate forces. Captain John Francis Tidball is credited with establishing the custom of playing taps at military funerals in 1862. Taps was officially recognized by the United States Army in 1874, and for use at military funerals in 1891. "I enclose on a separate sheet of paper three sets of words for Taps," he said. "The first is the best, I think. The third is for the last call over a soldier's grave. The sentiment of the second one more nearly reflects my nightly thoughts than the others. The words I use are best of all."

1.	2.	3.
Fades the light;	Love, goodnight;	When your last
And afar	Must thou go	Day is past
Goeth day,	When the day	From afar
Cometh night	And the night	Some bright star
And a star	Leave me so?	O'er your grave
Leadeth all,	Fare thee well,	Watch will keep
Speedeth all	Day is done	While you sleep
To their rest.	Night is on.	With the brave.

Late in the month he came back to revisit the letter he had received from a depressed Charlie, which he had forwarded to Marion for her comments. "It [the letter from Charlie] strikes me as quite sad. Possibly sub-conscious worry about James [their son who is overseas and presumably in harm's way] is the cause of the dejected tone of poor Charlie's thoughts. Of course, you won't let him know that I sent it to you, I think it true that both Charlie and Martha have been too self-centered to find much real happiness. They have planned everything for themselves and their family only, without conscious selfishness but merely leaving out of consideration other duties and interest. Now the great calamity finds them mentally ill-adjusted to meet it. 'Soul gaps' are frequently the result of too much self in the cosmos — and yet not quite enough to completely dull the spiritual perception. A selfish person can only be happy if so utterly selfish as to be quite blind to the fact. I must cultivate that kind of complete selfishness. It must be a joyous state! And Charlie congratulated me upon my role in life!

"I hope you will be very nice to Charlie and Martha. They must carry a heavy load of anxiety and apprehension, however little they may show it. Their habit is to control their emotions and suppress their display, but they love their boys very much, and must feel keenly the fact that James is going into dire danger for all they know. Think how we would feel if our little Corporal were crossing the sea to enter the great war! I do hope most fervently that they have had news of the safe arrival in England or France of the ship James is on."

On the last day of August he wrote that it had been six weeks now since he said his goodbye to her in the still-new Michigan Central Depot in Detroit after his leave home. He also treated her to a history lesson, comparing the unpreparedness of the country leading up to the War of 1812 with the current situation. An avid reader his entire life, he now quoted extensively from James Fenimore Cooper's 1846 History of the United States Navy. "He says (p.22), 'It is an axiom as true as it is venerable that a divided power becomes an irresponsible power.'" He went on to explain the causes leading up to the War of 1812, describing the incident between the British man-of-war HMS Leopard and the USS Chesapeake. The Chesapeake, rightfully refusing to allow the British to board her, was fired upon unexpectedly at point blank range, having to strike her colors after sustaining many dead and wounded. "That was England's way with weaker nations one hundred and ten years ago" he said, and continued, "On page 32, Cooper says 'To the wrongs inflicted on the American commerce by means of her illegal blockades and forced obstruction of colonial privileges England, however, added the intolerable outrage of impressment from on board American vessels on the high seas. England may find her justification for the practice in her necessity, perhaps, though necessity is but a poor apology for a moral wrong." So Germany, which had earlier that year re-instituted the heinous policy of unrestricted submarine warfare, and who also sanctioned the wholesale destruction of entire French and Belgian villages, was to be condemned in the same manner as his ancestral countrymen had condemned England 100 years before.

"And worst of all, the following," he continued to quote from Cooper's account of the treachery of the English: "'in the winter of 1812 a plot on the part of the English agents to sever the American Union was revealed to the government.' I wonder who the English Zimmerman was in 1812," he ponders, "and whether he promised to give part of our country to another power?

"All this was more than a century ago," he concluded, "but one can't help remembering! We taught England to abandon her illegal practices as we are now going to teach Germany to give up her infinitely worse habits."

By September he was getting daily passes to visit the nearby town of Beaufort, and beginning to make plans for Marion and the children to join him in South Carolina. He discussed at least four servants, including their 'driver', a man named Julius whom they had recently had to confront over certain irregularities.

Marion had written that she had found Julius taking the car in the evenings, unbeknownst to her, and that his motives were less than stellar. At first aghast, he exclaims, "I feel I ought to get mad at his using our car to cart around ….girls. If he can't do better than that he had better waive his exemption and go to war." On September 13 he wrote, "Your letter of yesterday made me proud of you, I know how hard it is for you to talk turkey to people and discuss their disreputable personal affairs. It must have been terribly trying to have it out with Julius but I am very glad that you did. I am glad, too, to remember," he confessed, "that I did give him permission to use the car as he said. I had forgotten it. So we can exonerate him on one charge at any rate. The treatment of his wife is another thing, and of course he ought not to use our car (and our gasoline) to drive bad girls around." The ultimate fate of Julius was unrecorded, but one might suspect that his Mrs. was no more amused than was Marion Denby.

He struggled at times with greater questions than chauffeurs and their peccadillos, and said that "I have been down in the dark places with my soul and prayed (I suppose it might be said) my way back." He wants her never to forget that "two thoughts only kept me going at times, one was of you, sweetest and dearest of women, and strongest of soldiers' wives, and the other was that my country needed all its gentlemen to offer their lives under its banner.

"Oh, but it has been rough at times!" However, the tide of lonely effort seems to be turning. "Now it all seems so easy. I can hardly realize how much I really suffered. All that is over. I am one of the non-comms." Given the immeasurable esteem in which he held these valiant citizens, it is impossible to exaggerate the significance of this statement. But he said more, "I like the boys, they like me. I have found many good companions among them — and I know 'that the backbone of the army is the non-commissioned man.' The life is easy now," and here he is speaking of the mental part necessary to endure all hardships past, present and future which a Marine in wartime must face. "I am accustomed to it. I am used to the men. I am one of them at last, so soldiers are made." How profound an epiphany this is for him comes in his next paragraph in which he once again extols the two passions of his life.

"With you coming," he said, "the last trifling hardship will disappear. So I feel that I am emerging from the valley and the hilltops are all glory crowned. How much I have gained! First, the deep and tender knowledge of the woman I love, how strong she is and how brave and cheery. Then, a tender intimacy with the flag, and with the dead of old and the dead and living of all time who have loved it and fought for it and for the ideals for which it stands. And the great, simple, beautiful thought that in 1917 as in 1861 [the year his father answered the call] and 1776 the flag did not call upon its gentlemen in vain. Is it presumptuous to feel that a golden chain stretches from Valley Forge through Gettysburg to Parris Island? Is not Washington still our leader? Is not Lincoln's gentle hand still guiding us onward? Those two, who have more profoundly influenced American life than any others, are they not immortal? They live today, beseeching, urging, restraining, inspiring their countrymen as effectively as though they spoke through living lips. The are not dead. They cannot die. They cannot die. They are immortal. And when all lips that today breathe their names in love and reverence are dust in the tomb, they still will be a living, triumphant force for good in the republic.

"Is that what the church means by immortality? If so, it is the truest fact in the universe," he concluded.

After many weeks of almost daily trips into tiny Beaufort (pop. about 2500 in 1917), and much walking back and forth to all parts of the town tracking down leads on rental properties, he had at last found a place suitable for his family to join him. In late September he was ready to return to Detroit and gather his little flock for the trip south. It would be a new adventure in all their lives, and one that none of them would forget.

(Note: *All Ned's letters from boot camp are found in the Edwin Denby, Jr. papers, Burton Collection, Detroit Public Library, Box #1*).

Chapter Sixteen

"When a man feels about his colors as he does about the reputation of his sister or his wife, and would give his life to save them from stain, why, then, he's a Marine!" letter to his brother

Garvin, 1918

Marine Corps; The Speech

At one point Ned mentioned in a letter that he had had something near 60,000 recruits pass before him through the Island. Parris Island was the major recruit training facility of the Marine Corps at this time, and so virtually all recruits after himself would have done just that, passed before him. Not only did he troubleshoot enlistment problems by acting as a godfather/guidance counselor, but he delivered the main indoctrination speech to all new recruits, mandated not only by the Marine Corps, but by the Secretary of the Navy. The Corps rose from 13,000 to over 70,000 men in a very short time. The United States was at war from April, 1917 to November 11, 1918, only nineteen months. Ned himself was dispatched to France in August of 1918, and so in a very short time, he must have delivered his speech a great many times. The primary function of the speech was to prepare raw recruits to acclimate themselves into a Corps at war.

He began with five general points of instruction, the first of which is the fact that from the moment they have set foot on Parris Island they are now subject to military discipline. Military law is different from civil law, and was first established by an act of the Continental Congress in 1775. Ned stressed for the men that they are to learn to take orders and to perform any task ordered. In addition, he sternly warned them never to shirk work — ever. His second point, emphasizing why it is he who is standing in front of them, is the location of his office, and his open invitation to make him their confidante. Most of them will respect this, and of the ones who do not, the experienced attorney is more than adept at spotting where the troublemakers reside. In his third point he carefully explained General Order NO. 312 of the Navy Department, warning them about unauthorized absences, sleeping on post, and his own pet peeve: drunkenness. He reminds them that Prohibition is the law of the land, and opines, "Keep away from in front of the bars if you want to keep out from behind the bars." (Edwin Denby Papers, DPL, Box #9)

Next he covered the subject of pay and allotments, insurance and savings programs. He told them that certain offenses, some of which he has just covered, include loss of pay, which will mean the loss of any allotment they may have elected for the assistance of loved ones. Base pay for a United States Marine in 1917 was a whopping $30.00 per month, from which $0.20 was automatically deducted for the hospital fund. If the Marine is married, his wife will automatically receive $15.00 from his base pay, plus $15.00 from the government. In addition, she will receive $10.00 if they have one child, another $7.50 if they have two, and another $5.00 for each child over two. A Marine's wife not needing her allotment needed to prove to the government that she does not, in writing. He further explained that in the case of an unfaithful wife, a Marine may make application to have the allotment denied, which means paperwork and an investigation. After covering insurance and war bonds, which the Marine may also have deducted from his pay, he cautions them not to cut themselves too short. He told them that it had been determined that the average enlisted man could survive on $7 to $10 per month, and he enumerated that this would cover such things as scrub brushes, soap, polish, clothing stops and other small articles, including tobacco, for those who used it.

His last major point of his opening remarks was to begin to explain to them the long and very proud history of the Marine Corps, and its unique relationship with the U. S. Navy. "The Navy never won a great battle that we did not help to win. The Navy never lowered its flag in defeat, and that it has done very rarely, but we stood by with bowed and sorrowing heads. You are about to join the Corps — never disgraced and unafraid." (Ibid.)

Next, he enumerated the peacetime duties of the Marine Corps, of which there are four.

First, the Marines furnish guard details for the capital ships of the Navy, as well as many other ships as well. The Marine guard usually makes up about 1/10 of the complement of the ship.

Second, the Marines furnish garrisons for our overseas possessions. He told them that only that very year, 1917, the United States had purchased the Virgin Islands for $25 million, and he said, "The day the flag of Denmark went down, and the flag of the United States went up, 500 Marines landed as garrison, and 500 Marines are there today. So, you will find Marines in Guam, the Philippine Islands, Hawaii, Samoa and other islands of the South Pacific. And you will find Marines in Panama and the islands of the Atlantic." (Ibid.)

The third duty of the peacetime Marine Corps is guarding Naval installations ashore.

The fourth duty he called "being the right hand of Uncle Sam. The Marine was, and is, and will again be, the right hand of the government for the protection of American lives and interests wherever they are threatened the wide world over, and for the carrying out of our foreign policies everywhere." (Ibid.)

Then he explained to them what they will face while they are on Parris Island. They have arrived and will remain at the Quarantine Station just as long as it takes for their papers to arrive, for them to be physically re-examined, and then to take the final oath. As soon as they take the final oath, they will receive their uniforms and then "go over the fence," meaning they will be fully "in" the Corps. He said that formerly they actually crossed over a fence which is no longer there, but the figurative term had remained.

As soon as they "go over the fence," they will be moved to the Maneuver Grounds, the first great training camp. He explained that the Maneuver Grounds are very different than they were just a year before when he came through. "When we went there we lived exactly like an army on the march. We lived in tents. We ate out of our mess gear, standing in long lines to receive our food from field kitchens. Then we searched the ground carefully to find places which looked as though they would not actually blister if we sat upon them, and there sitting on the ground, we ate our chow. Very shortly, of course, we could not eat at all unless our food was well seasoned with sand, but there was little trouble on that score because it generally was well seasoned with sand. We had no showers and we had no head. The head, by the way, is the term used in the service to indicate a water closet, or privy. Our head was simply a ditch which we would dig somewhere in the woods." (Ibid.)

With the pride of those who had gone before, he told them that when he arrived on Parris Island, "there was on this island no buildings of this character. There are now 280 such buildings at the Main Training Camp, and when I look back upon it, I feel quite sure that I personally built every one of those 280 buildings with my own hands for your comfort and luxury. At least my company, out of its brief training period of 10 days, under bitter sun, carrying lumber, manning the sawmills, unloading barges and loading and unloading trucks. We did not like it. We do not expect you to like it, but you will do it just the same if your company happens to be around when the work is to be done." (Ibid.) After certain basic skills are learned, they will then move to the Training Camp. Besides more of the same training and drill, they will take part in parades, reviews, battalion drills with other troops, in formations of up to 2000 men.

After Training Camp, they will go to the Rifle Range for three weeks of intensive instruction in the care and firing of their primary weapon, the rifle. He described in great detail what will be expected of them in qualifying, and the great emphasis which the Marine Corps places upon every Marine qualifying. He said that after their training is over they will have learned to do four things well:

1. Be obedient
2. Be disciplined
3. Shoot well
4. Use the rifle with the bayonet

He said that if they learn to do those four things, they will be Marines; all things else can be built upon that foundation. "Those are the four great elements of the foot soldier." (ibid.)

The speech covers 45 type-written, single-spaced, legal-sized pages, and he said that it had taken him over twelve hours to dictate it to a stenographer.

He concluded the speech in a manner characteristic of his well known, even famous, patriotism. "All through your service you will have the pride and glory of the thought that you are offering all for humanity, and for your country, and that is enough to make things seem easy. You may think me childish," he said, and then he admitted, "perhaps I am. But to me the sight of the flag takes the hurt and the pain out of most things. To me the flag seems like some beautiful spirit, lovingly brooding, always, over our ships at sea, and our camps at home, and the battle line of our men at war; the spirit of the nation looking down in sympathy on its sons." (Ibid.)

In January, 1918, Ned was discharged from enlisted service, and re-enlisted one day later as a 2nd Lieutenant. Scarcely a month later, the family received a telegram from Gilbert Wilkes in Paris via Charlie in Washington, D. C., that their sister Hattie had passed away on Monday February 11, 1918 from a long and unspecified illness. Her death had not been unexpected. Hattie had gone to Switzerland in 1911 right after Ned had left the Congress. She wanted to be closer to both of her boys who were in school there. At the outbreak of the war, the family had moved to Paris where Hattie involved herself in Red Cross work, while both boys became involved in the American war effort from France. Hattie was only 55 years old. (EC 2-14-1918)

By March Ned was promoted to 1st Lieutenant, and by July he was petitioning the powers that be for a chance to get overseas. On July 1, 1918, he received a polite but firm denial from Major General Commandant Barnett, assuring him that his usefulness at Parris Island was much too great to allow him to leave at that time. However, Barnett did add that "at a later date favorable action may be taken on your request, provided a relief is found who is suitable to General Cole." Nine days later he was promoted again, making Captain on July 10, 1918, and having found a suitable replacement, he received orders, and by August 15 was on his way to France aboard the USS Henderson troopship, which would figure prominently in his life in the coming years. In an ironic twist of fate, his replacement turned out to be Lieutenant Arthur Brennor Jacques, who had once served as a page in the House of Representatives at the time that Ned was a congressman. Before sailing for France, Ned penned a passionately patriotic letter to his younger brother, Garvin.

"I just watched 1,400 men marching to the dock to go away — Marines, trained and ready. I wish we had a million like them in France. Splendid youngsters, sun-burned (sun-baked would be a better term), hard as nails, their muscles like steel springs, good shots, full of love of the flag and the service, believing as I believe, that there is no organization in the world equal to their outfit, no fighting men as good as United States Marines — one's heart and eyes play queer tricks when they go marching by. And I am filled with gratitude when I think I have talked to all these men and have talked to at least two-thirds of the United States Marine Corps personnel and many of the officers and have tried to fill them with that love and pride in the service — that esprit de corps that drives men through hell and on to victory. When a man feels about his colors as he does about the reputation of his sister or his wife, and would give his life to save them from stain, why, then, he's a Marine — and all the world knows from Chateau Thierry what that is. Many of our casualties there were men to whom I lectured on thei arrival at Parris Island—poor boys; they followed the white road to duty, and now they are a part of the glorious traditions of their country and their corps. So we must go on and on, dogged, grim, relentless until the end, and many must die. And if I am dogged, grim and relentless and if I must die and leave my wife and babies—why, I, too, am on the white road and will walk it wherever it leads until the suffering world is at peace again and my country needs me no more." (DFP August 21, 1918)

Within days he was dispatched "on temporary duty as an observer of the methods of instruction for Depot and Division Replacements", which appears to have been another way of saying, "Thanks for your great work for us at Parris Island, and now as a reward, take a look around France before war is over." The Henderson put in at Brest, France on August 25. While in France he visited St. Aignan, Noyer, Toul, Nancy, Chalon-sur-Marne, Rheims, Banis and Headquarters of the Second Division at Somme Pi. At the time the Second Division was commanded by Major General John Lejeune who would later figure importantly in Ned's career. The two men and their wives would remain cordial friends for the rest of Ned's life and beyond. On October 24, 1918, he returned to the United States and on December 31, 1918, he was retired from active duty at his own request, the war having concluded on November 11th. On July 26, 1919, he was formally discharged from the Marine Corps with the rank of Major,

Though he did not know it at the time, Ned Denby was not finished with the United States Marine Corps, for he would become its head, as Secretary of the Navy, in only 20 months. He would never forget his service in the Corps, just as he had never forgotten his naval career, his Spanish-American War service, or his Yosemite pals. In the coming years he would make hundreds of new friends among the Naval and Marine Crops ranks, among officers and enlisted, and from the very top of the chain of command to the lowliest private, they would adore the "Seagoing Secretary" to the day he died.

Old Man Denby

Old man Denby, he was a Leatherneck, Damn good Leatherneck,
Number One Leatherneck,
Old man Denby served as a Leatherneck Five short years ago.
Five short years ago, Five short years ago,
And tho' now he ain't what he used to be, Still loves the old
Marines,
Still eats the pork and beans,
Pretty much the same as just what he used to be Leatherneck
five years ago!
Ditty sung to the Secretary of the Navy by the Marine Guard
of the USS Henderson during the Far East Trip, 1922
(Sung to the tune of 'The Ole Gray Mare')

Chapter Seventeen

"Never throughout history has a man who lived a life of leisure left

a name worth remembering."

Theodore Roosevelt

The Lull Before . . .

Somewhat of a challenge faced Ned Denby when, on January 1, 1919, he found himself an upstanding civilian once more. The Denby's had sold their spacious and comfortable home in Detroit's Indian Village during the war and were merely renting quarters not really suitable for a lengthy stay in Beaufort, South Carolina. After the harried pace of activity over the past nineteen months, it was time for the family to get reacquainted with and readjusted to civilian life. Most likely the idea of jumping back into the political and business milieu of Detroit was never far from Ned's mind, still, he owed it to himself and his patient, supportive family to spend some time at home. This they did, in Beaufort, for the following few weeks. Brother Garvin came down for a brief visit in January, while Ned busied himself with his most recent "mission": reforming the practices and procedures which governed the courts martial of the Naval personnel. The "Articles for the Government of the United States Navy" were the laws which governed the conduct of naval personnel from the time of the founding fathers, well over one hundred years earlier. They were not only antiquated, they were patently unfair, as Ned learned first-hand in the Marine Corps, and understood only too well by his training as a lawyer.

As with any other endeavor in his life, Ned took this challenge, to right inequities in the system, completely to heart, and went to any length necessary to achieve his goal. As an example of what some of these inequities were, in a letter from the Post Exchange Officer of Paris Island dated January 29, 1919, he learned that hundreds of recruits had been told they had enlisted "for the duration", only to find later, when the war ended abruptly, that they were obligated for a minimum four-year tour of duty. In February 1919, he went to bat for a Lieutenant Pay Master at Parris Island who, upon a sudden inspection of his books, was found to be short $20. Despite this lieutenant's unblemished record of over twelve years of service, he was charged with embezzlement, as Ned characterized it, "an offense of dishonor." In writing a letter of appeal to then Secretary of the Navy, Josephus Daniels, Ned pointed out that in civilian life the charge "if made at all" (over $20) would be petty larceny, not embezzlement. In a terse two-sentence reply, Daniels informed Denby that the lieutenant "is entitled to a hearing and will not be punished unless he is proven guilty." Hello. To which the exasperated ex-congressman replied, "if having the shortage was embezzlement, then he is guilty on the face of the record, The specification, under the charge of 'embezzlement', is that his books showed a $20 shortage. The shortage was there. He cannot explain it. Therefore, he is guilty of embezzlement. It is shameful that he be tried on such a charge for an incident so trifling."

But he continued, in his own inimitably passionate way, "Do you think it wise, Sir, to let a man be so needlessly dishonored at a time when the whole court martial system is under heavy and deserved attack?

"I have no particular interest in [this man], but I love the Navy and would protect it from deserved censure, as well as undeserved attack." This got him nowhere. (BHL, Edwin Denby Papers, Box #1)

There was more. From typed notes Ned made at this time, he transcribed information from an undisclosed Marine Corps officer source who stated

"When I was first asked to defend an accused person, I being then entirely ignorant of court martial methods, was surprised and somewhat perturbed. I went to the Judge Advocate and told him that I did not feel competent to defend a man for his liberty because of ignorance of military laws and court martial proceedings. He smiled and said in substance, 'That makes no difference. Convictions are almost certain. The best thing that the accused can do is to plead guilty as a rule. His case has been thrashed out at office hours and the charges and specifications examined at Washington, have been approved. He is almost certainly guilty. The court is a busy court and it does no good to consume its time.'" (Ibid.)

With information such as this to spur him, Ned carried the guidon straight to Headquarters, Marine Corps in April on his way home from Beaufort to Detroit. There he met and befriended Colonel Elisha S. Theall, who was at that time legislative legal advisor to the Secretary of the Navy, Josephus Daniels. Certainly his fame would have gained him immediate access to people who might be less available to others. Colonel Theall had graduated from Annapolis in 1897 and spent ten years in the Marine Corps until forced to retire because of heart disease. He then studied law at Columbia, practiced in Washington, D. C. and became an expert in "Congressional, Naval and international law." At the outbreak of the World War he had returned to active commission in the Corps at the rank of Colonel, and had remained after the War as a member of Secretary Daniels staff. (New York Times, January 29, 1921) When Ned came calling, Col. Theall was forty seven years old, just two years younger than Ned, and the two Marine officers obviously enjoyed attacking problems which interested them in common. Shortly after having met Ned, on April 15, Col. Theall wrote him in Detroit to request that Ned "drop me a memorandum suggesting changes in the system in order that I might have them at hand in case an opportunity should present itself to take it up with the Secretary of the Navy." (BHL Edwin Denby Papers, Box #1)

This was akin to asking Carter to supply the liver pills. In a little over two weeks Ned sent Theall a five and one half page typewritten document with his comments on the inequities he saw, as well as his recommendations for improvement. That there were problems with the old system no one in his right mind would deny. That seemed a given. But what stood out in Ned's letter of suggestions was his deep and genuine sympathy for the enlisted man. "One compelling reason why the military laws should be most carefully drawn and conscientiously administered, is the utter helplessness of the enlisted man. When he joins the service, he parts with control of his body and of his freedom of movement in every particular. He is in a sense, a helpless child in the hands of his superior officer. You know as well as I how difficult it is for an enlisted man to secure redress for grievances, in case his immediate superior officer is either unfair or prejudiced." Surely Ned was remembering here his first weeks at Paris Island as a lowly private, and though he most likely never had to fear unjust judicial punishment from the Marine Corps, certainly he was bunkmates with some who did.

So convinced was Ned that the system needed reforming, and that innocent men were being sent to prison, that he stated unequivocally to Theall that "I would at any time, after I became acquainted with the situation, have entered into an agreement with the Government, that if it would release and restore to duty, all those prisoners [then currently in the brig at Parris Island], I would give the Government $100 for everyone who was imprisoned again during the period of the war, or committed any offense of serious character, if the Government would give me $25 for every one that did not, but showed himself a good Marine or sailor thereafter. I should have made a handsome profit on the venture." (Ibid.)

In summary, Ned had several suggestions for Theall to present to his superiors, and they were primarily concerned with the fairness to, and safety of, the enlisted man. In calling for reform, his primary focus was on what he perceived to be overly harsh sentencing for trivial infractions.

"Punishment swift and sure is an aid to discipline, but punishment harsh and unnecessary is not. It is a rotten thing to break young men's hearts by injustice and it is a stupid thing to keep men idle in prison or disciplinary barracks at Government expense, without good reason." (Ibid.)

After not hearing from Theall for two months, and after writing another short letter asking why, Colonel Theall replied at length on July 31. He was career military, and though he tended to defend the ability of the system to "get it right" and to be fair, he did readily agree with Ned on some things that needed to be reformed. In the matter of the officer unfairly charged with embezzlement, however, neither he nor Daniels would budge. "No matter how small the shortage, if unaccounted for, embezzlement is chargeable in the Statutes and in order to remedy this condition Congressional action is necessary," he said. (Ibid.) Though Theall appeared to be sympathetic with Ned's aims, it does not seem that much was done at this time toward real improvement of the antiquated system. Unbeknownst to either of these men, Ned would become Secretary of the Navy, and thus have control of all of this, in just a little over nineteen months. However, Colonel Theall had been involved in an automobile accident on Thanksgiving night, 1919, which fractured his skull, entailing months of recovery, and eventually ended his life on January 29, 1921, only days before Ned was sworn in as his boss.

In mid March, Colonel Albert G. McLemore, assistant adjutant-inspector on the staff of the Major General Commandant, was in Detroit inspecting the local recruiting office. He spoke before the Detroit Board of Commerce, as well as to the Detroit Free Press. He had high praise for Ned Denby's achievement of addressing so many recruits at Parris Island, and in becoming so adept at spotting problem enlistments. "So efficient and so successful was Major Denby in this weighing of manhood that he never had a chance to face shells except for a short time as an observer. He was far too valuable at Parris Island." He further stated that "We in the Marine Corps, believe that Major Denby did more than any one man to inspire our officers and enlisted men with the spirit of service, integrity and cleanliness," High praise from a "regular". On the same day that McLemore was praising Ned in Detroit, the Evansville Courier reported that Ned's oldest brother, Graham, was seriously ill in Evansville.

The Denbys returned to Detroit in April and in an interview with the Detroit Free Press Ned emphasized how important he felt it was for the military in general, the Navy in particular, to reform the court martial system. "One thing I do want to say, without any undue emphasis, but in all sincerity in the world — I want to see a lot of progress made in the movement to change the court-martial system in the United States army. I know that system, as a lawyer, and one who represented many boys in service. The court-martial discussion is timely and necessary, and it should attract much attention." His reasoning was sound, and along definite lines: "The United States is going to build up a big volunteer army. If it is going to be successful, a guarantee that the man who volunteers for his country's service is going to get a square deal, is an elementary proposition.

"It must be settled, to guarantee the volunteer soldier that square deal in courts-martial," he emphatically declared. One wonders if the boys in Washington heard this salvo. As usual, he was in this case several years ahead of history in seeing America's need for a large volunteer army. It would not come until the boys went back to Europe a second time in 1944.

Within days of his arrival back in Michigan he was selected as State chairman for the Salvation Army's National Home Service Fund campaign which was attempting to raise $13,000,000 across Michigan from May 19 to 26. In June Ned was once more appointed to serve his fellow citizens this time as Detroit's representative to the National Advisory committee charged with the task of helping discharged servicemen find appropriate employment. One is led to wonder what civic jobs there might have been at this time without Ned Denby's name on the letterhead.

More seriously, however, was the fact that the brothers were called to Evansville in early June because Graham's illness had reached what appeared to be a critical stage. Arriving

June 10 just in time to preside over some improvement in their brother's health, by Wednesday evening, June 11th, Ned, Garvin and Wythe, who was then living in Chicago, had been able to return to their homes. Charlie had stayed in Washington. Six days later Wythe and his wife, Lucia, were back from Chicago as Graham's condition worsened, and at noon on Thursday, June 19th, Graham passed away at the family home on Upper 2nd Street of Bright's disease. He left his widow, Olga, and three daughters, Martha 17, Caroline 11, and Wythe 8. All four surviving brothers and their families attended the funeral. Graham, still six months shy of aged 60, was now the second of the siblings to pass away, Hattie having died in Paris the previous year at the age of 55. Two days after his death, the Evansville Courier ran a heartfelt tribute to Graham praising him for his generosity of time, legal expertise, and gentle manner. He had been sickly for much of his adult life, but it had never stopped him from sharing with and caring for others. Graham died as had his father, much loved and deeply mourned.

After the funeral, Ned and Garvin took Graham's oldest daughter, Martha, back to Detroit with them for a summer respite. Ned went on the regular summer cruise of the Board of Commerce, and as usual, was one of its principle speakers. In July, Ned's family joined Charles Jr.'s family, including his three sons, James, Charles Jr. and Edwin, at Garvin's estate called Denbrook, which was a few miles west of the city. The party also included their niece Martha, and her girl friend, Miss Dorothy Geissler from Evansville. The same family party gathered again six days later at Ned and Marion's farm near Pontiac. The farm, located in the lake-strewn area north of the city had been a source of great retreat for the Denbys for some years, and would continue to do so in years to come. Charles' family proceeded to Huron Mountain before their sons James and Charles Jr. returned to Princeton, and Edwin entered Harvard.

On Wednesday, August 6, after nearly ten years out of political office, Ned did an about face by throwing his derby into the governor's race. It was an early bid, "giving way to the pressure of friends throughout the state," and perhaps understandable given all the publicity his selfless Marine Corps service had generated. Still, the Free Press reported that "On his arrival in Detroit he refused to consider the matter, but since that time the pressure has been constant and growing." It must've seemed to Ned an offer he could not refuse.

"'Many disinterested persons from all over the state have urged me to become a candidate for the nomination for governor,' said Mr. Denby Wednesday. 'They have strongly represented it to be a duty. So I am yielding to their requests and my name will be on the ballot for the Republican nomination.'" (DFP 08-07-1919)

Most assuredly, the way one talked Ned Denby into running for office was to tell him it was his duty. Marines responded pavlovically to such an approach. The very next day the Grand Rapids Herald, "owned by popular Republican and former Michigan Senator William Alden Smith, commented very favorably upon the candidacy of Major Edwin Denby for governor today, saying 'Major Edwin Denby's entrance into the governor campaign is a wholesome sign, and his fitness for the office and splendid personality will be an inspiration to his friends throughout the state.'" (DFP 08-08-1919)

On August 25 he wrote to his friend Dr. Russell Hibbs who was vacationing at Huron Mountain. Hibbs was a world famous orthopedic surgeon who had pioneered many procedures which might be said to have created the modern field of orthopedics. He was the third surgeon-in-chief of the New York Orthopedic Dispensary and Hospital when barely in his thirties, and in 1918 became the first professor of orthopedic surgery at Columbia University College of Physicians and Surgeons. Impossible as it is to overstate Dr. Hibbs' contributions to medical science, it must be similarly stated that he loved nothing more than to get into the outdoors for a recreational hunting trip. In addition, he had served in the medical corps during World War I, and so he and Ned had much in common. Though Ned had friends whom he had known far longer, and relatives more intimate, there seemed to be no one in his life to whom he confided more of his inner feelings than Hibbs. In 1904 Dr. Hibbs had married Madeleine Cutting of the Massachusetts Cuttings, and the Hibbs and Denbys would remain friends for as long as any one of them remained alive.

"I guess you understand that I did not want this thing," Ned wrote Hibbs about the race for the governorship, "but there seemed no way out, so I am going after it now and I expect to get it," he spoke with unaccustomed bravado. "Possibly it may be worthwhile in the light of accomplishment. We can only wait an see. Anyway, I am not yet elected and just think what a vacation I will have in the winter of 1920 if I happen to have been beaten."

From there, however, he would wax philosophic with the doctor as he would with few other of his friends or acquaintances:

"You speak of not being afraid. There is something in what you say, but not being afraid is not a quality. It's a habit acquired with infinite pains and thought. There is not happiness in the mists except without fear. The white road I used to talk and think about while in the service runs on into peace and must be followed by us all if we are to justify our existence, or even enjoy it, so whether it leads to Lansing or to obscurity is a matter of comparative indifference. It's sticking on it that counts." (DPL Edwin Denby, Jr. Papers, Box #1)

Throughout September Ned made several speeches to different civic groups about his candidacy for the governorship, and a common theme upon which he spoke was his opposition to Wilson's League. Before the Detroit Engineering society in the familiar auditorium of the Board of Commerce building, "America stands best alone," he declared. "Mr. Denby said he had not found one American soldier or sailor who risked his life for the purpose of forming a League of Nations," and cogently pointed out that, "such a league would have resulted in the destruction of this country at the time of the Civil War." Fair-minded Ned then continued, "In regard to the League of Nations, it is unnecessary to call names. The issue is too important to be debased by mutual epithets. I know that I am honest in my opposition to the league as it stands and I know I love America quite as well as those who, as it seems to me, would throttle and destroy her in the silken bonds of league covenant, as it came across the sea. I cannot help feeling disturbed when I think of the contemplated surrender of a part of the independence of the United States and its freedom of action." (DFP 9-6-1919)

On the 10th he spoke in Monroe at the opening day of the harvest carnival, and on the 11th he spoke again to his own Rotary Club, of which he was still president. In this speech he urged his fellow rotarians to read their Constitution. "'It is our duty to Americanize ourselves,' he said. 'We should not lightly discard the ideas and ideals of the past. We should see to it that our instrument so sanctified by time and success shall not lightly be cast aside in the attempt to attain other ideas more distant, more doubtful and far from certain in their results.'" Frank Cody, his friend from the Detroit Board of Education and the Board of Commerce, was chairman of the Wayne County Constitution Day committee, and had talked the pastors of virtually all Detroit churches to preach Constitution Day sermons on the following Sunday.

On the 15th he spoke in Bay City to the local post of the American Legion, the growing World War I veterans' organization begun in Paris earlier in the year by, among others, Lt. Col. Theodore Roosevelt, Jr. Once again Ned warned against hidden provisions in the League which would bind America in ways not heretofore acceptable to freedom-loving Americans. On the 17th he was in Port Huron to speak at the Women's Benefit Association of the Maccabees, along with Governor Sleeper. On September 27 he spoke to a group in Richmond, Michigan, and on September 30, he spoke before an assembly of railroad and transportation men again in the auditorium of the Board of Commerce. His message was the same: joining the League of Nations as it was proposed would hamstring American choices, and destroy the Monroe Doctrine. As with most all Republicans of his day, Ned was one hundred percent against it.

October brought news of a new business venture, this time in partnership with Marion's younger brother, H. T. (Tom)

Thurber. Tom and Ned had formed the H. T. Thurber Company to franchise Barney Oldfield tires in the Detroit area. They had won the contract over fifteen other competitors. Young Thurber, formerly vice-president of a local real estate company, had just mustered out of the United States Navy, and would be president of the new tire company. Ned was vice president and Joseph A. Kennedy, a law partner of Ned's, secretary-treasurer.

To round out the important events of the year, in December the Evansville Journal reported that Ned, a "former Evansville man", had been elected 'President' (presumably of the United States) in a tongue-in-cheek 'campaign' at the fifteenth annual dinner of the Indiana Society of Chicago held that week in the windy city. The newspaper article gleefully reported that some of the opposing candidates were men such as Uncle Joe Cannon, Booth Tarkington, a couple of professional baseball players of the day, as well as a governor, a judge and a general. Also included was Will H. Hays, who had been born in Sullivan County, Indiana, was at that time Chairman of the Republican National Committee which would the following year, among others, get Warren Harding elected to the Presidency in a campaign managed by the capable Hays. He would go on to become Postmaster General in the Harding Administration, and later head the Motion Picture Production Code for over twenty years.

The newspaper reported that "the dinner convention was one of the happiest in the history of the society and many distinguished Hoosiers and ex-Hoosiers were present. "Denby and Barnhart [the man chosen as his veep], the ticket chosen, was 'railroaded' through," while the 'electoral commission' was headed by Wilbur D. Nesbit [famous humorist and poet]. Garbed in all the solemn pomp of the supreme court the commission quite autocratically elected Denby and Barnhart. Nesbit also was chairman of the platform committee, making the big plank one in which the society took a firm stand 'for Prohibition with mild reservations.'" (EJ 12-10-1919)

The year 1920 began with the Russian Civil War between the Whites and the Reds raging in Russia, and the first Red Scare reaching its height in the Western democracies, particularly the United States. The Treaty of Versailles, officially ending World War I, and effectively crippling the German state, took effect in January, the same month the League of Nations held its first council meeting in Paris. The same governments bent upon the humiliation of Germany were meeting to secure world peace and brotherhood in Paris. The United States was not among them. The Allied governments demanded the Netherlands surrender Kaiser Wilhelm II who had fled there at the end of the war, and were categorically refused one week later. He would retire at Huis Doorn, in considerably reduced splendor, and remain there for the next twenty-one years until his death in 1941. Americans officially swore off the 'demon rum' on January 17, and would spend the next thirteen years falling off wagons. America was in the midst of an economic downturn, facing strikes, inflation and massive unemployment, and also bracing for that great American quadrennial event, a Presidential election.

At the beginning of the year, the leading contenders of the two most powerful parties were General Leonard Wood, Senator Hiram Johnson of California, and Frank Lowden, governor of Illinois, for the Republicans, and, surprisingly, the President himself, infirm though he was, for the Democrats. It would take considerable coaxing discouragement from his closest friends and advisors to prevent this suicidal move. Politicos of the same party would not fare as well twenty-four years later when a dying FDR heartily fingered the entire country, and ran for his fourth term. But then, in 1944, there was no one from his party who had the courage to even try.

However much Ned had not wanted to enter the race for governor, it must have been particularly upsetting to him to have to withdraw from it as he did in early February, 1920. He did not meet with the press, he simply issued a statement:

"I am withdrawing today my candidacy for governor. August 7 last I announced that I would become a candidate. Since that time I have repeated that statement, both orally and by letter, to a great many persons. Now, however, I am compelled to withdraw, very sadly and reluctantly, but finally from the campaign. I wish at this time to thank most appreciatively the many friends who have encouraged me."

The Free Press added, "No reason is offered by Mr. Denby for this change of plans." (DFP Feb 4, 1920). It is hard to imagine anyone pushing Ned into something that he did not want to do, and yet, he was literally surrounded with people at all times who insistently wanted what they felt was best for him. It is difficult to gauge from this vantage point how much he was running on his own account, or for others. It is also hard to imagine what his life might have been had he stayed in this race and won it, as he was almost certain to do. But fate had other plans, and it is also certain that Ned was not one to look back with any regret.

Later in the same month, February 1920, he spoke before the Genesee County (Flint) Republican Club banquet, where he strongly urged the Wilson government to cancel European war debts owed to the United States by the Allies. He declared that it only made good business sense to forgive the debt which would go a long way toward restoring order to ravaged economies with which the United States did business. Then he completely took his audience by surprise by further "declaring that the terms of peace imposed on Germany were so heavy that it could never pay them. He advocated that all clauses of the peace treaty which aim at the permanent life of Germany be softened or annulled." He had sound and ulterior motives.

"The problem of problems, the one overshadowing world necessity, is the stabilizing and rehabilitation of Europe. Upon the recovery of Europe from its dreadful wounds and long sickness, absolutely depends the future prosperity of the United States. It cannot be doubted that unless Europe does speedily recover her political, moral and financial balance America will not long keep hers. If we forgive our war debts, and the other Allies follow suit among themselves, 20 billions of foreign debt falls from the shoulders of Europe—foreign war debts, dangerous as dynamite, poisonous to the future friendly relations of the world."
(DFP Feb 11, 1920)

If the Wilson Administration cringed to hear what Ned was saying about being a bit more lenient with Germany, they must have been appalled at his comments four days later concerning the invalided President himself. In an interview on Saturday, February 14, he pulled no punches in addressing the controversy over the firing of Wilson's Secretary of State, Robert Lansing. Lansing had taken over as the head American negotiator at the Paris peace talks, and had run afoul of his own administration for not appearing committed enough to the League of Nations. Furthermore, in the absence of leadership from the President, or from his Vice President, Lansing had called several meetings of the cabinet, and had had the effrontery to suggest that it might be time for Vice President Thomas Marshall to assume the presidency. Incurring the wrath not only of the invalid, but more importantly, of his little educated wife, Lansing was unceremoniously cashiered just the day before Ned spoke to the press.

"It is difficult to speak calmly of the recent developments in Washington." he opined. "The whole situation is medieval in its character. The president's theory seems to be that the wheels of government shall be stopped during the prolonged illness of the executive, or rather, that an informal, unofficial, wholly objectionable cabal shall administer the government, and be the intermediary between the other officials of the government and the ruler. Such things have been done before as a matter of court intrigue or in Oriental monarchies. They have never been done in free America.The President assumes that while he is ill and utterly incapacitated, the heads of the great departments of government shall not meet and discuss, even informally, the affairs of the government — even those which by their very nature demand immediate action and solution. The president's theory passes all bounds. He leaves representative government behind."

As any great orator or speech writer, however, Ned would save his best shot for the last:

"Such insolence, such utter disregard for the interests of the nation should be rebuked with a sureness and swiftness which will make its repetition impossible for all time to come."

Lost in all the fracas of politics, on Wednesday, February 18, Ned turned the big 5-0. There is no record of what he made of this, or if he made anything of it at all.

On March 2, General Leonard Wood was in Detroit for multiple appearances before the party faithful. At a Tuesday morning gathering for women only at the Detroit Opera House, he was introduced to the feminine crowd by Ned. The Nineteenth Amendment giving women the right to vote was being ratified by the States at this time, and became law by the vote of Tennessee on August 20, 1920. It then became certified on August 26 of that year, and changed the course of all political campaigns in the United States from that date onward.

In April he spoke before over two hundred former American officers from the Great War in the auditorium of the Elks Temple, once again arguing for the forgiveness of war debts, and also denouncing the peace treaty as "the most monstrous instrument ever invented".

In June occurred a curious affair which, though it did not directly involve or affect Ned at this time, would later when he took over the Department of the Navy. The Commandant of the Marine Corps served for a four year term. An exception to this rule was the current Commandant, George Barnett. Since his term would have expired in 1918 in the middle of the Great War, it had seemed prudent to extend his tenure for a second four years. At least, that is how George Barnett had viewed his second term. He had successfully turned the United States Marine Corps into an envied entity of the American military, presided over the exploding nature of its size and mission, and then just as successfully guided it through the always painful process of downsizing after the conflict. He had been decorated, feted, and showered with all manner of praise for the herculean accomplishments the Marine Corps had achieved under his command. But suddenly, in the middle of his second term, it was deemed time for him to go.

There is some evidence that Josephus Daniels, Secretary of the Navy through both of Woodrow Wilson's terms of office and a highly complex individual, had tried to meet with Barnett concerning his replacement as Commandant, but was forestalled by a claim of illness on the Commandant's part. There is some evidence as well that Barnett had had an inkling of what was to come. At any rate, claiming that it was now no longer convenient to meet in person, according to Barnett, Daniels dispatched a low-level messenger with the Commandant's letter of dismissal. Forever after, Barnett claimed utter and complete shock at the news of his removal in this manner, short of his full second term, and given days to move his family out of the Commandant's residence. He had faithfully served the Marine Corps for forty three years, six and a half of them as its decorated and successful leader. Four days later, on June 22, Barnett wrote an impassioned letter to President Wilson, urging a reconsideration of the decision, and if not that, at least allowing him to retain the rank of Major General for retirement purposes. Although he did not wish to retire at the time, he felt entitled to pick his own time, and at the higher rate of pay. Of course, Woodrow Wilson remained silent and unresponsive to Barnett's plea.

But why did Josephus Daniels do what he did at this time and to such an honored and respected high officer? There are two possible reasons, and a combination of them seems most probable. According to Smedley Butler biographer, Hans Schmidt, Barnett had "run afoul of Daniels by going behind his back in obtaining senatorial support for his own promotion during the 1918 Barnett amendment fiasco." (Schmidt, p. 110) Furthermore, a faction of the Corps' officers, with whom Daniels agreed, felt the leadership of the Corps was better off with "field officers", or officers who had seen far more field action than had Barnett. Barnett had been called a "rocking chair warrior" by the ultra decorated and flamboyant Smedley Butler. Graduating from Annapolis, Barnett was frowned upon by the action-fueled Butler who had not even graduated from high school. Furthermore, Butler was one of only two Marines ever awarded more than one Congressional Medal of Honor, and he was somewhat understandably prejudiced against desk-bound officers, which he felt Barnett to be.

Rightly or wrongly, both Butler, whose entire career was

abetted by a very influential congressional father, and Daniels, who claimed he had Wilson's agreement to do what he did to Barnett, greatly favored General John A. Lejeune for the commandant's office as a reward for his stellar performance on the battlefields of France. What Ned Denby made of all this wrangling, which became exceedingly public once the Senate got involved later in the year, is not recorded in so many words, but time would very shortly reveal what he DID about it, when he became Secretary replacing Daniels in less than one year.

Chapter Eighteen

"He who treads softly goes far."

Chinese Proverb

The Storm

In the same month that the Barnet putsch was playing out in the nation's capital, far to the west in the great "City of the Big Shoulders", in the Chicago Coliseum where Republicans had held their presidential scrap matches since 1904, they congregated once more on Tuesday, June 8, to select a man to lead their party in what they hoped would be a recapturing of the White House for the first time in eight years. No less than fifteen hopefuls crowded the field as voting for the all-important nomination began on the fourth day of the convention, Friday, June 11. Far and away the most important candidate who was NOT at the convention was the Rough Rider himself, Theodore Rex, who had passed away seventeen months earlier at Sagamore Hill, thus throwing the republican equation into the winds. Though the field was clear for new blood, it was equally clear from the start that the two most popular candidates, Leonard Wood and Frank Lowden, would almost surely cancel each other out, leaving the convention open for an unexpected result. Many rumors swirled around the windy city in the midst of a stifling heat wave, and following the convention and for decades to come, would tsunami into conjectures, then beliefs, then truth itself. Perhaps it was because of the startling outcome of the two day battle, which on the tenth ballot, during the second, long, sweltering day, nominated the movie-star good looking Warren Harding, that myths and rumors grew to such proportion as to be accepted as historical fact within a matter of a few short years.

The very first thing to know concerning Warren Gamaliel Harding, unequivocally and without exception, is the simple fact that 90% of what you think you know about him is probably false. Every school child has heard of the "smoke-filled room" where the Midwestern newspaper editor was supposedly selected by a senatorial cabal to run for the nation's highest office. Every casual student of presidential history knows how a willful, bossy, ambitious harridan virtually propelled her pliant husband into the candidacy. Another profoundly accepted bit of nonsense purveyed about Harding, then and later, was that he was a bumbling, incompetent lush without experience, without brains, and without ideas.

To the last mythical claim about the politician, let's take a look at one of the few biographies of his presidency that was written by a man who actually did research. In "The Harding Era" by Robert K. Murray, Mr. Murray categorically destroyed the idea that Harding was an "accident" who mysteriously happened at the convention.

"The success of Warren Gamaliel Harding at the Republican convention in 1920 was no mystery. Yet the fact that his nomination could come about so naturally, given the circumstances, prompted many to disbelieve its simplicity. After all, Harding was eminently available. He had been on the winning side of most national questions and had rarely taken a stand antithetical to political trends. He was small-town America personified— so much so that when the Lynds performed their famous study of Muncie, Indiana, they uncovered the exact beliefs which Harding displayed. He was genial and open, making few enemies and hosts of friends. He had political experience both at the state and national level. He was known personally—more than Wood or

Lowden, to the delegates, many of whom had seen him in earlier conventions. He had travelled the pre-convention presidential trail carefully and had displayed just the proper amount of reluctance and humility to offset his mounting ambition. He possessed a campaign manager who was quick and daring and complimented Harding's own affinity for conciliation and compromise. Finally, Harding was from Ohio, the mother of presidents and a pivotal state in any national election. Ohio had already provided six out of the ten presidents since 1869. Ohio candidates had a reputation for victory." (Murray, p. 41)

Next, concerning the willful shrew who supposedly drove him to the presidency and his death because of her maniacal ambition, the New York Times reported on June 21, 1920 under the heading, "Mrs. Harding's Foreboding" this fairly blunt quotation from the woman's own lips: ".....I cannot see why anyone should want to be President in the next four years. I can see but one word written over the head of my husband if he is elected, and that word is 'tragedy'." (NYT 6-11-1920, page 3) For those who would claim that Mrs. Harding was merely being coy for the big city reporter, here are the words of Harding's campaign manager concerning Mrs. Harding's presidential ambition: "She never once begged her husband to enter the race. She opposed it from the beginning.... She feared the tragic struggle in which he was entering with a dread that was pathetic." (Both quotations from Murray, p 35 and pp 23-4 respectively)

And up to the eve of the fateful day when he was nominated, let's examine the smoke-filled room cabal of Republican senators. At least this myth is based upon some modicum of fact. On the night after the first several ballots which had left the convention deadlocked, several senators, as well as many other convention delegates, visited the Will Hays, George Harvey two bedroom suite at the Blackstone Hotel to discuss the possibilities of the following day's voting. "They held a floating and freewheeling discussion not a formal cabal meeting." (Ibid. p37) Subsequently, after three Harding supporters made brief statements to reporters in the middle of the night, by morning "the rumor spread that a 'Senate cabal' had arrived at a decision for Harding." But the inconvenient facts happened to tell a different tale. "There were sixteen senators (including the ill Penrose) who were delegates to the 1920 convention. Thirteen of them voted AGAINST [italics added] Harding until the ninth ballot." (Ibid. p.38-9) Hard to understand a cabal which would succeed with its members voting against itself.

The gist of the matter was that Daugherty and Harding had both spent months of hard lobbying and preparation, letter-writing and arm-twisting, to get to this point. And the truth of the matter was that both of these men, whatever other faults each may have had, were tireless and savvy politicians. Far from a dark horse selected by cabal in a smoke-filled room, Harding was, as some have characterized him since, "the available man". So much so, in fact, that one writer entitled his book with this phrase. (Andrew Sinclair, The Available Man, 1965)

From the great city by the lake, Harding next repaired to Marion, Ohio, the hub of his universe. In this bustling cross section of midwestern life was his family, his business, his modest but comfortable home, and a great circle of friends and supporters. Unlike many busy commercial centers of its time, Marion was not located on one of Ohio's rivers, but instead enjoyed an almost unparalleled juncture of railroads for its size. From Marion, it was possible to get anywhere in the country, and vice versa. Undoubtedly, in deciding upon a front porch campaign such as three of his Ohio-born presidential predecessors, Harding and his staff took this significant railroad advantage into consideration. He spent the first weeks working on speeches, and by the third week of July, the flood of voters began to arrive at Marion's Union Terminal. By the end of September, it was estimated that over 600,000 citizens had swept into Marion for a glimpse of the candidate, a parade (daily), and a speech. Contrary to detractors' claims that Harding was kept on a "leash" by being chained to his front porch so he wouldn't shoot himself in the foot, the candidate also managed to give over a hundred speeches in nearly all parts of the country before the election. (Dean, p.72) But the primary pulse of the Harding campaign was the almost continuous speech-making from the porch. So many crowds of people came day in and day out that the entire front lawn had to be covered with stone to keep it from turning into a mud patch. One wonders how Harding's erstwhile neighbors viewed this daily intrusion and confusion. Professional sports teams came, women's groups, politicians, "and even a contingent from Hollywood led by Al Jolson, who serenaded Harding with a song he had written for the occasion." (Ibid. p.72)

On Saturday, September 11, the Michigan Republican party contingent boarded a special 6 car pullman train departing Michigan Central Depot in Detroit at 1250pm. Four days before in an article in the Press, Edward Lovely, chairman of the committee on arrangements, reported that "All of the available seating space in six pullman cars already has been reserved and it now appears it will be necessary to run a (second) special to accommodate the hundreds of Michigan Republicans who are signifying their intention of going." Among the distinguished Republicans on the train were the governor, Albert Sleeper, Alex Grosbeck, the candidate for governor, both Michigan Senators, Truman Newberry and Charles Townsend, Detroit Mayor James Couzens, former governor Fred Warner, former Senator William Alden Smith and, of course, Ned Denby. In fact, Ned was the program chairman. There was also a Women's committee, chaired by Mrs. Edith Dunk, which included the governor's wife, Mary Sleeper, and women from across the state. According to the Press, the train would make stops at Monroe and Toledo to take on additional Republicans, and "Each member of the delegation will be presented personally to Senator and Mrs. Harding." (DFP 9-7-1920) It was the first time that Ned Denby would walk the streets of Marion, Ohio, but it would not be the last. In three whirlwind, lightning fast years, he and the 29th President would return, one mourning, and the other being mourned. According to the schedule provided by the Free Press article, it was a little over three hour trip to Marion with a 1045pm projected return time which left the visitors about two and one half hours to traverse Marion's streets to Harding's porch, hear his speech, shake his hand, and return to their train for the ride home. It also made for a long and late day for the 54 year old candidate and his 59 year old wife. One contemplates a "front porch" campaign as being an easy one, and yet a closer look would seem otherwise.

At any rate, by election day, November 2, the country was poised to hand the reigns of government of the United States over to the opposing party. For the past seventeen months the ship of state had drifted aimlessly and disastrously about the seas of uncertainty, and Americans were heartily ready for a change. The latest polls were showing a 10-1 advantage to the GOP. The day dawned clear and chill in Marion as the candidate and his wife were driven to the polls. Florence Harding was the first woman to vote for her husband for President. It was one of many firsts that this adventurous and fun-loving woman would accomplish in the next three short years. Later that morning, Warren went to the Scioto Country Club near Columbus with Harry Daugherty for a round of golf. In the late afternoon at Harding's residence in Marion there was a small birthday party with staff and reporters to mark the candidate's 55th birthday. As the election results began to arrive, he had every reason to be thankful for the nation's unique birthday gift: he would win the presidency by a landslide unheard of up to that time.

By almost any standard, including the one which had stunned Teddy in 1904, Harding's victory was astonishing. It was the largest victory the Republican party had ever enjoyed.

"He had won thirty-seven states to Cox's eleven. Harding had even managed to crack the solid South by winning Tennessee. His coattails had proved long and strong, for he pulled with him an increase in the Republicans' majority in both the House of Representatives and the Senate. Most striking was the size of the popular vote: 16,152,200 for Harding and Coolidge; 9,147,353 for Cox and Roosevelt; and 919,799 for Socialist Eugene Debs." (Dean, p.77)

There would be many interpretations of the results, as there always are, but the bottom line was a thorough repudiation of Wilson's League, and his post-war non-involvement.

In Michigan, Ned had favored his old pal from House days, Frank Lowden, who had served Illinois' 13th District during Ned's last two terms in Congress. But Ned had dutifully supported candidate Harding during the campaign, and was sure to have been overjoyed at his party's smashing success.

Just before Christmas Ned "was unanimously appointed chief probation officer of the municipal court at a meeting of the Judges Monday [December 20]." The salary of the newly created position was only $4000 per year, "but Mr. Denby has not considered that," one of the judges reported to the Press. "I believe that he has shown himself interested in the affairs of Detroit and has shown that he is indeed a public spirited citizen in taking the position." (DFP Dec 21, 1920) He was given complete charge of all probation systems of the court, and full control of selecting his own staff. There is no question that Ned was thrilled. This was quite similar to the work which he had found so satisfying at Parris Island, and now he was given almost carte blanche in helping the troubled and less fortunate citizens of his beloved Detroit in the rebuilding of their lives. Ten days later Ned announced his first seven appointees for positions in the probation department, including three women and four men. The selections obviously reflected his experiences with Detroit charities, as one of his appointees was from the American Red Cross, one from the Bureau of Catholic Charities, and one from the Children's Aid Society. One man had twelve years' experience with the immigration service and spoke seven languages fluently.

Already in early February Ned submitted the first report of his newly created probation department. Of the 1,999 probationers on the books, 1,552 had shown improvement, while 226 had failed to do so. Over four thousand dollars in restitution had been collected in the first month alone. The report also specified that the largest number of cases fell within the 22 to 31 year old age group. His report further claimed that he felt his staff was already behind the curve in being able to address the number of cases under its care, and therefore, he was considering the use of volunteer probation officers — another innovation of his forward- thinking mind. Once more, one is forced at a juncture of Edwin Denby's life to muse about what might have been had he continued in his newest endeavor. Though without formal training in this area, Ned certainly possessed every life skill most necessary to make it succeed.

After his surprising election success in November, Warren Harding did something quite uncharacteristic of newly elected presidents: he not only went on vacation in Texas for some fishing and golf, but he and Florence took a cruise out of the country to Panama. Another little known fact about the supposedly incompetent Harding was that he was the most widely traveled president in history up to this time. Arriving back in the United States on December 4, the Hardings proceeded to Washington D. C. where they still maintained a residence as he would remain, until March 4, a member of the United States Senate. In fact, once again a first for Harding, he was the first sitting Senator ever elected to the Presidency.

From the moment he had won, Harding had contemplated his cabinet, and even while on vacation, had been working through his list of men whom he sought out for glory. The first member selected by early December was Secretary of State Charles Evans Hughes. From there he worked his way through his cabinet, sometimes getting his first choice, sometimes moving to his second or third. Much has been made of his choice for Secretary of the Navy, the uninformed claiming that he only picked Edwin Denby as an afterthought, and his last afterthought at that. The truth is that he had offered his close friend and active campaigner, John Weeks, the Navy portfolio, and been told by Weeks that he felt the Navy would be a conflict of interest for him since he had graduated from Annapolis in the class of 1881, and would become boss of those with whom he had gone to school and served. As early as January 24, 1921, the Free Press was reporting that it was Weeks who had given Harding Denby's name as his man for the Navy; but Harding demurred. He still felt an obligation to make room in his cabinet for Frank Lowden, as it had been Lowden's decision at the convention on the second day of the hopeless deadlock to release his delegates' votes to Harding. Never one to forget a debt, Harding offered Lowden the Navy job, but received Lowden's emphatic no — three times. Only then did Harding feel free to telegraph Ned on February 22nd,

"Please advise me by wire where I can communicate with you by telephone at two o'clock eastern time period.

Warren G. Harding"

Thus is history made.

Chapter Nineteen

"Wisdom in counsel is certainly desirable; battleships are good;
and the two together — matchless."

Edwin Denby

Secretary of the Navy

Given the truckloads of mire which have been heaped upon the entire Harding Administration for nearly a hundred years, the first days of the new era were actually quite bright, and full of promise. Following a modestly dignified inauguration, a succinct Inaugural Address which simply outlined his conservative agenda, the Hardings returned to 1600 Pennsylvania Avenue to their new home. The first official act of the new President was to order the gates of the White House to be thrown open, and left that way — the way they had always been up to the last two years of the gloomy, secretive Wilson administration.

The new Secretary of the Navy was already busy with his own agenda. In a telling gesture, he approached Major General Commandant LeJeune on the portico of the Capitol Building just after Harding's Inaugural Address. "General," he said, tapping the Commandant on the shoulder, "will you do me the honor of serving as Commandant of the Marine Corps during my term of office as Secretary of the Navy?" (LeJeune, p.472; in addition, in his book LeJeune explains that he had had the unique honor of being nominated Commandant by three successive Presidents, as he was asked by Coolidge, in 1924, to serve for an additional four years.) The following day, March 5, Harding submitted to the Senate the names of two Marine Corps Generals: that of LeJeune, to be confirmed as Major General Commandant (though appointed by Daniels/Wilson in June, 1920, the Senate had chosen not to confirm any further of the lame duck president's appointments), and of Barnett, to be promoted to the permanent grade of Major General, which Wilson and Daniels had inexplicably denied him. Thus Ned settled expeditiously the controversy which had been ignited by his predecessor over the leadership of his beloved Corps.

As early as February 27, the day after Ned had met with Harding in St. Augustine, Florida and accepted as Navy Secretary, perhaps the most important aspect of the process came swiftly with the announcement of Theodore Roosevelt, Jr., as Ned's Assistant Secretary. The eldest son and namesake of the most famous and popular Republican since Abraham Lincoln, Ted was just 33 years old, and became the third Roosevelt to assume the job, after his father (1897-1898) and his cousin (1913-1920). Following quite closely in his father's footsteps, Ted Jr. was decorated for his service in the World War, and was one of the founding members of the veterans organization which had become known as The American Legion. Bright and ambitious, from one of America's "royal" families, Ted was nevertheless loyal, intelligent and hard-working. One of the salient aspects of both men's characters was their shared and deep sense of humor. Both men came to have great respect for each other, so much so that when Ted's wife, Eleanor, wrote her memoirs nearly 40 years later (memoirs Ted was not given the opportunity to write for himself), she spoke of Ned Denby in the most glowing of terms. In fact, she said, "No man ever lived who was more honorable than Denby." (Roosevelt, p.155)

At the same time, in a New York Times article, Ned declared his surprise at being selected for high office: "To put it mildly, I was overwhelmed with surprise when I received a telegram on Washington's Birthday from Mr. Harding, requesting me to come here to discuss with him my entering the cabinet. February 22, strangely enough, is the birthday of both my wife and my mother," he told the Times.

"You ask me if I am glad to get the job? Frankly, I am. I have always loved the navy, for not only have I served there as a sailor and a Marine, but many of my family before me. I was named after my uncle, a Fleet Surgeon, who died in the line of duty, protecting his fleet against the ravages of yellow fever. My great-uncle commanded the mosquito fleet in the Indian River campaign during the Civil War."

Commenting upon the nomination of TRJr. as his assistant, Ned told the Times how pleased he was at the appointment, and recalled his first meeting with Ted's father in 1897 while he was still a member of the Michigan Naval Brigade and the young Teddy was Asst. Secretary. Tellingly, on the same day in 1921, the Times also ran a short article about mail train robbers in Pennsylvania Station who had the day before "attacked and fatally injured J. L. McCullough of Waynesburg, railway mail clerk on Panhandle Train 503 running from Pittsburgh to Washington and Waynesburg, and escaped with registered mail believed to be worth several thousand dollars." (NYT 2-27-1921) As this problem persisted, Ned would deal with this menace to the mails in just a few short months.

In a curious turn of events, Frank E. Doremus, the Michigan Democrat who had defeated Ned for his congressional seat in 1910, had elected not to run in 1920, and on the very day his tenure in Washington was closing, Ned was being sworn in for his second tour of duty in the nation's capital. Owing primarily to the generous nature of the incoming Secretary the Navy, the two men had managed to become good friends over the past few years, and when the banquet was scheduled in Detroit for Doremus' homecoming, Ned had to plead the press of his new duties as reason he could not be toastmaster for the event! Such were the politics and the gentlemanliness of the day.

On the first working day of the new administration, the

President met for over an hour with Secretary of State Charles Evans Hughes, Secretary of War, John Weeks, and Ned. The men discussed the growing controversy in the Caribbean between Panama and Costa Rica. It was a minor land dispute, but how the United States would respond, whose side the U.S. would choose, was being carefully watched by all of America's hemispheric partners. It was during this conference that the President was interrupted, per his instructions, with the arrival of his new dog, a six-month-old airedale terrier of exceptional breeding, given to him by a friend from Toledo. His official name was Caswell Laddie Boy, but he immediately and immortally became just "Laddie Boy" to a generation of children who adored him. In his day Laddie Boy was more famous than any Presidential pet before or after him. He fetched golf balls during Presidential golf outings, had his own chair in the cabinet room, was "interviewed" by more than one reporter, and had White House birthday parties complete with visiting canine guests. Taking the dog outside after his conference with Ned, the President joked with reporters about his new pal, "'You see,' he said laughingly, 'I am going to have near me at least one friend who won't talk." (NYT 3-6-1921)

It was said that Laddie Boy, who had not been taken on the President's western trip in 1923, had howled for three days before his master's untimely death. When Florence Harding left the White House, knowing she was too ill to take care of Laddie Boy, she gave the airedale to her secret service agent, Harry Barker, who had become like a son to her. Barker took Laddie Boy with his family to his new assignment in Boston. Laddie Boy lived a full life, passing away in 1929 of old age. Even then, six years after his life of notoriety, Laddie Boy was mourned by a generation of newsboys and other dog-lovers. (For those who feel that Laddie Boy did not live a full life of only eight years, one must remember that advances in veterinary medicine have allowed dogs to live far longer lives than one hundred years ago.)

Later that same day, at 3pm, there was a star-spangled swearing in at the Navy Department. Attending along with Ned's immediate family, were the new Assistant Secretary, Lt.Col. Theodore Roosevelt, Jr., the outgoing Secretary Josephus Daniels, Senator Charles Townsend of Michigan and the Michigan delegation from the House (thirteen — ALL Republicans!), Senator Carroll S. Page, Chairman of the Senate Naval Affairs Committee, Representative Thomas S. Butler, member of the House Naval Affairs Committee and father of the famed Marine Corps hero, Smedley Butler, and a host of naval and Marine corps officers. At this time Ned announced the retention of John LeJeune as Commandant of the Marine Corps, and the permanent promotion of George Barnett to Major General's rank. There is no mention of what Josephus Daniels made of this, and Ned almost certainly did not care. The Times rehashed the controversy in their article describing the swearing in of all the cabinet officers, reporting that Barnett had "received three hours' notice from Mr. Daniels to determine whether he would retire from active service or remain in the corps with the reduced rank of Brigadier General, which he held in the permanent establishment. He chose the latter, and was transferred to the Pacific Coast . Nothing has ever been disclosed as to the reasons for Mr. Daniels' action." (NYT 3-6-1921)

The same evening, March 5, the busy Secretary and his Assistant attended a dinner of the Navy League at the Willard Hotel. The Navy League, founded in 1902 after a suggestion by Theodore Roosevelt, and still in operation today, is a civilian group of over 50,000 members, both men and women, whose mission is to support America's Navy and Marine Corps personnel. Ned was a member of the League and Ted was a Director, and by attending they both signaled an end to the feud which had existed between Josephus Daniels and the League since 1917. In his speech to the League on that evening Ned spoke out boldly for the expansion of the Navy. He "declared for 'a fighting navy, a navy prepared for any contingency, a navy as large as that of any other country in the world.'" (NYT 3-8-12921)

The stakes were high. Toward the end of the Wilson years, the United States had embarked upon an ambitious naval buildup with the idea that the American Navy should be the equal of any. In the years leading up to the World War, the Germans had increased the size of both their land and sea forces, causing the British to nervously ally themselves with the Japanese. The idea was that Britain could rely on peace with Japan in the Pacific, and so concentrate on the perceived German threat in the Atlantic. But this caused the Americans, under Wilson and Daniels, to split the American Fleet in two, between the Pacific threat and the Atlantic threat, and to increase the overall size of America's naval force. These were the naval dynamics which existed at the dawn of the Harding Administration in March 1921. Ned, being Secretary of the Navy, came out wholeheartedly in favor of the impressive Wilson expansion. Others in the cabinet, including Harding himself, were not so sure. The press made some headlines over supposed rifts in the neophyte administration, but it would all come together in the fall.

Meanwhile, Ned selected Joseph A. Carey, a Washington attorney and former boatswain's mate in the Navy, as his private secretary. Like Ned himself, when the World War broke out, Carey re-entered the Navy and served in Brest, France, the sprawling American base on the French coast. The two had met while Ned was serving in Congress and Carey was a young attorney. They became lifelong friends as did most men who met the jovial giant. In another week, only sixteen days on the job, Ned boarded an evening train to Key West, Florida, and from there sailed on the destroyer USS Crowninshield to the great naval base at Guantanamo Bay. Reaching Cuba, he transferred his flag to the battleship USS Pennsylvania to observe target practice with Admiral Wilson. From Cuba he proceeded to Haiti and the Dominican Republic to inspect naval installations and Marine Corps facilities in both locations. On April 4 Ned stepped ashore at the Washington Navy Yard after making the astonishing 1600 mile run from the Dominican Republic to Washington D. C. in a record 55 hours. He had sailed in the brand new destroyer USS Pruitt, named for a 22-year-old Marine, John H. Pruitt, who had been awarded the Congressional Medal of Honor, posthumously, for actions which took place very near where Ned had been located in France in October, 1918. As he was departing Caribbean waters, the soon-to-be-dubbed "Seagoing Secretary" sent the following message to fleet and stations:

"The Secretary of the Navy, upon leaving Caribbean waters after a short, but instructive, tour of inspection, compliments the service on the highly creditable condition of the ships and shore stations. The men seem zealous and eager, the officers working hard for the good of the service. The Secretary deeply appreciates the uniform courtesy with which he has been welcomed during his visit. Good luck to you all." (NYT 4-5-1921)

In an editorial-information piece two days before, the Times had discussed how the new Secretary was making progress with the men of the service.

"He is big of body and happy of disposition, and while some of the old-timers among the officers of the Navy Department may have looked with a skeptical eye upon Denby when he first assumed office, there are few severe critics now. Mr. Denby did his best to fit in and try to make every one get along with him. He said that he wanted those associated with him in the navy to understand that there was going to be a fair deal all around and no bickering. Mr. Denby came out early in his career as Secretary as a "big navy man," and that made a popular hit with his coworkers."

To the end of his life, Ned would be revered by gobs and jarheads, officers and men. Every single one of them, even if and when they disagreed with him, knew that he was, at his very core, one of them.

Within one day of his return, he forwarded an eleven page tightly worded review of his trip through Haiti and the Dominican Republic at the request and for the benefit of Charles Evans Hughes. In measured, balanced and plainly spoken terms he made his observations and drew his conclusions. The United States at this time, had been continuously involved in Haiti since 1915, and in Santo Domingo (now known as the Dominican Republic) since

1916. The Harding Administration had inherited the previous several administrations' interpretation of the Monroe Doctrine, first formed in 1823 by the fifth President of the United States to make it clear once and for all that America was not going to be a battleground for warring and colonizing European Powers. Strongly backed by the British in the early years of its inception, for their own political and economic reasons, it was further expanded by Theodore Roosevelt, in 1904, owing to the perceived threat of the growing German influence in the Caribbean, and the United States' desire to protect its monumental investment in the Panama Canal.

Ned concluded that the Haitians were nowhere near self-government and that the United States would do well to continue its presence there in order to prevent further sectarian violence. He carefully and closely interviewed a wide variety of people while there, and was convinced that the majority of Haitians themselves desired the U.S. Marine government remain in place. Santo Domingo, on the other hand, was a horse of a different color. Here he found the great majority of the people earnestly yearning for the freedom of self government, certainly a heartstring which loomed large in the large breast of the Secretary. His recommendation was that the United States announce when it intended to leave, and do it quickly. "Uncertainty is dangerous," he warned.

"More dangerous than all, in my opinion, will in such case be the reaction upon the mind of the people of the United States. We have in Santo Domingo almost an extreme expression of the real meaning of the Monroe Doctrine. Our people do not grasp the full significance of the control exercised by our government over the republics to the south of us. They will not tolerate, and should not be asked to tolerate, the exercise of that control in any but the most beneficent and reasonable manner." (DPL, Edwin Denby Papers, Box #3)

It was clear from his remarks that he sympathized with the desires of the people for freedom and self government. There was also the problem of the Americans having started public works projects with government funds which, after a downturn in the economy, had not yet been completed. Ned estimated that it would take another $5 million for this task, and strongly urged that the U.S. not depart before these projects were finished. He then concluded,

"I feel an intense desire that the naval occupation shall prove to have been a success, which it cannot be unless the public works are completed; but I feel an even greater desire that the United States shall shake itself free from any just criticism as an arbitrary and autocratic master of small peoples. 'It is excellent to have a giant's strength, but tyrannous to use it like a giant.'" (Ibid)

Spoken as only a giant could and did understand it.

Ominously, as early as April 16, less than six weeks into the administration, Ned announced his intention to lease Navy oil reserve land. The press release, in the New York Times, deserves to be reported here, in full:

"Washington, April 16—To prevent the drainage of naval oil reserve lands in California by private drilling on the outskirts of the reserves, Secretary Denby has decided to lease drilling rights inside the reserves over a small area to private concerns, he announced today. Bids for the privilege of drilling on the naval oil lands will be advertised soon, the Secretary added. This is the first instance where any drilling has been permitted on the naval oil reserves, Mr. Denby said, and the step was taken only after it was found that the Government oil was being drained through the wells of private companies. Under the terms of the leases to be made the Government will reserve to itself a proportion of all the oil obtained, or the equivalent in cash. Efforts to open up the naval reserves in California for drilling by private companies have been made for several years, or practically ever since the reserves were created. The matter recently was seriously agitated in Congress, but Secretary Daniels stood out strongly against such a move, contending that the Navy must have the oil for future use in view of the rapid development of other available oil fields. The decision to leave parts of the reserves is not regarded as any change in the department's policy, Secretary Denby explaining that it was a precautionary measure to protect the navy supply." (NYT 4-17-1921)

So much for the later claims that oil leasing was done somehow in secret, or that Congress had not been fully consulted. Congress had been trying to get the previous administration to do just that. In addition, keeping the oil in the ground, unrefined, was leaving it completely unavailable in a time of emergency. Furthermore, on June 1, it was announced that the navy oil lands had been turned over to the Department of the Interior under the purview of Secretary of the Interior, Albert Fall. This action was accomplished by an executive order of President Harding, with full knowledge of everyone involved, in public, as recorded in the New York Times. (NYT 6-1-1921)

In late May, the President and Mrs. Harding entertained Madame Curie at a gala banquet held at the National Museum. The following day, Saturday, May 21, she was hosted by Marion Denby on the Presidential Yacht, Sylph, which was reserved for the use of the Secretary. They cruised down the Potomac to Mt. Vernon where the Mt. Vernon Ladies Association regents were holding their annual meetings that month. Both Ned's mother and grandmother had been regents of the Association in their day.

June brought the first jolt of political upheaval for the Secretary in the form of a publicity flap over remarks made by Rear Admiral William S. Sims before the English Speaking Union in London on Tuesday, June 7. Speaking extemporaneously before the luncheon, the outspoken Admiral who had been America's supreme naval commander in Europe during the War, and who had become well known for his blunt language in the past, made disparaging remarks about Sinn Fein, the Irish revolutionary political party. The American Admiral, an admitted Anglophile, felt that the war effort had been significantly damaged by the agitations of the the Sinn Feiners. Within one day of this news crossing the Atlantic to American newspapers, both the Senate and the House had passed resolutions to hold investigations into the speech, despite

Ned's immediate announcement that the Navy would investigate fully, and his demand that the Admiral explain himself forthwith. When the Admiral did not reply quickly enough, by June 11, Ned had cancelled the remainder of his leave and ordered him to return to America at once to explain himself in person. As events transpired, the Admiral was already booked on the Olympic, scheduled to sail in four days.

The irony in all of this was that Ned had found himself politically pressured into what may have appeared as a harsh response to the Admiral's exercise of his First Amendment right, and it had come only days after Ned had publicly lifted the "gag order" which had prevailed over naval officers in the past. He was now seen, and called for, appearing to reverse direction in his desire for a more open and "free" navy. On June 14, therefore, he issued a new general order to clarify his desire for more freedom, but with appropriate discretion.

Ned was almost certainly pleased to lighten up the situation when, on the 15th, addressing the graduating class of Georgetown University, he made fun of himself. "Every time we go to war," he said to them, "I lose twenty to forty pounds. But this country is so kind to me in peace times that I gain it all back again with interest. You can see for yourselves that I am faring pretty well now. I would hate to see another war for this nation, but we will have to engineer one if this thing keeps up." (NYT 6-16-1921)

Meanwhile, as Ned was fending off bad publicity and awaiting the arrival of Admiral Sims from England, Ted Roosevelt was busy reforming the navy. In a June article the Times noted that Ted had gone to bat for American citizens against the Civil Service Commission. Ted insisted that the Commission give preference to "citizens over aliens in the matter of selection of civil service employees of the naval establishment for retention during the reduction period that the Navy Department is facing" (following the war). The commission had taken the view that Roosevelt should not discharge aliens who were higher on the roster than citizens, and Ted strongly disagreed. So much so, that the

Commission reversed its stand, and the Times concluded that this reversal would be "far-reaching inasmuch as it sets a precedent to be followed in all other executive departments." (NYT 6-18-1921)

The same article continued to further reveal that with Ned's agreement, Ted was in the process of reorganizing navy yards to bring them all into the same measure of uniform management. Instead of the hodge-podge manner of the past, "Each navy yard will be in charge of a commandant clothed with both authority and responsibility under whom all the personnel will be placed. But under each commandant there will also be a yard manager with industrial experience, chosen from the commissioned personnel of the navy. This manager will have grouped under him in his respective yard the forces charged with building of ships, repair of ships and the civil personnel of the yard, leaving the commandant free to better handle the purely military functions of the yard, but the yard manager will be responsible to the commandant for results." Said Roosevelt: :"The keynote of the reorganization plan is economy and efficiency. It is all being done on the basis of trying legitimately to reduce expense and get at costs." (NYT 6-18-1921)

The overriding early theme of the Harding administration was cutting government costs. Naturally, during the long years leading up to and during the world war counting costs had fallen by the wayside. Harding campaigned on efficient government, and made it crystal clear to his cabinet that he was serious about it. Everyone was tasked with finding ways to save money, to do it quickly, and to run the government more efficiently.

Throughout the first one hundred and thirty years of the nation the government had operated without an office of the budget. Congress had passed such legislation during the Wilson years, but it had not been signed into law. Harding made it known to Congress that he would favor such a bill, and when Congress offered it to him early in his administration, he signed it in early June. He already knew whom he wanted to run the newly created Bureau of the budget, and he went directly to Charles Dawes, who had just recently turned him down for the post of Secretary of the

Treasury. Dawes knew the hole the country was in — "federal expenditures had risen from less than $1 billion in 1914 to $18.5 billion in 1919 (Murray, p.172), and he accepted Harding's offer to run Budget — but for exactly one year, no more. Under Dawes' and his successors' ministrations, federal expenditures steadily declined, and within two years were $2 billion below that spent in the last year of the Wilson administration.

So, it was real, and Harding was not joking. Cut costs, trim budgets, save money. Two members of the administration who heard the message loud and clear were the Secretary and the Assistant Secretary of the Navy.

So volatile had the Sims flap become that by Wednesday, June 22, when he arrived at the White Star Line docks in Manhattan on the Olympic, thirteen hundred New York police officers greeted the ship to prevent any demonstrations, either for or against, the Admiral. There were none. He proceeded to Washington, D. C. to meet with Ned. On June 24th it was announced that the Navy had once again reprimanded the brilliant but outspoken admiral, who was then enjoined to return to his regular duty post as head of the Naval War College without further penalty. Stopping by the White House to pay an unscheduled courtesy call, Sims was perhaps maddeningly glib with the press about the whole affair: "Would you like me to tell you what he said?" he asked reporters concerning the President. "You would? I won't." he rebuffed them. Then, "I think the incident ended. The Navy Department is giving out a statement on the subject. I've been reprimanded. I got what was coming to me. I spilled the beans. I'm very sorry to have caused the Administration any embarrassment. I didn't know it was loaded as much as it was." (NYT 6-24-1921)

A note of levity was introduced into all the high drama of the early days of the administration, when Ned, who had never needed prodding to pull off the practical joke, received an apparently valid letter from Secretary Mellon concerning his participation on "The Interdepartmental Social Hygiene Board." A quasi governmental/public organization for the education of the masses concerning social diseases and the necessity for hygiene as a foundation for their eradication, certain cabinet members were chosen to complete the list of officials committed and involved. However, Secretary Mellon had found, after consulting his Solicitor of the Treasury, that it was perfectly acceptable to appoint his Assistant to this prestigious post, if it proved that the Secretary was "prevented from serving personally on account of the pressure of other business." He mentioned that he was also writing a similar letter to John weeks at War. One can only imagine Ned receiving this communication and being handed the golden opportunity to pass it on to his Assistant. As a presage of things to come, he addressed his letter, "My dear Colonel" and then unloaded his gleeful message, "I now designate you to act in that capacity and rejoice in the opportunity of giving you so handsome an appointment." As if that were not quite enough, he signed, "with best wishes….." TRJr.'s response is too good not to quote it in full:

"My dear Mr. Secretary,

"This is to express my deep appreciation of your appointment of me to act as your representative on the interdepartmental social hygiene board. I am filled with delight at this thought. Before accepting the appointment, however, I feel that you should know my feelings insofar as the matter is concerned. I will use my earnest endeavors to disband the board at the earliest moment possible.

Believe me

Very truly yours,…   "

(DPL Edwin Denby Papers, Box #3)

Chapter Twenty

*"Peace cannot be kept by force; it can
only be achieved by understanding."*

Einstein

SecNav
Arms Limitation

The end of the First World War in 1918 had left the British Empire in near economic shambles. Britain had lost over a million dead, and had gone from being the world's premier economy with the largest and strongest extension of itself — its navy — to a debtor nation. More British workers were involved in strikes than in Germany and with unemployment in 1921 reaching 11.3%, the highest since records had been kept. (National Archives Article on Aftermath of War in Britain) The idea of arms limitation was not only not taboo in Britain, it was welcomed. Many thought that in the years following the war, it would be the British who would lead the world to the tables of limitation. It was not.

The Japanese, on the other hand, were not suspected of any ideas of peaceful coexistence, or arms limitation. Though the Japanese economy had been seriously hampered by the Russo-Japanese War, it had suffered little during the global conflict which had crippled Britain. Japan did not attempt to disguise its designs on hegemony, so much so that it was a miracle the United States was caught so flatfooted at Pearl in twenty years. In a letter from Ned's former congressional pal, J. Sloat Fassett , who had business interests in Japan and Korea, the message, even in 1921, was clear:

"I do not believe we need have war but I do believe we would be fools not to realize that it is a very easy thing to bring to pass by Japanese aggression, especially provided it finds us unprepared. Disarmament is great provided it is universal. We would be fatuous fools to begin, so long as Japan and England are desperately enlarging their armaments. There may be Chautauqua lecturers who would urge us to set a solitary example of complete military and naval inefficiency and unpreparedness but no sane man who has respect for and knowledge of history and its teachings can take such an asinine position." (DPL Edwin Denby Papers, Box #3)

If Warren Harding was not ahead of the curve on the desire for disarmament discussion, he was certainly in the forefront of it. "As early as the Marion talks following his election, Harding had discussed the conference idea with several persons...." (Murray, p.143) Several back channels were being pursued during the early first summer of the Harding administration. With the tacit interest of the British government, by July 8th Charles Evans Hughes had tasked his ambassadors in Great Britain, Italy, France and Japan with finding out if a favorable response to a conference would be forthcoming. Getting positive answers, by Sunday, July 10, Hughes had sent out the invitations to the world's first arms limitation conference, to be held in Washington, D. C. that autumn.

On June 2, Ned accompanied President Harding to Annapolis for the graduation of 260 naval cadets. Though the President had not been expected to speak, he was prevailed upon to make a few remarks after Ned had finished. The main speech, however, was Ned's, and it was given with his usual habit: straight from the shoulder.

"No one knows better than I," Ned told them, "with what great respect the enlisted man looks upon an officer who is 'every inch a man.' No one knows better than I with what contempt the enlisted man views an officer unduly burdened with the weight of his own importance. We need not worry about our rank. Our fitness for it will be justly appraised by those associated with us. The enlisted man will quickly size you up. He wants to like you. He wants to respect you. He properly feels that he is too much man himself to want to be commanded by one lacking any essential element of manhood. Go to your men simply and naturally, a man among men, giving the best that's in you and expecting good work in return. There is a smile in the navy and in the Marine Corps that men reserve for those they respect and like. It is better than any decoration. Try to win it." (DFP 6-3-1921)

In July, 1921, the Denbys moved into their new Washington, D. C. residence on R Street. Probably still not entirely unpacked, it was shortly time for Marion and the children to retreat to the farm in Pontiac, Michigan for the summer. Before joining his family in Michigan, the Secretary first observed the joint Army and Navy bombing exercises off the Virginia coast. Several ships were sunk with aerial bombs, dropped by both Army and Navy aviators. Ned was enthusiastic about the tests, especially the heroics of the aviators. However, Major General Charles F. Mencher, chief of the army air service, was somewhat gloomy over the results. "A cold, material fact has been demonstrated,' he said. 'That fact is that the battleship can be sunk by the aerial bomb." (DFP 8-21-1921) A completely new age in warfare was exploding before their eyes. It was going to take some getting used to.

Immediately after the tests, Ned joined the family at the Pontiac farm in the Oakland County lake district where hundreds of lakes are sprinkled throughout the near northern areas of Detroit. The Denbys had enjoyed their getaway farm for some years, and some of their relatives and friends owned property nearby. In an interview with the Free Press while on his vacation, Ned declared that he could easily see the boundaries of all the little northern suburbs one day touching each other as the area increased in population. In just a few years he would invest heavily in his own suburban development just to the south of his farm.

Only a short while after he had joined the family for vacation, however, tragedy struck in the form of a huge British dirigible which had been purchased by the United States Navy, and while on maneuvers with a mixed British-American crew had crashed over Hull, England. Only five men of the 49 member crew, one American and four British, survived the crash. It was the first, but was not to be the last, of the great dirigible disasters of the 1920's.

On Saturday, September 17, funeral services were held at the Brooklyn Navy Yard for the American victims of the ZR-2 disaster. They had arrived in New York the previous day aboard the British cruiser, HMS Dauntless. Ned attended the services, which had to be moved indoors account of heavy rains, dampening the size of the crowd that had been expected to be much larger. Of the sixteen Americans who lost their lives, three were sent to Arlington, one was buried at sea, and the remainder released to their families. On the day the Dauntless arrived New York harbor amidst a flotilla of American naval escorts, the National Advisory Committee for Aeronautics, consisting of Army and Navy personnel, as well as prominent civilians which included Orville Wright, recommended to President Harding that the development of rigid airships be continued by the United States. In light of the fact that the United States was in possession of the largest store of helium known to exist, it was believed that American efforts could continue with greater safety than that of other countries, such as Germany and England.

In late October the delegates for the Disarmament Conference began arriving in Washington. A total of nine nations would be represented at this, the first arms limitation conference in history: the United States, Great Britain, France, Japan, Belgium, China, Italy, Netherlands, and Portugal. The conference was held in the Memorial Continental Hall, built by the Daughters of the American Revolution as their headquarters in 1910. The American delegation to the conference consisted of four members: Secretary of State Charles Evans Hughes; Elihu Root, former Secretary of State under Roosevelt, Secretary of War under McKinley, and former Senator; Senator Henry Cabot Lodge of Massachusetts, Chairman of the Senate Foreign Relations Committee; and Senator Oscar Underwood, Senator from Alabama and Senate Minority Leader. The politically astute Harding had selected just the perfect mix of

Americans for the task at hand. They were in constant meetings in late October with the President, Secretaries Denby and Weeks, CNO Admiral Coontz and others. The American position was still being perfected up to forty-eight hours before the conference. But before it could begin, two items took President Harding and Edwin Denby's attention away from international matters.

As Secretary of the United States Navy Ned presided over an organization of well over one hundred thousand souls. The vast majority of them youngsters, hotheaded, careless, impulsive and often in trouble. Sometimes, deep trouble. As the highest authority in many of these cases, Ned was prevailed upon by the recalcitrants, their parents, relatives, friends, and quite often, politicians, for preferential treatment. In most all cases supplicants received a polite refusal from the Secretary, stating that for this reason, or for that, their requests could not be favorably answered. Sometimes Annapolis cadets, close to graduation, would have a change of heart and decide they didn't want to serve the Navy for four years in repayment for their free college education, and couldn't the Secretary see his way clear to release them from that inconvenient obligation? No. He could not. Ned was always fair, and sometimes, when he believed a cause just, went far out of his way to see, or to attempt to see, a situation corrected. This would go on in his life for years after he was no longer Secretary. And it really didn't matter who you were; good friends were as often turned down in unfair requests as perfect strangers.

But in early November, 1921, Ned received a letter from a Brooklyn widow whose only son and sole support had just died while enlisted in the Navy.

"Dear Sir,

"I take the liberty of writing you this letter in behalf of a poor boy who is held in the Brooklyn Navy Prison on charges regarding my son's death. This boy, William F. Harkness, and my son John Joseph Goddard, were two of the crew of the USS Eagle Boat 26. They got into a little dispute, decided to settle it on shore, and Harkness struck my son and killed him. It was an accident. Now, this boy's mother, a poor widow with only two

345

girls to support her, is breaking her heart over her boy. Now, I am earnestly appealing to you, in behalf of this boy's release. He never meant to kill my son. They were the best of friends. Think of what a disgrace it would be on that young man to be pointed out as a convict and the shame it would bring on his poor mother and sisters. Now, Mr. Denby, I beg of you to do what you can for him. If I can forgive him, why can't the Navy, for my son was a good boy and my main support. By sending the boy away, would not bring him back to me, but break another mother's heart.

"Hoping you will do all you can for him and I am sure his heartbroken mother will bless and pray for you.

"I remain,

"Mrs. M. Goddard"

Ned was so impressed with Mrs. Goddard's heartfelt plea that he not only took steps to grant her wish, but he forwarded the letter to the President. "Knowing how many unpleasant letters come to your attention I take great pleasure in enclosing to you one of the finest letters that I have ever read," he declared. "Needless to say, the Department has acted exactly in accordance with her wishes, and will in no way punish the young sailor who was the unintentional cause of her boy's death." (DPL Edwin Denby Papers, Box #3) By return letter, Warren Harding magnanimously agreed.

One further event of great national significance had yet to take place before the opening of the Washington Naval Conference. On Wednesday, November 9, the protected cruiser USS Olympia crept slowly up the Potomac River through fog and rain as seemed best to befit the solemn occasion. She was honored with cannon salutes at every fort along the way. She carried perhaps the nation's most cherished war casualty, known but to God. Decorated with the highest awards of many nations, honors reserved for the greatest in the land were lavished upon him. The Olympia slipped into her dock as a full regiment of cavalry awaited at the side of the ship. Secretary Weeks, Secretary Denby, General of the Armies Pershing, Chief of Naval Operations Admiral Robert Coontz, were also on hand for the arrival. A somber procession next made its way from the Washington Navy yard to the Capitol Rotunda where the body lay in state in the place previously reserved for the bodies of US Presidents Lincoln, Garfield and McKinley. President and Mrs. Harding arrived to pay their respects, followed by many high officials and dignitaries, including several from France, Great Britain and Canada, and many others who were already in town for the naval conference. On Saturday the 11th, the third observance of "Armistice Day" as it was then known, once again another somber procession filled with dignitaries from around the country and the world escorted the "unknown American" to his final resting place in Arlington National Cemetery. In a hallowed vault at the eastern side of the newly finished Memorial Amphitheater, a crowd of thousands gathered to hear President Harding eulogize the sacred dead. Said the President in part: "Ours are lofty resolutions today, as with tribute to the dead we consecrate ourselves to a better order for the living. With all my heart, I wish we might say to the defenders who survive, to mothers who sorrow, to widows and children who mourn, that no such sacrifices shall be asked again." (NYT 11-12-1921) With two small children and having served his nation in two wars, there was no one in the audience that day who could agree more fervently with the President than Ned Denby.

The International Conference on Naval Limitation held its opening session promptly at 1030 on a chilly Saturday morning, November 12. American journalist Mark Sullivan, once called by Time Magazine as "the Jeremiah of the United States Press", quoted Arthur Balfour's comment, referring to this first day, as "that inspired moment...that fateful Saturday...unique in history." (Sullivan, xi preface). Sullivan further set the tone of the opening day when he carefully described those attending, both delegates, and those observing from the galleries.

"The massive John W. Weeks came slowly down the steep steps of the gallery, his alert and vigorous attention divided between watching his step and casting a vigilantly appraising eye upon the forum below. Over Week's shoulder peered the homely and friendly face of the equally massive Denby. The simplicity of Denby's countenance, its typical American quality, brought out by the contrast with so many foreign faces else- where in the crowd, caused one of those curious and irrelevant leaps of memory which expressed itself in my jotting down in my notebook a line I once saw above an old hearthstone, 'East, West, Home's Best'." (Sullivan pp 2-3)

Sullivan further portrayed the arrival of the Conference's host: "Suddenly there was applause; it rose quickly in volume as realization for the occasion for it spread through the audience. Harding had entered. For the first time the crowd rose..." (Ibid.)

The delegates from each nation had been purposely kept to small numbers to facilitate the intricate negotiations and keep debate to a minimum. President Harding gave a short, opening speech, purposefully kept brief, so as not to spoil the grand effect that he and Charles Evans Hughes had prepared for the foreign delegates and the world. Just after Harding's speech and departure, the conference elected Hughes as its Chairman, and the Secretary of State then gave his opening speech. It was a blockbuster. One hundred years later, and after dozens of others have reiterated and evaluated what he said, suffice it to explain that Charles Evans Hughes, and by extension, Warren Harding, knocked the wind out of the sails of the navies of the world with the audacious scope of their plan. In one of the best held secrets of diplomacy in history, nothing had leaked to the press or to the other delegates about what was coming. It was a stunning coup for the Harding Administration, and all the attempts since to downplay its significance only point to how breathtaking it actually was. Hughes had challenged the British and the Japanese to either follow the bold designs of the United States' offer, or look like war-mongering fools if they chose not. He called for a moratorium on naval shipbuilding for ten years and the reduction of the overall tonnage of the three largest navies: United States, Britain, and Japan. "All in all, Hughes speech laid waste to

1,878,043 tons of the three finest navies in the world, and left the United States with 500,650 tons, Great Britain with 604,450, and Japan with 299,700." (Murray, p.151)

"At the conclusion of Hughes's speech the cheering lasted for ten minutes. Hats waved, handkerchiefs fluttered, men slapped, hugged and embraced one another." (Ibid, p.152) These were diplomats from all over the world. It was an astonishing piece of statecraft. Warned ahead of time by her husband not to miss the opening speeches, eighteen years later Mrs. Theodore Roosevelt, Jr., in her memoirs, wrote, "It was amid tumultuous cheering that Mr. Hughes finished laying the full American plan before the Conference for consideration, The whole world was surprised." (Roosevelt, p.143)

The conference lasted for three months, concluding on February 6, 1922 and establishing three major treaties. First, the Five Power Treaty which addressed the reduction in size of the principle navies; second, the Four Power Treaty, which pledged the United States, Japan, France and Britain to mutual understanding and nonaggression in the Pacific; and third, the Nine Power Treaty which codified the Open Door Policy, pledging the nine signatories to honor the territorial integrity of China. The treaties lasted for the next fifteen years, or until 1936, when Japanese militarism finally put them to sleep. As to the criticism that they did not last longer, it may be pointed out that that was not the fault of the Harding Administration, or even of Prince Tokugawa Iesoto, the head of the Japanese delegation. The Prince was a great friend of the United States and deeply committed to peace in the Pacific and the world. Unfortunately, he was no longer in power in later years, and he died in June, 1940, eighteen months before Pearl Harbor.

Throughout the three months of the conference Ned had kept a low profile. His work had gone before, presiding over a Navy which had to make sacrifices first to prove that America meant business, and before other nations could be expected to follow. The Americans were giving up 30 capital ships, nearly 900,000 tons. For a bluejacket who had spent significant parts of his life defending his country it was a lot to digest. For the many career naval officers who had spent their entire lives on the rolling decks of the country's warships, it had to be difficult. But Ned soldiered on, being quoted in the Times on the day following the opening, "I cordially approve the American proposals. I hope they will be approved by the conference and meet the wishes of the people represented in Washington." (NYT 11-13-1921) Ned Denby was nothing if not loyal to a fault.

During the early sessions of the conference a nuisance situation presented itself in the guise of the request by the Postmaster General, Will Hays, that something be done to stop the assault on the mails by unknown and increasingly daring thieves. The problem with mail theft had been going on for nearly two years and was getting out of control. The matter having reached the President's desk, it was referred to Ned to furnish U. S. Marines to guard the mails. Commandant LeJeune called one of his most famous Marines back from leave to head up the contingent who would protect the US Mail. He was Major General Logan Feland, one of the heroes of Belleau Wood in France. One thousand Marines were immediately dispatched to guard trucks, post offices and mail trains across the country. In a famous order from the Secretary of the Navy, Ned told his fellow leathernecks:

"There is no compromise in this battle with bandits. If two Marines guarding a mail car, for example, are suddenly covered by a robber, neither must hold up his hands, but both must begin shooting at once. One may be killed, but the other will get the robber and save the mail. When our men go as guards over the mail, that mail must be delivered or there must be a Marine dead at the post of duty. You must be brave, as you always are. You must be constantly alert and you must, when on guard duty, keep your weapons in hand and, if attacked, shoot, and shoot to kill." (NYT 11-13-1921)

Without surprise, by mid March the Marines had accomplished their mission. The attacks had ceased, and the newly appointed Postmaster General, Hubert Work (Will Hays had left the Harding Administration in January of 1922 to become the first head of the newly formed Motion Picture Producers and Distributors Association), wrote a highly laudatory letter of thanks to the Commandant of the Marine Corps via Ned's desk. In it he thanked by name Major General Feland for "the masterful and efficient methods" which were used by the Marines to accomplish their mission. Work concluded his letter by saying that he hoped to "again have the opportunity to be personally associated with your Corps, of which I have the highest regard." (DPL Edwin Denby Papers, Box #5) Of course Work could not know that the Marines would once again be involved in guarding the mails in just a few short years, however it would be after he had moved on to become Secretary of the Interior.

In early October the President, the First Lady, the Secretary of the Navy and wife, Assistant Secretary of the Navy and wife, Secretary of Agriculture and wife, the Commandant of the Marine Corps all journeyed from Washington the eighty some miles to the Wilderness Battlefield east of Fredericksburg, Virginia on a Saturday to observe the maneuvers of the east coast Expeditionary Force of the Marine Corps. Over 5000 Marines greeted the President and performed military maneuvers, including a simulated aerial attack on a mock dreadnaught.

In addition, the President also met with a group of Confederate veterans. The Washington party stayed in a tent complex, with wooden flooring, and inside plumbing. It was not luxurious, but better than the Marines' quarters. The President made a few brief remarks to the Marines on Sunday morning during religious services, and then reviewed the entire command. Before heading back to Washington, he visited the tiny graveyard where several unknown Civil War veterans are buried, including the arm of Stonewall Jackson which the great Confederate General had lost at the nearby battle of Chancellorsville in 1863. The New York Times article about the visit mentioned that the little cemetery had been found overgrown with weeds and the Marines did what they always do, requested permission, and then put the whole place in order, including white posts and wire fencing, in order to better honor General Jackson, and brothers-in-arms. The article also mentioned how pleased the Secretary of the Navy was to be once again among his beloved jarheads. (NYT 10-3-1921)

In the meantime, while the delegates from around the world were conferring over limitations, the Secretary of the Navy indulged himself in one of the more pleasant prerogatives of his office — he attended some Midshipmen and Marine Corps football games. On November 26, Ned and Marion joined the Coolidges, the Roosevelt Jr.s, the Weeks, and many other notables and government officials to watch Navy defeat Army 7-0 for the third straight year. One week later Ned watched the Marine Corps team from Quantico defeat the Army Third Corps team 20-0. Interestingly, the Army team was that year coached by 31-year-old Major Dwight D. Eisenhower. The Quantico Marines Devil Dogs, as they were called, won all of their games in 1921 and 1922 under head coach John Beckett who would spend 50 years in the Marine Corps coaching football teams and end his career as a Brigadier General. The hero of the 1921 team was backfield great, Frank Geottge, once praised by Walter Camp as being as good as Jim Thorpe or better. Goettge turned down an offer from the NFL in order to remain a Marine and was killed on Guadalcanal in 1942. The Marine Corps would field their college level football teams until 1972, when budget constraints ended the gridiron ambitions of the leathernecks. After the hard fought, but lopsided game against the army team, Ned wrote letters to both commanding officers of the teams, being especially pleased with how hard fought, but how gentlemanly both teams had played.

At the regular meeting of the board of Banker's Trust in Detroit on Wednesday December 21st, Ned was again reelected to the post of one of three Vice Presidents. On Saturday evening, the 24th, Ned's Christmas Greeting to the Navy went out to all installations afloat and ashore. In addition to Merry Christmas and Happy New Year, the Seagoing Secretary gave his men two of his favorite words of encouragement: "Carry on."

Chapter Twenty-One

"We'll let our friends be the peacekeepers, and the great country called America will be the peacemakers."

George W. Bush

The Opening Salvo

The social season in Washington, D. C. usually began in the early throes of winter, coinciding with the opening session of congress which took place in the first week of December. When General Washington selected the swampy area of tidewater Virginia for the location of the Republic's capital, it seems fairly certain that he did not take into consideration the stifling heat which would pervade his shining city during summer months. Fortunate that congress met from December to March. Even if a special session were to be called in March (not often, as it turned out), with some luck it could be adjourned before the worst of the steamy summer had descended, and members could repair to their homes or vacation spots for relief during the hottest months. But by late October, the society columns would once again begin to bristle with the names of the great, the famous, and sometimes the infamous, their doings, their comings and goings, their entertainments, frivolities, and fun. Senators, congressmen, cabinet members, their staffs, assistants, lobbyists and hangers-on all trickled back into the great beating heart of America. Due to the debilitating illness of the former chief executive, as well as the preceding years of world conflict, much of the gala atmosphere of the capital had been exceedingly curtailed during the previous administration. So it was, perhaps, with some additional excitement that, on Monday morning, January 2, 1922, thousands lined up outside the White House gates in bitter cold as 1400 diplomats and government officials were greeted by the President and the First Lady in the Blue Room between 1100am and 100pm. The doors were then closed for one hour for luncheon, and then reopened from 200pm to 430pm to allow over 5000 ordinary citizens to file through and shake the First Couple's hands for the first time in nine years. Not since William Howard Taft had greeted voters on New Year's Day, 1913, had the common folk been invited to press the Presidential flesh. Of additional interest in this particular social season was the fact that Washington was at present flooded with foreign dignitaries owing to the ongoing Arms Limitation Conference which would not conclude for two more months.

Ned and Marion held "a large and brilliant reception on Monday afternoon [while the Hardings were still greeting John Q. Public at the White House]....Mrs. Denby was extremely pretty in a gown of blue gray chiffon with touches of black and a smart black hat with lace brim. She wore some very long, old-fashioned gold earrings which were most becoming." Later, on Wednesday of that same week, the Denbys were entertained as the guests of honor at the home of Illinois Representative Fred Britten, a member of the naval affairs committee of the House. (DFP 1-8-1922)

The winter turned bitterly cold as January progressed, but the chill did nothing to slow the social whirl. Thursday, the 12th at 930pm the first of four official State Receptions took place at 1600 Pennsylvania Avenue, as 2,000 diplomats, and other invited dignitaries lined up to be greeted by the President and Mrs. Harding, again in the Blue Room. Of particular note on this occasion was the presence of the Prince and Princess Cantacuzene, in town to promote a favorite Russian charity, who joined the throng to greet the Hardings. The Princess, granddaughter of the late lion, U. S. Grant, was the first baby ever to be born in the White House.

On Tuesday afternoon, January 24, Ned and Marion hosted an open house reception for members of the Senate and the House of Representatives and wives in honor of the six years Ned had spent as one of their congressional colleagues. "Mrs. Townsend and Mrs. Newberry, the wives of the Michigan senators, presided over the tea table, and the wives of the Michigan delegation in the House of Representatives assisted through the drawing rooms and dining room. Mrs. Coolidge and Mrs. Gillett, wives of the vice-president and the speaker of the house, stood with Mrs. Denby to receive, making an altogether unique and very fitting affair." The writer could not help but recount, cattily, that Marion was adorned in pink, "which is much more becoming than her favorite blue." (DFP 1-28-1922)

In mid-January Ned's humorous side was once again fully exposed in the press when it became known that, apparently on one of his football weekends in Virginia, he had hunted without a valid Virginia hunting license. So inquired M. D. Hart of the Virginia Department of Game and Inland Fisheries in response to having received an 'anonymous' letter. Ned promptly produced the required permit and was just as promptly, and with some chagrin, invited to hunt in the State of Virginia whenever he chose. Unable to pass up an opportunity to make some fun of himself, the Secretary was quoted in the New York Times as being "reticent in telling the number of shells he used in bringing down each bird, but declared it was not over an average of fifty-eight. He only stopped shooting, he said, when he began to fear he was filling up the nearby river with lead and forming an obstruction to navigation." (NYT 1-13-1922) A week later, in replying to General Smedley Butler at Quantico, he reported gleefully that "benefits have even reached beyond, to the newspapers, which have had lots of fun over the allegations that I was shooting without a license. The returns from that poor little joke are still coming in, and I suppose I shall hear of it, always gladly, for some time to come." (BHL Edwin Denby Papers Box #5)

On Friday January 27, a snowstorm of unusual proportions struck the capital, burying motorists and snarling rail traffic while dumping over two feet of snow under gale conditions throughout Saturday, as well. The storm covered several states from the Carolinas to New York City, and various depths of snow measured as much as 33 inches with drifts in railroad cuts as deep as 16 feet. At 9pm on Saturday evening the entire roof of the recently constructed (1917) Knickerbocker Theater gave way under the weight of the snow, instantly crushing to death 98 people and injuring 133. A United States Congressman, Andrew Jackson Barchfield, a Republican from Pennsylvania, was among the dead. All Washington shivered in horror at the catastrophe, and even Congress closed because of the storm and the tragedy. Though numerous lawsuits would proliferate through the courts for years to come, liability was never established and no settlements were ever paid. In 1927 the theater's architect, and in 1937, its owner, both committed suicide.

Over a week later the Washington correspondent of the Detroit Free Press remarked that the city was still fighting its way out of the snowdrifts and the gloom of the tragedy and its aftermath. A celebration of President McKinley's birthday with attendance including the President and the First Lady, and the Congressional Club's reception in honor of Vice President and Mrs. Coolidge were both postponed, and many other events cancelled outright. The last of the funerals were held on Thursday, and official Washington then deemed it appropriate for the third of the official State Dinners to take place at the White House. That evening, no doubt with much conversation still devoted to the awful tragedy, President and Mrs, Harding entertained the beloved Chief Justice, William Howard Taft, and his equally popular wife, Helen, as well as other members of the judiciary and invited guests. Taft was entering upon his eighth month as Chief Justice, having been appointed by President Harding the previous June, after years of faithful service around the world in many capacities, to the only job he had ever really wanted.

Tragedy and state functions aside, that same week saw the federal bureaucracy once again sit down to brass tacks. "No presidential action by Harding was more discerning nor longer-

lasting than his imposition of business practices on government."
(Dean, p.105) After having appointed Charles Dawes Director
of the Budget Bureau the previous year, one thousand selected
department heads chosen from throughout the federal government
met for the second time on Friday, February 3, in the very same
hall where the Arms Limitation Conference was scheduled to
close in three days. In his opening remarks, President Harding
told the assembled that instead of a deficit of almost $25 million
for the fiscal year, it now appeared that the government would
show a surplus. The Budget Bureau was, in only six months,
realizing some significant results. Then the President turned the
meeting over to the often flamboyant Dawes. "Although he called
the gathering a business one, it had the earmarks of a religious
revival," commented the New York Times.

"The conventional sin of government extravagance was
pictured by Mr. Dawes with all the fervor with which 'Billy'
Sunday and similar revivalists assail a personal devil. He waved
two energetic arms. He loosened his collar, pointed his finger at
Cabinet members, and shook his fist at galleries filled with bureau
chiefs. He would stand facing one gallery and then spin rapidly
on his heel, without ceasing for an instant his flow of language,
and walk toward the other gallery. After the meeting, President
Harding observed that Mr. Dawes was the only public speaker
he knew who could speak with both feet in the air at the same
instant." (NYT 2-4-1922)

Gratifying for the Seagoing Secretary, T.R.Jr., and Admiral
Coontz, all of whom were in the audience that day, Dawes praised
the Navy chiefs for the job they had done to effect economies in
the Navy Department, but it appeared that he was setting them
up, for a moment later he reached beneath a table and produced
two identical-looking brooms, and then "demanded why it was
that the Navy Department had sought to purchase 18,000 brooms
when over in the War Department are 350,000 surplus brooms."
(Ibid.) Dawes spoke with such rapid-fire dialogue that several
hours later when reading stenographers' notes on what he had
said, "He announced that he would not give it out, saying that

it 'read like a mad-house.'" (Ibid.) Those listening that day must have agreed.

The following Monday Memorial Hall was once again packed to the rafters, as the delegates to the Arms Limitation Conference gathered there for the final time. In just over an hour, all the delegates from each country had signed each of the treaties in a ballet prepared carefully in advance. President Harding gave the closing speech. "The very atmosphere [of the conference] shamed national selfishness into retreat," the President said. "Viewpoints were exchanged, differences composed, and you came to understand how common, after all, are human aspirations; how alike, indeed, and how easily reconcilable, are our national aspirations." Following the President, the Rev. Dr. W. S. Abernathy of the Calvary Baptist Church, attended by both Harding and Hughes, gave the benediction. "As the prayer ended, Mr. Hughes thumped his gavel and announced that the Conference for the Limitation of Arms was adjourned sine die." (NYT 2-7-1922) Half a world away, the College of Cardinals had just elected Achille Ratti, Archbishop of Milan, as Pope Pius XI. The world went to bed that night with new hope, with a new pope, and in peace.

Then the storm broke. Two days later Ned announced the cessation of construction on fourteen capital ships, and two days following that, pink slips were handed out to 4,000 workers at Navy yards around the country. While Ned stated he was willing to drop 10,000 enlisted men from the Navy's rolls, Admiral Coontz, the Chief of Naval Operations, reported that the Navy would seek an appropriation some $250,000,000 less than would have been necessary without the Arms Treaty. The Navy would be content with an appropriation of $350,000,000. Getting into the spirit of 'slash and burn' the House naval affairs committee proposed on February 15 that the entire senior class of the Naval Academy, 540 strong, be released to the public without commissions, and that the overall naval budget be dropped to $250,000,000. However, even some of those proposing these economies agreed that it would result in a Navy of less effectiveness than even the 'treaty navy', as they were now calling it. This battle of numbers would ping-pong for quite some time, as members of congress jockeyed for political importance and headlines. Today we know them as "sound bytes".

Meanwhile, the Secretary of the Navy and his Assistant were forging a bond of friendship born of shared battles in the pressure cooker of Washington politics. As military men, both of them knew the irrevocable bonds often produced among men under fire. In his diary for February 15, 1922, TRJr. wrote,

"In the evening we dined with the Denby's. It was a pleasant dinner. At about ten-thirty, the President and Mrs. Harding, who were there, asked us about what we thought he should do. [There follows a discussion about naval appropriations, which were then ongoing.] "During the meeting Denby gave a typical example of the breadth of his character. When he presented the letter signed by him, he said — 'Mr. President, I am presenting a letter which I believe to be accurate and well written. I have signed it, but it was written by Colonel Roosevelt.' There are not many people who would do this." (TRJr. Diary, p.237)

Though many of Harding's and Denby's detractors would later strongly imply that there had been a falling out between these two valiant men, or that their relationship had never really been that close, it is obvious these are the fanciful speculations of writers who failed to do their homework. Furthermore, Ted was tireless in his cheerleading for the navy, as he revealed once again in a speech to the National Rivers and Harbors Conference in Washington on March 2. Arguing strongly for enough men to man the "treaty navy", he destroyed the idea that the scrapping of 27 capital ships would allow the navy to reduce its size, pointing out, correctly, that of the 27 to be scrapped, thirteen ships were then still under construction and there were no crews aboard them. Of the remaining fourteen ships, some were only partly commissioned or out of commission, so that a mere 850 sailors currently manned them. Five days later, this time Ned was again before a congressional committee, House Appropriations, arguing for his minimum 90,000 "working navy" number. The very next day the House Subcommittee on Naval Appropriations, headed by Patrick Kelley, unbelievably a Republican from Denby's home state of Michigan, emphatically called for a reduction in naval enlisted men to 65,000, commensurate with his suggestion of a $200,000,000 navy. By March 19 he was insisting that Denby's plea for a 90,000 man navy "would be ignored and that the bill would call for 60,000 men and proportionate reductions in vessels." (NYT 3-20-1922) At the same time John Weeks, Secretary of War, and General of the Armies Black Jack Pershing, were fighting similar proposals to gut the U. S. Army. Returning from a vacation in Florida, President Harding publicly backed both of his cabinet ministers' positions. To the stubborn House members, Harding pointed out that there would be little help from the Administration during upcoming congressional campaigns should the House insist upon numbers the Administration had deemed inadequate.

After all the posturing, the House Naval Affairs Committee reported out the Naval Appropriations bill calling for an 86,000 enlisted-man Navy, and recommended that the Navy accept only 200 graduating naval cadets from Annapolis' graduating class. In the same article, the Times reported that naval sources had indicated that even this reduction in the navy would almost undoubtedly call for the merging of American's two fleets, the Atlantic and the Pacific, into a single fighting force which would almost certainly be stationed in the Pacific. This immediately, as a matter of course, put every naval yard on the east coast in jeopardy.

On Wednesday, April 19, the House voted 279 to 78 in favor the the 86,000 man navy, with $251,360,000 in funding. The bill then went to the Senate. That evening the fourth and final of the official White House receptions was held, postponed from February 22 because of the crash of another dirigible. The Roma, an Army training craft purchased from the Italian government, and using hydrogen gas, had exploded and burned over Norfolk, Virginia killing 34 of the 45 personnel aboard. The reception on the evening of April 19 honored the nation's military, and in the reception line with the First Couple, were Marshal and Mme.

Joffre of France. Also assisting in the reception line in the Blue Room were the Secretary of War and Mrs. Weeks, and Ned and Marion.

While still battling with those in congress who wanted to defund the military, Ned joined Vice President Coolidge, John Weeks, and a host of other government officials at the dedication of the Grant Memorial on Thursday, April 27, the centenary of the General's birth. The celebrants were also once again joined by Grant's granddaughter, the Princess Cantacuzene. The gigantic memorial which faces the Mall on the western side of the Capitol was nearly twenty years in the making, and was, at that time, "one of the largest groups of statuary in the world, and the most ambitious piece of architectural statuary ever attempted in this country." (NYT 4-28-1922) Since celebrations concerning Grant's centenary were held in several locations, President Harding had chosen the humble sight of Grant's birth, Point Pleasant, Ohio, a tiny hamlet on the Ohio River, as the place where he would honor the late, beloved general. Perhaps he was remembering his own humble Ohio beginnings and, characteristically, taking a lower profile before the man whom he was honoring. Luckily for the President, an alert Secret Service agent of the advance team, E. W. Starling, had voiced concern over the planned trip from Cincinnati up the Ohio River to Point Pleasant aboard the riverboat, Island Queen, electing instead to transport the President on a different and safer craft. En route on that very day, a balcony for honored guests aboard the Island Queen, where the President would have been standing, collapsed, causing injury to some of the passengers. Those sighing with relief remembered also the time during the 1920 campaign when then candidate Harding's train had derailed in Ohio, injuring several, but not harming Warren Harding.

The very next day, on April 28, 1922, the irascible Senator from Wisconsin, Robert LaFollette, began the attack on the Harding Administration by introducing a call for an investigation of the Navy's oil leases. In a lengthy tirade which could serve as a handbook of investigation by innuendo, the lion-maned inventor of the meaning of the word RINO began by calling the oil leases "another Ballinger scandal" — conveniently forgetting that Ballinger was not a scandal at all, but was exonerated by the House Committee which had investigated him. Next, he claimed the Department of the Interior was "the sluiceway for 90% of the corruption in the country," once again completely forgetting that the country was in the midst of prohibition and literally drowning in illegal hootch. In concocting his spurious arguments, he cited both Admiral Dewey, the naval hero of Manila Bay, and Thomas Edison, the Wizard of Menlo Park, as somehow being experts on oil drilling, and claimed without a single shred of evidence whatsoever that "the supply of oil will be exhausted in a brief span of years." And just in case you missed his trump card, he returned once again to "The Ballinger-Pinchot investigation a decade ago [which] did not proceed upon more damning evidence that the public interest was being violated than is ready at hand at this time." But he was not finished. He further described the Secretary of the Interior "as one consistently opposed to government conservation." This was astonishingly rich since Senator LaFollette, and every single one of his senatorial colleagues had unanimously voted in favor of confirming Albert Fall to his Secretaryship a mere thirteen months in the past. He remembered Ballinger from "a decade ago," but he could not remember having voted to confirm "one consistently opposed to government conservation," just the year before. It was a masterpiece of mudslinging, and it was so good that his main tenets would be picked up by others as well as reiterated by himself, and form the basis of the entire Teapot Dome political farce. First you invent a narrative, then you repeat it and repeat it and repeat it until it becomes numbing — and then you quote it as BEING real, and then it BECOMES real.

On Saturday, April 30, LaFollette got his wish as the Senate voted to begin an investigation into the oil leases through the auspices of the Public Lands Committee. The next day in a prominent front page editorial article in Section 7 of the Times, the whole scope of the debate was rather fairly detailed. However, the article stated numerous times that drainage was not possible between the Teapot Dome and the Salt Creek Dome (the government land

and the public land in Wyoming), citing 'experts' as well as the Governor of Wyoming for this claim. What Governor Carey's qualifications for making this assertion were were not explained. The article ended with a curiously nebulous paragraph:

"'Extensive faults,' says a geological survey report, 'MAY have broken the oil bearing sands between the two domes, but their presence can be inferred only from the sharp bend in the anticlinal crest and from certain peculiarities in the distribution of the few outcrops which exist. IF faults are present, they would PROBABLY constitute a barrier that would prevent migration of oil from the Teapot Dome to the higher Salt Creek Dome." (NYT 5-7-1922)

So, it MAY, PROBABLY be that it was not possible to drain the Teapot Dome from adjacent lands by private contractors, i.e. — steal from the naval reserves. But then again, it may be that it WAS possible. Who does not know that you can hire an "expert" to subscribe to ANY position you like? (All emphasis above, including in the quotation, is mine.) The decades long campaign to bury Warren Harding, his Administration, his life, his lineage, his achievements, and anything and anyone associated with him by any means at hand and in any way possible, had well and fairly begun. Including efforts to destroy his Secretary of the Navy.

Chapter Twenty-Two

*"I believe the greatest thing a man can
do is live his life as a gentleman."*

Edwin Denby, Tokyo, 1922

Asian Adventure

The 1881 Senior Class of the United States Naval Academy at Annapolis, Maryland was 72 Cadets strong, from twenty-seven states, thirteen at-large, and three from the Empire of Japan. Most cadets entered the Academy at the age of seventeen or eighteen, but ten of these cadets had begun their studies at the age of fifteen, and four of them at the age of fourteen. Men became men at an early age in those days. The Academy was in its 32nd academic year, having been founded in 1845 by the Honorable George Bancroft, Secretary of the Navy under the Administration of James K. Polk, the President who filled out the borders of most of the Western half of the United States. The Academy in 1881 was superintended by Rear Admiral Christopher Raymond Perry Rodgers, nephew of brothers Commodore Matthew C. Perry who opened Japan for trade with the United States in 1854, and Commodore Oliver Hazard Perry, hero of the Battle of Lake Erie in 1813, two of the greatest figures of the early Naval pantheon. Among the many of the class of 1881 who reached notable stature were John Wingate Weeks, congressman, then senator from Massachusetts, and Secretary of War under Warren Harding and Calvin Coolidge; Ovington Eugene Weller, Senator from

Maryland; Brigadier General Charles H. Laucheimer, Adjutant Inspector General of the Marine Corps during World War I; Major General George Barnett, Commandant of the Marine Corps during the war; Admiral Baron Uryu Sotokichi who was an active participant in the Japanese naval victories against the Russian Fleet during the Russo-Japanese War. One further member of this class particularly close to Ned, was his brother-in-law, Gilbert Wilkes, who had married his sister Hattie and after a lucrative career in electrical engineering, had died suddenly at a young age. As Secretary of the Navy Ned had been invited to the 1881 Fortieth Class Reunion in June, 1921, at which someone (accounts vary) made the grand gesture of suggesting that the reunion for the following year be held in Japan. Everyone agreed that it would be a splendid gesture, and Ned was instantly urged to assist in making it happen, and invited to attend as well. Receiving the full support of President Harding, who saw the trip as a grand diplomatic endeavor, the reunion was set for Tokyo on the 146th anniversary of the independence of the United States, July 4, 1922.

The USS Henderson (AP-1), which would carry the party to the orient, was a United States Navy transport built at the Philadelphia Navy Yard, launched in June, 1916, commissioned May 24, 1917 just in time for World War I, and named, fittingly, after Archibald Henderson, long-serving Commandant of the Marine Corps for 39 of his 52 years in the Corps. She was 483 feet in length with a beam of 61 feet, and could carry nearly 1700 troops at a top speed of 12 knots. She made nine transatlantic crossings carrying American troops to the war and wounded back to the States, and enjoyed some colorful adventures. While never directly attacked, she survived a serious fire on one crossing, a collision incident with another transport on another crossing, and may have rammed a German U-boat off the coast of New Jersey in August, 1918. After the war, comparing notes with German naval forces it seems probable that she had rammed U-139, commanded by Lothar von Arnauld de la Periere, Germany's most successful submariner of the war. After the armistice Henderson again made numerous transatlantic crossings carrying over 10,000 troops home from Europe. She was then used as a troop rotation ship, carrying Marines to and from duty stations all over the Caribbean and the Orient. Just before the historic Japan cruise for the Class of 1881, she was given a refitting and repainting, sprucing herself up for the Seagoing Secretary and his important party, as well as a full complement of Marines who were being taken to duty stations in Asia.

But wait —! The United States Senate had something to say about this wasteful, and useless trip! They called it a "junket" — and well they should know one when they saw one — and declared it a waste of government money, completely unlike any of the junkets THEY had ever conducted! On July 17, with a very small number of members present, the Senate passed a resolution sponsored by Senator Medill McCormick of Illinois, a progressive Republican, objecting to the use of the government transport to conduct the Annapolis Class to Japan. No matter that Ned had written a lengthy and cordial letter to his friend, Senator Miles Poindexter of Washington on May 6, to alleviate any objections the Senate may have had. In his letter Ned explained that the Henderson was carrying replacement troops for Admiral Strauss' Asiatic Fleet, as well as stores, and would be making the trip whether the class went or not. In addition, all members of the class would pay a per diem rate ($1.50) for their passage, and that of their dependents. He explained that of the nearly 600 passengers the Henderson would carry, only about 58 of them were from the Class and their dependents. "I wish to make it clear to you," Ned told the Senator, "that the trip is costing the Government of the United States nothing and that it is regarded by the President of the United States and the Secretary of State as an unofficial diplomatic move designed to bring home to the Japanese people the friendly attitude of the Government and people of the United states." (BHL, Edwin Denby Papers, Box 2) The Saturday, May 20 edition of the Times reported that President Harding had weighed in on the propriety of the far eastern trip, via a spokesperson, saying that he "would almost be willing to pay for the cost of the fuel out of his own private purse, and would have been very sorry if Secretary Denby had decided not to go to Japan on the Henderson." The Times noted the President could not "understand the inexcusable fuss that had been made about" the trip. (NYT 5-20-1922)

Not to worry — when the anchors were weighed at Hampton Roads at precisely noon on Saturday, May 20, the Denbys, including 10 year old Edwin Jr., and seven year old Sue, as his sister was called, as well as Marion's younger brother, Henry Thurber, Jr., were aboard along with the Annapolis classmates and their families. Traveling in the Secretary's personal entourage were Captain Robert Blake, USMC, and Lieutenant J. S. Carey with wife and two daughters, his military aides; Charles Daugherty, confidential stenographer; Henry J. Baudu, USN, official photographer; and Mr. J. C. Brown, reporter with the International News. They were heralded with a nineteen gun salute of farewell as the Henderson headed for their first port of call, Port au Prince, Haiti. They were also sped upon their way by the good will of hundreds of American diplomats and military figures, as well as members of the press who had covered the recently concluded Arms Limitation Conference at which the Japanese had bent over backwards to lend themselves to compromise and cooperation. On the editorial page of the Times for the 13th, under the heading "Friendly Relations with Japan", the editors, after extolling the cooperation of the Japanese at the Conference concluded,

"What could be finer as contributing to the increasing good-will than the invitation of Admiral Uryu of the Japanese Navy to his fellow-members of the class of 1881 at the Annapolis Naval Academy to visit Japan this Summer as guests of the the Japanese Government at a reunion in Tokyo? Twenty-four of the Admiral's classmates will sail from Hampton roads on May 20, and with them will go Secretary Denby, detailed to the pleasant duty by President Harding." (NYT 5-13-1922)

Much has been made, all through the years, of Warren's Harding's "Ohio gang", and of his administration's "cronyism". The biggest 'crony', or in polite language, dear friend, of the 'Ohio gang" was without question his Attorney General, Harry

Daugherty. So it must have deeply chagrinned Ned, just before leaving on his historic trip, to have to step on the all- powerful AG's toes. In April a close friend of Mr. Daugherty's from New York, R. E. Breed, had written a letter to Ned requesting his son, a Lieutenant in the Navy, be granted a six months' leave of absence so that he might try his hand at a civilian business venture. But, hedging the Breed's bets, there was also attached the understanding that if the business venture did not pan out, the Lieutenant would resume his service with the United States government. Ned had denied this request. The Attorney General, just to make sure that Ned had considered all the facts of the case (i.e. that Breed was good friends with Daugherty), wrote Ned a second time, once again requesting that the leave of absence be granted. In his reply to the Attorney General, Ned was the picture of politeness, but also the soul of integrity. "I should very much like to do it," he said, "if it were at all compatible with the customs of the service and if it would not establish a most dangerous precedent. ...... I am very sorry indeed to refuse anything that you ask on behalf of as good a friend as Mr. R. E. Breed seems to be, but —-" (BHL Edwin Denby Papers, Box #5) This story is not related to show the 'cronyism' of Harry Daugherty, for any third grader knows that that is how Washington D. C. is operated under every administration, but to show the absolute integrity of Ned Denby. That Ned actually was sorry that he could not help the Attorney General was a given, for Ned loved nothing more than helping all people at all times.

The newly repainted little vessel steamed straight for the western half of the Caribbean island of Hispaniola, the long-troubled nation of Haiti. Ned had visited Haiti only the year before, and the U. S. Marines had been running the island nation since 1915. Although the Haitians had elected their own government recently, the ultimate authority of the nation rested in the hands of an American, Ambassador Extraordinary John Henry Russell, Jr. Typical of Marine Officers of that, or any, day, Russell had been dispatched to Haiti to command the brigade of Marines originally sent there by Woodrow Wilson, and was later recommended to President Harding to be named High Commissioner after a Senate investigating committee had visited the island. Russell would serve with distinction in Haiti until 1930, when he again took up his mantle of Marine General Officer, later to become Commandant.

Arriving in Haiti at noon on the 24th, the Henderson dispatched its small complement of Marines destined for duty at that port, while Ned, Marion, several members of the class of 1881, and a hand full of naval officers, went ashore. The following day, back at sea, Ned wrote a lengthy letter to President Harding describing his interpretation of Haitian affairs. The United States had "installed" the Haitian President, Philippe Dartiguenave soon after 1915, and the new President, after consolidating his power, had appointed the entire twenty-one man legislative body who were then, in April 1921, expected to re-elect him to a second term. So disliked was he by his own people, however, that the legislature elected an entirely different man, Louis Borno. "Having met both Presidents," Ned told Harding, "I am decidedly of the opinion that this little piece of double-crossing should prove highly beneficial to the Haitian people." He then went on to describe why he felt more hopeful for the Haitian future than he had the previous year, and in addition to the new president, his confidence rested with the enthusiastic and thorough administration of John Russell. Reporting that Marion had enjoyed herself thoroughly during their brief visit, he ended with warm regards for the President and Mrs. Harding.

After two days crossing the Caribbean, and traversing the Panama Canal, the Henderson next stopped at Balboa, Panama. The visit was described by Ned in his next letter to the President as 'hectic'. He inspected the naval installations which he admitted were 'very small', as well as Army installations. The chief concern at this time was the Pacific approach to the canal, the United States already having a distinct military footprint in the Caribbean. He admitted, though, that the current defenses on the western side of Panama are 'entirely inadequate.' and went on to say 'that some steps must be taken in the future to make certain our continued possession of this nerve center of the United States....It is a major problem," he confessed. Presaging Pearl Harbor 19 years into the future, he noted

"Possibly what we have with additional aeroplanes, especially of the sea-scout type, may be adequate. They must be supplemented, however, by large numbers of combat planes to meet attacks from the air, which might easily be made from ships at sea. The need for aeroplane carriers for air fleets could not be better illustrated than by the situation at Panama." (DPL Edwin Denby Papers, box #5)

But, being a 'big navy' man, he hedged in his next line: "This in no wise lessens the continued necessity for capital ships in the Navy." (Ibid.)

On the first day, the Denbys, as well as the Class of 81 and naval officers from the Henderson were treated to a reception from the Panamanian President Barahona and his wife. Ned conducted informal talks with the President whom he described to President Harding as 'not very well', and remarked that at the end of the very pleasant reception, "the President insisted upon sending my wife and me back to the Governor's House in his own carriage drawn by a pair of fine Kentucky horses and with an escort of mounted police. They are fine looking men well mounted on Jamaica ponies and made us feel quite regal as we trotted through the narrow streets of Panama and up to the Governor's house in Balboa." (Ibid.) In letters to both Secretary of State, Charles Evans Hughes, and Secretary of War, John Weeks, he lauded the professionalism and courtesies shown him and his family and his entire party by the United States Minister to Panama, John Glover South, and the United States Governor of the Canal Zone, Jay Johnson Morrow. He told Weeks how upset many of the class had been when learning that the Secretary of War was not able to make the trip.

One day out of Panama City on the broad swells of the great Pacific, the party celebrated their own Memorial Day. The holiday would have been sacred to Ned if he had never worn the uniforms of either the Navy or the Marine Corps, for he could never forget the gallant Colonel, his father, or the resplendent "Decoration

Days" of his youth. At noon, all hands were at quarters. The band played 'Nearer My God to Thee". As is naval custom, Marion cast a floral wreath upon the water, followed by a "floral ship' which was launched on behalf of the Class of '81, and other wreaths cast by wives and daughters of the Class. During the solemn firing of twenty-one minute guns, Ned spoke to the gathered:

"Hear the guns; the Navy's guns cry Peace! Peace to our comrades who travel now no earthly sea. Flowers are strewn upon the waters the world over, flowers not so beautiful or so fragrant as our thoughts of our dead. We must live true to the great past. Every officer and every enlisted man in the naval service has in his keeping his country's honor. The guns of the Navy today cry Peace to the dead and Peace among nations. God bless the dead and may they, and we, when we join them, rest in peace because we have done our duty and have served our country as they did." (DPL, Edwin Denby Papers, Box #10)

En route San Diego from Panama he also wrote Admiral Coontz, his Chief of Naval Operations, and several letters to TRJr. On June 2 he asked TRJr., "Are we being investigated for oil, or resoluted against for going to Japan?" He then wondered what was coming for the graduating class at Annapolis and says they should hear in the next couple of days. He also told Ted Jr. that "the splendors of the Canal are beyond words to praise. Perhaps you have been through, but I don't recall your having mentioned it. If you have not, you certainly ought to go. Your father's memory is revered on the zone in a way that would touch you deeply." (Ibid.)

The weather continued fine for tropical sailing and the party was enjoying itself immensely. However, Ned was not looking forward to San Diego. They had received wireless messages which indicated another extremely hectic and whirlwind stop. Not only would he be inspecting the large naval installations there, but the city fathers wanted to fete him and his party, as well. The Henderson arrived at San Diego on June 8, one day after Albert Fall delivered a report to the President on the oil contracts, and "At the same time Mr. Fall sent to the Senate copies of all contracts, documents and letter files bearing on the nation's petroleum reserves, both naval and those in other public lands, which were called for in a Senate resolution. The documents numbering 2,300 separate volumes, were sent to the Capital in a mail truck." (NYT 6-7-1922) The next day President Harding issued a statement supporting both his Interior and Navy Secretaries and again reiterating that everything that had been done with the leasing of naval oil reserves had been done with his prior knowledge and full approval. While in San Diego, Ned and party were feted by the town fathers at a luncheon where 1000 guests were seated at a table measuring over 2100 feet in length, stretching the entire length of the Marine barracks. He also spent some of his time flying over the installations in the area for the 'bird's eye view'. After the whirlwind days of June 8 and 9 in San Diego, Ned breathed a sigh of relief as his party departed California shores and headed for the Territory of Hawaii.

While on the way to the tropical paradise of Hawaii, Ned took time to pen an affectionate letter to one of his oldest and closest friends, his best man, Henry Lyster. Once again he mentioned how beautiful the weather had been, and added, "None of us have been seasick yet, nor had any excuse to be, as a matter of fact." Of particular interest to Henry, who had been on the Yosemite with Ned during the Spanish-American War, he mentioned that one of the members of the Class of '81 with whom he was traveling, had been on the Yosemite when she had met her end off Guam in 1900. He also relayed to Lyster that his nephew, Denby Wilkes, the oldest son of their former shipmate and mentor, Gilbert Wilkes, had just wired him news of the birth of his third son, "being another grandson of '81," he said. "The Class was quite excited about it." He further mentioned that, as Secretary of the Navy, he could have made his new nephew a lieutenant in the Navy, and then immediately rescinded his commission. But, he said, even though tempted in order to keep the 'Wilkes' name on the Navy rolls, it would not have been fair to those waiting for the honor. Ned also reminisced that it had been thirty-seven years previously when his father had taken his family from Yokohama to Taku Bar (on the China coast) on an American man-of-war, and that "I shall now take my son in an American man-of-war to visit the government of Peking. I hope the tradition may live and that in his turn he may keep our unusual connection with China unbroken." (DPL Edwin Denby Papers, Box #5)

Ned also kept up a lively correspondence with TRJr. about the appropriations bill which was now before the Senate, and other naval matters. That June the Army dropped the requirement that its officers appear in uniform at all times, allowing the men to wear civilian clothing at their discretion. TRJr. was in favor of the the Navy following this practice, believing that it would be a savings to officers who had to constantly launder their uniforms, and also, since the Navy men would be the only ones still in uniform, TRJr. worried that it would look like they had too many officers, and have a negative consequence with congressional appropriations. For some reason not specified, Ned was initially against the idea, but would later embrace it. In a letter dated June 19th, TRJr. brought Ned up to date with the appropriations bill, saying that he had been "in touch with the House confreres, particularly [their chief nemesis] Pat Kelley, and they have agreed to 'go the whole hog' on the Senate amendments. Indeed," he lamented, "they are behaving at this moment far better than our Senatorial friends. The Senators are so profoundly full of their own importance that devious circumlocutions are necessary whenever we have an idea, in order that they may think the idea is theirs, and therefore adopt it." Further, Ted reported that Medill McCormick, another congressional nemesis from their own Party, had been slinging barbs at him over the Henderson trip. But, he said, "they don't, however amount to anything. There is no feeling in Congress, let alone the country, that the Henderson should not have gone." (Ibid.)

Moreover, TRJr. went further: stating that he had been attending all the cabinet meetings, he noted that "We had one day wherein we all talked on the fact that Congress was rudderless and that there was a tendency to investigate everybody at random, without any particular rhyme or reason." (Ibid.) Little did this cabinet know what an avalanche was perched atop the Capital dome which was only waiting for the right moment to begin its rush down Pennsylvania Avenue. It would soon make every attempt to bury them all. Meanwhile, the Henderson sailed into Honolulu Harbor early on the morning of Saturday, June 17, to be greeted by Territorial Governor Wallace B. Farrington, and Mayor of Honolulu, John H. Wilson. In another of the many short visits, with great alacrity the Navy dispatched its materiel and human cargo, took on water and other supplies, while the Island entertained the noted party. Only the day before had the War Department finally ended inter-service bickering by decreeing that the senior naval officer on the Islands, Rear Admiral William S. Sims [yes, THAT Sims], would take precedence over the senior Army officer, Major General Charles Summerall. However, the Times article noted that "the dispute between the two departments, as to whether junior Rear Admirals are to be considered as equivalent to Major Generals in the Army and their relative rank for social purposes be determined accordingly, has not been settled." (NYT 6-17-1922) That knotty problem would be turned over to the Attorney General for a future and final determination. During the first day on Oahu, the party was driven around the island, stopping at Haliewa for luncheon, as guests of the Chamber of Commerce of Honolulu. Perhaps overwhelmed with the abundance of natural beauty found in the islands, in his luncheon remarks Ned said, "You don't like to think of the possibilities that make armies and navies necessary, but we do know such possibilities exist , and they cannot be forgotten by those responsible for the defense of the United States." (NYT 6-20-1922) Sunday evening the gallant Henderson departed the island paradise, proceeding westward toward the darkly mysterious orient.

Steaming at a steady 12 knots, the Henderson made good headway in reasonably good weather. On July 1, nearing Japan, Ned wrote John Weeks once again, remarking that the weather had been 'wonderful' except for 'the last day or two when a storm came up." Surely Ned recalled the tons upon tons of water which washed completely over the SS City of Rio de Janeiro when he had traveled these waters as a teenager, and the receding waves which had carried men out of the saloon and onto the open decks. He told Weeks that he and Class President, US Senator Ovington Weller, were a little bit afraid of the task at hand. At least, he decided, his task as center of attention would become somewhat alleviated by the ceremonies honoring the whole class. He also reported that at a dinner held shipboard during the voyage from Honolulu, the Class of '81 had made him "not an honorary, but an honored member of the Class of '81." He was obviously touched, but his humor still got the best of him as he next stated that since their action "I am beginning to recall incidents of our life at the Academy, and shall be able to tell as may things that never happened as any of them before we get through." He concluded with his hopes that they would be able to accomplish "a lot of good by this trip." (DPL Edwin Denby Papers, Box #5)

The following day, Sunday, July 2, twelve days out of Honolulu, the Henderson was met at the outskirts of Tokyo harbor by Japanese naval vessels, and airplanes, as well as a barge which carried their classmate Admiral Uryu and his wife, Japanese government officials, the Mayor of Tokyo, the Governor of the local province, as well as several American Embassy officials. Admiral Joseph Strauss, Commander of the United States Asiatic Fleet was also on hand for the greeting. No guns announced the arrival of the august party of visitors as official Japan was in mourning for Prince Fushimi, a member of the royal household, who had died recently of influenza at the age of 55. "The day was a bit overcast. For three days we had been sailing in a blow," Ned remarked in his unofficial stenographic notes. "There were no salutes, but up in the harbor daylight fireworks announced our presence. Bombs burst in the air freeing beautiful flags which drifted slowly to the water. It was a naval greeting with much color." After the official greeting party was aboard the Henderson, a second tug arrived filled with both Japanese and American reporters who also clambered aboard. Whereupon the Henderson raised anchor and slowly made its way into the harbor and to its pier. Many group photographs were taken, and then "all repaired to the dining saloon of the Henderson where luncheon was served." Following the repast, Ned chatted briefly with the press, commenting how pleased he was when they informed him that the Japanese Privy Council had that day approved the Washington Conference Treaties.

"Early in the afternoon Mr. Hanihara, the Vice Minister of Foreign Affairs, came on board. Mr. George H. Scidmore, American Consul General at Yokohama, and a number of American residents of the port city visited the Henderson. Mr. Scidmore was Vice Consul-General when Secretary Denby's father brought him to Yokohama on his way to China as American Minister from the United States." (DPL, Edwin Denby Papers, Box #10; private stenographic notes from the trip)

It is worth noting that George Scidmore at that time was one of the longest serving Americans in the consular service, having attained his 46th year of duty in 1922. He had not only been first appointed when the service was a haphazard, fly-by-the-seat-of-your- pants affair, he had demonstrably contributed to the rules and regulations which governed the service of his day. He would pass away four and one half months later, at the age of 68, and, according to his wishes, be buried in the Foreign Cemetery at Yokohama, the city in which he had spent so much of his life. A larger-than-life American who who served America by spending almost none of his life in America. Giants.

The party then boarded a train at 330pm which took them into Tokyo Central Station where another delegation of Japanese government officials and the United States Ambassador to Japan, Charles Warren and his wife met and greeted them. Warren and Ned had known each other since the 1890's in Detroit where the two of them had been renters at the famous "550 Jefferson", or, "the Bachelors". The party was then driven in a motorcade to the as yet uncompleted Imperial Hotel, designed by famed American architect, Frank Lloyd Wright. Ned's stenographic notes described the scene:

"Automobiles......conveyed us at once to the Imperial Hotel which had been put in readiness to receive its first guests. This hotel is built on the site of the old Imperial which was destroyed by fire. It is of oriental design, with a touch of southern California, and still preserving the unique patterns of the Orient in its decoration. As the Secretary turned from the desk after greeting the Management of the hotel, the orchestra broke into strains of the "Star-Spangled Banner" at the conclusion of which the guests were ushered to their rooms in the new home." (Ibid.)

The American party was treated to a dance at the hotel from nine to eleven. The Secretary and his family dined at a small dinner party at the American Embassy.

On the morrow, due to the funeral of Prince Higashi Fushimi, the prepared itinerary was necessarily altered. "One feature eliminated being a court dinner at the Imperial Palace in honor of the American Secretary and the classmates of Admiral Uryu."

"Soon after his arrival, Secretary Denby sent a large wreath of flowers to Princess Higashi-Fushimi with a message of sympathy. Secretary and Mrs. Denby, Major General and Mrs.George Barnett, and Mrs. Barnett's daughter, Miss Anne Gordon, Admiral Strauss, Brigadier General and Mrs. H. C. Haines, Rear Admiral and Mrs. John A. Hoogewerffe, and Senator O. E. Weller, accompanied by Commanders Hasegawa and Sakano, attended the funeral on Monday morning, leaving the hotel at 8:15 o'clock." (Ibid)

The rest of the party was provided a choice of automobile tours around Tokyo, visiting major parks and temples of interest. The balance of the day and evening were given to each guest's preference.

On the following day, July 4th, the regular program resumed with a luncheon given by Premier Baron Kato at his residence where over 150 guests were gathered. "The tables were beautifully decorated," according to Ned's dictated notes, "one striking feature of the decorations being flowers frozen in large blocks of ice." (Ibid.) Ned was effusive in his praise of the hospitality of the Japanese toward his party, and singled out Baron Kato for his excellent work at the Arms Limitation Conference in Washington. In veiled language, however, he cautioned that there "may come a time when in some crisis the ship of state of some other nation may be in danger of wreck. I believe that if such a time does come, Japan and the United States will be found working together to help the troubled ship to harbor and to safety." Here he was almost certainly speaking of Japan's past interference with China, and instead of threatening, he used the amity of the Arms Conference to plead for "mutual helpfulness as the best policy for nations to pursue." The Times referred to the Baron's luncheon as "one of the largest and most brilliant ever given in Japan." (NYT 7-5-1922) Unfortunately, heavy rains forced the cancellation of many of the sporting events which had been arranged by the hosts for the American sailors of the Henderson and the destroyer Alden on which Admiral Strauss, commanding the US Asiatic Fleet, had arrived. Ned spent some time in the afternoon conferring with the Admiral before attending a tea given by his old friend and fellow '550', Charles Warren. In the evening the Class of 1881, with its additional honorary member, was feted at its banquet at the Bankers Club. Ever the perfect hosts, the Japanese entertained the women of the group at a dinner party of their own at the Mitsui's Club with a visit to the Imperial Theater after dinner.

Of the toasts that evening at the 41st Anniversary of the Class of 1881, perhaps one of the most interesting ones was that of Major General, former Commandant, George Barnett, who noted that it was perhaps fitting that he should be selected to give such a toast. He recalled that whenever he had been posted to shore duty, he had requested to go back to sea, and nearly always to be posted to the Far East. "As you all know," the General said, "one who has once visited Japan desires to return." In a poignant nod to the passage of time, the General continued:

"The first time that I came to Japan I found all three of my admirable Japanese classmates living. Admiral Serata was then in command of the Naniwa-kan, a ship which I had visited when it was being constructed at the Cramp [William Cramp and Sons Shipbuilding Company] shipyards in Philadelphia.

"The next time that I came to Japan Admiral Serata was gone, but Rear Admiral Inouye and Admiral Uryu were alive. The next time, Admiral Inouye was dead. Fortunately, this time one of the class is alive, and we are here to do what we can to honor now one of the greatest officers of your navy, Admiral Baron Uryu, who has been beloved by us for the last 45 years."

The following morning, Ned, along with Admiral Strauss, Charles Warren and selected members of the party were formally presented to the regent, Crown Prince Hirohito, while Marion and members' wives were presented to Empress Sadako, the regent's mother. Crown Prince Hirohito had taken over most of the duties of his ailing father. According to the Times, the audience was "quite formal. The regent exchanged a few words with Secretary Denby and Senator Weller, and the Empress spoke briefly to Secretary and Mrs. Denby and to Senator Weller, The others simply approached the royal personages in the usual way, and backed away without speaking." (NYT 7-5-1922)

Ned's stenographic recollections were effusive in praise for the "stately ceremony," and confessed that "we all felt a sincere impulse of friendship and kindliness toward these august personages who seem to have kept their human touch as completely as though they have not dwelt in the seclusion of a palace." He concluded, "We earnestly wish them well."

After the audience the party was entertained by Baron Goto, Mayor of Tokyo at a luncheon at the Industrial Club. The Japanese were justly proud of their nation, their military prowess, and being an island nation like England, of their superb navy. The Baron paid tribute to naval men in his remarks, specifically those at the Washington Naval Conference who had given "evidence to the world that they loved their fellow men better than they loved their ships." He further praised: "With this conspicuous example from the naval men of the nations, our people have been inspired to hope that the fleets of America and Japan, — and not only they but all other fleets that may in future sail the Pacific, — will be the friendly fleets of right and generous countries." (DPL Edwin Denby Papers, Box #8)

In the afternoon, automobiles conveyed the party to the Akasaka Palace for a tea party. The Palace had originally been constructed between 1899 and 1909 as a residence for the Crown Prince. In later years, while his newer residence was being refurbished, it would again serve as Crown Prince Hirohito's residence from 1923 to 1928. Following World War II, it was confiscated by the Japanese Government, and is today used as one of two State Guest Houses of Japan.

In the evening of July 5th, the Americans were hosted at a dinner party by Count Uchida, the Foreign Minister. In his remarks that evening, Ned waxed philosophically upon mankind:

"I have always believed that the education of individuals is never complete until death comes to end the search for truth. Then, perhaps, the only real education begins. Of that we know nothing for we cannot follow beyond the grave. We do know, however, that character building and mind development are constant factors in the lives of men. "So, I believe, do nations change and grow better or worse according to the ethical and educational development of their peoples. At times, it has seemed, that vital elements of progress have been lost forever and that certain troubled nations could not recover from the reactions that appeared to bury their better thoughts." (Ibid.)

It is hard to imagine that the Secretary was not peering directly into the future of Japan, and yet here he was leading his audience to a greater appreciation of the accomplishments of the Washington Naval Conference, and to the very considerable and conciliatory contributions which had been made by the courageous men of Japan of that day.

On the morning of the third day of the official visit, July 6th, Ned and the Class of '81 motored to the Tokyo Peace Exhibition, given by the Exhibition's leaders and their Auxiliary. The exhibition had opened in March to celebrate the peace which followed World War I, and also to promote the development of agricultural, industrial and commercial enterprises in order to contribute to the prosperity and peace of the world. The organizers were more than happy to have the Americans visit their exhibition, and welcomed them with a luncheon and more of the well-known Japanese hospitality.

At 2:00pm Secretary Denby, Baron Uryu and his aide,

Commander Hasagawa, motored to the Imperial University where Ned was scheduled to address the law school students. While many were away on vacation, the attendance was reported at nearly a thousand. Ned began his speech by telling his young Japanese listeners that he had sat "many years ago" in the exact same seats in which they were now sitting - having attended the University of Michigan Law School. He said his graduating class was the largest that Michigan had ever had up to that time - 316 men and one woman. The reason, he explained to them, was that his class was the last time the university offered a two year law degree, that after his class it took three years for a degree in law. Furthermore, he told them, the dean of the law school in his day was "very easy", and if you showed up at all you were pretty sure of getting your diploma. After gaining some confidence of his audience with the details of his schooling, he next proceeded to shock them a bit, in case they weren't listening:

"I have always thought there are two professions more dangerous to true manhood than any other professions in the world. One is is the profession of law and the other public life — holding office." (Ibid.) He went on to explain that these two professions offered the greatest opportunities for temptation and error and furthermore, that the vast majority of men in public office had begun their careers in the law. At least, he explained, it was so in the United States Congress. Of course, there are good and noble facets of both professions, but the allurement to err are great. Next he brought the speech into focus:

"I have always thought there is a great comparison between the man and the nation. I believe the greatest thing a man can do is to live his life as a gentleman, and I mean by that a gentleman in the truest sense — a man who will not wrong his neighbor; a man who will not take undue advantage; a man who will not lie; a man who is true to the code of ethics of his country; and a man, above all, who is a patriot and will fight, if necessary, for his country, and do better than fight, live true to high ideals for the sake of his country. That is a gentleman, and that is the kind of men we want to people the earth with, and when we have succeeded in doing that and educating our young men so that they all try to live up to these high standards, then the rest is easy, And so it is with nations........." (Ibid.)

Later that same day, the Americans attended a tea party given by Kiujuro Shidehara, the Japanese ambassador to the United States who was home on leave at the time. The Shidehara's entertained their guests at the famed Iwasaki Gardens, the estate of Baroness Shidehara's father, founder of Mitsubishi. Baron Shidehara, a close friend of America, would become the first post World War II premier of Japan, and would remain a deeply devoted pacifist until his death in 1951.

In the evening the party attended a dinner at the American Embassy given for the visiting Americans and many high officials of the Japanese Government. One of the most brilliant banquets held at the Embassy for some time, the guest list exceeded 100 persons. The Embassy gardens were illuminated with Japanese lanterns; table decorations were in red, white and blue. After the banquet, Charles Warren proposed a toast to the Emperor, which was followed by a toast by Baron Kato to the President of the United States. The guests then danced in a large tent nearby on the embassy grounds until midnight, with music provided by the band of the Henderson.

The official events attending the anniversary of the Class of 1881 were now at a close. On the following day, a smaller contingent of the group which included Ned and his family, journeyed by train to Kamakura, an hour and a half to the south of Tokyo. At Kamakura, fifteen motorcars were waiting to drive the party the balance of the journey to Kurihama, the small coastal town where Commodore Matthew Perry, USN, had in 1853 opened Japan to trade with the United States. After centuries of isolation, the Japanese had so embraced joining the family of nations, that they revered the memory of Commodore Perry, and maintained the shrine to his honor with great care. The party had been amazed at the outpouring of affection shown by small towns and villages through which they had passed where families and school children held American flags and waved merrily in welcome.

Some pronounced it the highlight of their time in Japan. During short ceremonies at the monument near the very spot where Perry's squadron had anchored sixty-nine years before, Ned offered brief remarks, and Senator Weller planted a tree. While visiting the monument, the party was presented to Shozoemon Obitsu, a 93-year-old man who had been present when Perry and his ships had arrived in 1853. The group returned to Tokyo by 500pm. At 1000am the following morning Ned and his now much smaller party departed Tokyo by train for the two hour trip to the Japanese resort town of Nikko, where they vacationed and rested for the next three days. Nikko had become a tourist destination for western visitors during the past several years, popular for its hot springs, beautiful views, and plethora of beautiful temples and gardens. On Monday, July 10, the party traveled from Nikko back to Tokyo and thence to Yokohama in the afternoon where Ned toured the Yokohama Naval Hospital. In the evening the Denby party was hosted at a "Sayonara" dinner at the Oriental Palace Hotel given by the American Association of Yokohama.

The following morning Ned's now abbreviated party boarded naval transportation which took them to China. The Japanese visit had gone flawlessly. Much good will had been achieved to put a personal nature upon the progress which had been made at the Naval Conference earlier in the year. Japan and the United States would remain at peace with each other for nineteen years, and when that peace was shattered, it was not the Americans who would do the shattering.

Chapter Twenty-Three

*"How long are grown men in the Senate going
to permit this hamstringing to go on?"*

(NYT 11-27-1922)

The Darking Horizon

Following the impressive foreign policy achievement in Japan by the Seagoing Secretary and the Class of 1881, the party sailed from Yokohama on the Henderson to the far western Japanese port city of Nagasaki, where the two groups would part ways. The Class of 1881 continued with the USS Henderson on its mission to deliver troops to various locations, while Ned and his immediate family were met in Nagasaki by Admiral Strauss on the USS Huron. Admiral Strauss entertained the Secretary's family at dinner aboard the Huron, after which the Denbys sailed to Chinwangtao in China near the Manchurian border. Ned had been invited by the Chinese government to make an unofficial visit, and being this close to the wonderful experiences and memories of his youth, he could not resist. Once again with the blessing of the Harding administration including his Secretary of State, he visited the very troubled country of China, upon whose shores he had last set foot 28 years before. The Qing's were gone, swept away in a holocaust of "modern" and "progressive" revolution which converted 5000 years of continuity and culture into the "Republic of China". A government in little more than name only, it was various warlords who controlled vast expanses of the provinces, leaving tiny pockets to the "government" of the Republic.

But, of course, the Secretary, remembering fond days of his own youth, and more than likely thinking of his beloved parents as well, could not resist taking his family to mainland China. His visit being unofficial made it easier for different factions to communicate with him — and therefore the American government — and the most adventurous event of his entire trip took place on Wednesday, July 19 when he was offered and quickly accepted a chance to view Peking from the air. In a Chinese owned Vickers airplane piloted by American Charles Dolan and accompanied by two Naval officers, Ned was enjoying the sights of Peking from the air when it occurred to him that a flight over the Great Wall would be interesting. After following the path of the wall for some distance, the fuel line clogged shutting the engine down completely at an altitude of approximately 4,000 feet. According to the Times, "Realizing his danger, Dolan started to volplane, seeking a landing place. Finally, he located what appeared to be a comparatively clear space in the midst of the hills. Here the machine was brought to earth, only to be wrecked against the rocks that strewed the ground." (NYT 7-20-1922) Almost unbelievably, none of the four men were injured. They had to hike to the closest military station of Nankow where their fate was reported, and a special train was dispatched to retrieve the shaken but happy aviators. Before exact details of the accident had reached the United States, but indications being that Ned was fine, the Free Press could not help but note that "the Secretary is certainly built to bring an aeroplane down without loss of time." (!) (DFP 7-21-1922)

Due to the great distances and sketchiness of communications there was some consternation in Washington about Ned's fate — at least until solid word had been received. TRJr. dispatched an immediate cable through Admiral Simpson fairly demanding information, and at last on July 21 came the official word from Ned himself, "Aeroplane made forced landing. No one hurt." Ned further informed that details of his excitement had been cabled to Secretary of State Charles Evans Hughes by the American Minister at Peking, Jacob Gould Schurman. Hughes wasted no time in transcribing the cable into letter form for the President:

"July 20, 1922

My dear Mr. President:

I am sure you will be glad to see the following message from Ambassador Schurman with regard to Secretary Denby's accident and the happy impression that he is making in China:

"With regard to accident to Secretary of the Navy's airplane at Great Wall yesterday, it was a Vickers machine driven by American aviator Dolan whose skill and nerve in bringing disabled machine down 4000 feet and landing in mountainous region without loss of life or injury are highly praised by Secretary. Party were shaken up but Secretary showed no effects of it in the evening at dinner we gave here in honor him and Mrs. Denby at which sixty-eight Americans and Chinese sat down at table, nor at subsequent reception and garden party where he stood and shook hands with hundreds of people, Americans, Chinese and Europeans and remained till midnight. "Following sentence confidential. Secretary told me he had an exceedingly narrow escape. Chinese giving Secretary hearty welcome and splendid entertainment. He wins everybody by simplicity and democracy of manner and his massively frank and honest presence. His speeches are informal, happy, effective. His previous residence in China and well-known friendship for Chinese help him. Visit doing much good. Secretary leaves tomorrow morning by

train for Shanghai." "Faithfully yours,

Charles Evens Hughs"

(Harding Papers, Dartmouth College)

On Friday, July 21 the Denbys headed by train for Shanghai where they again met up with the USS Henderson. A portion of the Class of '81 had already departed on the USS Logan, and the balance would accompany the Secretary and his family for the remainder of the journey. By July 31 they were in Philippine waters arriving in Manila on August 1st. While there Ned inspected Philippine and American troops at Fort McKinley. He issued a fairly lengthy statement to the press concerning his views of the Japanese trip just concluded, and also on the hot-button topic of Philippine independence. Since the United States had fallen heir to the Philippines following the war with Spain in 1898, the question of the total independence of the Philippine people had been the foremost topic in Philippine minds. In fact, the United States had committed thousands of American troops to pacify the islands over a period of several years, continually finding itself in the precarious balance between beneficent assistance and imperialistic conquest. The official position of the United States' government, from the very beginning and up to Ned's day, had been that the Philippine people were not ready for self- government. Over one hundred and eighty languages were spoken in the Philippine Islands, and the mountain ranges as well as the islands themselves tended to isolate, rather than unify, the people. When the United States took over the Philippines in 1898, education was non- existent, literacy was extremely low when present at all, and agendas were plentiful. It simply was not time to rush headlong into what would have become a devastating civil war, with dozens of factions murderously wrestling for control. Twenty-four years later, when Ned was visiting, although conditions had improved, they were still not at the place where Americans felt comfortable in turning over the reigns of government. "I believe it to be many years away when the American flag will come down here," he said. (DFP Aug 2, 1922) He was correct. It did not come until July 4, 1946, following the successful conclusion of World War II, and the inability of the Truman Administration to delay it any longer. His visit included a trip to "the famous hot springs resort of Lost Banos, 32 miles from Manila, a luncheon in his honor by the Rotary Club of Manila and entertainment by the Masonic bodies of the city." (Ibid.) On August 1, TRJr. wrote he suspected that Ned had been forbidden to go in airplanes any more, adding, "Your accident in China very nearly got me in trouble here. Eleanor has taken it as a text a number of times for a sermon." After discussing navy business, he concluded, "As you unquestionably know, all kinds of dispatches have been received by the State Department, commenting in the most laudatory terms on your speeches, manners, and the effect of the visit. It couldn't have been timed better, and, as things have turned out, we were correct in supposing that nothing of moment would occur in the department."

After a short stop to drop off and pick up troops at Guam, the party sailed to Honolulu, arriving August 22. There, during a three day stop, according to the Times, he inspected military installations "afoot, afloat, from a plane and submerged." The seagoing Secretary became the first Secretary of the Navy to travel submerged in a United States submarine, the R-17, "winner of the submarine efficiency trophy," according to the Times. (NYT 8-25-1922) And apparently, he carried no lingering fears of flying, for he would avail himself of every opportunity to go aloft in the future, including in Hawaii, before his trip was even completed.

From Guam to Honolulu, with consummate graciousness which was pure "Denby", Ned spent some time cabling Secretary Weeks and Secretary Hughes, complimenting them on their diplomatic staff in Shanghai, Peking; and saving extra praise for General Leonard Wood, the Governor General of the Philippines. Ned obviously was exposed to primarily favorable information during his visit, as Wood's term as American proconsul was marred with unrest and considerable distrust among the Filipinos.

By Friday, August 25 the Henderson set sail for the mainland, and on August 31, Ned promulgated a bulletin to the entire crew of the Henderson, singling out the deck force, the Marine guard, the supply department, the medical corps, but reserving special mention for the engineering department for the flawless performance of the ship in meeting every destination on time. The Secretary glowed: "Altogether, in concluding this voyage I am glad to be able to say to you that the performance of the crew of the Henderson ashore and afloat has given me great pride and you, one and all, have my best wishes." Without incident, they reached San Francisco on Saturday, September 2. The Secretary had been out of the country for 105 days, and upon his return the most important thing on his mind was the hoped-for improvement in Japanese-American relations. However, he did not attribute this happy achievement to his own efforts but to the fact that the Four-Power Treaty had "cleared the atmosphere in the Far East." The Times correspondent continued, "The Washington Conference and the treaty resulted in a better understanding between Japan and China, according the Secretary Denby, and promised to bring about improved conditions in both countries. He said Japan showed every intention of living up to the provisions of the treaty." (NYT 9-3,1922) No matter the Secretary's hopes and dreams far outstripped later realities, no one could fault him for not heroically trying — or fail to applaud him for his persistent attempts to give all the credit to others.

The family rested in San Francisco for three days and then boarded train for Chicago. There they split ranks, Marion and the children taking the Michigan Central to Detroit for a further few days of rest with family and friends, while Ned boarded the Pennsylvania Railroad's "Pennsylvania Limited" at 630pm for Washington, D. C. As Denby men had always done, he headed straight to Washington to make his report in person.

While he had been out of the country, major problems had been disrupting and challenging the Harding Administration, in the form of unsettling coal and railroad strikes, and controversy, once again, over the tariff, as well as the Ship Subsidy bill. The Harding Administration, as Ned himself, was deeply committed to a stronger merchant marine, but as with so many good intentions, there were different avenues favored by different factions in pursuit of the correct result. Furthermore, the Administration was also mired, during the late summer months once again over the topic of payment of a bonus to the troops who had fought in the Great War. Against the President's strong opinion that the country could not afford the bill [there WAS once a time when some people

390

in government actually tabulated the cost of bills before simply passing them], in a selfishly political move, the Senate had voted favorably on the McCumber bonus bill on August 31. Virtually as Ned's family was regaining the western shore of the nation, the Congress was in the process of passing the expensive bill. Harding's objections were clear: the bill was set to pay money to a very small percentage of the populace at the expense of the entire country. It did not seem fair, or fiscally sensible. As Ned was speeding across the country on the finest railroad transportation of the day, Congress was sucking up its chest to pass the bill directly in the face of the handsome President from Marion, Ohio. The gauntlet bill was passed September 15, and four days later vetoed by the President. Harding's explanatory press statement is worth reviewing, it is so astonishingly removed from the current norm:

"Our heavy tax burdens reach, directly or indirectly, every element in our citizenship. To add one-sixth of the total sum of our public debt for a distribution among less than 5,000,000 of our 110,000,000, whether inspired by grateful sentiment or political expediency, would undermine the confidence on which our credit is builded and establish the precedent of distributing public funds whenever the proposal and the numbers affected make it seem politically appealing to do so." (Murray, p. 313)

Of far more importance than any legislation or presidential problem, however, had been the extremely grave illness of the First Lady during the waning days of August. Having lost one kidney to disease in 1905, she had been plagued by "severe uremic disturbances [which] had periodically placed her life in danger. This particular bout of hydro-nephritis was so serious that on September 7, one day after Ned had reached Washington, Dr. Sawyer had called in "Dr. Joel T. Boone, assistant White House physician, and two specialists, Dr. John M. T. Finney of Baltimore and Dr. Charles H. Mayo of Rochester, Minnesota, to the White House for urgent consultation." (Murray, p418-419) The President, in all probability at Ned's instigation, had been scheduled to go to Detroit in the third week of September for the laying of the cornerstone of Detroit's new Masonic Temple. Though Ned would have accompanied the Presidential party to his home town, now he would be tasked by the President to preside in his place. Dr. Boone would become very close to the Hardings, and would be there with the President at his demise. "Finally, on September 13 they could report that Dr. Mayo was on his way home and that the crisis was over." (Ibid.) However, the First Lady would remain bedridden for several weeks.

One of the seemingly endless critiques of Harding's Presidency was that he spent far too much time on his own correspondence, and it would appear that this observation was true. Instead of phoning his Secretary of the Navy with a succinct, "I'm tied up here, you're on...." which was all it would have taken, he wrote Ned a rather lengthy and quite thoughtful, letter. For those who enjoy claiming that Harding was an empty-headed boob, there seemed to be quite a few times when he was anything but. He was obviously a committed Mason who strongly urged Ned to convey to the Detroit fraternal orders his great regret in having to back out of his place in the ceremonies. But he saw a larger vision in the proceedings, one that corresponded with what he felt he and Ned and Hughes had accomplished with their efforts at the Washington Conference and the Japan trip.

"[T]he world at large will be much the better for the firmer establishment of the spirit of fraternity among all the peoples thereof. It would be perfectly futile, however, to exert ourselves in the promotion of fraternity among peoples and nations unless we were very sure of the firm establishment of a helpful and trusting fraternity among the citizens of our own republic. I believe our fraternal orders are exceedingly helpful in establishing this fraternity and I know that the Masonic Order plays its full part in consecrating men to helpfulness to one another and to devotion to country. It is good, therefore, to build temples which are symbolic of a great fraternal endeavor and the strength which comes of fraternal unity." (DPL Edwin Denby Papers, Box#5)

So off Ned and Marion went on Sunday, September 17, after a quick stop at the White House to pay their respects to an improving First Lady, arriving early enough in the afternoon for Ned to meet with event planners for rehearsal. Accompanying the Secretary and Mrs. Denby to Detroit was Ned's newly appointed Marine Corps aide, Major Maurice E. Shearer, a decorated hero of the world war. Interviewed by the Free Press on his arrival, Ned commented on the drastic change in the atmosphere in Washington since the First Lady's dramatic improvement, and sidestepped a question about the war in Greece, saying it was a matter for the State Department. (DFP 9-18-1922) The Denbys then retired to the Madison-Lenox Hotel for the night.

Early the following morning a veritable multitude of Detroiters and Michiganders were gathering from all points of the state to converge on the site of a truly wondrous building. Promptly at 1000 am the parade, consisting of 40,000 masons stepped off from their staging area at the old temple and proceeded through the streets to the new structure facing Cass Park on Temple Avenue. They followed on foot a phalanx of brand new Cadillac touring cars, in the first of which proudly rode Ned, with Governor Groesbeck, Mayor Lodge and Frederick Cooke, president of the Masonic Temple association. At the new temple a crowd estimated at 200,000, the largest gathering of any kind ever held in the city of Detroit up to that date, packed the park area and all side streets. Loudspeakers carried the ceremony throughout the area, WCX, the Detroit Free Press radio station, broadcasted the entire ceremony for those who could not attend, and the Metropolitan Picture Company produced a film of the proceedings which was shown that same day and all week in selected local theaters.

Ground had been broken on Thanksgiving Day, 1920, and the partially constructed edifice would not be finished and dedicated until Thanksgiving Day of 1926, but already the outlines of the gigantic structure could be perceived. When finished, it would become known as the largest Masonic Temple in the world, comprising some 1037 rooms, three theaters, the largest of which seated 5000 guests and boasted one of the largest stages in Detroit, three ballrooms and banquet halls, a 160X100 foot open span drill hall with a unique 'floating' floor. Designed in Neo-Gothic architecture, its very image not only soaring toward an Almighty Deity, but also celebrating the noblest achievements of the human spirit. Soaring sixteen stories above Temple Avenue, the building was designed not only with meeting space for scores of chapters of masons, but also with hotels rooms for visitors from out of town.

At noon the ceremony began, Ned sharing the honors of troweling cement for the cornerstone with the Grand Master MacKenzie. Ned wore the actual apron which had been worn by George Washington at the laying of the cornerstone of the Capitol Building, and shared with MacKenzie the trowel and Bible used by the Father of our Country. They had been graciously loaned for this special occasion by the Grand Lodge of Washington-Alexandria. Following the laying of the stone, speeches were the order of the day. Everyone remarked how each band in the procession had ceased playing upon entering the large square, and the mammoth crowd had followed suit, leaving a hushed silence throughout the solemn ceremony. But when Ned was introduced to the crowd to speak on behalf of the President, the cheering could be heard reverberating through the nearby buildings.

After the stone and speeches, five hundred masons repaired to the ballroom of the Statler Hotel where a reception was prepared to cap the event. The Toastmaster, you guessed it — Ned himself. He was the principle, but not the only speaker, as several Masons of high degree also spoke. After Ned had introduced, and the four principle Masonic speakers had spoken, the last to speak, Fred Cooke, President of the Masonic Temple association of Detroit presented Ned with a replica of George Washington's trowel made of pure gold as a gift to President Harding. Ned replied, "Mr. Chairman, I shall take back to Washington for myself a glorious memory, for the president a glorious message, of which this is the symbol."

On Tuesday, Ned spoke once more before his beloved Board

of Commerce, with an upbeat forecast for the future, "I feel quite strongly that the United States is on the threshold of another period of prosperity; all the signs have that prophecy to me," he said. Further, he stressed the great need for an organization such as this Board of Commerce and the principles it was designed to support. "More than ever before, perhaps, this is a time when not only in Detroit but everywhere in the country, there should be a greater spirit of mutual responsibility, of mutual forbearance, of mutual helpfulness and co-operation. I ask you business and professional men in Detroit who are today intent on the upbuilding of your Board of Commerce to keep that spirit in mind." (DFP Sep 20, 1922) Thursday Ned headed back to Washington while Marion and the children remained in Detroit for another week of visiting with relatives.

September 27, 12 Naval destroyers and a supply ship were ordered to the Near East to protect American interests during the intensifying war of independence in Turkey. Requested by the senior naval commandeer on station, they were to join with six American naval vessels already in the area.

By October 2 Marion was back in Washington with the children, in time to wish the Charles Denbys' a bon voyage, as they left Washington on Wednesday of that week for San Francisco from which they were to sail for the Orient. They would spend time in Japan with their son James, Secretary of the United States Consulate there, and also in China. Despite the governmental chaos in China, Charles still had business interests there. The following week TRJr. was in Detroit to kick off the fall mid-term campaign of the state Republicans. Ted reported he could never forget how Michigan Republicans had supported his father, and also praised his boss, Ned Denby, "a real American, as his record in the Spanish-American War and the Great War proved so splendidly and who today is vigorously carrying on my father's policy of an adequate navy, not for aggression but for the maintenance of American ideals." (DFP 10-11-22) All cabinet members were expected to make campaign appearances with the exception of Mellon, and of course, the president, who was yet hovering near his still- recovering wife.

In mid-October, Ned was back in Michigan to attend the air races at Selfridge Field north of Detroit. Named for Thomas Selfridge, a 26 year old Army pilot who was killed in the crash of a Wright Flyer being piloted by Orville Wright in September of 1908. Selfridge had been the first airman to die in a powered flight machine. Selfridge Field was so named when the United States began gearing up its Air Service just prior to World War I by establishing several training fields around the country. Later Selfridge was to serve as home base for the famed 1st Pursuit Group for over twenty years. Formed in France during World War I, both President Theodore Roosevelt's son, Quentin, and Ned's best friend, Henry Lyster, served with the 1st Pursuit Group. Also, some of the early members were young pilots Jimmy Doolittle, Carl Spaatz, Curtis Lemay and over 100 other pilots who all rose to become Generals in the United States Air Force.

Ned Denby, along with his friend Lyster, was also enamored with flight as his presence on this day in October 1922 attested. He was there to cheer on his navy pilots, though it seemed to be the army pilots who took the day. Two new world speed records were set, over 206 miles per hour over a specified course, and over 216 miles per hour on a single circuit. Advances in aviation had come so swiftly that only nineteen years after Kitty Hawk pilots during the Selfridge races were reporting periods of black-outs on some of their turns. The Times noted that in congratulating one of the winners, Ned had "burst into tears," in his excitement. (NYT 10-15-1922)

The following week Ned and Marion took a short trip into New England where Ned inspected the Naval bases at Boston and Portsmouth. They returned to Washington in time for the celebration of the new naval holiday: Navy Day. The brainchild of the Navy League, a civilian organization whose mission was, and is still, the promotion of the Navy, it was decided to hold the event on October 27, birthday of the late President Teddy Roosevelt, former Assistant Secretary of the Navy, and a strongly devoted Navy supporter. Naval ships at seaports on both coasts opened their vessels for touring by the public, shore stations were as well opened to the public, and wreath-laying ceremonies took place at several locations, the most prominent of which was Ned laying a wreath at the Tomb of the Unknown. Initially, approximately twenty-two states participated with proclamations and varying ceremonies, with seemingly the lone voice of opposition (there is ALWAYS one) that of Maine Governor Percival P. Baxter, who somehow worried that by such a national display of naval bravado that the world would be ready to believe we were not going to honor the Washington Naval Conference Treaties. Later in the day Ned was again wreath-laying, this time on the Washington Mall with a bevy of Navy and Marine Corps brass, he paid tribute at the statue commemorating John Paul Jones, father of the American Navy and its first and one of its most renowned heroes. So important to the Navy was his memory that Ned remarked it could have been called "John Paul Jones Day." (NYT 10-28-1922) In addition to the main ceremonies in Washington, Admiral Hillary P. Jones, commander-in-chief of the Atlantic Fleet, placed another wreath on the grave of the noble Teddy in Oyster Bay. Wreaths were also placed at the tombs of the "unknowns" in Paris and London in honor of the Yankee tar-boys.

Throughout October, as the football season got into full swing, the newspapers were full of stories of Ned and other cabinet members, as well as prominent military chieftains, who attended the more important games. Once again Marion joined in the fun which was played out against the autumn denouement of one of the most shameful episodes in Senatorial history. It was the complete and total vilification of one of the Democrats most hated foes: Truman Handy Newberry.

Born November 5, 1864, in Detroit, he was six years older than Ned. Beginning his career with railroads, he worked his way up the ranks to become manager of the Detroit, Bay City and Alpena Railway, then president and treasurer of the Detroit Steel & Spring

Company, and in 1902, he became one of the founding partners who organized the Packard Motor Car Company. Involved in other Detroit business interests as well, he helped organize the Michigan Naval Brigade in 1893, which is where and how his and Ned's paths converged. Newberry was commissioned a lieutenant in the United states Navy in 1898 and served as an officer on the Yosemite with Ned during the Spanish American War. The two, while never close, were life- long political and social acquaintances. A few years later he served as Assistant Secretary of the Navy under the Theodore Roosevelt administration, and after the resignation of Victor Metcalf, the ill Secretary, Newberry finished out his term as Secretary until March, 1909. Without a lot of previous interest in political office, he was persuaded by Michigan Republicans to oppose Henry Ford for one of Michigan's Senatorial seats in the election of 1918. Reportedly having spent well in excess of $200,000 dollars on the very close senatorial campaign (he won by a margin of about 4000 votes), he was promptly sued by one of the richest men who ever lived (his opponent Ford) for spending too much. Of course, having lost, the wealthiest man in America was precluded from having to reveal how much he had spent on his campaign. Only one thing was known for sure: Newberry had spent too much (i.e. he had won), and should be made to pay.

As though that were not enough, Mr. Newberry further had the temerity to become the tie- breaker in the U.S. Senate vote on the hallowed Treaty of Versailles, which included American entry into the League of Nations. The sacrosanct brainchild of the revered Woodrow Wilson, the treaty was voted down by the U. S. Senate on November 19, 1919. The Democrat fury in the Senate, as well as at large, was bottomless, beyond reason, and never-ending. It was mindless, spluttering hatred. Truman Newberry was sued under the Federal Corrupt Practices Act, tried and convicted. He took his appeal to the United States Supreme Court which, in May of 1921, reversed his conviction, making him eligible for his Senate seat. He was then investigated further by a committee of the Senate, which again exonerated him and ordered that he be seated. But that was not nearly enough torture to put one man through, and so the accusations and the editorials and the one and two and three-day speeches in the Senate continued. At one point Senator Thomas Walsh (D, Montana) offered a Resolution that neither Newberry nor Ford should be seated. The wrangling went on and on throughout 1921 and each time it appeared that a vote was close, one Democrat or another would thwart the entire process once again. Things grew so bad that even the decidedly anti-Newberry New York Times editorialized on November 27, 1921, under the title, "The Helpless Senate", over "the latest glaring illustration of the way in which the Senate of the United States deliberately disables itself so that it cannot transact business." It bemoaned that "the most august assembly on earth is left helpless before a single, obstinate member. It denies itself the elementary rights of a legislative body." Though much of the blockage occurred because of antiquated rules, the idea of changing them came only "half-heartedly", if at all, because "a rule forbidding a Senator to talk more than a week would be debated by him for at least two weeks." "Thus the Senate is caught in its own net. It cannot limit debate. It cannot vote to vote. It virtually transacts business only by unanimous consent, and this means that it is at the mercy of one or two unreasonable or truculent individuals. The managers of a Senate bill often have practically to go on their knees to opponents in order to get permission to pass it. They appeal to the 'courtesy' of Senators, but frequently this is merely like trying to call spirits from the vasty deep." (NYT ED. 11-27-1921)

Though the anti-Newberry forces were successful in postponing a vote until the next congressional session, finally, on January 13, 1922, a full three years after his election, the Senate voted to seat Senator Newberry by a margin of 46-41. All 46 yeas were Republican, and all 32 Democrats in the Senate were supplemented by the no-vote of nine Republicans.

But it was still not over. The very next day in an editorial, the Times was hand-wringing in agony over the triumph of the man "who helped THEM drag the country from its high and honorable place of moral leadership." Even worse: "He was a necessary part of the PLOT that in its success has kept the nations in turmoil, in prolonged disturbance and uncertainty; that has postponed indefinitely the day of economic healing." (NYT ED. 01-14-1922; emphasis mine) All of this from a businessman from Michigan who had served his country in the Navy, in war, as Assistant to and then Secretary of the Navy, and commandant of the third Naval District in New York, virtually his entire adult life. Who had spent most of his time during the senatorial campaign IN New York, had done very little campaigning himself, and paid scant attention to the money being spent in his campaign. Easily his most egregious error had been admitting that he had known little, and they used it as a bludgeon against him at every turn.

But it was not about Truman Newberry, it was not about money spent on any campaign, it was not about a senate seat from Michigan — it was about the hallowed, but rejected, League of Nations, and the memory of its holy, but senile, author. It was, in a word, politics.

To prove that point, the ink was not dry on the ballots cast in the midterms of November, 1922, when Woodbridge N. Ferris, the newly elected Democrat senator from Michigan, who had just unseated the Republican incumbent, Charles Townsend, announced he would re-open the Newberry case immediately. Noting that the Republicans had lost seats in the Senate, although still holding a slim majority, Ferris hinted that after unseating Newberry the Democrats might want to re-open the League of Nations question itself. It was too much for Truman Newberry, a 58 year old man who had been hounded for nearly four years, who, despite being exonerated by the United States Supreme Court, and being duly (and again) elected to his seat by the Senators themselves, nevertheless was vilified and crucified on the altar of political advantage. The United States Senators had proven themselves every ounce the children that even the New York Times' Editorial Board seemed to think they were. On

Sunday, November 19, 1922, Newberry wrote a letter to Alex J. Groesbeck, governor of Michigan, resigning his seat in the United States Senate. In a lengthy letter which mostly recounted the series of events as he viewed them, Newberry pointedly admitted the reason why it had all happened, and how he felt about it: "I am thankful to have been permitted to have served my state and my country, and to have the eternal satisfaction of having by my vote aided in keeping the United States out of the League of Nations." (NYT 11-19-1922)

Battered though he was, he had the last laugh for the Senate now had no further way to hound him. He had stepped onto a vast stage, cast a single ballot, and changed the course of history. They might hate him, they might have driven him from Washington, but Truman Newberry did not really care. He returned to Michigan, to his many business interests, and lived a very long and full life, dying at the age of 80, in October of 1945. He had lived just one month shy of twenty-three years, knowing that whatever he had lost — he had won far more. His story is recounted here at some length, for it was almost exactly this same Senate which would just months from now unequivocally prove that there were still lower lengths to which it would stoop.

Ned spent some time in late October stumping for the Republican Party candidates in Ohio and in several Michigan cities. A flap over raising taxes was quashed in early November as the administration let it be known that it would address the deficit expected that year by paring costs. Ned did his part in creating the furor by calling for an increase of Naval personnel from 86 to 96,000. "Denied" by President Harding, the Republicans got to look fiscally responsible once again, severely disappointing Kelley of Michigan who was spoiling for another fight. On November 14, Ned, TRJr., Admiral Coontz and Admiral Washington among others met with the House sub-committee on naval appropriations for a day-long conference on naval needs for the upcoming budget. Having publicly and loudly called for 96,000 men, Ned allowed the sub- committee to assure him that it had no intention of cutting the navy below the 86,000 men it already possessed, which is what he wanted. The following day, at the order of the President, Ned dispatched naval cruisers Cleveland and Denver to earthquake stricken Chile in South America, with medical and food supplies, and extra doctors.

Though President Harding had indicated that he would attend the Army-Navy game this season, at the last moment, he demurred, yet unwilling to travel outside Washington, even for a short distance and time, with Mrs. Harding still not fully recovered. On Saturday, November 25, Army rallied after trailing Navy twice in the game, to win 17-14. The Vice President attended in the President's place, as well as Ned on behalf of the Navy, and John Weeks on behalf of the Army. That evening the Midshipmen gathered for their traditional ball. The following day there was great consternation in the land as it was reported that several middies had overindulged, become boisterous, and had disgraced the uniform. There was even a report that Secretary Weeks had to call the front desk to complain about the noise. To top it all off, the cabinet had only recently been engaged in discussions about how to better enforce the Volstead Act in the midst of pressure from groups on both sides of the prohibition argument. Ned was furious, and announced immediately that a full investigation would take place. He seemed as angry with the Academy's leadership as he was with the cadets, and a full investigation was duly held. It developed that some of the reports had been exaggerated, and little came of it other than Ned's promise that it would never happen again. On Thanksgiving evening, Ned and Marion attended the Navy Relief Ball in Washington, heading the reception line. The ball was held at the Hotel Washington with music provided by the Marine Band. A supper was served at midnight.

News from the Middle East during the month of November was the blockbuster discovery of the tomb of King Tutankhamun in Egypt by the British archaeologist and Egyptologist, Howard Carter. As Carter began explorations of the many rooms of the tomb, newspapers around the world followed the progress of his discoveries. On Tuesday, December 6, former Prime Minister of France, Georges Clemenceau, visited Harding at the White House for a 40 minute talk. Two days later, the ex-Prime Minister was hosted by the President at an intimate luncheon in the State dining room of the White House, where former President Taft joined them, as well as two former ambassadors to France, Vice President Coolidge, and the entire cabinet. Speaking in other American cities, Clemenceau bent over backwards during his visit to claim that he had come for nothing, asked for nothing, wanted nothing. But the truth was, he would bend every ear possible toward a re-introduction of American interest in the League of Nations. Following the hour and a half luncheon, the President took Mr. Clemenceau and the French Ambassador Jean Jules Jusserand, in a private elevator to the second floor family residence for an introduction to the convalescing First Lady. Florence Harding might still not be feeling up to par, but there was nothing wrong with her curiosity.

The remainder of the year was filled with tales of American courage and assistance with the refugees fleeing from the Turkish War; with reports about the scrapping of what ships of what sizes by the Great Powers; how some countries were not scrapping yet but waiting for everyone to sign; more tales of valor on the beloved gridiron; and building up to holiday celebrations. On December 20, Vice President Coolidge, John weeks and Ned recorded special holiday messages to the nation at large via a new invention by Charles Hoxie, a researcher for General Electric. An early sound-on-film process, called the "pallophotophone", it allowed the men to pre-record their messages and be at home to listen to them. The Times skeptically reported, "Although the speakers will be hundreds of miles away from the broadcasting station, the assertion is made that their voices, which have been reproduced in advance on the films, will be heard as clearly as though they were speaking directly into the instruments." The broadcast was scheduled for 730pm and 1030pm on Christmas Eve.

Earlier in December Ned had made a fateful decision in the reorganization of the naval forces. On December 6th, 1922, he appointed Admiral Hilary P. Jones as Commander in Chief, United States Fleet. Instead of dividing naval forces more-or-less evenly between the Pacific, Atlantic fleets, the new plan combined the command structure into one fleet , comprised of the Battle Fleet, the Scouting Fleet, the Control Force, and the Fleet Base Force. The larger Battle Fleet was assigned to the Pacific with the newer battleships and aircraft carriers; the somewhat smaller Scouting Fleet was assigned to the Atlantic; the Control Force would take over after the Battle Fleet had established superiority over an enemy; and the Fleet Base Force was in support. The Special Service Squadron (responsible for the Caribbean), and the Asiatic Fleet were retained as separate entities. This battle order would prevail until just days after Pearl Harbor when the realities of the new war exploded upon the nation with the destruction at Ford Island.

President and Mrs. Harding spent a quiet Christmas alone at the White House. Ned traveled on Christmas Eve to Quantico to celebrate with his beloved Marines. He was able to return to Washington for Christmas Day celebrations with his family at their home on R Street. Mr. Victor Barnes, brother of Mrs. Truman Newberry, and Mr. and Mrs. Barnes Newberry of Providence, all gathered to spend Christmas with their parents, the Truman Newberrys, at their home. Mr. and Mrs. Newberry were scheduled to leave January 3, for a leisurely trip around the world. It would be a restful adventure, decidedly deserved.

Chapter Twenty-Four

"When men speak ill of thee,
live so as nobody may believe them."
Plato

The Cataclysm

Of course, there were many who wanted to see Ned Denby appointed by Governor Groesbeck as the man who would serve out Truman Newberry's term. Most people would jump at the chance to become a Senator, but many underestimated how much Ned really enjoyed being the Seagoing Secretary of his sailors-in-arms. And though there was not a great friendship between Ned and Truman Newberry, Ned could certainly not have missed what a snake-pit the U. S. Senate was. Throughout his political career and following life, it seemed that at almost every turn, his colleagues in Michigan were trying to draft him for a senatorial race. But it was not to be. Governor Alex Groesbeck, after staunchly declaring that he wanted nothing to do with the man he eventually picked, stunned many in Michigan when he selected James J. Couzens to join nerdy schoolteacher Woodbridge Ferris, as Michigan's second Senator. Couzens, born in Canada, emigrated to Detroit as a young man, began his career on the railroad as a clerk, worked his way up to an important job with the Alexander Malcomson coal business, and in 1902 when Henry Ford was organizing his third company, borrowed over two thousand dollars to invest in it. Seventeen years later, after again working his way up the Ford

Motor Company ladder to become vice-president and general manager, Ford would buy him out for $30,000,000 (over half a billion dollars in today's money). A progressive Republican, he would serve in the Senate until his death in 1936. As luck would have it, owing to his support for FDR's New Deal policies, he had been rejected by the voters of Michigan for another term just before his death.

New Year's Day arrived on a Monday in January, 1923, and on Tuesday, the White House announced the resignation of Interior Secretary, Albert B. Fall. The conservationists, still led by "Sir Galahad of the Woodlands" Gifford Pinchot (so brilliantly named by Harold Ickes, long-time Secretary of the Interior under FDR and Truman) had schemed and plotted and spied upon Fall from the day he had been appointed, and were thrilled with his resignation. Fall was a westerner, born in Kentucky, but a resident of the far west for all of his adult life, a two-fisted, no-nonsense rancher and political aspirant. "One old acquaintance, recalling how Fall once disarmed gunman John Wesley Hardin in an El Paso saloon, wrote, 'I have known many brave men. Fall was one of the most courageous of them all.'" (Noggle, p.10) Fall in no way fit in with the eastern elites, such as Pinchot, who believed that conservation was their sole prerogative. For little other reason, they had despised Ballinger over a decade before, wrecked his career and destroyed his reputation. They had again clashed with Wilson's Secretary of the Interior, Franklin K. Lane over the federal oil preserves, and in 1921, they had mounted an all out assault on the tenure of Albert Fall, and anyone connected with him. It is worth noting that in 1921 Pinchot and his friends "were also fearful over the selection of Edwin Denby as Secretary of the Navy. Pinchot recalled that as a congressman from Michigan during the Taft administration Denby had been a member of the committee which reported in favor of Ballinger. 'I went to Detroit afterwards,' he [Pinchot] said, 'and helped beat him [Denby] for re- election.'" (Burl, p.13) The self-selected conservationists stopped at nothing, never forgot, never forgave, and never turned the other cheek. They knew one mode and one mode only: destroy anyone in the way. Even after Fall's resignation, whether he resigned because as some claimed, he had been thwarted by his opponents, or because, as he had announced, his business interests had suffered enough and needed his closer attention, they relentlessly pursued their goal of getting their own way, and obliterating those who differed.

In late December Ned had received a formal invitation from Marion L. Burton. the president of the University of Michigan, his old alma mater, to speak in March, 1923, at the All-University Convocation. He coaxed Ned with the fact that Michigan, with over 11,000 students at that time, represented individuals from all over the United States and many parts of the world, and he would have a vast audience waiting to hear his words. On January 3, Ned replied with great regret that he would be in the Pacific at that time attending and observing the Navy's fleet maneuvers. However, Ned took the opportunity his reply afforded to pitch his idea for a football game the following autumn between his beloved Wolverine squad and General Smedley Butler's Marines of Quantico, Virginia. He had already broached the idea to one of his well-connected attorney friends from Detroit, James Murfin who had taken up the matter with famed coach, now athletic director, Fielding Yost, and been shot down cold because of conference regulations. Ned made a strong case for the Marines' visit by telling Burton of the huge crowds the Marines had drawn in eastern venues, and the great number of Marines who would be willing to make the trip to the midwest to watch the game. "I do not know that I have any particular right to trouble you with this matter, but I simply am full of it and cannot help mentioning it to Michigan men whenever I have the chance," he wrote, further pleading, "If I could only talk to you all I think you would see how much might be accomplished for the country and for the institutions concerned, by this game." (DPL, Edwin Denby Papers, Box #6) In mid-February, Ned found it necessary to invoke the old rule that Annapolis graduates serve a minimum of three years in the Navy after their graduation. From a surplus in the recent past, the navy at this time was facing a shortage of officers to man its ships at sea.

By the beginning of March, all Washington was preparing for the close of the congressional session so that vacations might be embarked upon, or other important adventures be undertaken. President Harding held an abbreviated cabinet meeting on Friday morning, March 2, two days before his scheduled Florida vacation. One cabinet member, the Times' did not specify who, asked if it would be alright if Secretary Hughes, as the senior cabinet official left in Washington after the President's departure, call the cabinet into session in case of emergency. Reportedly, Hughes leapt to his feet and declared that he did not care to have "his official head cut off," a reference to Wilson's wife's firing of his Secretary of State Lansing for doing just that. The meeting was the last cabinet appearance of Albert Fall, who stated that he was not saying good-bye, but merely, "'til we meet again." The Times further noted that more than half the cabinet would be leaving town on the same following Monday, Secretary and Mrs. Weeks and Attorney General Daugherty accompanying the President to Florida, while Ned was heading off to the Caribbean and South Pacific. (NYT 03-02-1923)

As the Presidential party was humming along the rails Florida-bound, Ned sailed once again on the gallant little Henderson in the early evening hours of Monday, March 5. In his party on this trip were 8 Senators, 34 members of Congress, eleven naval officials including his two military aides, his secretary John B. May, 24 newspapermen and 4 moving picture photographers. Absent from the group was the Navy's Michigan nemesis, Representative Patrick H. Kelley, who had elected not to run for re-election in 1923, but ran for a Senate seat, instead, and was defeated. After two days at sea, the Henderson grappled with furious seas off Hatteras "which kept all landlubbers close to their staterooms. Some of the naval officers on the transport said that the storm was the worst they had ever encountered. Secretary Denby," the Times reported, "proved to be a good sailor, spending part of the day on the bridge as the ship made its way slowly past Cape Hatteras." (NYT 3-7-1923) After five days at sea, the Henderson docked at Port au Prince, undoubtedly dropping off some Marines and giving congressmen an opportunity to meet with Commissioner Russell and observe for themselves the status of island politics. Three days later they arrived in Colon, the Caribbean entrance to the Panama Canal, met by seaplanes and a small portion of the fleet, guns booming in welcome for the Secretary of the Navy and CNO Admiral Coontz. The following day the entire party was feted by the President of Panama, Belisario Porras, who was in his third and final term as his nation's leader. After the diplomatic niceties, the Henderson plied the waters of Teddy's canal to the Pacific side where the combined fleet would gather for the largest naval maneuvers ever held up to that time by the American Navy.

By Thursday, March 15, the great ships of the combined fleet were all in place, 15 dreadnoughts and 57 destroyers, as well as many other attendant vessels which formed a veritable armada of seventy-two ships. The congressmen and reporters having been dispersed throughout the dreadnoughts for the best possible viewing platforms, the two-day exercise was commenced. The object of the first maneuver was to display for all to see the difficulty of defending the Pacific entrance to the canal with the meagre defenses that were in place. All were suitably convinced that the shore batteries and fortifications would not be able to withstand an all out assault by a determined enemy naval attack, especially one which might be accompanied by aeroplanes. On the return to Panama Bay, Ned transferred his flag from the battleship Maryland to the submarine 0-4 for another exhilarating dive off Panama. The following day the party reviewed shore defenses of the Pacific side of the canal from land, concluding that the shore defenses were woefully lacking. Everyone seemingly realized what the navy had been saying: that planes, submarines, and larger guns in the shore batteries and better placement were all to be desired.

On Saturday, March 17, the Navy department in the person of TRJr. in Washington, released information to the effect that Ned was shortly to ask for legislation from Congress which would eliminate the age-old distinction between line and staff officers in the Navy. Heretofore, staff officers of the supply, construction and civil engineering corps were separate from those officers who commanded bases, ships and fleets. "Officers of the Construction Corps are graduates of the Naval Academy at Annapolis. Those of the other two are generally appointed from civil life and are not trained in the duties of the line, the chief of which is the handling of warships in preparation for hostilities." (NYT 3-18,1923) As in any attempt to change the status quo, many feathers would be ruffled by this idea, and yet a modern navy was to become much more efficient by the new plan.

A subtle amusement occurred when on the 20th two New York Congressman, Albert Rossdale and Andrew Peterson, deciding they wanted a closer look at a sailor's life, donned uniforms of ordinary bluejackets, ate in the mess hall, drew shore passes and went ashore on liberty. Unfortunately, they were arrested some time later by a naval shore patrol for being out after curfew. "Wireless explanations from the battleship New York were necessary to effect a release," the Times gleefully noted. (NYT 3-21-1923) A much graver event began on the following day as the armada gathered for the naval artillery problems. The great Spanish- American War battleship, USS Iowa, BB-4, the most powerful ship in the American Navy of her day, was to be shelled and eventually sunk in an exercise of naval marksmanship, and the use and effectiveness of differing sizes of naval ordnance. After the first day of shelling with lighter shells, she was down by the bow, but holding her own. Crews worked feverishly to patch some of her holes to keep her afloat for the next day's engagement. On the following day, March 22, "surrounded by the super-dreadnoughts Maryland, California, Pennsylvania and Arizona, the Mississippi's guns began their deadly work [and] the Iowa looked like a diminutive plaything of another age," — as indeed, she was. "Iowa was dealt a death wound that sent her down within sixteen minutes from time the opening gun was fired in the second of two attacks. Nine salvos only were fired in this attack at a range of nine miles. Six of them scored hits."

"Secretary Denby ordered the Maryland's band to play 'The Star Spangled Banner while the Iowa was dying, and its last strains floated over the placid Pacific just as the tip of the Iowa's nose settled beneath the waves. While the Maryland's band played, the national salute of twenty-one guns was fired and 5,000 white- garbed officers and men manned the rails of the four super-dreadnoughts encircling the spot where the Iowa went down. The eyes of many were moist and the admiration for the clear-cut precision of the Mississippi's gunnery was almost blotted out momentarily by the sorrow that gripped all when they saw the Iowa go down to a heroic grave." (NYT 3-23-1923)

It turns out that a crew member of the Iowa from 1898 at Santiago Bay happened to work for the Canal Zone at Ancon, Panama. Charles C. Cameron of Union, Maine, was a member of Iowa's Marine guard, and when he learned of this, Admiral Jones, Captain of the Maryland, took him aboard to witness his old ship's demise. Though the gunnery exercises were a great success, it turned out to be a somber event for all.

The following day, on a much lighter note, the heavyweight boxing championship of the United States Fleet was won by a Sergeant Sneider of the Marines, serving in the guard detachment of the Mississippi, who knocked out C. G. Crowley, a cook from the Utah in ten seconds of the first round. Ned awarded the belts to the winners saying, "I am a firm believer in the great value of sports in our Navy." After a day of church services and rest, the Henderson and its congressional party departed Panamanian waters on Monday morning, March 26. Two days later, the Henderson stopped for a thirty hour visit to the island of Jamaica. The entire party was greeted by the British Governor, Leslie Robyn and treated to a banquet by the businessmen's association, followed by a ball. From Jamaica, the party next travelled to Santiago, Cuba

411

on March 30, going ashore long enough to take an automobile tour of many of the sites from the Spanish-American War. While serving aboard the USS Yosemite Ned had visited Santiago at least twice. After brief stops at Port-au-Prince once again, and Santo Domingo, the party docked in San Juan in early April in time to witness the swearing in of Puerto Rico's new Governor, Horace M. Towner. Appointed by President Harding, Towner had been a several term Iowa congressman, so it was fitting that many of his former colleagues from the House were on hand to cheer him. He would serve as Puerto Rico's governor until 1929, and be relieved in that position by Theodore Roosevelt, Jr. The final stop on this congressional Caribbean cruise was at St. Thomas, Virgin Islands on Sunday, April 8. The Dutch (now American) Virgin Islands had only been property of the United States' government for six years. In a meeting of the St. Thomas and St. Croix Municipal Council, it was strongly urged that the islands be exempted from United States prohibition law since exports from the islands had decreased 73% from the time of its implementation. Also urged was a water reservoir and irrigation projects as the islands had experienced several years of drought which had significantly hurt agricultural production. The Secretary immediately stated he would look into funding for the water project, "adding with a smile that 'water is more important than rum.'" (NYT 04-10-1923) That evening the Henderson pointed her bow toward Washington, and began the final leg of her journey.

By Thursday, sources in Washington were being advised by radio that the Henderson was making all speed toward the capital as the correspondent for the New York Sun, Thomas Dieuade, was seriously ill with a paralysis affecting his tongue, throat and jaw. Dieuade, a well-known correspondent for many years, had been aboard the USS Texas at the battle of Santiago during the Spanish-American War in 1898. At noon on Friday the 13th of April, the Henderson docked at the Washington Navy Yard, fourteen hours ahead of schedule. A little earlier, while passing Mt. Vernon in a driving rain, the ship's bell was rung, taps rendered and the band played the National Anthem. The party had traveled over 6000 miles on land, sea and air — and even under the sea.

In a newsy letter to TRJr., after the Panama exercises were completed, Ned wrote about how pleased he was at the manner in which his navy had performed — especially before such illustrious observers as they had entertained. He also complained about the perpetual naysayers,

"I have received a number of clippings talking about the low morale of the Navy being due to one cause or another, these clippings apparently emanating from the Department. From my observation, the morale of the Navy is extraordinarily good. The behavior of the men here has been beyond praise and their cheerful, contented attitude on ships tells the story of good treatment and of loyal devotion by all hands. We have every right to be proud of the Naval Establishment." (DPL Edwin Denby Papers, Box #6) His "we" of the last statement seems significant: he never failed to include others in his successes.

He rejoiced with his sportsman colleague in the fact that he had gotten in some pretty decent fishing with the American Minister and Senators Phipps and Oddie off the Pearl Islands in the Gulf of Panama. "We caught an almost disgustingly great number of a great variety of fish weighing from five to thirty-three pounds," he said, but best of all — "Not a speech so far!!" (DPL Edwin Denby Papers, Box #6)

But it would not be long before he would be called upon to speak once again before yet another group. On April 22, in a speech in Washington before the Government Club, after strongly supporting the role of the battleship in the current navy, he also tipped his hat to his Assistant Secretary. "Referring to the organization of the Navy Department, Mr. Denby paid a warm tribute 'to that splendid fellow citizen of yours, Theodore Roosevelt,' and said that he admired and respected Assistant Secretary of the Navy Roosevelt and was glad to see him 'where he is'." (NYT 4-22-1923) He also described for his audience that evening the "terrible and beautiful" sight of the sinking of the USS

Iowa, and further praised his bluejackets for behaving themselves on shore leave while in the Caribbean. In an introspective moment he also told his audience of the time when he had left his wife and children to travel far to the south to train as a United States Marine. He referred to himself as "the lonesomest boy in camp," and said "the only thing that had cheered him was to walk out to the center of the camp and look at the flag on the topmast." (NYT 4-22-1923) Later, after several others had also spoken that evening, a motion picture presentation was shown of the Iowa sinking, and the crowd did what all the sailors had done before them: they stood and sang the National Anthem.

It was a busy summer for the Secretary, and it seemed that several midshipman wishing to abscond from his obligation to the federal government which had paid for his four years' world class education had a friend in high places. He heard from Senator Frank B. Willis of Ohio, and even his good friend, John Weeks whom he respected greatly, seeking to allow certain young men to resign upon their graduation. He politely but firmly turned them down, particularly since the navy was no longer in a position to select only the top graduates to man its ships, but was in need of them all. Also in May, he received a somewhat tentative request from the President to at least review a court martial conviction of a pay clerk who had embezzled some thousands of dollars of government money, and after conviction, had appealed for clemency to the President. In his very thoughtful and carefully worded three page reply, Ned pointed out that the young man had been proven guilty of five charges in his court martial, that the court martial findings had been reviewed and found correct. He also stated that if the pay clerk's assertion that his lieutenant had brought charges against him because of his own culpability, that he needed to bring evidence of this fact forward for charges to be brought. He further negated the clerk's reason for clemency being based upon the fact that he was a husband and father, and also a Mason.

"As to the third statement, that he had a wife and family, I suppose that is true, most unhappily for him and for them. That is a condition frequently obtaining in civil life as well as in the military service.

"As to the fourth appeal, based upon the fact that he is a brother Mason, I am frank to say that such appeal prejudices the case in my estimation. I also am a Mason, and the abuse of Masonry in the effort to secure personal favors against the public weal is repellant to my understanding of the principles of the order.

"I cannot recommend a pardon for Pay Clerk . . ."

(DPL Edwin Denby Papers, Box #6 Harding did reply to Ned's letter to thank him, and seemed almost contrite that he had let himself be put into the position of asking. In the same month the President also wrote Ned of his pleasure that the USS Henderson would be available for his use on his upcoming Western trip. The President was setting the final plans in place for his ambitious tour of the western states, to include the then vast and mysterious territory of Alaska.

There were also outright kooks who often wrote the Secretary, offering all manner of goods and services, but usually with a hook. Some of them were addressed to the former Secretary, Josephus Daniels, and these Ned seemed to thoroughly enjoy forwarding to Daniels at his newspaper office in Raleigh, North Carolina as though they were serious correspondence. The former Secretary did not disappoint. Daniels had replied quite excitedly to a previous letter from a German citizen who requested to borrow several thousand dollars for some hare- brained scheme, which Ned had delightedly forwarded. In June, he received another, this time a somewhat irritable reply from Daniels concerning a letter from a "gentleman in Cuba offering to sell me a grape fruit farm. If you had read the letter through, you would have seen it was intended for you and not for me," he complained, "because it says 'I would run the whole outfit for you until you care to resign your post from the Navy and look after your own personal business.'" He carefully pointed out that since he had long since resigned that post, the letter could not be meant for him. It is a certainty that Ned thoroughly enjoyed sharing these replies with TRJr. and others.

In early June, the President was speaking at the dedication of the "Zero Milestone", a small monument which had been placed south of the White House to indicate mileage from a national point of departure. Ned was on the VIP stand with the President when a squadron of Navy fighters flew over the area, disrupting the President's remarks, To make matters even more embarrassing, it was the second time that year that it had occurred, the only redeeming feature being that the first incident had involved army planes. Ned was furious, and was seen leaving the ceremonies immediately afterward when he went directly to Navy Headquarters and issued an order that no naval or Marine Corps planes were ever to fly over Washington without his prior approval. In a letter of apology to the President shortly after, Ned assured Harding that the aviators had no idea they were buzzing the President, and that it would never happen again. In characteristic manner, Harding accepted his apology graciously, saying, "I knew, of course, that the interruption at the Zero Milestone dedication was due to a bit of thoughtlessness against which no one had thought to make provision." The next day the White House released the President's ambitious speaking itinerary for his western trip which was fast approaching, and two days after that, Ned gave the commencement address and passed out diplomas to 404 midshipmen at Annapolis. Garvin and his wife, in town visiting on vacation, accompanied Ned and Marion to the commencement ceremonies. The following weekend, Marion's brother, Thomas joined them for the weekend. On Saturday, the 16th, the party traveled to Princeton, New Jersey where Ned spoke at the dedication of 6 new elm trees on the campus to honor 6 naval heroes. On the following Monday, the Denbys were present when nephew Charles, Jr. graduated from the prestigious school.

On Wednesday, June 20, Ned took action to halt the escalating debate within the navy on the proposal to equalize the qualifications of line and staff officers. '"The time is not opportune for such a change,'"he said. (DFP 6-21-1923) Ever pragmatic, and unwilling to force an issue which entailed so much honest opposition, the Secretary relented. At 200pm on that same day, President and Mrs. Harding boarded their special train coach, the Superb, at Washington's Union Station, and departed on the seven week western and Alaskan trip which had been a dream of the President's since taking office two years before. Though the President had been complaining of the increasing strain of his office, and though Drs. Sawyer and Boone would accompany him throughout the trip, nevertheless "(a) trip to Alaska had long been considered necessary in order to resolve an administrative headache—no fewer than five cabinet officers and twenty-eight bureaus exercised authority over the territory. Many of these were in bitter conflict on how and by whom the natural resources of the area should be developed." There had been a bitter argument between Fall and Wallace in the cabinet, and Harding "desired to go to Alaska and investigate for himself before making up his mind." (Murray, p.440)

Two days later Ned boarded train and headed for Mill Pond Farm, the name the Denbys had given to their farm outside Pontiac. He had hardly arrived when he received a telegram from TRJr. notifying him that because of a clerical error, $4 million extra had been found in the budget numbers which they were preparing to submit to Congress. TRJr. said, with Ned's approval, that they would simply ask for three more mine-laying submarines, since the Navy was known to be light in this category, and Roosevelt had learned from the British experience in WWI that they were invaluable. In a following letter, dated the same date, Ted explained the situation further, added additional details of naval business and in closing mentioned that they were burying Admiral Charles Sigsbee that morning at Arlington. Sigsbee had the honor, or misfortune, to be in command of the USS Maine when exploded in Havana harbor in 1898 touching off the Spanish American War. Later in his career, he had the signal honor to command USS Brooklyn which brought the remains of John Paul Jones back to the United States in 1905, after his body had been re-discovered in a forgotten cemetery in Paris. Ned promptly answered TRJr. by return wire of his approval of the three submarines in the budget.

The next week Ned headed into Detroit for the 25th reunion of his beloved Yosemite crew pals, which was to take place on Thursday, June 28. On that same day, Ned sent off a lengthy letter to TRJr. Addressing it to 'the Acting Secretary of the Navy," he signified how greatly he esteemed and how little he feared the popularity of his more famous colleague. He first confessed himself "pretty tired" after all his recent travel, and mentioned his decision to remain in Detroit for the next few days, as he was scheduled to speak in Dayton, Ohio on July 4th and "do not fancy three [more] days on the sleeper." After discussing several office matters he wished Ted to take care of, he further explained,

"The weather changed while we were on the sleeper and we all nearly froze to death. I have a crick in my back and feel like an old man, but I am looking forward with great joy to meeting my pals of '98 tonight. I shall leave here whenever necessary to reach Dayton for the fourth." (DPL Edwin Denby Papers, Box #6) He ended his letter, "Be good, sweet child, and let who will, be clever, etc."

As Ned was heading down the rails into southern Ohio for his July 4th speech in Dayton, Marion and the children, escorted by her brother Thomas, left Washington on Tuesday for Detroit. They would spend the summer months at the Denby farm north of the city, nestled among the trees and lakes of southern Michigan.

After speaking at July 4th observances in Dayton, Ohio, Ned was back in Washington by Thursday, July 5 to resume his regular duties. On Thursday that week word was received from Paris that the French Chamber of Deputies had finally ratified the Washington Naval Treaties. Much speculation had been entertained as to why the French had seemed to be dragging their feet, and the Japanese had even appeared to be ready to drop the French from the agreement when the word came from Paris. It was speculated that there would be no further delay from the

French Senate, and authorities at the Navy Department and Foggy Bottom breathed easier. Ned led the life of a bachelor for just over a week, and then he, too, departed Washington on the 16th for the farm at Pontiac, Michigan. He took with him as house guests his Marine Corps aide, Major Maurice Shearer and his wife. On that same day the New York Times reported that President Harding, deep into the Alaskan leg of his journey, had gone further north than any other President in history, and that he had operated the locomotive of his train for about 26 miles. He was reported in a "gay" mood, meeting appreciative crowds, and seemingly making progress toward his goal of learning all he could about the vast wilderness of Alaska,

The Presidential party left Alaska on July 22, boarding the Henderson once again at the port of Sitka, once the Russian capital of the territory. They reached the Canadian city of Vancouver on Thursday the 26th for a whirlwind day of parade, golf, banquet and speech. Even for a younger man in better health, the President's schedule on this trip makes one pause. After the exhausting but very enthusiastic day in Canada, which was the first time a sitting President had ever visited that country, the Henderson sailed once again late in the evening for the U.S. port of Seattle.

On Friday the 27th, still several miles out from Seattle, the Henderson was involved in a minor collision with one of its escort destroyers in heavy fog. Though the destroyer sustained some significant damage, it was able to make port with the aid of other ships, while the Henderson was largely unscathed. It was like an omen, and in hindsight, there seem to have been many, for the very next day the President remained in bed on the Superb as it sped south toward San Francisco with what was reported to the press as "an attack of ptomaine poison described as slight." Details revealed that it had first occurred Thursday evening, had become more painful on Friday evening, but that the President was resting comfortably. George Christian, the President's secretary, said "that there was nothing alarming in the President's condition." (NYT 7-28-1923) Arriving in San Francisco on Sunday the 29th, the President's condition was said to have improved. The cause of the malaise had been identified as fresh crabs which had been served on board the Henderson.

Late Sunday evening, however, Dr. Sawyer was forced to issue a news bulletin indicating that the President was still very ill, and that consulting physicians were being summoned. Over the next two days the President's life seemed to hang in the great balance which lay beyond the abilities of the doctors of his day. By Wednesday morning, August 1, they were cautiously reporting some minor improvement in his condition. TRJr. wrote Ned that day almost surprised that "The President has apparently been really ill. I didn't appreciate how dangerous his condition was until about twenty-four hours ago," he admitted. "Fortunately, however, he has now definitely turned the corner. I got a telegram from George Christian late yesterday evening saying that he apparently was over the worst, and I am very much relieved." Further, TRJr. expressed his concern not only for the President's health, but also for Ned's. "What has happened in his case is the exact reason why I wanted you to go away and take these six weeks rest. I have been fearful all along that you would get run down and some slight turn of this sort would come which would be very serious on account of your condition. I do hope you are resting now." (DPL Edwin Denby Papers, Box #6) It is almost beyond irony that all three of these men, TRJr., Harding and Ned, would die of heart related disease at ages 56, 57 and 59, respectively.

Though special prayer services were being held throughout the nation, and sympathetic messages arrived from dignitaries around the world, though hope for improvement would rise, and optimism be born upon the collective breath of the nation, it was not to be. The telegram came via telephone from Washington at 1255am, August 3, HON EDWIN DENBY

PONTIAC, MICH

1927 FOLLOWING RECEIVED FROM SAN FRANCISCO QUOTE THE PRESIDENT DIED AT SEVEN TWENTY PM

FROM A STROKE OF CEREBRAL APOPLEXY THE END
CAME PEACEFULLY AND WITHOUT WARNING SIGNED
DAUGHERTY, WORK, WALLACE, HOOVER UNQUOTE

Ned dispatched two telegrams in heartfelt response: to Calvin
Coolidge, and to his friend, Florence Harding. To the newly-sworn
President he cabled "You have my sympathy and best wishes in
your time of trial. I leave at once for Washington." And to his
friend, the grieving widow, he cabled, "Dear Mrs. Harding, Our
hearts go out to you. You have always been so strong and fine.
May God give you courage to bear this great affliction. The whole
world mourns with you. With affection and deep sympathy,
Edwin and Marion Denby."

In shock and searing grief, the entire nation would now
proceed solemnly with the rituals of catastrophic mourning,
beginning with the fallen leader's crepe-draped train on its 2810
mile journey from the Palace Hotel to the White House.

Chapter Twenty-Five

"I delight in the fact, however, that when the history of these transactions shall be written there will be found no word of mine indicating that at any time I cringed before the blast of political hostility or failed to reiterate upon all occasions that what I had done was just and right and for the best interests of the United States."

Edwin Denby to Will Hamilton, 16 February 1924

Destructive Destiny

In the weeks leading up to Warren Harding's untimely demise in the Palace Hotel in San Francisco, California, the political climate in the country was anything but stable. The Filipinos were once again on the warpath, this time demanding the immediate recall of the American Governor General Leonard Wood, a demand which would go unheeded by the President; one political columnist was proclaiming that Harding's wonderful majority from the 1920 election was all but gone; the Republican candidate in a special senatorial election in Minnesota that July lost to Magnus Johnson of the Farmer's Labor Party, a blow to the Republican party, and a serious disappointment to Harding; several influential politicians from the progressive side were calling for a special session of congress to deal with the "farm issues"; an all out revolt of mid-western politicians was predicted by noted columnist William Allen White, something he said the President was soon going to have to deal with; boisterous Bobby LaFollette was threatening a possible third party bid for the 1924 elections; Republican Senators Brookhart from Iowa and Borah from Idaho were pressing hard for recognition of the new Bolshevik government in Russia. Also in July the French Government created a shrine to the American dead at Belleau Wood, one of the many American cemeteries in France which the French would one day conveniently forget. The President's former Baptist pastor died in Marion at age 58 on July 20, and on the same day, the President's 95 year old aunt, Mrs. Clara Van Kirk Mitchell died in Columbus, Ohio, the first two of the proverbial bad things which come in threes. The very next day, the President's chauffeur, Mr. Edward White was notified by cable of the birth of his daughter weighing seven pounds four ounces, mother and daughter doing well.

Clearly the bloom was off the Harding Administration's political rose, and despite many positives from the past two and one half years, the critics seemed ascendent. Beginning at 730pm August 2, 1923, the critics, however, would take a very brief vacation while the rituals of civilized bereavement were duly indulged by an entire nation and much of the world. While the Presidential train which had brought the President to San Francisco days before was being decorated with the black bunting of mourning, the Harding procession was being assembled, literally, from coast to coast. Millions would line the tracks along the train's route, over one and a half million in Chicago alone. On Friday, August 3, the Free Press caught up with Ned before he had departed for Washington. In speaking of the President, his friend, he said, "He died because he would not spare himself in working for his country." He continued, "I can think of nothing at present except the loss of a dear friend and chief. Everyone loved President Harding and Mrs. Harding, who so nobly supported him in the trials of his great office. and to whom the heart of the world will go out in sympathy." (DFP 8-4-12923) As he had advised the new Commander-in-Chief, Ned left that day for Washington. Marion followed him on Tuesday of the next week, arriving in time to be on hand with Mrs. Hughes and Mrs. New to officially meet Florence Harding's return to the White House with the body of the late President.

The machinery of the United States Government being what it is, Calvin Coolidge, despite finding himself far out of touch in rural Vermont at the death of President Harding, was sworn in as the new President by his father in a mere four hours and seventeen minutes. The following day, the 30th President of the United States was in Washington holding a conference in the Willard Hotel with cabinet members concerning the details of the funeral arrangements. President Harding's train arrived Washington on Tuesday, August 7. He was escorted with great solemnity to the White House where he lay in state in the East Room until Wednesday morning. He was then once again solemnly escorted by the new President, cabinet officers and military contingents to the Capitol Rotunda where his funeral service took place that day, and the body lay in state for public review until that evening. He was then transferred to Washington's Union Station where his Presidential train departed at 730pm for Marion, Ohio, for his final internment. Ned and Marion attended the funeral in the Rotunda and then later in the afternoon boarded the President's train for the trip to Ohio.

Traveling over the B&O, the Pennsylvania, and finally, the Erie Railroad leading into Marion Thursday morning. President Harding's body was removed to his father's home on East Center Street for viewing by his friends and neighbors from Marion. Mr. W. H. H. Piatt. a Kiwanian from Kansas City, Missouri had been tasked by Kiwanis International to attend and to describe the scenes of this last ceremony in the life of Warren Harding, a brother Kiwanian. Mr. Piatt's article appeared in the Kiwanis Magazine for September, 1923. He arrived in Marion on Friday morning, August 10, and by that time thousands had passed by the president's bier in his father's home.

"For hours and hours a line of people more than half a mile in length, eight to twelve abreast, walking as closely one after the other as possible, pressed forward to the home of Dr. Harding, father of the President, there to take a last loving leave of all that was mortal of the first citizen of these United States."

After the very public and pomp-filled ceremonies in the nation's capital, Mrs. Harding had strongly and purposefully insisted that the obsequies in the President's home town be kept simple, and quietly dignified. Marion, Ohio had had a great deal of practice in entertaining large crowds during the months of campaigning in 1920, and though small and humble, was more than capable of handling the 200,000 visitors who descended upon her for the solemn occasion. About noon on Friday, the President was borne by funeral motor coach to the Marion Cemetery where he was interred in a holding vault, pending the construction of a fitting memorial tomb.

"Large as was the crowd and strange to the city, confusion was almost negligible, discomfort unobservable, and complaint thereof unheard.

"At the cemetery thousands found a place outside that reserved for the immediate family and distinguished visitors. When the funeral cortege arrived, the waiting thousands bared their heads to the glaring sun and stood uncovered to the conclusion of the final rites, most eloquent in their simplicity.

"When the casket was borne within the vault and a bugler, stepping to position in its portals, sounded taps in notes clear and silvery, no eye was undimmed with tears nor voice un-choked with emotion."

One wonders if Ned, standing there with Marion at his side among the other dignitaries outside the vault did not remember such a short time ago when he had shared those immortal words for "Taps" with her in a letter from Parris Island.

"Marion's people were wonderful in their courtesy," Piatt continued, "and their hospitality to the strangers within their gates. All were guests in all that is comprehended within that word. Hundreds parked their motor cars on private lawns in response to hospitable signs. "Park here - no charge." All business save supplying food to the hungry and water to the thirsty, was closed. The hotel where I had a room during my brief stay refused my preferred payment for its use, the landlord saying it was his pleasure and privilege to give for the occasion the use of the room without charge." (DPL Edwin Denby Papers, Box #6)

Thus was the 29th President of the United States laid to rest by his grieving countrymen. Perhaps the suddenness of his tragedy called forth the great national outpouring of love and respect that for a brief time seemed to blanket the land. It was not to last. There had already been rumblings of problems in the Veterans Bureau, and there would be much more to come. Because of this precipitous plummeting of Warren Harding's reputation, the permanent memorial for him, so quickly planned, would not be completed until 1927 nor dedicated until 1931. Considered the most elegant of Presidential memorials outside of Washington, D. C., it would be the last of the large shrines built to honor the memory of America's greatest men.

In one of the earliest communications between the new President and his Seagoing Secretary, President Coolidge wrote Ned proclaiming himself thoroughly pleased that the Navy intended to hold the second annual Navy Day on the upcoming anniversary of Theodore Roosevelt's birthday, as it had the previous year. In fairly strong words, the President applauded "the traditional devotion of the navy to the highest usefulness and efficiency [which] makes it especially fitting that Navy Day be observed so as to show the country's appreciation of this splendid service." Though Ned returned to the farm in Pontiac to finish the vacation which had been interrupted by the death of the President, TRJr. kept him well informed about navy business. Concerning the upcoming budget talks which he and Ned would engage in with the President, Ted indicated, "I think he is rather favorably inclined toward us." Ted also reported Senator Henry Cabot Lodge "pledging his support to us all the way through." And again, on August 30, Ted reported, "I think it [budget preparation] is all going well and Coolidge has indicated as much to me in his conversations." (DPL Edwin Denby Papers, Box #6)

By September 5, Florence Harding had returned to Washington, packed, and prepared to leave the capital city. Her plans were still ambiguous at this point, as she had good reasons for living in both Marion and Washington. But for the moment, it seemed appropriate for her to remove to the background. Because her home in Marion was still under lease, and because of the precarious nature of her health, she took up residence at Dr. Sawyer's private sanitarium, White Oaks Farm, on the outskirts of Marion, and except for brief trips, was to remain their for the rest of her life. Before leaving, however, she took the time to say good-bye to some of her closest friends. To "My dear Secretary and Mrs. Denby," she wrote, "I cannot leave Washington without an expression of my deep appreciation of these years of close association with you both. There has never been anything to mar the feeling of sympathy and congeniality which Mr. Harding and I both so much enjoyed in all our relations with you, and I could wish nothing that would mean more to me than that the friendship that was begun so happily may always continue to be a part of my life."

Later that same week came disastrous news from the west coast where a flotilla of fourteen destroyers were traveling from San Francisco to San Diego on the evening of September 8. Navigating by dead reckoning since the radio navigation aids of that day were not trusted by many sailors of the time, the lead destroyer of the fourteen in column, turned east in heavy fog to enter the Santa Barbara Channel, and shortly after plowed into the rocks off Honda Point at 20 knots. Within five minutes, six following destroyers piled into the same rocks. Two more grounded, but were able to back off, and the remaining five were able to steer clear. Twenty- three sailors lost their lives, and the seven destroyers on the rocks had to be sold for scrap, a $13,000,000 loss to the navy. It was the single greatest loss of naval ships outside of war in the Navy's history. The board of inquiry would later establish that compounding the errors made in dead reckoning were the additional factors of dense fog, and unusually heavy currents believed to have been caused by the recent, massive Great Kanto Earthquake in Japan which had devastated Tokyo, Yokohama and surrounding areas. Against the extensive loss, the Navy could take some solace in the heroism of the sailors who survived and gallantly risked their lives to help others in peril. Also of note was the bravery of the Squadron's Commanding Officer, Captain Edward H. Watson, who fearlessly claimed the entire fault for himself, selflessly exonerating all the officers and men under his command.

On September 13, Ned sent a birthday telegram to TRJr. who was at American Legion Headquarters in Saratoga, New York. "Congratulations Ted," his telegram read, "May you have one hundred more." The following week Ted was denying reports that Ned was about to resign as Secretary, and that he, Ted, would replace him. Several New York politicians had been seen conferring at the White House during the week, and thus was the speculation by the press. In early October Ned received a letter from Charles Evens Hughes about the cabinet chair which had been used by President Harding, and which the cabinet had elected to present to Mrs. Harding. A new chair had been purchased to replace it, at a cost of $110, $11 of which was Ned's share of the cost.

Also in early October came the christening of the USS Shenandoah (ZR-1), the first of the Navy's gigantic rigid construction airships to be built in the United States. The ZR-1 had completed its trials, and had returned to Lakehurst, New Jersey on October 3. Great care had been taken to extend invitations to all and sundry who might be interested in the event. Not only government officials, but dozens of aircraft manufacturers, and other government suppliers had been invited. In the morning hours of October 10th, Ned, Marion, Ned Jr., Marion's Aunt Mary Canfield and Ned's Marine Corps aide, Major Shearer, all boarded the train in Washington, D. C. for the trip to Philadelphia where they were met by Captain Hayne Ellis and his wife to be driven to Lakehurst. A large group of invited guests gathered about the gondola just aft of the nose of the massive craft at 200pm to hear Marion repeat the words, "I christen thee Shenandoah", after which she pulled a ribbon connected to a trap door beneath the ship which released three doves which oriented themselves, and then flew off to Washington, D. C. In the time of prohibition, the traditional champagne bottle was taboo. Ned gave a short speech, and read telegrams from the President and TRJr. Then the christening party, including Ned, Marion, Ned, Jr., Ned's brother Garvin and Marion's aunt, as well as a host of naval brass boarded the giant ship's gondola for a short flight. Out over the Atlantic, Marion was asked if she would like to steer, and with her life-long sense of adventure, gladly took the helm. Asked how she had liked it, Marion replied, "It was great, but I'd rather drive my own car and leave the piloting of airships to the Navy." (NYT 10-11-1923) Eleven year old Ned, Jr. would hold a life-long fascination with airships, and only after several disasters had occurred to make the Navy re-think the program, would he elect to join the submarine service instead. Indeed, in 1925, on a good-will tour of the midwest, the Shenandoah crashed in rural southeastern Ohio killing fourteen of the forty-three crew members, including the commanding officer, Zachary Lansdowne. The wisdom of pursuing this technology may be easily questioned today, in hindsight, but to the military officers of the day, only two things were absolutely known: the future of warfare was aloft, and the Germans led the world in airship experimentation. Later that afternoon aboard a train carrying him to New York City, Ned told reporters, "We propose to keep up with every development of aviation. We expect to equal and hope to surpass all other nations." (Ibid. p 23)

While Marion and Ned, Jr. headed back to Washington, Ned took a train to New York to the orthopedic hospital run by his close friend, Dr. Russell Hibbs. Ned had injured the achilles tendon in his right leg playing baseball, and Dr. Hibbs had scheduled surgery. On the morning of Thursday, October 11, Ned underwent a successful operation, and as was the custom of the time, his right leg was encased in a plaster cast for ten days. During this time that he remained in the Orthopedic Hospital he received several updates from TRJr., as well as flowers and letters from a host of his friends. He received, however, no letter in his entire career any more delightful and entertaining than the one from his friend, Major General Smedley Butler, commanding officer at Quantico, and thus, CO of the Marine football team which was to play the University of Michigan in November. Ned had requested the General visit Detroit on his behalf while he was in the New York hospital to make sure all was prepared for the Marine Corps-University of Michigan football game. Obviously, wishing to cheer a friend in the hospital, the irrepressible comedic nature of Smedley Butler seeped through in almost every line. "Our train wandered around Pennsylvania and New York all night, avoiding the hills but none of the bumps, and after a night of pain, we reached Buffalo, where the affable agents of the Pennsylvania Railroad turned us over to the District Passenger Agent of the Michigan Central." (DPL, Edwin Denby Papers, Box#7) So much for romanticizing the rails. Arriving Detroit, the Marines were met by "a Mr. Henry, Mr. Macauley, Mr. Chapin, Mr. Hines, a Colonel Waldron, the acting Mayor of the city whose name, I think, is Hodge; four railroad representatives, a Mr. Metzgar who once built an automobile called the 'Flanders', the ownership of which about ruined me financially and morally; a representative of the General Motors Company whose name I cannot recall, the usual collection of small boys and large automobiles . . . The first inspection having been passed satisfactorily apparently, and the Acting Mayor having relieved himself of a speech evidently written by a funeral director, we proceeded in column of mobs." (Ibid.)

As Smedley Butler had been courted for the job of heading up the American Automobile Association, and apparently was still toying with the offer, he reported to the convalescing Secretary, "I admit frankly that the more they talked, the dizzier I got, and the interview wound up by my passing the 'buck' to Bunny [Mrs. Butler]. I was pretty groggy and holding onto the ropes for support, but by singing 'The Halls of Montezuma' quietly and soothingly, I was able to keep my gas mask adjusted, and was therefore not overcome." The following day he was treated to a tour of automobile facilities around Detroit and flatly stated,

"I really was overcome at the conditions under which Detroit struggles for an existence, it seeming to me incredible that all this work could be done in such a small number of measley looking shacks, particularly that woe-begone edifice used by the General Motors Company as its office." (Ibid.) The once famous General Motors Building on West Grand Boulevard had been completed the year before, and GM had moved into it that very year. After offending as many of the people of Detroit as he could think of, Butler continued with another page and a half of actual details of arrangements for the game and the 1500-2000 troops which they intended to transport to Detroit, and hence, Ann Arbor for the contest. Not probably the letter one would expect from a ground-pounding war-dog who had fought and drunk and scrapped his way around most of the continents of the globe, won two Medals of Honor in the process, and only lacked a third because some of his early adventures occurred before officers were allowed to receive the highest medal of the land.

Monday, October 22, with the aid of crutches, Ned left the New York Orthopedic Hospital and traveled directly by train to Washington, D. C. Though he didn't immediately return to the Navy Department, he did attend Tuesday's regular cabinet meeting, the new President keeping up Harding's weekly cabinet tradition.

It was now, in October, 1923, that the tenacious vitriol of four men came to a boil and thus began the political downfall of Edwin Denby. We have seen how Ned had run afoul of Sir Galahad of the Forests, Gifford Pinchot, as early as ten years previously, because of his belief in the innocence of Richard A. Ballinger - a man who was never charged or tried, much less convicted, of anything, but was hounded out of Washington by a political cabal so vicious that it stopped at nothing whatever until he was destroyed. Pinchot provided the conservation movement with Harry Slattery, a Washington, D. C. attorney, for three years his secretary and lifelong devoted lackey, who poked and prodded Bobby LaFollette into calling for the senate resolution which would begin the investigation into the navy oil reserves. At this point, the entire focus of the conservationists' hostility was directed at Albert Fall, whom they despised, and whom they were determined to prove had done something illegal. LaFollette, at first not seeing enough publicity in the adventure, tried to palm Slattery off onto two other insurgent Republican Senators, Hiram Johnson of California, and William Borah of Idaho, neither of whom wished to become involved. Finally, when Slattery returned to LaFollette to once again plead his case, Bobby told him, "Harry, we will go ahead." (Noggle, p.34) As has been noted, LaFollette did bring his resolution to the senate in April of 1922, which voted it unanimously into being; but for several reasons, nothing was done about it for nearly eighteen months. Politically astute LaFollette requested that the oil reserves be investigated by the Public Lands Committee, rather than the Naval Affairs Committee which would seem to be the logical choice, but which was "weighted with administration supporters." (Ibid. p.43)

Although there were some heavyweight Republican senators on the Public Lands Committee as well, LaFollette correctly surmised that it was his best chance to uncover dirt on Fall. So little importance, however, did the Public Lands Committee place upon this investigation that it selected its most junior member, Senator Thomas James Walsh of Montana to lead it. In the beginning, even Walsh had very little inclination to waste his time on a seemingly non-issue, and "already holding more committee assignments than any other man in the senate, [he] accepted with reluctance and hesitation." (Ibid. p. 46) Furthermore, in June 1922, Fall in response to the senate's request, sent literally a truckload of documents to the Senate. At a meeting with Slattery, LaFallotte and Walsh, it was agreed that Slattery would spend the rest of the summer combing through the documents, and be ready for hearings in the autumn. Thus, on October 22, a year a a half after the resolution creating the investigation, the hearings finally began.

Thomas J. Walsh, the senator from Montana, was an

exceedingly complex man. Of the principle characters mentioned so far, he was the only Democrat. Over the course of subsequent events, he would be joined by others, but the fact is, the insurgent Republicans, eleven years after the debacle of 1912, were still very much a factor in Washington, in national politics, and in the senate in particular. And insurgent Republicans made their reputations by making life miserable for regular Republicans. Walsh had always been a Democrat, but he had not always been an insurgent liberal. He had gotten there over a period of time, with a great deal of help from others. Educated as a lawyer, he quickly became known as one of the finest prosecutorial senators the Democrats had, then, or perhaps, ever. Yet, in his own words Walsh said of himself: "I sometimes accuse myself of coming to conclusions and forming resolutions without due reflection and then afterwards endeavoring to support them by specious arguments having only possibilities for their bases." (Bates, p. 7) This was the character, in his own words, of the man who now took control of the hearings of the senate concerning the matter of oil leases.

We can trace the history of the oil lands, when they were first set aside, by which administration, for what purpose, and with what legal means it was done. We can follow the changes from one administration to the next, from Teddy Roosevelt through Warren Harding. We could see that some people changed their minds over what should be done, and how it should be done, and some decidedly did not. All of this has, however, already been written, and to an exhaustive degree, in many fine books of the past, albeit, most of them pro- conservation, and decidedly anti-Harding Administration. But for our purposes in discussing the life of Edwin Denby, let's begin in 1921 when it was first brought to Ned's attention that some of the naval oil reserves were being drained away by private operators who were drilling offset wells. An important factor in the whole affair also resided in the fact that, for whatever reason, there was a great fear in the United States at this time that our oil sources were extremely limited and might go dry at any moment. In addition to the already near-hysterical fears of the conservationists and the almost pathological distrust of anyone not of their own clique, there was this additional, and we now know by hindsight, completely irrational, fear of the country running out of oil. This at the exact time in history that the navies of the world were as rapidly as possible converting all naval vessels from coal to oil as a means of propulsion. This, also at a time when the congress was once again cutting our land army to the barest bone, and relying on a reduced navy to shoulder the burden of defending our shores in the event of future conflict. Therefore, as David Stratton explained in his excellent book on Fall and Teapot Dome, "Quite simply, the big stakes were in oil during the early 1920's. That is why Teapot Dome became the 'aristocrat' of all the Harding scandals." (Stratton, p.230)

In previous administrations, government department heads had often squabbled mightily over "turf". It is age-old, the petty controversies and arguments over who is responsible for, and/or who is in charge of this or that. The Executive branch continuously debates with Congress in the same manner. Warren Harding wanted to change this, and absolutely, as we have seen, desired to reign in government spending which had gone catastrophically out of control during World War I. He had signed the bill creating the Office of the Budget. He had hired Dawes to sledge-hammer his way through the bureaucracy in order to save money. Not only did Ned Denby hear this message, but he also discovered that "the Navy Secretary's office was responsible for 45,000 acres of public land; the Department of the Interior managed some 3.5 million acres of public land. 'Interior had developed the Bureau of Mines with 150 officials expert in handling oil lands, making technical leases, measuring oil, metering gas, determining proper royalties, disposing of the royalty products, conserving such properties and keeping the accounts.' Interior's U.S. Geological Survey enjoyed a national reputation in matters of oil exploration and petroleum reserve estimates. The Navy Secretary's office, by contrast had minimal staff, limited resources, and a nodding acquaintance with real estate transactions." (Irwin, p. 40-41)

In 1920, before the Harding Administration or the Denby Secretaryship, Congress had been concerned that the oil lands were being drained, and so passed the Minerals Leasing Act. It provided that the "Interior Department, in concert with the navy, would lease navy reserves to private oil firms—the companies paying a royalty or compensation for such leases. The lawmakers' legislation assigned the Interior Department to manage the oil lease arrangements." (Ibid. p. 20) But this did not sit well at all with Josephus Daniels, Secretary of the Navy during the Wilson administration, and he requested and received the "Daniels Amendment" to a Navy appropriations bill, which "accorded the Secretary, not the Interior Department, as manager of the petroleum set aside, specially to use, store, exchange, sell oil at the Secretary's discretion." (Ibid. p.21) So, the basic structure of leasing oil reserves to private concerns had already been set — by Congress — well before the Harding Administration.

Learning all this in his first weeks on the job as Navy Secretary, and knowing how deeply his President felt about saving money, what is surprising about Ned Denby's decision to go to Harding with the suggestion that the meager naval reserves (by comparison with the land which Interior already managed) be transferred back to the Department of the Interior, to be managed by the dozens of government experts already on the payroll, and with more expertise than their naval counterparts? If there was ever such a thing as a "no-brainer", this certainly appeared to be it.

At least, to Ned Denby it seemed so.

If all of this backdrop did not furnish enough skies of gray for Cole Porter's proverbial "Russian play", there was even more. On March 5, 1921, one single day after Ned was sworn in as Secretary, Senator Walsh of Montana had written a letter. A very common, and yet a very curious letter. Common in that he was asking someone in authority for a favor, and curious as to how he went about it, and to whom it was addressed. Thomas Walsh did not know Edwin Denby — yet. So he did not direct his inquiry to the novice Secretary, he addressed it to an old Senate colleague, fellow

Democrat and fellow Westerner, Charles Belknap Henderson of Nevada, who had just been defeated in his re-election bid to the senate and had left his seat two days before. But with all his other qualities which certainly endeared him to the Senator from Montana, he had a singular and very important one: he had attended the University of Michigan Law School with, and was a friend of — Ned Denby. And Senator Walsh needed a favor from the new Secretary because he had a single offspring — his beloved daughter, Genevieve Walsh Gudger, who had a husband, Emmet Caryle Gudger, a Commander in the United States Navy, who was looking for a job. Commander Gudger had graduated from the Naval Academy and had served in Brest, France during World War I as Paymaster. He had returned to the United States in 1920, and was now, through his father-in-law, aspiring to the position of Chief of the Bureau of Supplies and Accounts of the Navy, a job previously held by an admiral who had retired. Senator Henderson's letter to Ned was little more than an endorsement of the accompanying two-page letter from Senator Walsh extolling the qualities and the experience of his daughter's husband. The letter is filled with innuendo and implication, making it sound as though Gudger had single-handedly kept the war going in Brest. Walsh even alludes to Admiral Frank Fletcher's recall from France over procedural difficulties, claiming that Fletcher's entire staff was fired with him, with the single exception of the hallowed Gudger. In a marginal note, however, written on Ned Denby's copy of this letter, was the emphatic notation, "NO. (capitalized and underlined) Lieut. Carey, Lieut. Anderson and all other officers on staff were retained." (DPL, Edwin Denby Papers, Box #6) The Lieut. Carey mentioned here was none other than Ned Denby's private secretary, Joseph Carey. Makes one wonder what other details of the letter may have been exaggerated by an overly effusive father-in-law. Needless to say, Ned "replied that it was his policy to appoint bureau chiefs from the Captains and Admirals list alone. Commander Gudger did not receive the appointment his father-in-law sought for him." (Weisner, p.172)

If this was still not enough, "Walsh had been a leading advocate of the Treaty of Versailles and had often tangled with the irreconcilable Fall in Senate debates on the League issue. It is impossible to say how much partisan revenge Walsh was now exacting against Fall for the treaties' defeat, but this old grudge cannot be overlooked as one of his motivations." (Stratton, p.277) This was the man, thirty-one months after Ned turned his son-in-law down for an inappropriate promotion, this Senator from Montana, who held the reins of the senate investigation into naval oil leases.

Though the hearings plunged onward, nothing much had come to light, and as the October leaves colored, turned and began falling into November, the excitement started to build for the one-time United States Marine Corps vs the University of Michigan football game to be played at Ferry Field in Ann Arbor. A huge parade and celebration was prepared at Detroit. The Free Press had located 35 wounded Marines from Belleau Wood, bought them special tickets for the game, planned their transportation in automobiles donated by Packard Motor Company. All stops were being pulled, as the first contingent of the team boarded an airplane on Thursday to fly to Detroit. Ned, Marion, Commandant LeJeune, General Butler, several admirals and approximately 75 other officers with 50 of their wives, and an additional 1500 Marines boarded trains Friday afternoon for the overnight travel to Detroit.

The big day of the game was scheduled for Saturday, November 10th, the birthday of the United States Marine Corps, the solemn celebration of which had just been established by Commandant LeJeune two years before. Though the Marines had always distinguished themselves in battle, the holocaust of German machine gun nests in Belleau Wood had seared the Leathernecks for all time with the memory of its ferocity and their own heroism in overcoming it. Commandant LeJeune had worked hard, both in World War I, and later as Commandant, to forge his men into one of the most elite fighting forces in the world, and a part of that was celebrating its history, and a part of that was remembering for all time the fateful day of its birth. Every Marine since John LeJeune was Commandant, knows what November 10th means, and Edwin Denby was certainly aware of its significance when he asked for the game with his alma mater. Unfortunately, many of the planning committee in Detroit had no idea of the Marine Corps Birthday, and had begun to call the event, "Denby Day". In his reply to Smedley Butler's letter about the preparations, Ned had emphatically stated, "Under no circumstances can I consent that they shall call the 10th of November 'Denby Day' in Detroit or Ann Arbor, It's 'Marine Day' and that's enough for me. I have very urgent and satisfactory reasons for not consenting to any such foolishness as called that great day 'Denby Day', so I hope you will discourage it in any way you can." (DPL Edwin Denby Papers, Box #7)

The day having arrived, five special trains consisting of 42 sleepers and 11 dining cars, pulled into the station at Detroit at 730am, disgorging hundreds of U. S. Marines, their Seagoing Secretary and his party. After the parade and luncheon, all boarded trains again for the short trip to Ann Arbor. During the first half the Secretary sat with his alma mater, and then at halftime, the Marine band crossed the field. "The band halted before his box and a beaming sergeant stepped forward, saluting. 'Edwin Denby' he said 'the Marines want you to come home.' And then, after the Secretary had walked to the other side of the gridiron, there was another smiling officer who came out of the ranks and said in an echoing voice, 'Edwin Denby, us Marines were lonesome without you. Where have you been all the time?'" The Free Press writer, overcome by the spectacle then wrote, "Imagine saying that to Woodrow Wilson. You imagine it — no one else can." (DPL 11-11-1923) But it was not to be the Marines' day after all, as they could only score 6 points against Michigan's undefeated, Yost-led and highly talented eleven. Ned's alma mater won the game 26-6. The crowd that day was estimated at 42,000, and so excited did the timekeeper get at the beginning of the game that he allowed the first quarter to run past the established fifteen minute allotment all the way to thirty-three. In the evening over 750 attended the Marines' Ball at the Board of Commerce ballroom, in what the locals reported to be the most brilliant military fete in the history of the city. The Red Cross, the Salvation Army, the YMCA, churches and other civic organizations all contributed to feeding and housing the Marines, who then departed Detroit early Sunday morning for Niagara Falls, where they again detrained and enjoyed the local sights for another day. Leaving Niagara Falls on Monday, the Marines were finally back at the base in Quantico by Tuesday morning. It was reported that most of the enlisted men had spent a month's salary on the trip.

In the first weeks of the Public Lands Committee's hearings, however, nothing much seemed to come to light. But in December Walsh began to hear rumors from some New Mexico enemies of Fall's, that the former Secretary had appeared to have come into a large sum of money during the time of the leasing of the oil lands, and just the hint was all it took to unleash the ravenous bulldog which Thomas Walsh had become. Like pouring gasoline onto an open flame, Walsh began pursuing threads and soon learned that Fall had been given a $100,000 loan, originally reported to have come from Ned McClean, the publisher who was a friend of Walsh's. For the balance of the month, Walsh sniffed like a bloodhound, all the way to Florida where Ned McClean and Albert Fall were both confined to beds with illnesses. Fall flatly denied everything. McClean wasn't saying much, and there, once again, the whole sordid affair seemed to stagnate.

In early December the Navy Department announced plans for an all-out exploratory expedition to the North Pole, approved by President Coolidge. The first announcement reported that although ships would be used in an auxiliary role, the primary thrust would be in the air, with conventional craft, as well as the new Shenandoah. The New York Times article described the "over a million square miles on unexplored territory in the Arctic regions between the North Pole and Alaska," and stated that "as much as possible of this and other polar territory will be explored." Furthermore, "An attempt will be made to discover whether or not the theory now held by scientists that a large continent exists in this region is correct." (NYT 12-4-1923) On the same day, in another article, the Times also noted that the inspiration for this adventure had come from Robert Bartlett, a member of Admiral Peary's famous 1909 Polar expedition which claimed to be the first ever to reach the North Pole. The article explained that some months previously Bartlett had urged the Navy Secretary to agree to attempt the undertaking by re-purchasing Peary's original steamer, the Roosevelt, then in commercial service. When discussions followed in the navy department about such an expedition, it was quickly pointed out that by using the old technique of "drifting" through the ice, a process which often took months, a rival nation could easily outmaneuver such an attempt by simply flying to the Pole. (Ibid.) Thus, the plan to use airplanes and, possibly, the Shenandoah. Rear Admiral William A. Moffatt, Chief of the Bureau of Naval Aeronautics, and called today the father of Naval Aviation, was named to head the navy board which was tasked with planning the expedition. By December 26, the Navy had identified the two bases from which it would operate, Nome, Alaska, and Spitsbergen, Norway. In each would be moored a naval vessel fitted with a mooring mast, and accompanied by three fixed wing aircraft, which would augment the principle exploratory services of there Shenandoah. A back-up to the Shenandoah would be the ZR-3, still at present being built in Germany. The expedition was being scheduled for the summer of 1924. It was heady stuff, the very type of adventure which seemed to flow through the veins of the Seagoing Secretary.

The day after Christmas the court in charge of trying the officers in the Honda Point Disaster released its findings. Captain Edward Watson, Commodore of the squadron of destroyers, and Lt. Commander Donald Hunter, commander of the destroyer Delphi, the lead ship which led the others off course, were assigned the loss of places on the promotion lists. Captain Watson to lose 150 numbers, effectively meaning that he would be denied promotion before mandatory retirement, and Lt. Commander Hunter to lose 100 places. Eight other officers charged were acquitted, and the conviction of a ninth was set aside. It was noted that the sentences appeared to be light owing to the fact "that the court [had] evidently taken into consideration the long and meritorious services of the two officers." (NYT 12-27-1923) On December 29, Ned and Marion joined several other political, military and family guests aboard President Coolidge's yacht, Mayflower, for a supper and short cruise on the Potomac River. Plans were developing rapidly for the polar expedition, as a full page article on December 30 in the Times, complete with map and large photograph of the Shenandoah, explained the goals of the quest.

On January 2, the navy announced the plans for 1924's fleet maneuvers to be held from January 12 through the 22nd again in the waters off Panama. The largest American armada ever assembled to that date was scheduled to include "15 battleships, 4 light cruisers, sixty- three destroyers, eleven submarines, one airplane carrier, one airplane tender, eighty-seven aircraft, four destroyer tenders, three submarine tenders, five mine force and thirty-three train vessels." (NYT 1-2-1924) Ned planned to join the fleet during these maneuvers, rather than sailing with them from the beginning. On Tuesday, January 8, Ned joined President Coolidge and John Weeks in laying a wreath at the equestrian statue of Andrew Jackson which stands in Lafayette Square across the street from the White House. "Old White House attaches could not recall any previous Republican President having observed Jackson Day by paying tribute to one of the greatest Democrats." (NYT 1-9-1924) Perhaps "Silent Cal" was hedging his bets before the storm which was about to break.

And break it did, and with an explosion which threatened to engulf not only the Harding Administration and the Republican Party, but the Democracy and the Republic itself! On January 21, TRJr.'s younger brother, Archie, who had been working for the Sinclair Consolidated Oil Company, volunteered that he had been told by G. D. Wahlberg, Harry Sinclair's private secretary, about a payment to a foreman who worked for Albert Fall in the amount of $68,000. Wahlberg further told Archie that he had the cancelled checks to prove this. Archie, knowing quite well what political poison the oil mess was, quit his job and went straight to his brother for advice, TRJr. told his younger brother that he had to go to the committee immediately and testify. Three days later, Edward Doheny read a prepared statement before the investigating committee admitting that he was the source of the $100,000 loan to Fall which heretofore had been attributed to Ned McClean. In other words, Albert Fall had lied to the committee when he had claimed the loan had come from McClean. Doheny, a small, unassertive multi-millionaire surmised that Fall had been trying to keep his name out of the investigation, knowing exactly what would happen when it was known. The problem was that Albert Fall had signed, and Ned Denby had co-signed oil contracts to both Harry Sinclair and Edward Doheny.

On that same day, Thomas Walsh, "declared that the testimony before the investigating committee disclosed TO HIS MIND that the great naval oil reserves protected by three successive presidents, Roosevelt, Taft and Wilson, as an indispensable element to the future national defense, were 'UTTERLY GONE' (emphasis added), and the navy, under the terms of the leases, would get but 6 percent of the oil." What basis in fact for this dramatic claim, or the accuracy of the percentage quoted, was never produced by Senator Walsh. It was not necessary. Senator Walsh was protected by 'senatorial privilege', and he could — and he DID — say anything he pleased. Any of them could. Most of them did.

Fall explained until he was blue in the face that Ed Doheny had been his friend for years, and when land adjacent to Fall's New Mexico ranch had come up for sale, Fall borrowed the money from Doheny to purchase the property. But Walsh and the Democrats were having none of this. They had found the 'smoking gun', the holy grail for a party in the minority facing Presidential elections in just ten months. Elections which also involved that of the erstwhile Walsh himself. It was time to make some hay.

But Fall had already resigned from the cabinet. Of course, the smear had to start with Fall, and Fall had made it easy for them, but there was so much more to do, to accomplish. So the vitriol now swung to the Secretary of the Navy, the OTHER cabinet member responsible for the leases, the man who had allowed, nay — encouraged, nay — had INVITED all of this to happen. Walsh's extravagantly exaggerated attacks now became deadly, personal and cruel. Even the Chicago Tribune noted "that disclosures thus far were 'sordid and ominously ambiguous' [and] criticized 'the strident demands for instant action and the ludicrous scramble to get into the limelight' as being 'plainly cheap politics.'" (Noggle, p.207) In the early stages Walsh had called Ned "stupid" and "careless", but later "he turned on Denby and said 'he should be driven out of public life with all the odium that could possibly attend his going.'" (Weisner, p.172) Though Ned vigorously defended himself, there were few who were listening. At one point during Ned's testimony before the committee when he could not recall exact figures and dates fast enough for Walsh's questioning, Ned offered to answer any questions in person or in writing when he had had a chance to consult the navy records. The committee chairman then asked Senator Walsh if he desired the answers after the Secretary had consulted the records. His reply: "No, that will not do me any good at all. I wish the record to show that the Secretary does not know anything at all." (Weisner, p.171) Put bluntly: "No thanks, I don't want the answers. I just want to make this honorable man look like a fool." Thus the Senator from Montana, job-hunter for an ill-qualified son-in-law, got even with the man who had refused him.

On January 28, 1924, Walsh, at it again, charged Ned with "negligence in his duty; and unless Denby's resignation was in Coolidge's hands by sundown, Walsh promised to 'ask action of this body appropriate to the occasion.'" (Noggle, p.97) On the same day, Senator Joseph T. Robinson of Arkansas, a progressive Wilson Democrat, beat Walsh to the punch, introducing the 'Robinson Resolution' calling for Edwin Denby's resignation from the cabinet. The very next day on the steps of the White House following the Tuesday cabinet meeting, Ned "told reporters that he had no intention of resigning, despite growing demands in the Senate that he do so. He thought that the oil leases were legal and wise. He resented intimations that he was guilty of malfeasance, and he challenged all Senators who thought otherwise to place their sentiments on record. 'I want a record vote in the Senate,' he said." (Ibid.)

By this time a growing group of dear friends, co-workers, and many just plain Denby supporters were beginning to avalanche the Senate with telegrams and letters on Ned's behalf. The effort of support was headed by long time friend, auto magnate Roy Chapin, one of the founders of the Hudson Motor Company and later Secretary of Commerce under Herbert Hoover, the letters and telegrams ranged from the famous Fielding Yost, to John Q. Citizen. Addressed to many of the Senators, a fair amount of them were sent to Woodbridge Ferris, Michigan's Democrat Senator. Nite-letters signed by over fifty people cajoled Senators to consider the facts, to consider the magnificent character of the man these Detroiters and Michiganders knew so well, and loved even more.

Though Republicans had called for some modicum of fairness in the continuing vituperation of their Democrat fellows, they called in vain. So out of control was the downhill racer of Democrat destruction that one of their own, Senator James A. Reed, Democrat of Missouri, now provided the Republicans with Teapot ammunition of their own. Reed, with Presidential aspirations, called for Doheny to be summoned before the committee again to be asked very specifically if he had ever employed any government official, while that official had been serving or after serving. Republican Senator Lenroot was prompted by Reed ahead of time, and had calculated precisely the information he wished to be revealed. Yes, Ed Doheny replied to the question, as luck would have it, he had once employed Wilson's Attorney General, Thomas W. Gregory, who had just days before been appointed by President Coolidge as Special Counsel to investigate — Ed Doheny, oil leases, Teapot Dome. Furthermore, he had also employed the California legal firm of McAdoo, Cotton and Franklin, and had paid William Gibbs McAdoo, Wilson's Secretary of the Treasury and also his son-in-law, approximately $250,000. Most damaging of all, William McAdoo was far and away the favorite candidate for the Democrat nomination for the presidency of the 1924 election, and in one fell swoop, James Reed had nearly removed him from contention. Though McAdoo and others of his supporters would work tirelessly on damage control, it soon became clear that his Doheny association would not only destroy his own political plans, but could jeopardize the investigation as well. In one of the great "what ifs" of American politics, one is left to contemplate how different history might have been had a clean and popular William McAdoo run against an ill-equipped, self-effacing, oil-scandal-smeared Silent Cal Coolidge. Thomas Gregory quietly withdrew his name from consideration as Special Counsel, and eventually, William McAdieu, as the Republicans were now calling him, was rejected at the Democratic National Convention.

All of Ned's thousands of Michigan supporters, and telegrams from virtually all over the country notwithstanding, on Monday, February 11, in the early evening the Senate voted on the Robinson Resolution to demand President Coolidge fire Edwin Denby from his cabinet. The vote was 47 in favor, including the votes of 10 Republicans (Brookhart, Capper, Frazier, Herald, Johnson of California, Ladd, LaFollette, McNary, Norbeck and Norris), with only 34 against. Only one single Democrat, William Cabell Bruce of Maryland (father of David K. E. Bruce of OSS fame, and later U. S. Ambassador to France, West Germany and the United Kingdom), had the courage to vote against the lynch mentality. Woodbridge Ferris, the school marm from Michigan voted against his fellow Wolverine. William Borah, Republican from Idaho, stated flatly on the Senate floor that the only reason he was opposed was because he disagreed with the Senate's right to interfere in the President's appointees. Within hours Silent Cal fired back. "I do not propose to sacrifice any innocent man for my own welfare," flatly declared the President of the United States in open defiance of the Senate. But it was mostly for show.

What the embattled President really meant was he would gladly sacrifice anyone and anything on the sacred precept of re-election. Though Ned, too, publicly avowed he would never resign, but would fight to the end, the negotiations had already begun between him and the White House. Coolidge selected Ned's closest friend in the cabinet, John Weeks, to deliver the message, and once it was clear to Ned that his liability trumped the truth, the outcome was decided. Eight days after the Senate vote, Ned tendered his resignation to the President. But he qualified it, however insignificantly, for his own dignity: "It will always be gratifying to me that neither you nor anyone else has at any time advised me to resign," he said, and though he cordially thanked the President for his support after the vote, he picked his own day to resign. "As there are a few pending matters which should receive my personal attention, I suggest that my resignation be accepted as of the date of March 10th, 1924." He once again reiterated his thanks, "I assure you again of my appreciation of the many courtesies you have shown me and of your last great act in refusing to accede to the demand of the Senate that you ask my resignation. With cordial regards to you and Mrs. Coolidge and best wishes always........." the Seagoing Secretary, with unparalleled graciousness in the face of calumny, bowed his great, scarred head, and quietly left the stage.

Chapter Twenty-Six

And how can man die better
Than facing fearful odds
For the ashes of his fathers
And the temples of his gods?

Old Roman lay

Bitterness Be Gone

The principle reason Ned Denby resigned on February 18, but made his resignation date effective March 10, 1924 was to dare Thomas Walsh and the other rabid Democrats of the Senate to impeach him. Many of them had brought serious charges, not to overlook completely false and slanderous accusations, against him. They had done their best to smear him with the taint of incompetence and corruption. But of course, there was no one in the Senate, including, perhaps, especially, Mr. Walsh, who was ready to bring impeachment charges against Ned Denby. Not the cagey Bobbie LaFollette, nor the pugilistic Joseph Robinson of Arkansas, nor any one of the others who had voted against Ned on February 11th, and the main reason why they were not a very simple one: they knew perfectly well that he was guilty of nothing whatsoever. "Inviting attention to the fact that he will remain in office until March 10, Mr. Denby declared that in the interim there is 'plenty of time for impeachment proceedings to be begun,' and that anyone who says he is resigning for fear of impeachment 'simply lies.'" (NYT 02/18/1924) On the same day as receiving Ned's resignation, Coolidge replied in tones so carefully measured as to chill the soul. He would be cordial, he would be correct, but there would be no mercy in the sentence. He would "treasure and reciprocate your expressions of friendship," and "remember the fine sense of loyalty which you have always exhibited toward me with much satisfaction," but there would be no reprieve, and there would be no warmth. A day later Ned dropped the President a note saying he would not be attending any more cabinet meetings. Two days later Coolidge replied that he was sure he and the other cabinet members would like to have Ned attend "until the end of your term". As though he were finishing up a semester at the Bryn Mawr. Awkwardly, on the same date, Ned sent a thank you note to Mrs. Coolidge, in appreciation of the flowers she and the President had sent Ned on his birthday, two weeks before.

Perhaps another reason Ned had for resigning when he did was the fact that the President had unceremoniously called for the cancelling of the much-heralded Polar Expedition just the week before, citing certain nebulous opposition he had detected in congress. Given how deeply committed to the adventure Ned was, it almost certainly felt to him like a double blow of infamy. He tried vainly to convince the President to reconsider, but it was to no avail. Though he faithfully carried out his orders to halt the expedition, he made it crystal clear in his press release who was cancelling and why:

"Memorandum for the Press Navy Department
15 February 1924

Orders to cease preparation for the polar expedition were issued today by the Secretary of the Navy. The President, having been informed that considerable opposition existed in Congress, instructed the Department not to proceed with the expedition at this time nor until the naval bills have been considered and Congress given an opportunity, if it desires, to express its views upon the Polar expedition." (DPL, Edwin Denby Papers, Box #8)

One can almost feel the brittleness and bitterness of the words which the Secretary selected to inform the world of yet this one additional indignity. And this is not Edwin Denby feeling slighted for Edwin Denby, it is the Seagoing Secretary furious over the slight to his beloved Navy.

Ned had received a great deal of mail in support of his cause during the days leading up to his resignation, but after it, he was deluged with letters of indignation, surprise, and support from all across their country. From the cabinet in which he still served he received condolences from Charles Evans Hughes ("Will you permit me to congratulate you on the manly attitude you have taken during the trying ordeal of the past months......through it all you have maintained a personal dignity and bearing which have made a lasting impression upon the American people,") John Weeks ("I shall always have for you the affection which has resulted from close association, and admiration of your career and of your many high personal characteristics." and Herbert Hoover: "There is so little that men can say on these occasions, but I cannot let these three years of kindly associations with one of such sensitive perception of duty and conscience, so complete devotion to our country and its best service, go by without just a personal note of affection and confidence." (DPL EDP, Box #7)) From Garvin came a handwritten note of love which surely warmed him greatly: "I can't help telling you what you must already know, that you have more than ever the affection and confidence of your brothers." (Edwin Denby Papers DPL, Box #7) Many letters came from avowed Democrats:

"The undersigned was a follower of Grover Cleveland and a democrat in politics before most of the present breed were ever heard of...the man who tells me that you, who wore the uniform in two wars, could be guilty of robbing his Government — is a liar!" (from Franck Taylor of Virginia, a manufacturer of wagon spokes; (DPL Box #7). From Standard Furniture Company, Bisbee, Arizona: "Our good old U. S. is with you. You are one of the truly big men and your resignation will reflect immensely to your future popularity and happiness. Yours very truly, C. W, Allen, a Democrat." (Ibid.) An unusual handwritten and heartfelt note came in late February from an unexpected source. "...there has never been any doubt in my own mind or that of any other Washington correspondent with whom I have talked concerning your own entire honesty, sincerity, and patriotism... concerning the leases opinions differ. Concerning your own good faith they don't. Your character has not been impeached. Your patriotism is unquestioned. You will leave many friends in Washington, including myself......With warm regards and best wishes always, believe me, Sincerely, Theo A. Huntley, Washington Correspondent, The Pittsburgh Post." (Ibid.)

In late February he received a letter of condolence from his longtime friend, Winifred Lyster, mother of one of his closest friends in Detroit since the early days. Mrs. Lyster was just shy of her 82nd birthday when she lost her only daughter, Eleanor Lyster Parker on February 10th, but still had time and heart to pen a letter to her "fourth son", as Ned fondly remembered in his reply. "Please don't worry about me," he pleaded with her. "I have acted for what I always thought was for the best," he said, and though he was going through dark times, "I have had a buoyant, glorious, unreasoning support so cheering that I am left without even bitterness but in reality, with confidence and with a greater love of humanity than ever. Your letter received today will be the most treasured souvenir of a period hideous but glorious. My little trouble is nothing. It does not hurt me," he assured her. "Sharing your grief, and grateful for your love. PS You have believed in me. Please think only that my resignation was the bravest act of my life." (Ibid.) As well as life-long friends, Ned also heard from old friends from his past. "You might not recall my name," one began, "Thought your memory may run back among your classmates of Michigan '96 Law to the small chap with a Van Dyke beard who sat near you and roomed with little Dan Williams at the Delta Chi house." A. C. McCaughan had done well for himself since Michigan Law and took the time to write Ned an affectionate letter from Corpus Christi, Texas, where he managed business interests in Texas and Mexico. In his reply Ned was effusive: "More than I can tell you I appreciate your letter of March 12th. It was friendly, considerate and courteous of you to write to me. Please accept my cordial thanks," (Ibid.)

Someone sent Ned a clipping of "Breakfast Table Chat", a

regular column written by the famous Free Press columnist/poet, Edgar Guest. Four lines of Guest's installment were particularly important to Ned.

"Whichever way the squabble goes,
Whichever way the scandal ends,
I know that old Ned Denby knows,
That here at home we're all his friends."

Ned wrote Guest a short note to thank him for his support and the very meaningful words of his poetry. On February 28, Guest responded.

"It may be some consolation to you to reflect that many good men, in our country's history, have been sadly wronged; that personal integrity is a bigger thing than political preferment and that as the years go by personal integrity has always outlived the petty conquest of the self-seeking demagogue.

"You need have no fear about coming home. You are coming home to such a friendship as the greatest man in Washington today might well envy. You are coming home to a garden of hearts in which grow abiding faith and trust and confidence. In a word, you are leaving the city of sneers for the City of understanding and true devotion. You remember what Uncle Joe Cannon once told you about Politics? 'Well, let me tell you this, there is no glory in the world to equal the love of the friends at home' and you have that in boundless measure." (Ibid.)

A strong group of about twenty businessmen from Detroit, headed by Roy Chapin, and including his closest and longest friends, Harry Lyster, Will Hamilton, Hugh O'Brien among many others, had worked tirelessly for the past several weeks to stir up as much support as possible from all over the country. They were stunned when Ned seemed to throw in the towel so precipitously. Particularly since Ned was adamantly telling everyone that no one had asked for or suggested his resignation. However, as each of them took time to reflect, the majority almost immediately understood that Ned was taking the only course which he felt was honorably open to him, and they once again supported him, and his decision, with unbound openheartedness. Within days of the resignation, they were urging him to come home as soon as possible, and they had already formed a committee consisting of members of the Detroit Board of Commerce, the Detroit Athletic Club, the Detroit Bar Association, the American Legion, the Army and Navy Club, and the Detroit Council of Churches to plan his homecoming celebration.

Newspapers across the country, as well as private citizens, were now climbing on the bandwagon of praise for the bloodied but unbowed Seagoing Secretary. The Corpus Christi Caller said, "Had Denby deliberately set out to gain public sympathy, he could have adopted no better policy [than to resign]. Of all the emotions except for hate, sympathy is the most powerful. The former secretary's courage, before and after he had relinquished his post, his professed desire not to embarrass the administration, and the complete absence of even a whimper of protest, have made him, in the public view, almost a hero." (Corpus Christi Caller, Mar 12, 1924) The Washington Evening Star called him "a man who has been guided consistently in his public duties by consideration for the public welfare.," and said that "the services rendered by Mr. Denby for his country are now to be recognized as worthy of the highest praise and approval." (The Washington Evening Star, March 14, 1924) The Houston Post editorialized "No evidence has been adduced to show that he had the slightest knowledge of the money transactions between Mr. Fall and Sinclair and Doheny.....It is not proven yet that his judgment was at fault......the search for the truth should discriminate between fact and common gossip, and the exigencies of politics ought not require the damnation of upright men along with those who have betrayed the public." (The Houston Post, February 20, 1924) Even the vaunted New York Times said, "....it should be borne in mind that nothing in the whole investigation has left a smirch upon Secretary Denby's character or official integrity.......The fact is that he leaves office in some respects very like a victim." (New York Times 2/19/1924) An undated Wall Street Journal editorial found in Edwin Denby's papers stated ".....no one has ever questioned the personal integrity or the courage or the patriotism of Edwin

Denby. Mr. Denby was in Congress in the day that Cannonism was a burning issue, when many [others] were being elevated on the sole propositions of opposition to Cannon. Congressman Denby one day called a reporter of a Detroit newspaper to him and gave him a statement that was the broadest kind of an endorsement of Speaker Cannon. The reporter told Mr. Denby it meant his defeat. Mr. Denby replied that he knew that well. The statement was printed and Mr. Denby did not come back to Congress. But he kept the Denby record straight." (DPL Edwin Denby Papers, box #7) Three days before he left office, Ned received a letter from the publisher of the Democrat Chronicle of Rochester, New York. He had been one of the citizens whom Ned always invited to the great events involving the United States Navy, having just returned from the fleet exercise in the Caribbean. After thanking Ned for his opportunity and praising the Navy for its efficiency, he added a more personal note to his thanks:

"I cannot let the opportunity pass without expressing to you my personal regret at the most uncalled for and unfair conditions that have surrounded you of late, and at the same time wish to say - what you undoubtedly know - that you occupy a remarkably affectionate place in the hearts of all of the officers and men of the Navy." (Ibid.)

Not all newspapers, by any means, were in Ned's corner. In early February, the New York Herald, notoriously Democrat, and as vehemently anti-administration as any Senator in Washington, ran an article on its front page declaring, "President Should Remove Denby as Dangerous Man". Like much of Walsh's accusations, those of this particular newspaper article were based on assumption and opinion rather than any fact, and concluded in all capital letters. "DENBY SAYS THAT IF THE MATTER CAME BEFORE HIM HE WOULD DO IT ALL OVER AGAIN." This statement which Ned had truly, and proudly, made seemed to drive the diehards even zanier in their hatred of him. Some Senators used this quote of Ned's as the exact reason they voted against him in the Robinson resolution.

Navy and Marine Corps men, almost universally, stepped

up to support their Seagoing Secretary. Though Ned had spent much of his time in the cabinet sincerely trying to streamline and modernize the Navy, and had possibly stepped on some toes in the process, the feeling of most naval officers and men was decidedly in his favor. From the 'Florida Gator', the onboard newsletter of the U. S. S. Florida came the following editorial, "The commissioned personal as well as the enlisted men and civilian employees of the Navy looked upon the tenth of March with tear dimmed eyes. This was caused by the resignation of Hon. Edwin Denby, former Secretary of the Navy.........Mr. Denby knew his job, the success he achieved will be of lasting benefit for the Navy and Marine Corps. He still has our interests at heart which is obvious from the contents of his farewell message.

"0010 SEVEN ALNAV to officers and men of the Navy and Marine Corps and to the civilian members of the establishment, Goodbye, God bless you. Edwin Denby 1100

"We too, bid you, Mr. Denby, however with regret, farewell and with united strength we of the Navy pray that God may ever bless you." (DPL EDP Box#7)

Perhaps no letter of goodbye would mean more to Ned than the one he received from his Assistant Secretary. In later years historians, and particularly some biographers of TRJr. would intimate an estrangement between the two men. Allow TRJr.'s own words to dispel that myth:

Undated, Washington

"Dear Ned,

"It came as a very great surprise to me this morning when I heard you had resigned.

"We have been very close during the last three years doing what I like to believe is valuable work for the country and the navy. Never in my life have I known anyone whom I thought had a finer character and higher ideals. I have never known you in any action taken by you while here consider for an instant anything other than the interests of the country. You have never thought for an instant for yourself. Your record is one that your children and the country may well be proud of in unselfish patriotism. But a short time will go by before everyone will realize this.

"It will always be one of my proud memories that I served under you."

Theodore Roosevelt" (DPL, EDP, Box #7)

A familiar theme in many of the letters Ned received at this time was that in time, and many believed not much time, Ned would be completely vindicated. Some, particularly the lawyers, tended to remark that this would surely come though the courts. Since Ned had been tried and convicted and banished in the non-judicial Senate, and without a trial or an opportunity to fully answer his critics, most people, it seemed, felt that once all the facts were known, he would be exonerated. Though no charges would ever be brought against him in an actual court for any reason, let alone for oil leases, his well-wishers were primarily wrong in believing that history would vindicate him. History does not write itself, nor does the truth possess a printing press. Men write history, and then print what they have written, and the bulk of all 'history' written about the Harding Administration and the majority of all that has been written about Teapot Dome to this day tends to give Edwin Denby short shrift.

Another common theme in the aftermath of Ned's resignation was once again the widespread desire of those who knew him, particularly his friends in Michigan, that he run for the Senate. Michigan at this time was possessed with two anemic Senators in Woodbridge Ferris and James Couzens, neither one of whom seemed to have much personality or direction, or certainly, influence in the Senate. Politicians and the general public as well almost clamored for Ned to run. Yet none of them seemed to stop to ask themselves why Ned Denby would want to return to Washington to join the very pit of vipers which had just tarred and feathered, insulted and destroyed him. At this exact point in time, it is highly doubtful Ned would have cared to fill any elective post, and that is exactly what he did: shy away from any overture in that direction. Another consideration which had certainly evaded those wishing for him to run for office was that Ned had actually lost money while in Washington as the Secretary of the Navy, His law partner and business manager, Joseph Kennedy, wrote him more than once about the depletion of his fortunes. The fact of the matter was that it was very expensive to entertain, let alone live, in the nation's capital, and yet that was exactly what a high post in the government required one to do. Ned had just turned fifty-four, and it was time for him to get back into the business world and begin to plan for his and his family's future.

Three days after Ned had given up his post, President Coolidge offered the Secretaryship to former Iowa Senator and then district federal judge William S. Kenyon, who declined. Next the President offered the job to Curtis D. Wilbur, chief justice of the California supreme court, who accepted. Wilbur, an 1888 graduate of the Naval Academy, had resigned his commission upon graduation at a time when that was acceptable, and thus had never served in the Navy. Ned, in Detroit at the time, was effusive in his approval: "I regard the appointment as an exceptionally good one," he said. "Judge Curtis is a man of broad experience, and his early training in Annapolis naval academy equips him splendidly for the responsibility he is to assume." Ned also sent a congratulatory telegram to his successor. "Cordial congratulations to you, the navy and the country. Earnest wishes for your success." (DFP 3-15-1924)

At the same time TR Jr. was back on the stand in the senate investigation being grilled about his order to send Marines to clear squatters out of the Teapot Dome reserve. Further, the Senatorial inquisitors wanted to know about Archie's employment by Sinclair, how he got the job and what he was paid. In a separate article in the same newspaper on the same day Ed Doheny reiterated that his $100,000 loan to Albert Fall had been just that - a loan to an old friend - and that if Albert Fall needed another $100,000 loan he would gladly supply it. The probing and the questioning and the relentless pursuit of the smallest detail of purported perfidy had become so bizarre that in early March, in response to a poetical parody read into the Congressional Record by Senator 'Cotton Tom' Heflin of Alabama called "The Golden Fleece", Senator Henry Cabot Lodge responded with his own poetry, a parody on Longfellow:

"Absolute knowledge have I none
But my aunt's washerwoman's sister's son
Heard a policeman on his beat
Say to a laborer on the street
That he had a letter just last week -
A letter which he did not seek -
From a Chinese merchant in Timbuktoo
Who said that his brother in Cuba knew
Of an Indian chief in a Texas town
Who got the dope from a circus clown
That a man in Klondike had it straight
From a guy in a South American state
That a wild man over in Borneo
Was told by a woman who claimed to know
Of a well known society rake
Whose mother-in-law will undertake
To prove that her husband's sister's niece
Has stated plain in a printed piece
That she has a son who never comes home —
Who knows all about the Teapot Dome."

(Noggle, p.122-3)

After Ned had left the cabinet, the denouement of the Teapot Dome affair would play itself out over many years into the future. In May, 1924, bowing to purely political pressure, and as mindful of the November election as the Democrats, Calvin Coolidge appointed Owen Roberts (R) and Atlee Pomerene (D) as special prosecutors to investigate the legality of the oil leases. On June 6, the majority report of the Public Lands Committee of the Senate issued its report on its investigation, written by the principle senatorial investigator, Thomas Walsh. Harry Slattery, the Washington attorney who had first prodded LaFollette to begin the investigation, was disappointed. "As one editorialist suggested, 'After the thunder and the earthquake, the still small voice. After the months of resounding inquiry.....the report of Senator Walsh.'" (Noggle, p. 155) After the dog-and-pony show —

phffffft! But the real affront which was hardest for the diehards to swallow, "he had exonerated Denby." (Ibid.) So the Torquemada of Teapot Dome, after months of vicious and demeaning attacks now admitted publicly to his Senate colleagues and to the nation, and in writing, that he had no evidence against Ned for anything.

However, that minor technicality had not stopped the onslaught of abusive verbiage against the Attorney General, Harry Daugherty, toward whom the full ire of the Senate had been directed the moment that Ned had left the cabinet. Daugherty was being investigated by the Wheeler Committee using the exact same tactics that the Lands committee had used against Fall and Denby. It was largely due to the Wheeler Committee headlines that the itinerant liar Gaston Means was popularized. In a syndicated editorial in the Chicago Herald Examiner, the great independent editorialist Arthur Brisbane wrote, "Mr. Daugherty brought legal proceedings against a collection of war profiteers and grafters, and talked plainly about them. Some powerful men are included among those that have good reasons to hate him,." (DPL, ED Papers, Box #9) Harry Daugherty, acquiescing to pressure from the re-election-minded President, finally submitted his own resignation May 28, and it was immediately accepted. He was later tried on charges that he had illegally profited from the sale of a company which had been seized during World War I (which had nothing to do with oil leases), and would be acquitted — twice. Harry Daugherty was a rough-hewn, savvy politician who had made many enemies in Washington for several different reasons — none of them ever proven to be illegal. Yet he was swallowed up, chewed to pieces and spit out in the same Democrat witch hunt which had destroyed Edwin Denby.

Summing up the balance of the teapot Dome story, the oil leases were eventually declared in court to be illegal under civil actions with judges rendering the verdicts. Calvin Coolidge needed the leases to be declared illegal in order to maintain his claim of cleanliness in the time when most others were being found so "dirty". In a rendering made by a single judge, the leases were declared illegal on May 28, 1925. On November 22, 1926, Edward

Doheny and Albert Fall were tried for conspiracy to defraud the government. After a trial lasting less than one month, they were both acquitted. In April of 1928 Harry Sinclair was tried and acquitted of charges of conspiracy to defraud the government. In a report by the Navy in February, 1929, it was revealed that Sinclair and Doheny together had lost over $47,000,000 on their government oil leases. In October of 1929 Albert Fall was finally charged with the bribery of Edward Doheny, in spite of the fact that five months previously, the Doheny company had forced the sheriff's sale of the Fall ranch in order to pay off the $100,000 debt of Doheny's loan to Fall. A debt is repaid. A bribe is not. Albert Fall was convicted, the first cabinet member ever convicted of a felony in the United States, was sentenced to one year and a day in prison and fined $100.000. Fall was so ill he was transported to prison in an ambulance, and so broke that he was never able to pay the fine. In the supreme irony of Teapot Dome, five months later, before the exact same judge, Edward Doheny was acquitted of the charge of having bribed Albert Fall. "Fall and Doheny were tried in the same court, with the same judge, with the same two federal prosecutors, and with much of the same evidence." (Stratton, p.330) But the results were exactly opposite. Of course it did not make any sense. It was not meant to make any sense. It was politics. Simply, politics.

It is difficult today to asses the real significance of Teapot Dome when the scandals of the present dwarf into oblivion the numbers which were involved. By 1944 the government (under another conservationist Democrat) "had drawn up and signed a full-fledged unit plan contract that would make Standard Oil of California (now Chevron) the navy's operational agent on Elk Hills [the reserves #1 and #2] for the next fifty years. Responding to the Arab oil embargo of the early 1970's, Congress contracted all three California and Wyoming reserves [which included Teapot Dome] for full commercial productions at their 'maximum efficient rates' to help offset American reliance on imported petroleum, and, in 1977, transferred their management from the navy to the newly created Department of Energy. Only then did the Teapot Dome reserve confirm long-held suspicions that it was a lemon and would never fulfill Harry Sinclair's grandiose expectations for it." (Ibid., p.346) In 1997 the federal government sold its 78% share of the Elk Hills reserves saying 'The Navy no longer needs Elk Hills and this sale helps get the government out of the oil and gas business.'" (Ibid. p.347) Edwin Denby and Albert Fall were not, it turns out, stupid and incompetent, they were simply seventy years ahead of the times.

———————————————

On Saturday evening, March 8, the Navy and Marine Corps held a banquet in Ned's honor attended by over 200 men. TRJr. attended, as did Commandant LeJeune, Admiral Coontz and Admiral Hilary P. Jones. "White, clean and pure, inside and out," declared the Commandant of there Marine Corps. "Upright, fair and everlastingly honest," said Admiral Coontz. While TRJr. called him "courageous, and his integrity unswerving."

"I am trying to die with my face toward the enemy," Ned told them. "I am trying to be brave and go through with this. I am leaving in body, but my spirit will always be with the navy." Ned told them this was the third war in which he had served. The Spanish-American War, World War I, and the oil investigations. "This third war has been more bitter than any I've been through those three years." (DFP 03-10, 1924) In ceremonies in his office on his last day, Commandant LeJeune re-instated Ned's commission as Major in the Marine Corps Reserve. The Marine Band, too large to fit in the office, played "Semper Fidelis" in the courtyard below his window. During the day, as the band continued to play, Ned stood in his office and shook hands with several hundred employees of the navy department. The Chief Clerk, F. S. Curtis, who had served the navy for thirty-three years, presented Ned with an engraved booklet of over 2,000 signatures of civilian navy personnel. The inscription read:

"To Hon. Edwin Denby:

"We, the undersigned civilian employees of the Navy

Department submit to you this declaration of our high regard and steadfast confidence and our appreciation of your uniform justness and considerate courtesy in all your acts as Secretary of the Navy. We beg to express our hopes and prayers for your future happiness. March 10, 1924."

Ned spent the remainder of the day signing letters to family and close personal friends. He also met with members of the press as his habit was to address them nearly every day he was in Washington. The press had always liked the Seagoing Secretary, and the feeling was mutual. Ned knew, despite many of the things which had been said about him over the past months, that the beat reporters were his friends.

Wednesday evening he and Marion boarded the train for home. It was to be Ned Denby's homecoming. At 240pm their train pulled into the Michigan Central Depot to the roar of a tumultuous crowd which met them at the station. Thousands upon thousands of Detroiters had turned out to welcome the Denbys and to let them know that a different kind of justice prevailed here in the Midwest. Ships whistles from the Detroit River blared, planes flew overhead, the Detroit City Police Department band was on hand, and hundreds of cars were festooned with signs which read, "Welcome Home, Ned". The interior of the station had been decked out with bunting and flags and the movement through the throng was slow, owing to the great number of people whom Ned knew, recognized, and wanted to thank. His brother, Wythe, was trackside with the Acting Mayor and officials from the committee organizing the event. At the curb outside the station Marion was met by the Hamilton's oldest daughter who whisked her away to a private luncheon, and an opportunity to rest before the evening's gala events. Ned was placed into a large touring car, and the whole procession moved down Lafayette Boulevard where throngs lined both sides of the street. There was a short ceremony of official welcome at the City Hall, and then the procession moved to the Detroit Athletic Club where Ned was given some time to confer with close friends in private.

That evening nearly 600 tickets had been sold for the dinner in the banquet hall of the Board of Commerce Building which Ned had helped to build. The galleries were packed with over 400 more interested bystanders, including Marion and many other wives. Speeches all around, but the only one remembered, and the one they all wanted to hear, was Ned's. Given the great patriotism which engulfed Ned Denby like the very air he breathed, he would himself probably tell you that his speech to the recruits at Parris Island during World War I was the most important speech of his life. Yet the speech which follows, certainly would be a very close second:

"When the secretary of the Navy takes his oath of office he assumes an obligation as lofty as can be given to any citizen except the president of the United States.

When he has spoken the few words embodied in that oath — "to support and defend the constitution of the United States against all enemies, foreign and domestic," to "bear true faith and allegiance to the same,." and to "faithfully discharge the duties of the office on which I am about to enter, so help me God," he has taken upon himself the burden and the lofty privilege of controlling and directing, under the Congress and the commander-in-chief, the first and greatest agency of defense.

"Thereafter he has no interest in life as compelling, no duty so stern, as to direct that agency so that it may always be ready to discharge its splendid mission, the defense of our country. In the navy politics has no place. In the navy, self-seeking must not exist. To the secretary and to all officers and men there must be but one thought, how best to make sure that our country shall be able always to repel invasion and to prosecute successful war.

"To the navy, all nations are friends, and all nations potential enemies. For it must make the country safe from attack from every quarter. In an efficient navy ships and guns and mechanisms must be of the latest and best insofar as national policy , evidenced by treaties conceived in mutual confidence and respect may limit armament. An efficient navy must be a happy but disciplined force. Morale must be high, and the men of the service must be ready to die both in war and in peace for their country or their fellow men. And that is true of the American navy.

"Our records are filled with the tales of daring that excite the imagination and bring back the days of romance. There is not upon this earth a finer, cleaner thinking, more unselfish body of men and women. No matter what the order, whether the command of a superior, or the decree of fate, it is taken with a cheerful 'Aye, Aye, Sir,' by the navy. I had the honor recently as secretary of conferring upon an enlisted man the medal of honor. This is what he had done: He was on a submarine. She was rammed and was sinking. The men all escaped but one who was trapped below, and would have died by the inrush of water through an open hatch. This man himself safe on the deck of the submarine, saw the danger, re-entered the vessel, closing the hatch behind him and sharing the risk of almost certain death with the comrade whose life he saved. The ship sank but both most happily were rescued after many hours' imprisonment. He got what he richly deserved, the highest honor the navy can confer. He is typical of the glory of the service. So much for the men.

"The women of the service are imbued with the same great spirit of acceptance of that which comes in the line of duty. Not long ago one of our cruisers went on the rocks and was lost. The captain in an effort to help some of them men, after long exposure, was beaten down by the crushing waves and lost his life. I wrote to the widow to offer her sympathy and to speak of the honor of his passing in the line of duty. This was her reply:

'Letters expressing appreciation of my husband bring me deep joy, for we are comforted in knowing that the fine qualities of our loved ones are recognized by all. His new 'post of duty' has taken him temporarily a bit far from us, but he used to ask me not to cry when he went to sea—and so I am trying constantly not to cry now. There is so much to be thankful for—H. G. Junior and I try to think only of that.'

"And she was only typical of the women of the service. They 'try not to cry' when their husbands go to sea, and that is morale. The navy has it, and it is part of the secretary's duty to stimulate that glorious spirit that puts the country first, a shipmate second and self last.

"There is another thing a secretary must try to do, and that is to see that proper provision be made that the outer walls may hold, the walls of steel, against attack at any time, from any quarter. That needs thinking ahead and providing for the needs of the fleet. In trying to to do that I have been overthrown. But I rejoice in the belief that the work is done. Fuel oil will be found in Hawaii for the onrushing fleet if it ever is needed. And along the eastern and western coasts of our nation great reservoirs will be found should we ever again need the services of our combined fleets. They will be created by exchange or sale or storage of the underground deposits which, had it not been brought to the surface, would have been lost to the navy forever.

"I will not mar this occasion by any argument explanatory or defensive in regard to the matter that has clouded my days and shadowed my nights. Only this will I say, lest you think I come home a repentant prodigal to receive your forgiveness for wrongs I may have done. I come neither asking forgiveness nor bowed down with shame, but proudly to proclaim to you that I have done no wrong nor aught that merits rebuke from you, my dearest friends, nor from them, my ruthless enemies.

"Rather let me say to you now that I have endeavored to do my duty as fully as God has given me power to do. If it be wrong to try to save that which I was charged to guard, then I have done wrong, not otherwise. If it be wrong to try to protect the homes of the American people from external attack and to place this country in a position for defense such as it had not had before, then I have done wrong, not otherwise.

"I believe that what I did was just and lawful and sound and for the best interests of the United States. It would be idle to answer those who say that I, who have loved my country and served it twice in military uniform, that I, who cherish for the great service of which I had the honor for three years to be the chief, the warmer affection and pride, that I, who look into your faces tonight and find there confidence, affection and esteem could have betrayed my country, the navy, and you. There is an old verse, Byron's, I think, which I like to think of—

'Here's a tear for those that love me, And a smile for those that hate,

And whatever sky's above me, Here's a heart for any fate.'

"So you shall not find me wearing my grievances, if I have any upon my sleeve. You shall not be asked for sympathy, and I pray you do not give it, for I do not need it. You shall not be bored now or hereafter, collectively or individually, with the recital of woes, for I have none. It may be that the list of those persons whom I hold in contempt has been somewhat extended in recent weeks, but you shall not know from me who those persons are. I would, were I able, however, tell of the myriads who have won into my heart by their tenderness and faith.

"Some things have been deeply impressed upon me that it is well for me to know of my own bitter experience. We have all read and thought somewhat upon them, but not all have had the rare and great privilege of testing their truth in their own lives. Long has it been said that 'sweet are the uses of adversity.' Now I know what that strange phrase means. For from adversity has come strength to endure and courage to act. Strength to endure the gibes of calumny, courage to do the hardest, and I think, the bravest thing I have ever done, to resign high office while still the malicious shafts of shame and ridicule were hurtling round my head.

"Twice before I have come home from war, back to Michigan, back to friendship, back to confidence and kindness. Now for the third time I come from war, made hateful by poisoned gas and base stratagems, from defeat without shame, to welcome without flaw. By innuendo and even direct attack, for the first time in my life, my integrity has been assailed, vainly assailed. I make bold to believe, in the ears of those who hear me now, or who will read my words in that greater voice, the press, anywhere in this well-loving state of Michigan.

"But do you think I could have lived bathed in filth from day to day, if I had not known there was no joint of the armor of my honor? We talk about good conscience, but we do not understand until the enemy is trying to crush heart and soul. Then between us and shame and despair good conscience and simple faith stand like guardian angels. These angels and a third, stood ever keeping open the door of happiness and keeping out the demons of hate and bitterness. The third was my wife, born and living always in Detroit. When your wife can read day after day columns of abuse and denunciation and keep always a smile and never complain and never regret loss of honors, place and position, so long as honor is unimpaired, the world has no weapon to break or embitter the soul. And from her, too, there will be no complaints. "Of another thing, too, have I deep cause for sincere rejoicing— my faith in my brother men is strengthened, not weakened, by this political tempest which has broken down my little house and strewn it upon the ground. You cannot imagine how immense the influence, the comfort of your letters and your messages.

"It has seemed as the letters and messages have fluttered in, in a veritable storm of kindness and confidence, as though all Michigan, moved by a kindly, tender impulse, had determined to give comfort to my wife and me in the hour of our trial.

"And Michigan has not been alone in this brotherly crusade. The poison of each day has had its antidote, and through it all the star of loyalty has illumined the darkness. Thousands of whom I have never heard have voiced their resentment.

"I am so egotistical tonight that you will scarce bear with me longer, I fear, but tonight is my night, is it not? And for Auld Lang Syne, you will let me tell you how you have helped me and how I think you have honored yourselves.

"Believe it or not, as you will, you have made me a better man. You have strengthened my love for my fellow man. You have proved that the world is good, that the eternal verities still govern the affairs of men.

"From a heavy heart, laden with the joy of this homecoming, I thank you and pledge you that you will not regret your faith." (DFP 3-14-1924)

There is so much more which could be said about Teapot Dome, and Ned Denby's, and for that matter, Warren Harding's,

468

part in it. It was almost all said in those times, and it did not matter then, and it would not matter any more now. Except to say — 17 years, 8 months and 25 days later, when the Kate bombers, the Val dive bombers and the Zero fighters came out of the rising sun on Sunday morning over Pearl Harbor, though the destruction they wrought was horrific and the loss of life most poignant, one million, five hundred thousand gallons of naval fuel oil was sitting there in some of the finest tankage found anywhere in the world, unmolested, brooding — waiting. It would propel the great armada of freedom moving forward, the greatest armada the world had ever seen. Courtesy of the courage, the integrity, the honesty, and the patriotism of Ned Denby.

Chapter Twenty-Seven

"More than half-beaten, but fearless, Facing the storm and the night;
Breathless and reeling, but tearless, Here in the lull of the fight,
I who bow not but before Thee, God of the fighting clan,
Lifting my fists I implore Thee, Give me the heart of a Man!"

from "Battle Cry' by John G. Neihardt

Civvies, Sun and Sanctuary

Harry Daugherty submitted his resignation to the President less than three weeks after Ned had left, on March 28, 1924. It was not an amicable parting. Having successfully defended himself through everything so far, he could not overcome Silent Cal's jitters over his reelection. When the President demanded his resignation, he had no choice but to acquiesce. Having now witnessed three of Harding's original cabinet members depart, the congressional democrats knew they were on a roll. They called TRJr. in to testify once again all about his employment by Harry Sinclair, which was before World War I. They grilled him all over again about his holding stock in the company while oil leases were being signed, hardly listening to his statements that his wife had held the stock and had divested herself of it, at a loss, before any lease had been signed. In vain he told them over again that he had not had anything to do with the leases. In her charming memoir, "Day Before Yesterday," Mrs. Theodore Roosevelt, Jr. stated bluntly, "Ted went through hell." (Roosevelt, p. 157) In Congress representative William F. Stevenson of South Carolina attacked the Roosevelt's over their Sinclair stock and demanded that he resign immediately. Ted had been in Albany on business, and when he heard what had happened, he "arrived early the next morning and refused breakfast, saying he was going to beat up Stevenson before doing anything else." Mrs. Roosevelt continued,

"Ted said no man could assail me in Congress or anywhere else and get away with it, and to bloody hell with the consequences. "I reached for the telephone and called Alice [Roosevelt Longworth, Ted's older sister], waking her from a sound sleep. "'Sister? Ted is back. He's just leaving to go and beat up Stevenson.' Alice caught on at once. 'Let me talk to him.....Ted? I hear you're going to beat up Stevenson.... Yes, of course, he deserves it.....I know he's a rat.....By the way, he's a little elderly man and wears glasses. Remember to have him take them off before you hit him.' 'Are you sure of that,' asked Ted, who did not know Stevenson. 'Positive.' 'Oh, damn,' said Ted. 'Then I guess I can't do it.'" (Ibid.)

So crucial was the timing of the sale of the oil stock to the Roosevelt political aspirations that even years after TRJr. was gone, Eleanor included a photostatic copy of the sale in her memoirs. Ted survived the congressional onslaught and remained the Assistant Secretary under Wilbur until later in the year when he resigned of his own volition in order to run, unsuccessfully, for Governor of New York.

The ink was not dry on Daugherty's resignation letter when Senator Kenneth McKellar (D) of Tennessee was calling for another resolution, this time to investigate whether or not Andrew Mellon was holding office in violation of law, in that he was still engaged in trade or commerce. Oddly that seemed to have just dawned on someone three full years into the Secretary's term of office. Despite the fact that some of the Senate Democrats wanted to pursue Mellon's ouster, as well as that of Hoover and Wallace, there was little support for the McKellar resolution, and by the next day the Times was reporting that it had collapsed. Short-lived as the attack on Mellon was, it created a revulsion across the country which tended to put a damper on further attacks on the cabinet. The country had had it.

On Sunday April 6, Ned was back in Washington, D.C. to speak at the commemoration of the fifteenth anniversary of Robert Peary's discovery of the North Pole. In days far preceding the idea of space exploration, Ned declared, "His was the last supreme adventure that great souls like him could embark upon," and "His deed was one that told the whole story of the duty of a man, especially when that man wears the uniform of his country." The observance was held at Peary's gravesite in Arlington National Cemetery.

Letters continued to pour into Ned's mailbox from naval and Marine corps officers stationed around the world. Several mentioned not knowing of the resignation until receiving the "ALNAV" message released on March 10. All were disturbed with the news of the loss of the beloved chief, many deeply so. Some mentioned that when Ned had arrived as their new Secretary in 1921 they were overjoyed to realize how deeply he cared for the affairs of the Navy, some contrasting his with a rather callous attitude of certain predecessors. To those Ned stated in his replies that they were receiving a great new chief in Wilbur, and that he, Ned, would always miss them all.

On April 10, Ned received a minor but important recognition from the Commandant of the Marine Corps in the form of an overlooked Good Conduct Medal which had for some reason never been given him during the War. Apologizing for the "omission that was inadvertently committed at Headquarters," LeJeune continued, teasing his good friend, "It gives me the greatest pleasure to have the opportunity of officially informing Mrs. Denby and the other members of your family that the Marine Corps authorities have put the stamp of approval on your military conduct and have pronounced it one hundred percent perfect." (DPL Edwin Denby Papers, Box #9) The citation came complete with mock orders of a thoroughly hilarious nature, and hand delivered by a Lt. Colonel Turner. In his thank you reply Ned claimed, "I value it almost more than any other service medal I have," and pointed out, "It is a medal which you have never had the right or opportunity to earn. I like it because it is exclusively for enlisted men." All enlisted men who had ever served under or with Ned Denby knew of his esteem.

The Denbys returned to Washington for the remainder of March, April and into late May to take care of Washington affairs, and to put their Washington home on the market for sale. In a supreme gesture of goodwill Marion joined Mrs. Theodore Roosevelt, Jr. in a tea which Eleanor was giving for the wife of the new Secretary of the Navy, Mrs. Curtis Wilbur. Mrs. Eberle, Mrs. Coontz, Mrs. Jones, wives of admirals and Mrs. LeJeune, wife of the Commandant assisted. It seemed like a subtle way for Eleanor Roosevelt to stand support for the wife of her husband's disgraced chief. On May 6, Ned once again put a lid on his supporters by declaring in a terse statement that he would not be a candidate for the United States Senate in the coming elections. It was blunt and there was no explanation. The very next day, the Free Press commended his decision as wise, believing that the great good will shown him by the citizens of Michigan was primarily "personal rather than political." (DFP 5-9-1924) At the same time he wrote his good friends, the Gibbs in New York, "Now that the sulphur is floating away and more or less peace reigns, I begin to feel almost normal again though the lack of someone to fight or something to fight for still gives me exceeding pain." He further reported that he would leave "tomorrow for Chicago to speak at the University of Michigan Alumni dinner, thence to Detroit to speak at a banquet, thence to Ann Arbor to speak on Cap Night, the Freshmen's big blow-out. I return to Washington about the 20th and we prepare to leave for the farm [in Pontiac], approximately June 1." (DPL, Edwin Denby Papers, Box #9) The Free Press reported some days later that at his Chicago speech before the Michigan Alumni Club the audience was standing on their chairs and cheering him with such gusto that it could be heard throughout the Hotel LaSalle.

Also at this same time, Ned and the family made a day trip over the fields of Gettysburg. As luck would have it, he had recently received a letter of support from a member of the Union

Army which warmed his heart. He told the man that his family "all felt a new inspiration of loyalty and respect for the men who served the Union." His remarkable patriotism was undamaged by his calumnious enemies.

In the Senate, heated debate still raged over the oil leases, and would for some time to come. Prior to his leaving office, Ned had been given a questionnaire by Representative Fred Britten, chairman of the House Naval Affairs Committee, and a close friend, whose purpose was to give the outgoing Secretary an opportunity of officially answering questions about the oil leases which Senator Walsh had denied him. The questionnaire came too late to change the outcome of Ned's tenure, but was later attempted to be entered into the record of the Walsh investigation by Republican Senator Selden Spencer, a member of the Public Lands Committee. This was blocked, however, by Senator Walsh, who had no interest in hearing any real answers from Ned Denby, as he had already stated plainly, weeks before. On May 13, "with E. C. Finney, assistant secretary of the interior on the stand. Spencer produced the questionnaire which Edwin Denby, former secretary of the navy, answered for the house naval affairs committee." Naturally, Walsh vehemently objected, and the committee room was up for grabs for a few minutes while tempers were sorted out. "After fully ten minutes of heated controversy, Ladd [committee chairman] decided in favor of Walsh, but Spencer was permitted to present the Denby questionnaire to Finney, WHO UPHELD DENBY'S DEFENSE IN THE LEASING POLICY." (Emphasis mine) On the same day TRJr. was a witness before the federal grand jury investigating the oil scandal. (DFP 05-14-1924) Two days later, Michigan Democrats, meeting in Flint, worked out a party platform, one plank of which described the Republican party as having "enthroned, big business and chicanery. Daugherty, Fall and Forbes were condemned, but Edwin Denby, former secretary of the navy, was unscathed in the resolutions." (DFP 05-16-1924) At least Michigan Democrats seemed to have an opinion of their own.

In the first week of June the Denbys departed Washington, D. C. as a place of residence for the final time. They went to the farm outside Pontiac for the coming summer, with plans to spend the following winter months in Detroit. Ned, however, was called back to Washington to testify before the grand jury of the president's special prosecutors on June 10. Indictments had been handed down by the District of Columbia Supreme Court against Albert Fall, Harry Sinclair, Edward Doheny and his son, Edward Doheny Jr. Admirals J. K. Robison and L. G. Gregory also testified, agreeing with Ned about the leases. On the 24th the Democrats opened their National Convention in New York's Madison Square Garden. "The fourteen day spectacle of family bickering was a tragedy for the Democratic party." (Noggle p.163) It would be the longest convention in history, requiring 103 ballots to nominate John W. Davis, another dark horse, the only candidate of a major party for president from the State of West Virginia. The Republicans, having had a less complicated selection to make, had completed their convention in Cleveland in three days in early June. The Denby family spent the summer on the farm outside of Pontiac, enjoying the pastoral quietude provided by the rolling, lake-strewn Michigan countryside. In August Ned allowed his name to be added to a committee supporting William R. Kales' bid for his old 1st Congressional seat in Detroit. Two of his closest friends, Hank Lyster and Hugh O'Brien, were already on the committee, and enlisted Ned in an attempt to help wealthy industrialist Kales, who was president of Whitehead & Kales Company, steel fabricators. Kales would lose in the primary to another Republican, John Sosnowski. Later that same month, Ned moved the family into the Whittier Residence Hotel on Burns Avenue overlooking the Detroit River. Just a year old at the time, the Whittier would quickly become one of the premier residence hotels in the city. With jaunts to the South, and to the beloved "farm" near Pontiac, the Whittier would be Ned's place of residence for the remainder of his life.

During the first week of September Ned and Marion once again visited Washington D. C. to finalize the sale of their Washington home. The home had been purchased as a church rectory. According to the Free Press' society column, "Mr. and Mrs' Denby saw a number of their old friends and enjoyed them quietly, for it was not generally known they were in town until after their departure." The article graciously went on to add, "They are deeply regretted in Washington and will be greatly missed in the society in which they were so active and so popular. They were most charming hosts and delightful dinner and dancing guests." (DFP 9-7-1924) Given the treatment of the virulent elements in the Congress and certain members of the press, and also the uncertainty of future litigation, it would not seem surprising that the Denbys would keep a low profile, or that Ned would shun politics. In fact, the Denbys had no intention of any course except leading a quiet life, at least for the foreseeable future.

In mid-October Ned received a thoughtful, somewhat poignant, letter from older brother, Charlie, who had by now given up his employment with Hupmobile and returned his family to a Washington, D. C. address which was much closer to the center of power. Charlie, now semi- retired, reported that their youngest brother, Garvin, who had also left his lucrative automobile job in Detroit and moved back to New York, had recently become involved in the beginning of a new "investment bank". Garvin was the Secretary-Treasurer, and was, Charlie claimed skeptically, "to have a salary — sometime!" But the problem was needing "to float $6,000,000 of stock. I am, of course, invited to take a front pew, and I, of course, gratefully declined." Charlie continued, tentatively, "I hope it's alright, and I hope Garvin makes a living out of it." But Charlie did not seem terribly confident in their younger brother's sincerity or ability. "He wants money but does not work for it. The trouble is that only a lot would help him. Too bad! if he had only 'dug in' 20 years ago he would easily have had an income more [than] enough for his simple life." After discussing local fishing conditions, Charlie told him, "Many people speak of you with affection and good will and predict a glorious comeback some day - " but it is said in a manner which conveyed how little either of them truly believed it. In the midst of his sign- off, he further added, "Garvin's outlook is bleak," as though that were the message he intended all along, but couldn't bring himself to put on paper. It appeared that Garvin would play the baby of the family for all of his life, and the brothers would always feel the need to look out for him — or at least hope for the best and hold their breath. (DPL, EDJr. Papers, Box#5)

By October 19, Ned was in Los Angeles for the first of the oil lease trials, this one brought by Coolidge's special prosecutors, Pomerene and Roberts, to break the lease held by Edward Doheny's Pan American Petroleum Corporation. Ned travelled west on the train with his old Department secretary, Joe Carey, and the two of them met and had dinner with his brother Wythe and sister-in-law, Lucie, in the Dearborn Station in Chicago. Joining Ned in Los Angeles were former Secretary of the Navy Daniels, current Secretary Wilbur, as well as TRJr., and selected admirals. The trial coincided with the last several days of the national election, and when asked by reporters, Ned told them, "Yes," if he were home and could vote, he would most certainly be casting his ballot for the President who had accepted his resignation. By October 22 he told Marion he had been sightseeing and had seen several stars' homes and some still-standing movie sets. On October 23 he wrote her, "My dearest, Yesterday was a day of rejoicing. Your first letter came." After thirteen years of marriage he still wrote her letters like a love-sick college boy. He also told her, "It [her letter] was handed to me personally in the court room by the Postmaster of Los Angeles. How's that for a mailman?" He further reported having dinner with old friends from Evansville high school days and that they had gone to Grauman's Egyptian Theater, opened merely two years before, to see "The Thief of Baghdad". He didn't seem terribly impressed with the Egyptian decor — "very elaborate and ornate — too much so. Little girls in Egyptian costumes as ushers, etc., etc." He further remarked, "Confidentially, I do not think the government is faring very well in its case so far. The Detroit papers will of course feature everything as sensational. Use your salt cellar freely on their reports. I am not worried." (DPL Edwin Denby Jr. Papers, Box #2)

In his next daily epistle he reported that he had been visited by Admirals S. S. Robison, Commander-in-Chef of the Battle Fleet stationed at San Pedro, and retired Admiral Frank Bostwick. The Admirals had left their cards at his hotel, and then proceeded downtown to the courtroom to look him up. The following day, two more admirals from the fleet had sought him out. "It is going to be a big round up before we're done," he told her. (Ibid.) On October 25 he reported that it did not look like he would be able to get away from the west coast before the following week. He was being reimbursed by the government "for my travel expenses at the rate of 5 cents per mile and $1.50 per day while in attendance as a witness. The latter will pay about one tenth of the cost (hotel), but the former will about meet railroad fare and costs." Two days later he lunched aboard the USS California, flagship of the Battle Fleet, off San Pedro with Admiral and Mrs. Robison. "They are charming people and very friendly to me, for I gave the Admiral his present command (Commander-in-Chief, Battle Fleet, rank admiral) after he did such good work as Military Governor in Santo Domingo. He is a fine officer. She [Mrs. Robison] spoke of some note you had written her which evidently made a deep impression." (Ibid) Three days later he turned philosophical:

"There is much meat for moralizing in my present position. One year ago this city would have been en fete in my honor. Now even Navy Day passed off without my being invited to speak or even attend any function. "Thank God for an equable temperament, a modest spirit, and a full realization of American public life....if I should not - after these varied and harrowing experiences of the past year, turn out a well-rounded philosopher - nothing could make me one." (Ibid)

He further mentioned Charlie's letter about Garvin's "investment banking, "Garvin's situation seems pathetic. I wish he would find a way out. What a world!" (Ibid)

The day before the election he reported that he had taken a motor trip to San Diego over the previous weekend. He travelled with a Dr. Haworth, a former friend whom he had met in Beaufort, South Carolina during the war. They had lunch in the U. S. Grant Hotel in downtown San Diego which had been built under the auspices of Ulysses S. Grant, Jr. in 1910. "Then we crossed the bay on the ferry to Coronado and went to Uncle Joe Pendleton's house." [Major General Joseph Henry Pendleton who served in the Marine Corps for over 40 years and had just retired the previous June; he would serve as mayor of Coronado from 1928-1930 and die in 1942 at age 81.] "He and Mrs. P were almost childish in their delight at seeing us. They are nice old people. The General showed us every inch of the house and grounds and babbled joyously about everything. It was a great pleasure to give them so much pleasure." The day after the election he reported that he had attended a fairly large party to hear election returns. "So a great nation quietly did its most important job, and answered the calumnies of Davis and LaFollette. I note that T. R. was beaten [TRJr. defeated for Governor of New York State}. The voters 'ran out' on him, It was a wonderful victory for Coolidge and Dawes. I sent each a message of congratulations this morning. That will fill their cup of bliss," he noted with his undaunted sense of humor. He described the day before when he was grilled by Doheny's attorneys for four hours about his testimony. "Hogan's office is in the bowling alley at Mr. Doheny's wonderful place. The house and grounds are simply splendid. The bowling alley is in a building apart from the house, huge conservatory, and other places. It has been converted into an office and a brass plate on the door styles it 'Hogan's Alley'. It appears Mr. Doheny also had a pretty good sense of humor. On November 7 he reported that he would surely be on the stand the next day, and that is his last letter from Los Angeles.

His pal Cal had not needed his vote, for he won resoundingly over both of his opponents, the Democrat John Davis, and boisterous Bobby La Follette. With 54% of the popular vote, the

Sphinx carried 35 states earning him 382 electoral votes and his own, single term as President of the United States. Though John Davis would live to see Dwight Eisenhower in the White House, Robert La Follette would be dead in just over seven months. Silent Cal's Teapot Dome strategy - to say as little as possible at any time ever - had served him well. The Republicans, though battered daily in the press for over a year, gained three Senate seats and picked up an additional 22 seats in the House, to retain firm control on both houses of congress. It was a stunning rebuke.

After a fairly short illness beginning in late October, former First Lady Florence Harding succumbed to her kidney disease in Marion, Ohio on Friday morning, November 21, 1924. She died at White Oaks Farm, just one month after her good friend and doctor, Charles Sawyer, had passed away, an event which had upset her terribly, and from which she never recovered. Two days after Mrs. Harding's death, her girlhood friend, Mrs. Lucie Daugherty, wife of the former Attorney General, passed away at her home in Columbus, Ohio. Ned, having just returned to Detroit from the Los Angeles trial, and Marion, made the trip south into central Ohio one more time.

Under a deep and steely autumn sky sprinkled with gentle snow flurries the casket was taken to the receiving vault where the President had been waiting for her since August of the previous year. The white pillared, marble tomb at the edge of Marion would not be ready for another three years, and so Florence would be carefully guarded by the same contingent of U.S. Army troops who had been there since Warren's funeral, and whom she had visited, and personally greeted each individually, only the month before. The Republican Glee Club of Columbus serenaded her with her favorite song, "The End of A Perfect Day", and all heads were bowed when the burglar sounded taps. Joining Ned from the cabinet, and as honorary pallbearers, were Hubert Work, Secretary of the Interior, John W. Weeks, Secretary of War, Harry S. New, Postmaster-General. (Sibley, p.264) Captain Adolphus Andrews, military aid to President Coolidge and the latter's personal representative, also attended. The former President's father, two of his sisters, and both of Florence's brothers, among other relatives, also attended. The following day, along with Work, Weeks and New, as well as George Christian, President Harding's private secretary, Ned and Marion journeyed the forty-five miles south to Columbus for the funeral services of Lucie Daugherty.

Back home in Detroit, Ned shared thoughts in a letter in early December with his close friend, Dr. Hibbs in Manhattan. "I am getting on speaking terms with my own affairs," he told the doctor, "which has not been the case for many years. It is a distinctly pleasant experience, and it is also distinctly pleasant to take things easy, as I am now doing. I walk about three miles every day — part of the way home from the office, and I am really in fine physical condition." Ned seemed to be coming to terms with what had happened to him in the previous year, at least to the extent that he would ever come to terms with it. It was not in his character to curry national favor, and he would not, - but he missed it. Though the admirals, as well as the able seamen and the Leathernecks would always seek him out, always defer to him, always hold him in the highest respect, his life was not ever going to be the same.

It certainly was a formula for whining and self-pity, but that would never be his way. His way would always be the way of adventure, of looking ahead, of seeking the greener grass just over the very next hill. And that is just what he did.

Chapter Twenty-Eight

Young and Old
When all the world is young, lad, And all the trees are green,
And every goose a swan, lad, And every lass a queen,
Then, hey for boot and horse, lad, And 'round the world away!
Young blood must have its course, lad, And every dog his day.

When all the world is old, lad, And all the trees are brown, And all the
sport is stale, lad, And all the wheels run down,
Creep home and take your place there, The spent and maimed among;
God grant you find one face there, You loved when all was young
Charles Kingsley

The Quiet Years

Ned was more than ready for the next chapter of his great adventure, wherever it might lead and take him, but his fellow Detroit citizens and his multitude of friends had some plans of their own for the direction of his life. After allowing him a period to adjust himself to his abrupt return to the regular world, they did what they had always done with Ned Denby: they invited him to lead them. On January 4th he was called upon to speak before The Gristmill Club of Old-Timers, which was an organization of 600 members of Detroiters, either Detroit-born, or having resided in Detroit for twenty years, who came together "to renew old associations, carry on the traditions of the city, and foster new ideas along the old lines of patriotism, honesty, courage and thrift." (DFP 9-23-1923) Formed only four months before, the group had rapidly grown, and was now meeting once a month in the Book-Cadillac. Ned spoke on the necessity of a strong Navy, and particularly about developing the air arm of the military. Two weeks later he was on the dais at a banquet honoring the first year in office of the Rt. Rev. Herman Page, D.D., Episcopal Bishop of the diocese of Michigan, where it was announced that Ned would be the church club speaker for the meeting on February 19. He would speak on the Far East. The very next day, February 20, the Walsh Report was released which "held Edwin Denby, as Secretary of the Navy, and Theodore Roosevelt, as Assistant Secretary, blameless in connection with the granting of the celebrated Teapot Dome and California oil leases," In reply to the majority report, Senator Spencer, of the minority opinion said "that during his experience in public life there had been no more patriotic man in the cabinet than Denby." (DFP 1-21-1925)

On Thursday evening, March 5, he and Marion were honored with a banquet at the Metropolitan M. E. Church at which Ned was the principle speaker. He spoke about the great Pacific nations, China, Russia, Japan and the United States and his vision for peace and harmony among them. The next day he spoke at the Windsor, Ontario Chamber of Commerce noting that he regretted the passage of the latest Immigration Act which had been signed by Coolidge the preceding year and would take effect in the coming May. Remaining the guiding immigration law until 1952, it was so unpopular in Japan as to be known as 'the Japanese Exclusion Act'. The immigration controversy at this time involved the great unrest which had overwhelmed both China and Russia, and whose outcome was as yet far from clear in either country, as well as the great cultural changes taking place in an ever more militaristic Japan. Ned, having lived in, traveled in and befriended the far east advocated giving the benefit of the doubt to nations struggling to define themselves in the modern world. Prophetically, the editorial writer for the Free Press, attempting to elucidate the dangers as well as the opportunities of American interest, concluded "The Oriental menace of which so much is heard need never reach American shores at all if America keeps its eyes squarely on the danger spots. Unheeded at the outset, it will develop all the more speedily and may catch this country unawares." (DFP 3-7/1925) Prescient words.

The following Tuesday, the Sons of the American Revolution entertained as guest of honor and principle speaker, John LeJeune, Commandant of the Marine Corps. LeJeune was well received by the audience, speaking out against the spate of anti-war books, plays and even silent movies unfairly depicting, the Commandant felt, the average American fighting man. Ned and Marion joined the Commandant at the speaker's table, and Ned spoke of his admiration for the Marine Commandant, and urged Detroiters to keep out of the active controversy in the air squabble now going on in Washington. Following the war, the argument raged over one air wing, as was the British model, or separate naval aviation and army air forces, as eventually developed in the United States. Though Ned did not say it that evening, he was solidly on the side of advancing naval aviation as a separate entity. Three days later, at a large meeting of the Aircraft Club of Detroit in the General Motors building, on the one year anniversary of his triumphant return to Detroit after his resignation, "And I repeat what I said one year ago," he boomed out in his fullest baritone, "'Had I to do again, what I had to do then, I would do it!'" The crowd surged to their feet in thunderous applause, reported the Free Press. "In token of the esteem with which Mr. Denby is regarded, the Aircraft Club amended its by-laws and, by acclamation, elected Mr. Denby its first honorary member." In after meeting comments to the local press, Ned said emphatically, "I do not, however, favor unification of the several air services." Fortunately for America, this view would prevail and foster the competition which would eventually create far superior air weapons in the conflagrations of the coming years. (DFP 3-11-1923)

In early April the Young Men's Christian Association announced that Ned had been selected and had accepted the challenge of heading up a $5,000,000 (just under $80 million in today's dollars) fund raising campaign aimed at constructing seven neighborhood YMCA's throughout the Detroit area. As soon as Ned's name was announced, the Free Press reported that "several prominent Detroiters" had volunteered to serve with him. A little over a week later he addressed six hundred delegates at "a one day sales congress under the auspices of the Life Underwriters' Association of Detroit," representing about 75 insurance companies of the state of Michigan. Among several topics he covered, he told them that he bought his first life insurance policy in 1898, that he had paid off the policy with the two months' discharge pay he received from the navy. "When my first policy matured, " he told them, "I bought three fine pictures with the proceeds. These pictures are in my home now," he said. (DFP 4-17-1925) On Wednesday afternoon, the regional executive secretary of the national council of the Y.M.C.A., A. G. Knebel, speaking to the executive committee of the fundraising campaign in Detroit's Statler Hotel, said that the associations of America and Europe were watching closely the progress of the campaign because it was "being conducted on a scale hitherto unattempted by any 'Y' in the world." (DFP 4-23-1925) The Free Press article continued in explaining the significance of the Detroit campaign. "If you win in this campaign, and I know you will," said Mr. Knebel, "the cause of public giving — the work of making our communities a better place to live in, through community effort and the upbuilding of the community spirit — will have been put forward by a full quarter century. You will have got a new standard in conducting an undertaking the essence of which is public welfare. You will have set a new and higher value on character building. Your success will inspire organizations throughout the world to conduct their programs on the basis set by the city of Detroit." (Ibid.) As in everything Ned Denby did in his life, he was leading this campaign with the highest of goals.

The following day the Press carried an article about a fourteen year old Detroit youngster and YMCA participant, who had written Ned asking what he could do to help in the campaign. Instead of writing a letter in reply, Ned grabbed hat and coat and went to the "Y" where the young man was playing in the gymnasium. "You boys want to know what you can do in this campaign," he addressed the assembled youths who surrounded him, "Well, I'll tell you. Just let people take a look at you. You're the finest advertisements of the Y.M.C.A. I've seen yet." (DFP 4-24-1925) The 'Y' campaign held daily meetings, luncheons, pep rallies of their day, to stir the troops into successful action, and the campaign kicked off on May 5th. It was a textbook for campaign drives of the future. Ten days later, on Friday, May 15, the drive came to its thrilling conclusion. During the campaign, Henry Ford and his son, Edsal, had each given $750,000, while Ned and Marion themselves had contributed $5,000. On the last day, five and dime magnate and fellow Detroiter, S. S. Kresge, added another half million. In the crowded, raucous ballroom of the Book-Cadillac on Friday evening, "over and over again," the Free Press reported, "Edwin Denby pounded a locomotive bell …and with each ring the figures of the Y.M.C.A. building and expansion campaign climbed—mounted past the $5,000,000 goal, and stopped at $5,471,323." Over 2,000 workers then marched out of the hotel up Washington boulevard and down Woodward avenue to the signboard on the Campus Martius where Dr. A. G. Studer, general secretary of the Detroit "Y" painted in the last picture of the seven Y.M.C.A branches that are to be built with the money." Mr. Charles Van Dusen, President of the Y board said, "Mr. Denby has been a strength to this campaign that few of you can realize. Each of you has been responsible for this success, but back of it all stands a spirit placed in this work by your general chairman." Added Ned, "The Y campaign has brought out a spirit in Detroit never found here before." (DFP 5-16-1925) Two days after the campaign had ended, the Y.M.C.A. directors were meeting to discuss plans for the construction of the seven branch facilities, Dr. Studer reported, "Harvey Firestone, the tire manufacturer, dropped into our directors' meeting on the last day of the campaign and said he wanted to take a look at the bunch of men who had nerve enough to go out and ask $5,000,000 for a public welfare project. He said they were figuring on a campaign in Akron, but were doubtful as to how much they could raise. He saw how our campaign was going and left us a check for $5,000 and said he was going back home to tell the boys that the largest sum they had discussed was by far too low. That is the way the success of the Detroit campaign is influencing welfare work the world over." (DFP 5-17-1925) On the same day Ned was busy denying, once again, that he was running for something that someone seemed to think he should be. This time is was for mayor of Detroit. "I am busy with my own affairs, which require my entire attention," he told them. He did not add that it was the first time in years that he had had the luxury of minding his own business.

At the end of the month Federal Judge Paul J. McCormick released his findings in the trial in Los Angeles to declare the Doheny lease of the Elk Hills oil lands null and void. Judge McCormick did decide that the lease was void by the fraud committed between Fall and Doheny in the matter of $100,00 which passed between them. However, McCormick upheld the right of the Secretary of the Navy to lease the lands, and further trade the crude, in part, for the fuel tanks filled with refined, usable fuel oil at Pearl Harbor. It was a huge vindication of Ned and what Ned had done.

Furthermore, Admiral John K. Robison, head of the navy's bureau of engineering, whose job it had been to effect the leases once they were negotiated and signed, received unqualified approbation from Judge McCormick. "The latter [Robison] manifested an ardent and patriotic desire to construct reserve oil fuel stations at Pearl Harbor, Hawaii, and other strategic points in order to strengthen the national defense." And further, "The testimony of Admiral Robison, together with all the circumstances in proof, convince me that Admiral Robison had no ulterior motive or mercenary purpose in any of the transactions involved in this case." (DFP 6-6-1925) Admiral John Keeler Robison, the General Micheal Flynn of his day, was an 1891 graduate from Annapolis. He had, by 1925, admirably and faithfully served the United States Navy for 34 years. At the time of Teapot Dome he was a Captain, with the temporary rank of Rear Admiral because of the job he held. Nothing was ever shown that Robison did which was against any rules or any law, except that he had had the great misfortune to be in the wrong place at the wrong time. Because of the stigma attached to his name, he was passed over for promotion twice. When he requested the right to retire with his temporary rank (a significant difference in retirement pay), Calvin Coolidge refused him. He was never promoted, and when he finally did retire in 1926, it was at the lesser rank of Captain.

Robbed not only of his dignity and integrity, but of his rightful pay grade, he was smeared, insulted and crushed for political expediency, and for absolutely no other reason.

Ned's good friend, Own Rippey, wrote him on June 16, beginning with: "I see by the paper that you have been elected Second Vice-President of something or other. Congratulations.

"Congratulations also, very much belated, on the success of the splendid Y drive. I don't believe any other person in Detroit could have gotten such gratifying results. It was a glorious victory.

"Congratulation on the Oil Lease Case vindication. As I read the newspaper account of the decision, the leases would have been upheld had not our friend Fall accepted favors......That must be a great relief to you, though of course your own conscience was clear in the meantime." (DPL, Edwin Denby Papers, Box#9) Then, in a startling verdict in Cheyenne, Wyoming, Judge T. Blake Kennedy, in the government's case against Harry Sinclair's leasing of the Teapot Dome, found in favor of Sinclair "on every point raised by the Federal counsel." (NYT 6-20-1925) The congratulations, however, were premature. Both of these decisions would be overturned upon appeal. Throughout, however, the merry-go-round of courts and trials and appeals and verdicts, no one ever found a single infraction for which to convict Edwin Denby. After Edward Doheny, wearied by the months of constant legal struggles, had made public further information which he called 'his own story', Ned was confronted by "the New York Times representative," in Detroit. "I have nothing to say concerning Mr. Doheny's assertions," Ned responded in what the representative reported as "his courteous manner." "The entire matter is a closed incident as far as I am concerned." (NYT 7-2-1925) You can almost see Ned's 'courteous' smile as he said this. Curiously, in a short paragraph just below the story about Ned, the Times reported that it had also attempted to track down Senator Walsh, who had the previous day traveled to New York, checked into the Waldorf, "but left there almost immediately, saying that he was going to visit friends and would probably return today. The Senator, meantime, left no address," lamented the Times. (Ibid.)

In the first week of July Ned also received a letter from Admiral Robert E. Coontz, the man who had been the Chief of Naval Operations during most of his tenure as Secretary. After being relieved of CNO, Coontz had been made C-in-C, U. S. Fleet, and was currently taking an American armada of naval vessels on a cruise to Australia and New Zealand, in the largest demonstration of American naval power since the circumnavigation of the Great White Fleet in 1908-9. The Admiral began by reminding Ned how they had attempted such a cruise in 1922, only to be held up by the State Department. Yet, as he wrote, he was commanding a force of over 25,000 personnel on fifty-six ships, including, as he proudly notes, "eleven battleships." As any seasoned sailor, he noted that they had crossed the equator, and initiated nearly 22,000 of their complement in the rite of passage known as "Crossing the Line". Sailors who have crossed the equator are known as "Shellbacks", and are entitled to initiate those who have not who are called "Pollywogs". Poignantly, he referenced the sad fate of his comrade, John Robison, saying, "I cannot see how the President failed to nominate him [for promotion to Admiral], although he must have some precedent......This should not be so and I hope is an error." Sadly, it was not.

Just a week later, Ned received a letter from another of his former naval comrades, this time from Admiral Julian Latimer, who had been Judge Advocate General of the Navy during most of Ned's time in office. In 1925 he was named Commander of the Special Service Squadron, a segment of naval vessels dedicated to protecting the Panama Canal, as well as patrolling the Caribbean and the Pacific coast of Central America. Established in 1920, it was headquartered in Balboa, Panama Canal Zone, and was abolished in 1940 as part of a reorganization of fleet assets. Ned had written the Admiral in June, reassuring him that he was back on his feet and doing well. Latimer, in his response, mentioned wistfully Ned's description "of life on the farm in June, with the bees humming and the grasshoppers jumping," and said it "made me very envious. How I would enjoy being with you for a few afternoons of real good fishing with one rod and one line and much conversation." Clearly the two men had spent recreational time together, and Latimer had previously been to visit Ned on his farm. "Tell Sister [the young Marion's family nickname] that I expect her to learn to milk the cow this summer, as well as I was able to when I was with you." (DPL Edwin Denby Papers, Box #9)

In August he received a lengthy letter from Anna Drew, wife of a British diplomat with whom Ned had worked in China some thirty-two years before. It appears they had corresponded during the years, but not on a regular basis. The Drew's were the parents of five children when Ned knew them in China, and later a sixth. Dora Drew, their oldest daughter, was the young lady with whom Ned rode horses, along with her father, of course, and whom he mentioned in his letter to his mother in 1893 about looking for a bride. He had told her how striking the young Dora was on horseback with her hair "up" in the manner of a young lady who was no longer a child. Now Mrs.Drew mentioned to him all those years later that "scarcely a day is recorded in Dora's and Elsa's journal without a mention of you or Garvin." Even after the many years which had passed, their China ties were strong, almost unbreakable. After a sojourn in Italy, Mrs. Drew told him of returning to London, and having seen "more than sixty of the old China friends!!" They had then retired to their seaside cottage which had been selected and readied by Dora, but had only enjoyed it for six weeks when her husband had passed away at the age of 81. They had been married fifty years. Her letter was full of ennui, of the nostalgic glances into a past that had left them both long before. There were surely many fond and beautiful chords plucked on Ned's heartstrings with her musings.

Thursday, September 3 brought the terrible news of the crash of the U.S.S. Shenandoah in the rolling, partially wooded fields of southwest Ohio. On a promotional tour of some Midwest fairs, Shenandoah was that day en route to Dearborn, Michigan where Henry Ford had just completed the construction of a new mooring mast at his private airport and was eagerly awaiting a ride himself. The great ship had been caught in a sudden and violent updraft which carried it to a height which its gas bags could not withstand, and it was torn to pieces. Fourteen members of its crew, including its commanding officer, Lt. Cmdr. Zachary Landsdowne, were killed. The news hit Ned and Marion particularly hard as they had just been so instrumental in the launch of the Shenandoah less than two years before, and knew many of the crew members who were involved and lost their lives. Ned was, in fact, waiting at the Dearborn Airport for the arrival of the Shenandoah when he received the news. It was Ned who had given Lt. Cmdr. Landsdowne his appointment as commander of the airship. Ned called the stricken men, "martyrs of progress," and said "they would be the first to say that the conquest of the air should go on. Not for one moment should the development of lighter than air craft be retarded by this catastrophe," declared Ned. (DFP 9-4-1925) Once again, it was simply not yet understood that lighter than air dirigibles were not going to pan out as viable air transportation.

In the same issue of the Free Press was another article in which it was claimed by Mrs. Landsdowne, the wife of the deceased commander, that her husband had warned Secretary Wilbur of the possibility of inclement weather in the area of Ohio in which the dirigible had crashed. Mrs. Landsdowne was reported to have talked to reporters with complete calm, and told them that her husband knew the violence of Ohio thunderstorms because he had been born in Ohio. Mrs. Landsdowne also told the press that Zachary Landsdowne was killed on the twentieth anniversary of his joining the Navy. Also interviewed by the press, Secretary Wilbur categorically denied that he had insisted the Shenandoah make the trip against the protestations of Commander Landsdowne. He was coming quickly to learn what a hot-seated job he had accepted.

Mid September saw Ned declared as honorary chairman of the Detroit Convention and Tourist Bureau which was attempting to raise a war-chest of $150,000 to aid in continuing to attract tourists and conventions to the city. Detroit at this time was one of the major players in the lucrative convention business, indeed, had been the number one convention city in America for fifteen years, and it was estimated that tourists brought upwards of $15 million into the economy annually. Two days later he was also reported on the committee of the World War Orphans Campaign. We can safely forgive Ned Denby for thinking that the taps on his shoulder were never going to stop, because they weren't. In addition, he had his law practice, and along with business partner John Baker, another Yosemite pal, was quickly developing a 'planned community' northwest of Pontiac, called Drayton Woods, only one of Ned's substantial real estate holdings. September was the month the Denbys usually began shutting up the farm in preparation to returning to the city, but this year they had decided to do something different. Having packed up the household goods and shipped them off on the Pennsylvania Railroad, on September 15, they boarded train themselves and headed for Beaufort, South Carolina. Having to change trains in Washington, D. C., Ned took the time to stop in and visit Curtis Wilbur, perhaps to commiserate with him on the bad press he had been getting over the Shenandoah, among other things.

The Denbys had spent time during Ned's Marine Corps years living in Beaufort, just minutes from the recruit training base at Parris Island. Ned certainly must have seen the potential for development in the area, and after becoming involved with Drayton Plains he undoubtedly had property in mind in Beaufort. Of even more importance, perhaps, to Ned at this point in his career, the area around Beaufort offered immense opportunities in the hunting and fishing arenas which had always been important to him. Indeed, as he began to formulate business plans in his head, advertising the 'outdoor life' aspect of Beaufort would take the forefront of his thinking. The Denbys also still had friends in the Beaufort area, so that destination made perfect sense for a winter headquarters. On September 16 Garvin wrote to him using letterhead from a different job, and saying how surprised he had been to hear of the decision to winter in Beaufort, "but it appeals to me as a darn good idea from all points of view except that of the quails, and I am sure that your friendly absorption will convert even them.

"I have not written sooner," Garvin said, "because my letter would not have been much pleasure to either of us, but things are looking a little better now." DPL, Edwin Denby Papers, Box #9)

A few days later he received a short note from his friend, the University of Michigan Regent and former 'Bachelor', James Murfin, in which he enclosed an article from the Detroit Times from thee days before. "I do not know how the newspapers got on to it," he said, but then told Ned that the Board of Regents on which he sat had "extended a formal invitation to your successor to be present" at the upcoming Michigan/Navy football game. The same game which Ned had worked so assiduously to promote two years before. Apparently Mr. Wilbur could not make up his mind, and so Michigan Congressman John Sosnowski "made a personal appeal to him to come on." The word came back that Mr. Wilbur would indeed join them for the gridiron festivities IF Michigan paid his expenses, and conferred upon him an honorary degree! "My reply to this I cannot quote at this time because I wish to send this letter through the mail," blustered his exasperated buddy, "but I assure you it was plenty. It takes all sorts and kinds of people to make up this world and, as Dooley says - 'Every now and then I am glad I am not one of them'." (DPL Edwin Denby Papers, Box #9)

In October he received news from John Baker, his owner/partner in the Drayton Woods development, to tell him about how the street grading was going. Further, he reported that 57 lots had been sold, and then gushed "Drayton Woods is beautiful and every time I see it I want to add to the price of each and every lot — especially the ones that are sold." (Ibid.) The following month, after the Michigan football team of Fielding Yost had pulverized Navy 54 to 0, he heard again from his old friend Murfin, who always and after all the years, still called him 'My dear Duke'. He detailed some after-the-game comments by Michigan's famous coach, saying, "Yost said this not alone was the best team he ever had but it was the best team he ever saw. There certainly is praise enough for eleven men." (Ibid) That year's Michigan team outscored their eight opponents by a score of 227-3; and still lost one game to Northwestern 2-3. Such was football in 1925.

Toward the end of November he received a letter from another of 'his' admirals — men whom he had promoted or whom he had placed in their present commands, Charles Butler McVay, Jr.. McVay had just returned to Washington duty after several months on the China station where "[t]hings were pretty thick during my entire time and particularly so for the last 18 months when I was unable to get more than ten minutes distant from my flagship. For 7 1/2 months of the last 13 I was at Shanghai and had nearly all of the vessels of the Asiatic Fleet there as well as Marines from Guam and Manila. During the last trouble I was Senior Flag Officer for the first week or so and the others placed all vessels at Shanghai and on the Yangtze under my control, so I had between 60 & 70 vessels of various nationalities!" Since the time Ned had lived in China, over thirty years before, foreign powers were still meddling in Chinese politics. Remembering the Boxers, however, they did so with enormous firepower. McVay mentioned getting consensus decisions from Americans, British, Japanese, French, Italian and Portuguese, and told his old chief that "You have lots of friends out there and I 'made much face' through knowing you." McVay also mentioned how envious he was, now stationed in Washington, of the Denbys in Beaufort, "my old stomping ground — and yours. I had a wonderful time there." (Ibid)

On September 30, J. K. Robison's four year term as head of the Navy Engineering Department came to and end. The Free Press duly noted this, and stated the bare facts — that Robison had been passed over for promotion, and that Calvin Coolidge had personally denied his retirement at admiral's rank, a fact glossed over by the New York Times. One month later, a banquet was held in Detroit by the University of Michigan Club and the Detroit Athletic Club to celebrate the recent polar flight of Commander Donald MacMillan. Robison, a Detroit native, attended. "Robison paid glowing tribute to Edwin Denby his former chief," the Free Press article declared. (DFP 10-31-1925) The article did not say that Ned Denby was no longer in Washington to defend himself and his men. Nor did it state what was not known for years — that Curtis Wilbur had attempted to get Robison to abridge his testimony in one of the Teapot Dome trials. Robison refused.

As mentioned, Curtis Wilbur was finding his job more contentious than he probably had thought before accepting it. On Tuesday, December 1, 1925, the New York Ties wrote:

"Secretary Wilbur recently has faced severe criticism from various quarters as a result of the loss of the airship Shenandoah, the accident to the submarine S-51 [submarine sunk in collision] and the forced descent of Commander Rodgers and the crew of the PN-9-1 during the Hawaiian flight [Navy seaplane attempting to set a long distance record, ran out of fuel at sea]. Following that came the Mitchell criticisms of the navy and Mrs. Zachary Lansdowne's allegations that the Shenandoah was dispatched to the Middle West on a political flight, and that an attempt had been made to influence her testimony." (NYT 12-1-192

Ned would have sympathized with the secretary's woes; it simply was not in his nature to gloat.

Toward the end of 1925 another annoying matter flared up as it was reported in the Detroit press that Ned and J. Walter Drake had somehow been involved in an Internal Revenue Service fraud charge, involving his long time friend, Jim Inglis, president of the American Blower Company. In their indomitable quest for truth and justice, one Detroit paper (The Detroit Times) ran a front page story under the heading, "Tax Charge Hits Denby." Of all people, Michigan's own Senator Couzens was leading yet another Senate investigation, this one into irregularities involving reporting to the IRS. The bottom line, which it would take some days and weeks to shake out, was that an employee of Inglis, had submitted incorrect estimates of the value of certain of the company's assets; right or wrong, this had been done without Mr. Inglis' knowledge. When rumors appeared that Mr. Inglis was being investigated, J. Walter Drake, Ned's Yosemite shipmate and current Assistant Secretary of Commerce, had written a letter stating that "he did not believe James Inglis.....would file a fraudulent return." (DFP 12-13-1925) Later, it was determined that Ned's entire participation in this affair involved a hand-written notation in the margin of a document stating "Denby telephoned." How exasperated this must have left Ned when it came to light is completely understandable. Drake was livid. Although many of his friends wrote to him commiserating over the ridiculousness of the accusation and the total disregard for the barest minimum of American fairness, not only in the press, but once again by a member of the Senate, Ned seemed to consider the source, and move on.

He literally did have bigger fish to fry.

Note: The PN-9-1 mentioned above was one of two PN-9 Navy Patrol Flying Boats dispatched from San Francisco to Hawaii on August 31, 1925, during Wilbur's tenure as Secretary of the Navy. The flight was designed to test the range of the flying boats, as their flight was scheduled over 2400 miles distance. The first of the two planes landed on the ocean after only 300 miles with engine failure, and the crew rescued by a pre-positioned Navy destroyer. The second PN-9 commanded by Commander John Rodgers literally ran out of fuel hundreds of miles short of landfall and was forced to ditch in the sea as well. However, since both engines failed, the plane had no way to contact its closest naval escort, and the PN-9 crew were on their own. But not to worry. These were navy men, sea-dogs, and so they tore fabric from the wings of their plane, fashioned crude sails and sailed the airplane 450 miles toward the Hawaiian Islands. After nine days, the sailing plane was spotted a few miles off the coast of Kauai and the crew was rescued. Commander Rodgers was subsequently promoted to Assistant Chief of the Navy's Bureau of Aeronautics.

Chapter Twenty-Nine

For age is opportunity, no less,
Than youth itself in another dress,
And as the evening twilight fades away
The sky is filled with stars invisible by day.

Longfellow

A Very Busy Man of Leisure

Beaufort, South Carolina is the second oldest city in that coastal state, founded in 1711 by the Board of Trade of the British Government. Nestled on Port Royal island, one of the "Sea Islands", of which there are over sixty in the county, Beaufort is the county seat and though small, an important entity throughout the area's history. It is most probable that had Ned not joined the Marine Corps in 1917, that he would have never heard of Beaufort, let alone left Detroit to live there. Yet there was a stillness, and a languid southern charm (one almost struggles to refrain from using the word, 'ambiance') in the locality as completely opposite of the northern bustle of the booming auto capital as it was possible to be. In the insouciance of Southern society, Ned surely felt again the chords first struck in his teenage breast in the subservient ether of colonial China. In addition, the semi-tropical climate of Beaufort provided the sportsman far more opportunities in nature and more time of the year to enjoy them. Ned knew how to vacation, and was certain to make the most of an area where 'vacation' could be every day.

The Beaufort of Ned's time was a classic ante-bellum town,

hardly more than a village of approximately three thousands souls. During the Civil War — the dominant event of Beaufort's history — Union forces had early occupied the area around Port Royal, building forts, and hospitals, a forge, naval facilities, as well as constructing schools to indoctrinate and educate the thousands of freed slaves who flooded the area for safety and to join the Union Army. It became an even more important place in reconstruction times as northern teachers flocked to the area to teach freed slaves, and so developed a dichotomy of experiences which most other southern towns and cities never knew. It had been a rich, cotton-producing area as dependent upon the slave population as anyplace in the south, and yet produced Robert Smalls, an educated slave owned by wealthy planter Henry McKee, who was so intelligent, and so industrious that he ended up years later buying his former master's mansion. Smalls was trained as a harbormaster, and during the war had commandeered a Confederate gunboat in Charleston harbor, and before the Confederate troops realized what he was doing, had loaded up his family and some friends and sailed the gunboat out of the harbor right under the guns of Fort Sumpter. Sailing the craft to Beaufort, the US Navy was so impressed they made him the permanent captain of the vessel. After the war, Smalls became a businessman, involved in many ventures, civic projects and politics. A Republican (because at this time ALL African Americans were Republicans), Smalls was elected to the United states House of Representatives for multiple terms.

Ned stayed in weekly contact with his law partner and business agent, Joe Kennedy, sometimes receiving multiple page letters detailing dozens of ventures, deals, contracts and stock trades. He also heard from John Baker, his partner in Drayton Woods, as well as several other business associates. All in addition to his lively correspondence with his admirals and many other military contacts, relatives, and just plain friends. As the Edwin Denbys were settling nicely into their new surroundings, in January, 1926, his older brother, Charles, headed back to China for an extended business trip. At home with Charles' wife Martha was their youngest son, Charles, Jr., who had recently become secretary to Associate Supreme Court Justice, Oliver Wendell Holmes, Jr.

On January 30, 1926, Ned was notified by the Marine Corps that he had been promoted to Lieutenant Colonel in the Marine Corps Reserves, pending a physical examination at nearby Parris Island. A February 20 article by Free Press "private leased wire" reported Ned and Marion with some Detroit friends on a visit to the Charleston area. The article stated that "Mr. Denby became interested in this section of the country through his service during the war when he spent much time as an officer in the Marine Corps at Parris Island. He was favorably impressed with the natural beauty and pleasant climatic conditions of the lower Carolina coast that he recently purchased a large tract of land between here and Beaufort, where it is expected he will spend much of his time." (DFP 2-20-1926) There seems to have been a real estate venture among Ned and seven other businessmen in February 1926, which purchased a total of 5000 acres of land in the Beaufort/Port royal area. At least part of the program called for an 18 hole golf course and the construction of a hotel. On February 21, Charlie, just returned from China, dropped him what, for Charlie, was a talkative letter. And the news was not good, and he couldn't wait to tell his brother what was going on in China. Charlie reported, "I had an awful time in China. I was worried literally crazy for one month. Chaos reigns there.....What I fear is a long time, perhaps 25 to 100 years, of slow adjustment of east to west which will leave the foreigner out. Certain it is that the China of our day is gone forever." At first Charlie had been told that all his Chinese holdings were worthless, but he told his brother that after some "telegraphic correspondence between Shanghai and Tientsin, I was able to get a fair price for my holdings and sold out." He then went on to describe just how bad it was:

"I did not go north from Tientsin as there are no trains and rare ships. The trip is dangerous and subject to great hardship. My friends advised me not to go until I had settled my business because active warfare is on between Tientsin and the sea, and, as my banker said "if you go you are liable to be killed or captured

and your objective coming to China will be defeated as well as causing great anxiety to your friends and costing your family thousands of dollars' [in ransom].......I saw so many deplorable things and heard so many sad stories in Shanghai that I was glad to get away." He further told Ned that he would like to visit him, "but shall not be able to. I have to reorganize my affairs, adjust my establishment to a smaller income and try to recover my moral and physical equilibrium which was badly shattered."
(DPL Edwin Denby Papers, Box #9)

A week and a half later Charlie was back writing to Ned about business deals. "I note that you are in a syndicate for subdividing. Can you let me in for say $5000 cash on that?" Ned had always led the way in business deals, and Charlie seemed to be the only brother who had the money to participate in them. But he was still not over the shock of seeing the sad state into which China had sunk. "I am getting a little more at ease but am still jumpy," he said. In January Ned also received a poignant note of thanks from Margaret Rose Lansdowne, wife of the commander of the Shenandoah who had been killed over Ohio the previous September. "In giving my husband the Shenandoah," she told him, "you gave him the pride of his naval career." Further, she asked, "Permit me to add that Zach had always a tremendous admiration for you, and felt always that things would have been very different had you remained his chief. He spoke of you always with great affection and respect." (Ibid.)

Some time in March Ned became aware, undoubtedly from conversation with Ned Jr., that there were no photographs of the President of the United States in the local school which he was attending in Beaufort. Never one to miss an opportunity to have some fun, Ned immediately wrote a letter to Stonewall Coolidge — a very 'crafted' letter. So much so, that it's penciled practice version remains in Ned's papers today. "Things are progressing in the South," he began innocuously. "I have been spending the winter with my family in this delightful little city and have been much interested in several developments. For example," you can almost hear him chuckling as he writes, "a resident Southerner may now call himself a Republican on national issues or a national republican and not be lynched. Progress!" he exalted. "Similarly, while the public schools have on their walls no picture of a Republican President, the school authorities have told me that if I could get the pictures they would welcome [them] and gladly place them on the school room walls. Your photograph," he explained in case Cal didn't get it, "—one in the High School and one in the Grammar School. So unless you prefer for any reason not to do so, I have the honor to request that you will sign the two photographs that will accompany this letter [he did not even require the President of the United States to furnish his own photographs] and give me permission to present them to the respective schools." He then continued to suggest the exact inscription which he desired the Sphinx to affix to each photograph, and concluded with the piece de resistance: "I am sure you will not object to sharing wall space with Jefferson Davis and Robert E. Lee." And one may be equally sure Ned Denby had a huge grin on his face as he licked the stamp!

Calvin Coolidge, responded to Ned on April 3 on White House Stationary, with his customary hollow note of interest and insincere good wishes. "It was a pleasure to hear from you, and I have been very much interested....." When a man uses the word, "very" three times in a three sentence communication, you might want to read it with perhaps a skeptical eye.

In late March, in response to a short letter from Garvin, Ned wrote that he wished Garvin would come down to visit and help him "deplete the fishing supply." He further related that "our quail shooting season is over and our sea bass, drum and other fishing including the festive crab, is just beginning." He told him he had, with three others, chartered a fine boat, and "do not know how we ever got on without it here before, or how we will get on without [it] hereafter, for she is a great convenience and a great delight." Russell and Madeleine Hibbs were due from New York the following day, and Charlie was to come "sometime around the first half of April." Just in case anyone mistook that Ned's current penchant was toward loaf and leisure, he added, "let me spin you yarns about the fortune I propose to make in Beaufort realty when the city is on the map."

By March, Ned had only been in the area for about six months, but he is hard at selling the place to his friends. Since he was not a salesman by nature, nor a swindler, it seems a measure of just how deeply he felt about the future of the Beaufort area that he would so strenuously promote it not only to others, but to dear friends. On specially printed stationary which read "E.D. Beaufort, South Carolina", Ned wrote to his friend Walter Briggs, a Detroit entrepreneur who owned the Detroit Tigers and was a patron of the Detroit Zoo, Eastern Michigan University and the Detroit Symphony Orchestra. "This is the first time in my life," Ned wrote, "that I have ever felt so absolutely confident of the outcome of an investment that I ventured to recommend, even to urge, a friend to put his money into anything that I am organizing and which he cannot study at first-hand." He added, "I have never had a failure in real estate investments." In Ned's own words, he sounded like a member of Beaufort's Chamber of Commerce: "It has a soft, balmy climate during the greater part of the year, is located amid scenes of great natural beauty and has an unsurpassed historical background." Ned was so enthusiastic about his plans, and also about the upcoming ceremonies on Parris Island, he may be forgiven for giving Briggs more of a history lesson than he had probably had since college. "On the 27th of this month, for example, there will be dedicated on Parris Island. nearby, a monument to the Huguenots who, in 1562, there founded the first attempt at a permanent European settlement in what is now territorial United States." Whether Ned was successful in recruiting Briggs for his real estate venture is not known. But he accosted anyone and everyone who would listen, and probably some who didn't care to listen. Dr. Hibbs jumped in for $7000 and brother Charles for another $5000 which he stipulated was from his wife, Martha's, funds. His business manager in Detroit, Joe Kennedy, also signed on for $2000, apologizing that he was so tied up with other projects that that was all he could afford. Additionally, J. Walter Drake added his intention to invest $3000.

Ned could be forgiven for probably boring Walter Briggs with more Beaufort history than he ever wanted to hear because Ned had been instrumental in getting Congress to pass legislation to fund a $10,000 monument to French settlers which was duly erected at the the site of Charlesfort, the first white European settlement in North America. Situated on Parris Island, the ancient fort had been re-discovered by military men, and completely verified as to its authenticity by archeological experts. The story of the dedication was carried nationally in the New York Times, the Washington Herald, the New York World, the Baltimore Sun, Portsmouth (VA.) Star, and Newport News (VA.) Press, and others. The ceremonies of dedication were under the auspices of the Huguenot Society of South Carolina, and hundreds of descendants of French Huguenots attended, along with dignitaries from both France and the United States. Thomas McLeod, Governor of South Carolina, Curtis Wilbur, Secretary of the Navy, John LeJeune, Commandant of the Marine Corps, Jules Henry, first secretary of the French Embassy at Washington, all spoke. Ned was present, and for one of the few times he was not the principle speaker. He enjoyed himself thoroughly, however, as he told several of his friends. He donned his old Marine Corps uniform and presented himself to his successor as "adjutant" for the day. Curtis Wilbur, a jurist through and through, gave probably the most meaningful remarks. Speaking of the uncommon courage of those who had originally built the fort, Wilbur said,

"We are here to dedicate a memorial to their valor and to record the fact that the spirit which they here manifested survived in others who also fled to this continent to secure liberty and today we bear joyful witness that nowhere on this continent from Point Barrow to Cape Horn, from the Atlantic to the Pacific is it now necessary for earnest, honest, liberty-loving, God-fearing folks to imprison themselves within fortifications in order that they may exercise the humble privilege of worshipping God in accordance with the dictates of their own consciences.

"We do not fully appreciate the rich blessings which we enjoy because it is humanly impossible to put ourselves in the place of those who here built the fort to secure their liberty, nevertheless there is one word above all others which appeals to the American mind and heart. We wrote it in our Declaration of Independence, in our national and state Constitutions, in our law books and

judicial decisions— we have it inscribed upon our coins — Liberty!" (BHL Edwin Denby Papers, Box #1)

It is impossible to imagine that after hearing those stirring words Ned did not heartily shake the judge's hand, the man who had supplanted him in the job he loved and still deeply missed. For they were the words of his father, of his grandfathers, and of all the Denby men who had risen to the call of their nation's colors, including Ned himself. In those days giants walked among us, or certainly men who had known the giants. In those days they built monuments to the valorous dead and the hallowed precepts by which they lived — and died. Today we tear them down.

Throughout the early months of 1926 Ned kept up a very lively correspondence with many people of hugely varied backgrounds. He corresponded with and tried to help a Marine imprisoned in Leavenworth; with a Detroit mother whose Marine son was a shirker, and who specifically asked Ned to write her a letter explaining why he could not help her son, that the son had to step up and help himself, so that she might show it to her son— and Ned did, in three typed pages. He heard from both of his nephews, Hattie's boys who were still living abroad, making their livings in France. Ned felt a great affection for these nephews whom he had helped raise while they lived with him in Washington. He corresponded with a Mr. Fred Kent of Asheville, N.C. about how he needed to proceed to form a Rotary Club in Beaufort. He received a warm and respectful letter from Representative John Sosnowski, the man who currently held his old congressional seat from Detroit, in reply to Ned's request for a current Congressional Directory. "I am endeavoring to keep up with the work and the reputation established when you so ably represented it," Sosnowski told him. "From time to time I run across matters here recalling your very excellent work.....I have always held you in the highest esteem." (BHL Edwin Denby Papers, Box #1) He corresponded with a young Marine stationed in Haiti whom he had helped to get appointed to the Haitian police force, and who told him in gratitude, "I will tell you all the news from this place and how I am getting along and I want you to know that I will make good." (Ibid.) He also heard from a George Hunter who worked for the Cable Piano Company of Chicago and Detroit, concerning anything he might be able to do for an employee of theirs who was in trouble with narcotics. Ned and Hunter had been tent- mates together at Parris Island, both having been from Detroit, and Hunter felt their employee could be resurrected if only Ned could get the Michigan Attorney General to quash his indictment. Ned declined to become involved in this way, but things turned out well for the employee anyway, as he pled guilty to one charge and the other was dismissed. He served a short sentence and was doing well. In a follow-up letter, Hunter told Ned "I have met many of the boys that were there at the time that we were and they have always asked for you and thought of you with nothing but love in their hearts for the help and uplift which you were responsible for." (Ibid.) In addition, of course, he also received weekly, and sometimes more frequently, updates from his business manager, Joe Kennedy.

Once more, in April, he received a letter from a brother in financial trouble, this time, his older brother, Wythe. Ned had co-signed a note which was due which Wythe could not pay, and Wythe had driven from Chicago where he lived, to Detroit to talk things over with Ned's business manager, Joe Kennedy. Joe provided enough funds to buy Wythe some time. Wythe then wrote his brother in Beaufort, as if in confession, but sent the letter via Kennedy. It's difficult to parse the family dynamics of a hundred years ago, but Ned, while waiting a full month to reply to his brother, basically told him not to worry about it, and that Kennedy had been in Beaufort visiting him and had already told him all about it. At nearly the same time he received a letter from Charlie ruminating over the possibility that the two of them would need to "pension" Garvin, and speculating on how much per month he could afford. Charlie, still smarting over the devastation of his business interests in China, and the resultant loss of income, was, nevertheless, the family poor-mouth. Interestingly, in Ned's next letter to Charlie he failed to discuss financial help for Garvin. Almost surely no one in the family, including Charlie, knew he was already sending Graham's widow, Olga, in Evansville, a monthly check.

As if to bear out Charlie's foreboding about Garvin, Ned next received another catharsis from his little brother concerning the still woeful state of his finances. It seems that Ned had a second mortgage on Garvin's house in the amount of $3000 which, again, Garvin could not pay. This time Ned's response was rather more prompt, as he reassured his brother that he did not require the payment of the mortgage he held until Garvin was in better financial position to pay it. As if he feared his brother had not visited him in Beaufort because of his finances, Ned finished his letter, "I am sorry you are unable to come to see us. Remember, that when you can come, we are here and you are welcome. Later we shall be there [Pontiac farm] and you will be welcome. Wherever we are you will be welcome." (Ibid.) Garvin wasted no time in replying to his indulgent brother's leniency, "Many thanks for your last letter. It's contents relieved me considerably," he wrote on April 23. He also mentioned Charlie had been suffering from bladder trouble, and that he had seemed "deeply depressed, the last time I saw him, which is a correlative symptom, because he has really little to be depressed about." (Ibid.) Spoken by a man who's chief care was his income. Later in the same letter he told his brother that they had sold $250 worth of dogs that month, but in an earlier letter he had admitted that the dogs were their only income at the time.

In late April Ned was in Charleston once again, this time as part of the seventeen member Detroit delegation to the National Foreign Trade council convention. "The foreign trade convention is attended annually by 2500 industrial leaders from all corners of the world, and is eagerly fought for by cities of this country." (DFP 5-16-1926) The Press went on to explain that Ned & co. had won out for the location of 1927's convention over representatives from Houston, Honolulu, Mobile, Norfolk, Va., and Oakland, California." This was an extremely important industrial trade feather in Detroit's cap, and the article ended by saying that "Denby was later asked to appear before the body of industrial leaders to deliver the farewell address of the meeting." In early May Ned wrote a long letter to Joe Kennedy about Detroit area business decisions, and then told him of a town meeting to be held in Beaufort that evening to discuss plans to turn the old double-turreted USS Amphritrite into a floating hotel. "I went over it in Charleston the other day and needed no imagination to see how attractive the hotel will be, swinging to the tide in mid-stream [in the river off Beaufort]." He further admitted to Joe that he had been bitten by "the golf bug but have had only one opportunity since you left to play." (BHL Edwin Denby Papers, Box #1)

In late April Ned heard from another one of his regular correspondents, his former private secretary from the Navy Department, Joe Carey. Carey had remained in Washington after Ned's resignation and formed a lucrative law practice. The two had been and remained close, with an abiding and affectionate respect for each other. Carey mentioned escorting a "Beaufortite" whom he referred to as "Tillie the Toiler" to the Mayflower Hotel for lunch. Tillie must have been unusually tall for Carey remarked that "Fortunately we were sitting down most of the time so that after she resumed her journey I was not troubled with a stiff neck." Carey further reported that "She told me a great deal of interest about Beaufort, and the Denbys, not overlooking the real estate 'wizard'." More significantly, however, was Carey's next bit of information:

"I am sending herewith a prospectus of Detroit's new airport which is being promoted by Carl Fritsche and a crowd who are in the Aircraft Development Corporation. You might look it over and if you are interested you might get more than a speaking acquaintance with it. I suggested to Carl Fritsche, when he was here a short while ago, that this is the sort of proposition that requires someone of your experience, ability and prestige to help put it over in the right way. Carl replied that if you are interested

he would see that you were made President of the Corporation."
(BHL Edwin Denby Papers, Box #1)

Fritsche was general manager of the Aircraft Development
Corporation, a group of Detroit businessmen and engineers who
had formed to promote the air industry in general, and lighter
than air ships in particular, and were at this time also developing
Detroit's first commercial airport, which in another year would
become known as Detroit City Airport. It would remain the
principle Detroit airport for twenty years, and handle scheduled
commercial flights until 2000. It would seem, however, that Ned
did not "bite" on this bone, being more interested in the wizardry
of real estate. One thing was certain about Ned Denby, however,
— if he didn't think of it first, his friends would. To his dying
day they were ready to put him up for something, and usually
something big. Almost as big as he was.

The Denbys found that they had to delay their return to the
Pontiac farm until after the opening of the floating hotel which
Ned had worked so hard to obtain for the purpose of advertising
the Beaufort area. The hotel opened on June 12th. "I have had so
much to do with getting it here that it would be very hard for me to
leave before that date," he wrote to Joe Kennedy. They once again
travelled through Washington, stopping for a short visit with the
Hayne Ellis' family. Rear Admiral Ellis had served as a liaison
officer during the arms Limitation Conference in Washington in
1921-22, and as Naval Aide to Ned for his last two years in office.
In October plans were announced concerning the construction of
a seven story apartment building in Pontiac listing Ned as one of
the principle parties involved. Toward the end of the month Ned
was in Philadelphia for a reunion of 50 years worth of University
of Michigan graduates at the Bellevue-Stratford hotel. On the eve
of what was now becoming an annual game between Michigan
and Navy, the guests sang Bye, Bye, Navy, and "jibed their fellow
alumnus Edwin Denby, former secretary of the navy, of the fate
that awaits the navy's mascot, the traditional goat. 'You may sink
the Navy tomorrow,'" Ned told them, "'but not with the ease and
flippancy that your songs indicate. The Navy will at least cross

Michigan's goal line." The following day in Municipal Stadium in Baltimore, the Jack Tars shocked the Wolverines by handing them their only defeat of the season, 0-10. Dean of the Engineering Department, Mortimer Cooley, a former shipmate of Ned's on the Yosemite in the Spanish American War, "voiced the warning that Michigan must beware when it meets the Navy tomorrow. 'We all know the fighting spirit of the Navy,' he said, 'and the Navy is never whipped.'" (DFP 10-30-1926) He turned out to be right.

Invited to be the principle speaker at the Armistice Day celebrations in Pontiac on November 11, Ned insisted that he march on foot in the parade. "If I am going to be in the parade, I want to be with the boys." (DFP 11-11-1926) Ned spoke at the dedication of a war memorial to the high school students of Pontiac who had served in the war. He had a very clear message: "When we cease to follow the flag," he warned his audience, "then will the decay of our nation begin." (DFP 11-12-1926)

A day later brought other significant business news for the Detroit area and for Ned. An announcement was made by prominent businessmen and leaders of the aircraft industry of the formation of the Chateau Voyageurs, a recreational club on Grosse Ile. The club, designed to feature facilities for golf, tennis, horseback riding, yachting and water sports, was also to feature an airport. "A 100 acre harbor adjoining the property will furnish an ideal landing place for seaplanes," noted the Press article. The Club had already purchased the summer home of R. E. Olds, completely furnished, for use by club members. Ned was chosen as 'first commodore and honorary president of the club," while Olds became chairman of the board, and Carl Fritsche became temporary secretary. The airport was to be ready by the following May and had been offered to Detroit for use until its own municipal airport could be constructed. Over the years in the future, the airport transitioned into a Naval Air Station, and trained pilots for both World War II and the Vietnam War, closing only in 1969. R. E. Olds fabulous summer home which became for a time the Clubhouse for the Chateau Voyageurs still stands as a private residence.

On Tuesday, November 16 it was announced that Ned had sold an 1100 acre parcel of land a mile south of Trenton, Michigan in the southern Detroit suburbs to a Detroit real estate man.

The price speculated upon by the Free Press was "within the neighborhood of "$2,200,000." (DFP 11-16-1926) All throughout this remaining half of the year Ned waited, in all probability, with some suspense, as the papers were still carrying stories every week of this oil trial and that. Due to the skill of attorneys, both prosecuting and defending, and the debilitating illnesses of Albert Fall, the oil litigations would continue into the early 1930"s. Ned appeared on behalf of the defense in the Fall-Doheny oil conspiracy trial in Washington, D. C. on Wednesday, December 8. On the stand for two and one half hours undergoing what the Press referred to as a "pummeling" by prosecuting attorney Owen Roberts, the trial lasted barely two weeks, ending somewhat abruptly, and found both Albert Fall and Edward Doheny not guilty.

Three days before Christmas, Ned was on hand at the Ford Airport in Dearborn, Michigan, along with Edsal Ford, Joseph Carey, William B. Mayo and six members of the First Pursuit Group of military aviators from Selfridge field, as well as newspaper men, to greet the arrival of Richard E. Byrd's airplane. Byrd, a naval aviator, had overflown the north pole the previous May 9, and after a triumphant tour of the country's airfields, the plane had been purchased by the Ford Motor Company and was coming to its final and permanent home. "We have no museum as yet, but when we get one," Edsal Ford told the newsmen, "this plane will be an important part of it." The plane in question, a Fokker F.VIIa/3m tri-motor monoplane was named The Josephine Ford after Edsal Ford's three year old daughter, Josephine, and because Edsal had contributed heavily to help fund Byrd's flight. True to his word, the fabulous museum, today known as 'The Henry Ford', was built in 1929 directly across the street from the Ford Airport, and The Josephine Ford took her place as a permanent fixture where it stands today, in the early air exhibit.

Ned was once more the guest of honor, as he had been so many times in his life at banquets just such as these, on December 27 at the Detroit Athletic Club where 200 friends gathered to honor and recognize his forty years of service "to city, state and nation, from the time he served in China in Harrison's and Cleveland's administrations, to the time he became Secretary of the Navy.... under eight presidents of the United States in peace and in war." Ned received greetings from eleven admirals and the commandant of the Marine Corps, among many others. Rev. Merton S. Rice of the Metropolitan Methodist church introduced him, saying, "Ned Denby is an American. I can hardly think of him without thinking of the country from which he comes. So many times he has answered the call of service to his country, and so many times has he acquitted himself nobly in that call, that he is America personified." When called upon to speak, Ned did so with great gusto in his own defense;

"I have no shame whatever, but only pride, with regard to what was done in storing oil in the Hawaiian Islands. I would rather today face a firing squad than to undo what I did at that time. What was done was dictated by the highest motives, and with the defense of the United States in mind. "Hawaii is the stronghold of power for America in the Pacific. The presence of that oil there means that a fleet can find its lifeblood in the islands and be equipped for an 80 days' campaign." (DFP 12-28-1926)

Ned, of course, was preaching to the choir. But it made no difference to Ned whether friend of foe was in his audience. He would never apologize. He did not have to. Fifteen years later the American fleet, traveling on contract oil, sank four of the six Japanese carriers at the historic Battle of Midway, the same carriers which had attacked Pearl Harbor only six months before. Ned was right about the adversary. He was right about preparedness. He was right about the strategic importance of Pearl Harbor, and he was absolutely right about the advantage of a million and a half gallons of navy fuel oil stored there, and not in the ground in Wyoming, but ready for immediate use.

Chapter Thirty

"Then sow; — for the hours are fleeting, And the seed must fall today;
And care not what hands shall reap it, Or if you shall have passed away
Before the waving cornfields Shall gladden the sunny day.
Sow; and look onward, upward, Where the starry light appears—
Where, in spite of the coward's doubting,
Or your own heart's trembling fears,
You shall reap in joy the harvest You have sown today in tears."

from "Sowing and Reaping" by Adelaide Proctor

The Fruits of Civic Labors

January 4, 1927, the Denbys set out from Detroit on their return to Beaufort, leaving the frozen icebox of the north for the sunnier and more moderate temperatures of the south.

Counting his Marine Corps service on Parris Island during the war, this marked the tenth year that Ned had been visiting Beaufort. "In 1919 Denby was so charmed by Beaufort that he bought the house on Bay Street that had long been the home of George Gage and his children." (Rowland, Wise, p 206). Gage was, like Ned, a northerner who had come south as a missionary with his mother, a noted abolitionist. They had settled in Beaufort to take part in the Port Royal Experiment, a project by northern missionaries to help educate and empower freed slaves. The Experiment was ended in 1865 by President Andrew Johnson, a southern Democrat. George Gage had gone on to become wealthy from lumber, and lived the remainder of his adult life in Beaufort, a very prominent citizen involved in several important aspects of Beaufort life. In many respects, George Gage personified the new wealth of the old south — entrepreneurial and inventive men, some, like Gage, driven by highly laudable morals, and others, of course, who became known as 'carpetbaggers' and had no morals at all.

Ned naturally fit into the category of moral entrepreneurs, genuinely smitten by the beauty of the low counties, but also smitten by the opportunity he saw to make significant amounts of money. By this time Ned had begun selling properties for another sub-divided housing development, this one known as, "Sea Island Homes".

In February two of his nephews, both sons of his brother, Charlie, were married in highly publicized society weddings in the north. James Orr, the eldest son, aged 31, wed Phyllis Cochran in Philadelphia on February 19. The bride and groom were shortly to leave for Asian climes, as James was soon to take his place as the third generation of Denbys to serve the United States State Department in China. James had been named our Legation's second secretary, a job his father had once held forty-one years earlier. Furthermore, "James was the only Denby child to have been born in Peking." (Washington Evening Star, February 26, 1927) But before sailing, James stood best man to his next youngest brother, Charles III, aged 26, who wed Rosamond Reed, daughter of Pennsylvania Senator David Reed, in what was described as the wedding of the season. No less than the President and Mrs, Coolidge, the entire cabinet, and hosts of other dignitaries attended the event held in the Bethlehem Chapel of the National Cathedral on Wisconsin Avenue. The papers noted, perhaps snidely, that the President failed to show at the reception at the Reed home, choosing instead, after announcing that he would attend, to visit the temporary home the Coolidges would soon occupy while some major renovations took place at 1600. The dignitary most notable for his absence at both functions, was the boys' uncle Ned. Characteristically of Ned, not wishing to spoil the event, he knew that with the oil trials still bubbling over in the nation's capital, if he were to attend, he would undoubtedly steal the press from the principle characters. There is no correspondence between the two brothers who remained close all their lives — it was almost as if it were not necessary to discuss it. It was simply the right thing to do, and so it was done.

One of the most significant events of the 20th century took place on May 20-21, 1927 as Charles Lindbergh, who had been born in Detroit in 1902, and whose mother had taught chemistry at Cass Technical High School there, piloted his Ryan NYP monoplane from Roosevelt Field on Long Island, to Le Bourget Aerodrome seven miles northeast of Paris, France. Lucky Lindy had just become arguably the most famous person of the 20th Century.

The most significant event of 1927, in Ned's life, was the great upheaval of the local economy in the low counties. As far back as June of 1926, his friend, law partner, and business agent, Joe Kennedy, had remarked about the shaky reputation of the Beaufort Bank, and had speculated openly about its long term viability. Ned had been somewhat offended at the time, and had become almost peevish with Kennedy about the whole arrangement.

Kennedy, having obsequiously admired and supported his far more famous boss, suddenly was questioning his judgment in a financial matter, and Ned was not happy about it. Kennedy had actually called the Beaufort Bank "weak", and when Ned telegraphed him, he replied in his next letter, "I judge from your telegram which I received today [June 1, 1926] that you do not like to have me make such insinuations as that and I assure you it did not afford me any particular pleasure to do it, but it would make a very embarrassing situation if something did happen to the bank....." (BHL Edwin Denby Papers Box #1) The bottom line was, Kennedy pulled out of the real estate deal, Sea Island Homes, being backed by the Beaufort Bank. Ned's reply to this, dated June 2nd was blunt, "I bank at the Beaufort Bank which your letter shows you distrust, and my associates are men in whom you have no confidence." (Ibid.)

It is difficult to understand how someone as astute in business could have missed, or chosen to ignore, the signs of trouble which appeared obvious to Joe Kennedy from over 800 miles away. Ned was undoubtedly still recovering from the shock and the sensation of the public flogging in the U. S. Senate and the nation's newspapers, which to only a slightly reduced way, still continued. He had had fond memories of his time in the Marine Corps, and his time with his family in Beaufort. He was a man of the deepest loyalty, and undoubtedly wished to cling almost desperately to this loyalty in the face of the calumny which had been heaped upon him, even by some he had thought his friends.

As Lawrence Rowland and Stephen Wise, in their book, "Bridging the Sea Islands' Past and Present" so aptly point out, "The institution at the heart of business was the Beaufort Bank, which had been founded in 1908." By 1914 the bank had built a fine new office building on Bay Street in Beaufort, and by 1915 the bank was operating five branches. "The Beaufort Bank continued to grow and by 1920 its assets at $723,201.35 surpassed the older People's Bank." The bank paid dividends every year and "in 1922 the Beaufort Bank became the first bank in the county to exceed $1 million dollars in total assets." (Rowland, Wise, p. 254)

"But trouble was brewing for the Beaufort Bank and for the local economy." (Ibid) Markets were changing, whole business models once viable, were suddenly disappearing. The Marine Corps, whose explosive expansion during World War I, was cutting back, downsizing as the Marine Corps always did in peacetime. "In July 1924 the Beaufort Bank reached its pinnacle with assets of $1,391,321.95. Deposits were $822,451. But it would be another twenty years before any Beaufort bank reached that level. Ninety days after July 1924 deposits shrank 13 percent and assets declined 6.5 percent, never to rise again…   by 1926 the bank was in distress." (Ibid) How could the auto tycoon, the real estate "wizard" have missed this?

A large town meeting took place on Sunday July 11 and the situation was explained. Apparently the officers did a good job because the citizens basically accepted what they had to say. Despite this, however, the bank closed its doors the next day for thirty days to prevent a run. This act triggered the entrance of the state bank examiner, and events ran swiftly from there. By September indictments were being handed down, and after some frenzied attempts by some of the citizens to save the bank, it closed for good.

"The fallout from the Beaufort Bank collapse affected the region for years." (Ibid, p.255) The simple fact was that Ned had had difficulty believing several of his "friends" were lying, but this is exactly what they did. One of the glaringly illegal procedures the bank had engaged in was the failure "to cancel properly several notes and mortgages that had been paid off by local property owners," thus on paper claiming 'assets' which no longer existed. It was fraud, it was cruel, and it was catastrophic for the local economy. It would take the Beaufort citizenry years to recover from the mess. Nor was it simply a Beaufort problem. "In 1926, 120 South Carolina banks were in the hands of receivers." (Ibid) In all fairness to Ned Denby, few, if any, saw a catastrophe of this magnitude coming. Many of Beaufort's leading and well-to-do citizens lost everything and many lost significantly, including Ned. Though the Denbys were due to return to the Pontiac farm in June, as was their habit, Rowland and Wise note that "Denby returned only once to Beaufort after the bank failure." The idyll of the South was over for Ned. "It was the end of the business and commercial legacy of reconstruction," claim the authors of Bridging the Sea Islands' Past and Present, "and the local beginning of the Great Depression." (Ibid p. 256)

Not long after the Denbys return to Pontiac, a formal dinner dance was held for the opening of the Chateau Voyageurs Club on Elba Island. The officers and their ladies from Selfridge were the guests of the club members, which included, of course, the new President of the Club, Ned Denby. Still "in preparation" according to the Free Press' account, were the two golf courses, riding stables, swimming and yachting facilities, "and a landing field for aviators". (DFP 7-3-1927) The following month, on Monday July 25, at 730 in the evening, city, Y.M.C.A., and religious officials gathered at the corner of Jefferson Avenue and Garland Street on Detroit's east side to hold the cornerstone laying exercises for the new Hannan Memorial Branch of Detroit's Y.M.C.A. A $700,000 (eleven and a half million in 2022 dollars) facility, it was to be one of the seven regional centers to be constructed from the fundraising campaign of which Ned had been the highly successful chairman.

Ned attended and gave the principle address, among those of several Y.M.C.A. officials. A cornerstone, "which will contain a Bible, an American flag, a history of the Y. M. C. A.,.... copies of city and community newspapers and the branch constitution and bylaws will be sealed by Charles B. Van Dusen, chairman of the board of directors of the Y. M. C. A. of Detroit." (DFP 7-24-1927)

In early August Ned joined Detroit Mayor John W. Smith and other dignitaries who traveled to Camp Custer, Michigan near Battle Creek, "in connection with the final program of the annual Citizens Military Training Camp." The camp was built in 1917 to train men for World War I. By authority of the National Defense Act of 1920, military training camps were established to provide training on a voluntary basis. Unlike the Reserves or National Guard, these camps provided military training without the obligation of being called up for service. Between the years of 1921 and 1940 approximately 400,000 men received military training. It was an alternative to conscription, and an offshoot of pre-World War I Preparedness Movement which sought to provide officers and men in advance of necessity. CMTC training lasted one month each year at several bases around the country. Two Presidents of the United States were CMTC graduates: Harry Truman and Ronald Reagan.

On Friday evening, September 30, Ned was principle speaker at a banquet once again, but this time at a very unusual ceremony celebrating two extremely unusual young men. At the Palestine Lodge No,159, "an event believed to be unique in Masonic affairs," took place when "worshipful master" Edward S. Evans conferred upon his twin sons the degree of Master Masons. (DFP 9-25-1927) The Press article went on to remark that the senior Evans "gained fame in the aviation world when, with Linton Wells of New York, he achieved a new around-the- world speed record, making the trip by airplane, automobile, ship and train in twenty-eight and a half days." (Ibid) So, take that, Phineas Fogg! What the article could not know was that in the future, all three Evans men would become glider enthusiasts and experts, and that their expertise would be of great use for their country in a future world conflagration.

At nearly the same time that Ned was speaking before the Masons, his brother Garvin and wife's dog, Denbrook Balaclava won best male Irish Terrier in the Ladies Kennel Association of America dog show cat the Westchester Biltmore Country Club in Rye, Long Island, New York. It was only one of several awards that the Garvin Denbys' dogs would win that season. On a more serious note, and also at just the same time Rear Admiral Thomas P. Magruder, then Commandant of the Fourth Naval District at Philadelphia wrote an article which was published in the Saturday Evening Post entitled, "The Navy and Economy." In it he complained of abuses in the lack of economy, but the real controversy over the article stemmed from the fact that it was written at all, not as much as what it actually said. In addition to the embarrassment to Secretary Wilbur, the Navy Department and the administration itself, the biggest problem was that it appeared to be within the rules and guidelines established by Ned back in 1921, which basically stated that an "officer may publish anything he wishes if he does to violate the proprieties, such as by revealing naval secrets or misrepresenting conditions.
(NYT 9-25-1927)

In another Times article two days later, Magruder, in response to Secretary Wilbur's request for him to submit his plan for the Navy's reorganization, stated that he had not intended to reorganize the navy. "My article was an effort to have carried out the naval policy approved by former Secretary Denby. That contained a number of well-thought-out ideas which have never been entirely carried out, and it was my purpose to focus attention on these subjects." By this time Magruder had become golden to certain politicians, especially those who viewed their jobs, Republican or Democrat, to stir up the fires of controversy thus acquiring for themselves any modicum of power which might be so gained. Bobby LaFolette may have gone to his reward, but William Borah in the Senate, and Thomas Butler, Chairman of the House Naval Affairs Committee in the House, were quick to jump to Magruder's defense.

With such powerful allies, Wilber had to proceed with caution. He ordered Magruder to vacate his post upon arrival of his relief, and to report to the Secretary of the Navy in Washington. Though Magruder appealed to President Coolidge, in effect, he was outmaneuvered, as Coolidge did what he always did during controversy, he looked the other way and pretended he didn't see anything. Wilbur left Magruder hanging in Washington for nearly two years before reassigning him to active duty in 1929. The admiral quietly retired in 1931.

In early October Ned was once again called upon by fellow Detroiters to assist in the dedication of a solemn memorial. The University of Detroit, founded in 1877 by Jesuits, was celebrating its 50th birthday, the establishment of its new facilities at the McNichols Campus, and also dedicating a memorial plaque embedded into the base of the World War I Memorial Clock Tower. Three companies from each of the three services, paid tribute to the twelve war dead who had been students at the university before the war. The brothers of two of the honored removed the American flag draped over the plaque commemorating the names of the twelve. Ned spoke, and a bugler played taps. Once more the old sailor/Marine in Ned stood at rigid attention as taps was rendered while certainly he remembered many comrades who had died in the service of the country.

On Monday October 10, the Supreme Court rendered its verdict on the Harry Sinclair lease of the Teapot Dome tract of the naval reserves. The Court returned the tract to the ownership of the government, as was expected, and did not allow damages to Sinclair. Though highly critical of Albert Fall, the Court had little to say about Ned. It needs be said that there were two types of trials which came out of the whole escapade, the civil cases which were decided by a judge, and the criminal cases which were   decided by a jury of peers. With little exception the civil cases went for the government, and the criminal cases tended to exonerate the charged. The exception, of course, was the last trial, that of Albert Fall for bribery, where he was found guilty of bribing Edward Doheny, while Edward Doheny was acquitted of BEING bribed! Four days later a judge in Wayne circuit court ordered a Mr. Wayne Ellis to pay Edwin Denby $1,805,869.90 "before January 5. The order was a consent decree rising out of a suit brought against Ellis to keep a contract." Apparently, after paying a $30,000 down payment for some parcels of land, Mr. Ellis defaulted upon paying the remainder. The following Monday the trial of Albert Fall began. Ned certainly must have thought that these trials were going to continue forever. Many Democrats were trying very hard to accommodate him.

November brought the now annual game between the Naval Academy and the University of Michigan football teams. Michigan was ready for the midshipmen, well remembering the devastating loss they had suffered in Baltimore to the sailors the previous year. In addition to that drama, the brand new Michigan Stadium, a monster built with the initial capacity of 72,000, but with footers which would allow expansion up to 150,000 (a size envisioned by the legendary Fielding Yost; the stadium today has been enlarged to 107,601), had been dedicated only three weeks before on October 22. Furthermore, the Wolverines had, for the first time in twenty-five years, a new coach in the person of Tad Wieman. The Midshipmen, on the other hand were coming off their National Championship Year of 1926 (which they shared with Alabama and Stanford), and it appeared that a very good game was brewing for the 1927 contest.

As in previous years, Ned attended a pre-game banquet as one of many guests of honor, and then proceeded into the new behemoth on the corner of Main and Stadium Streets to watch the Wolverines win 27 to 12. Only a week later, the Y.M.C.A. was once again celebrating the building campaign, this time with a week-long series of events to showcase the newly refurbished Main Y.M.C.A. building and the Elizabeth branch. Both facilities had been entirely rebuilt to the most modern specifications, and on the final day of celebration, several famous Detroit flyers were recognized, including Edward S. Evans who had circumnavigated the globe in 1926, and two other flyers who held world records, and Ned Denby, of course, as the man who had organized the campaign to raise the funds for the buildings being showcased.

On December 2, Ned "was elected chairman of the newly organized Detroit Salvation Army advisory board at a luncheon meeting in the Hotel Statler," the Free Press reported. "The purpose of the board, as explained by Colonel Albert S, Norris, divisional commander, is to have the members serve in an advisory capacity with reference to all Salvation Army activities in Greater Detroit; to give special advice on real estate matters, such as offers for the purchase of army property, the selection of location for any of the army's activities; to serve on any committee at any time former to present the army's interests to the Detroit Community union, and to consider any capital account program made necessary by plans for new buildings." (DFP 12-3-1927) It was that last part that seemed most important, for the Salvation Army leaders had seen what Ned Denby could do with a fund-raising campaign for capital structures, and they wanted him to do the same for them.

The next day, the Y. M. C. A. was at it again, this time dedicating the Northern Branch of the organization at the corner of Woodward Avenue and Winona Streets. A four-story edifice it contained "complete gymnasium facilities, swimming pool, game rooms, reading rooms, cafeteria, private dining rooms and housing facilities for nearly 200 residents." (DFP 12-5-1927) Once again, Ned attended the ceremonies.

Disaster struck swiftly and without any warning whatever on the afternoon of December 17 as the Coast Guard destroyer Paulding stationed at Boston, Massachusetts, while on rum patrol off Provincetown, Mass., accidentally struck and sank the United States Navy submarine S-4. The S-4 had just run a submerged measured mile test, and inadvertently surfaced directly in front of the Coast Guard ship. Despite immediately lowering a lifeboat, the Paulding found no survivors on the surface. Hampered by heavy weather, the navy responded with pontoons from New London, Connecticut and Brooklyn, New York, which were restricted in getting to the stricken submarine by the adverse conditions. Fully twenty-four hours after the crash, navy divers were able to establish contact with six survivors trapped in the forward torpedo room, six men who had water, no food, and approximately 48 hours worth of good air until suffocation. The entire nation held its collective breath as the navy and its heroic divers bravely faced the deteriorating weather conditions, even at the peril of their own lives, and made several attempts to attach air lines to the submarine, and later worked on a plan to force food and air canisters through a torpedo tube. Nothing worked. One diver was caught in lines 100 feet below the surface and hours were lost in extricating him. Conditions were so hazardous that the diver who rescued the trapped man was awarded the Congressional Medal of Honor. The weather did not in any way cooperate, poor at best for days after the crash. At some point during the first two days, while another nearby submarine, the S-8, was still receiving messages pounded on the interior hull of the craft, it was learned that the officer who was sending the signals was Lt.j.g. Graham Newell Fitch, son of retired Army Colonel Graham Denby Fitch, and cousin of Edwin Denby. Lt. Fitch was newly married, 25 years old, and according to the New York Times, "one of the youngest officers in the submarine service." (NYT 12-19-1927)

Congressmen began lining up to hoist Wilbur on their petards, one claiming, by the Navy's own calculations, that there had been "seventeen mishaps to Navy ships since 1923; eight accidents to submarines." (NYT 12-28-1927) Finally, on December 27 the Navy "officially recognized that the 40 officers and men on the ill-fated submarine S-4 were dead." (Ibid.) The weather off Provincetown continued difficult for some time and the Navy did not revisit the salvage effort until March, 1928. On March 17, the S-4 was finally raised, towed to Boston Navy Yard. She was decommissioned, refurbished and recommissioned as a test vessel, and served until January 1936.

Being an old sea-dog himself, Ned knew dangers which sailors faced every day of their service. It is virtually certain that almost no one mourned young Fitch, and all of his 39 shipmates, more than the Seagoing Secretary.

Chapter Thirty-One

"You have enemies? Good.
That means that you've stood up for something,
sometime in your life."

Sir Winston Churchill

The Final Year

The year 1928 was a presidential election year. Following the turnaround of the economy in the shortened presidency of Warren Harding, the nation had enjoyed several years of unbridled prosperity. You would never know this if you listened to any Democrat campaigning for office in 1928. For this reason primarily, for the benefit of political advantage, the Democrats kept up the drumbeat of Teapot Dome throughout the decade, and into the following one. Since they had had little political success on a national level after Woodrow Wilson, it may be one of the principle reasons that Teapot Dome remained a resonating scandal for decades to come. Certainly there were abuses. There has never been an administration free of them. But Teapot Dome was hammered into the American psyche with such sledgehammer blows that it became truly a self-perpetuating legend.

Early in 1928, and with the upcoming election clearly in mind, the New York Times breathlessly and dramatically, ran a full page article on the front page of their 'special features' section entitled, "WIDER SPREADS THE ELUSIVE FILM OF OIL; The Trail from Teapot Dome Now Leads to Political Campaign Funds and Opens Up Another Chapter of Mystery in the Six- Year Old Romance of

Investigation by a Senate Committee." (NYT 2-19-1928) And so, the MYSTERY and the ROMANCE were to continue. Even if there really was nothing new, but simply a rehash of old information.

In January the retired John J. (Black Jack) Pershing, formerly generalissimo of all American forces in the World War, made a one day trip to Detroit. The city had always treated the General with the utmost pomp — but most American cities did and would until the day he died. He arrived by private rail car late Friday evening, and was then officially greeted Saturday morning by the Mayor and other dignitaries. Then off for luncheon with the Board of Commerce. "Before the Board of Commerce defense committee he lauded Detroit's leadership as the 'nation's air capital.'" (DFP 1-29-1928) Which was great, because that was how many Detroit businessmen were now seeing their city, and more importantly, wanting others to see it. Next Pershing went to the still new Masonic Temple, for which Ned had laid the cornerstone, and spoke to a huge audience in the 5000 seat auditorium. That evening, in the Crystal Ballroom, a banquet was given in his honor. Beside Ned on the dais with all the Detroit dignitaries sat the tiny form of a white-haired, 85-year-old spinster, Mrs. Henry L. Lyster who had adopted Ned over thirty years before, and always called him her "fourth son". When the toastmaster introduced her to the audience that evening, he detailed the men in her life who had served in the nation's armed forces from the Mexican War to World War I. She was given a standing ovation. A little while later when Pershing rose to give his address to the assemblage, he first turned and bowed to Mrs. Lyster and remarked,

"'One of my special pleasures, Madam, is to have been present at this board with you this evening,' said the man who had led 2,000,000 men to war, numbering in his command those three sons and one son-in-law of the woman he addressed.

'I wish to thank you for what you have been to your family, and for what you are to us today.'"

The Free Press writer went on to add:

"And that was the keynote of the episode—the thought that ran through the mind of every person present and made it just a bit hard to keep back the tears. The white haired figure at Mr. Denby's right was not only the daughter of a soldier, the wife of a soldier and the mother of warrior sons. She was the spirit of the womanhood of these United States, a living chapter of the nation's history that shall stand, valiant and undaunted, as she has stood, to the end." (DFP 1-30-1928)

The United States Navy had another serious scare at the same time that Pershing was saluting Mrs. Lyster. The submarine, S-3, sister of the S-4 which had recently been lost just before Christmas, had been traveling with the Control Force en route to Cuba for winter maneuvers when she disappeared into the stormy mists of the Atlantic. Apparently, the ship's radio masts had been damaged by the storm and the sub was unable to radio her location, and became lost in the storm. Other subs in the formation reported "fighting their way through high seas in the teeth of a heavy gale and rain squall," which had separated the S-3 from the group. The search consisted of "more than two score naval surface craft" and lasted nearly 48 hours before she was found. Almost certainly there was a huge sigh of relief in the office of the Secretary of the Navy.

On February 8, Ned addressed the Export Club on the subject of China. "We need have no anxiety about the China of today," he said. "She is merely experiencing the birth pains of liberty. Americans should remember that it took us 13 years to formulate our constitution. The achievement of liberty is not to be expected immediately for the asking. Too, China has a more complex problem than that which confronted our forefathers. They are subjected to outside interference, whereas America's liberators had none. They have a population of more than 300,000,000 to satisfy, which is many more times larger than the population of America at the time of the revolution." (DFP 2-9-1928) Americans as long ago as Ned, and even before, have never understood, too, that some cultures simply do not place the premium on individual liberty that Americans do; or at least that Americans have in the past.

In April the government prosecution of Harry Sinclair was in full swing in the nation's capital. As part of his defense, Ned was called as a witness to testify to what he had always freely and openly and loudly proclaimed over and over again in the past six years — that he, and he alone, being concerned about protecting the navy's oil reserves, had originated the idea of leasing them to private companies. That it was he who had originated this idea, and that he had then taken it to Albert Fall. On April 18, Admiral J. K. Robison had testified extensively to these particulars and had been "put through a grueling cross examination by Owen J. Roberts, special government prosecutor." (DFP 4-19-1928) Next, the defense called Ned to verify what Robison had already said. But after only a few preliminary questions, the prosecution objected to Ned's testimony "because Robison had testified that Denby had not talked with Fall or seen him about the lease in any way." (Ibid.) The judge sustained Roberts' objection, and Ned was dismissed, having made a trip to Washington for nothing.

On April 21, in a surprise move, Harry Sinclair's defense rested — without calling Harry Sinclair to the stand to testify in his own behalf. After weeks of testimony and drama, the jury was out for one hour and fifty-five minutes. The verdict was stunning. Absolute acquittal. The recent judgments of the Supreme Court and the Court of Appeals were totally rejected, and in later jury interviews, it was revealed that at no time during deliberations was there a single vote to convict. "The verdict was the greatest surprise Washington has had in years," moaned the New York Times (4-22-1928) The Times article even predicted, incorrectly, that now in all probability Edward Doheny and Albert Fall would not be further prosecuted.

Monday evening, April 30, 61 members of the USS Yosemite crew met at the U.S. Naval Reserve armory to celebrate the 30th anniversary of their departure for Newport News, Virginia. Among those who were in attendance were Truman Newberry, Mortimer Cooley, the retired dean of the engineering college at University of Michigan, and Ned's life-long friend, Henry Lyster. Two weeks later Ned attended a private luncheon at the Detroit club sponsored by F. J. Haynes, chairman of the board of directors of Dodge Brothers, to honor Dr. Alberto Pirelli, president of the International Chamber of Commerce. Dr. Pirelli was a proud and successful Italian businessman, quite enamored of the administrative and economic gains that Italy had achieved under Benito Mussolini. "'Italy is forging ahead with wonderful strides under the leadership of Mussolini,' Dr. Pirelli said. 'His handling of all problems confronting Italy during the last few years have been just what Italy needed and has strengthened its position among world nations.'" (DFP 5-15-1928) While Mussolini didn't fare so well in the coming years, the Pirelli tire company of Milan is still in business today with assets of over 12 billion euros. The following day Ned attended a banquet in the Statler Hotel given by twenty prominent businessmen and military officers on behalf of the visiting Army Chief of Staff, Major General Charles Summerall. Ned was still vitally interested in the United States government's war plans and preparedness. Though he talked of peace and prosperity and strongly believed in brotherhood, he never lost sight of being prepared with a strong military.

He had company. The members of the Aircraft Development Corporation were like-minded men who wanted to see Detroit developed as a major player in the aircraft industry. Just as Detroit's legendary machine shops — those which had fueled the massive outpouring of interchangeable parts for weapons — had powered the allied offensives which won World War I, many Detroit industrialists and businessmen now saw Detroit as the bassinet which would cradle the exploding aircraft industry. Men such as one of the greatest industrialists the world had ever seen — Henry Ford, who firmly believed that his "Flivver" was going to become everyman's private aircraft, just as the Model T had become the world's land vehicle. Men such as Edward Evans, and men such as Ned's fellow club members at Chateau Voyager, who thought it completely normal when they built their club that it should have facilities for an airport, as well as nearby water for amphibious aircraft. Men such as the members of the defense committee of the Detroit Board of Commerce. Men such as Ned Denby.

He was close friends with John A. LeJeune, Commandant of the Marine Corps, who was at this time formulating the revolutionary new role for the Corps: amphibious warfare. He remained friends with many of the admirals who were involved with the war planning for the future, such as the famous War Plan Orange. He did not miss any of the local gatherings of these men because he remained interested in and deeply committed to the preparedness which he had been preaching for years. And so, on May 30, he was once again present at the noon meeting of the defense committee of the BOC which entertained the eleven members of the French Flying Mission. "A group of France's most representative airmen, soldiers, bankers and industrialists" who spent three weeks touring the industrial centers of the United States. Including many trips about the country by air.

On Monday evening, June 11, Ned joined 500 members of the Michigan Alumni Association at a testimonial dinner in the Book Cadillac ballroom for retiring Dean of the Michigan School of Engineering and Architecture. Dean Mortimer E. Cooley, a shipmate on Yosemite and life-long friend of Ned's was hanging up his spurs after 47 years at the university. When it came time for Ned to speak, he called for a "rising tribute to Dean Cooley, which was accompanied by prolonged applause, college yells and whistling. This tribute exceeded the welcome given the dean as he entered the banquet room."

"Denby related personal anecdotes concerning his association with Dean Cooley aboard the battleship Yosemite [no one seemed to mind that the lowly Yosemite was on this night promoted to a first class battleship] during the Spanish-American War. He eulogized him as....a man 'with deep love and personal interest in those with whom he mingled.'" (DFP 6-11-1928) In July Ned and Marion did some vacationing touring down the course of the St. Lawrence River, returning to the Pontiac farm by July 29.

In June both political parties once again celebrated that all-American quadrennial party known as conventions. The Republicans went first in Kansas City's Convention Hall from June 12 to 15. On the first ballot they nominated Herbert Hoover, who was Secretary of Commerce under Harding and Coolidge, and had served as Director of the United Sates Food Administration under Wilson. He had always been a popular man; more importantly, he had successfully sidestepped any taint or whiff of oil, and it seemed that it would take a very popular Democrat to beat him. Along with Hoover, the convention nominated Senator Charles Curtis of Kansas, the first person with Native American ancestry to achieve this rank in the government. The Democrats, followed two weeks later with a similarly brief conclave in Sam Houston Hall, in Houston, Texas, nominating Alfred E. Smith, the Roman Catholic governor of New York for President, and the pugilistic Joseph T. Robinson, Senator from Arkansas, as his veep. Robinson had several times nearly come to blows with other Senators while on the Senate floor, and once punched a guard in the face at the 1920 Democrat convention for questioning his credentials. This was also the same Robinson whose resolution had called for President Coolidge to fire Ned Denby in February 1924. So the stage was duly set for the national contest — and the democrats wanted to talk about oil!

On September 27, Ned again spoke before the defense committee of the Board of Commerce, once more concerning the need for a strong merchant marine and a strong navy to protect it. He was extensively quoted in his eloquent plea, saying,

"There is just as much sense in employing a competitor to deliver your goods as in shipping your products under a foreign flag.

"It has happened, and may happen again, that a nation with a stronger navy would blockade our ports during a war with us, or in case of war with a third country, we being neutral, would attempt to regulate trade routes and ports of call to the detriment of our trade. With an adequate navy, no nation would dare try either.

"The merchant marine delivers the goods, the navy affords it protection. Michigan sent abroad in 1926, automobiles and other products to the value of $262,594,218. Assume that this trade stopped suddenly. How many families would be affected by the cessation of employment, in the plants, the railroads, the dry goods and grocery stores?

"In maintaining police forces to control crime, health departments to protect health, fire departments to save property, we do not thereby encourage criminals, disease and fire loss. Nor in main- taining an adequate navy as a protection against possible enemies do we precipitate war.

"Thieves do not come to a city because it maintains an adequate police force. Nations do not attempt to dictate to others which have adequate defenses. Navies no more cause war than police forces cause crime.

Insurance against disaster may only be provided by adequate defense preparations." (DFP 9-27-1928)

Ned would find a willing audience before this group, but not beyond it. The United States would not wake up to the inadequacy of its merchant marine until the Germans and the Japanese were hard against us, and then a man named Henry J. Kaiser would go to work, providing nearly 3000 liberty ships during the war years. Ned was advocating such an industry many years before Kaiser brought it into being.

During the third week of September the family closed up the summer home near Lake Angelus and returned to the Whittier. All except Ned, Jr., now 16, who was bound for the Severn School in Severna, Maryland, a private boys only high school which functioned as a preparatory school for the Naval Academy.

Early in October Ned and Truman Newberry presented new colors (flags) to the Gilbert Wilkes Camp of veterans of the Spanish American War. The same flags which had been carried in that war were still being used, and Ned and Newberry felt the original flags should be preserved for posterity. Additionally, a contingent of 30 of the Wilkes' Camp left the following day for the convention which was scheduled in Havana, Cuba, and new flags seemed appropriate. "Mr. Newberry eulogized the veterans for their ardor and patriotism in the Spanish-American War and for their civic and national services since then." (DFP 10-3-1928) Ned also gave brief remarks. Later in October, Ned and Detroit welcomed Evangeline Booth, commander of the Salvation Army in the United States, and daughter of the founder, William Booth. The often fiery, sixty-three year old evangelist was described by the Free Press as "still militant and enthusiastic," as she sat in the armchair of her suite in the Statler hotel for the interview. Having become a United States citizen in 1917, she was asked how she was going to vote in just a matter of days, to which she replied, "A woman mustn't tell her politics," yet then declared that she favored the candidate of prohibition (Hoover). That evening, braving an autumn downpour, over 5,000 people were admitted to the Masonic Temple auditorium (another thousand were turned away) where Ned, as chairman of the Salvation Army Advisory Board, introduced her. Speaking without intermission for two hours, she held the crowd spellbound, "until in a dramatic finale she flung herself at the foot of an electrically lighted cross, proclaiming the power and the love of God, while her tattered shawl fell about her shoulders. Many in the huge audience wept." On the front page of the same newspaper which carried the story of Evangeline Booth, the banner headline proclaimed, 'VAST NEW YORK CROWD GOES WILD OVER HOOVER." Having that success in Al Smith's home town boded somewhat ill for the Democrat candidate. Also on that same front page was another story about the fact that Henry Ford had declined an invitation from the German dirigible, Graf Zeppelin, for a ride home from New Jersey, as the great ship, on a good will tour, was en route to Detroit as its next stop. And just below that story was the brief announcement that the Ford Motor company had signed a contract with The Transcontinental Air Transport, Inc., for an $800,000 order of "ten tri-motored monoplanes for the airmail service to be inaugurated next spring." (DFP 10-23-1928) Detroit truly was at the very epicenter of the air industry.

Which was again demonstrated just four days later when Amelia Earhart, 'Queen of the Air', on an exhaustive speaking tour about the United States, arrived in Detroit. She was fresh off her trans-Atlantic flight with Wilmer Stultz and Louis Gordon, having become the first woman to traverse the Atlantic by air. Ms.

Earhart spoke to the Adcraft Club noon luncheon meeting at the Detroit-Leland Hotel, and insisted that flying was getting safer all the time. Ned was on the dais once again with other notables from Detroit.

On Tuesday, November 6, 1928, the voters of the nation did what was expected of them — they elected Herbert Hoover to the office of the Presidency in a resounding victory, the third straight Republican landslide of the decade. The former Commerce Secretary captured 444 electoral votes to 87 for his opponent, including several southern states which had traditionally gone Democrat. Hoover's landslide was so large that he swept both houses of congress for the Republicans, increasing even the majorities which had prevailed under Coolidge, as well as most of the State of Michigan and Wayne County political offices.

By December, Ned travelled to Washington D. C. to once more watch a football game in which he had vested interests on both sides of the field, as the Quantico Marines, undefeated in 19 starts, fell 10-0 to the Navy sailors from the Newport, R.I. naval training station. Secretary Wilbur, John LeJeune, Senator Hale of Maine and Representative Britten of the House, chairmen of the senate and house naval committees watched the proceedings along with Nicholas Longworth, then speaker of the house, and Ned. The Quantico jarheads had won the trophy, previously, three years in a row.

On December 4, the Michigan Supreme Court found in Ned's favor in the lawsuit which he had won in lower courts, but which had been appealed. Ned's adversary claimed that Ned had misrepresented the parcel of land as being 1000 acres when it was actually only 873. "The supreme court ruled that the property was not sold on an acreage basis and no statement concerning its size was contained in the contract." (DFP 12-5-1928) The following day Ned spoke before the Veterans of Foreign Wars on the subject of the cruiser bill which was then before congress. Several days later, he was present at the Masonic Temple when nearly one hundred new 32nd degree Masons were added to the list. Residing principally in Detroit now allowed him to become involved once again in organizations from which he had had to be absent for some time.

In early January, 1928, Ned acted again as chairman of the general committee, this time for the three day convention of Protestant Laymen's Missionary movement, to be "participated in by laymen from all Protestant denominations in Detroit and also by laymen from churches within a radius of forty miles." (DFP 1-9-1929) All sessions of the convention took place in the Metropolitan United Methodist Church, newly constructed in 1922 with a large bequest from Sebastion S. Kresge who lived just up prestigious Woodward Avenue in the exclusive Boston- Edison neighborhood. Just over a week later Ned was one of the speakers at a Sons of the American Revolution function in the Statler Hotel honoring the birth date of Benjamin Franklin.

While those in congress were nastily debating a naval bill for the construction of fifteen new cruisers and an aircraft carrier, the citizens of Detroit were busily preparing to launch another civic fundraising campaign, this time in the amount of $3,025,000 to benefit Grace Hospital, the Salvation Army and the Narcotic Educational Association of Michigan, Inc. Naturally, they were going to ask Ned Denby to lead it. "Rapid growth in the city's population and accompanying increased need for service have taxed facilities of all three organizations, it is said, to the point where new buildings must be erected and extensions made to plants if they are to function effectively." (DFP 2-3-1929) Joining Ned on the fundraising committee, among others, were William T. Barbour, husband of one of Marion's dearest friends; Edward S. Evans, the glider enthusiast; Mrs, Alfred G. Wilson, otherwise known as Matilda Dodge, one of the wealthiest women in the world; Mrs. Helen B. Joy, wife of the head of the Packard Motor Car Company; and Dr. A. G. Studer, general secretary of the Detroit Y. M. C. A. It was a prestigious group, led by the one man in Detroit above all others who was renowned not only for his civic- mindedness, generosity and integrity, but for his ability to get the job done. On the same date that the Salvation Army funds campaign was announced, Ned was named as toastmaster for the "annual members' dinner at the downtown Y. M. C. A. to be held on February 28. Who else could possibly be more pertinent to such a gathering?

But it was not to be.

On the evening of February 7, 1929, Ned spent the evening, according to a short biography written after Word War II by his wife Marion, "playing cards with his wife.....and went to bed at the usual time and in his usual health." Around 5 in the morning Marion later would say that he became restless, but that, without waking up, he settled down again in sleep. At eight o'clock, she found him unresponsive in his bed, and he was gone. Ten days short of his fifty-ninth birthday. As Marion understated in the biographical sketch, "an ideal way to go, but very hard on those who were left behind." (DPL Edwin Denby Papers) The great heart which had powered his enormous physique for so long had simply and unexpectedly stopped.

The news surged throughout Detroit with seismic reverberations — "What?! What!? Ned Denby?! But I just saw him..."

So, death, uncaring, creeps in unaware and snatches from us our most beloved.

Chapter Thirty-Two

When your last Day is past
From afar Some bright star
O'er your grave, Watch will keep
While you sleep With the brave.

From "Taps"

The Family

The sudden and unexpected death of Ned Denby caused a sensation in Detroit, and in many circles around the world, particularly in the Navy and the Marine Corps. The effusion of grief, the unutterable sense of loss, was immense. One question resounded: "Who could possibly replace this man?" The answer was a reverently hushed: "No one."

The "king" of Detroit was dead. But there was no, "Long live the King" — for there was no one to take his place.

All Detroit seemed to galvanize into action. The defense committee of the Board of Commerce where Ned had concentrated much of his last efforts, led by Colonel Walter Cole, took up the lead in funeral planning. For this man, a funeral was going to take careful consideration, for Ned Denby was not merely a husband, father, and brother, Ned Denby was institutional Detroit itself. Literally dozens of organizations needed, or felt they needed, to be represented, and yet the affair must be kept dignified at all costs. So complicated would the preparations be, simply because of the great number of people needing to be accommodated, that Cole set up a temporary planning headquarters in the Book Cadillac. The widow made her wishes known, for Marion would become now the backbone of her family, cut from that mold which said she would always remain true to the memory and honor of her husband, but also staunchly chart her own course. The funeral would not be military, and yet hundreds of Detroit police would escort the cortege to the cemetery, blocking off whole streets to facilitate its progress, and there would be several hundred soldiers, sailors and Marines lining the route from the gates of Elmwood cemetery to the place of burial. City hall was draped in black, and all flags in the state were flown at half mast. Curtis Wilbur ordered all flags on all naval vessels and stations around the world flown at half staff on the day of the funeral.

The funeral was planned for Monday, February 11, at Christ Episcopal on Jefferson, just a few doors from the 550 where Ned had spent some of his young bachelor days. Officiating would be Ned's friend, the pastor of Christ Episcopal, the Rev. William D. Maxon. Since the seating capacity was limited, it was imperative that the crowd be closely monitored. Charles arrived from Washington, and Wythe from Chicago, but Garvin was ill and not able to travel. A nephew, Gilbert Wilkes, came from Reading, Pennsylvania, and several officers and friends made the trip from Washington. Marion received condolences from virtually all the mighty of the land, some friend in name, some friend in deed, but perhaps the most touching came from John LeJeune, still the Commandant, who reported himself "inexpressively grieved and shocked. I loved Colonel Denby as a friend and admired him as a man. He was greatly beloved by all Marines." (NYT 2-9-1929)

Another poignant tribute to Ned came from the man who then occupied his former seat in Congress, Robert H. Clancy. Clancy had had an interesting career, graduating from UofM, working for Detroit newspapers and then becoming secretary to Frank Doremus, the man who unseated Ned in the 1910 election for the 1st Congressional District seat. Clancy went on to work in various capacities for the next several years, finally winning the same 1st District seat for himself in 1922 as a Democrat. Four years later he was himself defeated by the Republican John Sosnowski, and four years after that, Clancy switched parties, became a Republican, defeated Sosnowski in the primary, and the Democrat in the election, serving once again in the 1st District seat for three more terms, from 1927 to 1933, as a Republican. Just as Doremus had become good friends with Ned, so had Clancy genuinely come to a warm, personal friendship. On the day Ned passed, Clancy rose on the floor of the House to make these remarks:

"'It is with deep sorrow," said the Detroit member, "that I rise to announce the death of a friend and constituent, a former member of this house and a former secretary of the navy, Honorable Edwin Denby.......My statement must be brief," continued Clancy, "but I believe it is proper to note on the record now that Mr. Denby was of noble cast of mind and that his sufferings as a public servant contributed to his early death. Both as a congressman and as a cabinet officer he endured the outrageous slings of political fortune.

"Friend and foe have always given him credit for absolute honesty, unflinching integrity, the highest patriotism and utterly unselfish ideals of service. Added to this, he had a lovable personality. His geniality and kindliness set off well his huge physical stature.'" (DFP 2-9-1929)

Clancy went on in private to say that he had had lunch with Ned only a couple of months previously and that Ned had stated that he intended to run for congress once again "when reapportionment gave Detroit more seats and he would not have to run against me." (Ibid) Whether Ned would have run again is mute, but ironically, after reapportionment took place, Clancy lost the next election from the newly established district.

According to Colonel Cole's list, the following organizations were given space for the services: Governor Green; Mayor Lodge; the entire City Council; Wayne County Officers; Probation Officers; Bar association; Y.M.C.A.; Federal Motor Truck Company; Hupp Motor Car Company; University of Michigan Alumni and Regents; Bankers Trust Company; Detroit Rotary Club; several Masonic organizations; Detroit Athletic Club; Board of Commerce; Salvation Army; Detroit Community Fund; Prismatic Club; Detroit Newsboys Association; Michigan National Guard; Reserve

Officers Training Corps; Michigan Naval Force; representatives of eleven different military commands; Committee on National Defense, BOC; American Red Cross; Colonial Dames of America; veterans of the Yosemite; local officers of the Navy and Marine Corps, and many, many others as well. It was going to be a full house.

Marion selected eight of his closest friends to be the actual pallbearers, including Henry Lyster (Yosemite), J. Walter Drake (Yosemite), John E. Baker (Yosemite), William Hamilton (long time friend), Joe Kennedy (law partner), Dr. Russell Hibbs (long time hunting partner, doctor and friend), and Joe Carey (his assistant as SecNav). There were no honorary pallbearers since that list would have been so numerous no one wanted to take the chance of forgetting someone.

The only viewing was under military guard from 9:30 to 10:30am Monday in Christ Episcopal. The church was then cleared to allow invited guests to take their seats. The service started promptly at 1100, following which the cortege moved up East Jefferson Street to McDougall and into Elmwood Cemetery. Established in 1846, its grounds were designed in 1890 by famed landscape artist, Frederick Law Olmsted. The Denby plot was reverently selected on a rise overlooking a picturesque pond, and small stream which is the last visible remnant of "Bloody Creek", so named during Pontiac's uprising of 1763, when 20 British soldiers lost their lives and 41 more were wounded in a night ambush. For all time Ned would lie in a place of stunning tranquility and beauty, overlooking the verdant and now peaceful scene.

As the bier was carried to the gravesite, planes from Selfridge flew overhead in tribute. After the Episcopalian prayers were spoken, one more shipmate from Yosemite, Dr. H. J. Higgs, blew taps. Higgs was known far and wide for the sweetness of his rendition of taps, and at a function in the past when Ned had heard him, it was reported that he asked Higgs to be sure to play it at his funeral. The doctor obliged, at both of his services. One can only imagine if Marion remembered the day Ned had written her with the lyrics of the song which he had discovered while at Parris

Island. He had told her then that the third verse "is for the last call over a solider's grave," But it was the "sentiment of the second [verse which] more nearly reflects my nightly thoughts...." he had told her from the loneliness of boot camp. Surely that would be the verse which Marion would remember and cherish:

"Love, goodnight
Must thou go
When the day
And the night
Leave me so?
Fare thee well,
Day is done,
Night is on".

Though the king lay in his vault, the mourning ceremonies were not over. One week later, on what would have been Ned's 59th birthday, Monday, February 18, several hundred more of his closest friends and family gathered once again in the Cass Theater in downtown Detroit. Built originally as the auditorium for the Board of Commerce, it was a venue in which Ned had spoken on dozens of occasions. It also accommodated more of his friends for whom there had not been room in Christ Episcopal. The services were held under the auspices of the Board of Commerce, the beloved organization which had meant so much throughout Ned's adult life. Victor Kolar, assistant conductor of the Detroit Symphony Orchestra, led the entire string group of over 50 musicians in providing the music. Kolar, Hungarian born, had studied composition under Antonin Dvorak, composed many pieces of his own, and later became the orchestra's conductor, 1940-1942. Again the flags on all city buildings were lowered to half mast during the ceremony, which took place from 1pm to 2pm. S. Wells Utley, then current president of the Board of Commerce, in introducing the principle speaker, said of Ned,

"In the millions who come and go in this great city of ours, others will come as great in business ability as he, others will come who answer the call to arms with the same spirit of patriotism as he, others will come who serve us in the state and the nation with the same devotion that he did, but I suspect that there is no one of us here today who will ever live to see the time when these qualities will be so intermingled in any one man that we can say that one has come to Detroit to take and accurately fill the place left vacant by Ned Denby's going." (DPL Edwin Denby Papers, Box #11)

For those in Detroit who knew him, and that was almost everyone, there was a void that was never going to be filled.

Utley then introduced Abner Larned, former president of the Board of Commerce, successful businessman, civic leader on a scale to nearly equal that of the man he would eulogize, and beloved humanitarian. From the tone of his remarks, it quickly became obvious how deeply moved Mr. Larned was over Ned's passing, and how completely he respected and admired him. After a short summary of Ned's life of service, he ended with the story of the Y.M.C.A. fund raising campaign which had concluded so successfully for the city and for Ned.

"I recall the great campaign he led that resulted in the subscription of five million dollars for the Y.M.C.A. and kindred projects. It was the last night of the campaign and every inch of space in the great ballroom of the Book-Cadillac Hotel was filled with an eager, tumultuous crowd. The last report was in and victory had perched on the banners of the workers. Then Ned rose to speak. He was superlatively happy that night. As he got to his feet he was greeted with a bedlam of welcoming cheers. I can see him now; his great beautiful smile swept that audience like a benediction, and then he spoke as only he could speak, his voice like the tone of a deep organ. He stretched out his arms as though he would take every man in the room in his arms and he said, 'You, you splendid men of Detroit, you have done this wonderful thing for the young manhood of our city and I am so proud and so grateful that you have permitted me a part in your great accomplishment.' Was it any wonder that those he led loved him?" (Ibid.)

The associated Building Campaign of Grace Hospital, Salvation Army and the Narcotic Education Association, moved quickly to name a successor to Ned's Chairmanship in late February. He was "Phelps Newberry, vice-president of the Guardian Trust company, lieutenant colonel of the army air reserve and civilian aid to the secretary of war." (DFP 2-24-1929) Less than a month after Ned's Cass Theater service, his longtime friend, Will Hamilton, president of the Clinton Woolen Manufacturing Company, passed away suddenly on Friday, March 15 at his home of a paralytic stroke. Marion and Mary would lean on each other and remain friends until Mary's death in 1942. Following Will's passing, Mary wrote Marion on the back of the family thank you card literally days after Ned's death: "Dear Marion, You are a wonderful help and comfort to us in our sorrow and we love you more than ever. Affectionately, Mary." Marion was cut from the exact cloth of her husband — thinking of others rather than dwelling on her own great loss.

She had help. Ned Jr. was home from Severn, and though he would return to finish his senior year, he would quickly develop into the man of the house, and fill that roll lovingly and respectfully, for the rest of his life. Sue, or Sister, as they mostly called his sibling, was also with Marion, now an exuberant, poetry-writing typical teenager, full of all the slang of the day and the fun-loving nature of her father which had made him so beloved.

Teenage Sue had a saying, and she used it so much in conversation and especially at the closing of letters that her mother adopted it, and signed all her letters to Annapolis, "Gils and tons of love...." Translation: "gils" was the abbreviated form of "gillions", a slang invention of measurement far superior to millions. Both children, Ned Jr. and Sue, would lovingly refer to their father as "Fad" until the day they died.

Only days after Ned's services in Detroit, his former SecNav personal secretary, Joe Carey, had written a letter to Calvin Coolidge, enclosing a photograph of his late chief, sitting at his desk in the naval headquarters. On his desk in plain site was a campaign prop which read, "Keep Coolidge", right next to a desk calendar which showed the date to be March 5, five days before his resignation was final. Joe pointed out to the President that at no time had Ned's loyalty to him every wavered in the slightest. Believing Marion would enjoy having the photograph, Carey then mailed a copy to her and explained what he had done with it, and also mentioned that he was working on an article for publication as to why the oil storage tanks were so necessary in Hawaii. Marion replied almost immediately on February 25, thanking Carey for the letters and the photographs he had enclosed, and asked him if he had any others, particularly of Ned standing. She explained that the city wanted to do a statue of Ned for Belle Isle, and she did not have too many photos of her husband in that position. She particularly remembered one, she said, in which Carey and Ned were standing together, and asked if he had a copy of that. She then went on to say that she thought it "a good idea to get the material together, [for Carey's magazine article] but I feel that anything published right now might detract from the wonderful impression; that has been left by the beautiful write-ups at the time of the funeral." She explained to Carey that "I   have a strong feeling that Ned would rather bury the past as is, than have anyone try to vindicate him. I feel that he has already been vindicated and that anything further on the subject at this time, might detract from his wonderful memory." After   thanking him profusely for his care in the matter, she continued, "I am trying to guide my whole future career through Ned's eyes, and I know how he would feel about the matter just now." (DPL Edwin Denby Papers, Box #8)

In September of that year, Lucia Denby, wife of Ned's older brother Wythe, died in Chicago of 'malignancy of the stomach' in the vernacular of the day. Wythe seems to have been the sibling who had always gone his own way, the more aloof of the Denby offspring, and after years of living in many locations, he would bring Lucia to his home in Evansville, to be buried on the little knoll with his family in Oak Hill Cemetery. He would join her there thirteen years later.

By late October, 1929, coinciding almost precisely with the cataclysm on Wall Street, and timed precisely to the observance of Navy Day which his father had initiated, Representative Robert Clancy, then holding Ned's 1st Congressional District seat in

Congress, appointed Ned Jr. to the Naval Academy at Annapolis. Still at the Severn Preparatory School in Maryland, Ned would take the entrance exam for the Academy the following Spring and enter the Academy as a plebe on July 8, 1930. At almost the same time as Ned Jr. was matriculating, another beloved figure which had loomed eloquently throughout his father's life, departed the scene. Winifred Lyster, the grand dame of Detroit, passed away quietly at her home in the same Whittier Residence/Hotel on Wednesday, May 7th, 1930. She was eighty-eight years old, and had outlived Ned by fifteen months. All Detroit was again in mourning.

Though the stock market had crashed and many had suddenly lost their fortunes, it did not spell immediate doom for everyone. Marion was a proud, intelligent and industrious woman, who watched her security dwindle away over the next several months, when she found it necessary, by 1932, to find employment with Mason Brothers Realtors. The work was slow, very time-consuming and usually discouraging, but Marion kept up a strong front for Ned Jr. in her letters to the Academy. In August, 1932, she informed Ned Jr. of the serious illness of Dr. Russell Hibbs, the New York orthopedic pioneer who had been one of his father's closest friends. In September she told him that even though Hibbs' condition was grave and Madeleine, his wife, was living "from hour to hour", that she still found time and the kindness to send Marion a check to help with Sue's schooling. Sue had entered the Warrenton School for Girls in Virginia, and as funds evaporated, despite her proud inclination to refuse all help, Marion was forced to accept Madeleine Hibbs' assistance. The one thing which trumped her pride was caring for her daughter. Only a week later she informed Ned Jr. that "Uncle" Hibbs had passed away on September 16.

By October she wrote Neddie (she called him "Bebo") that the Lysters had sold their Detroit home and had apparently moved back to Washington. She was speaking of William John LeHunte Lyster, Colonel, United States Army retired (1932), the oldest child of Winifred Lyster, and older brother of Ned's Yosemite pal, Henry Lyster. Colonel William, who had invented the Lyster Bag, a rubber-lined canvas bag used in water purification during both World War I and II, had one child, a daughter, Elizabeth who was best friends with Sue Denby. Later Marion would tell Ned Jr. that the Lysters were still maintaining a residence in Detroit at The Whittier. By this time, her resources dwindling, Marion had left the Whittier and moved into a far more modest apartment in asmall building just across Jefferson Avenue. Her loyal maid Nellie would accompany her, no matter her plight.

On October 6, 1932, Marion met with representatives of the banks which held mortgages on Denby property, or had other financial claims on Ned's estate. Her younger brother Cleveland, with whom she was closest, was an attorney and acted as unofficial auctioneer at the proceedings which began at half past ten in the morning and lasted until four fifty in the afternoon. "We are completely washed up," she reported to   Ned what she could never bring herself to reveal to Sue, "not an asset remaining to us, but we did clean up some heavy loans at the banks," she told him with almost a tone of relief. After explaining where most of the property went, she continued, "It seems so strange not to own a foot of property anywhere after all the 'rounding out' that was done and the quantity of land owned at one time." It was sadly the closing of a chapter in her life with Ned, and ever pragmatic, Marion looked primarily into the future for her son and daughter.

In November of this year, the New Deal was elected.

Somewhere in December of 1932, Elizabeth Lyster metamorphosed from "Sue's girlhood friend", and after her visit to Annapolis that month, she became in Marion's letters, "your girl". It was a romance which would make many people in both families very happy. Marion was forty-seven years old, and for the first time in her life she was fully in control of her own destiny and making her own decisions. Even with much loss, there seemed to be silver linings, and almost an adventurous feeling to the progress of her life, and her family. Then, things turned ugly, and very quickly.

The banks in Detroit, some of the largest in the nation, began to crumble. Or, more specifically, the public's trust in them began to evaporate. The governor of Michigan declared a bank holiday in February of 1933, and Marion was caught completely helpless, as were all the people of Michigan. On the fifteenth she wrote to Neddie, "As I pay cash for everything and have no charge accounts anywhere, and having only about five dollars cash on hand, it looked pretty serious. I did not expect to eat much during the coming week." But her loyal maid had not left her. "I told Nellie I might never be able to pay her another cent, and on top of that, the good old stand-by went off and bought a ham and other food supplies with what cash she had and brought it home to tide us over the bank holiday." They were getting by, but only just. "Everyone is worried stiff," she admitted to him.

It was at this juncture that another principle actor of the era suddenly departed the mortal stage. Thomas J. Walsh, scourge of the oil leases, super-prosecutor of the senate, destroyer of innocent lives as well as the guilty, had been selected by the new administration to become the attorneys' dream: Attorney General. Prosecutor for the nation. But first, Thomas had gone to Florida for vacation, and from there slipped over to Cuba where he married a Cuban woman he had apparently been seeing for some time. The couple were married in Cuba on February 25, and then returned to Miami. Walsh became ill with something like indigestion, though doctors suspected a diagnosis more serious and recommended bed rest. But Walsh was only days from the inauguration, from assuming the prize of a lifetime of political quest. He insisted they go north, and so he and his wife boarded the ACL for Washington, D. C. When the new wife awakened on the train on the morning of March 2, she found her husband lying on his face on the stateroom floor. First a porter was summoned to find a doctor, and then a conductor arrived to assist, and cradling the aged senator's head in his lap, he observed the senator breathe his last. Though his son-in-law, the office-seeking Gudger whose petition Ned had denied, felt that there had been foul play involved in his father-in-law's death, his wife, the senator's only child, disagreed — and no autopsy was performed. After services in the senate, Walsh's remains were taken to Montana for a local service and burial beside his first wife. His widow did not go to Montana, but returned to Cuba, and disappeared into history. (Bates pp 329-330)

Almost like one of the cliff-hanging Hollywood movies of the 1930's which all Americans were so fond of attending, Marion reported to Neddie that she had applied for a Spanish- American War widow's pension, and that one night she had prayed fervently for something good to happen. "Strange as it may seem," she told him, "next morning a letter was in the mail..." She was to receive $30 a month - a veritable fortune in those times. However, before the pension arrived, she was living with much less. "Cash is the scarcest thing in Michigan, and all cheques are rubber," she told him. Between her and her maid Nellie, all their money had to go for food. She had nothing left with which to pay bills or pay her rent. She agonized over her inability to pay her landlord, who had been so good to allow her to live in her apartment without paying. April 1st, 1933 she received her first Spanish-American War widow pension check for $34.50 and she was overjoyed. Within days, however, she saw in the paper that congress had just passed a law to cut the Spanish American pensions in half. "Can you beat my financial luck of the last three years?" she lamented to her son.

Still in early April, news broke of the crash of the the USS Akron, several miles out in the Atlantic Ocean, with the loss of 73 of the 76 crewmen aboard, including Rear Admiral William Moffett who was at that time Chief of the Navy's Bureau of Aeronautics. The Bureau, only 12 years old at the time, had been headed by Moffett since its inception in 1921, having been promoted to the position by Ned Sr. Ever since he had watched his mother christen the behemoth Shenandoah at Lakehurst as a young boy, Neddie had dreamed of his own career in the noble giants of the skies. Marion and Neddie had a running disagreement about his participation in such endeavors, and she now flatly stated, "This ends your career in the lighter than air division of the Navy." She could not have known then that her only son would move from this dangerous pursuit to enter the almost equally dangerous submarine service

The Family

only a handful of years later.

By 1933 she had started looking desperately for somewhere cheaper to live, her inability to pay her landlord at the Chalfonte having bothered her immensely. She also told Neddie she saw no way she would be able to raise enough money to get to Warrenton, Virginia for Sue's graduation from high school in June. She had not shared all of her financial woes with Sue, hoping to spare her the worry, and Sue had begged her to come, even if just for one day. Then, again in the manner of the old cliff-hangers of the day, she reported that her younger brother Cleveland was going to donate the money for her to come as his graduation present to Sue. Even better, when she arrived home that very day, she found an anonymous New York bank draft for fifty dollars (almost certainly from Madeleine Hibbs). "Can you beat that for Santa Claus?" she asked. In addition, in a postscript of the same letter, she reported that the bank, which had been holding the bulk of her money over some technicality, had phoned to tell her that the matter had been cleared up, and her money was now cleared to her again. "If I live through the night after such a day of glad tidings and good breaks, it'll be because I am in the home of a physician (her friends, the Jennings) — no heart could stand such a strain without medical aid. — Mother"

In May, 1933, she had finally located a cheaper place to live: it was in the tiny apartment above the garage at the home of Dr. Alpheus Jennings. Marion was getting the doctor's breakfast in the morning because Mrs. Jennings was ill. The doctor left for a business trip and Marion found herself taking care of the ill wife full time. "Mrs. J is laid up and it's lucky I am here. I've really been quite useful for once in my life," she said with extreme modesty. In June she drove the 550 miles to Annapolis to pick up Neddie and both of them then attended Sue's graduation in Warrenton, Virginia.

After arriving back in Detroit she reported her expenses to him, which included both herself and Sue: Her bill for one night's lodging for both, including their breakfast, was $2.40! "It cost me $6.87 to get to Washington, and it cost us each $7.82 to get home."

In another month, and to Marion's great pleasure, Neddie and Elizabeth Lyster announced their engagement.

On Sunday, September 17, 1933, news reached Marion that brother-in-law Garvin had succumbed after an operation for acute appendicitis in Amityville, New York. Garvin and Ester had been married for thirty years and had no children. Only Charlie in Washington, D.C. and Wythe in Chicago were left of the six Denby children.

After about four months in their cramped quarters in the garage attic apartment, Marion's fortunes finally took a wonderful turn for the better. She accepted a job as a house mother at the Cranbrook Schools, a part of the Cranbrook Educational Community, located in Bloomfield Hills, a northern suburb of Detroit. Founded in the early twentieth century by newspaper publisher George Booth on an original farm of 174 acres, the facility came to include the Cranbrook Schools (originally for boys only), Cranbrook Academy of Art, Cranbrook Art Museum, Cranbrook Institute of Science, and later, the Cranbrook House and Gardens, the former home of the Booths. Marion's job would be to supervise boys' after hours regimen, as well as inspect the dormitories first thing in the morning. A benefit to the job, of course, was her own room and board, but additionally attractive was a room for Sue.

On Thursday, October 19, she had her first day off, and she spent it by going downtown and meeting with two men from the Denby Club who were organizing for a marker to be placed in Grand Circus Park on the exact spot where Ned had taken the oath to become a 47-year-old private in the Marine Corps, sixteen years ago. She told Neddie the men wanted her to speak at the next Edwin Denby Club meeting, but "I'd be scared to death," she admitted. "It seems as though the interest in and admiration for father would never die, and naturally, I want to do all I can to stimulate it. Isn't it splendid that they feel that way?" [This, six years after Ned's demise.] By November Marion could report that she had been able to get her former maid, Nellie, a job at Cranbrook. Loyalty ran very strong in Denby family. By the following January, 1934, she had also gotten Concetta, the wife of their former caretaker at the farm a job at Cranbrook, as well.

On her wedding anniversary in 1934 she wrote him, "....with us, each year added to our happiness and that is why it is so hard to have one year together cut off so abruptly, and I shall never be reconciled to father's being taken, but if he has been spared suffering of any kind, mental or physical, I can, and must stand it. That is the thought I try to bear in mind and what I have tried to do."

As his graduation day loomed in 1935, the last rigid airship dirigible in the Navy, the USS Macon, crashed off the coast of California. Owing to modifications of equipment after the crash of the Akron, the Macon carried life jackets and inflatable rafts, and only two crewmen were lost, while 81 were safely rescued by naval ships in the area. "Now the Macon!" Marion exclaimed in her February 13 letter to Neddie. "Do you wonder that I have qualms about your lighter than air service?" She would not have to worry about the airships. On Monday, July 1st she wrote to inform him that her brother Tom, had passed away in San Francisco. "It was very sudden as he was getting ready to go to work when he commenced to feel badly. They called a doctor and before he could get there, Uncle Tom was gone. He died very quietly without much pain." The body was to be shipped back to Detroit for burial in Elmwood Cemetery in the family lot. He would join his older brother Don who had passed in 1927.

In a February, 1936, letter she mentioned the recent death of Major General Billy Mitchell, sometimes known as the father of the United States Air Force. After an extremely bitter divorce from his first wife, Mitchell had married Elizabeth Trumbull Miller from Detroit. "You of course remember Mrs. Mitchell," she prompted him. "Betty Miller — that was Uncle Tom's girl!." Small world.

In June Sue and Marion once again drove to Annapolis, this time for Neddie's graduation ceremonies. They stayed at the home of Admiral and Mrs. David Sellers, once naval aide to his father, and now superintendent of the Academy. Following graduation, Ned was assigned duty on the USS Oklahoma (BB37), a Nevada Class battleship, where he would spend the next two years of his career. During part of this time, the Oklahoma was dispatched to Spain to rescue refugees left homeless by the Spanish Civil War, and in one, Ned Jr. gave a harrowing description of the naval launches moving back and forth between the ships at sea and the shore, though perilous surf. He proudly told her he made many trips back and forth through the treacherous seas and not only didn't lose a single refugee, but had no one else injured or lost. It was a remarkable feat. In August 1936 he listed the ports they had made since leaving Annapolis: "Portsmouth (England), Goteburg (Sweden), Cherbourg (France), and then in Spain, Bilbao, Santander, Bayonne, Bilbao again, St. Jean de Luz, Bilbao, St. Jean de Luz, Vigo, Cadiz, Gibraltar, Cadiz, Gibraltar, Malaga, Palma, Barcelona, Marseilles (France), Valencia, Malaga, and Gibraltar." "I'm an old Gibraltar pilot from way back, now," he reported. Two months later they were traversing the Panama Canal en route the West coast, when he told her he had just "discovered the other night that the ship's dentist, Commander T. L. Sampsell, served with father on Parris Island during the war.......He lived in Beaufort, on Bay Street, but couldn't remember where....."

After over eighty years of liberal bias in our history departments and our news media, it is hard to conceive of anyone of that era who did not view Franklin Roosevelt as the savior of all mankind. But following FDR's 1936 pulverizing victory over Republican challenger, Alf Landon, Ned Jr. was none too happy, "Well the United States has chosen," he wrote in disgust. "Never before in her history has her destiny rested so completely in the hands of one man. What he chooses to now do with her, will be her ultimate fate, or at least will be her course for many, many years, as it will be too risky to change in four years. The international situation will not permit it. So we shall be irrevocably committed to Mr. Roosevelt's policies, regardless of what his successor in office thinks—if he HAS one in four years! He actually has the power today to make himself 'Dictator of Newdealia' if he wants to. The people have said, in effect, 'Roosevelt can do no wrong,' and it lies entirely with the President what course he chooses to steer the United States, whether we're to continue as a democracy, or become something else — where the government is Roosevelt, and the nation dares not think otherwise." Prescient words.

By January 1937, he had put in for sub school in New London, Connecticut, and informed his mother that he and Betty were planning a June wedding that year. On March 16, he wrote Marion that he had received a telegram from Betty saying, "New London definite. Am writing. Betty." He bemoaned the fact that the daughter of a retired Army Colonel could find things out about the Navy before he got the word. "The sweet, little magician," he called her, and then asked, "Mother, who am I marrying?"

The wedding was held in St. John Episcopal Church on Lafayette Square, for years known as the "Church of the Presidents", on June 8, 1937. Betty's maid of honor was none other than the groom's sister, Sue. 'Aunt' Madeleine Hibbs. perhaps understanding how difficult a day it would be for Marion to experience alone, sent the newlyweds an extremely generous wedding gift, and then provided the HIbbs' private cabin at the exclusive Huron Mountain Club in northern Michigan for their honeymoon. By October Betty was pregnant, and Ned Jr. started referring to his mother as "Old Granny Denby". On May 11, 1938, Marion received his telegram, "Your granddaughter Elizabeth Lyster Denby weighing six pounds twelve ounces arrived five fifty tonight both mother and daughter splendid condition arrival very prompt please notify Cleve and the rest of the family much love from all three of us, NED."

After her graduation from Warrenton, Sue stayed with her mother at Cranbrook, eventually taking a job there as a secretary. Being a pretty, light-hearted and vivacious young lady, she was naturally a great hit at a boys' school. By March 1937 Marion had begun to intimate in her letters to Ned Jr. that there was one boy in particular who seemed to be stepping to the fore. As events unfolded, it became apparent that Sue's 'special' interest was Louis Bemis Wetmore from Glen Falls, New York, who was at Cranbrook studying architecture in the Art Academy. By March 29, she said, "That's [the developing relationship] a very heavy case. I am glad you are coming home here in May so that you can give him the O.O. It begins to look serious."

Marion was quite right about the relationship between her daughter and young Louis. They became engaged on Sunday, May 28, 1939, and were married later that same year, on December 18. The service was held at Christ Church in Detroit where both children had been baptized, and their beloved father had been eulogized. Ned was home for the event and served as an usher. Marion certainly must have been filled with a great sense of relief that both of her children had married so well. Undoubtedly, there was sadness that this great happiness could not be shared with her beloved husband. That Ned Jr. had become the man he was a testament to the father they all missed, and to the woman his father had married. In a February 1935 letter from the Academy, written on the day before what would have been his father's 65th birthday, Ned had said to her: "18 February 1870, sixty-five years ago tomorrow. That day there was born into this world a man whom I shall always regard as the greatest, biggest, finest, kindest, most honorable, most honest, most upstanding, wisest, most lovable man who ever lived, or ever will live. To say that I am proud to call him father would be true, but putting only a small portion of my actual feelings and sentiments on paper. He was so much more than that to me, and to all of us, and to every who knew him........Each year.....as I observe other people I can appreciate the difference between him and other men, and the Providence which was so kind as to give him to you for a husband, protector, provider, lover and all the other wonderful things he was and is to you, and represents, and to me for Father, friend, guide and guardian angel. The best I can do will be none too good for him... and if I can be half the man that father was, I shall not have lived in vain. I think that on his birthday we can all do well to pause and reflect, and rejoice that the world had such a man, and that it was our supreme and wonderful privilege to all be his."

But the time for hero worship, however due and noble, was slipping away. Young Edwin was making his own name and way for himself. In a letter from his commanding officer on the

Oklahoma to a naval friend in Detroit, "You don't have to worry about young Denby," Commander Doyle told his friend. "He is a smart naval officer. He would stand on his own anywhere, but you know in what respect and admiration his illustrious father was held by the service. The result is that everyone is interested in the son and immediately he is able to show them that he has the stuff. The boy has a grand future. Has all the equipment to reach the 'top of the pile'. We are all fond of him and the Denby family and Detroit can be proud of such a fine representative in the Navy." By September 1937, he had completed sub school, and by January 1938 he was assigned to the Navy's submarine, USS R-13. In January 1939 he was promoted to Lt.jg and assigned to the newly launched USS Sculpin (SS-191). He sailed in Sculpin to San Diego, California, and thence to Hawaii by March, 1940. In June he was transferred to USS Shark (SS-174). On December 3, 1940, Shark was dispatched to the Asiatic Fleet based in Manila.

Marion had worried so deeply about her son aloft in a dirigible, and instead, he was in the Philippine Sea on Pearl Harbor Day at the outbreak of the war. By February, Shark was patrolling in Indonesian waters, and on February 7, she reported chasing an empty cargo ship which had escaped her. She was never heard from again. By March 7, she was reported lost. Only then, because of wartime restrictions, could Marion be notified. After the war a great effort was made by the United States Navy to comb through the records of the Imperial Japanese Navy in order to solve the mysteries of what had happened to several missing US ships. A guess was made that she had been caught on the surface by the destroyer IJN Yamakaze at 0137 on February 11, and sunk with 5 inch gunfire. A total of fifty-two American submarines were lost during World War II, many of them are yet to be found. Over 3500 American submariners remain on eternal patrol. May God rest them all.

Chapter Thirty-Three

*"And this is the eternal law. For evil often stops short
at itself and dies with the doer of it. But good - never!"*

Charles Dickens

Until The End

Perhaps Marion's salvation was that she was surrounded with the boys of Cranbrook—and they needed her. Though her grief must have been immense, she was a child of duty, born into the velvet shackles of public rectitude, and public service — above all else, service. Sue and Louis were living in New York, but she had a great circle of deeply devoted friends, and she had her 'rock', her younger brother Cleveland who had always been there to support her. Eleven years her junior, and the 'baby' of their family, Cleve was anything but the typical baby of the family. A highly respected and accomplished attorney from a prestigious law firm, an almost indefatigable servant of the public welfare, Cleve may have been his father's favorite child, if the elder Thurber had lived to know all of his children as adults. Cleve would live to become one of the most respected bankers in the city of Detroit, and assisted his frugal and industrious sister with her modest investments, which would one day pay dividends for her family.

At the close of the Cranbrook school session for 1944, Marion received a very complimentary letter from her boss, the assistant headmaster: "As someone once said to me, 'Mac Denby always does her part and more!' I fully agree and add a 'Hallelujah.'" He closed his warm letter with a note about Marion's upcoming trip to Silver Springs, Maryland, where Sue and Louis were living. Sue was pregnant with their first child, and Marion was headed, as always, to where she would be needed most. On Tuesday, June 20, 1944, Sue gave birth to their first son, whom the young couple lovingly honored both deceased father and brother with the name Edwin Denby Wetmore. By April, 1947, the young Wetmores delivered their second son, John French, in Providence, Rhode Island. It seemed to be at this juncture, mid-1947, that Marion decided it was time to sever her long ties with Cranbrook. At the age of sixty-two, Marion had spent her entire life, from her girlhood with the death of her parents, to the present time. taking care of others. Now she could devote herself to the Wetmore's own growing boys' school. In 1950, Peter came along, and in 1954 Dan was added to the Wetmore clan. For the first time in her life, as well, Marion could at least think about how she would like to spend her own time.

During these years of upheaval and change, Charles Jr., perhaps one of the greatest sinologists our country has produced, after years of decline, succumbed in Washington, D. C. on February 15, 1938, at the age of 76. The last Denby sibling of the Charles Harvey Denby clan of Evansville, Indiana, Wythe, passed away in Chicago in February 1942, also at the age of seventy-six, and thirteen lonely years after the death of his beloved Lucia. Wythe's death brought to a close a great chapter in Denby lore, and it seems one that was not soon to be repeated.

Elizabeth (Betty) Lyster Denby, a thirty year old mother and war widow, spent the years after Ned, Jr.'s death living with her parents in Washington, D. C. and raising their daughter, who was called Lisa. Four years later, Betty married Jean Louis Caillouet, Jr., a commander in the United States Navy, in a private ceremony conducted at home on January 5, 1946. Cherished daughter Lisa had her coming out party at the age of sixteen, on June 15, 1955 at the Chevy Chase Club in Maryland. Marion was able to be there and enjoy the festivities. Lisa was a graduate of the Holton-Arms School of nearby Bethesda. She planned to attend Wheaton College in the fall. (Washington Evening Star, June 16, 1955) Three years later Lisa married John Gibboney Lewis, an aspiring architect from Leesburg, Virginia in St, Margaret's Episcopal Church in Washington. Her step-sister, Miss Julie Bissell Caillouet, was her maid of honor.

Marion retired to a duplex apartment in Detroit's northern suburbs in 1947. By then, her 1938 Ford V-8 Coupe was already nine years old and she would drive it for at least another eleven years, turning down flat all offers from strangers to buy the iconic and perfectly maintained automobile. She was "tight-fisted" her grandsons would describe her, but a "spitfire" with strong opinions about women's rights and equality for African Americans. They still tell the story with pride and ironic amusement of the time when Marion was deeply concerned over the illness of her African American maid who lived with them in Washington while Ned was Secretary of the Navy. Marion called Bethesda to secure a room for her employee but was told that she could not be accepted at Bethesda because it was segregated at that time. "Oh, really?" Marion replied. "Well, then let me get hold of my husband who is the Secretary of the Navy...." A car was dispatched from Bethesda to pick up Marion's maid, and no more was said about the matter. (Conversation with the Wetmore Brothers, September 15, 2022) As sturdily frugal as she was about herself and her own expenses, when college approached for her two oldest grandsons she contributed liberally to the fund. Her time was amply filled with her myriad friends — like her husband Ned, she kept many girlhood friends throughout her entire life — and, of course, her beloved family. A fearless adventuress, she didn't hesitate to navigate the often treacherous roads of her day to make trips to the East Coast or to the upper reaches of Michigan where she continued to vacation with Madeleine Hibbs at Huron Mountain. Marion Thurber Denby, like her husband, was never a person to allow her circumstances to detain or detour her course as she saw it. One by one, the Wetmore grandsons would get their turns to visit 'gran', and when they weren't visiting her, she would often come to visit them.

Louis Bemis Wetmore had studied architecture at M.I.T., but when he continued his studies at Cranbrook, the staff there steered him into an abiding interest in city planning. A shy man by nature, he was attracted to, but didn't quite know what to make of, the vivacious and popular Sue Denby, who invited him one day to walk with her while she distributed the mail to various departments at the school. When he hesitated, she told him in exasperation, "Well, I'm not going to walk you to the altar!", and then, later, she proceeded to do just that. (Conversation with the Wetmores, Sept 2022) By the nature of Louis' career in city planning, the Wetmores lived in many locations throughout the early years of their marriage, until Louis finally accepted a job teaching at the University of Illinois in Urbana. There Louis and the family remained from 1955 to 1976 at his retirement. However, during this time, Louis became one of three people selected to set up the Department of Urban Affairs for the U. S. government, and also was singled out by the elder Mayor Richard Daly of Chicago to update Chicago's City Plan from 1965 to 1967.

As Marion declined in her later years she took up residence in an assisted living home, and later a nursing home, and she passed away from old age on November 2, 1973 at the age of eighty-eight. From writing to Ned, Jr. in 1932 that they were "wiped out" following the banking catastrophes of the great depression, Marion had put away her Spanish American War pension, small as it was, and had invested it wisely through the years. When she passed, she left her descendants just over $300,000, or something north of $2 million in today's money.

The precious orphan who had become the backbone of her family at the age of nineteen had acquitted herself with an integrity and grit that few are called upon to display. The long life that both of her Neds had been so abruptly denied, she lived for them with great fortitude, faithfulness and dignity. And then she died in peace.

Denby Family
Photo Album

McGary's Landing, 1812

Charles Denby - Aged 20
Graduated 1850
In Uniform of Virginia Military Institute.

Charles Denby - Age 20

Battle of Perryville from Harper's Weekly

The City of New York

James Butler (Wild Bill) Hickok

Hiram Rhodes Revels

"Old" Vanderburgh County Court House,
Evansville, now an office building

Willard Library

SS City of Rio de Janeiro

U. S. sailors on the USS Trenton cheering the
Vandalia, Apia Harbor

USS Marion in Chinese waters

Mixed doubles in China as drawn by
one of Ned's correspondents

Gilbert Wilkes

Charles Jr. in Pekin

Michigan's 1895 Football squad wearing their
game faces; Ned in rear with very thin hair

Center Rush: "I became a football player.
I have my picture in togs to prove it."

Mrs. Henry F. Lyster

Naval Reserve Training Ship "Yantic, Detroit, Michigan

Michigan Naval Militiamen awaiting
orders aboard Yantic in 1898

A model of "El Sud", Morgan Line, Southern
Pacific Railroad, soon to be USS Yosemite

USS Yosemite, fitted for war and glory

Michigan Naval Militia on parade
in Detroit, Michigan

Naval Armory, Detroit, Michigan

Pen & Ink Drawings by Ned's artistic friend,
Mary Hamilton (DPL)

St. George Hotel, Evansville, Indiana

Ned's thank you letter to members of the Edwin
Denby Club for their help in getting
him elected to his first term in Congress

576 Wedding photos of Alice Roosevelt and Nicholas
Longworth, 1906

Major General Alexander Macomb, hero of the
Battle of Plattsburg, War of 1812, which stands at
the foot of Washington Blvd, Detroit, Michigan

Hotel Tivoli, Ancon, Canal Zone, Panama

Commemorative Coin Struck for
Dedication of the Macomb Statue

President-elect Taft riding hatless to
his snowy Inauguration

The Henry Thomas Thurber Family,
1895; Marion standing, far right

Congressman Longworth of Ohio at bat
during the 1911 Congressional Game

Halley's comet, first photographed
in its 1910 appearance

Marion Bartlett Thurber on her
wedding day, March 18, 1911

The newlyweds in Italy with
Count Pecorini and his family

Palace of Fine Arts, San Francisco

Ive had about enough of this"
says Uncle Sam, chasing
Pancho Villa into Mexico

Detroit Board of Commerce Building,
Detroit, Michigan

Ned raising his right hand to be
sworn into the Marines, 1917

Ned finally in the uniform of a sergeant

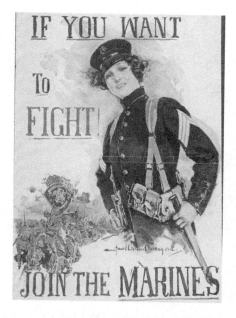

Marine Corps recruiting poster from World War I

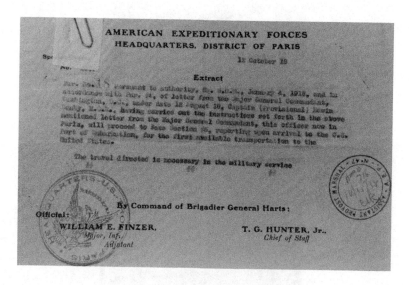

Ned's Order Home, October 1918

Dr. Russell Hibbs

Prohibition

Major General Commandant George Barnett

Republican National Convention, Chicago Coliseum, 1920

Harding campaigning from his
front porch in Marion, Ohio

Campaign parade decorations on a Marion Street, 1920

Union Depot, Marion Ohio, 1920's

Harding's Inauguration, March 4, 1921

Ned being sworn in as Secretary of the Navy, with
outgoing Secretary, Josephus Daniels, looking on

USS Pruitt

The Sylph

Laddie Boy

The Denbys' Washington home at 2224 R Street

Memorial Continental Hall, site of the
Washington Naval Conference

John Weeks, Ned, General Pershing, Admiral
Coontz salute the Unknown American

Harding Speaking at the Dedication of the
Tomb of the Unknown American

The remains of the Knickerbocker Theater,
Washington, D. C.

The Ulysses S. Grant Memorial,
Washington, D. C.

Admiral Baron Uryu Sotokichi

The Seagoing Secretary and a few dozen
pals en-route Japan 1922

Imperial Hotel, Tokyo, Japan

Akasaka Palace, Tokyo

Commodore Perry Monument, Kurihama, Japan

Postcard of Detroit's Masonic temple
in the 1920's

Statue of John Paul Jones in Washington, D. C.

Truman Handy Newberry

Former Prime Minister George Clemenceau (left)
with French Ambassador Jusserand
in Washington, 1922

USS Iowa, BB-4

Zero Milestone south of the White House

The President and the First Lady leaving USS Henderson

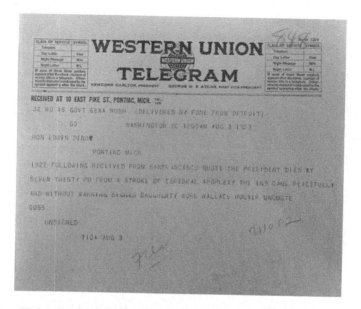

Telegram to Ned announcing the death of the
President, from Daugherty, Work, Wallace, Hoover

Harding funeral train

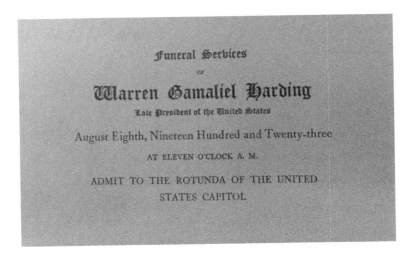

Ticket of admittance to the Capitol Rotunda
for the President's funeral service

The holding vault in Marion Cemetery

Harding Memorial, Marion, Ohio, final
resting place of Warren and Florence Harding

Ned, Marion, Ned Jr. board the
gondola of Shenandoah

Marion at the christening; Ned Jr. to her right

Newly occupied General Motors Building,
New Center, Detroit, 1923

General Smedley Butler left, and
Commandant John A. LeJeune

Typical political cartoon of the 1920's

Ned in his Washington office on
his last day as Secretary

President Coolidge presents Henry Breault with CMOH,
while Ned and the brass observe, March 8, 1924

To This High Standard

Ned in 1923

Ned and Admiral Peary's daughter, Marie, April 6, 1924
Admiral Peary monument, Arlington National Cemetery

The Whittier, Detroit

The Doheny Residence, Chester Place, Los Angeles, California

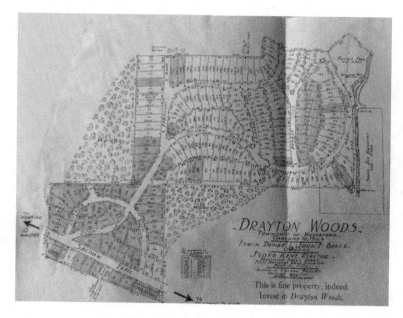

Plots for Dayton Woods

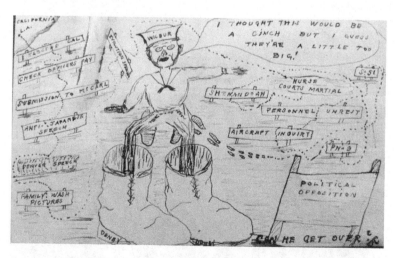

Ned may have respected his successor, but
this was too good not to save in his files

Monument to French Huguenots at
Parris Island, South Carolina

The USS Amphritrite Hotel moored
in the river near Beufort

R. E. Olds' summer home, Grosse Ile,
Clubhouse for the Chateau Voyageurs

The "Josephine Ford" Fokker tri-motor in the
Henry Ford Museum, Dearborn, Michigan

The 1914 Beaufort Bank Building, now
a restaurant in Beaufort, May, 2022

The Hannan Memorial Branch of the
Detroit Y. M. C. A.

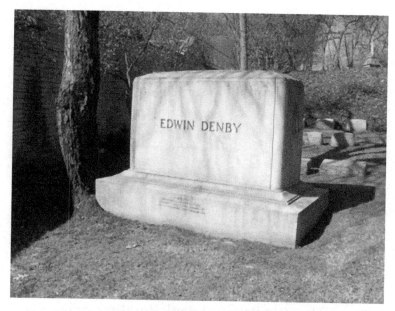

Denby Tomb, Elmwood Cemetery, Detroit; at the bottom is the tribute added commemorating the life and death of Edwin Denby, Jr. lost at sea

Elmwood Cemetery

Ensign Ned Denby and his teenaged sister, Sue

Young ladies going riding, Warrenton Country School

Ned Jr. and 2 year old Elizabeth

American Cemetery, Manila, where the
lost of the Pacific are remembered

Plaque erected at Christ Church Detroit
in honor of Edwin and Edwin, Jr.

Edwin Denby's grandsons, John,
Edwin and Dan, April 28, 2019

Bibliography

1. Hall, Sheryl Smart; Warren G. Harding & the Marion Daily Star; the History Press, Charleston, South Carolina; 2014

2. Irwin, Manley; Silent Strategists, Harding, Denby and the U.S. Navy's Trans Pacific Offensive, World War II; University Press of America; Lanham, Maryland; 2008

3. Stratton, David; Tempest Over Teapot Dome, The Story of Albert B. Fall; University of Oklahoma Press, Norman; 1998

4. Murray, Robert K.; The Harding Era. Warren G. Harding and his Administration; Copp Clark Publishing Co.; Toronto; 1969

4a. Murray, Robert K.; The Politics of Normalcy. Government Theory and Practice in the Harding-Coolidge Era; W. W. Norton & Co., Inc.; New York, 1973

5. Ashby, Leroy; The Spearless Leader, Senator Borah and the Progressive Movement in The 1920's; University of Illinois Press; Chicago; 1972

6. Robert W. Walker; The Namesake: the Biography of Theodore Roosevelt, Jr. by Robert W. Walker; A very excellent biography of one of the great Americans, cursed by being the oldest son of one our greatest citizens and leaders, yet his own man who made his own mark

7. Bredon, Juliet; Sir Robert Hart: the Romance of a Great Career; Dodo Press; 1910

8. Successful Men of Michigan, a Compilation of Useful Biographical Sketches of Prominent Men, written and edited by Newspapermen, published by St. U. Colins, 1914

9. Tiffen, Mary; Friends of Sir Robert Hart, Three Generations of Carrall Women in China; Crewkerne, Tiffania Books, 2012

10. Brady, Tim. His Father's Son, the Life of General Ted Roosevelt, Jr.. New York, New American Library, 2017

11. Jeffers, H. Paul. Theodore Roosevelt Jr. The Life of a War Hero: Novato, CA. Presidio Press, Inc., 2002.

12. Lejeune, John A. Major General. The Reminiscences of a Marine. Philadelphia. Torrance and Company, 1930

13. Penick, James, Jr., Progressive Politics and Conservation: The Ballinger-Pinchot Affair, Chicago, The University of Chicago Press, 1968

14. Bates, J. Leonard, Senator Thomas J. Walsh of Montana, Urbana and Chicago, University of Illinois Press, 1999

15. Philbrick, Nathaniel, Sea of Glory, America's Voyage of Discovery; the U. S. Exploring
Expedition 1838-1842, NewYork, Penguin Group, 2003

16. Weisner, Herman B.. The Politics of Justice: A. B. Fall and the Teapot Dome Scandal, A new Perspective: Albuquerque, Creative Designs, 1988

17. Irwin, Manley R.; Paper: U. S. Navy, Brest France, 1917: The Search for an Optimum Command Structure, September 15, 2017

18. Chang, Jung; The Concubine Who Launched Modern China, Empress Dowager Cixi, Toronto, Anchor Books, 2013

19. Davis, Donal Finlay, Conspicuous Production, Automobiles and Elites in Detroit 1899-1933; Philadelphia, Temple University Press, 1988

20. Smith, Richard J., China Cultural Heritage, The Qing Dynasty 1644-1912, Boulder, Westview Pres, 1983

21. Denby, Charles, LL.B.; China and Her People, Being the Observations Reminiscences, and Conclusions of an American Diplomat; Boston, L. C. Page & Company, 1906

22. Brown, Ervin A., The Rev.; Christ Church Detroit - A Beacon of Hope, Ann Arbor, Edwards Brothers, Inc., 1995

23. Simon, Joseph Arthur, The Greatest of All Leathernecks, John Archer Lejeune and the Making of the Modern Marine Corps; Baton Rouge, Louisiana State University Press, 2019

24. Zimmermann, Warren; First Great Triumph, How Five Americans Made Their Country A World Power; New York, Farrar, Straus and Giroux, 2002

25. Gwinn, William Rea; Uncle Joe Cannon, Arch-foe of Insurgency, a History of the Rise and Fall of Cannonism; Bookman Associates, 1957

26. Donald, Aida D.; Lion in the White House, A Life of Theodore Roosevelt; New York, Basic Books, 2007

27. Wolraich, Michael; Unreasonable Men, Theodore Roosevelt and the Rebels Who Created Progressive Politics; Palgrave Macmillan, New York, 2014

28. Cordery, Stacy A.; Alice - Alice Roosevelt Longworth from White House Princess to Washington Power Broker; Penguin Books, New York, 2007

29. Roosevelt, Mrs. Theodore, Jr.; Day Before Yesterday, the reminiscences of; Doubleday & Co., Inc.; Garden City, New York, 1959

30. Morris, Edmund; Theodore Rex; Random House, New York, 2001

31. Rosen, Jeffrey; William Howard Taft; The American President Series; New York, Henry Holt & Company, 2018

32. Merry, Robert W.; President McKinley, Architect of the American Century; Simon & Schuster, New York, 2017

33. O'Toole, G. J. A.; The Spanish War, An American Epic 1898; W. W. Norton & Co., New York, 1984

34. Guest, Edgar A.; All That Matters; Pantianos Classics; first published 1922

35. Asher, Michael; Khartoum, The Ultimate Imperial Adventure; Penguin Group, New York, 2005

36. Boulger, Demetrius Charles, Gordon, the Career of Gordon of Khartoum, originally

published in two volumes in 1896

37. Daugherty, Harry M.; The Inside Story of the Harding Tragedy, The Churchill Company, New York, 1932

38. Cannadine, David; Mellon, An American Life; Alfred A. Knopf, New York, 2006

39. Noggle, Burl, Teapot Dome, Oil and Politics in the 1920's, W. W. Norton & Co., New York, New York

40. Ward, James A.; Three Men in a Hupp, Around the World by Automobile, 1910-1912; Stanford University Press, Stanford, Ca, 2003

41. Lea, Homer; The Valor of Ignorance, Harper and Brothers, New York and London, 1909

42. Kaplan, Lawrence, M.; Homer Lea, American Soldier of Fortune; The University Press of Kentucky, 2010

43. Schmidt, Hans; Maverick Marine, General Smedley D. Butler and the Contradictions of American Military History; The University Press of Kentucky, 1987

44. Barnett, George; George Barnett, Marine Corps Commandant, A Memoir, 1877-1923; edited by Andy Barnett; McFarland & Company, INc.; 2015

45. Dean, John W.; Warren G. Harding, Times Books, Henry Holt & Co., New York, 2004

46. Bettez, David J.; Kentucky Marine, Major General Logan Feland and the Making of the Modern USMC; University Press of Kentucky, Lexington, 2014

47. Allen, Frederick Lewis; Only Yesterday, An Informal History of the 1920's;Harper & Row, New York, 1931

48. Anthony, Carl Serrazza; Florence Harding, The First Lady, The Jazz Age, and the Death of America's Most Scandalous President,William Morrow & Co., New York, 1988 (this is a smear campaign piece of trash; whatever bad impression could be drawn, was drawn and then emphasized; no good was shown.)

49. Miller, Char; Gifford Pinchot and the Making of Modern Environmentalism; Island Press, Washington, 2001

50. Lockwood, Charles A.; Adamson, Hans Christian; Tragedy at Honda; Valley Pioneer Publishers; Clovis, California; 1997

51. Frothingham, Robert; Songs of Men, An Anthology Selected and Arranged by; Houghton Mifflin Company, Cambridge, 1918

52. Helsley, Alexia Jones; Beaufort, South Carolina, A History; The History Press, Charleston, 2005

53. Rowland, Lawrence S, and Wise, Stephen R.; Bridging the Sea Islands' Past and Present; University of South Carolina Press, Columbia, 2015

54. Walters, Ryan S.; The Jazz Age President, Defending Warren G. Harding; Regenery History, Washington, D. C., 2022

55. Sullivan, Mark; The Great Adventure at Washington, The Story of the Conference; Doubleday, Page & Co.; New York, 1922

56. Sibley, Katherine A.; First Lady Florence Harding, Behind the Tragedy and Controversy; University Press of Kansas, 2009

57. Thomas, Lowell; Old Gimlet Eye; Soldier Press, Los Angeles,

2018

58. Irwin, Manley; Dedicated to Scientific Management, Edwin Denby, Secretary of the Nav, 1921-1924; University of New Hampshire, Durham, New Hampshire; paper

59. Laws and Regulations, State and National relating to the Naval Militia; Washington, D.C.; Government Printing Office, 1895

Made in the USA
Columbia, SC
27 July 2024

39490256R10343